Computational Neuroscience for Advancing Artificial Intelligence:

Models, Methods and Applications

Eduardo Alonso
City University London, UK

Esther Mondragón
Centre for Computational and Animal Learning Research, UK

MEDICAL INFORMATION SCIENCE REFERENCE

Hershey · New York

Director of Editorial Content:	Kristin Klinger
Director of Book Publications:	Julia Mosemann
Acquisitions Editor:	Lindsay Johnston
Development Editor:	Joel Gamon
Publishing Assistant:	Jamie Snavely
Typesetter:	Michael Brehm
Production Editor:	Jamie Snavely
Cover Design:	Lisa Tosheff

Published in the United States of America by
Medical Information Science Reference (an imprint of IGI Global)
701 E. Chocolate Avenue
Hershey PA 17033
Tel: 717-533-8845
Fax: 717-533-8661
E-mail: cust@igi-global.com
Web site: http://www.igi-global.com

Library of Congress Cataloging-in-Publication Data

Computational neuroscience for advancing artificial intelligence : models, methods and applications / Eduardo Alonso and Esther Mondragon, editors.
      p. cm.
   Summary: "This book argues that computational models in behavioral neuroscience must be taken with caution, and advocates for the study of mathematical models of existing theories as complementary to neuro-psychological models and computational models"-- Provided by publisher.
   Includes bibliographical references and index.
   ISBN 978-1-60960-021-1 (hardcover) -- ISBN 978-1-60960-023-5 (ebook) 1. Computational neuroscience. 2. Neurosciences--Mathematical models. 3. Artificial intelligence. I. Alonso, Eduardo, 1967- II. Mondragon, Esther, 1965-
   QP357.5.C634 2011
   612.80285'63--dc22
                              2010018588

British Cataloguing in Publication Data
A Cataloguing in Publication record for this book is available from the British Library.

Table of Contents

Section 3
From Neuroscience to Robotics and AI

Section 4
Neuroscience and Business

Detailed Table of Contents

Section 1
Neuroscience and Computation

Chapter 1

Robert C. Honey, Cardiff University, UK
Christopher S. Grand, Cardiff University, UK

Here the authors examine the nature of the mnemonic structures that underlie the ability of animals to learn configural discriminations that are allied to the XOR problem. It has long been recognized that simple associative networks (e.g., perceptrons) fail to provide a coherent analysis for how animals learn this type of discrimination. Indeed "The inability of single layer perceptrons to solve XOR has a significance of mythical proportions in the history of connectionism." (McLeod, Plunkett & Rolls, 1998; p. 106). In this historic context, the authors describe the results of recent experiments with animals that are inconsistent with the theoretical solution to XOR provided by some multi-layer connectionist models. The authors suggest a modification to these models that parallels the formal structure of XOR while maintaining two principles of perceptual organization and learning (contiguity and common fate).

Chapter 2

Rosemary A. Cowell, University of California - San Diego, USA
Timothy J. Bussey, University of Cambridge, UK
Lisa M. Saksida, University of Cambridge, UK

The authors present a series of studies in which computational models are used as a tool to examine the organization and function of the ventral visual-perirhinal stream in the brain. The prevailing theoretical view in this area of cognitive neuroscience holds that the object-processing pathway has a modular organization, in which visual perception and visual memory are carried out independently. They use computational simulations to demonstrate that the effects of brain damage on both visual discrimination and object recognition memory may not be due to an impairment in a specific function such as memory or perception, but are more likely due to compromised object representations in a hierarchical and continuous representational system. The authors argue that examining the nature of stimulus representations and their processing in cortex is a more fruitful approach than attempting to map cognition onto functional modules.

Chapter 3

Standard associative learning theories typically fail to conceptualise the temporal properties of a stimulus, and hence cannot easily make predictions about the effects such properties might have on the magnitude of conditioning phenomena. Despite this, in intuitive terms we might expect that the temporal properties of a stimulus that is paired with some outcome to be important. In particular, there is no previous research addressing the way that fixed or variable duration stimuli can affect overshadowing. In this chapter we report results which show that the degree of overshadowing depends on the distribution form - fixed or variable - of the overshadowing stimulus, and argue that conditioning is weaker under conditions of temporal uncertainty. These results are discussed in terms of models of conditioning and timing. We conclude that the temporal difference model, which has been extensively applied to the reinforcement learning problem in machine learning, accounts for the key findings of our study.

Section 2
Computational Models in Neuroscience

Chapter 4

Schmajuk, Lam, and Gray (SLG, 1996) introduced an attentional-associative model able to describe a large number of classical paradigms. As other models, the SLG model describes blocking in terms of the competition between the blocker and the blocked conditioned stimulus (CS) to gain association with the unconditioned stimulus (US) or outcome. Recent data suggest, however, other factors together with competition might control the phenomenon. For instance, Beckers et al. (2005) reported that blocking and backward blocking are stronger when participants are informed that (a) the predicted US is submaximal than when it is maximal, and (b) the predictions of the US by the CSs are additive than when they are sub-additive. Submaximality refers to the evidence that the predicted US is weaker than its maximal possible value. Additivity denotes the fact that two CSs, each one independently predicting a given US, predict a stronger US when presented together. Beckers et al. suggested that their results are better explained by inferential accounts, which assume involvement of controlled and effortful reasoning, than by associative views. This chapter shows that a configural version of the SLG attentional-associative model is able to quantitatively approximate submaximality and additivity effects on blocking while providing a mechanistic explanation of the results. In general, the chapter illustrates the potential of associative models to account for newly discovered properties of known psychological phenomena.

Chapter 5

Edgar H. Vogel, Universidad de Talca, Chile
Fernando P. Ponce, Universidad de Talca, Chile

Pavlovian conditioning is a very simple and universal form of learning that has the benefit of a long and rich tradition of experimental work and quantitative theorization. With the development of interdisciplinary efforts, behavioral data and quantitative theories of conditioning have become progressively more important not just for experimental psychologists but also for broader audiences such as neurobiologists, computational neuroscientists and artificial intelligence workers. In order to provide interdisciplinary users with an overview of the state of affairs of theoretically oriented research in this field, this chapter reviews a few key mechanisms that are currently deemed necessary for explaining several critical phenomena of Pavlovian conditioning. The chapter is divided into several sections; each referring to a particular theoretical mechanism and to the type of phenomena that it has been designed to account. The progression of the sections reveals phenomena and mechanisms of increasing complexity, which is an indication of the theoretical sophistication that has been reached in this domain. Since there is not a single theory containing all mechanisms, they are described separately from their originating theories, emphasizing thus the fact that they might be used in almost any theoretical implementation.

Chapter 6

Elliot A. Ludvig, University of Alberta, Canada
Marc G. Bellemare, University of Alberta, Canada
Keir G. Pearson, University of Alberta, Canada

In the last 15 years, there has been a flourishing of research into the neural basis of reinforcement learning, drawing together insights and findings from psychology, computer science, and neuroscience. This remarkable confluence of three fields has yielded a growing framework that begins to explain how animals and humans learn to make decisions in real time. Mastering the literature in this sub-field can be quite daunting as this task can require mastery of at least three different disciplines, each with its own jargon, perspectives, and shared background knowledge. In this chapter, the authors attempt to make this fascinating line of research more accessible to researchers in any of the constitutive sub-disciplines. To this end, the authors develop a primer for reinforcement learning in the brain that lays out in plain language many of the key ideas and concepts that underpin research in this area. This primer is embedded in a literature review that aims not to be comprehensive, but rather representative of the types of questions and answers that have arisen in the quest to understand reinforcement learning and its neural substrates. Drawing on the basic findings in this research enterprise, the authors conclude with some speculations about how these developments in computational neuroscience may influence future developments in Artificial Intelligence.

Chapter 7

In this chapter the author will first give an overview of the ideas behind Adaptively Parameterised Error Correcting Learning (APECS) as introduced in McLaren (1993). It will take a somewhat historical perspective, tracing the development of this approach from its origins as a solution to the sequential learning problem identified by McCloskey and Cohen (1989) in the context of paired associate learning, to it's more recent application as a model of human contingency learning.

Section 3
From Neuroscience to Robotics and AI

Chapter 8

Myoelectric signal is known as an alternative human-machine interface (HMI) for people with motor disability in dealing with assisting robots and rehabilitation devices. This chapter examines a myoelectric HMI in real-time application and compares its performance with traditional tools. It also studies the manifestation of fatigue in long-term muscular activities and its impact on ultimate performance. The core of applied HMI is built on the support vector machine as a classifier. The experiments confirm that the myoelectric HMI is a reliable alternative to traditional HMI. Meanwhile, they show a significant decline in the dominant frequency of myoelectric signals during long-term applications.

Chapter 9

Mobile robotics can be a useful tool for the life scientist in that they combine perception, computation and action, and are therefore comparable to living beings. They have, however, the distinct advantage that their behaviour can be manipulated by changing their programs and/or their hardware. In this chapter, quantitative measurements of mobile robot behaviour and a theory of robot-environment interaction that can easily be applied to the analysis of behaviour of mobile robots and animals is presented. Interestingly such an analysis is based on chaos theory.

Chapter 10

Phil Husbands, University of Sussex, UK

Andy Philippides, University of Sussex, UK

Anil K. Seth, University of Sussex, UK

This chapter reviews the use of neural systems in robotics, with particular emphasis on strongly biologically inspired neural networks and methods. As well as describing work at the research frontiers, the paper provides some historical background in order to clarify the motivations and scope of work in this field. There are two major sections that make up the bulk of the chapter: one surveying the application of artificial neural systems to robot control, and one describing the use of robots as tools in neuroscience. The former concentrates on biologically derived neural architectures and methods used to drive robot behaviours, and the latter introduces a closely related area of research where robotic models are used as tools to study neural mechanisms underlying the generation of adaptive behaviour in animals and humans.

Section 4
Neuroscience and Business

Chapter 11

David Bisset, iTechnic Ltd, UK

This chapter explores the challenges presented by the introduction of robots into our everyday lives, examining technical and design issues as well as ethical and business issues. It also examines the process of designing and specifying useful robots and highlights the practical difficulties in testing and guaranteeing behaviour and function in adaptive systems. The chapter also briefly reviews the current state of robotics in Europe and the global robotic marketplace. It argues that it is essential, for the generation of a viable industry, for the Academic and Business sectors to work together to solve the fundamental technical and ethical problems that can potentially impede the development and deployment of autonomous robotic systems. It details the reality and expectations in healthcare robotics examining the demographics and deployment difficulties this domain will face. Finally it challenges the assumption that Neural Computation is the technology of choice for building autonomous cognitive systems and points out the difficulties inherent in using adaptive "holistic" systems within the performance oriented ethos of the product design engineer.

Chapter 12

Nick F Ryman-Tubb, City University London, UK

Neural networks are mathematical models, inspired by biological processes in the human brain and are able to give computers more "human-like" abilities. Perhaps by examining the way in which the biological brain operates, at both the large-scale and the lower level anatomical level, approaches can be devised that can embody some of these remarkable abilities for use in real-world business applications. One criticism of the neural network approach by business is that they are "black boxes"; they cannot be easily understood. To open this black box an outline of neural-symbolic rule extraction is described and its application to fraud-detection is given. Current practice is to build a Fraud Management System (FMS) based on rules created by fraud experts which is an expensive and time-consuming task and fails to address the problem where the data and relationships change over time. By using a neural network to learn to detect fraud and then extracting its' knowledge, a new approach is presented.

Epilogue

Chapter 13

    Eduardo Alonso, City University London, UK
    Esther Mondragón, Centre for Computational and Animal Learning Research, UK

The authors propose in this chapter to use abstract algebra to unify different models of theories of associative learning -- as complementary to current psychological, mathematical and computational models of associative learning phenomena and data. The idea is to carry out a comparative study of recent researches in associative learning so as to identify the symmetries of behaviour. This approach, a common practice in Physics and Biology, would help us understand the structure of conditioning as opposed to the study of specific linguistic (either natural or formal) expressions that are inherently incomplete and often contradictory.

Preface

Notwithstanding the integrative and interdisciplinary nature of Computational Neuroscience (and Artificial Intelligence) research in the field is still carried out by working neuro-scientists and working computer scientists who inevitably, and thankfully, bring with them their own distinctive methods, goals, theories and, of course, prejudices.

On taking on this editorial project we did not want to edulcorate this basic fact. On the contrary, we aimed at presenting the reader with a panorama of what people investigating in the area of Computational Neuroscience really do. More often than not the alleged commonalities get diluted when we get into the details of an algorithm or the intricacies of a neuro-psychological model. More often than not we discover that sharing an ontology hides important differences in the way Computational Neuroscience is understood and approached by the different communities that fall under that name.

We can thus claim that this volume gives a true account of the area's heterogeneity. As a side-effect coherence in style and presentation were not a priority and for that we apologise to the readers: Following the chapters may be challenging but we believe it is a challenge worth taking.

This book is different from others in that we have not sought the collaboration of computational neuroscientists who dwell in middle ground, that is, of computer scientists who have never set foot in a lab or neuro-scientists who use but barely understand the complexities of computational models. But rather of specialists in neuro-science and computer science who for one reason or another are compelled to crisscross their areas of expertise.

As editors we have been as flexible as possible. Some chapters are predominantly technical and assume previous knowledge whereas other authors have followed a more didactic and openly interdisciplinary style. We have opted for a free-hands editorial approach: We understand that in so doing any reader would find something of interest in this book, be it a professional computer scientists or an undergraduate psychology student. This unorthodox approach in which surveys appear along with experimental reports and theoretical analyses makes the book demanding yet, we hope, entertaining.

The overall layout of the book is classical though: On the one hand, it exposes the extent to which neuro-scientists use computational methods and tools in building accurate neuro-psychological models; on the other hand, it reports on how computer scientists use neuro-psychological theories in developing efficient learning algorithms. Following this general scheme we have structured the book in four sections:

Section 1 presents examples of the kind of empirical work carried out by behavioral neuroscientists who use computational tools to facilitate the description and integration of results and to assist in elaborating new predictions.

We start this section with Honey and Grand's chapter, in which a multi-layer artificial neural network (ANN) is used to model how animals may learn configural discriminations related to the XOR problem.

Cowell, Saksida and Bussey also use ANNs, this time to examine the organization and function of the ventral visual-perirhinal stream in the brain. More specifically they run computational simulations to demonstrate that the effects of brain damage on both visual discrimination and object recognition memory may not be due to an impairment in a specific function such as memory or perception, but are more likely due to compromised object representations in a hierarchical and continuous representational system.

However useful they might be, ANNs are not the only computational method neuro-scientists make us of. As an example, Jennings and collaborators introduce in the third chapter a model of overshadowing and temporal phenomena using Temporal Difference –a well-known algorithm in machine learning.

Section 2 is a compendium of different theoretical approaches to learning and behaviour built directly upon computational models and methods.

Schmajuk and Kutlu's chapter presents a complex ANN that models attentional-associative processes and is able to describe a large number of classical paradigms.

Along the same line, McLaren proposes a connectionist model, the Adaptively Parameterised Error Correcting System (APECS) that provides insights in several learning problems from sequential learning to human contingency learning.

Vogel and Ponce give a theoretical overview on the mechanisms underlying Pavlovian conditioning, with an accent on how computational models have been shamelessly merged with psychological ones. The integration of various models in explaining such fundamental phenomena is a success story in computational neuroscience.

This chapter is ideally complemented with Ludvig, Bellemare and Pearson's, who take a computational problem, Reinforcement Learning, and investigate it from different inter-related perspectives, computer science, neuroscience and even economics.

The third section of the book is dedicated to illustrate how neuro-science models have contributed to solve computational problems in Artificial Intelligence and Robotics.

Asghari-Oskoei and Hu's chapter explores how in building robots for the disabled precise psychological models and methods must be taken into account. The authors advocate that in building such robots engineering or purely computational aspects are necessary but not sufficient.

Nehmzow's contribution offers an innovative approach to the modeling of computational entities, agents and robots, in which quantitative approaches take precedence. We think it is instructive to draw parallelisms between his work, inspired in the study of complex systems and their typically non-linear dynamics and recent studies on networks, neural or not, natural or artificial.

The third chapter, by Husbands, Philippides and Seth, reviews the use of neural systems in Robotics with particular emphasis on strongly biologically inspired neural networks and methods. It starts with an elegant historical introduction on the subject and then proceeds in a two-fold manner: First it gives examples of applications of artificial neural systems in Robotics then on Robotics tools used in neuroscience.

The fourth section reports work rarely accounted for in Computational Neuroscience handbooks that tend to focus on research carried out in academic institutions. We dedicate two chapters to the views of researchers working in Industry on how Computational Neuroscience can be applied to real-life domains. Interestingly, their opinions diverge.

Bisset's contribution expresses serious doubts about the role played by Neural Computation in engineering and Robotics, a critical view that will no doubt provoke a lively and necessary debate about Computational Neuroscience research, its hype and claims, and how things work in down-to-earth industrial applications.

On the contrary, Ryman-Tubb reports on several neural approaches in Fraud Management Systems that are already in place in the banking sector with an emphasis on the integration of symbolic and connectionist methods –which proves that, at least in some cases, research is driven by business.

Finally, we have taken the liberty of adding a chapter of our own, since the content fitted the purpose of the book in an intriguing way. In it we argue that computational models in behavioral neuroscience must be taken with caution --a strange epilogue from the editors of a book on Computational Neuroscience-- and advocate for the study of mathematical models of existing theories as complementary to neuro-psychological models and computational models.

We would like to finish with a note of thanks to all who made this book a reality. To Joel Gamon, who promptly and efficiently answered our many questions, and of course to the authors.

Sadly, we shall close this preface with sorrowful news: Ulrich Nehmzow died of cancer shortly after submitting his final draft. His attitude and commitment were, to the very last moment, an inspiration. This book is a tribute to him. *Requiescat in pace*.

Eduardo Alonso
City University London, UK

Esther Mondragón
Centre for Computational and Animal Learning Research, UK

Section 1
Neuroscience and Computation

Chapter 1
Application of Connectionist Models to Animal Learning:
Interactions between Perceptual Organization and Associative Processes

Robert C. Honey
Cardiff University, UK

Christopher S. Grand
Cardiff University, UK

ABSTRACT

Here the authors examine the nature of the mnemonic structures that underlie the ability of animals to learn configural discriminations that are allied to the XOR problem. It has long been recognized that simple associative networks (e.g., perceptrons) fail to provide a coherent analysis for how animals learn this type of discrimination. Indeed "The inability of single layer perceptrons to solve XOR has a significance of mythical proportions in the history of connectionism." (McLeod, Plunkett & Rolls, 1998; p. 106). In this historic context, the authors describe the results of recent experiments with animals that are inconsistent with the theoretical solution to XOR provided by some multi-layer connectionist models. The authors suggest a modification to these models that parallels the formal structure of XOR while maintaining two principles of perceptual organization and learning: contiguity and common fate.

INTRODUCTION AND SCOPE

Learning can be viewed as an adaptive process that allows the melee presented to an animal's senses to be organized according to certain principles in the service of that animal's future interactions with the world. Viewed in this light, understanding the principles of learning is a core objective for artificial intelligence, ethology, neuroscience and psychology. The study of learning in nonhuman animals (henceforth animals) has provided us with a unique stage upon which to investigate these principles in action, under experimentally controlled conditions, and at a variety of levels of analysis: from molecular mechanisms to behavioural ones. This chapter illustrates how evidence from laboratory-based behavioural studies in animals can inform our understanding of some long-standing issues surrounding the nature of the

DOI: 10.4018/978-1-60960-021-1.ch001

mnemonic structures that underpin learning. Our focus will be on configural learning problems - problems that require animals to be sensitive to the presence of patterns of stimulation as opposed to the presence of any individual stimulus. Analysis of the mnemonic structures that underlie an animal's ability to solve such problems has been at the heart of debates concerning the nature of learning across a broad range of disciplines.

PRINCIPLES OF PERCEPTUAL ORGANIZATION AND LEARNING

What sort of principles might underpin how information is organized in the service of future behaviour? The Gestalt school of psychology identified a set of such principles in the context of, among other things, perceptual organization. According to these principles, things that are presented in close *temporal proximity* will be grouped, as will things that are *visually similar* to one another; and the elements of dynamic patterns that have a *common fate* (or move in the same direction) will also be grouped (for a review, see Wertheimer, 1923). These principles of perceptual organization echo the *laws of learning* from associationist psychology (see Warren, 1921). For example, for the associationists, temporal continuity and similarity were held to influence the process of association - influence the strengthening of a mental link between the memory of one stimulus and another (for a recent review, see Hall, 1994). In fact, as Rescorla (1985) has noted, Kohler (1947, p. 163) suggested "the association of two processes is only the aftereffect of their (perceptual) organization." We shall return, in closing this chapter, to the specific suggestion that association can be reduced to an aftereffect of perceptual organization. For now, it is sufficient to note that the way in which perceptual organization and learning interact has been (e.g., Gibson & Gibson, 1955; Postman, 1955) and continues to be a contentious issue (e.g., Hall,

Blair & Artigas, 2006; McLaren & Mackintosh, 2002; Mundy, Honey & Dywer, 2007).

CONTIGUITY, SIMILARITY AND COMMON FATE

There is good evidence that temporal proximity and similarity are influential parameters in studies of simple Pavlovian conditioning: The development of conditioned responding during pairings of one stimulus with another is often more rapid when both stimuli are presented in close temporal contiguity (e.g., Schneiderman & Gormezano, 1964; Mahoney & Ayres, 1976) and when the two stimuli are similar to one another (e.g., Grand, Close, Hale & Honey, 2007; Rescorla & Furrow, 1977; Rescorla & Gillan, 1980). That is, the Gestalt psychologists' observations concerning perceptual organization find obvious empirical analogues in studies of a form of learning that has been interpreted in associative terms since its original description (see Pavlov, 1927).

The idea that stimuli with a common fate will be grouped also finds analogue within the associative tradition: Patterns of stimulation (let us call them A and B) that have been paired with the same outcome come to be regarded as similar, and those that have been paired with different outcomes become less so (James, 1890). There is now abundant empirical support for this basic suggestion (e.g., Honey & Hall, 1989; Zentall, Steirn, Sherburne, & Urcuioli, 1991). Moreover, this process of grouping does not simply reflect the fact that stimuli with a common outcome have come to evoke the same response (Hull, 1939; Miller & Dollard, 1941) or the same associate (Honey & Hall, 1989): There is now clear evidence that such effects reflect the fact that stimuli that have been paired with a common outcome are more likely to be *perceptually* grouped than those paired with different outcomes (e.g., Allman, Ward-Robinson & Honey, 1994; Close, Hahn, & Honey, 2009; Delamater, 1998; Honey

& Ward-Robinson, 2002; Honey & Watt, 1998; for a review, see Honey, Close & Lin, 2010). Later on, we will outline the way in which this process of stimulus grouping can be implemented within a connectionist analysis; but we will begin by describing the procedure and results from a simple unpublished experiment from C. Grand's doctoral thesis (Grand, 2007). This experiments shows how the principles of temporal contiguity and common fate operate in studies of simple conditioning. Taken in isolation, the results of this experiment are unremarkable; but they do serve as an illustrative counterpoint for later experimental work that is of direct relevance to answering a central question: How do animals solve XOR?

The upper panel of Table 1 depicts the design of this unpublished experiment. Inspection of this table reveals that the design allows the principles of temporal proximity and common fate to operate in concert. In the first stage, rats received two pairs of stimuli (A, B and C, D; that were visual, olfactory, thermal and tactile stimuli). Whenever the members of one pair were presented, either in isolation (A or B) or in combination (A and B), the same outcome (food) was delivered. With the result that A and B are often (but not always) contiguously presented, and A and B are always paired with the same outcome (food in this case). Similarly, whenever the members of the other pair were presented, either alone (C or D) or compound (C and D), the same outcome (no food) was presented. In fact, each trial involved placing animals in an experimental chamber with the designated stimulus (A, B, C, D, AB or CD) for five minutes; and on food-rewarded trials, pairs of reward pellets were delivered to a food well every thirty seconds (i.e., each reinforced trial involved twenty food pellets). Learning was assessed by recording the tendency of the rats to enter to the food well during the first thirty-second period of each trial, in which no food pellets were delivered. Unsurprisingly, rats acquired this simple discrimination, approaching the food well more frequently during the opening thirty seconds of

Table 1. Experimental designs

Training	Revaluation	Test
A→food		
B→food		
AB→food	A→shock	B
C→no food	C→no shock	D
D→no food		
CD→no food		
A→food		
B→food		
AB→no food	A→shock	B, AB
C→no food	(C→no shock)	D, CD
D→no food		
CD→food		

Note: The individual stimuli used (denoted here as A, B, C and D) were taken from domains (visual, thermal, olfactory and tactile) that could be readily combined to produce stimulus compounds (AB and CD). All rats received the identified trial types during the three stages of the experiments (training, revaluation and test); and the outcomes that followed each trial type during training (i.e., food and no food) and revaluation (i.e., shock and no shock) were counterbalanced across stimulus pairs (A, B, and C, D; see text for further details).

reinforced trials (A, B, and AB), than during the equivalent periods on trials on which no food would be delivered (C, D and CD).

To assess whether the training outlined in the previous paragraph had resulted in rats grouping A with B (and C with D) the rats then received a revaluation treatment in which A was paired with mild footshock and C was not. If the contiguous pairings of A with B, or the fact that both had signaled the same outcome (food), resulted in them being grouped, then pairing A with footshock should result in not only A eliciting a fear reaction (in this case freezing or inactivity), but also B eliciting a fear reaction. During the test, stimulus B elicited significantly more fear than D. This result was not restricted to the case in which A, B and AB were paired with food, and C, D and CD were paired with no food; the same was true when it was A, B, AB that were paired with no food and C, D, and CD that were paired with food. So, the fact that B elicited more fear than D must reflect the fact that either A had been grouped with B - either because they had been presented together during the first stage of training (on AB trials; see Rescorla & Cunningham, 1978) or because they had predicted the same outcome (i.e., food) whenever they were presented (on A, B, and AB trials; see Honey & Hall, 1989). Given the fact that there is independent evidence for the influence of each of these principles – contiguity and common fate - it seems reasonable to assume that the results of this simple experiment reflected the combined influence of the two.

In fact, there is a continuing debate concerning the appropriate interpretation of these effects of contiguity (often called *sensory preconditioning*; e.g., Brogden, 1937) and having a common fate (known as *acquired equivalence*; e.g., Hull, 1939) that we shall come back to in due course. However, it should be apparent already that there are discriminations (e.g., negative patterning) that would be impossible to learn if these two principles of grouping operated and were of equal importance. In a negative patterning discrimination, when A and B are presented separately they are paired with the same outcome (e.g., food) and when they are presented together they are followed by a different outcome (e.g., no food). At face value, this arrangement should ensure that A and B are grouped, and thereby make it difficult to show a conditioned response whenever A or B are presented separately, but not when they are presented together. We now turn our attention to patterning discriminations, first considering the broader systematic importance of the finding that animals can learn them, and then by considering further the paradox that this finding brings with it.

Patterning Discriminations

There is one principle of organization that both defines the Gestalt school of psychology and divides contemporary (elemental and configural) theories of associative learning in animals. Namely, the principle that the whole pattern of stimulation (or Gestalt) is more than the sum of its parts. Both elemental (e.g., Rescorla & Wagner, 1972) and configural theories (e.g., Pearce, 1994) of associative learning assume that separately pairing of two stimuli (A and B) with an outcome (e.g., food) results in the growth of independent associations. In the case of elemental theories, these associations are direct, with the input provided by A and B becoming directly linked to the memory of the outcome (i.e., A→outcome and B→outcome). In contrast, in the case of configural theory, the associations between the inputs and outcomes are mediated by configural units (i.e., A→A→outcome and B→B→outcome); the explanatory significance of these configural units will become more apparent in the next paragraph. According to the elemental position, if following the formation of the A→outcome and B→outcome associations one were to present A and B together, the associative strength of the resulting compound AB (and its tendency to activate the memory of the outcome) should equal the sum of associative strengths of A and B independently: The whole is equal to the sum of its parts. According to the configural analysis, however, the presentation of AB will activate a configural representation (AB) that differs from that activated by A or B alone; and the memory of the outcome will become active to the extent that associative strength generalizes from A (and B) to AB: The whole is not equal to the sum of its parts.

On the face of it, there is a simple discrimination learning problem that should allow one to adjudicate between the elemental and configural analyses outlined above: arrange that the presentation of a compound stimulus (A and B) predicts one outcome (e.g., no food) and the separate presentation of each of its components (A or B) predicts another outcome (e.g., food). This negative patterning discrimination is equivalent to an XOR problem: the input vector (A, B) predicts food when either input is present (i.e., 1, 0; or 0, 1), but predicts no food otherwise (i.e., 1, 1; or 0, 0). It should, therefore, come as no surprise that animals operating according to simple elemental associative principles should not be able to solve the discrimination: They should never come to show less conditioned responding to the pattern AB than to its components (A or B). A configural animal, however, should be able to acquire the discrimination, by virtue of acquiring the following types of configural associations: A→A→outcome, B→B→outcome, A→AB→no outcome, and B→AB→no outcome (see next section for further details). In fact, it is already well established that animals can successfully acquire the just-described negative patterning discrimination (e.g., Rescorla, 1973; Woodbury, 1943), and the results depicted in Figure 1 confirm this fact.

Figure 1 shows the results from the training stage of the experiment (outlined in the lower half of Table 1) that was given to rats by Grand and Honey (2008). There were four blocks of training, each block consisted of four days, and on each day rats received each of the six trial types shown in Table 1. The experiment used the same general procedures and stimuli as the experiment shown in the upper half of Table 1 (mentioned earlier), with notable exception that the training stage now involved patterning discriminations. In particular, all rats received both a negative patterning discrimination (i.e., A→food, B→food, AB→no food) and a positive patterning discrimination (i.e., C→no food, D→no food, CD→food) during the first stage of training. Inspection of Figure 1 reveals that rats came to approach the food well more often when A and B were presented alone than when they were presented together; and to approach the food well more often when C and D were presented together than when they were presented alone. The fact that animals can acquire patterning discriminations (and in particular negative patterning) is clearly more compatible with a configural approach than with an elemental approach. Although it should be acknowledged that it is possible to supplement the elemental approach with additional principles that allow it to explain how ani-

Figure 1. Mean rates of food well entries (in responses per minute, RPM, standard error of the mean, ±SEM) during negative patterning (A→food, B→food, AB→no food), and positive patterning (C→no food, D→no food, CD→food); closed symbols indicate pooled rates of responding to single stimuli (i.e., A, B and C, D) and open symbols indicate rates of responding to compounds (i.e., AB and CD; combined results from Experiment 1 and 2 in Grand & Honey, 2008).

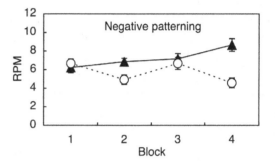

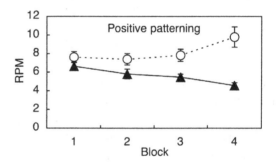

mals acquire patterning discriminations (e.g., McLaren & Mackintosh, 2002; Wagner & Rescorla, 1972; Wagner, 2003), the resulting elemental models do not provide a satisfactory account for other facets of configural learning (see Honey et al., 2010).

Configural Analysis

A configural analysis of the associative structure that underpins the ability of rats to solve a negative patterning discrimination is shown in the left-hand upper panel of Figure 2. This panel depicts a simplified multi-layer network of the form developed in Pearce (1994; see also, Maki, 1993; Maki & Abunawass, 1991). Here, input units activated by A and B are connected to an output unit activated by food (and no food) via a set of configural or hidden units (A, B and AB). Once the discrimination is acquired, it is assumed that whenever A or B are presented they will fully activate configural units A and B (and the food output unit), respectively, and will both partially activate configural unit AB. In contrast, when A and B are presented together they will fully activate AB (and the no food output unit; see Konorski, 1967; Honey & Ward-Robinson, 2002; Honey & Watt, 1998) and partially activate A and B. This state of affairs can be achieved by allowing the pattern of stimulation present on each trial (A, B, and AB) to recruit a different configural unit; by allowing the A→A and B→B links to be strengthened to an asymptotic value of 1, and by constraining the A→AB and B→AB links to have values of above.50 (otherwise A and B would become fully active on an AB trial) but below 1 (else AB would become active on A and B trials; cf. Pearce, 1994). The relative strengths of the links is depicted in the upper half of Figure 1 by using continuous and broken arrows (denoting links) between the input units and configural units. This general form of analysis has received support from a variety of sources (e.g., Redhead & Pearce, 1995; Williams, Dumont, & Mehta, 2004; Williams, Mehta, Poworoznyk, Orihel, George & Pearce, 2002).

The analysis of patterning offered by the configural model outlined above is one of a class of multi-layer networks that were adopted in the wake of the failure of simpler networks to provide a satisfactory solution to the XOR problem (see Rumelhart & McLelland, 1986). This particular analysis is localist, in the sense that a pattern of input becomes represented by a single configural unit that becomes fully activated only upon re-presentation of the same pattern (see Page, 2000). It embodies the principles of temporal proximity and similarity: contiguous patterns of inputs and their outcomes are represented by their shared links with a specific configural unit; and similar patterns will tend to activate the same configural units (cf. Grand *et al.*, 2007). However, this configural analysis of patterning is one that requires that although A and B have separately predicted the same outcome (i.e., have had a common fate) they do not get grouped at the configural layer. This analysis of how negative patterning is solved is, therefore, inconsistent with findings suggesting that that pairing stimuli (e.g., A and B) with the same outcome results in them coming to activate the same hidden-layer unit within a localist multi-layer network (e.g., Honey & Ward-Robinson, 2002). For a more complete review of this evidence the reader is referred to Honey et al. (2010), but we briefly present an illustrative experiment below.

Rats were first given a configural discrimination in which pairs of similar patterns (i.e., AX and BX; CY and DY) are followed by one outcome (food) and others (AY and DY; CX and DX) are followed by a different outcome (no food). This design equates the various binary associations between each of the critical test stimuli (A, B, C and D), the stimuli that accompany them (X and Y), and the outcomes with which they are paired (food and no food). Once rats had acquired this discrimination, pairing A alone with footshock resulted in B eliciting greater conditioned fear than D (e.g., Honey & Watt, 1998). This finding, and many supplementary findings, provide converging support for the suggestion that the components (A, B and X) of similar patterns (e.g., AX and BX) that have been followed by the same outcome (e.g., food) become linked to the same hidden unit (ABX) within a multi-layer network: Activation of this hidden unit by both A and B will allow the mediation of fear between A, that has been directly paired with footshock, and B at test. If this connectionist analysis of the influence of common fate is accepted, then how do animals solve XOR?

Figure 2. Connectionist networks in which input units (A, B, C, D) activated by stimuli have become linked to output units (Food, No food, Shock) via intervening units. Upper panel: conventional configural structure, after negative patterning training (left) and revaluation (right; see the lower panel of Table 1 for the experimental design). Lower panel: novel dual node structure with two types of hidden unit, after negative patterning training (left) and revaluation (right; adapted from Grand & Honey, 2008).

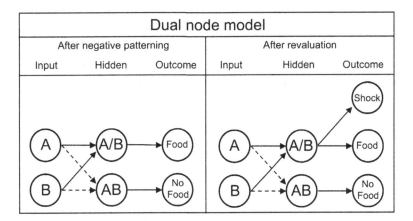

The paradox identified in the previous paragraphs might be moot: During a patterning task, in which the stimuli (A and B) are equally often followed by two different outcomes (food and no food), the principle of common fate might not influence the final state of a connectionist network. Instead the network might eventually recruit a different hidden unit for each of the three patterns (i.e., A, B and AB) and link these units to the appropriate outcome units (i.e., food, food, and no food, respectively; cf. Pearce, 1994). This is certainly one possibility. However, Grand and Honey (2008) proposed an alternative theoretical analysis for how animals solve patterning problems that retains the principles that stimuli which co-occur, on the one hand, and those that predict the same outcome, on the other hand, come to activate the same hidden unit within a connectionist network.

RESOLVING THE PARADOX

How could rats solve patterning problems in a way that retains the principle that when stimuli are followed by the same outcome they come to activate the same hidden unit? One possibility rests on the supposition that the hidden layer contains two types of unit. A (dual node) model with such units is depicted in the lower left-hand panel of Figure 2. This model has a conventional AB unit that becomes active upon presentation of A and B together, but does not become fully active when either A or B are presented alone; and it has a second type of unit (A/B) that has an activation profile that is quite different. The A/B unit becomes active whenever A or B are presented alone, but does not become fully active when A and B are presented together. This model supposes that negative patterning is solved by the presentation of A with B activating AB, which is linked to no food, and by the presentation of A or B activating A/B, which is linked to food. This state of affairs can be achieved in a variety of ways. For example, for the sake of simplicity, one could allow all links to be strengthened in accordance with a Hebbian learning rule (Hebb, 1949, Stent 1972), but suppose that once the activation that an A/B unit exceeds some value (e.g., 1) then it will become inactive and that only when the activation value of AB exceeds some value (e.g., 1) then it will become active. However, for the sake of consistency with the upper panel of Figure 2, the pattern of links shown in the lower panel of Figure 2 indicates that the strength of the links to the AB unit as weaker (broken arrows) than those to the A/B unit (continuous arrows). The way in which the nonreinforced AB compound and its reinforced components, A or B, become linked to their respective AB or A/B units can be achieved through a simple local feedback processes that operate between the output units and the hidden layer (see Allman *et al.*, 2004). The details of this feedback process need not concern us here, but it is worth noting that there is now

evidence that is consistent with the suggestion that the delivery of outcomes (like food and no food) do influence hidden-layer activity (see Honey & Ward-Robinson, 2002; Honey & Watt 1998).

It might strike some readers that appealing to a second type of hidden unit is contrived. However, there is some indirect evidence to support it from single-cell recording studies in macaques (Peirce, 2007). There is, in fact, a large population of cortical visual neurons that have a property that is analogous to the hypothetical A/B units: at high levels of contrast they supersaturate, ceasing to fire, rather than exhibiting saturation, their firing reaching a plateau (Peirce, 2007). This parallel is intriguing. However, as alluring as the analogy between real neurons and the units within hypothetical neural networks has proven, there is clearly a significant gulf between evidence from single cell recording studies in macaques and behavioural evidence showing that rats can solve patterning problems involving stimuli from different modalities. What is needed is a way of experimentally discriminating between a conventional configural network and the dual node model described above. Grand and Honey (2008) described a series of experiments that did just this.

Experimental Analysis

The logic behind the experiments was straightforward, and each used the same type of stimuli and procedures that have already been described in the context of the simple unpublished experiment presented above and outlined in the upper panel of Table 1; with the notable exception being that the first stage of training involved rats acquiring negative and positive patterning discriminations. In fact, as can be seen from comparing the experimental designs in the upper and lower panel of Table 1, the sole difference between the experiments is that the outcomes associated with the presentations of the outcomes of the two compound stimuli (AB and CD) have been reversed. Once the rats had acquired the patterning discrimination (e.g., A→food, B→food, AB→no food, C→no food, D→no food, AB→food; see Figure 1) they received revaluation trials on which A was paired with footshock and C was not (see lower panel of Table 1).

According to a conventional configural model (see upper right-hand panel of Figure 2), pairing A with footshock should allow hidden unit A to become linked to the corresponding output unit. Future presentations of A will therefore activate the footshock output unit and result in rats showing fear. To the extent that the presentation of AB might also activate the A configural unit, then the presentation of AB might also result in rats showing some fear. However, the presentation of B should be incapable of activating configural unit A and it should not elicit fear. In contrast, according to the dual node model, pairing A with footshock should result in the A/B unit, but not the AB unit, becoming linked to the outcome unit activated by footshock (see lower right-hand panel of Figure 2). This will mean that when A is presented alone it should elicit fear, because it will activate the A/B unit that is linked to the footshock output unit, and when B is presented alone it should also be capable of eliciting fear, because it too will activate the A/B unit. However, presenting the compound AB should not activate the shock output unit as it will activate the AB unit – this unit should not have been active when A was paired with shock.

The pattern of results observed by Grand and Honey (2008) is summarized in Figure 3. Inspection of this figure shows that the results are inconsistent with the configural analysis and consistent with the dual node model: The presentation of B elicited greater fear than the presentation of AB. Moreover, B also elicited greater generalized fear than both a control stimulus, D, that had originally been trained in a positive patterning discrimination, and a compound stimulus (CD) that had been paired with the same outcome as B during training (in this case food; cf. Delamater, 1998; Honey & Hall, 1989). This pattern of results

Figure 3. Mean percentages of time freezing (i.e., showing fear; ±SEM) during presentations of B, D, AB and CD (adapted from Grand & Honey, 2008; see the lower panel of Table 1 for the experimental design).

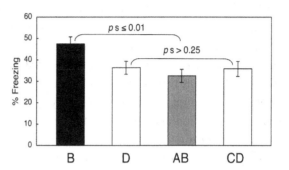

was not restricted to the case in which A, B and AB were the stimuli for a negative patterning discrimination and C, D and CD were the stimuli for a positive patterning discrimination; the same pattern of results was observed when the stimuli were assigned in the opposite fashion. The fact that the (C→no shock) trial is in brackets indicates that a critical aspect of these results (that B elicited more fear than compound CD) was also observed when the C→no shock trials were omitted during the revaluation stage. Thus, B did not elicit more fear than CD because C had become associated with the absence of footshock during the revaluation stage. The dual node connectionist network uniquely predicts the pattern of results depicted in Figure 3. Thus, the behavioural evidence supporting the artificial neural network outlined in the lower panel of Figure 2 is at least consistent the properties of real neural networks (cf. Peirce, 2007).

Occam's Razor

On the one hand, our appeal to two types of hidden entity will no doubt strike many people as extravagant: two types of such entity will be judged as at least one type too many. On the other hand, to others this development will seem modest in the context of the known properties of real neural networks: appealing to one type of entity was surely always doomed to fail to provide an adequate account of even the relatively simple forms of learning under consideration here. In contrast, we both think that our appeal to two types of hidden entity does no real violence to Occam's razor: *entia non sunt multiplicanda praeter necessitatem*; but recognize that our analysis is likely to be incomplete. Shanks and Darby (1998) provided behavioural evidence that is consistent with the suggestion that humans acquire rules during patterning discriminations: humans given patterning training seem to abstract the general rule that when stimuli are presented alone they signal the opposite outcome to when they are presented together. There is nothing in the network that we have outlined that would, in and of itself, predict that patterning training will results in such rule-based behaviour. As its stands, the network learns that when *specific* stimuli are presented alone (e.g., A or B) they predict the opposite outcome to when they are presented together (e.g., AB). We have no evidence concerning whether nonhuman animals would show evidence consistent with the acquisition of a general rule when given an equivalent form of training to humans (see Shanks & Darby, 1998), but we should not like to rule out this possibility at this juncture.

CONCLUDING COMMENTS

Animals can solve problems that are both more complex and certainly appear to be more interesting than those that we have considered in this chapter. Indeed, recent issues of influential science journals are replete with tales of animals acting in ways that are purported to be beyond the scope of the types of connectionist analyses under scrutiny here (e.g., Blaisdell, Sawa, Leising, & Waldmann, 2006; but see Dwyer, Starns, & Honey, 2009). Also, there is something quite contrived and artificial about a negative patterning problem, and it is perhaps fitting that our analysis of how animals solve it might seem to be similarly contrived. The fact that animals often require many trials to learn such discriminations might make some people wary about using them as test beds for theoretical analyses of learning and memory that are intended to have much broader significance. However, even if one acknowledged that these views have some merit, the fact that animals can solve negative patterning/XOR means that any model of learning must also do so. We hope that the results that we have presented here have illustrated how behavioural experiments with nonhuman animals have the potential to bring us a little closer to understanding the form that such a solution might take. At a more general theoretical level, the results presented in this chapter suggest that associative processes tune perceptual organization - that there is an interaction between perceptual organization and associative processes (cf. Kohler, 1947). We share the view that connectionist networks provide a coherent theoretical medium in which this interaction can be characterized and believe that the evidence from behavioural experiments in animals can provide a bridge between artificial neural networks and the real thing.

ACKNOWLEDGMENT

The authors thank the BBSRC (UK) for funding the research upon which parts of this chapter are based.

REFERENCES

Allman, M. J., Ward-Robinson, J., & Honey, R. C. (2004). Associative change in the representations acquired during conditional discriminations: Further analysis of the nature of conditional learning. *Journal of Experimental Psychology. Animal Behavior Processes, 30,* 118–128. doi:10.1037/0097-7403.30.2.118

Blaisdell, A. P., Sawa, K., Leising, K. J., & Waldmann, M. R. (2006a). Causal reasoning in rats. *Science, 311*, 1020–1022.doi:10.1126/science.1121872

Brogden, W. J. (1939). Sensory pre-conditioning. *Journal of Experimental Psychology, 25*, 323–332. doi:10.1037/h0058944

Close, J., Hahn, U., & Honey, R. C. (2009). Contextual modulation of similarity in the rat. *Journal of Experimental Psychology. Animal Behavior Processes, 35*, 509–515.doi:10.1037/a0015489

Coutureau, E., Killcross, A. S., Good, M., Marshall, V. J., Ward-Robinson, J., & Honey, R. C. (2002). Acquired equivalence and distinctiveness of cues: II. Neural manipulations and their implications. *Journal of Experimental Psychology. Animal Behavior Processes, 28*, 388–396. doi:10.1037/0097-7403.28.4.388

Delamater, A. R. (1998). Associative mediational processes in the acquired equivalence and distinctiveness of cues. *Journal of Experimental Psychology. Animal Behavior Processes, 24*, 467–482.doi:10.1037/0097-7403.24.4.467

Dwyer, D. M., Starns, J., & Honey, R. C. (2009). "Causal reasoning" in rats: A re-appraisal. *Journal of Experimental Psychology. Animal Behavior Processes, 35*, 578–586.doi:10.1037/a0015007

Gibson, J. J., & Gibson, E. J. (1955). Perceptual learning – differentiation or enrichment? *Psychological Review, 62*, 32–41.doi:10.1037/h0048826

Grand, C., Close, J., Hale, J., & Honey, R. C. (2007). The role of similarity in human associative learning. *Journal of Experimental Psychology. Animal Behavior Processes, 33*, 64–71. doi:10.1037/0097-7403.33.1.64

Grand, C. S., & Honey, R. C. (2008). Solving XOR. *Journal of Experimental Psychology. Animal Behavior Processes, 34*, 486–493.doi:10.1037/0097-7403.34.4.486

Hall, G. (1991). *Perceptual and associative learning*. Oxford, England: Clarendon.

Hall, G. (1994). Pavlovian condition: Laws of association. In N. J. Mackintosh (Ed.) *Handbook of perception and cognition. Vol 9: Animal learning and cognition* (pp. 13-43). San Diego, CA: Academic Press.

Hall, G., Blair, C. A., & Artigas, A. A. (2006). Associative activation of stimulus representations restores lost salience: Implications for perceptual learning. *Journal of Experimental Psychology. Animal Behavior Processes, 32*, 145–155. doi:10.1037/0097-7403.32.2.145

Hebb, D. O. (1949). *The organization of behavior*. New York: Wiley & Sons.

Honey, R. C., Close, J., & Lin, T. E. (2010). Acquired distinctiveness and equivalence: A synthesis. In Mitchell, C. J., & Le Pelley, M. E. (Eds.), *Attention and associative learning: From brain to behaviour* (pp. 159–186). Oxford: Oxford University Press.

Honey, R. C., & Hall, G. (1989). Acquired equivalence and distinctiveness of cues. *Journal of Experimental Psychology. Animal Behavior Processes, 16*, 178–184.doi:10.1037/0097-7403.16.2.178

Honey, R. C., & Ward-Robinson, J. (2002). Acquired equivalence and distinctiveness of cues: I. Exploring a neural network approach. *Journal of Experimental Psychology. Animal Behavior Processes, 28*, 378–387.doi:10.1037/0097-7403.28.4.378

Honey, R. C., & Watt, A. (1998). Acquired relational equivalence: Implications for the nature of associative structures. *Journal of Experimental Psychology. Animal Behavior Processes, 24*, 325–334.doi:10.1037/0097-7403.24.3.325

Hull, C. L. (1939). The problem of stimulus equivalence in behavior theory. *Psychological Review, 46*, 9–30.doi:10.1037/h0054032

James, W. (1890). *The principles of psychology.* New York: Holt.

Kohler, W. (1947). *Gestalt psychology.* New York: Liverright.

Konorski, J. (1967). *Integrative activity of the brain: An interdisciplinary approach.* Chicago: University of Chicago Press.

Mahoney, W. J., & Ayres, J. J. B. (1976). One-trial simultaneous and backward fear conditioning as reflected in conditioned suppression of licking in rats. *Animal Learning & Behavior, 4*, 357–362.

Maki, W. S. (1993). From elementary associations to animal cognition: Connectionist models of discrimination learning. In Zentall, T. R. (Ed.), *Animal Cognition: A tribute to Donald A. Riley* (pp. 293–312). Hillsdale, NJ: Erlbaum.

Maki, W. S., & Abunawass, A. M. (1991). A connectionist approach to conditional discriminations: Learning, short-term memory, and attention. In Commons, M. L., Grossberg, S., & Staddon, J. E. R. (Eds.), *Quantitative analysis of behavior: Neural network models of conditioning and action* (pp. 241–278). Hillsdale, NJ: Erlbaum.

McLaren, I. P. L., & Mackintosh, N. J. (2002). Associative learning and elemental representation: II. Generalization and discrimination. *Animal Learning & Behavior, 30*, 177–200.

Miller, N. E., & Dollard, J. (1941). *Social learning and imitation.* London: Kegan Paul, Trench, Trubner & Co.

Minsky, M. L., & Papert, S. A. (1969). *Perceptrons: An introduction to computational geometry.* Cambridge, MA: MIT Press.

Mundy, M. E., Honey, R. C., & Dwyer, D. M. (2007). Simultaneous presentation of similar stimuli produces perceptual learning in human picture processing. *Journal of Experimental Psychology. Animal Behavior Processes, 33*, 124–138. doi:10.1037/0097-7403.33.2.124

Page, M. P. A. (2000). Connectionist modelling in psychology: a localist manifesto. *The Behavioral and Brain Sciences, 23*, 443–467.doi:10.1017/S0140525X00003356

Pavlov, I. P. (1927). *Conditioned Reflexes.* London: Oxford University Press.

Pearce, J. M. (1994). Similarity and discrimination: A selective review and a connectionist model. *Psychological Review, 101*, 587–607. doi:10.1037/0033-295X.101.4.587

Peirce, J. W. (2007). The potential importance of saturating and supersaturating contrast response functions in visual cortex. *Journal of Vision (Charlottesville, Va.), 7*, 1–10.doi:10.1167/7.6.13

Postman, L. (1955). Association theory and perceptual learning. *Psychological Review, 62*, 438–446.doi:10.1037/h0049201

Redhead, E. S., & Pearce, J. M. (1995). Stimulus salience and negative patterning. *Quarterly Journal of Experimental Psychology, 48B*, 67–83.

Rescorla, R. A. (1973). Evidence for a "unique stimulus" account of configural conditioning. *Journal of Comparative and Physiological Psychology, 85*, 331–338.doi:10.1037/h0035046

Rescorla, R. A. (1985). Pavlovian conditioning analogues to Gestalt perceptual principles. In F.R. Brush., & J.B. Overmier (Eds.) *Affect, conditioning, and cognition: Essays on the determinants of behavior* (pp. 113-130). Hillsdale, NJ: LEA.

Rescorla, R. A., & Wagner, A. R. (1972). A theory of Pavlovian conditioning: Variations in the effectiveness of reinforcement and nonreinforcement. In Black, A. H., & Prokasy, W. F. (Eds.), *Classical conditioning II: Current research and theory* (pp. 64–99). New York: Appleton-Century-Crofts.

Rosenblatt, F. (1958). The perceptron: A probabilistic model for information storage and organization in the brain. *Psychological Review, 65*, 386–408.doi:10.1037/h0042519

Rumelhart, D. E., & McLelland, J. L. J. L. (1986). Parallel distributed processing: Explorations in the microstructure of cognition: *Vol. 1. Foundations*. Cambridge, MA: MIT Press.

Schneiderman, N., & Gormezano, I. (1964). Conditioning of the nictitating membrane of the rabbit as a function of CS-US interval. *Journal of Comparative and Physiological Psychology, 57*, 188–195.doi:10.1037/h0043419

Shanks, D. R., & Darby, R. J. (1998). Feature- and rule-based generalization in human associative learning. *Journal of Experimental Psychology. Animal Behavior Processes, 24*, 405–415. doi:10.1037/0097-7403.24.4.405

Stent, G. S. (1973). A physiological mechanism for Hebb's postulate of learning. *Proceedings of the National Academy of Sciences of the United States of America, 70*, 997–1003.doi:10.1073/pnas.70.4.997

Wagner, A. R. (2003). Context-sensitive elemental theory. *Quarterly Journal of Experimental Psychology, 56B*, 7–29.

Wertheimer, M. (1923). Principles of perceptual organization. In Beardslee, D. S., & Wertheimer, M. (Eds.), *Readings in perception* (pp. 115–137). Princeton, NJ: Van Nostrand-Reinhold.

Williams, D. A., Dumont, J.-L., & Mehta, R. (2004). Conditions favoring superconditioning of irrelevant conditioned stimuli. *Journal of Experimental Psychology. Animal Behavior Processes, 30*, 148–159.doi:10.1037/0097-7403.30.2.148

Williams, D. A., Mehta, R., Poworoznyk, T. M., Orihel, J. S., George, D. N., & Pearce, J. M. (2002). Acquisition of superexcitatory properties by an irrelevant background stimulus. *Journal of Experimental Psychology. Animal Behavior Processes, 28*, 284–297.doi:10.1037/0097-7403.28.3.284

Zentall, T. R., Steirn, J. N., Sherburne, L. M., & Urcuioli, P. J. (1991). Common coding in pigeons assessed through partial versus total reversals of many-to-one conditional and simple discriminations. *Journal of Experimental Psychology. Animal Behavior Processes, 17*, 194–201. doi:10.1037/0097-7403.17.2.194

KEY TERMS AND DEFINITIONS

Acquired Equivalence: Learning theorists and computational neuroscientists have appealed to the idea that when two stimuli are paired with the same consequence or outcome they will be grouped, either in terms of their capacity to elicit the same response (e.g., Hull, 1939; Miller & Dollard, 1941), the same associate (e.g., Honey & Hall, 1989), or the same configural/hidden unit within a multilayer neural network (e.g., Coutureau, Killcross, Good, Marshall, Ward-Robinson & Honey, 2002; Honey & Ward-Robinson, 2002).

Common Fate: The Gestalt psychologists developed a set of principles of perceptual organization, one of which was the idea that the elements of dynamic patterns that have a *common fate* or move in the same direction (e.g., a flock of birds), will be grouped (for a review, see Wertheimer, 1923).

Configural Representation: A pattern of stimulation can be represented by each of its elements or components coming to activate a separate, configural entity. A configural representation can be allied to a Gestalt, but within connectionist theorizing configural representations find a natural home in the connections between the input layer units and a hidden layer unit in multilayer neural network (e.g., Page, 2000; Pearce, 1994).

Contiguity: Contiguity is a principle of perceptual organization, on the one hand, and a principle of associative learning, on the other hand. It refers to the idea that when stimuli occur close together in time (or space) they will be perceptually grouped, or grouped by virtue of an association forming between them.

Elemental Representation: A representation of a pattern of stimulation might involve the elements or components of that pattern becoming linked directly to one another. This view is allied to Hebb's (1949) notion of a cell assembly, and has been more fully developed in the context of learning theory by, for example, McLaren and Mackintosh (2002).

Multilayer Neural Network: A network in which input units are connected to output units via weighted connections to an intervening layer or layers of hidden units.

Patterning Discriminations: A discrimination learning problem involving two stimuli (A and B) in which the individual presentation of either A or B predict one outcome (e.g., food) and their joint presentation (A and B) predict the absence of that outcome (e.g., no food).

Perceptron: An artificial neural network involving, at its simplest, a set of input units connected to an output unit (Rosenblatt, 1958; for a detailed critique, see Minsky & Papert, 1969).

XOR: The exclusive or (XOR) is a disjunctive operation in which an input vector (A, B) gives an output (i.e., 1) when either input is present (i.e., 1, 0; or 0, 1), but not when both are present (i.e., 1, 1) or absent (0, 0); a patterning discrimination is an example of an XOR problem.

Chapter 2
Using Computational Modelling to Understand Cognition in the Ventral Visual–Perirhinal Pathway

Rosemary A. Cowell
University of California - San Diego, USA

Timothy J. Bussey
University of Cambridge, UK

Lisa M. Saksida
University of Cambridge, UK

ABSTRACT

The authors present a series of studies in which computational models are used as a tool to examine the organization and function of the ventral visual-perirhinal stream in the brain. The prevailing theoretical view in this area of cognitive neuroscience holds that the object-processing pathway has a modular organization, in which visual perception and visual memory are carried out independently. They use computational simulations to demonstrate that the effects of brain damage on both visual discrimination and object recognition memory may not be due to an impairment in a specific function such as memory or perception, but are more likely due to compromised object representations in a hierarchical and continuous representational system. The authors argue that examining the nature of stimulus representations and their processing in cortex is a more fruitful approach than attempting to map cognition onto functional modules.

INTRODUCTION

Research in cognitive neuroscience seeks to understand the biological – specifically, neural – foundations of mental phenomena. Most theories in cognitive neuroscience seek to explain a particular cognitive function by specifying which parts of the brain contribute to that function and describing, at some level, the putative neural mechanisms that underlie their contribution. It seems clear

DOI: 10.4018/978-1-60960-021-1.ch002

that investigating a cognitive process from the standpoint of a well-specified theory can speed the acquisition of our understanding immeasurably. Well-specified theories give concrete predictions, are falsifiable and are explicit enough to be tested and refined; they therefore lend themselves to a systematic process of development into an ever more accurate model (Popper, 1999). The process of testing and refinement narrows down the number of experiments that are required in the investigation, focuses the research direction, and encourages a thorough, mechanistic understanding of the cognitive and neural phenomena. When it comes to hypothesizing about both cognitive function and the neural mechanisms employed by the brain – be those mechanisms specified at the level of synapses, localized networks of neurons, or whole neural systems – computational models can be very useful as a method of creating a well-specified theory with clear predictions.

In this chapter, we will describe a computational modeling framework for the investigation of visual cognition in the brain. Broadly speaking, we seek to understand the brain-based cognitive processes that enable us to apprehend, discriminate and remember visual objects, and how and why those cognitive processes break down following brain damage. In particular, we focus here on the *functional organization* of the brain regions devoted to processing visual objects. We ask, are the brain areas that underlie object processing functionally distinct from one another, such that they can be described as 'cognitive modules' for individual functions such as visual memory and visual perception? Or, are these cognitive functions in fact intimately linked and subserved by common neural substrates and mechanisms? As the report of our computational investigations will reveal, we favour the latter view, in which a single brain region is capable of participating in multiple cognitive functions and a single cognitive function finds its neural basis across multiple brain regions.

In addition, through a description of our proposed computational framework for understanding visual object processing, we will illustrate and advocate our modeling philosophy. In general, we adhere to the principle of Occam's Razor and we place an emphasis on the correct choice and explicit declaration of the problem space that a model attempts to address. According to our view, a theoretician should first define clearly the target data of the theory (the problem space) in order to avoid any misunderstanding about the phenomena that one should expect the model to capture, and in order to restrict the scope of the model to a reasonably-sized and tractable domain. Within that problem space, the theoretician should account for the data using the simplest possible model (Occam's razor). This is particularly applicable in cognitive neuroscience, where the aim is to understand how high-level cognitive processes emerge from systems-level or network-level processes: the explanatory power of a model is maximized when the mechanism driving the behavioural trends in the simulation data is clearly defined and observable, rather than obscured by having many complex computational details operating in parallel. In addition, the model should be formulated at the appropriate level of biological organization.

The program of research we describe in this chapter has been reviewed in several articles, each of which focused in detail on a particular topic, such as the original formulation of the perceptual-mnemonic/ feature-conjunction model (Bussey, Saksida, & Murray, 2005), the medial temporal lobe (Bussey & Saksida, 2005) the implications of this work for hippocampal function (Bussey & Saksida, 2007), or the translation of results relevant to amnesia from the animal to the human domain (Saksida & Bussey, 2010). This chapter is to some extent a consolidation of those diverse reviews, augmented with some new results (Cowell, Bussey, & Saksida, 2010) and reexamined with a view to providing a case study of the use of computational models in cognitive neuroscience. The objectives of the present chapter are thus threefold: to argue for a functional organization of the visual processing areas of the brain in terms of a continuum rather than as 'cognitive modules'; to provide an illustration of our modeling philosophy, with specific examples; and to show how computational models – formulated in accordance with our modeling philosophy – can help advance scientific understanding in the field of cognitive neuroscience.

COMPUTATIONAL INVESTIGATIONS IN COGNITIVE NEUROSCIENCE

Here we provide a brief introduction to the connectionist modeling approach that we have used in our investigations of the ventral object processing pathway. We favour computational models of cognitive function over verbal hypotheses because they constitute concrete theories, which provide explicit predictions that can drive experimental work. In addition, computational models are mechanistic, and in the case of neural network models, the mechanisms are inspired by and in line with the information processing characteristics of neural tissue. Further, the instantiation of a theoretical account in computational terms can reveal hidden assumptions and novel predictions that the theorist might not have anticipated. That is, running simulations can help us understand our own theories more fully. Finally, computational models can be useful for demonstrating a proof of concept, in order to make a theoretical point more easily understood than is possible with a verbal account.

We will discuss four principles to which we adhere in building our computational models, addressing: the level of biological organization at which the model attempts to address data, the problem space within which the model operates, the issue of parsimony, and the biological plausibility of the model. The degree of biological plausibility exhibited by a model is in large part determined by the first three principles.

Levels of Biological Organization

Levels of biological organization in neuroscience refer to the hierarchy of structural components comprising an organism. Churchland and Sejnowski (1988) discuss the specific levels of organized structure at which research can be conducted in neuroscience: each level exists at a different scale, ranging from molecular interactions within and between cells to large-scale interactions at the level of the central nervous system (see Figure 1).

The level, or scale, of biological organization of a theory should not be confused with the *levels of analysis* defined by Marr and Poggio (1977), which refer to the conceptual content of a scientific explanation. The levels of analysis of a cognitive phenomenon comprise: *computational*, asking what are the goals of the cognitive operation; *algorithmic*, asking what formal function transforms inputs into outputs in the service of the computational goals; and *implementational*, asking what physical substrate is used to carry out the algorithmic operations, and how. As Churchland and Sejnowski (1988) point out, an analysis at the implementational level is possible at any one of the biological scales in Figure 1, and each alternative implementational explanation may be associated with its own algorithmic description. That is, the spectrum of biological levels and the spectrum of levels of analysis are, in principle, orthogonal. One key difference between the levels of analysis and the levels of biological organization is that the former are formally independent, whereas the latter are not. That is, a given algorithm can solve a task whether it is implemented in brain tissue or in a computer; however, the details of the nervous system at the level of networks are constrained by its details at the level of neurons and synapses.

Cognition may be investigated at any scale of biological organization illustrated in Figure 1. Indeed, explanations of the same cognitive phenomenon may exist at several levels of biological organization. For example, memory can

Figure 1. The levels of biological organization at which a model may be formulated. After Churchland and Sejnowski (1988)

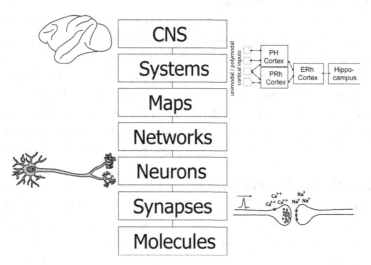

be explained at the level of individual synapses in the form of long-term potentiation, or across multiple brain systems in the case of a rich episodic memory trace. It is perhaps difficult to find any cognitive phenomenon that can be said to reside wholly at one level of biological organization. Because many cognitive phenomena are spread over several levels, and because the details at each biological level are inter-dependent, it may in fact be useful to construct a model at a biological level that is somewhat "fuzzy", being formulated mainly at the level of, say neural systems, but drawing inspiration and loose constraints from what is known about networks and neurons.

Problem Space

The problem space of a model can be thought of as the scope of its explanatory power. This includes the number of phenomena (behavioural, neural, synaptic, etc.) that the model attempts to explain, and the number of levels of organization at which it attempts to explain them. The two dimensions of problem space are illustrated schematically in Figure 2.

Choosing a given point on the biological organizational ladder, whilst still allowing the model to be sensitive to constraints from the level below and the level above, constrains the problem space enormously. Often this is necessary because extra details from other levels are irrelevant and would reduce the clarity of model's mechanism. Building a complex model that tries to include everything can sometimes mean that the simulation ends up as poorly understood as the nervous system itself (Sejnowski, Koch, & Churchland, 1988). Even when we have constrained our problem space in terms of levels of biological organization, in order to come up with a computationally tractable problem, we may still need to limit the number of phenomena that we attempt to simulate. A disadvantage of the pursuit of a large problem space is that it can produce a model that is not at all parsimonious. Additionally, the problems addressed by connectionist models in cognitive neuroscience are often poorly understood; attempting to model several phenomena at once can be prohibitively ambitious and, as with including too many levels of organization, might reduce the clarity of the demonstration being made by the model.

Figure 2. A schematic illustration of two different problem spaces that a model in cognitive neuroscience may span. The left diagram represents a model that attempts to account for several phenomena (for example, recognition memory, visual discrimination, and perceptual learning) at only one level of biological organization: the systems level. The right diagram illustrates a model that accounts for only one cognitive phenomenon, but attempts to explain the mechanism at several levels of biological organization. Modified from Cowell (2006), unpublished dissertation.

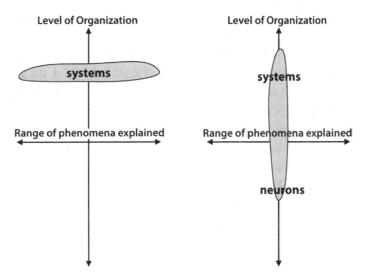

Parsimony

Following Occam's Razor, any scientific model should aim to provide the most parsimonious version of events that will account for the available evidence. For investigators of artificial intelligence, and indeed 'purely cognitive' theorists, who have no interest in the nature of the hardware in which their discovered algorithms will eventually be implemented, parsimony should always be a priority. Certainly, parsimony is a sensible guiding principle when attempting to engineer the most efficient machine. But the task of the cognitive neuroscientist, concerned with the brain, is rather one of reverse engineering: we are interested in how nature came upon her solutions to the problems presented to our biological ancestors, through natural selection. The process of natural selection does not, of course, have an *a priori* purpose to build the most efficient machine, with the end goal of modern humans in its sights.

Instead, humans and other animals are the product of an evolutionary process in which our cognitive ability has been augmented in a step-wise manner by building on pre-existing structures. This process does not necessarily yield the most elegant computational solutions, and so we must be open to the possibility of a lack of parsimony in the brain's design. We therefore caution against a slavish adherence to Occam's Razor in the face of neurobiological or behavioral evidence that counters the simplest possible explanation.

However, a cognitive neuroscientist still needs a good, brain-based reason to construct a model that is more complex than is necessary to explain the data. It is not useful to include biological facts not relevant to the phenomenon being modeled, or the mechanism by which the processing is simulated. This principle relates to the discussion of problem space, above, because there often exists a trade-off between the parsimony of a model and the size of its problem space.

Biological Plausibility

Since we are cognitive neuroscientists rather than researchers of Artificial Intelligence, the present discussion is constrained to brain-based models of cognition. All such models necessarily strive for some degree of biological plausibility. O'Reilly (1998) argues persuasively in favour of biological plausibility: "Biological realism lies at the foundation of the entire enterprise of computational modeling in cognitive neuroscience. This approach seeks to understand how the brain… gives rise to cognition, not how some abstraction of uncertain validity does so. Thus, wherever possible, computational models should be constrained and informed by biological properties of the cortex. Moreover, computational mechanisms that violate known biological properties should not be relied upon."

This philosophy is advocated by most connectionist modelers interested in problems of brain-based cognition. When employing this principle, however, it is important to keep in mind the pre-defined level of biological organization and the pre-defined problem space of the model. For example, Rolls and Deco (2002) take the legitimate view that while connectionist approaches can make an important start in understanding how complex computations such as language could be implemented in brain-like systems, if the model uses back-propagation, or too few neurons, it can provide only a guide as to how cognitive functions might actually be implemented in the brain. Theorists who take this view to an extreme, choosing to work with only models that operate according to strict rules of biological plausibility, and attempting to incorporate as many of those low-level details as possible, are applying a bottom-up research strategy. The models they prefer are those in the *realist* tradition, which can be contrasted with *simplifying* models.

Realistic models involve large scale simulations that attempt to include as much cellular detail as is available (Sejnowski et al., 1988). These can be pitched at the neuron level or the network level, but cannot feasibly be couched at a level of any organization any higher than this, since incorporation of cellular detail in a model of systems-level processes would result in a model so complex as to make analysis of its mechanisms intractable. When attempting to understand more abstract cognitive phenomena, realistic models should give way to simplifying models that capture the important principles underlying brain function without incorporating all known neurobiological detail. Most connectionist models of brain function fall into this category, and in drawing inspiration from realistic models of information processing in neurons they constitute an extremely powerful tool for theorizing. As cautioned by Churchland and Sejnowski (1992), critics of connectionism should not assume that a high degree of realism always equates to a high degree of scientific value.

The modeling work that we will present in this chapter adheres to the general principles just outlined. In presenting the models, we will provide illustrative examples of these principles. But first, we outline the debate within the cognitive neuroscience literature that the models were designed to address.

Memory and Perception: Cognitive Modules or a Continuous Hierarchy of Representations?

The standard paradigm in cognitive neuroscience assumes that the brain can be best understood as consisting of modules specialized for different psychological functions. Within the field of memory research, the influence of a modular approach has been particularly powerful. One of the earliest studies that lent support to the notion of cognitive modules in memory was the examination of the amnesic patient, H.M., by Scoville and Milner (1957). H.M. underwent bilateral removal of the medial temporal lobes, as a treatment for intractable epilepsy, and was subsequently unable to store new information about facts and events

(Bussey, Saksida, & Murray, 2002; Scoville & Milner, 1957). H.M.'s cognitive deficits were selective, however, since he did not appear to have any gross perceptual deficits and he even showed "perceptual priming" (E. K. Warrington & Weiskrantz, 1968) which led researchers to suggest that his perceptual capacities were intact. This dissociation reinforced the already popular idea that the brain is organized into separate functional systems, in this case for perception and memory. The study of H.M. sparked much experimental work investigating animal models of human amnesia (e.g., Mishkin, 1982; L.R. Squire & Zola-Morgan, 1983). Most of these experimental investigations assumed that mnemonic processes could – and should – be studied independently of perceptual processes.

In the present chapter, we will focus on visual memory and visual perception, and the issue of modularity as it relates to object processing. The brain regions at the centre of the debate over the functional organization of visual object processing are the ventral visual stream (VVS) – along which information flows in a posterior to anterior direction, from occipital V1 through to inferotemporal cortex – and the medial temporal lobe (MTL), which comprises several multi-modal brain structures and lies downstream of the VVS. Following the study of H.M., there developed a substantial empirical literature not just investigating amnesia, but also searching for evidence that visual memory and perception are functionally and anatomically distinct. Many studies of the latter type were published in the 1960s and 1970s, and used a task known as "visual discrimination learning" to investigate the effects of lesions in both anterior and posterior areas of the VVS in monkeys. Often, the studies revealed a dissociation between the behavioral effects of damage to the two regions. The dissociation was interpreted as evidence for a functional distinction, with memory carried out in anterior areas and perception in posterior areas. Some of these visual discrimination learning studies reported only a single dissociation, either

because the authors included in their experimental design lesions of just one area instead of several, or because only one type of discrimination task was used rather than two (Butter, 1972; Dean, 1974; Iversen & Humphrey, 1971; Kikuchi & Iwai, 1980; Manning, 1971a, 1971b; M. Wilson & Kaufman, 1969). However, several authors found double dissociations within one study, by using two or more lesion groups with ablations at different points in the VVS and two or more discrimination tasks (Blake, Jarvis, & Mishkin, 1977; Cowey & Gross, 1970; Gross, Cowey, & Manning, 1971; Iwai & Mishkin, 1968; M. Wilson, Zieler, Lieb, & Kaufman, 1972). This work likely constitutes a major contribution to the origins, at least in animal neuropsychology, of the modular view of memory and perception.

The modular view continues to prevail in modern neuroscience and psychology (e.g., Buffalo et al., 1999; Sakai & Miyashita, 1993; Tulving & Schacter, 1990). For example, Squire and Zola Morgan (1991) have made the functional and anatomical distinction between declarative memory and visual perception a central aspect of their highly influential theory of memory. In their seminal 1991 paper, they proposed that human declarative memory is mediated by a group of brain structures in the medial temporal lobe (MTL). Importantly, they suggested a functional dissociation between inferotemporal cortex (IT), thought to mediate perception, and structures within MTL thought to support declarative memory (E. A. Buffalo et al., 1999; E. A. Buffalo, Ramus, Squire, & Zola, 2000; Levy, Shrager, & Squire, 2005; Shrager, Gold, Hopkins, & Squire, 2006; Stark & Squire, 2000; Suzuki, Zola-Morgan, Squire, & Amaral, 1993). Thus, the MTL memory system was contrasted with another cognitive module – a "perceptual representation system" (Tulving & Schacter, 1990) in the ventral visual stream – which is critical for visual perception and perceptual learning. The MTL memory system has become the dominant theoretical construct in memory research (Squire, Stark, & Clark, 2004).

However, the idea that memory and perception are sub-served by discrete cognitive modules is not without its opponents (Bussey, 2004; Fuster, 2003; Gaffan, 2002; Palmeri & Gauthier, 2004). When considering the possibility that the functional distinction between perception and memory is blurred, an obvious place to look, in the brain, is the interface between the regions presumed to support memory and those thought to underlie perception. This interface is a brain structure in the medial temporal lobe known as the perirhinal cortex. Damage to perirhinal cortex consistently causes deficits in object recognition memory (E.A. Buffalo, Reber, & Squire, 1998; Eacott, Gaffan, & Murray, 1994; Meunier, Bachevalier, Mishkin, & Murray, 1993; Mumby & Pinel, 1994). Object recognition memory – defined as the ability to identify which of two or more objects has been previously encountered – has been taken as the canonical test of declarative memory in animals (e.g., Manns, Stark, & Squire, 2000). Since object recognition depends on perirhinal cortex, this brain structure has been named as a critical component of the MTL memory system that is damaged in amnesia.

More recently, some researchers have argued that perirhinal cortex is important not just for declarative memory, but also for object perception. The earliest indication that perirhinal cortex may be important for perception came from Eacott, Gaffan, and Murray (1994), who tested the object recognition memory of macaque monkeys. Eacott et al. observed that monkeys with removal of perirhinal and entorhinal cortex showed a delay-dependent memory deficit relative to control monkeys (with no brain lesion). That is, the monkeys with perirhinal cortex damage showed severe impairments when there was a long delay between study of the objects and test of recognition memory, but no impairment when the study-test delay was short. A lack of impairment at short delays is usually taken as evidence that perception is intact (Holdstock, Shaw, & Aggleton, 1995). However, when Eacott et al. increased the percep-

tual difficulty of the task, lesioned monkeys were impaired even in the zero-delay and shortest delay conditions. Since, in these conditions, there was a minimal or zero memory component to the task, this finding implied a role for perirhinal cortex in perception. Inspired by the results reported in this important study, other authors began to examine perirhinal cortex function in novel ways. For example, Buckley and Gaffan examined the role of perirhinal cortex in perception in a series of studies using visual discrimination learning tasks. The results they obtained (Buckley, 2005; Buckley & Gaffan, 1997, 1998a) led these authors to argue that perirhinal cortex has a role in cognition that extends beyond object recognition memory. These and other studies provided evidence that perirhinal cortex is important not only for memory, but more generally for "object identification" (Buckley & Gaffan, 1998b; Eacott & Gaffan, 2005; Goulet & Murray, 2001; Murray, 2000; Murray & Bussey, 1999; Murray, Málková, & Goulet, 1998).

With some researchers claiming an exclusive role for perirhinal cortex in declarative memory, and others suggesting that this structure also contributes to object identification, Bussey, Saksida and colleagues proposed a new paradigm for understanding the function of perirhinal cortex (Bussey & Saksida, 2002; Cowell, Bussey, & Saksida, 2006; Murray & Bussey, 1999). They suggested that it may be fruitful to consider perirhinal cortex as an extension of VVS, rather than as belonging exclusively to the MTL memory system. More recently, we have additionally proposed that the ventral visual-perirhinal stream may contribute to both visual perception and visual memory all along its length (Bussey & Saksida, 2005, 2007; Cowell et al., in press; Saksida, 2009), implying a blurring of the functional distinction traditionally assumed.

In sum, the general controversy that we will address in this chapter is whether perception and memory are distinct or whether they overlap, in terms of both cognitive processes and anatomical locus within the MTL and VVS. But, we will begin our discussion by examining a specific controversy over the role of perirhinal cortex, a structure that lies at the interface between MTL and VVS. We will describe a computational modeling framework that began life as an investigation of visual discrimination learning in perirhinal cortex. This formal theoretical framework was subsequently developed to span both perirhinal cortex and VVS, and simulate behavioral data from tests of object recognition memory, as well as visual discrimination. We will chart its progress, and thereby demonstrate the utility of computational modeling to our account of visual object processing as a hierarchically organized functional continuum.

A REPRESENTATIONAL-HIERARCHICAL VIEW OF MEMORY AND PERCEPTION

The Perceptual-Mnemonic Feature-Conjunction Model

Several animal studies have shown that although damage to perirhinal cortex can lead to impairments in visual discrimination, it does so only under certain circumstances (Buckley & Gaffan, 1997, 1998a, 1998b; Gaffan & Murray, 1992). The findings concerning which circumstances were necessary for a visual discrimination task to depend on perirhinal cortex were initially somewhat puzzling. In an attempt to make sense of the findings, Bussey, Saksida and colleagues (Bussey & L.M. Saksida, 2002; Bussey et al., 2002; Bussey, Saksida, & Murray, 2003; Murray & Bussey, 1999) began to think about the perirhinal cortex, not only as a structure in the MTL memory system that contributes solely to declarative memory, but also as part of the VVS. This hypothesis assumes that perirhinal cortex has visual information processing properties similar to those of other regions within the VVS, and that it may be the final station in this brain pathway. Under this account, the

puzzling pattern of deficits caused by perirhinal cortex lesions can be understood by considering the hierarchical organization of representations in the VVS, as illustrated schematically in the left panel of Figure 3. Posterior regions in the VVS are assumed to represent simple features, whereas more anterior regions in the VVS are assumed to represent more complex conjunctions of features. According to this scheme, a lesion in perirhinal cortex destroys or compromises the highly complex visual representations, which are formed from the conjunction of large numbers of features. Without complex representations, the animal must rely on representations of simple features, housed in more posterior regions of VVS, in order to solve visual discriminations. To test this idea, the scheme was instantiated in a neural network model: the perceptual-mnemonic/feature-conjunction (PMFC) model. The model is shown in the right panel of Figure 3. The model simulates behavioural experiments, and suggests that impairments in visual discrimination learning are caused by perirhinal cortex lesions because lesioned animals have impoverished representations of complex stimuli, and the remaining representations of simple features are inadequate for making certain types of discrimination between visual objects. To test the model, a "lesion" was made by removing the layer of the network corresponding to perirhinal cortex, and the effects of this lesion were compared with previously reported effects of lesions in perirhinal cortex in monkeys (Bussey & Saksida, 2002). The model was able to simulate the effects of lesions of perirhinal cortex on visual discrimination behaviour in a range of different experimental contexts.

Modeling Philosophy behind the PMFC Model

The PMFC model is formulated at a high level of biological organization, namely the neural systems level. Psychologically, the model addresses how representations are organized and associated dur-

Figure 3. The left panel illustrates the putative hierarchical organisation of visual representations in the ventral visual-perirhinal stream. A single letter represents a visual feature, which are assumed to reside in posterior regions; with progression along the hierarchy, simple features get combined into increasingly complex conjunctions, reaching a maximum in perirhinal cortex (anterior). The right panel shows the architecture of the PMFC model. The hierarchical scheme in the left panel was instantiated in a network with 2 layers of 'representation' nodes, each of which can become associated with an outcome such as reward. Simple visual features are represented in the 'feature layer' and conjunctions of those features in the 'feature conjunction' layer, which corresponds to perirhinal cortex. Modified from Bussey et al. (2002)

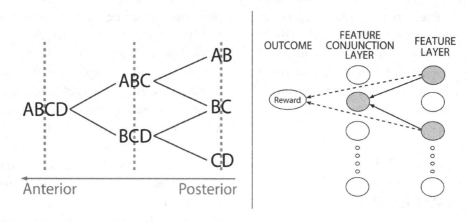

ing learning, in line with the 'parallel distributed processing' school of computational modeling (McClelland & Rumelhart, 1986; Rumelhart & McClelland, 1986), and the 'associative' tradition of learning theory (e.g., Dickinson, 1980; Mackintosh, 1974). The units in the network represent visual representations and, although the model is influenced by lower levels of biological organization, such as data from electrophysiological studies of neurons, the units do not represent individual neurons. The neural entity that might be said to correspond to a unit in the network is a population of neurons that, as an assembly, codes for a visual representation of an object or an object-feature. No attempt is made to explain how exactly these representations are formed or coded at the neuronal level. Furthermore, the problem space is constrained to data from visual discrimination learning within perirhinal cortex. Properties of neurons that are not necessary to model these data (such as back-projections or 'repetition suppression' mechanisms) have not been included in the

model, in keeping with the principle that a model should be no more complex than is necessary to account for the target data. Finally, although it is known that perirhinal cortex has anatomical connections not shared by other regions in VVS, giving it access to non-visual sensory information, including auditory and somatosensory information (Murray & Bussey, 1999) the model focuses on the role of perirhinal cortex specifically in visual learning and memory. Accordingly, the PMFC model is based on the properties of perirhinal cortex thought to be shared with other visual areas in the VVS, and non-visual information entering the perirhinal cortex is not included in the model.

PMFC Model: Simulating the Effects of Feature Ambiguity

The PMFC model was first used to simulate extant data, but it has also made novel predictions that have been tested experimentally. The most important of these predictions concerns the central theoretical tenet of the PMFC account: the idea that animals with perirhinal cortex lesions will be impaired on any task which requires representations of complex conjunctions of features at the object level for its solution. One example of this would be a visual discrimination problem in which *combinations* of features predict the correct item in a pair of to-be-discriminated objects, while the individual features of the objects are uninformative. The features are uninformative because they appear as part of both the correct (S+) and the incorrect (S-) objects in a pair. Such a discrimination problem possesses "feature ambiguity", a property that emerges when a feature is rewarded when it is part of one object but is not rewarded when it is part of another object. Feature ambiguous discrimination problems are so-called because individual features are ambiguous in terms of the predictions of reward that they make; only a combination of features will give unambiguous predictions and correctly guide the subject's responses.

Specifically, the PMFC model predicts that animals with perirhinal cortex lesions will have difficulty acquiring any visual discrimination which possesses feature ambiguity. This prediction was explicitly demonstrated with a simulation of visual discrimination learning, in which networks were trained to discriminate pairs of "objects", each consisting of two "features". Networks were tested in three conditions: maximum feature ambiguity, intermediate feature ambiguity, and minimum feature ambiguity. In the maximum condition, all objects were constructed from a set of just four features, in such a way that all four features were explicitly ambiguous (AB+, CD-, BC+, AD-; where each letter represents a feature, a pair of letters represents an object, a plus sign represents that the object was rewarded and minus that it was unrewarded). In the intermediate feature ambiguity condition, six features were used to construct the four objects, so that only two features were explicitly ambiguous (AB+, CD-, CE+, AF-). In the minimum feature

ambiguity condition, no features were explicitly ambiguous (AB+, CD-, EF+, GH-). The results of this simulation are shown in Figure 4. It can be seen that as the degree of feature ambiguity of the visual discrimination task increases, networks with the perirhinal cortex layer removed become increasingly impaired.

PMFC Model: Testing the Predictions for Feature Ambiguity

Bussey et al. (2002) directly tested this prediction of the PMFC model in monkeys, by using stimuli that were specially constructed to systematically vary the level of feature ambiguity in the same way as it was varied in the neural network simulations.

Figure 4. Simulation data generated by the PMFC model, from Bussey et al. (2002). Data are mean errors to criterion in the acquisition of a pairwise concurrent discrimination problem with three levels of Feature Ambiguity: minimum, intermediate and maximum. Error bars indicate ±SEM. Asterisks indicate a significant difference between groups at the level p < 0.00001. Modified from Bussey et al. (2002)

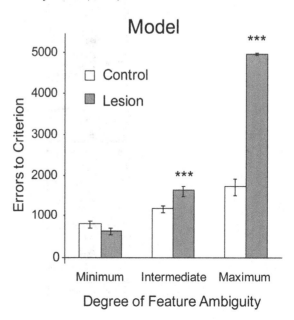

Each visual "object" was constructed from a pair of grayscale photographic images, with one photographic image being considered as a "feature" (see left panel of Figure 5). As shown in the right panel of Figure 5, the pattern of results closely matched that predicted by simulations using the connectionist network: Monkeys with perirhinal cortex lesions were unimpaired in the minimum feature ambiguity condition, mildly impaired in the intermediate feature ambiguity condition, and severely impaired in the maximum feature ambiguity condition.

These results allow interpretation of some puzzling findings in the literature. For example, Buckley and Gaffan (1997) had previously reported that monkeys with perirhinal cortex lesions were impaired relative to control monkeys when concurrently learning a large but not a small number of visual discriminations between pairs of objects. The model provides an explanation of this "set size" effect. According to the PMFC model, it is not the number of objects that is the critical factor, but rather the degree of feature ambiguity. However, large sets of object pairs possess more feature ambiguity than small sets

Figure 5. Left panel: stimuli from the Maximum Ambiguity condition of the visual discrimination task given to monkeys in Bussey et al., 2002. Stimuli had the same structure as described for networks in the text. Each stimulus was composed of two conjoined grayscale photographs (two 'features'). Stimuli were grouped into pairs; in each pair, one stimulus was consistently rewarded and the other unrewarded. In the maximum ambiguity condition (shown), all stimulus features were explicitly ambiguous because they appeared equally often as part of rewarded versus unrewarded stimuli. Only the conjunction of two features – i.e. the whole stimulus – provides the information necessary to solve the task. Right panel: acquisition of visual discrimination by control monkeys and monkeys with lesions of perirhinal cortex, from Bussey et al. (2002). Error bars indicate ±SEM. * p < 0.00001; **P= 0.01. Compare to Figure 4. Modified from Bussey et al. (2002)

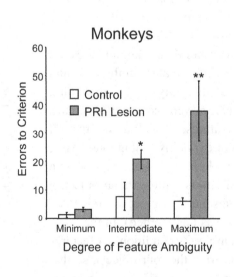

of object pairs, because as the number of object pairs to be discriminated becomes larger, the probability increases that a given object feature will appear both as part of a rewarded object, and as part of an unrewarded object. Bussey et al. (2002) provided a clear demonstration of this point, because they varied only feature ambiguity, while holding set size constant, showing that it is feature ambiguity that is critical, rather than the number of object pairs to be discriminated. This account also explains why Buckley and Gaffan (1997, 1998a) observed an impairment in monkeys with perirhinal cortex lesions on a "configural" discrimination task, using only a small number of stimuli, whereas a much larger stimulus set was required to reveal an impairment on a standard concurrent discrimination learning task. In configural discrimination problems, feature ambiguity is explicitly arranged to be at a maximum (as in the maximum feature ambiguity condition of Bussey et al., 2002). By contrast, in concurrent discrimination problems, feature ambiguity increases with increasing set size because features become ambiguous by chance. In terms of feature ambiguity, concurrent discrimination tasks using a large set size can be thought of as partial configural discriminations, equivalent to the intermediate condition of Bussey et al. (2002).

Animal models are critical in the search for the neural underpinnings of cognitive processes for many reasons; for example they allow us to examine the effects of circumscribed, focal lesions, unlike the brain damage seen in humans, which rarely respects anatomically defined boundaries. A complete account of human brain function, however, requires additional evidence demonstrating the translation of animal results into the human experimental domain. Barense et al. (2005) have investigated the function of perirhinal cortex – specifically the feature ambiguity hypothesis – in a study with amnesic patients. Barense and colleagues assessed the performance of two groups of patients on the 'feature ambiguity' discrimination task described above (Figures

4 and 5), on which monkeys with perirhinal cortex damage were impaired as a function of degree of feature ambiguity. One group of patients had damage to the hippocampus, and a second group had more extensive damage to MTL that included perirhinal cortex. Both patient groups had previously performed normally when tested on general neuropsychological tests of perception (Osterrieth, 1944; E. Warrington & James, 1991), which suggested that none of the patients had impaired perceptual abilities as traditionally assessed. The discrimination task structure used by Barense et al. was identical to that used in the Bussey et al. monkey study; there were three levels of feature ambiguity – minimum, intermediate, and maximum – and the number of object-pair discriminations was held constant. However, the stimuli were adapted for the human subjects, by presenting them as coherent objects such as "blobs" and "bugs". To do this, the stimuli were based on the same underlying structure as in the monkey study, but each stimulus object was composed of two explicitly defined components (e.g., shape and fill for blobs, or body-type and legs for bugs). Barense et al. (2005) found that the patients with selective hippocampal lesions – that is, with no perirhinal cortex damage – performed no differently from their age-matched controls on all conditions. However, the patients with more extensive MTL lesions including damage to perirhinal cortex showed the same pattern of results as the lesioned monkeys in Bussey et al. (Bussey et al., 2002): they were significantly impaired in the intermediate and maximum feature ambiguity conditions, but performed normally on the minimum feature ambiguity conditions. Importantly, the deficits observed in the MTL patients were unlikely to be a result of task difficulty, because control subjects performed equally well across all conditions.

These findings, along with others in which the learning component of the visual discrimination task was minimized (Lee, Bandelow, Schwarzbauer, Henson, & Graham, 2006; Lee, Buckley et al., 2006; Lee et al., 2005; Lee, Scahill, & Graham, 2008), support the claim that perirhinal cortex has a role in visual perception, as well as in memory. The PMFC model suggests that the contribution of perirhinal cortex to visual perception can be explained in terms of feature ambiguity. The model helped to establish this theoretical account by providing explicit predictions, and demonstrating how the puzzling and contradictory results obtained with different set sizes could be explained in terms of a single underlying factor – feature ambiguity. Moreover, the model provided a clear and concrete exposition of a theory that would have been hard to describe verbally.

Contributions of the PMFC Model to Understanding Visual Cognition

We provide here a specific example of a way in which this model – couched at the neural systems level – has been used to guide experimental work in neurophysiology, aimed at determining the neural processes underlying visual cognition. When building the PMFC model, Bussey & Saksida (2002) found that it was necessary to include an assumption that, for conjunctive representations, "the whole is greater than the sum of the parts". That is, in the perirhinal cortex layer, the presentation of a whole object possessing several features elicits more activation than the sum of the activation that would be produced by presenting each feature individually. Moreover, it was necessary to assume that for a given object, even if completely novel to the network, it would be possible to recruit such a whole-preferring conjunctive representation upon first presentation of the object. At the time, there was no empirical evidence to support this a priori assumption. Following publication of the model, Baker, Behrmann and Olson (2002) tested this idea in a single unit recording study with monkeys. These authors found neurons in inferotemporal cortex that, with experience, responded selectively to the feature conjunctions necessary for solving visual discriminations on which the

monkeys had been trained. If the behaviourally relevant stimulus was AB, for example (where each letter stands for a visual feature and the pair of letters stands for their conjunction), neuronal selectivity developed whereby the influence on neuronal activity of A and B together was greater than predicted by the additive influences of A and B individually. These data suggest that conjunctive stimulus representations are indeed recruited during training and honed so that the whole is greater than the sum of the parts. The use of this a priori assumption in a computational model, in order to bring about a certain behavioural outcome in the model, thus influenced the experimental research by constraining the search space for potential neural mechanisms. This outcome demonstrates that a certain degree of speculation by computational modelers about neural mechanisms can be useful; the speculative assumptions can be tested, and occasionally they may turn out to be correct!

While the PMFC model has enjoyed considerable success in advancing our understanding of perirhinal cortex function, its problem space was deliberately constrained in at least two ways. First, it is limited to data from visual discrimination learning. And second, only the effects of lesion experiments, and specifically those involving perirhinal cortex, are addressed by the model. If there is, as the model suggests, a blurring of the functional distinction between perception and memory in perirhinal cortex, perhaps the perirhinal cortex – previously assumed to contribute solely to memory – shares some functional properties with other brain regions thought to be critical for visual perception? Perhaps the problem space of the PMFC model can be expanded to include earlier stations in the ventral visual stream, by applying the same account of cognition to these areas. The PMFC model proposes that perirhinal cortex plays an important role in perception by providing complex conjunctive representations of stimuli that are necessary for visual discriminations in which the stimuli possess ambiguous features. These high-level representations are thought to help resolve what has been referred to as "feature ambiguity". However, as noted above, we do not claim that perirhinal cortex is the only region of the brain in which conjunctive representations exist. We propose that there is an important role for conjunctive representations in other areas, for example in regions upstream of the VVS. According to the hierarchical scheme illustrated in Figure 3, these conjunctions are simpler and composed of fewer features. To investigate the contribution of these simpler conjunctive representations, we extended the PMFC model in a posterior direction (Cowell et al., in press). In the next section, we describe how an extended version of the PMFC model can account for data from studies contrasting the effects of lesions in both anterior and posterior regions of the VVS.

Extending the PMFC Model

We extended the PMFC model to test whether the function of not only perirhinal cortex, but the whole of VVS, can be understood in terms of conjunctive representations and the resolution of feature ambiguity. The hypothesis is that even simple representations are useful to the extent that they resolve feature ambiguity. In the original PMFC model, there is only one layer that possesses conjunctive representations: the perirhinal cortex layer. In extending the model, we added further layers to represent a range of stimulus complexity; at each successive layer a greater number of features is integrated into a conjunction. Thus, the extended PMFC model continues to assume the hierarchical organization of visual representations in VVS, with simple visual features or simple conjunctions of features represented in posterior regions and more complex conjunctions of features represented in anterior areas. The new architecture allows explicit simulation of the effect of posterior VVS lesions on the visual discrimination of simple stimuli, as well as the effect of anterior VVS lesions on complex visual discriminations.

The three layers of stimulus representations in the extended PMFC model can each resolve feature ambiguity at a certain level of stimulus complexity. The central claim of our account of VVS function is that stimulus representations at a certain stage of processing in the VVS provide the optimal solution for a given discrimination problem, according to the level of complexity of the stimuli in that problem (Ullman, Vidal-Naquet, & Sali, 2002; Zhang & Cottrell, 2005). However, other stages of VVS outside of the optimal processing stage may also provide sub-optimal solutions for the discrimination. In general, the closer a processing station lies to the optimal stage, the better its solution will be: there is a continuous gradation in the ability of different VVS regions to solve a particular discrimination, reflecting the continuous gradation in the complexity of stimulus representations along the VVS (Tanaka, Saito, Fukada, & Moriya, 1991). Thus, the relative difference in the complexity of representations in any two brain regions can be mapped onto the relative difference in the functional contributions of those two regions. That is, if one brain region contains more complex representations than another, it will play a more critical role in discriminating complex objects than that region. Conversely, the region containing less complex representations will be more important in the discrimination of simple objects.

Lesion effects can be explained according to this scheme just as they were for the original PMFC model. When a monkey learns a particular visual discrimination, if the "optimal" stage in the VVS for solving the discrimination is damaged, discrimination performance will be severely impaired. Since the function of VVS is claimed to be continuous, the closer a brain lesion falls to the processing stage best able to resolve ambiguity in the to-be-discriminated stimuli, the worse will be the resultant discrimination performance.

Modeling Philosophy of the Extended PMFC Model

As in the case of the original PMFC model, we do not include low-level properties of neurons that are unnecessary to the proposed mechanism for visual discrimination. We define our problem space as the data from neuropsychological studies investigating the role of VVS in visual discrimination. In keeping with Occam's Razor, we use the simplest model that can explain the data. For example, we have not appealed to top-down processing from higher cortical areas because such details are not needed to capture the important patterns in the target data. Since our account of the target data is centered on the complexity of stimulus representations at different points in VVS, we have chosen a computational model appropriate to this level of analysis and level of biological organization: a simple connectionist network in which the properties of the representations are clearly defined and play a critical role in determining discrimination performance. To include details of top-down processing known to exist in the brain would expand our problem space, in terms of the number of biological levels modeled, but at a cost: it would decrease the parsimony of the account, and obscure the key mechanism at work in the model.

Extended PMFC Model: Revisiting Iwai and Mishkin (1968)

As stated above, any theory of human cognition is best tested in human subjects. In the case of the continuous processing account we propose, the optimal empirical target data for the theory would come from groups of human patients with brain damage in sequential regions of the VVS. The VVS hypothesis we advocate predicts that a continuous pattern of deficits in visual discrimination and memory performance would be revealed across the groups, if the complexity of the stimulus material were carefully manipulated.

However, neuropsychological patients with clean focal damage in these brain regions are very rare. As an extremely useful substitute, an abundant source of behavioural data is available in the monkey neuropsychology literature, in the studies of visual discrimination learning described above. Iwai and Mishkin (1968) provides an excellent representative example of that literature; it was a comprehensive study in which both anterior and posterior lesions were tested on two different tasks and a double dissociation found.

Iwai and Mishkin trained five groups of monkeys; two of the groups served as controls and the remaining three experimental groups received lesions in VVS that ranged from posterior to anterior in their placement. The first experimental group received ablations of a small region of cortex in anterior VVS (Group III+IV), the second experimental group received a lesion more posterior than that of the first group (Group I+II) and the third experimental group received the most posterior lesion, which overlapped with that of the second group, but extended further into occipital cortex to a point posterior of the inferior occipital sulcus (Group O+I). The monkeys learned several different visual discrimination tasks, two of which we simulated: a task termed "Pattern Relearning" and another named "Concurrent Object Discrimination Learning". Pattern learning was first presented to all groups pre-operatively. Monkeys were trained on a single-pair discrimination of two white patterns – a plus sign and the outline of a square – on a grey background, until attainment of criterion. After surgery, animals were retrained on the same problem, yielding a "relearning" score. For the concurrent object discrimination learning task, all monkeys learned the task post-operatively. Subjects were trained on eight object-pair discriminations concurrently, with five daily presentations of each pair, administered in random order, until a criterion was reached. The results of this study are shown in the top panel of Figure 6. On the "Pattern Relearning" task, the two posterior groups (O+I and I+II) relearned the

Figure 6. Top: acquisition of visual discriminations by monkeys in the two tasks of Iwai and Mishkin (1968). Placement of the brain lesion is indicated on the x-axis; number of trials taken by monkeys to reach criterion is indicated on the y-axis. Monkeys with posterior lesions were relatively impaired on the Pattern Relearning task, whereas monkeys with anterior lesions were relatively impaired on the Concurrent Discrimination task. Middle Panel: Simulation data generated by the extended PMFC model on the two tasks of Iwai and Mishkin (1968). Bottom Panel: Simulated acquisition of visual discriminations between stimuli of intermediate complexity by the extended PMFC model. Modified from Iwai and Mishkin (1968) and Cowell et al., (in press)

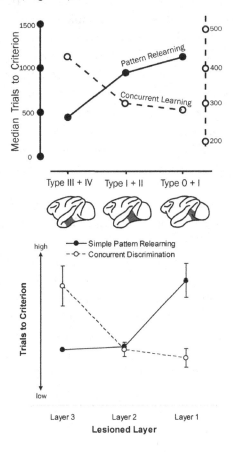

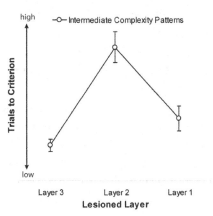

task more slowly than the anterior group (III+IV), following surgery. On the concurrent object discrimination task, the trend was reversed: monkeys with anterior lesions learned more slowly than animals in groups I+II and O+I. Thus, there was a clear double dissociation between location of brain lesion and cognitive impairment. Iwai and Mishkin concluded that this double dissociation arose from "two qualitatively different disorders: (1) a sensory, perceptual or attentional loss and (2) a defect in memory or associative learning". In Cowell et al. (in press), we used the Extended PMFC model to examine whether this modular model provides the only account of these data.

With the Extended PMFC model, we explored the possibility that the effects of VVS lesions on visual discrimination learning performance are due to the animals possessing compromised representations of visual stimuli, rather than an impairment of a specific function such as memory or perception. To simulate the Pattern Relearning task, networks were trained to discriminate a single pair of similar simple patterns, represented in the model by a pair of input stimuli possessing two features each, with one feature shared by the two input stimuli. To simulate Concurrent Discrimination Learning, networks learned to discriminate eight pairs of complex objects. A complex object was represented in the model by an input stimulus possessing four features. In all simulations, lesions of the network were effected by completely removing the layer corresponding to the cortical area lesioned in Iwai and Mishkin (1968). The simulation results are remarkably similar to the data of Iwai and Mishkin. As is shown in the middle panel of Figure 6, networks lacking layer 1 (Group 'Posterior') were impaired relative to networks lacking layer 3 (Group 'Anterior') on the Pattern Relearning task. However, on the Concurrent Discrimination Learning task, Group 'Anterior' was impaired relative to Group 'Posterior'. Networks lacking Layer 2 (Group 'Middle') showed performance levels between

those of Groups 'Posterior' and 'Anterior' on both tasks.

According to the Extended PMFC model, the area of VVS critical for a given visual discrimination task depends on the level of complexity of conjunctive representations required to disambiguate the stimuli used in that task. If animals are required to discriminate simple patterns possessing simple conjunctions of few visual features – as in the Pattern Relearning task – the conjunctive representations in posterior regions are critical for good performance. Conversely, if they must discriminate complex objects possessing complex conjunctions of many visual features – as in the Concurrent Object Discrimination task – representations in anterior regions are needed to solve the task efficiently.

Extended PMFC Model: Predictions of Continuous Cognitive Function

We claim that, in the Extended PMFC model, cognitive function in the ventral visual stream and perirhinal cortex is continuous: progression through successive stations in VVS should reveal a gradual change in the functional contribution of brain regions, rather than a sharp boundary where perceptual function ends and mnemonic function begins. However, the simulation results in Figure 6 seem to indicate that the 'continuous' model of cognition in fact gives rise to modular cognitive function. After all, the results display a double dissociation, just like the one observed in the monkey data. This counterintuitive result is exactly what the model was designed to demonstrate: the data look as though they have emerged from a modular underlying system, but they have not. The model therefore suggests that the same may be true in the brain. Others have remarked on the difficulties inherent in the interpretation of double dissociations. For example, Shallice (1988) cautions that "If modules exist, then double dissociations can reveal them. However, finding double dissociations is no guarantee that modules exist". This property of the Extended PMFC model echoes Plaut (1995), who simulated a double dissociation between concrete and abstract word reading in dyslexia, using a single-system connectionist model in which functional specialization arises without an assumption of modularity.

However, to demonstrate explicitly the continuous nature of the account, we report a further simulation. The specific claim is that the degree of discrimination impairment caused by a lesion in VVS should reflect the extent to which the to-be-discriminated stimuli are optimally represented in the brain region that is lesioned. Therefore, in this simulation, networks were trained to discriminate stimuli of complexity intermediate between those in the Simple Pattern and Concurrent Discrimination tasks of Iwai and Mishkin. In the spectrum of complexity that we defined, intermediate stimuli possessed three features. We therefore expected the greatest discrimination impairment to occur for networks with a lesion of the middle layer, where stimuli with three features are best represented. It can be seen from the bottom panel of Figure 6 that the model indeed predicted a deficit – for Layer 2 lesioned networks – in the concurrent acquisition of eight pairwise discriminations between stimuli of intermediate complexity. This simulation demonstrated explicitly the prediction that a lesion in any point of the VVS should cause impairments in visual discrimination learning, if the to-be-discriminated stimuli are at a level of complexity best represented by neurons in the lesioned region.

Extended PMFC Model: Testing the Predictions in Human Subjects

In order to find empirical data in humans that speak to the foregoing predictions of the Extended PMFC model, we need to look for studies that tested human patients with damage in both posterior and anterior lesions in the ventral visual-perirhinal stream. Although there are currently no human studies in which the effects of both anterior and

posterior lesions were examined and two tasks were administered to both groups – as in Iwai and Mishkin (1968) – there do exist some data that hint at how the results of such a study would look. First, an investigation of the effect of anterior VVS lesions on complex visual discriminations was reported by Barense et al. (2005), as described above, and, second, patients with posterior VVS lesions were tested on simple visual discriminations by Rosenthal & Behrmann (2006).

The 'Concurrent Discrimination' task of Iwai and Mishkin can be thought of as equivalent to the 'Maximum' or 'Intermediate' feature ambiguity conditions of Barense et al. (2005). This is because, as demonstrated in the original PMFC model, asking subjects to learn concurrently to discriminate between several pairs of complex stimuli introduces feature ambiguity into the discrimination problem (the "set size" effect). As we saw in Barense et al. (2005), patients with damage to perirhinal cortex were impaired on such visual discriminations, in line with the extended PMFC model's account.

Rosenthal & Behrmann (2006) used a visual discrimination learning task with simple stimuli to test a patient, JW, who has an extensive bilateral lesion of V2 and no evidence of damage in more anterior VVS. The patient JW and age-matched controls were trained to discriminate between three classes of visual stimulus, with feedback. Stimuli from all categories were composed of a pair of white stripes on a grey background. The three categories differed only in the width of the white stripes, being either narrow (category A), intermediate (category B), or wide (category C). Thus, the stimuli were simple but they shared many perceptual properties, making their category membership highly ambiguous. According to the extended PMFC model, the resolution of a discrimination task such as this should require representations of simple feature conjunctions in posterior VVS. In line with the model, JW was impaired in the acquisition of this discrimination, requiring many sessions of learning to attain good discrimination performance, in contrast to controls who acquired the discrimination in one training session. This study indicates that, in human subjects just as in non-human primates, damage to early stations in VVS causes impairments in the classification of simple visual stimuli.

Thus the PMFC model and its extension suggest that, rather than there being a functional distinction between more anterior regions in MTL and more posterior regions in VVS, these two regions perform a very similar function, but operate on stimulus representations at a different level of complexity. In this account, all regions in the ventral visual-perirhinal stream contribute to visual discrimination whenever the representations needed to perform the discrimination are housed there. Simulations from the PMFC model and its extension have helped to make the case for this hypothesis. However, so far we have only considered data from visual discrimination studies. As discussed above, it is well-established that perirhinal cortex plays a critical role in object recognition memory. If we are to claim that the VVS and perirhinal cortex have truly shared functional roles, and that the anatomical and functional distinction between visual perception and visual memory is a false one, we must show that the computational framework can account for recognition memory data, too.

A Model of Object Recognition Memory in Perirhinal Cortex

Expanding our problem space to encompass object recognition memory involves asking whether the feature ambiguity hypothesis can explain the classic finding that this function is impaired by perirhinal cortex lesions. In order to investigate this possibility computationally, we require a model that can simulate object familiarity, the cognitive index upon which object recognition memory is presumed to depend. The original PMFC model (Bussey & L. M. Saksida, 2002) possessed only static representations of stimuli,

which were associated with reward during training in the service of visual discrimination. However, a familiarity mechanism necessitates the use of flexible representations, which can develop from a novel to a familiar state during exposure to the stimulus. We therefore adapted the original model, retaining the same representational-hierarchical paradigm, but allowing for familiarity to develop through tuning of the stimulus representations with experience (Cowell et al., 2006). A stimulus representation becomes sharper as that stimulus is presented to – and repeatedly sampled by – the network, and the sharpness of the representation is used as the basis of familiarity judgments (as in Norman & O'Reilly, 2003).

Using this model, we simulated several empirical results (Cowell et al., 2006), including the canonical finding that impairments following damage to perirhinal cortex are exacerbated by lengthening the delay between presentation of to-be-remembered items and test (Figure 7). The mechanism in the model for this delay-dependent deficit is as follows. When a subject is presented with a complex object in the study or "sample" phase of the task, the object becomes familiar and its representation sharpened over the course of the sample period. Following the sample phase, there is a delay before testing the subject's recognition memory. We assume that, during the delay, the subject perceives many visual stimuli, both real and imagined; these stimuli are presented briefly to the model. We also assume that commonly encountered objects share simple features such as lines, shapes and colours, and so these features will occur repeatedly and become highly familiar. Then, during the test or "choice" phase of the task – in which the subject must indicate which of two objects is novel and which is familiar – many features possessed by the novel object will be familiar from experience with other objects during the delay. As a result, these individual features – represented in the "caudal" layer of the model, corresponding to posterior VVS – will not be useful for discriminating the novel from

Figure 7. Simulation of object recognition memory using the connectionist network of Cowell et al. (2006). The longer the simulated delay, the greater the impairment of networks lacking a perirhinal cortex layer, relative to control networks which possessed an intact perirhinal cortex layer. Modified from Cowell et al. (2006)

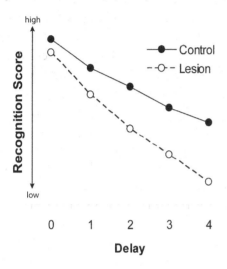

the familiar object. In other words, there is feature ambiguity in the discrimination of the novel and familiar objects. In contrast, the conjunctive representations in perirhinal cortex remain useful following the delay. This is because perirhinal cortex houses complex conjunctive representations that are unique to each object. These complex representations can be used by the subject in the choice phase, because even if all of the features of the novel object have been experienced during the delay, the specific, unique conjunction of features that constitutes the novel object has not. Therefore the novel object can be discriminated from the familiar object, despite the fact that many or all of its features are familiar. Thus, the model suggests that the role of perirhinal cortex in object recognition is the same as its role in visual discrimination: in object recognition, an intact animal uses object-level representations in perirhinal cortex to resolve feature ambiguity. A subject with a damaged perirhinal cortex must rely

only on spared representations in earlier regions of the VVS to try to judge which object is novel. As the delay increases, a greater number of commonly occurring features are encountered and a greater degree of feature ambiguity arises (much like the set size effect in visual discriminations), producing larger impairments in recognition memory.

The adapted computational model not only accounts for the canonical findings in object recognition memory, it also generates some novel predictions. For example, the model predicts that if object recognition is tested with no delay between study and test, but the novel and familiar objects are made more perceptually similar, animals with perirhinal lesions will be impaired. Since there is essentially no memory load in this task when there is zero delay, such a result would be a demonstration of a perceptual impairment in a classic "memory" experimental paradigm. Another prediction the model makes is that a "configural" version of the object recognition task – created by constructing a novel stimulus in which all features are familiar but the conjunction of them is novel – will lead to recognition impairments in subjects with perirhinal cortex damage.

We tested these novel predictions in rats (Bartko, Winters, Cowell, Saksida, & Bussey, 2007a, 2007b). To do so, we used a Y-apparatus for testing rats on the standard spontaneous object recognition task, to mitigate spatial confounds (Forwood, Winters, & Bussey, 2005; Winters, Forwood, Cowell, Saksida, & Bussey, 2004). A modification of this apparatus allowed us to present the choice objects immediately after the sample objects, that is, with almost no delay (Figure 8). This procedure corresponds to the immediate delay condition used in delayed matching- and non-matching-to-sample tasks in monkeys, thought to reflect perceptual rather than mnemonic function (Buffalo et al., 1999; Eacott et al., 1994). Using this procedure, we found that rats with lesions in perirhinal cortex were impaired relative to controls when the novel and familiar stimuli presented in the choice phase were highly perceptually similar,

Figure 8. Apparatus used in the 'zero-delay' spontaneous object recognition task of Bartko et al., (2007a). All objects are placed in the Y-shaped maze before the trial begins. At the start of the object recognition trial, the rat is placed in the maze and released from the start box (at left) by raising the guillotine door, depicted here raised. In the sample phase, the rat explores two identical copies of the 'sample' object. At the end of the sample phase, the sample objects are removed, along with the inner pair of walls, allowing the rat to proceed immediately to the choice phase. In the choice phase, the rat explores a third copy of the now familiar sample object, in one arm of the maze, and a novel object, in the other arm. Healthy rats will show a preference for exploring the novel object, indicating recognition memory for the familiar object. Modified from Bartko et al. (2007a)

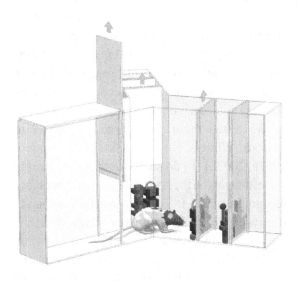

but not when the novel and familiar stimuli had low similarity. Next, we developed a version of the spontaneous object recognition task that allowed us to test rats on a configural object recognition task (Bartko et al., 2007b), structured similarly to the "maximum feature ambiguity" condition of the visual discrimination task of Bussey et al. (2002). In this experiment, we used two sample phases, one after the other, followed by a choice phase. All stimuli were a compound of two stimulus features; here, we represent each feature by a letter and each object by a pair of letters. In each sample phase, a compound stimulus – either BC or AD – was presented. Both of these compound stimuli thus became familiar. A third compound, AB, was presented as the novel stimulus in the choice phase, to be discriminated from one of the familiar sample objects. Thus, the novel stimulus in this case was simply a novel recombination of features that were present in the sample stimuli. This meant that all of the features (A, B, C, and D) appearing in the novel and familiar stimuli of the choice phase were familiar. Therefore, the novel stimulus could not be identified using feature representations alone; only the conjunction of features, AB, was novel. As predicted by the model, rats with perirhinal cortex lesions were impaired in the configural condition, but performed no differently from controls when the novel stimulus could be determined on the basis of simple features. These data support the model's suggestion that perirhinal cortex is critical for resolving feature ambiguity not only in visual discrimination tasks, but also in object recognition.

Thus far, we have used the computational framework to make three important demonstrations. First, it has provided an account of cognitive processing in perirhinal cortex that can explain a series of puzzling results from visual discrimination studies (Bussey and Saksida, 2002); second, the model has enabled us to demonstrate that the cognitive mechanisms underlying visual discrimination in perirhinal cortex may also underlie visual discrimination in posterior VVS (Cowell et al., in press); and third, the framework has demonstrated that the contribution of perirhinal cortex to visual discrimination may depend on the same mechanism as its well-established role in object recognition memory (Cowell et al., 2006). That is, we began with a constrained problem space: the model addressed only visual discrimination learning and only in perirhinal cortex. We first expanded the problem space in terms of brain regions, to deal with visual discrimination learning in not only in perirhinal cortex but also in VVS. Then, we expanded the problem space in terms of cognitive paradigms, to deal with object recognition memory in perirhinal cortex. By providing a common theoretical framework to address these different problems, the model has allowed us to argue for a unified account of cognition in these brain regions.

FUTURE RESEARCH DIRECTIONS

Having extended the model in a posterior direction, and adapted it to simulate object recognition memory, an obvious next step in developing and testing this computational framework would be to address object recognition memory in posterior VVS. The overarching theoretical approach claims that a brain region may contribute to any cognitive function that requires the representations housed in that region. According to this view, representations in posterior VVS may be critical not just for visual discrimination – as is widely accepted – but also for recognition memory. Interestingly, López-Aranda et al. (2009) have recently demonstrated the involvement of area V2 in extrastriate visual cortex in recognition memory. As argued by Saksida (2009), this finding is consistent with the representational-hierarchical view, rather than the modular approach. Determining the exact nature of the contribution of posterior brain regions, such as V2, to recognition memory is a direction for future research.

More generally, we hope that future research in the field of cognitive neuroscience will benefit from the use of explicit computational models like those described in this chapter. Of course, the use of computational models in neuroscience is widespread already. But we have two specific

recommendations: first, that such models should be used more widely in *cognitive* neuroscience, by experimental researchers; and second, that the models thus used should be pitched at an appropriate level, such that they have explanatory power, yet are simple and clear enough to be understood by researchers with areas of expertise not centred on computational modeling. We recommend this because models in cognitive neuroscience are perhaps at their most useful when situated at the interface of multiple scientific disciplines, where they can exert a real influence on the work of researchers who necessarily spend much of their time immersed in the techniques and literature of behavioural neuroscience, cognitive psychology, human neuropsychology, neurophysiology, anatomy, or any combination of these. Essentially, for a model in cognitive neuroscience to be useful, it needs to speak to cognitive neuroscientists sufficiently clearly that it drives experimental research. We believe that the computational framework expounded in this chapter provides a good example of such a model. It has certainly driven a large body of experimental work, including studies in rodents (Gilbert & Kesner, 2003; G. Norman & Eacott, 2004), monkeys (Baker et al., 2002) and humans (Barense, Gaffan, & Graham, 2007; Devlin & C.J., 2007; Hartley et al., 2007; A.C. Lee, Bandelow et al., 2006; 2006; 2007; 2008; Levy et al., 2005; Moss, Rodd, Stamatakis, Bright, & Tyler, 2005; Preston & Gabrieli, 2008; Shrager et al., 2006; Stark & Squire, 2000; Tyler et al., 2004; van Strien, Scholte, & Witter, 2008). This list of studies includes tasks such as visual discrimination, recognition memory, "oddity tasks", scene perception, and categorization, and employs techniques as diverse as animal neuropsychology, fMRI, electrophysiology and human cognitive neuropsychology. The model has also been reviewed in a number of recent articles on the present topic (Baxter, 2009; Hampton, 2005; Squire et al., 2004; Suzuki, 2009; Suzuki & Baxter,

2009). While the 'representational-hierarchical' view remains controversial, and whether its account of cognitive function ultimately turns out to be correct, it is clear that the model has played an important part in recent advances in our understanding of visual cognition in the temporal lobe.

CONCLUSION

We have presented a computational framework for understanding cognitive processing in the ventral visual-perirhinal stream. While the model has three different instantiations, all three emerge from a common computational framework, which assumes a continuous hierarchy of object representations and uses those representations to resolve feature ambiguity in visual tasks. The account was first established as a simple model that resolved a puzzle over the role perirhinal cortex in visual discrimination learning. Subsequently, the model was extended in a posterior direction to demonstrate that the idea of a continuous representational hierarchy is useful for understanding brain function in the whole of VVS and not just in perirhinal cortex. Finally, we showed that the idea of a continuous hierarchy of representations can be extended to account for empirical data from a different cognitive paradigm: object recognition memory.

In sum, we have demonstrated that computational modeling can be an extremely useful tool for cognitive neuroscientists. However, we argue that for theorizing in cognitive neuroscience, models should be kept simple, in order to make clear the mechanism and assumptions driving the trends that emerge in the simulation results. When a model is formulated thus, it becomes accessible to a wide and multi-disciplinary audience, within which it can facilitate discussion, encourage theorists to clarify opposing positions, and drive experimental research. We hope that the work reviewed in this chapter has achieved these aims.

REFERENCES

Baker, C. I., Behrmann, M., & Olson, C. R. (2002). Impact of learning on representation of parts and wholes in monkey inferotemporal cortex. *Nature Neuroscience, 5*, 1210–1216.doi:10.1038/nn960

Barense, M. D., Bussey, T. J., Lee, A. C., Rogers, T. T., Davies, R. R., & Saksida, L. M. (2005). Functional specialization in the human medial temporal lobe. *The Journal of Neuroscience, 25*(44), 10239–10246.doi:10.1523/JNEUROSCI.2704-05.2005

Barense, M. D., Bussey, T. J., Lee, A. C. H., Rogers, T. T., Davies, R. R., & Saksida, L. M. (2005). Functional specialization in the human medial temporal lobe. *The Journal of Neuroscience, 25*, 10239–10246.doi:10.1523/JNEUROSCI.2704-05.2005

Barense, M. D., Gaffan, D., & Graham, K. S. (2007). The human medial temporal lobe processes online representations of complex objects. *Neuropsychologia, 45*(13), 2963–2974.doi:10.1016/j.neuropsychologia.2007.05.023

Bartko, S. J., Winters, B. D., Cowell, R. A., Saksida, L. M., & Bussey, T. J. (2007a). Perceptual functions of perirhinal cortex in rats: zero-delay object recognition and simultaneous oddity discriminations. *The Journal of Neuroscience, 27*(10), 2548–2559.doi:10.1523/JNEUROSCI.5171-06.2007

Bartko, S. J., Winters, B. D., Cowell, R. A., Saksida, L. M., & Bussey, T. J. (2007b). Perirhinal cortex resolves feature ambiguity in configural object recognition and perceptual oddity tasks. *Learning & Memory (Cold Spring Harbor, N.Y.), 14*(12), 821–832.doi:10.1101/lm.749207

Baxter, M. G. (2009). Involvement of medial temporal lobe structures in memory and perception. *Neuron, 61*(5), 667–677.doi:10.1016/j.neuron.2009.02.007

Blake, L., Jarvis, C. D., & Mishkin, M. (1977). Pattern discrimination thresholds after partial inferior temporal of lateral striate lesions in monkeys. *Brain Research, 120*, 209–220. doi:10.1016/0006-8993(77)90901-5

Buckley, M. J. (2005). The role of the medial temporal lobe in memory and perception: evidence from rats, nonhuman primates and humans. *Quarterly Journal of Experimental Psychology, 58B*, 246–268.

Buckley, M. J., & Gaffan, D. (1997). Impairment of visual object-discrimination learning after perirhinal cortex ablation. *Behavioral Neuroscience, 111*, 467–475. doi:10.1037/0735-7044.111.3.467

Buckley, M. J., & Gaffan, D. (1998a). Perirhinal cortex ablation impairs configural learning and paired-associate learning equally. *Neuropsychologia, 36*, 535–546. doi:10.1016/S0028-3932(97)00120-6

Buckley, M. J., & Gaffan, D. (1998b). Perirhinal cortex ablation impairs visual object identification. *The Journal of Neuroscience, 18*, 2268–2275.

Buffalo, E. A., Ramus, S. J., Clark, R. E., Teng, E., Squire, L. R., & Zola, S. M. (1999). Dissociation between the effects of damage to perirhinal cortex and area TE. *Learning & Memory (Cold Spring Harbor, N.Y.), 6*, 572–599. doi:10.1101/lm.6.6.572

Buffalo, E. A., Ramus, S. J., Squire, L. R., & Zola, S. M. (2000). Perception and recognition memory in monkeys following lesions of area TE and perirhinal cortex. *Learning & Memory (Cold Spring Harbor, N.Y.), 7*(6), 375–382. doi:10.1101/lm.32100

Buffalo, E. A., Reber, P. J., & Squire, L. R. (1998). The human perirhinal cortex and recognition memory. *Hippocampus, 8*, 330–339. doi:10.1002/(SICI)1098-1063(1998)8:4<330::AID-HIPO3>3.0.CO;2-L

Bussey, T. J. (2004). Multiple memory systems: Fact or fiction? *Quarterly Journal of Experimental Psychology, 57*, 89–94.

Bussey, T. J., & Saksida, L. M. (2002). The organization of visual object representations: a connectionist model of effects of lesions in perirhinal cortex. *The European Journal of Neuroscience, 15*(2), 355–364. doi:10.1046/j.0953-816x.2001.01850.x

Bussey, T. J., & Saksida, L. M. (2002). The organization of visual object representations: A connectionist model of effects of lesions in perirhinal cortex. *The European Journal of Neuroscience, 15*, 355–364. doi:10.1046/j.0953-816x.2001.01850.x

Bussey, T. J., & Saksida, L. M. (2005). Object memory and perception in the medial temporal lobe: An alternative approach. *Current Opinion in Neurobiology, 15*, 730–737. doi:10.1016/j.conb.2005.10.014

Bussey, T. J., & Saksida, L. M. (2007). Memory, perception, and the ventral visual-perirhinal-hippocampal stream: thinking outside of the boxes. *Hippocampus, 17*(9), 898–908. doi:10.1002/hipo.20320

Bussey, T. J., Saksida, L. M., & Murray, E. A. (2002). Perirhinal cortex resolves feature ambiguity in complex visual discriminations. *The European Journal of Neuroscience, 15*, 365–374. doi:10.1046/j.0953-816x.2001.01851.x

Bussey, T. J., Saksida, L. M., & Murray, E. A. (2003). Impairments in visual discrimination after perirhinal cortex lesions: Testing 'declarative' versus 'perceptual-mnemonic' views of perirhinal cortex function. *The European Journal of Neuroscience, 17*, 649–660. doi:10.1046/j.1460-9568.2003.02475.x

Bussey, T. J., Saksida, L. M., & Murray, E. A. (2005). The PMFC model of perirhinal cortex function. *Quarterly Journal of Experimental Psychology, 58B*, 269–282.

Butter, C. M. (1972). Detection of Masked Patterns in Monkeys with Inferotemporal, Striate or Dorsolateral Frontal Lesions. *Neuropsychologia, 10*, 241–243. doi:10.1016/0028-3932(72)90066-8

Churchland, P. S., & Sejnowski, T. J. (1988). Perspectives on Cognitive Neuroscience. *Science, 242*(4879), 741–745. doi:10.1126/science.3055294

Churchland, P. S., & Sejnowski, T. J. (1992). *The Computational Brain*. Cambridge: MIT Press.

Cowell, R. A. (2006). *Modelling the effects of damage to perirhinal cortex and ventral visual stream on visual cognition*. Unpublished dissertation, University of Oxford, UK.

Cowell, R. A., Bussey, T. J., & Saksida, L. M. (2006). Why does brain damage impair memory? A connectionist model of object recognition memory in perirhinal cortex. *The Journal of Neuroscience, 26*(47), 12186–12197. doi:10.1523/JNEUROSCI.2818-06.2006

Cowell, R. A., Bussey, T. J., & Saksida, L. M. (2010). Functional dissociations within the ventral object processing pathway: cognitive modules or a hierarchical continuum? *Journal of Cognitive Neuroscience, 22*(11), 2460–2479. doi:10.1162/jocn.2009.21373

Cowey, A., & Gross, C. G. (1970). Effects of foveal prestriate and inferotemporal lesions on visual discrimination by rhesus monkeys. *Experimental Brain Research, 11*(2), 128–144. doi:10.1007/BF00234318

Dean, P. (1974). Choice reaction times for pattern discriminations in monkeys with inferotemporal lesions. *Neuropsychologia, 12*, 465–476. doi:10.1016/0028-3932(74)90076-1

Devlin, J. T., & C.J., P. (2007). Perirhinal contributions to human visual perception. *Current Biology, 17*(17), 1484–1488. doi:10.1016/j.cub.2007.07.066

Dickinson, A. (1980). *Contemporary animal learning theory* (1st ed.). Cambridge: Cambridge University Press.

Eacott, M. J., Gaffan, D., & Murray, E. A. (1994). Preserved recognition memory for small sets, and impaired stimulus identification for large sets, following rhinal cortex ablations in monkeys. *The European Journal of Neuroscience, 6*, 1466–1478. doi:10.1111/j.1460-9568.1994.tb01008.x

Eacott, M. J., & Gaffan, E. A. (2005). The roles of the perirhinal cortex, postrhinal cortex, and the fornix in memory for objects, contexts, and events in the rat. *Qaurterly Journal of Experimental Psychology, 58B*, 202–217. doi:10.1080/02724990444000203

Forwood, S. E., Winters, B. D., & Bussey, T. J. (2005). Hippocampal lesions that abolish spatial maze performance spare object recognition memory at delays of up to 48 hours. *Hippocampus, 15*, 347–355. doi:10.1002/hipo.20059

Fuster, J. (2003). *Cortex and Mind*. Oxford: Oxford university Press.

Gaffan, D. (2002). Against memory systems. *Philosophical Transactions of the Royal Society of London. Series B, Biological Sciences, 357*, 1111–1121. doi:10.1098/rstb.2002.1110

Gaffan, D., & Murray, E. A. (1992). Monkeys (*Macaca fascicularis*) with rhinal cortex ablations succeed in object discrimination learning despite 24-hr intertrial intervals and fail at matching to sample despite double sample presentations. *Behavioral Neuroscience, 106*, 30–38. doi:10.1037/0735-7044.106.1.30

Gilbert, P. E., & Kesner, R. P. (2003). Recognition memory for complex visual discriminations is influenced by stimulus interference in rodents with perirhinal cortex damage. *Learning & Memory (Cold Spring Harbor, N.Y.), 10*(6), 525–530. doi:10.1101/lm.64503

Goulet, S., & Murray, E. A. (2001). Neural substrates of crossmodal association memory in monkeys: the amygdala versus the anterior rhinal cortex. *Behavioral Neuroscience, 115*(2), 271–284.doi:10.1037/0735-7044.115.2.271

Gross, C. G., Cowey, A., & Manning, F. J. (1971). Further analysis of visual discrimination deficits following foveal prestriate and inferotemporal lesions in rhesus monkeys. *Journal of Comparative and Physiological Psychology, 76*(1), 1–7. doi:10.1037/h0031039

Hampton, R. R. (2005). Monkey perirhinal cortex is critical for visual memory, but not for visual perception: Re-examination of the behavioural evidence from monkeys. *Quarterly Journal of Experimental Psychology, 58B*, 283–299.

Hartley, T., Bird, C. M., Chan, D., Cipolotti, L., Husain, M., & Vargha-Khadem, F. (2007). The hippocampus is required for short-term topographical memory in humans. *Hippocampus, 17*(1), 34–48. doi:10.1002/hipo.20240

Holdstock, J. S., Shaw, C., & Aggleton, J. P. (1995). The performance of amnesic subjects on tests of delayed matching-to-sample and delayed matching-to-position. *Neuropsychologia, 33*(12), 1583–1596.doi:10.1016/0028-3932(95)00145-X

Iversen, S. D., & Humphrey, N. K. (1971). Ventral temporal lobe lesions and visual oddity performance. *Brain Research, 30*(2), 253–263. doi:10.1016/0006-8993(71)90077-1

Iwai, E., & Mishkin, M. (1968). Two visual foci in the temporal lobe of monkeys. In Yoshii, N., & Buchwald, N. (Eds.), *Neurophysiological basis of learning and behavior* (pp. 1–11). Japan: Osaka University Press.

Kikuchi, R., & Iwai, E. (1980). The locus of the posterior subdivision of the inferotemporal visual learning area in the monkey. *Brain Research, 198*(2), 347–360.doi:10.1016/0006-8993(80)90749-0

Lee, A. C., Bandelow, S., Schwarzbauer, C., Henson, R. N., & Graham, K. S. (2006). Perirhinal cortex activity during visual object discrimination: an event-related fMRI study. *NeuroImage, 33*(1), 362–373.doi:10.1016/j.neuroimage.2006.06.021

Lee, A. C., Buckley, M. J., Gaffan, D., Emery, T., Hodges, J. R., & Graham, K. S. (2006). Differentiating the roles of the hippocampus and perirhinal cortex in processes beyond long-term declarative memory: a double dissociation in dementia. *The Journal of Neuroscience, 26*(19), 5198–5203. doi:10.1523/JNEUROSCI.3157-05.2006

Lee, A. C., Buckley, M. J., Pegman, S. J., Spiers, H., Scahill, V. L., & Gaffan, D. (2005). Specialization in the medial temporal lobe for processing of objects and scenes. *Hippocampus, 15*(6), 782–797. doi:10.1002/hipo.20101

Lee, A. C., Levi, N., Davies, R. R., Hodges, J. R., & Graham, K. S. (2007). Differing profiles of face and scene discrimination deficits in semantic dementia and Alzheimer's disease. *Neuropsychologia, 45*(9), 2135–2146.doi:10.1016/j. neuropsychologia.2007.01.010

Lee, A. C., Scahill, V. L., & Graham, K. S. (2008). Activating the medial temporal lobe during oddity judgment for faces and scenes. *Cerebral Cortex, 18*(3), 683–696.doi:10.1093/cercor/bhm104

Levy, D. A., Shrager, Y., & Squire, L. R. (2005). Intact visual discrimination of complex and feature-ambiguous stimuli in the absence of perirhinal cortex. *Learning & Memory (Cold Spring Harbor, N.Y.), 12*(1), 61–66.doi:10.1101/lm.84405

Mackintosh, N. J. (1974). *The psychology of animal learning*. London: Academic Press.

Manning, F. J. (1971a). Punishment for errors and visual-discrimination learning by monkeys with inferotemporal cortex lesions. *Journal of Comparative and Physiological Psychology, 75*(1), 146–152.doi:10.1037/h0030675

Manning, F. J. (1971b). The selective attention "deficit" of monkeys with ablations of foveal prestriate cortex. *Psychonomic Science, 25*(5), 291–292.

Manns, J. R., Stark, C. E., & Squire, L. R. (2000). The visual paired-comparison task as a measure of declarative memory. *Proceedings of the National Academy of Sciences of the United States of America, 97*(22), 12375–12379.doi:10.1073/pnas.220398097

Marr, D., & Poggio, T. (1977). From understanding computation to understanding neural circuitry. *Neurosciences Research Program Bulletin, 15*, 470–488.

McClelland, J. L., & Rumelhart, D. E. (Eds.). (1986). *Parallel Distributed Processing: Explorations in the Microstructure of Cognition* (*Vol. 2*). Cambridge, MA: MIT Press.

Meunier, M., Bachevalier, J., Mishkin, M., & Murray, E. A. (1993). Effects on visual recognition of combined and separate ablations of the entorhinal and perirhinal cortex in rhesus monkeys. *The Journal of Neuroscience, 13*, 5418–5432.

Mishkin, M. (1982). A memory system in the monkey. [Biology]. *Philosophical Transactions of the Royal Society of London, 298*, 83–95. doi:10.1098/rstb.1982.0074

Moss, H. E., Rodd, J. M., Stamatakis, E. A., Bright, P., & Tyler, L. K. (2005). Anteromedial temporal cortex supports fine-grained differentiation among objects. *Cereb Cortex, 15*(5), 616–627. doi:10.1093/cercor/bhh163

Mumby, D. G., & Pinel, J. P. (1994). Rhinal cortex lesions and object recognition in rats. *Behavioral Neuroscience, 108*(1), 11–18.doi:10.1037/0735-7044.108.1.11

Murray, E. A. (2000). Memory for objects in nonhuman primates. In Gazzaniga, M. S. (Ed.), *The new cognitive neurosciences*. London: The MIT Press.

Murray, E. A., & Bussey, T. J. (1999). Perceptual-mnemonic functions of perirhinal cortex. *Trends in Cognitive Sciences, 3*, 142–151.doi:10.1016/S1364-6613(99)01303-0

Murray, E. A., Málková, L., & Goulet, S. (1998). Crossmodal associations, intramodal associations, and object identification in macaque monkeys. In Milner, A. D. (Ed.), *Comparative Neuropsychology* (pp. 51–69). Oxford: Oxford University Press.

Norman, G., & Eacott, M. J. (2004). Impaired object recognition with increasing levels of feature ambiguity in rats with perirhinal cortex lesions. *Behavioural Brain Research, 148*(1-2), 79–91. doi:10.1016/S0166-4328(03)00176-1

Norman, K. A., & O'Reilly, R. C. (2003). Modeling hippocampal and neocortical contributions to recognition memory: a complementary-learning-systems approach. *Psychological Review, 110*(4), 611–646.doi:10.1037/0033-295X.110.4.611

O'Reilly, R. C. (1998). Six Principles for Biological Based Computational Models of Cortical Cognition. *Trends in Cognitive Sciences, 2*(11), 455–462.doi:10.1016/S1364-6613(98)01241-8

Osterrieth, P. (1944). Filetest de copie d'une figure complex: Contribution a l'etude de la perception et de la memoire [The test of copying a complex figure: A contribution to the study of perception and memory]. *Archives de Psychologie, 30*, 286–356.

Palmeri, T. J., & Gauthier, I. (2004). Visual Object Understanding. Nature Reviews. *Neuroscience, 5*, 291–304.doi:10.1038/nrn1364

Plaut, D. C. (1995). Double dissociation without modularity: evidence from connectionist neuropsychology. *Journal of Clinical and Experimental Neuropsychology, 17*, 291–321. doi:10.1080/01688639508405124

Popper, K. (1999). *All Life is Problem Solving*. London: Routledge.

Preston, A. R., & Gabrieli, J. D. (2008). Dissociation between explicit memory and configural memory in the human medial temporal lobe. *Cerebral Cortex, 18*(9), 2192–2207. doi:10.1093/cercor/bhm245

Rolls, E. T., & Deco, G. (2002). *Computational Neuroscience of Vision.* New York: Oxford University Press Inc.

Rosenthal, O., & Behrmann, M. (2006). Acquiring long-term representations of visual classes following extensive extrastriate damage. *Neuropsychologia, 44*(5), 799–815. doi:10.1016/j.neuropsychologia.2005.07.010

Rumelhart, D. E., & McClelland, J. L. (Eds.). (1986). *Parallel Distributed Processing: Explorations in the Microstructure of Cognition* (*Vol. 1*). Cambridge, MA: MIT Press.

Sakai, S., & Miyashita, Y. (1993). Memory and imagery in the temporal lobe. *Current Opinion in Neurobiology, 3,* 166–170. doi:10.1016/0959-4388(93)90205-D

Saksida, L. M. (2009). Remembering Outside the Box. *Science, 325*(5936), 40–41. doi:10.1126/science.1177156

Saksida, L. M., & Bussey, T. J. (2010). The Representational-Hierarchical View of Amnesia: Translation from Animal to Human. *Neuropsychologia, 48*(8), 2370–2384. doi:10.1016/j.neuropsychologia.2010.02.026

Scoville, W. B., & Milner, B. (1957). Loss of recent memory after bilateral hippocampal lesions. *Journal of Neurology, Neurosurgery, and Psychiatry, 20,* 11–21. doi:10.1136/jnnp.20.1.11

Sejnowski, T. J., Koch, C., & Churchland, P. S. (1988). Computational Neuroscience. *Science, 241*(4871), 1299–1306. doi:10.1126/science.3045969

Shallice, T. (1988). *From neuropsychology to mental structure.* New York: Cambridge University Press.

Shrager, Y., Gold, J. J., Hopkins, R. O., & Squire, L. R. (2006). Intact visual perception in memory-impaired patients with medial temporal lobe lesions. *The Journal of Neuroscience, 26*(8), 2235–2240. doi:10.1523/JNEUROSCI.4792-05.2006

Squire, L. R., Stark, C. E., & Clark, R. E. (2004). The medial temporal lobe. *Annual Review of Neuroscience, 27,* 279–306. doi:10.1146/annurev.neuro.27.070203.144130

Squire, L. R., & Zola-Morgan, S. (1983). The neurology of memory: The case for correspondence between the findings for human and nonhuman primate. In *The physiological basis of memory* (pp. 199–267). Academic Press.

Squire, L. R., & Zola-Morgan, S. M. (1991). The medial temporal lobe memory system. *Science, 253,* 1380–1386. doi:10.1126/science.1896849

Stark, C. E., & Squire, L. R. (2000). Intact visual perceptual discrimination in humans in the absence of perirhinal cortex. *Learning & Memory (Cold Spring Harbor, N.Y.), 7*(5), 273–278. doi:10.1101/lm.35000

Suzuki, W. A. (2009). Perception and the medial temporal lobe: evaluating the current evidence. *Neuron, 61*(5), 657–666. doi:10.1016/j.neuron.2009.02.008

Suzuki, W. A., & Baxter, M. G. (2009). Memory, perception, and the medial temporal lobe: a synthesis of opinions. *Neuron, 61*(5), 678–679. doi:10.1016/j.neuron.2009.02.009

Suzuki, W. A., Zola-Morgan, S., Squire, L. R., & Amaral, D. G. (1993). Lesions of the perirhinal and parahippocampal cortices in the monkey produce long-lasting memory impairment in the visual and tactual modalities. *The Journal of Neuroscience, 13,* 2430–2451.

Tanaka, K., Saito, H., Fukada, Y., & Moriya, M. (1991). Coding Visual Images of Objects in the Inferotemporal Cortex of the Macaque Monkey. *Journal of Neurophysiology, 66*(1), 170–189.

Tulving, E., & Schacter, D. L. (1990). Priming and human memory systems. *Science, 247*(4940), 301–306.doi:10.1126/science.2296719

Tyler, L. K., Stamatakis, E. A., Bright, P., Acres, K.,Abdallah, S., & Rodd, J. M. (2004). Processing objects at different levels of specificity. *Journal of Cognitive Neuroscience, 16*(3), 351–362. doi:10.1162/089892904322926692

Ullman, S., Vidal-Naquet, M., & Sali, E. (2002). Visual features of intermediate complexity and their use in classification. *Nature Neuroscience, 5*(7), 682–687.

van Strien, N. M., Scholte, H. S., & Witter, M. P. (2008). Activation of the human medial temporal lobes by stereoscopic depth cues. *NeuroImage, 40*(4), 1815–1823.doi:10.1016/j.neuroimage.2008.01.046

Warrington, E., & James, M. (1991). *The Visual Object and Space Perception Battery*. Bury St Edmunds, UK: Thames Valley Test Company.

Warrington, E. K., & Weiskrantz, L. (1968). New method of testing long-term retention with special reference to amnesic patients. *Nature, 217*(132), 972–974.doi:10.1038/217972a0

Wilson, M., & Kaufman, H. M. (1969). Effect of inferotemporal lesions upon processing of visual infomation in monkeys. *Journal of Comparative and Physiological Psychology, 69*(1), 44–48. doi:10.1037/h0027923

Wilson, M., Zieler, R. E., Lieb, J. P., & Kaufman, H. M. (1972). Visual Identification and Memory in Monkeys with Circumscribed Inferotemporal Lesions. *Journal of Comparative and Physiological Psychology, 78*(2), 173.doi:10.1037/h0032819

Winters, B. D., Forwood, S. E., Cowell, R. A., Saksida, L. M., & Bussey, T. J. (2004). Double dissociation between the effects of peri-postrhinal cortex and hippocampal lesions on tests of object recognition and spatial memory: heterogeneity of function within the temporal lobe. *The Journal of Neuroscience, 24*(26), 5901–5908.doi:10.1523/JNEUROSCI.1346-04.2004

Zhang, L., & Cottrell, G. (2005). *Holistic processing develops because it is good.* Paper presented at the Proceedings of the 27th Annual Cognitive Science Conference, Stresa, Italy.

KEY TERMS AND DEFINITIONS

Cognitive Neuroscience: The scientific field concerned with the investigation of the psychological, computational, and neurobiological bases of cognition.

Connectionist Model: A computational model in the artificial neural network tradition, that aims to understand human intellectual or cognitive abilities as processes that *emerge* from the interactions of many interconnected simple processing units.

Level of Biological Organization: The physical scale at which a scientific problem is studied, ranging from small-scale molecular interactions up to large-scale phenomena observed at the level of large brain systems, e.g., the 'medial temporal lobe', or even the entire central nervous system.

Problem Space: The target data of a model, which determine the type and number of phenomena that the model addresses, and the type and number of levels of biological organization at which they are addressed.

Cognitive Module: A functionally, and often anatomically, distinct brain system, the processing within which is presumed to underlie a single, specialized cognitive ability.

Ventral Visual Stream (VVS): A pathway of interconnected structures in the visual cortex that extends along the ventral aspect of the mammalian brain, bilaterally. It is thought to encompass areas from V1 in occipital cortex through to anterior inferior temporal cortex in the temporal lobe, and possibly beyond.

Hierarchical Continuum: A description of the putative functional organization of the VVS, in which the complexity of visual representations builds up in a hierarchical manner with progression from posterior to anterior regions, such that both representational complexity and concomitant cognitive function change in a continuous, graded fashion.

Visual Discrimination Learning: A task in which subjects are trained to learn to discriminate between pairs of visually presented stimuli, typically by presenting pairs multiple times and rewarding one item in the pair consistently while never rewarding the other.

Object Recognition Memory: The ability to state whether a given object has been encountered before. Tests of object recognition memory have become the canonical measure of declarative memory in animal models of amnesia.

Chapter 3
Temporal Uncertainty during Overshadowing:
A Temporal Difference Account

Dómhnall J. Jennings
Newcastle University, UK

Eduardo Alonso
City University London, UK

Esther Mondragón
Centre for Computational and Animal Learning Research, UK

Charlotte Bonardi
University of Nottingham, UK

ABSTRACT

Standard associative learning theories typically fail to conceptualise the temporal properties of a stimulus, and hence cannot easily make predictions about the effects such properties might have on the magnitude of conditioning phenomena. Despite this, in intuitive terms we might expect that the temporal properties of a stimulus that is paired with some outcome to be important. In particular, there is no previous research addressing the way that fixed or variable duration stimuli can affect overshadowing. In this chapter we report results which show that the degree of overshadowing depends on the distribution form - fixed or variable - of the overshadowing stimulus, and argue that conditioning is weaker under conditions of temporal uncertainty. These results are discussed in terms of models of conditioning and timing. We conclude that the temporal difference model, which has been extensively applied to the reinforcement learning problem in machine learning, accounts for the key findings of our study.

INTRODUCTION

Overshadowing is a procedure in which a target conditioned stimulus (CS1) is conditioned together with a second stimulus (CS2), usually in a simultaneous compound which co-terminates with the delivery of an unconditioned stimulus (US). This training results in attenuated (or *overshadowed*) responding to CS1 when it is subsequently tested alone, compared to the case in which CS1 is con-

DOI: 10.4018/978-1-60960-021-1.ch003

ditioned in isolation. A key variable in determining the degree of overshadowing is the relative salience of the two stimuli: the more salient the overshadowing stimulus relative to the target, the more overshadowing is observed (Mackintosh, 1976). This observation may be interpreted theoretically in terms of learning models such as that proposed by Rescorla and Wagner (1972): the limited amount of associative strength that may be supported by the US must be distributed between the two competing CSs; as speed of acquisition depends on stimulus salience, this distribution is affected by the relative salience of the two stimuli.

However, pairing a CS of fixed duration with a US is a procedure that informs the animal not only *that* the US be delivered, but also *when* it is to be delivered, and there is good evidence to suggest that animals are indeed able to time the delivery of a US (e.g. Kirkpatrick & Church, 2000). This observation makes little contact with standard associative models of conditioning (e.g. Mackintosh, 1975; Pearce & Hall, 1980; Rescorla & Wagner, 1972) which, despite accounting for the magnitude of conditioned responding to a CS, generally fail to provide a comprehensive account of how animals learn about the temporal properties of the CS. More detailed discussion of theories of timing will be postponed until the general discussion; at this point it is sufficient to note that standard associative theories typically fail to conceptualise the temporal properties of a stimulus, and hence cannot easily make predictions about the effects such properties might have on the magnitude of overshadowing. Despite this, in intuitive terms one might expect these temporal aspects to be important. As noted above, the most important determinant of the degree of overshadowing is usually thought to be the ease with which the overshadowing stimulus can acquire associative strength. One can, however, make a parallel argument about a stimulus' temporal properties; given that better predictors of the US acquire associative strength more easily than unreliable predictors, then one might expect a fixed stimulus to be a

better overshadowing stimulus than a variable one. This is because, in some sense, a stimulus of fixed duration is a more reliable predictor of US outcome than one of variable duration, as the fixed stimulus gives precise information about the time of US delivery while the variable one does not.

There is no previous research addressing the way in which fixed and variable CSs can produce overshadowing; however, Kohler and Ayres (1979) examined the ability of fixed and variable duration CSs to produce blocking. They conditioned animals to a tone-light compound; for two groups of animals both tone and light were fixed, and one group was pretrained with a fixed light. For another two groups both tone and light were of variable duration and one group was pretrained with a variable light. They found equal blocking in both groups, suggesting that a fixed stimulus was no more able to produce blocking than a variable one. However, this conclusion is complicated by the fact that the treatment of the pretrained stimulus was confounded with the distribution of the to-be-blocked stimulus: the fixed stimulus blocked a fixed target and the variable stimulus a variable target. Moreover, subsequent work has suggested that a fixed CS may after all be a more effective blocking stimulus than a variable (D. Jennings and K. Kirkpatrick, unpublished data). It should be noted, however, that neither of these studies included any groups trained to the target alone. As a consequence, it is impossible to assess what effect the temporal distribution of the stimuli had on their ability to produce an overshadowing effect. This was, therefore, the purpose of the present experiment.

The experiment employed six groups of Lister hooded rats (Harlan UK, Table 1) maintained on a restricted diet at 80% of their free feeding weight. Since we used a houselight as one of the stimuli the boxes were normally not illuminated. All six groups were trained with a light CS that produced diffuse illumination of the conditioning chamber of about 200 lux when operational; three groups (Fc, VF and FF) experienced the light for a fixed

Table 1. The design of the overshadowing experiment (N= 8 per group).

Group	Treatment	
	Training	Test
Absent-Fixed (Fc)	CS2→US	CS2
Fixed-Fixed (FF)	CS1CS2→US	CS2
Variable-Fixed (VF)	CS1CS2→US	CS2
Absent-Variable (Vc)	CS2→US	CS2
Fixed-Variable (FV)	CS1CS2→US	CS2
Variable-Variable (VV)	CS1CS2→US	CS2

CS2 = Light; CS1 = 70db white noise; F = Fixed 30s; V = Variable 30s

duration and three for a variable duration (Groups Vc, FV and VV). For one of each of these triplets of groups the light was conditioned alone (Groups F and V), for another it was conditioned with a fixed noise (Groups FF and FV) and for the third it was conditioned with a variable noise (Groups VF and VV). In this way we could compare the ability of fixed and variable stimuli to produce overshadowing, independent of whether the overshadowed stimulus was itself fixed or variable.

The basic experimental approach is described in Table 1; training was conducted over six sessions and consisted of 26 trials per session, and each trial comprised presentations of the houselight followed by the delivery of a single food pellet. Each head entry into the food cup was recorded by interruption of a photobeam; therefore, the rate and distribution of responding during the CS constituted the measure of learning (for further details see e.g. Jennings, Bonardi and Kirkpatrick, 2007). In the control groups the light was presented alone, whereas in the experimental groups it was accompanied by CS1, the 70-db white noise. Critical to the present experiment was the distribution form of the stimuli; two different distributions were employed - either a *fixed* stimulus that was 30 s in duration, or a *variable* stimulus, whose duration was drawn from an exponential distribution with a mean and standard deviation of 30 s

(so that the average level of exposure to the fixed and variable duration stimuli was the same; Evans, Hastings & Peacock, 1993). The inter-trial interval (ITI), measured from food delivery to onset of the next CS, consisted of a fixed 60 s, plus an additional variable duration period with a mean of 60 s. Following training we conducted ten test sessions during which three reinforced probe trials of the light (all groups) and noise (the four experimental groups only) stimuli alone were presented to assess any overshadowing effect.

Compound training with the six different groups outlined in Table 1 was conducted without incident over six consecutive daily sessions. An initial inspection of responding during training indicated that there was no difference between the groups. We also conducted an examination of the timing functions; groups that were conditioned to a compound containing a fixed duration stimulus displayed an increase in response rate from stimulus onset to the expected time of food delivery, consistent with them having learned the time to reinforcement. Conversely, groups that received only variable duration stimuli during conditioning responded at a steady rate over the course of the CS.

Following training we investigated overshadowing by examining responding during test trials of the light stimulus (CS2) presented alone. Data recorded during this phase are presented for all six groups in Figure 1. It is evident that in general there was more responding to the light when the stimulus was of a fixed duration than when it was variable. Moreover, responding was lower in the overshadowing groups than in the control groups, and this overshadowing effect was larger when the overshadowing stimulus was fixed than when it was variable. Essentially, groups trained with a fixed overshadowing stimulus (FF and FV) responded at a significantly lower rate than the control groups (F and V), whereas groups trained with a variable duration overshadowing stimulus (VF and VV) did not differ from either the control or the other overshadowing groups. Although there

Figure 1. Elevation scores displaying the mean level of responding (± SE) to the light (CS2) dependent on whether the overshadowing stimulus was absent (Groups F and V), variable (Groups VF and VV) or fixed (Groups FF and FV). Groups trained with a fixed light are shown in the left half of the Figure, and those trained with a variable light are shown on the right.

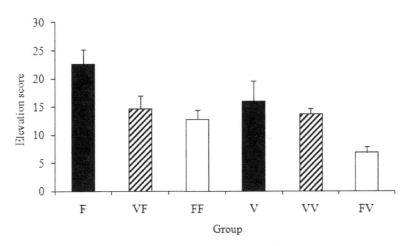

was some indication of higher response rates when the noise was fixed than when it was variable, this was not statistically reliable.

Groups that received the fixed duration probe trials displayed an increase in their rate of responding from stimulus onset to the time when food was delivered at stimulus offset (Figure 2, top panel), whereas those experiencing variable duration probes tended to respond at a steady rate throughout CS presentation (Figure 2, bottom panel). These data are by no means unusual in that it has been shown that fixed and variable distributions tend to generate this form of responding; yet it should be remembered that, at least for the compound groups with mixed distributions (FV and VF), there were two sources of competing temporal information. Our analysis indicates that the rats in these two groups were able to track these different distribution forms despite this competition. We will return to this issue shortly following a theoretical discussion of the data set as a whole.

A brief recap of the main finding of this experiment shows that the degree of overshadowing that was observed depended on the distribution

form of the overshadowing stimulus: overshadowing was more profound when the overshadowing stimulus was fixed than when it was variable. At face value the implication of this finding is that a fixed duration stimulus acquires associative strength more effectively than one of variable duration. This suggestion is consistent with our additional observation of greater conditioned responding to the target CS when it was of fixed duration than when it was variable.

It is not immediately clear how these results are to be explained. Standard associative models do not incorporate any mechanism for explaining timing effects, and so it is far from obvious how they could accommodate these data. It should be noted, however, that one interpretation of our results is that a fixed stimulus acquires associative strength more than a variable one because it is a better predictor of the US. Mackintosh (1975) proposed a model of conditioning according to which the associability of a stimulus is directly related to its predictive power, such that better predictors have higher associability. One possibility, therefore, is to argue that the variable stimulus varies from trial to trial, whereas the fixed does

Figure 2. The probability of responding as a function of time since CS onset during light probe trials, for groups that received a fixed target stimulus (top panel) and a variable target stimulus (bottom panel).

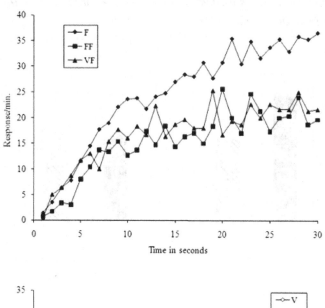

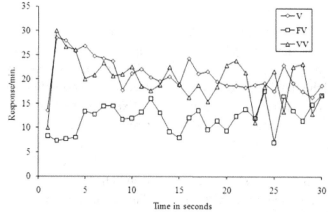

not; the model then predicts that the associability of the variable stimulus should fall below that of the fixed simply because the fixed, being the same from one trial to the next, will acquire more associative strength. His model could thus predict that a fixed stimulus would have greater associability than a variable stimulus, and that this is the source of the results that we observed. Although logical, however, this account fails to capture any of the temporal characteristics of responding and so on these grounds must necessarily be regarded as incomplete.

An alternative approach is to look to hybrid models that have been developed to account for both conditioning and timing, such as rate expectancy theory (RET: Gallistel & Gibbon, 2000, 2002; cf Gibbon, 1977). RET proposes that conditioning and timing are dependent on a timing-like mechanism, with timing occurring after conditioned responding has been established – a serial process account. Conditioning requires a comparison of the rate of reinforcement during the CS with that during the background: when the CS is perceived as elevating the rate of reinforcement over that occurring in the CSs absence, then conditioned responding to the CS emerges. However, RET predicts that responding during the fixed and variable duration CSs of our experiment should be identical, as their average duration, and hence the average reinforcement rate during fixed and variable CS presentation, is identical - and yet in our experiment this was clearly not the case. For the same reason it would predict no difference in the ability of fixed and variable duration stimuli to produce overshadowing, and yet we observed that the fixed CS was the better overshadowing stimulus. In fact RET cannot easily explain overshadowing *per se*; the overshadowing process lies outside the scope of the model, and requires the introduction of additional principles, such as stimulus salience. In short, then, RET cannot provide a satisfactory explanation of our results.

An alternative model of conditioning and timing is the temporal coding hypothesis (Savastano & Miller, 1998). This is a form of single process model which asserts that conditioning and timing arise simultaneously, as a consequence of pairing a CS and a US together. Specifically, when an association is formed, a temporal map detailing the predictive relationship between the CS and US is established, and the match or mismatch of the temporal maps associated with any two stimuli will affect the way in which they interact associatively (Barnet, Grahame & Miller, 1993; Blaisdell, Denniston & Miller, 1998). In the present experiment this account would predict that overshadowing should be most profound between two stimuli that share the same temporal map - specifically in Groups FF and VV (Blaisdell, et al., 1998). However, this was not what was observed; rather, overshadowing was greater in Groups FF and FV than in Groups VV and VF. This suggests that matching temporal maps is not an important determinant of the overshadowing effect, and that our results that do not, therefore, support the temporal coding hypothesis.

One further model of timing and conditioning is the temporal difference (TD) model (Sutton &

Barto 1987, 1990), a single process model that emphasises an integrated approach to conditioning and timing. It employs a conditioning mechanism that is a modification of the Rescorla-Wagner (Rescorla & Wagner, 1972) model, but which incorporates a temporal component enabling it to accommodate the fact that delayed reinforcers are less effective than immediate ones. This may be adapted to deal with CSs of varying durations by assuming that a stimulus of given duration is comprised of a series of time steps that condition independently of each other, and that is reinforced by a punctate US (cf. Moore & Choi, 1997); the model then describes how later portions of the CS will condition more effectively than earlier ones. This permits an explanation of how responding can gradually increase over the course of the CS (Moore & Choi, 1997; Sutton & Barto, 1990), and has successfully predicted conditioned performance in serial-compound experiments (e.g. Egger & Miller, 1962) and blocking studies (e.g. Gaioni, 1982; Jennings & Kirkpatrick, 2006). This model can account for our results, because it predicts that a variable stimulus will acquire less associative strength than a fixed, even though the mean duration of the two stimuli is the same. The reason for this lies in the way in which reinforcement accrues to CS time steps that are removed from the US. The model assumes that the time step closest to the US acquires associative strength in the normal way, but that delayed time steps acquire strength *not* through direct association with the US, but recursively via second-order conditioning to the unit closer in time to the US, and the amount of associative strength each delayed time step receives is determined by a discounting parameter *gamma* (γ), which has a value between 0 and 1. For example, let us assume that the final time step acquires an associative strength of 1 unit. The first delayed time step will acquire this strength, discounted by γ, and thus acquire 0.9 units of strength. The second delayed time step will acquire the first step's strength (γ), also discounted by γ, meaning it acquires γ^2 (0.81

units) the third delayed step acquires γ^3 (.73 units) and so on. Effectively this means that units more contiguous with the US acquire substantially more associative strength than temporally distant units (Sutton & Barto, 1990). This is important because although the variable CS will comprise the same total number of time steps as the fixed, on some trials the variable CS will be either shorter or longer than the fixed stimulus. Consequently, when the CS is shorter, fewer units will be available to receive reinforcement and where longer, some time units will be far removed from the US and will, therefore, receive negligible associative strength.

For example, consider a fixed duration CS of two time steps, and a variable CS drawn from a uniform distribution, that can range between 1 and 3 steps. Over three trials a total of six steps will be reinforced: the fixed CS is two steps long on each trial, whereas the variable (let us assume) is one step on one trial, two on another, and three on a third. Let us again say the final unit on each trial acquires an associative strength of 1. Setting gamma to 0.9, associative strength acquired on the first trial with each delayed time step is effectively directly proportional to gamma. Thus for the fixed CS the first step (defined as that closest to the US) will accrue 1 unit of strength on each trial (3 after three trials), and the second step 0.9 on each trial (2.70 after three trials), yielding a total of 5.70 units after three trials. The first step of the variable stimulus will also acquire 1 unit per trial (3 after three trials). However, the second step is only present on *two* of the three trials, and so will acquire a total of $0.9 \times 2 = 1.8$ over three trials. On the trial in which the variable stimulus is longer than the fixed, there will be a third time step, which will acquire $(0.9)^2 = 0.81$ units. This yields a total of 5.61 units, which is less than the 5.70 units acquired by the fixed CS. In short, this difference arises because the fixed CS differs from the variable CS only in that a time step from position 2 has been moved to position 3, and time steps further from the US acquire less associative

strength. The TD model can, therefore, account for the key findings of the present study.

A further aspect of our data concerns the form of responding (timing) that we observed during the various stimuli. To date, most models of conditioning and timing have tended to focus on conditioned responding during fixed duration stimuli, and as a consequence are silent about performance during variable duration CSs (although see the TD model referred to above). An analysis of the timing functions in the present study indicated that rats responded quite differently to the target stimuli depending on whether they were of fixed or of variable duration. When the target was a fixed 30-s there was a gradually increasing rate of responding which reached a peak at about the time of US delivery (Figure 2a) and a slope that differed significantly from zero; when it was of variable duration, on the other hand, responding was relatively stable and the slope did not differ from zero (Figure 2b). Although the different patterns of responding during stimuli of fixed and variable duration have been demonstrated before (Kirkpatrick & Church, 2003), one further marked feature of the present results was that this pattern was unaffected by whether the target stimulus had suffered overshadowing or not. Whether or not this is a general feature of response form during cue competition will require further investigation; however, these results are consistent with previous reports that demonstrate that stimuli of differing fixed durations were tracked accurately by rat subjects during both blocking and overshadowing (Jennings & Kirkpatrick 2006; Jennings et al., 2007).

Hybrid accounts of timing and conditioning usually implicitly assume that attenuation of responding during cue competition tasks will also lead to disruption of timing. For instance, the temporal coding hypothesis argues that conditioning and timing emerge directly as part of the learning process, whereas according to RET timing may only emerge after conditioning has occurred; according to both these accounts therefore, disruption of conditioning must necessarily be accompanied by a disruption of timing. One account that might not predict such a deficit is the TD model; according to this account cue competition and, therefore, overshadowing occurs between the units that comprise the stimulus, according to Rescorla Wagner principles. Timing occurs because of the asymmetric distribution of associative strength over the course of the CS, with units close in time to the US acquiring the most strength. Even if the total associative strength acquired by the CS were reduced, as long as the proportion acquired by the later time steps relative to the earlier ones were preserved, then one would expect similar timing functions regardless of whether overshadowing was obtained or not.

Both conditioning and timing are known to occur in many basic conditioning procedures, and are often studied using highly similar experimental procedures; it is the dependent measures of responding that differ (Kirkpatrick & Church 1998). Yet surprisingly little attention has been paid to understanding the relationship between measures of the magnitude of responding (conditioning) and the time of responding (timing), and the nature of the relationship between these two forms of learning. What attention there has been has tended to come from students of timing who have sought to model the conditioned response within a variety information processing accounts of learning (e.g. Gallistel & Gibbon 2000). While this approach shows imagination and a willingness to address the thorny issue of how these two core psychological processes interact, such an approach also requires that a great many advances in associative theorising should necessarily be abandoned. The alternative (and arguably more parsimonious approach) is to incorporate timing within a model that is at least, in part, associatively based; based on the experimental results presented above, the TD appears to make a step in this direction.

In summary, we have provided further evidence that the temporal properties of the stimulus can affect the outcome of classical conditioning procedures. Standard associative theories cannot easily accommodate findings of this type, as by and large they fail to conceptualise the temporal properties of the stimulus. Hybrid models, which attempt to accommodate both timing and conditioning within a single framework, fare no better, in part because they have no principled account of associative phenomena such as the overshadowing effect. The account that provides the best explanation of our data is probably the temporal difference (TD) model (e.g. Sutton & Barto, 1987; 1990 cf., Vogel, Brandon & Wagner, 2000) - a model that uses incorporates a modified Rescorla-Wagner conditioning rule within a framework that has a principled conceptualisation of the temporal properties of the stimulus. This type of approach is probably that best suited to account for the phenomena of conditioning and timing within a single theoretical framework.

REFERENCES

Barnet, R. C., Grahame, N. J., & Miller, R. R. (1993). Temporal encoding as a determinant of blocking. *Journal of Experimental Psychology. Animal Behavior Processes*, *19*, 327–341. doi:10.1037/0097-7403.19.4.327

Blaisdell, A. P., Denniston, J. C., & Miller, R. R. (1998). Temporal encoding as a determinant of overshadowing. *Journal of Experimental Psychology. Animal Behavior Processes*, *24*, 72–83. doi:10.1037/0097-7403.24.1.72

Egger, M. D., & Miller, N. E. (1962). Secondary reinforcement in rats as a function of information value and reliability of the stimulus. *Journal of Experimental Psychology*, *64*, 97–104. doi:10.1037/h0040364

Evans, M., Hastings, N., & Peacock, B. (1993). *Statistical Distributions*. New York: Wiley.

Gaioni, S. J. (1982). Blocking and nonsimultaneous compounds: Comparison of responding during compound conditioning and testing. *The Pavlovian Journal of Biological Science*, (January-March): 16–29.

Gallistel, C. R., & Gibbon, J. (2000). Time, rate and conditioning. *Psychological Review, 107,* 289–344.doi:10.1037/0033-295X.107.2.289

Gallistel, C. R., & Gibbon, J. (2002). *The symbolic foundations of conditioned behavior*. Mahwah, NJ: Erlbaum Associates.

Gibbon, J. (1977). Scalar expectancy theory and Weber's law in animal timing. *Psychological Review, 84,* 279–325.doi:10.1037/0033-295X.84.3.279

Jennings, D. J., Bonardi, C., & Kirkpatrick, K. (2007). Overshadowing and stimulus duration. *Journal of Experimental Psychology. Animal Behavior Processes, 33,* 464–475.doi:10.1037/0097-7403.33.4.464

Jennings, D. J., & Kirkpatrick, K. (2006). Interval duration effects on blocking in appetitive conditioning. *Behavioural Processes, 71,* 318–329. doi:10.1016/j.beproc.2005.11.007

Kirkpatrick, K., & Church, R. M. (1998). Are separate theories of conditioning and timing necessary? *Behavioural Processes, 44,* 163–182. doi:10.1016/S0376-6357(98)00047-3

Kirkpatrick, K., & Church, R. M. (2000). Stimulus and temporal cues in classical conditioning. *Journal of Experimental Psychology. Animal Behavior Processes, 26,* 206–219.doi:10.1037/0097-7403.26.2.206

Kirkpatrick, K., & Church, R. M. (2003). Tracking of the expected time to reinforcement in temporal conditioning procedures. *Learning & Behavior, 31,* 3–21.

Kohler, E. A., & Ayres, J. J. B. (1982). Blocking with serial and simultaneous compounds in a trace conditioning procedure. *Animal Learning & Behavior, 10,* 277–287.

Mackintosh, N. J. (1975). A theory of attention: Variations in the associability of stimuli with reinforcement. *Psychological Review, 82,* 276–298. doi:10.1037/h0076778

Mackintosh, N. J. (1976). Overshadowing and stimulus intensity. *Animal Learning & Behavior, 4,* 186–192.

Moore, J. W., & Choi, J.-S. (1997). The TD model of classical conditioning: Response topography and brain implementation. In Donahoe, J. W., & Dorsel, V. P. (Eds.), *Neural-networks models of cognition* (pp. 387–405). New York: Elsevier Science.

Pearce, J. M., & Hall, G. (1980). A model for Pavlovian learning: Variations in the effectiveness of conditioned but not unconditioned stimuli. *Psychological Review, 87,* 532–552. doi:10.1037/0033-295X.87.6.532

Rescorla, R. A., & Wagner, A. R. (1972). A theory of Pavlovian conditioning: Variations in the effectiveness of reinforcement. In Black, A. H., & Prokasy, W. F. (Eds.), *Classical conditioning: II. Theory and research* (pp. 64–99). New York: Appleton-Century-Crofts.

Savastano, H. I., & Miller, R. R. (1998). Time as content in Pavlovian conditioning. *Behavioural Processes, 44,* 147–162.doi:10.1016/S0376-6357(98)00046-1

Sutton, R. S., & Barto, A. G. (1987). A temporal difference model of classical conditioning. In *Proceedings of the Seventh Annual Conference of the Cognitive Science Society* (pp. 355-378). Erlbaum.

Sutton, R. S., & Barto, A. G. (1990). Time derivative models of Pavlovian reinforcement. In Gabriel, M. R., & Moore, J. W. (Eds.), *Learning and computational neuroscience: Foundations of adaptive networks* (pp. 497–537). Cambridge, MA: MIT Press.

Vogel, E. H., Brandon, S. E., & Wagner, A. R. (2000). Stimulus representation in SOP II: An application to inhibition of delay. *Behavioural Processes*, *110*, 67–72.

KEY TERMS AND DEFINITIONS

Conditioning: The mechanism of learning about contingencies between environmental events.

Timing: The ability to accurately anticipate the time at which a predicted outcome will be delivered.

Overshadowing: Interference in learning about the relationship between an event and an outcome due to the presence of a second stimulus that predicts the same outcome.

Temporal Variability: The distribution of a stimulus' temporal properties indicating whether it is fixed or variable.

Temporal Difference Learning: An approach to learning how to predict a quantity that depends on future values of a given signal. The name TD derives from its use of changes, or differences, in predictions over successive time steps to drive the learning process. The prediction at any given time step is updated to bring it closer to the prediction of the same quantity at the next time step.

Section 2
Computational Models in Neuroscience

Chapter 4

An Associative Approach to Additivity and Maximality Effects on Blocking

Néstor A. Schmajuk
Duke University, USA

Munir G. Kutlu
Duke University, USA

ABSTRACT

Schmajuk, Lam, and Gray (SLG, 1996) introduced an attentional-associative model able to describe a large number of classical paradigms. As other models, the SLG model describes blocking in terms of the competition between the blocker and the blocked conditioned stimulus (CS) to gain association with the unconditioned stimulus (US) or outcome. Recent data suggest, however, other factors together with competition might control the phenomenon. For instance, Beckers et al. (2005) reported that blocking and backward blocking are stronger when participants are informed that (a) the predicted US is submaximal than when it is maximal, and (b) the predictions of the US by the CSs are additive than when they are sub-additive. Submaximality refers to the evidence that the predicted US is weaker than its maximal possible value. Additivity denotes the fact that two CSs, each one independently predicting a given US, predict a stronger US when presented together. Beckers et al. suggested that their results are better explained by inferential accounts, which assume involvement of controlled and effortful reasoning, than by associative views. This chapter shows that a configural version of the SLG attentional-associative model is able to quantitatively approximate submaximality and additivity effects on blocking while providing a mechanistic explanation of the results. In general, the chapter illustrates the potential of associative models to account for newly discovered properties of known psychological phenomena.

INTRODUCTION

In the last four decades, powerful computational models of associative learning have been developed which are able to describe in great detail a large number of classical conditioning paradigms (Schmajuk, 1997, 2010). Many of these models assume that conditioned stimuli (CS) compete to gain association with the unconditioned stimulus (US). Recently, competition between cues to be-

DOI: 10.4018/978-1-60960-021-1.ch004

come accepted as the cause of certain outcome has become a major topic in the field of causal learning (De Houwer and Beckers, 2002; Shanks, 2007). Cue competition has been traditionally studied in forward blocking (Kamin, 1968), a classical conditioning paradigm that consists of presentations of CS A and CS X (the putative causes in causal learning) followed by the US (the outcome in causal learning), following A-US presentations. The procedure results in a weaker conditioned response to X than that attained when A-X-US presentations follow reinforced presentations of another conditioned stimulus, B.

According to traditional associative theories, forward blocking is the consequence of stimulus A winning the competition with X to predict the US, because the US is already predicted by A at the time of A-X-US presentations (e.g., Rescorla and Wagner, 1972), or because stimulus A is a better predictor than X of the US (e.g., Mackintosh, 1975). In contrast with these views, Beckers et al. (2006) proposed that blocking is the consequence of an inferential process which verifies that both additivity and submaximality assumptions are true. Additivity denotes the fact that two causes predict a stronger outcome when presented together than when presented independently. Submaximality refers to the evidence that a single cause does not predict the possible maximal outcome value. Therefore, according to the inferential process view, a relative weak response to X (blocking) is justified only when cause A by itself predicts an outcome that is smaller than the possible maximal outcome, thereby allowing a potential additive effect of X on the outcome to be detected. If no increment in the outcome is detected, X is said not to be a cause of that outcome.

Beckers et al. (2005) used a food allergy task in which participants were shown that the effect of stimuli other than A and X can be added (G and H additivity training) or the maximal possible value of the outcome (US maximality training) before blocking. They also tested the effect of G and H additivity training before backward blocking or

recovery from overshadowing, and of G and H additivity training after blocking. Subsequently, participants were asked to rate how likely it is for a patient to develop an allergy after eating different food items. According to Beckers et al. (2005, 2006), their results can be explained in inferential terms (which might involve syllogistic logic, natural logic, inference schemes, or causal Bayes nets). Blocking is not present if either the submaximal premise (the predicted US is weaker than its maximal possible value) or the additivity premise (the predictions of the US by the CSs can be added) are not satisfied. In contrast, Beckers et al. (2005) applied the Rescorla-Wagner (1972) model to the description of outcome maximality and showed that, assuming a maximal outcome, the model incorrectly predicts more blocking with an intense than with a moderate outcome. Similar results to those reported by Beckers et al. (2005) were found both in humans (Lovibond et al., 2003) and rats (Beckers et al., 2006).

In this chapter, we show that a configural version of the Schmajuk, Lam, and Gray (1996) attentional-associative model (see also Schmajuk and Larrauri, 2006; Larrauri and Schmajuk, 2008) describes maximality effects on forward blocking, and additivity effects on forward and backward blocking.

AN ATTENTIONAL-ASSOCIATIVE MODEL OF CONDITIONING

Schmajuk, Lam, and Gray (SLG, 1996; Schmajuk and Larrauri, 2006) proposed a neural network model of classical conditioning. The network incorporates (a) an attentional mechanism regulated not only by Novelty (difference between the actual and the predicted magnitude) of the US as in the Pearce and Hall (1980) model, but also by Novelty of the conditioned stimuli (CSs) and the context (CX), (b) a network in which associations are controlled by a modified, moment-to-moment (vs. trial-to-trial) version of the Rescorla and

Figure 1. Simplified circuit of the Schmajuk-Lam-Gray (1996) model. CS: conditioned stimuli; US: unconditioned stimulus; τ_{CS}: trace of CS; B_{CS}: Predicted CS; z_{CS}: attention to CS; X_{CS}: internal representation of the CS; $V_{CS,US}$: X_{CS}-US association; B_{US}: predicted US; CR: conditioned response; Novelty': detected novelty. Triangles: variable connections (associations) between nodes that modulate the activation of the node. Arrows: inputs that control the associations of the node.

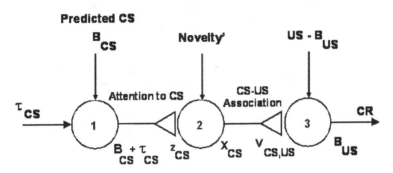

Wagner (R-W, 1972) competitive rule, and (c) feedback from the associative network to the input. Schmajuk et al. (1996), Schmajuk and Larrauri (2006), and Larrauri and Schmajuk (2008) offered a detailed description of the model in terms of differential equations.

Figure 1 shows a simplified diagram of the SLG model that illustrates the different mechanisms involved in the generation of a CR when a given CS is presented. Node 1 receives input from a short-term memory trace of the CS, τ_{CS}, and the prediction of that CS, B_{CS}, by other CSs or the CX. In order to modulate attention to the CSs in proportion to the novelty detected in the environment, the output of Node 1, ($\tau_{CS} + B_{CS}$), becomes associated through z_{CS} with the normalized value of the total novelty detected in the environment, Novelty'. Importantly, z_{CS} can change either when the CS is present or is absent but predicted by other CSs through B_{CS}, a property that is used to explain additivity pretraining effects on backward blocking and additivity post-training effects on blocking described later in this chapter.

Node 3 receives input from Node 2, X_{CS}, as well as from the error term (US - B_{US}). The synaptic weight connecting Node 2 to Node 3, $V_{CS,US}$, reflects the (excitatory or inhibitory) association

of X_{CS} with the US. Changes in $V_{CS,US}$ are given by

$$dV_{CS,US}/dt = K X_{CS} (\lambda_{US} - B_{US}) (V_{MAX} - |V_{CS,US}|), \tag{1}$$

where X_{CS} is the internal representation of the CS, λ_{US} is the intensity of the US, V_{MAX} the maximum value that $|V_{CS,US}|$ can attain, and B_{US} is the aggregate prediction of the US by all X's active at a given time. Changes in $V_{CS,US}$ are proportional to a common error term ($\lambda_{US} - B_{US}$), which reflects the difference between predicted, B_{US}, and the real value of the US. Through this error term, CSs compete to become associated with the US, a device used to explain overshadowing and blocking. Changes in $V_{CS,US}$ are also proportional to the individual error term ($V_{MAX} - |V_{CS,US}|$), which has been extensively used to account for the differences in compound conditioning of two CSs with different initial $V_{CS,US}$ (e.g., Brandon, Vogel, and Wagner, 2002; Le Pelley, 2004; Rescorla, 2000, 2001, 2002). In the present chapter, this individual error term is used to explain maximality effects on blocking (i.e., the fact that blocking is weaker when the prediction of the US by the blocking stimulus has reached a maximum value which is unable to match the value of the actual US).

Figure 2. A simplified diagram of the Configural form of the SLG model. τ: traces of A, X, G and H; z: attention to A, X, G, and H; X: representations of A, X, G, H, and C; Out: Outcome; V: A-Outcome, X-Outcome, C-Outcome or C'-Outcome associations. When simultaneously active τ_A and τ_X activate configural stimulus C, and when simultaneously active τ_G and τ_H activate configural stimulus C'. The dashed arrow connecting C and C' represents the generalization between them. Through that generalization τ_A and τ_X can activate the $V_{C',OUT}$ association, and τ_G and τ_H can activate the $V_{C,OUT}$ association. Triangles: variable connections between nodes, z and V. Arrows: fixed connections between nodes.

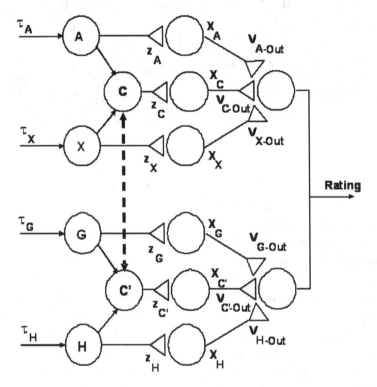

THE CONFIGURAL FORM OF THE SLG MODEL

Figure 2 presents a simplified diagram of a configural version of the SLG model, as applied to the maximality and additivity experiments in blocking described here. According to Figure 2, simultaneously active τ_A and τ_X activate a configural stimulus C, and simultaneously active τ_G and τ_H activate configural stimulus C'. Attention to τ_A, τ_X, C, τ_G, τ_H, and C' varies with Novelty'. Configural stimuli C and C' can be associated with all other simple and configural CSs. As shown by

the dashed double arrow in Figure 2, we assume generalization between compounds C' (GH) and C (AX) to be complete, based on Young and Wasserman's (2002) experimental data showing that generalization between compounds is much stronger than generalization between simple stimuli. In addition, the model implements (a) generalization between elements and their compounds by simultaneously activating the elements (e.g., A and X) and their respective compound (AX), and (b) generalization among elements through the presence of a common contextual stimulus.

SIMULATION METHODS

This section summarizes the parameter values, simulations values, and the way ratings were computed in the simulations.

Parameter values. All simulations adopted the same parameters values: K_1=.2, K_2= 2, K_3=.4, K_4=.1, K_5=.02, K_6=.005, K_7=.005, K_8=.005, K_9=.75, K_{10} = 0, and K_{11}=.15. This set of parameters is identical to that of the original version of the model (Schmajuk et al., 1996; Schmajuk, Buhusi, and Gray; 1998a; Buhusi, Gray, and Schmajuk, 1998; and Schmajuk, Cox, and Gray, 2001), except for K_{10} = 0 (originally.7), which eliminates the inhibitory effect of the OR on the CR. Also, the maximum value of z_{CS} is 1.5, z_{CS}/dt = (τ_{CS} + K_3 B_{CS}) (K_5 Novelty' (1.5 - z_{CS}) - K_6 (1 + z_{CS})), in order to increase the effect of Novelty' on attention; and V_{MAX} = 0.5 in Equation 1, in order to show maximality effects with the CS saliences used in our simulations (see Beckers et al.'s (2005) Experiment 1).

Simulation values. Like in the Beckers et al. (2005) experiment, the number of maximality pre-training trials (10 CX-, 10 CX+, and 10 CX++ trials), as well as the number of additivity pre-training and post-training trials were identical in all our simulations (10 G+, 10 H+, and 10 GH+ or GH++ trials). Furthermore, like in the experimental design the number of trials (10 A+ and 20 AX+ trials) was identical in all blocking simulations (Experiments 1, 2, and 4). However, in contrast to the experimental design used in Experiment 3, we used different number of trials in the simulation for backward blocking (10 AX+ and 80 A+ trials) and in the simulation for recovery of overshadowing (30 AX+ and 10 A+ trials). These differences are due to the different rates of change in associative and attentional mechanisms, which are differentially involved in each case. Similar differences were reported in the past by Schmajuk and Larrauri (2006) for forward and backward blocking.

In Beckers et al.'s (2005) food allergy task the intensity of the allergy developed by the fictitious patients was denoted by a red bar on the computer screen. Because a red bar is not a biologically significant US (e.g., food or pain), in our simulations the Outcome is equivalent to another CS and therefore able to establish Outcome-CS associations with the CSs that represent the causal foods.

Ratings. In the experiments, participants were asked to rate the probability (between 0 and 9) that a patient would develop an allergy after eating different food items. Therefore, we transformed the predictions of the outcome generated by the model into probability rates.

This was accomplished by describing with the sigmoid function Rating= (Predicted Outcome)^n/((Predicted Outcome)^n + β^n), where β= Average of Predicted Outcomes by A, X, K, L, and Z, and n = 12, that extends the ratings over a 0-1 range.

APPLICATION OF THE CONFIGURAL FORM OF THE SLG MODEL TO THE EXPERIMENTAL RESULTS

In this section we apply the configural form of the SLG model to the Beckers et al. (2005) data.

Maximality Training Preceding Blocking

Experimental data. In Beckers et al.'s (2005, Experiment 1) maximality study, one maximal and one submaximal group were used. The maximal group received 24 CX–/CX+/CX++ alternated trials (prior training), followed by 16 alternated A++/Z- trials (elemental training), and finally by 24 AX++/KL++/Z- alternated trials (compound training). Whereas CX denotes the context alone; Z, A, X, K and L denote neutral stimuli; and symbols –, + and ++ respectively indicate no outcome, or the same outcome with different intensities. Stimuli were pictures of different foods on a computer screen, and the outcome (an allergic reaction) was represented by a red bar of different lengths on the screen. Responses to X and K (and L) were then compared. Submaximal groups received A+/Z- trials during elemental training, and AX+/KL+/Z- alternated trials during compound training. As shown in Figure 3 (Upper Panel), although blocking was present in both groups, it was stronger in the submaximal than in the maximal case.

Simulated results. Simulations for Becker's (2005) Experiment 1 included 5 Z-, 10 CX-, 10 CX+, and 10 CX++ trials. The intensity of Outcome was 0.8 for CX+, and 1 for CX++. After CX pretraining, 10 A+ or A++ trials were followed by 20 AX+ or AX++ trials. Salience of compound C was 1. The Outcome was simulated as another CS (equivalent to the red bar), able to form both Outcome-Outcome and Outcome-CS associations. The value of the maximal Outcome was 1.0 and the submaximal Outcome was 0.8. Notice that the value of V_{MAX} in $(V_{MAX} - |V_{CS,US}|)$ (see Equation 1), is kept constant with both maximal and submaximal outcomes.

Figure 4 illustrates how the term $(V_{MAX} - |V_{CS,OUT}|)$ explains maximality and how the value of V_{MAX} was selected. In the maximal case (Left Side in Figure 4), assuming that all the CSs equal 1, the blocking effect is given by the difference between responding to K and X, i.e., $\text{Blocking}_{MAX} = V_{K,OUT} - V_{X,OUT} = V_{K,OUT} - (\text{Out}_{MAX} - V_{A,OUT})$. Assuming for simplicity, that both $V_{K,OUT}$ and $V_{A,OUT}$ have reached a value close to asymptote V_{MAX} (with $V_{K,OUT} < V_{A,OUT}$ because the common error term in Equation 1 during KL++ training is smaller than during A++ training), $\text{Blocking}_{MAX} = 2 V_{MAX} - \text{Out}_{MAX}$.

In the submaximal case (Right Side in Figure 4), assuming again that all the CSs are equal to 1, the blocking effect is given by the difference between responding to K and X, i.e., $\text{Blocking}_{SUB} = V_{K,OUT} - V_{X,OUT} = V_{K,OUT} - (\text{Out}_{SUB} - V_{A,OUT})$. In this case, $V_{A,OUT}$ approximates V_{MAX} during A+ trials and $V_{K,OUT}$ will tend to $V_{K,OUT} = 0.5 * \text{Out}_{SUB}$ during KL+ trials. Therefore, $\text{Blocking}_{SUB} = 0.5$

Figure 3. Maximality training preceding blocking. Ratings of stimulus A, X, Z, and average rating for stimuli K and L for the Maximal and Submaximal cases. Upper Panel: Data from Beckers et al.'s (2005) Experiment 1. Lower Panel: Simulated rating with the configural-attentional version of Schmajuk-Lam-Gray (1996) model.

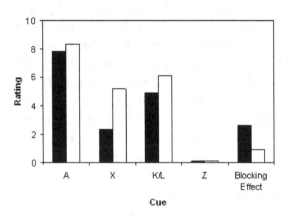

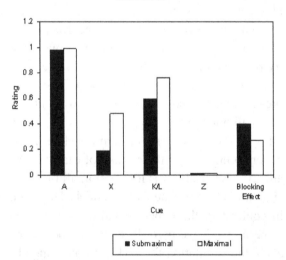

$* \text{Out}_{SUB} - (\text{Out}_{SUB} - V_{MAX}) = - 0.5 * \text{Out}_{SUB} + V_{MAX})$.

In order to find the value of V_{MAX} that makes $\text{Blocking}_{MAX} < \text{Blocking}_{SUB}$, we write $2 V_{MAX} - \text{Out}_{MAX} < -.5 * \text{Out}_{SUB} + V_{MAX}$, and therefore $V_{MAX} < \text{Out}_{MAX} -.5 * \text{Out}_{SUB}$. For the selected $\text{Out}_{MAX} =$

Figure 4. Associative mechanisms during maximality and submaximality. Asymptotic values of associations $V_{X,OUT}$ $V_{A,OUT}$ and $V_{X,OUT}$for the maximal and submaximal cases. V_{MAX} is the value in the limiting term (V_{MAX} - $|V_{CS,US}|$ $|$) in Equation A9. All CSs are assumed to be equal to 1.

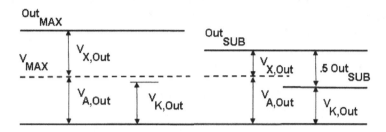

1.0 and Out_{SUB} = 0.8, it results V_{MAX} <.6, and we choose V_{MAX} =.5.

Figure 3 (Lower Panel) shows that computer simulations with the configural form of the SLG model reproduce Beckers et al.'s (2005) results. As mentioned above, the model incorporates an individual error term, (V_{MAX} - $|V_{CS,OUTCOME}|$), Equation 1). According to this term, A-Outcome associations are limited to a maximum value so that A cannot fully predict the Outcome of maximal strength, and therefore is unable to prevent X from becoming associated with that Outcome (see Figure 5, Top Panel). Figure 6 shows that X_X is similar, $V_{X,US}$ is larger, and CR is stronger, in the maximal than in the submaximal case. As shown in Figure 4, because the A-Outcome association, $V_{A,OUT}$, is limited by V_{MAX} it leaves more room for the X-Outcome association, $V_{X,OUT}$, to grow when the Outcome is maximal than when the Outcome is submaximal. Instead, because the submaximal Outcome is relatively weak, even a limited A-Outcome association can fully predict the Outcome thereby blocking the formation of X-Outcome associations.

Because the maximal values of the Outcome seem to be learned (see Beckers et al., 2006, Experiment 3, for an example in rats), V_{MAX} in Equation 1, should be able to change with different maximal values of the Outcome experienced by the participants. As explained in detail in Figure 4, V_{MAX} can be expressed as a function of $Outcome_{MAX}$ and $Outcome_{SUB}$, which guarantees that blocking is weaker with the maximal than with the submaximal outcome. Because the value of V_{MAX} increases as the maximum experienced value of Outcome increases, an initially maximal Outcome might become submaximal and show increased blocking. With increasing V_{MAX} values, $V_{CS,OUT}$ will be able to increase (V_{MAX} - $|V_{CS,OUT}|$), and blocking, weak or absent at first, will be clearly present (see Beckers et al., 2006, Experiment 3).The exact form of function V_{MAX} = f($Outcome_{MAX}$, $Outcome_{SUB}$) is an empirical issue that can be explored with experiments similar to Beckers et al.'s (2006).

One justification of the limits imposed on associations $V_{CS,US}$ is the intuition that the neurophysiological representation (for example, number of postsynaptic receptors, available presynaptic neurotransmitter) of both excitatory and inhibitory magnitudes of $V_{CS,US}$ cannot surpass certain values. In addition, a CS with a weak X_{CS}, will result in a weak B_{US}, given by

$$B_{US} = \Sigma_{CS} B_{CS, US} = \Sigma_{CS} X_{CS} V_{CS,US.} \qquad (2)$$

Because a weak B_{US} results in a very strong $V_{CS,US}$ according to Equation 1, a non-salient CS would accrue unlikely powerful associations. Limits on associations were proposed by Blough (1975, Page 20) in order to avoid an unrealistic perfect discrimination in his simulated psychometric

Figure 5. A simplified diagram of the Configural form of the SLG model illustrating the effect of maximality training preceding blocking. When the $V_{A,OUT}$ association is constrained to a maximum value, then when the Outcome (Out) is maximal (Upper Panel), $X_A*V_{A,OUT}$ is much smaller than the value of Out and therefore $V_{X,OUT}$ can grow, which results in a decreased blocking effect. When the Outcome (Out) is submaximal (Lower Panel), $X_A*V_{A,OUT}$ approximates the value of Out and therefore $V_{X,OUT}$ cannot grow, which results in a blocking effect.

MAXIMAL

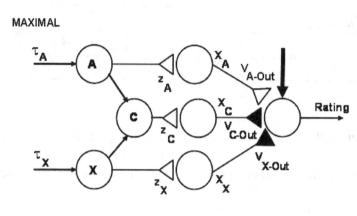

SUBMAXIMAL

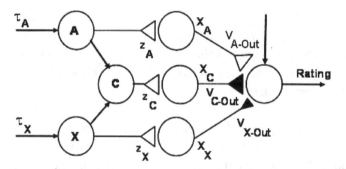

function. A similar constraint was introduced in a classical conditioning model by Schmajuk and DiCarlo (1992) and Schmajuk et al. (1996), and later used in the conditioning models presented by Brandon et al. (2002) and Le Pelley (2004). Importantly, this widely accepted constraint has been used to explain Rescorla's (2000, 2001, 2002) results regarding the reinforcement or non-reinforcement of a compound of stimuli with different initial associative values. This is especially relevant in blocking experiments, because the constraint modifies the Rescorla-Wagner (1978) common error correction and allows that equation to describe the greater increase in X-US associations than in A-US associations during AX+ trials

observed by Rescorla (2001). Finally, Schmajuk and Larrauri (2008; see also Haselgrove, 2010) showed that even the original Rescorla-Wagner (1972) rule is able to described maximality effects when an individual error term is incorporated.

Interestingly, it is possible to assign psychological meaning to the limiting term (V_{MAX} - $|V_{CS,OUT}|$). The value of V_{MAX} establishes whether a potential cause can be considered or not the exclusive cause for a given outcome. It implies that a relative weak cause will not be able to fully predict an Outcome ($CS_{WEAK} * V_{MAX}$ < Outcome), that is, it cannot be accepted as the only cause of a strong (maximal) outcome, thereby becoming unable to block other potential causes. However, if the strength of the

Figure 6. Maximality training preceding blocking. Values of X_X, $V_{X,OUT}$ and the CR on the test trial for non-additive and additive groups. Submaximal blocking is stronger than Maximal blocking because $V_{A,OUT}$ cannot increase proportionally to the maximal Outcome, thereby allowing increases in $V_{X,OUT}$ in the second case. The phenomenon is explained in associative terms.

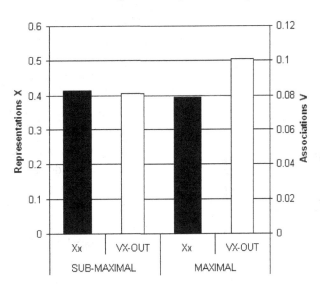

cause increases, it will be able to fully predict an Outcome ($CS_{STRONG} * V_{MAX} = Outcome$) and able to block other potential causes. Also, by limiting the value of associations $V_{CS,OUT}$ to V_{MAX} the system preserves its sensitivity and its ability of increasing the prediction of the outcome when the magnitude of the cause increases.

Additivity Training
Preceding Blocking

Experimental data. In Beckers et al.'s (2005, Experiment 2) additivity pretraining study, one additive and one subadditive group were used. The additive group received 40 G+/H+/GH++/ I+/Z- alternated trials (prior training), followed by alternated 16 A+/Z- trials (elemental training), and finally by 24 AX+/KL+/Z- alternated trials (compound training). Whereas G, H, I, Z, A, X, K and L denote stimuli, symbols + and ++ indicate the same outcome with different intensities. The

probability, assigned by each group, of X and K (and L) to cause the outcome (ratings) were then compared. Subadditive groups received GH+ instead of GH++, and in order to maintain constant the maximal outcome, presentations and I++ instead of I+ presentations. As shown in Figure 7 (Upper Panel), although blocking was present in both groups, it was stronger in the additive than in the subadditive case.

Simulated results. Simulations for Becker's (2005) Experiment 2 included 30 additive (5 Z-, 10 G+, 10 H+, 10 GH++) or subadditive (5 Z-, 10 G+, 10 H+, 10 GH+) pretraining, 10 A+, 20 AX+ trials, and 20 KL+ trials. Stimulus duration was 10 time units, stimulus intensity was 1, C intensity was 1, the Outcome was 2 for additivity and 1 for subadditive training. We did not include I+ or I++ trials because, as mentioned in the section describing Experiment 1, the model is not sensitive to changes in the maximal outcome. However, within-group simulations including I+

Figure 7. Additivity training preceding blocking. Ratings of stimulus A, X, Z, and average rating for stimuli K and L for the Additive and Subadditive cases. Upper Panel: Data from Beckers et al.'s (2005) Experiment 2. Lower Panel: Simulated rating with the configural-attentional version of Schmajuk-Lam-Gray (1996) model.

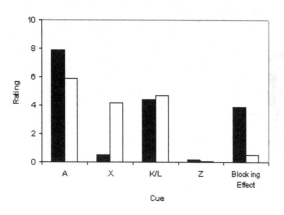

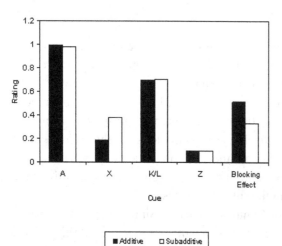

and I++ trials show results similar to the ones reported in this section.

Figure 7 (Lower Panel) shows that the configural form of the SLG model is able to correctly describe the experimental results. Like the Rescorla-Wagner (1972) model, the SLG model explains blocking because, at the time of the pre-sentation of X, A already predicts the Outcome (or US). As shown in Figure 2, compound stimulus C', activated by τ_G and τ_H and associated with the Outcome during pretraining, fully generalizes to compound stimulus C when it is activated by τ_A and τ_X (Figure 8). The $V_{C,OUT}$ association, together with the blocker stimulus A, contributes to predict the Outcome thereby increasing blocking. Because the $V_{C,OUT}$ association acquired during pre-training is stronger in the additive than in the subadditive case, blocking is stronger in the former than in the latter case (Figure 9). In addition, an attentional mechanism also contributes to increasing blocking in the additive case. Attention to X is weaker in the additive case because the stronger $V_{C,OUT}$ association results in less Novelty' and a weaker z_X and X_X. Interestingly, such decrease in attention to the blocked CS has been reported by Mackintosh and Turner (1971) and Kruschke and Blair (2000).

It is important to notice that the increased blocking in the additive case is not simply the result of a larger Outcome presented on GH compound trials, but truly the consequence of the Outcome being larger on compound GH++ than in elemental G+ and H+ trials. Computer simulations show that when a G++, H++, and GH++ trials are used, facilitation is not present. The lack of a blocking facilitation is explained in terms of the relatively small C-Outcome association achieved when the Outcome is well predicted by both G and H during pretraining.

Livesey and Boakes (2004) suggested another associative explanation for absence of blocking in the subadditive case. They proposed that when the combined effect of two stimuli, A and X, is less than the sum of their individual effects, those stimuli are combined into a single stimulus. Blocking would not be present in the subadditive case because the A-Outcome association is not activated by the A-X configural stimulus, which gains a strong association with the US. However, as Livesey and Boakes (2004, page 376) point out, further assumptions are needed to explain how a

Figure 8. Variables during the AX+ phase of blocking, following additive training. Following additivity pretraining the $V_{C,OUT}$ association is stronger (Upper Panel) than after subadditivity pretraining (Lower Panel), and therefore $V_{X,OUT}$ is weaker during AX+ trials (more blocking), in the additive (Upper Panel) than in the subadditive (Lower Panel) case. Also contributing to an increased blocking, the stronger $V_{C,OUT}$ association results in less Novelty' and a weaker z_X and X_X in the additive (Upper Panel) than in the subadditive (Lower Panel) case.

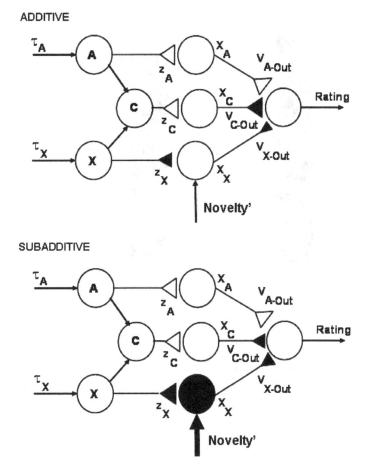

response to X is produced, when the strong association is formed between the A-X configuration, and not X, with the US.

Additivity Training Preceding Backward Blocking and Release from Overshadowing

Experimental data In Beckers et al.'s (2005, Experiment 3) additivity pretraining study, one additive and one subadditive group were used.

The additive group received 40 G+/H+/GH++/I+/Z- alternated trials (prior training), followed by 24 AX+/KL+/Z- alternated trials (compound training), and finally by alternated 16 A+/Z- trials (elemental training). Subadditive groups received GH+ instead of GH++ presentations and I++ instead of I+ presentations. Beckers et al.'s (2005, Experiment 3) also included a release (recovery) from overshadowing experiment, identical to backward blocking except that the elemental training consisted of 16 A-/Z- trials. As shown

Figure 9. Additivity training preceding blocking. Values of $V_{C,OUT}$ $V_{X,OUT}$ X_X and the CR on the test trial for the non-additive and additive groups. Following additive pretraining blocking is stronger than following non-additive pretraining because both X_X and $V_{X,OUT}$ are weaker in the first case. The phenomenon is explained both in attentional and associative terms.

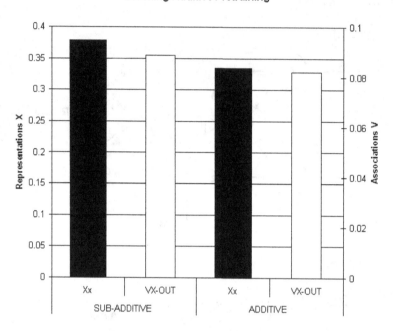

in Figure 10 (Upper Panel), although backward blocking was present in the additive case it was absent in the subadditive cases, no differences were found in release from overshadowing. Beckers et al. (2005) pointed out that the result contradicted models (Dickinson & Burke, 1966; Van Hamme & Wasserman, 1994; Miller and Matzel, 1988) that assume that the same associative principles underlie both backward blocking and recovery from overshadowing, because they predict that any manipulation affecting one should affect the other.

Simulated results. Simulations for Becker's (2005) Experiment 3 consisted of 5 Z-, 10 G+, 10 H+, and 10 GH+ (subadditivity) or GH++ trials (additivity) followed by 10 AX+ trials, 70 A+ trials and 10 KL+ trials (backward blocking), or 30 AX+ trials, 11 A- trials, and 30 KL+ trials (release from overshadowing). All other parameters were as those used in Experiment 2. As in

the case of Experiment 2, we did not include I+ or I++ trials, but within-group simulations including I+ and I++ trials show results similar to the ones reported in this section.

Figure 10 (Lower Panel) shows that the configural form of the SLG model predicts that additivity pretraining results in stronger backward blocking (AX+ followed by A+ training) than subadditivty pretraining. Notice that the Beckers et al. data show no backward blocking in the subadditive case. According to the SLG model, backward blocking is the result of the Outcome-X associations activating the representation of X during A+ presentations. During this period, Novelty' in the experimental group first increases and then decreases because X, predicted both by the Outcome and by A, is absent. Therefore, the representation of X becomes associated with Novelty' and attention to X slightly increases. In

Figure 10. Additivity training preceding backward blocking and release from overshadowing. Ratings of stimulus A, X, Z, and average rating for stimuli K and L for the Additive and Subadditive cases. Upper Panel: Data from Beckers et al.'s (2005) Experiment 3. Lower Panel: Simulated rating with the configural-attentional version of the Schmajuk-Lam-Gray (1996) model.

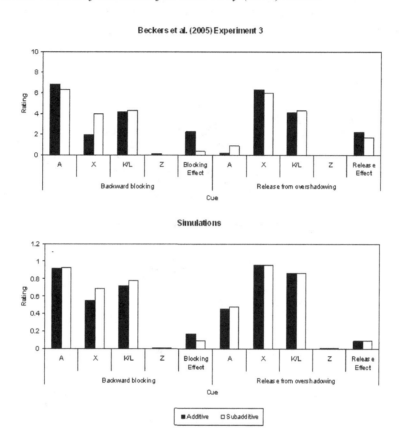

the control group, Novelty' increases even more because K and L, both predicted by the Outcome, are absent. Therefore, the representation of K (and L) becomes more strongly associated with Novelty' and attention to K is stronger in the control than in the experimental group. Correspondingly, during testing, responding to K is stronger in the control than responding to X in the experimental group, that is, backward blocking is present.

According to the model, following additivity training, the $V_{C,OUT}$ association is stronger than after subadditivity pretraining, and therefore $V_{X,OUT}$ and $V_{A,OUT}$ are weaker during AX+ trials (more overshadowing), in the additive than in the subadditive case (see Figure 11). During AX+

trials, the stronger $V_{C,OUT}$ association decreases Novelty', z_X and X_X more in the additive than in the subadditive case. During A+ trials, Novelty' increases, and the prediction of X, B_X, activated by the Outcome through $V_{OUT,X}$ associations, increases z_X and X_X, which remain weaker in the additive than in the subadditive case. In addition, during A+ trials, the stronger subadditive X_X activates and partially extinguishes its $V_{X,OUT}$ association (because X_A also increases and activates $V_{A,OUT}$ thereby making negative the common error term, see Equation 1), which becomes weaker in the subadditive than in the additive case (see Figure 13, Left Panel). Blocking is observed because Novelty' increases more in both additive and sub-

Figure 11. Variables during the AX+ phase of backward blocking, following additive training. Following additivity training, the $V_{C,OUT}$ association is stronger (Upper Panel) than after subadditivity pretraining (Lower Panel), and therefore $V_{X,OUT}$ and $V_{A,OUT}$ are weaker during AX+ trials (more overshadowing), in the additive (Upper Panel) than in the subadditive (Lower Panel) case. During AX+ trials, the stronger $V_{C,OUT}$ association decreases Novelty', z_X and X_X more in the additive (Upper Panel) than in the subadditive (Lower Panel) case. During A+ trials, z_X increases but still remains weaker in the additive than in the subadditive case.

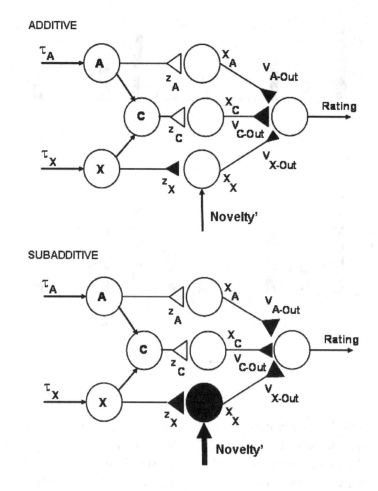

additive control groups than in the experimental groups (A+ trials). In consequence, responding to X (proportional to the product $X_X V_{X,OUT}$) is stronger, and blocking is weaker, in the subadditive case than in the additive case (see Figure 13, Left Panel).

Notice that, as in the case of forward blocking, the increased backward blocking in the additive case is not simply the result of a larger Outcome presented on GH compound trials, but the conse-

quence of the Outcome being larger on compound GH++ than in elemental G+ and H+ trials.

Figure 10 (Lower Panel) also shows that the configural form of the SLG model is able to describe the effect of additivity pretraining on recovery (release) from overshadowing (AX+ followed by A- training). According to the model, recovery from overshadowing is the result of the increased attention to X during A- presentations following AX+ pairings. According to the model,

Figure 12. Variables during the A- phase of recovery from overshadowing, following additive training. Following additivity training, the $V_{C,OUT}$ association is stronger (Upper Panel) than after subadditivity pretraining (Lower Panel), and therefore $V_{X,OUT}$ and $V_{A,OUT}$ are weaker during AX+ trials (more overshadowing), in the additive (Upper Panel) than in the subadditive (Lower Panel) case. During A- trials, A activates the prediction of X, B_X, which becomes associated with Novelty'. In the absence of the Outcome and the stronger $V_{C,OUT}$ association Novelty', z_X and X_X are stronger in the additive (Upper Panel) than in the subadditive (Lower Panel) case.

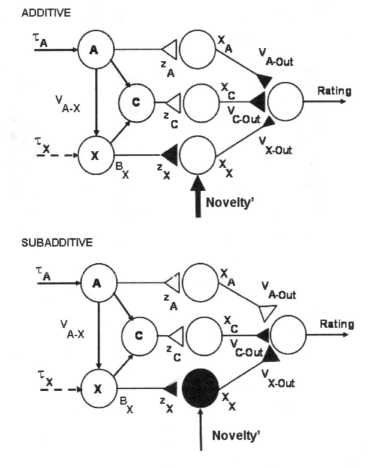

in absence of the stronger Outcome during A-presentations in the additive case, X_X is slightly stronger than in the subadditive case (see Figure 12, and Figure 13, Right Panel). Also, $V_{C,OUT}$ is stronger and, therefore, $V_{X,OUT}$ is weaker in the additive than in the subadditive case (Figure 12). In consequence, because responding to X is a function of the product $X_X V_{X,OUT}$, recovery from overshadowing is similar in subadditive and additive cases (see Figure 10, Lower Panel).

In addition to describing the facilitatory effect of additivity pretraining on backward blocking, computer simulations show that the model also describes the facilitatory effect of subtractivity pre-training on backward blocking (Mitchell et al., 2005). According to the inferential view, G+/ H+/GH- training following backward blocking (AX+, A+) leads to the logical inference that X is not causal –because X does not decrease the outcome produced by A– thereby increasing

Figure 13. Additivity training preceding backward blocking and release from overshadowing. Values of X_X and $V_{X,OUT}$ on the test trial for the non-additive and additive groups. Left Panel: When training precedes backward blocking, responding to X is weaker (and blocking is stronger) in the additive than in the non-additive case because attention to X (and its representation X_X) is weaker in the additive case, even when associations $V_{X,OUT}$ are similar. Right Panel: When training precedes recovery from overshadowing, responding to X and recovery is similar in both cases because in the additive case a slightly stronger representation X_X is compensated by a slightly weaker association $V_{X,OUT}$

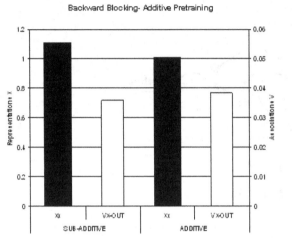
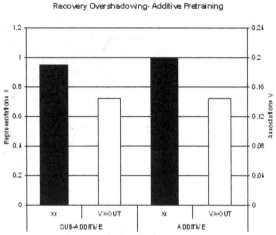

backward blocking. Our simulations of the effect of subtractivity pre-training on backward blocking used the same number of trials used to simulate Beckers et al.'s (2005) Experiment 3, but 10 GH- trials replaced the 10 GH+ (subadditive) trials, and a total 50 A+ trials. Our simulated results correctly show a stronger blocking effect for the subtractivity case (10%) than for the nonadditive case (4%). According to the model, this is the consequence of the increased Novelty' when configural stimulus C associated with Outcome = 0 encounters Outcome =1 during AX+ presentations. However, possibly because our simulation design is very different from the complex experimental design used by Mitchell et al. (2005), whereas these authors reported that responding to X in the subtractivity group was lower than in the nonadditive group, simulations show a higher X responding in the subtractivity group than in the nonadditive group (even if blocking was the strongest in the first case).

Additivity Training Following Blocking

Experimental data. In Beckers et al.'s (2005, Experiment 4) additivity posttraining study, the additive group received 40 G+/H+/GH++/I+/Z- alternated trials, and the subadditive group 40 G+/ H+/GH+/I++/Z- alternated trials, following total 40 blocking trials. As shown in Figure 14 (Upper Right Panel), although blocking was present in both groups, it was stronger in the additive than in the subadditive case.

Simulated results. Simulations for Beckers et al.'s (2005) Experiment 4 included 5 A+, 20 AX+, 20 KL+, and additive (5 Z-, 10 G+, 10 H+, 10 GH++) or subadditive (5 Z-, 10 G+, 10 H+, 10 GH+) post-training trials. Other parameters were identical to those used for Experiment 2. As in the case of Experiment 2, we did not include I+ or I++ trials, but within-group simulations includ-

Figure 14. Additivity training following blocking. Ratings of stimulus A, X, Z, and average rating for stimuli K and L for the Additive and Subadditive cases. Upper Panel: Data from Beckers et al.'s (2005) Experiment 4. Lower Panel: Simulated rating with the configural-attentional version of the Schmajuk-Lam-Gray (1996) model.

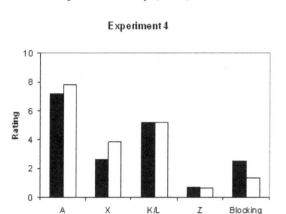

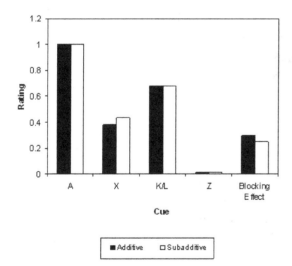

ing I+ and I++ trials show results similar to the ones reported in this section.

In agreement with those data, Figure 14 (Lower Panel) shows that the configural form of the SLG model shows that additivity posttraining results in stronger blocking than subadditivty pretraining.

As Mitchell et al. (2000) correctly observed, in the absence of pretraining, the C compound is already associated with the Outcome during post-training and, therefore, C-Outcome associations cannot be used to explain increased blocking. However, the configural form of the SLG model provides an attentional interpretation for the result. In terms of the model, during the AX+ phase of blocking, Outcome-X and C-X associations are formed. During post-training, Novelty' increases because the Outcome predicts the absent A and X, and G an H are novel. In the additive case, during GH++ trials, X is predicted by the relatively strong Outcome through $V_{OUT,X}$ associations. In the subadditive case, during GH+ trials, X is predicted by the relative weak Outcome through the same $V_{OUT,X}$ associations. Because $V_{OUT,X}$ associations extinguish faster with the stronger, additive Outcome (GH++), the prediction of X, B_X, becomes less associated with Novelty' and therefore z_X is weaker in the additive than in the subadditive case (see Figure 15). Thus, as shown in Figure 16, the representation of X, X_X, is weaker in the additive case than in the nonadditive case. Because X predicts the Outcome in proportion to the product $X_X V_{X,OUT}$ (see Equation 2) rating is lower (and blocking is stronger) in the additive than the non-additive case (see Figure 14, Lower Panel).

Interestingly, because it assumes that biological USs do not predict other CSs (Schmajuk and Larrauri, 2006), the SLG model predicts that additive/subadditive post-training would not affect blocking, a result observed (under some conditions) when rats were trained with water as the US (Ralph Miller, personal communication). According to the model, additivity effects might be observed in animals if the US was represented by another CS (a surrogate US) and that CS was associated to a biological US. Such approach was used by Miller and Matute (1996) to demonstrate backward conditioning in rats.

Figure 15. Variables during the GH+ trials of blocking, following additive training. During GH trials, because the representation of the Outcome, X_{OUT} is stronger during additive than subadditive post-training, $V_{Out,X}$ association formed during AX+ presentations extinguishes faster, which results in a weaker B_X. Therefore z_X proportional to the association of B_X (activated by both C and Out) and Novelty' is weaker in the additive than in the subadditive case. A weaker z_X translates into a weaker X_X and lower X rating.

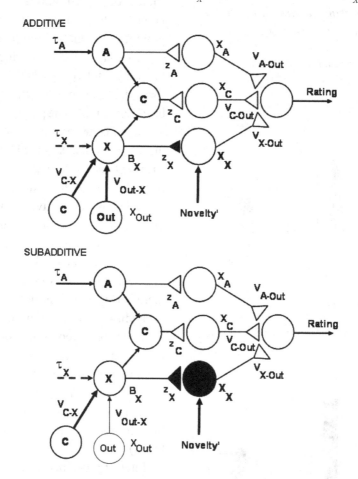

DISCUSSION

We have shown that a combination of configural, attentional and associative mechanisms is able to approximate the effects of (1) maximality pretraining on forward blocking, (2) additivity pretraining on forward blocking, (3) additivity pretraining on backward blocking and recovery from overshadowing, and (4) additivity post-training on forward blocking, as described in the Becker et al (2005) report. In addition to the Becker et al's

(2005) experiments, the SLG model describes the facilitatory effect of subtractivity pre-training on backward blocking (Mitchell et al., 2005).

COMPARISON BETWEEN INFERENTIAL EXPLANATIONS AND THE MODEL EXPLANATIONS

Our model's explanations for the results differ from those offered by the inferential approach. How-

Figure 16. Additivity training following blocking. Values of X_x, $V_{X,OUT}$ and the CR on the test trial for the non-additive and additive groups. When training follows blocking, rating of X is weaker (and blocking is stronger) in the additive than in the non-additive case because attention to X (and its representation X_x) is weaker in the additive case, even when associations $V_{X,OUT}$ are similar.

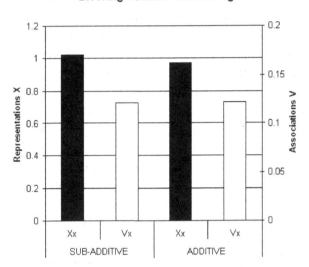

ever, comparisons are difficult because whereas our model describes the results in mechanistic terms, the inferential approach describes the results in terms of higher cognitive processes. In this section, we compare both types of explanations by replacing the model mechanistic descriptions by the participant views of (a) the relations between causes and outcomes, and (b) how much attention should be given to a cause in order to explain a given outcome.

According to the inferential view, because in the submaximal case (A+, AX+) a larger outcome is expected when A and X are presented together (the additive assumption), the fact that the outcome does not change leads the participants to decide that X is not an effective cause (blocking). Instead, because in the maximal case (A++, AX++) the outcome is not expected to increase when A and X are presented together (ceiling effect), the fact that the outcome does not change leaves the

participants unable to decide if X does or does not contribute to the outcome (no blocking). In contrast, according to our model, the maximality results are the consequence of the participants not accepting (due to previous experience) that a single cause A can produce the strongest (maximal) outcome, thereby judging that the added X is an effective cause of the outcome. Notice that, in the maximal case, whereas according to the inferential approach participants make a decision of not discounting X as an effective cause (no blocking), according to our model participants judge X as an effective cause (no blocking).

According to the inferential view, because in the additive case the outcome is expected to increase when A and X are presented together, the fact that the outcome does not change leads the participants to decide that X does not contribute to the outcome (blocking). Instead, because in the subadditive case the same outcome is expected when A and X are presented together, the fact that the outcome does not change leads the participants to believe that X might be an effective cause too (no blocking). In contrast, our model offers different explanations depending on the experimental situation. When additive training precedes blocking, (a) participants believe that the AX compound, but not X alone, is an important cause of the outcome, and (b) participants pay less attention to X during the AX+ trials, in the additive case than in the subadditive case. When additive training precedes backward blocking, participants pay more attention to the added X during the AX+ trials in the subadditive than in the additive case, and that attentional difference persists during the A+ trials. Finally, when additive training follows blocking, participant increase more their attention to the added X during the GH trials in the subadditive than in the additive case. Therefore, in all three cases, blocking is stronger in the additive than in the subadditive case.

Whereas in the cases of maximality and additive training preceding blocking the results are explained in terms of X-Outcome associations, the other cases are explained in terms of the attention directed to X. Schmajuk and Larrauri (2008; see also Haselgrove, 2010) have shown that, with slight modifications, even the simple competitive rule proposed by Rescorla-Wagner (1972) is able to describe the effects on blocking of maximality – when a constraining rule is added – and additivity pretraining – when a configural stimulus is added–. Therefore, the present results confirm that the additional attentional mechanisms incorporated into the SLG model are necessary to describe the other experimental results.

Interestingly, our model correctly predicts that blocking is present in an attenuated form in the subadditive and maximal cases. As pointed out by Beckers et al. (2005), this is not the situation with the inferential approach, which predicts that blocking is absent in the subadditive case. The observation of blocking in the maximal case,

however, could be inferentially explained by assuming that larger outcomes were experienced (or are innately known) previous to the experiment. Furthermore, only the inferential approach expects backward blocking to be completely eliminated by subadditive pretraining. Importantly, however, our model is able to reproduce the graded results observed for the cases of maximality and additivity.

Besides providing a combination of configural, attentional and associative explanations for the effects of maximality and additivity on blocking and backward blocking, simulations with the model suggest some experimental questions. Is it necessary to use different values of outcome in the maximality experiment, or is the maximal value sufficient? How many presentations of the maximal outcome are needed to change from a given maximal value to another (i.e., how do they affect V_{MAX}?). Would the presentation on GH++ trials of an outcome that exceeds the sum of the outcomes presented on G+ and H+ trials (++ outcome more than twice the strength of the + outcome) increase the facilitatory effect of additivity, as our simulations suggest?

Simulation Procedures

We verified that, in addition to the simulation values used here (e.g., number of G+, H+, GH+, GH++, A+, AX+, KL+ trials, CS intensity and duration) simulated results are robust under a wide range of values. For example, Schmajuk and Kutlu (2009) reported equally good simulated results for Beckers et al.'s (a) Experiment 2 using 90 additive or subadditive pretraining trials, 20 A+, 40 AX+ trials, and 40 KL+ trials, and (b) Experiment 4 using 20 A+, 20 AX+ trials, 20 KL+, and 90 additive or subadditive post-training trials. In both cases, stimulus durations were 10 time units, stimulus intensities were 0.6, C intensity was 1, and Outcome was 2 for additivity and 1 for subadditive training. In general, simulation results can be obtained within a wider range of simulation values for the effects of (a) maximality and (b) additivity training preceding blocking than for the effects of (c) additivity training preceding backward blocking and (d) additivity training following blocking. This might not be surprising given that Beckers et al. (2006) reported that only the two first effects are present in rats, and that the model was originally developed to describe animal conditioning.

However successful, the designs used in our simulations were simpler than those used in the experiments. In order to facilitate the understanding of how the model arrived at the results, our simulations were carried out with a simplified design that (a) uses between-group designs instead of within-group used by Beckers et al. (2005), and (b) does not include I+ and I++ trials that the Beckers et al. (2005) experiments included to control for maximality. Nevertheless, qualitatively similar results were found when (a) within-group simulations were used, and (b) I+ and I++ trials were also included. Unfortunately, the complexity of this design made extremely difficult the identification of the mechanisms responsible for the results. The use of between-group simulations might be justified because between-group designs were used in experiments similar to the ones described in this chapter that were carried out in rats (Experiments 1 and 2 in Beckers et al., 2006) and were accepted as equivalent to those carried out in humans.

Other differences between simulations and experiments should be noticed. Whereas all simulations used the same number of G, H, and GH trials –as in the experiments–, different numbers of trials were used in blocking, backward blocking, and recovery from overshadowing –in contrast to the experiments. The different number of trials is the consequence of most parameters being identical to those used in all previous applications of the SLG model. Furthermore, the fact that the model needs more trials than humans do might be evidence that the model was initially developed to

describe learning in animals. In sum, although our results might be considered only an approximation to Beckers et al.'s human data, even so, the model provides a clear qualitative explanation of the results in term of the different mechanisms that integrate the model.

Other Applications of the Model

In addition to the Beckers et al's (2005) causal learning experiments, computer simulations show that the configural version of the SLG model can also account for higher-order retrospective revaluation (De Hower and Beckers, 2002). For this experiment, the model correctly shows that following 100 CT1+ and 140 T1T2+ simulated trials, 80 presentations of C+ result in weaker responding to T1 (and stronger responding to T2) than 80 presentations of C- (CS salience was 1 and duration 10 time units, ITI 500 time units).

CONCLUSION

The results presented in this chapter support the notion that a version of the SLG model, which incorporates a combination of configural, attentional and associative mechanisms, is able to describe the effects of maximality and additivity training on forward and backward blocking. Importantly, the SLG model describes a large body of other classical conditioninig paradigms, including the multiple properties of latent inhibition (Schmajuk, 2002), super-latent inhibition, recovery of overshadowing, forward blocking, and backward blocking (Schmajuk and Larrauri, 2006), and the multiple properties of extinction (Larrauri and Schmajuk, 2008). In addition, the model is compatible with current neuroscientific evidence regarding error correction (Schultz, 2006) and attentional (Schmajuk, 2005; Dunsmoor and Schmajuk, 2009) mechanisms in the brain.

REFERENCES

Beckers, T., De Houwer, J., Pineno, O., & Miller, R. R. (2005). Outcome additivity and outcome maximality influence cue competition in human causal learning. *Journal of Experimental Psychology. Learning, Memory, and Cognition, 31*, 238–249.doi:10.1037/0278-7393.31.2.238

Beckers, T., Miller, R. R., De Houwer, J., & Urushihara, K. (2006). Reasoning rats: forward blocking in Pavlovian animal conditioning is sensitive to constraints of causal inference. *Journal of Experimental Psychology. General, 135*, 92–102. doi:10.1037/0096-3445.135.1.92

De Houwer, J., & Beckers, T. (2002). Higher-order retrospective revaluation in human causal learning. *The Quarterly Journal of Experimental Psychology, 55B*, 137–151. doi:10.1080/02724990143000216

Dickinson, A., & Burke, J. (1996). Within-compound associations mediate the retrospective revaluation of causality judgments. *Quarterly Journal of Experimental Psychology, 49B*, 60–80.

Dunsmoor, J., & Schmajuk, N. A. (2009). Interpreting patterns of brain activation in human fear conditioning with an attentional-associative learning model. *Behavioral Neuroscience, 123*, 851–855.doi:10.1037/a0016334

Dunsmoor, J., & Schmajuk, N. A. (in press). Interpreting patterns of brain activation in human fear conditioning with an attentional-associative learning model. *Behavioral Neuroscience*.

Haselgrove, M. (2010). Reasoning Rats or Associative Animals? A Common-Element Analysis of the Effects of Additive and Subadditive Pretraining on Blocking. *Journal of Experimental Psychology. Animal Behavior Processes, 36*, 296–306. doi:10.1037/a0016603

Kamin, L. J. (1968). "Attention-like" processes in classical conditioning. In M. R. Jones (Ed.), *Miami Symposium on the Prediction of Behavior: Aversive Stimulation* (pp. 9-33). Miami, FL: University of Miami Press.

Kruschke, J. K., & Blair, N. J. (2000). Blocking and backward blocking involve learned inattention. *Psychonomic Bulletin & Review, 7*, 636–645.

Larrauri, J. A., & Schmajuk, N. A. (2008). Attentional, associative, and configural mechanisms in extinction. *Psychological Review, 115*, 640–676. doi:10.1037/0033-295X.115.3.640

Livesey, E. J., & Boakes, R. A. (2004). Outcome additivity, elemental processing and blocking in human causality judgments. *The Quarterly Journal of Experimental Psychology. B, Comparative and Physiological Psychology, 57*, 361–379. doi:10.1080/02724990444000005

Lovibond, P. E., Been, S. L., Mitchell, C. J., Bouton, M. E., & Frohardt, R. (2003). Forward and backward blocking of causal judgment is enhanced by additivity of effect magnitude. *Memory & Cognition, 31*, 133–142.

Lubow, R. E., & Moore, A. U. (1959). Latent inhibition: The effect of non-reinforced preexposure to the conditional stimulus. *Journal of Comparative and Physiological Psychology, 52*, 415–419.doi:10.1037/h0046700

Mackintosh, N. J. (1975). A theory of attention: variations in the associability of stimuli with reinforcement. *Psychological Review, 82*, 276–298. doi:10.1037/h0076778

Mackintosh, N. J., & Turner, C. (1971). Blocking as a function of novelty of CS and predictability of UCS. *The Quarterly Journal of Experimental Psychology, 23*, 359–366. doi:10.1080/14640747108400245

McCall, R. B. (1970). *Fundamentals of statistics for psychology*. New York: Harcourt Brace Jovanovich.

Miller, R. R., & Matute, H. (1996). Biological significance in forward and backward blocking: Resolution of a discrepancy between animal conditioning and human causal judgment. *Journal of Experimental Psychology. General, 125,* 370–386. doi:10.1037/0096-3445.125.4.370

Miller, R. R., & Matzel, L. (1988). The comparator hypothesis: A response rule for the expression of associations. In Bower, G. H. (Ed.), *The psychology of learning and motivation* (*Vol. 22*, pp. 51–92). Orlando, FL: Academic Press.

Mitchell, C. J., Lovibond, P. F., & Condoleon, M. (2005). Evidence for deductive reasoning in blocking of causal judgments. *Learning and Motivation, 36,* 77–87.doi:10.1016/j.lmot.2004.09.001

Pavlov, I. P. (1927). *Conditioned reflexes*. London: Oxford University Press.

Pearce, J. M., & Hall, G. (1980). A model for Pavlovian learning: variations in the effectiveness of conditioned but not unconditioned stimuli. *Psychological Review, 87,* 532–552. doi:10.1037/0033-295X.87.6.532

Rescorla, R. A. (2000). Associative changes in excitors and inhibitors differ when they are conditioned in compound. *Journal of Experimental Psychology. Animal Behavior Processes, 26,* 428–438.doi:10.1037/0097-7403.26.4.428

Rescorla, R. A. (2001). Unequal associative changes when excitors and neural stimuli are conditioned in compound. *The Quarterly Journal of Experimental Psychology. B, Comparative and Physiological Psychology, 54B,* 53–68. doi:10.1080/02724990042000038

Rescorla, R. A. (2002). Effect of following an excitatory-inhibitory compound with an intermediate reinforcer. *Journal of Experimental Psychology. Animal Behavior Processes, 28,* 163–174. doi:10.1037/0097-7403.28.2.163

Rescorla, R. A., & Wagner, A. R. (1972). A theory of Pavlovian conditioning: Variations in the effectiveness of reinforcement and nonreinforcement. In Black, A. H., & Prokasy, W. F. (Eds.), *Classical conditioning: Current theory and research* (*Vol. 2,* pp. 64–99). New York: Appleton-Century-Crofts.

Schmajuk, N. A. (1997). *Animal learning and cognition: A neural network approach*. New York: Cambridge University Press.

Schmajuk, N. A. (2010). *Mechanisms classical conditioning: A computational approach*. New York: Cambridge University Press.

Schmajuk, N. A., & Kutlu, G. M. (2009). The computational nature of associative learning. *The Behavioral and Brain Sciences, 32,* 223–224. doi:10.1017/S0140525X09001125

Schmajuk, N. A., Lam, Y., & Gray, J. A. (1996). Latent inhibition: A neural network approach. *Journal of Experimental Psychology. Animal Behavior Processes, 22,* 321–349.doi:10.1037/0097-7403.22.3.321

Schmajuk, N. A., & Larrauri, J. A. (2006). Experimental challenges to theories of classical conditioning: Application of an attentional model of storage and retrieval. *Journal of Experimental Psychology. Animal Behavior Processes, 32,* 1–20. doi:10.1037/0097-7403.32.1.1

Schmajuk, N. A., & Larrauri, J. A. (2008). Associative models can describe both causal learning and conditioning. *Behavioural Processes, 77,* 443–445.

Schmajuk, N. A., Larrauri, J. A., & LaBar, K. S. (2007). Reinstatement of conditioned fear and the hippocampus: An attentional-associative model. *Behavioural Brain Research*, *177*, 242–253. doi:10.1016/j.bbr.2006.11.026

Schmajuk, N. A., & Thieme, A. D. (1992). Purposive behavior and cognitive mapping: An adaptive neural network. *Biological Cybernetics*, *67*, 165–174.doi:10.1007/BF00201023

Schultz, W. (2006). Behavioral theories and the neurophysiology of reward. *Annual Review of Psychology*, *57*, 87–115.doi:10.1146/annurev. psych.56.091103.070229

Shanks, D. R. (2007). Associationism and cognition: human contingency learning at 25. *Quarterly Journal of Experimental Psychology*, *60*, 291–309. doi:10.1080/17470210601000581

Sherman, J. E., & Maier, S. F. (1978). The decrement in conditioned fear with increased trials of simultaneous conditioning is not specific to the simultaneous procedure. *Learning and Motivation*, *9*, 31–53.doi:10.1016/0023-9690(78)90025-5

Van Hamme, L., & Wasserman, E. (1994). Cue competition in causality judgments: The role of nonpresentation of compound stimulus elements. *Learning and Motivation*, *25*, 127–151. doi:10.1006/lmot.1994.1008

Wagner, A. R. (1981). SOP: A model of automatic memory processing in animal behavior. In Spear, N. E., & Miller, R. R. (Eds.), *Information processing in animals: Memory mechanisms* (pp. 5–47). Hillsdale, NJ: Erlbaum.

Young, M. E., & Wasserman, E. A. (2002). Limited Attention and Cue Order Consistency Affect Predictive Learning: A Test of Similarity Measures. *Journal of Experimental Psychology. Learning, Memory, and Cognition*, *28*, 484–496. doi:10.1037/0278-7393.28.3.484

KEY TERMS AND DEFINITIONS

Blocking: Conditioning to CS1-CS2 following conditioning to CS1 results in a weaker response to CS2 than that attained after CS1-CS2-US pairings.

Backward Blocking: Conditioning to CS1 following conditioning to CS1-CS2 results in a weaker response to CS2 than that attained after CS1-CS2-US pairings.

Overshadowing: Conditioning to CS1-CS2 results in a weaker response to CS2 than that attained after CS2-US pairings.

Recovery from Overshadowing.: Following overshadowing, extinction of CS1 results in increased responding to the overshadowed CS2.

Additivity: When CS1 and CS2 (causes) predict a stronger US (outcome) when presented together than when presented independently.

Additivity Training: Showing that the effects of two CSs, not used in the experiments, can be added.

Submaximality: When a single CS (cause) does not predict the possible maximal US (outcome) value.

Maximality Training: Showing the maximum possible value of the US (outcome).

Chapter 5
Empirical Issues and Theoretical Mechanisms of Pavlovian Conditioning

Edgar H. Vogel
Universidad de Talca, Chile

Fernando P. Ponce
Universidad de Talca, Chile

ABSTRACT

Pavlovian conditioning is a very simple and universal form of learning that has the benefit of a long and rich tradition of experimental work and quantitative theorization. With the development of interdisciplinary efforts, behavioral data and quantitative theories of conditioning have become progressively more important not just for experimental psychologists but also for broader audiences such as neurobiologists, computational neuroscientists and artificial intelligence workers. In order to provide interdisciplinary users with an overview of the state of affairs of theoretically oriented research in this field, this chapter reviews a few key mechanisms that are currently deemed necessary for explaining several critical phenomena of Pavlovian conditioning. The chapter is divided into several sections; each referring to a particular theoretical mechanism and to the type of phenomena that it has been designed to account. The progression of the sections reveals phenomena and mechanisms of increasing complexity, which is an indication of the theoretical sophistication that has been reached in this domain. Since there is not a single theory containing all mechanisms, they are described separately from their originating theories, emphasizing thus the fact that they might be used in almost any theoretical implementation.

INTRODUCTION

Pavlovian conditioning is one of the most basic and well-studied varieties of learning. In its simplest form, a target stimulus, designated as conditioned stimulus (CS), is repeatedly paired with a reflex-eliciting stimulus, designated as unconditioned stimulus (US), resulting in a progressive change in the response to the CS, designated as conditioned response (CR). The classic example is dogs learning to salivate in the presence of a bell that has been paired with food (Pavlov, 1927), but several other more efficient procedures have been developed, such as eyeblink conditioning in

DOI: 10.4018/978-1-60960-021-1.ch005

Figure 1. Basic connectionist representation of Pavlovian conditioning. Presentation of the US and the CS provokes the activation of their respective units, a_{US} and a_{CS}. The adaptive unit represents the output responsible for the generation of the CR and is unconditionally activated by the US, via λ, and conditionally by the CS via V_{CS}. The link between the CS and the adaptive unit can be modified by learning, which depends on concurrent CS-US processing.

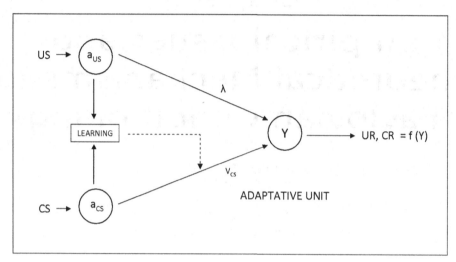

humans (Hilgard & Campbell, 1936) and rabbits (Gormezano, Schneiderman, Deux & Fuentes, 1962), fear conditioning in rats (Estes & Skinner, 1941), pigeon autoshaping (Brown & Jenkings, 1968), and taste aversion in rats (Garcia & Koelling, 1966).

The fundamentals of the process of CR acquisition, as well as of its natural counterpart, extinction, along with several other related phenomena, have been intensively studied since the pioneering work of Pavlov (1927). After more than a century of research, a great deal of empirical work has been cumulated and the theoretical interpretations are still subjected to intense theoretical debate (Wagner & Vogel, 2009).

One of the hallmarks of Pavlovian conditioning theories is their marked preference for associative explanations and quantitative formulations, where learning is viewed as changes in CS-US associations. The goal of quantitative theoreticians is to develop algorithms to describe the dynamics of these changes (learning rules) and to conceive theoretical structures in which they take place (stimulus representation and association between the representations).

Given that the predominant outcome of CS-US pairings is the development of a CR that resembles some aspects of the unconditioned response (UR) elicited by the US, several authors have adopted the simple schema outlined in Figure 1, in which the CS and the US are connected to a common response unit or adaptive unit (Sutton & Barto, 1981; Vogel, Castro & Saavedra, 2004). It is assumed that the CS and the US activate their respective representational units, which in turn influence the activity of the adaptive unit in proportion to their associative links, V and λ. The CS link is assumed to be modifiable, starting with a value of zero prior to conditioning but with the possibility of developing positive (excitatory links) or negative (inhibitory links) values after CS-US pairings. The US link, λ, is assumed to be non modifiable and capable of producing substantial activation of the response unit. Learning is normally assumed to be Hebbian; that is as a function of simultaneous CS and US processing.

The network depicted in Figure 1 contains the three basic structural elements of any connectionist theory for conditioning: stimulus representation units, response generation unit and links between units. Moreover, an algorithm to change the association or learning rule must be also stated. A large number of theories have been proposed in this tradition; each of them with mayor or minor differences in their architectures and learning rules, focusing in somewhat different subset of phenomena, and expressed with different degrees of mathematical sophistication.

In this chapter, instead of reviewing theories, we focus on a sample of the most important categories of phenomena and on the respective theoretical mechanisms that have been proposed. The assumption is that over the years some insights have been gained about a few critical mechanisms of Pavlovian conditioning necessary for any theory addressing certain phenomena. We selected a few general mechanisms and describe them independently from the theories in which they were originally implemented, in an attempt to show that almost all can be used in a broad range of models.

In order to keep the focus on the conceptual rationalization behind each mechanism, the description of empirical evidence is restricted to a minimum of details. Thus, some critical experiments are described only in terms of their general rationale and major conclusions. To simplify the description of the designs, we use a common nomenclature, in which CSs are designated with capital letters and the presence or absence of the US with the signs "+" and "-", respectively (e.g., A+ designating CS A paired with the US and B-designating CS B without the US). Compound trials involving two or more simultaneously presented CSs are designated with the letter corresponding to each CS followed by the corresponding sign (e.g., AB+, BCD-). Occasionally, the expression "reinforcement" or "reinforced trial" is used to refer to the presence of the US.

ERROR CORRECTION MECHANISMS: SATURATION VS. AGGREGATED PREDICTION

As shown in the network outlined in Figure 1, a fundamental requirement for leaning is concurrent CS-US processing. However, although necessary, this simple Hebbian mechanism is not sufficient to account for the fact that over a number of CS-US pairing, the size of the increments in CS-US association becomes smaller as the cumulated associative strength of the CS increases towards an asymptote. This fact, commonly referred to as a *negatively accelerated learning curve*, was managed by early theoreticians of Pavlovian conditioning (e.g., Atkinson & Estes, 1963; Hull, 1943; Bush & Moesteller, 1955) by assuming what Wagner (1969) called a *"saturation principle"*, in which each CS can acquire only a limited amount of association with the US, which is provided by the US itself.

The saturation principle is equivalent to assume that learning is due to an error correction mechanism in which the US acts as a supervisor that teaches the CS how to produce the CR, via a progressive diminution of the difference between λ and V. Panel a of Figure 2 depicts a graphical representation of this mechanism, in which it can be seen that leaning accrued to each CS depends on the amount of its own error term. Formally, the change in the associative strength accrued to CS_i, ΔV_i is given by the equation $\Delta V_i = \theta(a_{US}\lambda - a_{CS}V_i)$, known as "linear rule". The symbol θ represents a learning rate parameter and $(a_{US}\lambda - a_{CS}V_i)$ is the error term or reinforcement. According to this equation, CR acquisition occurs in those trials in which the internal representation of the CS and the US are active (i.e., a_{CS} and a_{US} are greater than zero) and the error term or reinforcement is positive (i.e., $a_{US}\lambda > a_{CS}V_i$).

With the linear rule is possible to predict the negatively accelerated acquisition curve, since the increments in V decrease as the net V value increases. Learning reaches its asymptote when

Figure 2. Two approaches to error computation in Pavlovian conditioning. Presentation of the US and the CSs provokes the activation of their respective units, a_{US}, a_{CS1} and a_{CS2}. The adaptive unit represents the output responsible for the generation of the CR and is unconditionally activated by the US, via λ, and conditionally by the CSs via V_i. According to the saturation mechanism (panel a) the error is computed independently for each CS, while that for the aggregated prediction mechanism (panel b) there is common error term.

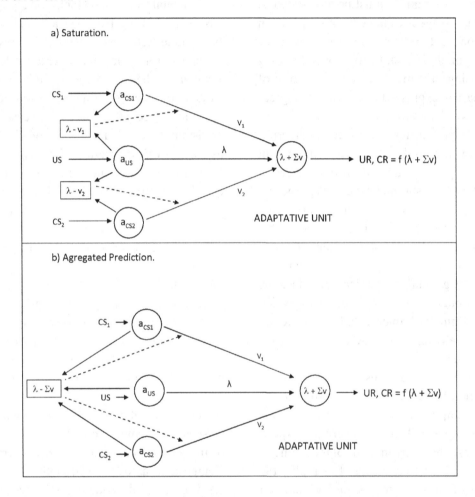

the error equals zero (i.e., $a_{US}λ=a_{CS}V_i$). The error correction mechanism involved in the linear rule easily accounts also for the progressive disappearance of the CR occasioned by the presence of a well trained CS in the absence of the US or extinction. In this case, since $a_{US}λ=0$ and $a_{CS}V>0$, the error term becomes negative and V_i decreases in a negatively accelerated fashion towards an asymptote of zero.

A situation that rapidly becomes evident with the linear rule is that it cannot account for the formation of inhibitory associations, whose reality has been demonstrated in a number of studies (see Rescorla, 1969, 1979; Wagner & Rescorla, 1972). The most common procedure to obtain inhibitory associations is by a certain type of discrimination training where a CS A is followed by the US when isolated, but not when is presented in association with another CS, B (i.e., A+AB-), resulting in B obtaining the capacity to inhibit the response elicited by any other excitatory CS, C, when they are compounded (i.e., BC). Since the error correction mechanism involved in the linear rule computes incremental changes up to an asymptote of λ and decremental changes down to an asymptote of zero, it is expected that A will develop excitatory associative strength in A+ trials towards lambda and will lose some of it in AB- trials towards and asymptote of zero. Since B is already at the asymptote for negative trials, the rule predicts incorrectly that it will not develop any association with the US, neither excitatory nor inhibitory. In other words, since the linear rule assumes no interaction between A and B during the negative trials, the amount of associative strength accrued to B depends only on its initial value of 0, irrespectively of the positive values acquired by A in the positive trials.

Given these difficulties, it can be assumed that inhibition develops trough other mechanisms independently from the development of excitation (see, Hull, 1943; Estes, 1950). Another possibility is to assume that the CSs interact or interfere with one another during learning, such as the amount of associative strength accrued to a CS depends on the amount of associative strength acquired by all concurrently active CSs. In order to effectively solve the discrimination involved in the conditioned inhibition paradigm, B could develop negative associative strength in the AB- trials to counteract the excitation obtained by A in the positive trials.

Several experiments published in the late sixties provided compelling support for the later possibility. The most commonly cited study is the demonstration of the so called *"blocking phenomenon"*, in which the prior reinforcement of A alone, reduces (blocks) the acquisition of conditioned response to another CS, B, if it is reinforced together with A (A+/AB+). The conclusion of blocking and of other similar findings, like overshadowing (Pavlov, 1927) and relative validity (Wagner, Logan, Haberland, & Price, 1968), is that what is learned to one of the cues on a trial appears to depend not only upon its own current associative value, but also upon the asso-

ciative value of the other cues present in the trial. This fact is sometimes called *stimulus selection* or *stimulus competition* (Wagner, 1969).

Several theoretical alternatives have been proposed for this competition among CSs and all of them share the common feature of assuming that the amount of reinforcement to a given CS varies as a function of another existing association. The general assumption is that the change in the associative value of a given CS does not depend only of its own associative value, but upon the aggregate value of all CSs present on the trial. Panel b of Figure 2 illustrates the first and most influential alternative, proposed by Rescorla and Wagner (1972). As can seen in the Figure, the only difference with the saturation principle, is in the common, instead of independent error term for all CSs. Formally, the Rescorla-Wagner rule posits that the change in associative strength accrued to CS_i, ΔV_i is given by the equation $\Delta V_i = \theta(a_{US}\lambda - \Sigma a_i V_i)$.

The Rescorla-Wagner rule represents a very simple modification in the computation of the error term used in the linear rule, but it meant an enormous conceptual change in the way in which Pavlovian conditioning is viewed. After this model, Pavlovian conditioning began to be considered as one of the mechanisms by which animals learn predictive relationship among stimuli. Since the activation of the adaptive unit by the US becomes ineffective in producing reinforcement as similar amounts of activation are obtained by conditioned sources, the Rescorla-Wagner model is regarded as using a "variable reinforcement mechanism".

An alternative explanation of stimulus competition is that the associative failure, rather than being caused by a diminution of the reinforcing properties of the US (i.e., variation on US processing, as assumed by the Rescorla-Wagner model), is due instead to a diminution in the associability of or attention paid to the target CS (i. e., variation in CS processing). Models using this approach, referred to as "attentional theories," (Mackintosh, 1975) state that stimuli compete for a limited attentional capacity and hence competence for learning. According to this view, stimulus competition does not occur because the reinforcement becomes ineffective, but instead because animals "ignore" a CS in presence of another CS that is more predictive of reinforcement.

Both approaches are able to account for a broad range of phenomena quite accurately despite of their different conceptions of stimulus competition, since both consider the relative rather than the absolute value of stimuli in predicting the US to be the critical component of conditioning. The debate as to whether it is US processing or CS processing that changes over the course of learning (that is, whether stimuli compete for available reinforcement or for attentional resources), has not been resolved, and it is in part reflected in the formulation of some mixed models that rely on both CS and US variation processes (Pearce & Hall, 1980; Harris, 2006).

Finally, there is still another more radical approach to stimulus selection, called "Comparator Theory" (Miller & Matzel, 1988). It assumes that there is no competition among CSs for learning (like the linear operator rule) but for performance. According to this approach, the level of conditioned responses to a given CS is a function of the comparison of the CS's associative strength with the associative strengths of any other cue with which the CS has become associated. Thus, for instance, the low level in initial responding seen in a blocked cue would not be due to its low associative strength, but to the comparison with the similar or greater associative strength of the blocking cue with which it was associated in the compound phase. Some evidence showing that the detrimental effects of stimulus selection can be reversed by extinguishing one of the cues, has been assumed as an encouraging fact for this hypothesis (Cole, Matter & Miller, 1995) but there is also no supportive evidence (e.g., Williams, 1996).

As it will be shown below, although competitive versus non competitive learning is an unresolved issue, there is enough grounds for preferring the *aggregated prediction* mechanism. Likewise, the variable reinforcement alternative seems to have a greater heuristic value to be combined with some additional mechanism that will be discussed in the next sections.

TIME VARYING STIMULUS REPRESENTATION

There is substantial evidence suggesting that what is learned in Pavlovian conditioning depends not only on the informational value of the CS, but also in temporal factors. Several phenomena demonstrating the influence of temporal variables have posed a number of theoretical puzzles, which have been solved by implementing computational strategies of increasing complexity. In this section we describe the most basic temporal phenomena and the simplest theoretical strategy which implies incorporating a *time varying stimulus representation*.

The simplest temporal phenomena are the ones related to the manipulation of the CS-US interval or ISI. This has been studied by means of two temporal arrangements, delay conditioning, in which the CS precedes and overlaps the US and trace conditioning, in which one of the stimuli terminates before the onset of the other. Depending on the order of presentation of the CS and the US, trace conditioning is referred to as "forward conditioning" (the CS precedes the US) or "backward conditioning" (the US precedes the CS).

There are two major outcomes with these procedures that have captured the attention of researchers. The first is the observation that the temporal features of the CR, such as its latency of initiation and peak, depend on the ISI employed in training. Response onset latency, defined as the time interval between CS onset and the beginning of the CR, and latency to CR peak, defined as the time between CS onset and an the moment of maximal CR amplitude, have shown to increase with the ISI (Bitterman, 1964; Davis, Schlessinger & Sorenson, 1989; Gallistel & Gibbon, 2000; Kimmel, 1965; Mauk & Ruiz, 1992). The second phenomenon is the demonstration that there is an optimal intermediate duration interval in which the rate and possibly the asymptote of learning is maximal, which decreases with longer and shorter intervals, suggesting that the relationship between the strength of conditioning and the ISI follows and inverted U function (Kehoe, 1990; Schneiderman, 1966; Schneiderman & Gormezano, 1964; Smith, Coleman & Gormezano, 1969).

In order to approach these phenomena, it is necessary to assume a temporally varying representation of the CS or trace. The concept of trace, first proposed by Pavlov (1927) and further developed by Hull (1943), refers to the change over time in the activity of the CS, which may continue after its offset. According to Hull (1943), the learning that accrues to a CS in a given trial depends on the strength of its trace at the US locus.

The transition from this general notion of trace to modern quantitative formulations came with the first generation of "real time" models of Pavlovian conditioning (e.g., Moore & Stickney, 1980; Sutton & Barto, 1981; Wagner, 1981), which assumed that the trace is an unitary or molar representation of the CS controlling only a global association with the US. Following Hull (1943), those models have in common the assumption that the amount of learning and the strength of the CR at each moment of the CS duration would depend on the strength of the trace at those moments.

The top plot of Figure 3 presents one example of molar trace used by a real time rendition of the Rescorla-Wagner (1972) model by Schmajuk (1997). As it can be seen, the CS- trace follow a curvilinear function, which includes an exponential grow to a maximal value following CS onset, an adaptation phase in which the trace remains constant, and an exponential decay towards zero after CS offset. If this molar trace is used in conjunction with a learning rule that computes increments in associative strength in the portion

of the trace in which the CS and the US overlap, and decrements (extinction) in those moments which they do not overlap, the basic temporal phenomena can be easily managed.

The three bottom plots of Figure 3 illustrate how the molar trace notion accounts for the inverted U-shaped ISI function appealing to differential incremental and decremental processes for short-, medium- and long-duration ISIs. In this example, learning accrues faster to medium than longer ISIs despite of sharing the same amount of increments because there are more decrements in the longer condition. Likewise, faster conditioning for ISIs of intermediate duration than shorter ISIs is a consequence of the lesser strength of the trace at the shorter ISI meaningless increments. The superiority of the decremental process in the medium over the short ISI is assumed to be overcome by its differences in the incremental process (Wagner & Rescorla, 1972).

Furthermore, if it is assumed that the initiation of the CR depends on the associative strength carried by the trace at each moment; molar trace models predict longer latency of CR and of peak for those ISIs with poorer conditioning, which are consistent with the empirical evidence of training with relatively long ISIs.

Thus, according to this view, the basic temporal phenomena of conditioning depend exclusively on the associative strength acquired by the CS, where CR latency and peak latency are inversely correlated with the strength of conditioning. It is important to emphasize that this simple mechanism works identically with either the aggregated prediction (e.g., Rescorla-Wagner rule) or the saturation (e.g., linear rule) mechanisms, since the two approaches compute increments at the locus of reinforcement and decrements at every other loci. However, the aggregated prediction mechanism is better suited to account for the fact that under some circumstances backward conditioning may result in small amounts of excitatory learning (Siegel & Domjan, 1971) but also in notable inhibitory learning (Burckhardt &

Figure 3. Time courses of the CS in a trial in which the CS is followed by a binary US, according to a real-time rendition of the Rescorla-Wagner model by Schmajuk (1997). The top plot presents the general shape of the trace and the bottom plots depict incremental (dark shaded area) and decremental (clear shaded area) learning for s short (left plot), medium (middle plot) and long duration CSs.

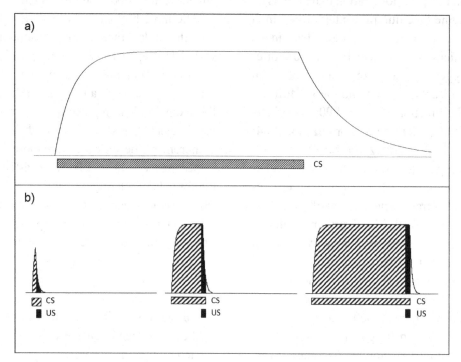

Ayres, 1978). Although it is not very intuitive to rationalize how the molar trace in combination with the aggregated prediction notion can produce a CS with net inhibitory associative strength, some computational strategies appealing to differential values of lambda at US onset versus offset has been offered by Wagner and Rescorla (1972) and Sutton and Barto (1981).

Finally, it should be noticed that there are some alternative accounts of timing outside the associative approach, which posed that timing is learned by a different mechanism than conditioning (Gibbon & Balsan, 1981) or even the most extreme tack that both conditioning and timing are acquired through some kind of temporal processing of the cues (Gallistel & Gibbon, 2000). Since the focus of the present paper is on associative models, these approaches are not treated here.

COMPONENTIAL STIMULUS REPRESENTATION

As indicated in the previous section, a time varying representation of the CS is a necessary condition to explain some temporal phenomena; but it is not sufficient to explain many others. Although rudimentary CR timing and inverted U-shaped ISI function can be obtained with the molar trace mechanism, there are a number of empirical observations that pose unsolvable problems to this notion.

Most of these problems are associated with the fact that temporal phenomena not always are correlated with the strength of conditioning, as it would be predicted by the molar trace mechanism. One example is the phenomenon of inhibition of delay, in which the latency of the CR increases over training without noticeable decrements in

CR amplitude, indicating that both measures can be uncorrelated (Pavlov, 1927; Rescorla, 1967; Vogel, Brandon & Wagner, 2003). A further, related problem with the molar trace mechanism is that it predicts that the peak of the CR should occur at the point of maximal strength of the trace, which is inconsistent with data showing that the predominant time of occurrence of the CR is at the US locus (Biterman, 1964; Ellison, 1964; Kimmel, 1965; Smith, 1968; Sheffield, 1965; Williams, 1965).

There are two additional pieces of evidence leading to reject the idea that CR timing varies simply as a function of the strength of conditioning. The first can be seen in experiments of eyeblink conditioning, in which training is conducted simultaneously with two different ISIs in inter-mixed trials. The typical result is that, in test trials of long duration, the animals produce two CRs, each resembling the CR normally exhibited by animals trained with each ISI separately (e.g., Hoehler & Leonard, 1976; Kehoe, Graham-Clarke & Schreurs, 1989; Millenson, Kehoe & Gormezano, 1977). The second evidence is the demonstration that training with one interval followed by a shift to a shorter o longer interval produces an abrupt change in CR latency and peak (e.g., Boneau, 1958; Coleman & Gormezano, 1971; Prokasy & Papsdorf, 1965). In these circumstances, the change in the timing of the CR is discrete, reflecting an abrupt jump from its previous location to the new location. Since the strength notion predicts that the topography of the CR would entirely depend on the associative strength accrued to the CS (and the intensity of the stimulus trace) mixed training with two ISIs should produce only one CR, with a topography that should look like the average topography of CRs which would normally develop when each ISI are trained separately. Likewise, the molar trace mechanism predicts that instead of a discrete change in the topography of the response observed when the ISI is shifted, the change should appear gradually, reflecting the lost

or gain of associative strength which is expected to have developed with the new ISI.

A possible solution for these challenges had already been envisioned by Pavlov in 1927, who, in an attempt to account for inhibition of delay, proposed that training with a single CS can be seen as a situation where animals learn to discriminate among a complex combination of hypothetical elements present during the CS duration. Although several early theorist adhered to Pavlov's "temporal discrimination" hypothesis (e.g., Kimmel, 1965; Konorski, 1948; Sheffield, 1965), it has only recently been quantitatively implemented to describe the several temporal phenomena outlined in this section, in which is known as *"componential models of Pavlovian conditioning"* (Vogel, Castro & Saavedra, 2004).

Figure 4 presents an example of how a componential mechanism can be incorporated into an associative network. Panel a depicts a typical network in which it is assumed that the conditioned stimulus is made up of a number of components that establish separable associations with the adaptive unit. A critical aspect of this CS representation is the assumption that the pattern of activity of each element varies in time following CS initiation, such as they are differentially eligible for reinforcement and non reinforcement depending on their temporal location with respect to the US. For simplicity, the figure does not show a realistic pattern of activity of the elements but instead a mere sequence of elemental activation in time.

A number of ways to rationalize the temporal dynamics of the CS-elements have been proposed. As an example, Panel b of Figure 4 presents a "tap delay line" in which the presence of the CS is assumed to initiate a sequence of activation of elements that share exactly the same pattern of activity but spread in time (Moore, Desmond & Berthier, 1989). Panel c depicts a similar example, the gamma functions, which assume that after the onset of the CS, a set of elements is activated in series with strength that is directly proportional to their respective position in the series (Killeen

Figure 4. Componential representations of the CS. Panel a presents the common assumption that the CS activates a sequence of elements (the circles connected by arrows) which develop separate associations with the adaptive unit. Each element gives rise to non-monotonic courses of activity. Three examples of componential CS representations are depicted in panels b (More, Desmond & Berthier, 1989), c (Killen & Fetterman, 1988) and d (Grossberg & Schmajuk, 1989)). Panel a presents an example of binary elements whose state of activity varies between off (white circles) and on (dark circles) sates over the duration of the CS. The black rectangle at the bottom of panels b, c, d and e represents the duration of the CS.

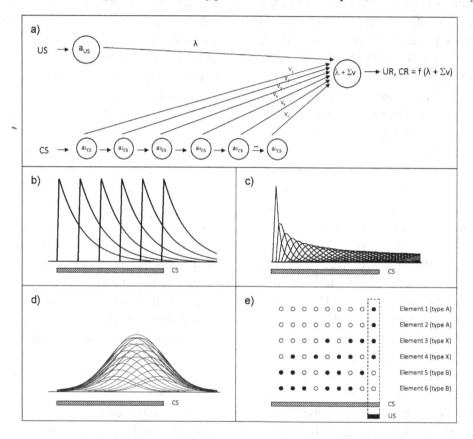

& Feterman, 1988). A further possibility is shown in panel d, where all elements are activated at the same time but vary considerably in the duration and strength of their respective patterns of activation over the duration of the CS (Grossberg & Schmajuk, 1989). In these three examples, it is assumed that conditioning accrues to each element depending on its strength at the locus of reinforcement.

Putting aside differences in details among the different componential stimulus representations, they share essentially the same assumption that every element has a preferential locus or distinctive pattern of activity over the CS duration. This implies that some elements have a more positive correlation with reinforcement across trials that other elements do, in such a way that they may develop comparatively more associative strength. A simpler way to describe this general principle of temporal discrimination is shown in Panel e of Figure 4. Here, it is assumed that the processing of the CS is represented by a set of binary elements, which can be in an "on" a state of activity (represented as a black circle) or in an "off" state of activity (represented as a white circle), at any time of the CS duration. The figure depicts the pattern of activity of six elements in a training situation in which the US is presented in the last moment of the CS. Although the elements differ in their loci of activity, they can be classified roughly into three categories. The "A-elements" that are solely activated at the US locus, The "X-elements" that are activated in both the US locus and at some other moments, and the "B-elements" that are activated only when the US is not present. Thus, temporal discrimination is similar to an AX+BX- discrimination in which A, B and X are explicit cues instead of elements.

With the simple schema shown in Figure 4 e, one can easily see that, regardless of the learning rule employed, componential models are equipped to predict that the uniquely reinforced A-elements will develop more associative strength than the partially reinforced X-elements and the non reinforced B-elements, such that a maximal CR would be predicted at the US locus. Likewise, the problem posed by the double peaked CRs and the shifting ISI observations can be solved by assuming that different CRs may develop with different ISIs by virtue of associative strength accruing with relative independence to different constellations of A-elements.

It should be pointed out that in the description of the componential CS representation outlined in Figure 4, we deliberately omitted the error term, avoiding any commitment with the saturation or the aggregated prediction alternatives. However, there is a few temporal phenomena, like the inverted U shaped ISI function and inhibition of delay, which strongly depend on which learning rule is used. For instance, if a componential representation is used in combination with a non competitive learning rule (i.e. saturation mechanism) an inverted U shaped ISI function will be gracefully predicted (Grossberg & Schmajuk, 1989; Kirkpatrick & Church, 1998; Machado, 1997). In noncompetitive learning, the asymptote for a given element is independent of the value of every other simultaneously active element, such that learning stops when every element has reached its asymptote. The more elements at a given temporal locus, the greater the asymptote for the CS at this locus. Consequently, if the number of active elements is assumed to vary nonmonotonically across the CS duration, the predicted ISI function is also nonmonotonic. Although this description is based on binary elements, this can be generalized to the functions described in panels b, c and d of Figure 4.

Conversely, if a componential CS representation is used in combination with a competitive learning rule (e.g., the aggregated prediction mechanism) the inverted U shaped ISI function is not predicted. According to this mechanism, the aggregated associative strength at a given temporal locus, rather than the individual elements, approach to the asymptote provided by the US, so learning stops when the summed associative strength reaches its asymptote. In this case, the number of elements influences the asymptote of each element, but does not affect the final values of the collection. Since the net associative strength developed at the US locus is independent of the number of active elements at this time, this notion predicts a relatively flat ISI function at asymptote (see Brandon, Vogel & Wagner, 2003).

Although a nonmonotonic ISI function at asymptote has not yet been clearly demonstrated, there is a simple modification in any competitive learning rule that may lead to such a prediction. The solution consist in constraining the associative strength that each element may acquire, such that the net learning accrued at each ISI will be a function of the number of elements at the time of reinforcement (Blought, 1975; Brandon et al., 2003; Desmond, 1990; Schmajuk & DiCarlo, 1992; Schmajuk, Lam & Gray, 1996). Such a mechanism, merge two principles for limiting learning described in the first section of this paper: saturation and aggregated prediction.

Consequently, the alleged inverted U function at asymptote, if real, does not demand a particular kind of learning rule, but indicates instead the need of constraining the amount of learning accrued to each CS element. Apart from this, there is a number of further reasons to consider a constraining mechanism in componential models of Pavlovian conditioning. One of them is an experimental observation done by Rescorla (2000) demonstrating that, although the associative strength of stimuli trained in compound is incremented by reinforcement and decremented by nonreinforcement, the amount of change depends on the starting associative values of each stimulus. One of the specific finding of this study was that reinforcing a compound made of an excitor and an inhibitor, resulted in a greater grow in associative strength for the inhibitor than for the excitor. The fact that excitors and inhibitors do not share a common fate when reinforced in compound is contrary to the common error term of the aggregated prediction mechanism. Rescorla (2000) and others (Brandon et al, 2003; Schmajuk, 2009) have suggested that this phenomenon can be explained by a competitive rule if it is further assumed that (1) nominal excitors and inhibitors are composed by a large number of elements of varying strengths, and (2) the total associative strength of the excitors and inhibitors is unlimited, but each of their respective elements is constrained. Thus, when the excitor and the inhibitor are reinforced in compound, despite of being updated by a common error term, the elements of the inhibitor are less likely to be at their limit than the elements of the excitor, and are, therefore, more likely to develop excitation.

A further advantage of competitive over noncompetitive componential mechanisms is the ability of the former to account for inhibition of delay. The noncompetitive notion assumes that any CS element who is active at the moment of reinforcement will develop positive associative strength, independently of the strength of the rest of the elements that compose the CS. In terms of elements depicted in Figure 4 e, inhibition of delay does not develop with a non competitive mechanism because those CS elements that are active only during the nonreinforced part of the CS (the B-elements) do not develop the required inhibition to counteract the excitation developed by the partially reinforced X-elements. On the contrary, the competitive mechanism predicts inhibition of delay, since its resolves the AX+BX-discrimination with elements A and X becoming excitatory and the B-elements inhibitory.

Naturally, the use of a competitive learning rule in addition with a componential representation of the CS has the additional advantages of accounting for the stimulus selection phenomena described in the first section of this paper.

PRIMING PHENOMENA AND THE RECURRENT INHIBITION MECHANISM

As we already described above, one of the ways in which the aggregated prediction mechanism can be implemented is by assuming the variable reinforcement posture (Rescorla & Wagner, 1972). According to this notion, the effectiveness of the US to produce reinforcement diminishes as the aggregated associative strength of the CSs increases. Apart from the evidence of diminished learning seen in the stimulus competition phenomena, there is an important corpus of evidence demonstrating other ways in which a stimulus becomes less effective as it becomes more predicted. These observations are grouped under the term *"priming phenomena"*, meaning that predicted or primed stimuli are less effectively processed, as they would be otherwise.

Priming phenomena can be divided into three types. The first refers to experimental situations in which the presentation of the CS or the US by themselves prior to conditioning retards learning. Although Pavlov offered the hypothesis that mere exposure of the CS renders it inhibitory, there is substantial evidence suggesting instead that preexposure effects are associated with a loss of salience or diminished processing of the stimuli.

For instance, Rescorla (1971), demonstrated that a preexposed CS is retarded in the subsequent acquisition of both excitatory and inhibitory learning. Likewise, Reiss and Wagner (1972) demonstrated that CS preexposure reduced rather than increased the tendency of the CS to produce a response decrement when compounded with another excitatory CS.

Similar findings have been reported in which US-preexposure appears to retard or block the acquisition of an association between a non exposed CS and the US (Hinson, 1982). Since it has been commonly found that these sorts of decrements in learning depend upon the use of the same context in the preexposure and conditioning phases, preexposure effects have been interpreted as being the result of the stimuli becoming predicted or primed by the context (Hall & Channel, 1985; Hall & Minor, 1978; Hinson, 1982).

The second class of observations is the decrease in the amplitude and frequency of the unconditioned response after repeated presentations of a stimulus (Thompson & Spencer, 1966). In the procedure known as short-term habituation, the decrements are observed in responding to the second one in a pair of identical stimuli. The decrement is denominated as "short-term" because the difference in responding to the second stimulus decreases as the interval between the two stimuli increases (Whitlow, 1975). One interpretation is that the second presentation of the stimulus is less effective because it is already predicted by the first presentation. In the procedure known as long-term habituation, repeated presentations of the stimulus produce a more persistent decrement, which is more pronounced with longer inter stimulus intervals (Davis, 1970). Some studies demonstrating context specificity of long term habituation support a contextual priming explanation of this effect (Jordan, Strasser, & McHale, 2000; Rankin, 2000; Tomsic, Pedreira, Romano et al., 1998).

There is still another phenomenon, called "conditioned diminution of the UR", which might be included in the same category as habituation. It refers to the fact that a US that is preceded by an excitatory CS with which has previously been paired, elicits a UR that has a diminished amplitude in comparison to an unannounced US (Donegan, 1982; Kimble & Ost, 1961). According to Wagner (1976, 1978, and 1979) the only difference between long term habituation and conditioned diminution of the UR is that while in the later case the US is predicted by and explicit CS in the former case it is predicted by the context.

The last type of evidence is related to the fact that learning can be disrupted by certain stimuli or distracters. For instance, it has shown that an "extra US" or an "extra CS" prior to regular CS-US pairings provokes diminished learning (e.g., Kalat & Rozin, 1973; Terry, 1976, Pfautz & Wagner, 1978). Similarly to short term habituation, the effectiveness of the distracters diminishes as the distracter to trial interval increases. Interestingly, it has been demonstrated that the distracters can lose this property once they become expected (Wagner, Rudy & Whitlow, 1973).

One general conclusion that might be drawn from priming phenomena is that capability for a stimulus to act as a distracter, to form associations and to generate an unconditioned response depends inversely on the degree to which the stimulus is expected. In this line of reasoning, Wagner (1976, 1978, and 1979) proposed that expectancies or "priming" of a stimulus in short-term memory can be brought forth by two instances: the presentation of the stimulus itself, as it is the case of short-term habituation and distracter effects; or by presentation of another stimulus that associatively acquires the ability to retrieve the representation of the target stimulus, as it is the case of long term habituation, conditioned diminution of the UR and preexposure effects. To theoretically capture these ideas, Wagner proposed a model of associative learning, SOP, whose most distinctive feature is the use of a *recurrent inhibition mechanism*.

In order to illustrate how the recurrent inhibition mechanism works, Figure 5 presents a simplified rendition of SOP. It is assumed that all stimuli, CS and US, activate a pair of processing units, a primary unit, Al, (according to the parameter p1) and a secondary unit, A2 (according to the parameter pd1). The activity of the secondary unit recurrently inhibits the primary unit, making it transiently less susceptible to activation by its initiating stimulus. Activity in A2 eventually decays, releasing the A1 unit (according to the parameter pd2, which is not shown in the figure). Consequently, the activity of each stimulus across time may be represented by two traces: the trace of the activity of the primary unit, and the trace of the secondary unit, defined as the momentary proportion of elements active in each unit, respectively. SOP assumes that pl is a function of relatively stable properties of the stimulus (e.g., intensity) taking a value greater than zero in the presence of the stimulus and zero in its absence. The values of pdl and pd2 are assumed to be independent of the presence or absence of the stimulus but are critical with respect to the duration of the effective representation of stimuli.

SOP assumes that excitatory and inhibitory links between CS and US are established separately. Changes in the excitatory CS-US connections, ΔV_i+, at any moment are assumed to be proportional to the momentary product of concurrent $A1_{CS}$ and $A1_{US}$ activity. Analogously, changes in the inhibitory CS-US connections, ΔV_i-, at any moment are assumed to be proportional to the momentary product of concurrent $A1_{CS}$ and $A2_{US}$ activity. The learning rules of SOP suggest that the activation of the CS-representation acquires the associative tendency to produce US-secondary activity (net V+), or to acquire an opposing influence (net V-) depending on whether the net associative tendency is excitatory or inhibitory.

SOP assumes that the presentation of the US generates a two folded sequence of response, the first being dependent on the activity of the US-primary unit, and the second on the US-secondary unit. The CSs have a direct influence in behavior by activating the US secondary unit by means of their associative links, and an indirect behavioral consequence by means of the inhibitory effect that the activation of the US secondary unit has over the activation of the US primary unit.

According to SOP, the acquired CS-US association influences not only the probability of the response, but also the processing of the US. By this reasoning, if the A2 node of a US is activated by the precedence of an associated CS (associatively-generated priming) or by itself (self-generated priming), the A1 node of that US will be less susceptible to activation, so as to produce not only a diminished UR as seen in short-term habituation, conditioned diminution of the UR and distracter effects, but also less associative learning, as seen in long-term habituation and preexposure effects, which are the typical priming phenomena described in this section.

COMPLEX REPRESENTATION OF THE US AND MODULATION MECHANISMS

Most of the mechanisms described so far have been designed to account for phenomena in which the representation of the US no needs to be especially complex. In this section we describe a few phenomena that have encouraged authors to propose a more sophisticated conception of the role of the US in the associative process.

The first piece of evidence to be considered refers to the fact that several measures of the same CS-US association are not always correlated. A good example is the study by Schneiderman (1972) who measured conditioned eyeblink and conditioned heart-rate responses in rabbits trained with a paraorbital shock US and different CS-US intervals. He found that the ISI function for the two responses diverged, such that, for instance, the optimal ISI for the conditioned heart rate response is not equally effective for the conditioned eyeblink response. Likewise, Tait and Saladin

Figure 5. A simplified representation of the SOP model. The CS and the US activate their respective primary units ($A1_{CS}$ and $A1_{US}$) which in turn activate the corresponding secondary units ($A2_{CS}$ and $A2_{US}$). The dotted lines ending in a horizontal line represent recurrent inhibition from each secondary unit to its corresponding primary unit (self generated priming). The CS influences the activity of the US-secondary unit by means of its associative value, V_{CS} provoking associatively generated priming and the CR. The activity in the A1US units is responsible for the generation of the primary UR, whereas the activity in A2US is responsible for the generation of the secondary UR and the CR.

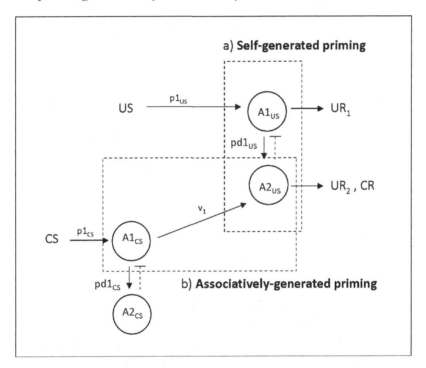

(1986) demonstrated that backward pairings of a paraorbital shock US and a CS resulted in inhibitory learning when assessed through conditioned eyeblink but resulted in excitatory learning when assessed through conditioned suppression of drinking. This sort of findings is consistent with the common observation that some procedures of Pavlovian conditioning such as fear conditioning and taste aversion are much less dependent on short CS-US intervals than other procedures such as eyeblink conditioning and pigeon autoshaping.

The dilemma posed by the divergence of response measures phenomenon can be solved by assuming that different types of conditioned responses would depend on associations formed between the CS and different aspects of the US.

This type of solution was originally outlined by Konorski (1967) who distinguished between emotional and sensory representations of the US. More recently, Wagner and Brandon (1989) and Grossberg (1989, 1991) have incorporated *dual representations of the US* into their respective quantitative models to account for several facts of Pavlovian conditioning.

Apart from separating emotive and sensory aspects of the US and assuming different temporal dynamics for each representation, there is a number of additional properties to each of these responses that must be captured by models. One of them refers to the fact that emotive responses have general influences over behavior, while sensory responses are specific to the sensory system in

Figure 6. A complex representation of the US in Pavlovian conditioning. The presentation of the US produces activation of a sensory unit ($Y_{sensory}$) and an emotive unit ($Y_{emotive}$) via its $\lambda_{sensory}$ and $\lambda_{emotive}$ links, respectively. The sensory unit is associatively activated by the CS via the link $V_{sensory}$ and produces a specific sensory response like eyeblink. The emotive unit can be associatively activated by the CS via $V_{emotive}$ and controls generalized emotive responses like fear. The emotive unit modulates its corresponding sensory unit and the sensory units of other USs (e.g., startle response).

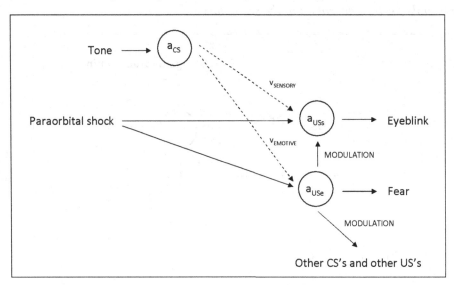

question. For instance Brandon, Bombace, Falls and Wagner (1991) demonstrated that paring a long CS with a paraorbital US, although did not result in appreciable development of a conditioned eyeblink response to the CS, it granted the CS with the ability to potentiate another unconditioned responses, such as the startle response elicited by an air puff delivered into the rabbit's ear.

The ability of a CS to potentiate other responses are not confined to unconditioned responses, but also to sensory conditioned responses produced by another CS. An example of the later is a study by Brandon and Wagner (1991) in which rabbits received alternated pairings of a paraorbital shock with a long CS in some trials and with a short CS in other trials. As expected, testing showed considerable conditioned eyeblink response to the short CS but none to the long CS. However, the amplitude of the CR to the short CS was reliably incremented when presented in association with the long cue, indicating that the long cue

acquired potentiating properties. This finding is congruent with the so called *"occasion setting"* phenomenon (Ross & Holland, 1981), observed in certain discriminations involving both compound and unique cues. For instance, when the A+ AB- discrimination (or feature positive discrimination) is conducted with a long feature (cue A) and a short target (cue B), the task is solved by forming an excitatory association between the feature and the US, whereas the target remains neutral. In interpretation, it is said that the feature acts as an occasion setter or modulator, since it sets the occasion for responding to the target cue, without producing itself any conditioned response.

Regarding that conditioned and unconditioned sensory responses can be notably influenced by emotive associations, some authors have deemed necessary to incorporate a *modulation mechanism* into their models. Figure 6 presents an example of a network with a dual representation of the US that incorporates a modulation mechanism.

The rationalization is that (a) the presentation of any US gives rise to the activation of two units: a sensory unit and an emotive unit, (b) the CS forms separate associations with each US unit, (c) Sensory conditioned responses, like eyeblink, are commanded by the association of the CS with the sensory unit, while emotionally conditioned responses, like fear, are controlled by the association of the CS with the emotive unit, and d) The emotive unit not only controls the production of emotional responses but also modulates the activity of several other sensory units (like the startle response elicited by a puff or the conditioned eyeblink itself).

In order to account for the fact that the emotive and sensory associations not always correlate, it is necessary to assume differential temporal processing of the sensory and emotive US units. Wagner and Brandon (1989), in an attempt to account for the data with eyeblink conditioning and conditioned emotional responses in rabbits, articulated an extension of their recurrent inhibition model by assuming that the sensory association responsible for the conditioned eyeblink depends on a "rapid" processing of the US, whereas the emotive association responsible for the conditioned emotional response depends on a "slower" processing of the US. With a single variation in the parameters that regulate the activity of sensory and emotive US units, their theory is able to account for an impressive set of differences between emotive and sensory CRs and the majority of modulation effects.

Emotive modulation is a powerful mechanism to account for the several situations in which a CS may influence other's CSs and USs levels of sensory responding, even when the CS itself is unable to produce its own discrete CR. However, there is some evidence suggesting that this is not the full picture. The problem in this case is that it is grounded in the fact that conditioned emotional responses are assumed to have general modulatory effects over a broad range of behaviors, which is contradicted by some instances of occasion setting in where the occasion setters rather than modulating the CR of any CS, exert control only to the specific CS that were trained in compound. Brandon and Wagner (1991) remarked that in these circumstances, the occasion setter may combine with the target as a configural cue rather than acting as a modulator. The importance of configurations is discussed in the next section.

CONTEXT SENSITIVE STIMULUS REPRESENTATIONS

Several lines of converging evidence suggest that the effective stimulus representation that controls learning and performance in Pavlovian conditioning is sensitive to the stimulation context in which it occurs. For instance, it has been shown that rabbits (Whitlow & Wagner, 1972), rats (Harris et al. 2008), and humans (Ludwig & Lachnit, 2003) can learn negative patterning discriminations, in which two cues, A and B, are reinforced when presented by themselves (A+B+) and nonreinforced when presented in compound (AB-). Since in reinforced trials A and B develop their respective excitatory associations with the US, the representation of AB should be somewhat different than the mere sum of its elements in order to solve discrimination. Likewise, same animals can learn a biconditional discrimination, in which the compounds AB and CD are reinforced and the compounds AC and BD are nonreinforced (Harris et al. 2008; Saavedra, 1975; Harris & Levesey, 2008). Since differential responding to negative versus positive compounds in the biconditional discriminations cannot be predicted by the association formed by the partially reinforced components A, B, C and D, the representation of each compound should be different from the aggregation of its elements. Thus, in negative patterning and biconditional discrimination responding seems to be controlled by conjunctions of cues rather than by the component cues.

Figure 7. Three componential approaches to configural learning. The rows present a set of elements that can be active (dark circles) or inactive (white circles) during A alone, B alone and AB compound trials. Notice that the added elements, inhibited elements and replaced elements approaches are identical in their presentation of A and B alone differing only in the pattern of activity assumed for the AB compound.

Element	a) Added Elements			b) Inhibited Elements			c) Replaced Elements		
	A-Alone	B-Alone	AB-Compound	A-Alone	B-Alone	AB-Compound	A-Alone	B-Alone	AB-Compound
a1	●	○	●	●	○	●	●	○	●
a2	●	○	●	●	○	○	●	○	○
ab	○	○	●	○	○	○	○	○	●
b1	○	●	●	○	●	●	○	●	●
b2	○	●	●	○	●	○	○	●	○
ba	○	○	●	○	○	○	○	○	●

The predominant explanation of these findings is that animals code not only for the presence and absence of stimuli but also for stimuli conjunctions or configurations. For instance, Rescorla (1972) and Whitlow and Wagner (1972) suggested that when stimulus A and B are compounded, the resulting AB cue contains all the elements of A and B, plus some "configural" element that is unique to the conjunction of A and B. Alternatively, Pearce (1987, 1994 and 2002) emphasized a more central role of configurations by assuming that compound stimuli are processed as unique exemplars that form associations independently of those formed by their elements. According to Pearce's view, configurations develop unitary associations with the US and their component elements only play a role in determining the degree of generalization between configurations.

Wagner and his collaborators (Brandon, Vogel & Wagner, 2000; Wagner & Brandon, 2001; Wagner, 2003) used a componential representation of the CS to describe the similarities and differences between these alternative views of configural learning. Their rationale can be appreciated in Figure 7, which presents examples of the representation of cues A and B when presented alone or in compound (AB) according to the different approaches. The shared assumptions are: (1) each nominal CS activates a number of elements that form separate associations with the US (i.e., componential stimulus representation mechanism), and (2) the activation of a given element depends not only on the stimulus that it represents but also on the presence or absence of other cues (i.e., context sensitivity mechanism). Panel a, presents what Brandon, Vogel and Wagner (2000) called the "added elements view" of Whitlow and Wagner (1972), in which compound AB contains not only the full representation of cue A isolated (elements a1 and a2) and the full representation of cue B isolated (elements b1 and b2) but also a pair of configural elements (ab and ba) that are activated only when both A and B are present. Panel b, presents what Wagner and collaborators described as the "inhibited elements" strategy proposed by Pearce (1987), meaning that when the stimuli A is compounded with B, some elements are assumed to remain active (a1 and b1) but other are assumed to be "deactivated" or "inhibited" (a2 and b2), such that the AB compound would contain half of the element of A isolated and half of the elements of B isolated.

The principal difference between these two approaches to configural learning is their differential predictions with respect to experiments in which a compound is formed by stimuli that have been trained separately. The added elements notion always assumes a summation of associative strength of the elements forming a compound, whereas the inhibited elements notion assumes instead a subtraction of the associative strength of each element when presented in compound. A number of experiments have been designed to distinguish between these two approaches. One critical but simple experiment is the so- called "summation test", in which responding to a novel compound AB is tested after training with A and B separately. The added elements notion predicts a summation of responding to the compound while the configural approach predicts an "averaging" of the degree of responding to the elements.

The prediction of the added elements notion is additive because each element contributes its whole associative strength when forming a compound with another stimulus. This can be seen in the example depicted in Panel a of Figure 7 in which training with A+ and B+ produces excitatory associative strength for a1 and a2, and for b1 and b2, respectively. Since AB contains all four excitatory elements (a1, a2, b1 and b2), responding is predicted to be greater than to A and B alone. In contrast, according to the subtractive principle of the inhibited elements approach, each stimulus A and B contributes only half of its associative strength when forming the AB compound (a1 and b1), so that responding to AB is predicted to be similar to that of A and B (Panel b).

The empirical evidence with the summation test is controversial. While several experiments conducted with a variety of species, stimuli and procedures have found evidence of summation (e.g., Collins & Shanks, 2006; Rescorla, 1997; Whitlow & Wagner, 1972; Soto, Vogel, Castillo & Wagner, 2009) other studies have shown absence of summation (e.g., Aydin & Pearce, 1995). In addition to these experiments, several other more complex tasks have been designed, encountering

the same level of ambiguity (Kudney & Wagner, 2004; Pearce & Wilson, 1991). Furthermore, there have been a number of demonstrations where one or another stimulus processing strategy can be encouraged by some pre-experimental treatments or by specific instructions (e.g., Melchers, Lachnit, Üngör & Shanks, 2005; Williams & Braker, 1999).

For some authors, this corpus of contradicting evidence suggests the need for models with flexibility of processing (Melchers, Shanks & Lachnit, 2008). Panel c of Figure 7, presents a way in which this flexibility can be instantiated. This proposal, suggested by Wagner (2003), assumes that *context sensibility* involves both additive and subtractive mechanisms, such that when stimuli A and B form a compound (AB), some of their elements are inhibited (a2 and b2) but others are added (ab and ba). Since the addition of elements is compensated with the inhibition of others, Wagner (2003) nominated his solution as "replaced elements" strategy. Note that in this solution there are some "context independent" elements that are activated whenever their respective stimulus is presented, regardless of any other present stimuli (e.g., a1 and b1), while "context dependent" elements do depend on the presence or absence of other stimuli (e.g., a2, b2, ab and ba). Thus, flexible processing (e.g., different degrees of summation) can be obtained by varying the relative proportion of context dependent and context independent elements.

Two final remarks should be added in this section, both pointing to some interesting theoretical developments in the domain of configural learning. The first refers as to whether context sensitive stimulus representation can be rationalized in other ways different from assuming configural units. For instance, Harris (2006, 2009) has defended the idea that negative patterning and biconditional discrimination can be described without appealing to any sort of configural representation of the CS, but simply assuming that CSs are composed by a large number of elements that vary in their capability of being processed or attended to when the CS that they represent is presented isolated or in compound with other CSs (see also Mc Laren & Mackinstoh, 2000, 2002).

The second remark refers to the fact that in all theoretical alternatives depicted in Figure 7, configural elements (i.e., those elements whose activity depends on the presence or absence of other cues apart from the one that they represent) do not receive a special treatment and enter into the associative process under the same conditions just like any other element. Several authors have questioned this view, mainly on the grounds that it involves the non economical assumption that there should be as many configural elements as possible combinations of cues (Gluck & Myers, 2001; Honey & Ward-Robison, 2002; Kehoe, 1990; Schmajuk & Dicarlo, 1992). Rumelhart, Hinton and Williams (1986), proposed one alternative in which configural units stay on an intermediate layer or hidden units layer, where they are connected to the adaptive unit (output) and to the representation of the CSs (inputs).

Schmajuk and his collaborators (e.g., Schmajuk & Dicarlo, 1992; Schmajuk, Lamoureux & Holland, 1998) have elaborated several variations of this hidden-units approach to account for a number of phenomena of Pavlovian conditioning, especially in the domain of configural learning and occasion setting. According to these renditions, nominal CSs influence directly the activity of the adaptive unit by their respective associative links and indirectly via links between the hidden-units and the adaptive unit. The common assumption is that direct and indirect links to the adaptive unit are updated by a common error term based on the aggregated prediction assumption. The distinctive feature of this notion is that CSs establish also modifiable links with the hidden units, which are updated by a backpropagation rule (Rumelhart et al., 1986), which basically computes a second error term once the links at the output level have been updated via the first error term. Leaving aside computational details of this strategy, the important aspect to be emphasized here is that

according to this mechanism, "configurations" are not assumed to be hard-wired but susceptible to be reinforced by learning.

CONCLUSION

Quantitative tradition in theories of conditioning is almost a hundred years old. The first attempts were either very specific learning equations trying to describe the course of acquisition (Gulliksen, 1934; Gulliksen and Wolfe, 1938; Thurstone, 1930) or broad spectrum theories seeking to describe the general laws of Pavlovian and instrumental learning (Estes, 1950; Hull, 1943; Spence, Farber & McFann, 1956). Over this period, the field has witnessed important advances in the understanding of the behavioral mechanisms underlying simple learning, and much of this is due to the strong commitment of early theoreticians to formulate quantitative theories with testable predictions.

This virtuous circle between theoretical predictions and experimental evidence is well represented by the first theory that focused specifically in Pavlovian conditioning, the model proposed by Robert Rescorla and Allan Wagner (Rescorla & Wagner, 1972; Wagner & Rescorla, 1972). The heuristic value of this theory is founded in the fact that many of the observed phenomena and subsequent theoretical developments described in this chapter are in some way or another linked to the success and shortcomings of this theory. Although it is difficult to keep track of all the contributions, most researchers would acknowledge the integrative efforts of these two leaders in the field. There are no doubts that many other theories and contributions have been left out in this review, but it is clear that the work of these authors has dominated theorizing and research in the field for more than 30 years.

This chapter presents an overview of the major mechanisms that have been proposed in the framework of connectionist theories of Pavlovian conditioning. In order to provide a general and

Table 1. Summary of mechanisms and their corresponding phenomena

	Stimulus Selection	Timing	Common Fate	Priming	Divergence of Responses Measures	Configural Learning	Occasion Setting
Saturation		•	•				
Aggregated Prediction	•	•	•	•	•	•	•
Time Varying Stimulus Representation		•		•	•		
Componential Stimulus Representation		•	•			•	•
Recurrent inhibition				•			
Complex US-Representation					•		•
Context Varying Stimulus Representation						•	•

conceptual view of the field, the choice was to focus on a few critical mechanisms rather than in the theories themselves and in the quantitative details of their implementation. Table 1 presents a summary of the seven mechanisms discussed in the chapter, along with the category of phenomena that they address. The order in which the mechanisms appear in the table is an attempt to show how certain mechanisms that were regarded as sufficient and necessary to account for certain phenomena became necessary but not sufficient for other phenomena leading to the need of additional mechanisms.

It should be emphasized that none of these mechanisms is universally accepted. Indeed, controversy is yet alive in every phenomena and mechanism discussed in this paper and even the usefulness of the associative approach altogether has been put into question by some authors (e.g., Gallistel and Gibbon, 2000). However, we believe that some consensus has been reached with respect to some mechanisms, such as the need for learning rules that compute the aggregated prediction of the US, componential and context sensitive representation of the CS, and some more complex ways of representing the multiple roles of the US as a reinforcer and a modulator.

Theories proposed within the last few decades have progressively grown in complexity incorporating several of these mechanisms. Furthermore, the field is moving rapidly and it is becoming increasingly interdisciplinary. Although the mechanisms described in this chapter are logical entities that have been invented to account for behavioral data, several advances in the neurobiological basis of conditioning are posing new challenges to purely behavioral theories, but, at the same time they are providing additional source of support for some of the theoretical ideas. Of curse, it is not just that learning theory is benefiting from the research in neuroscience, but the other way around too. If computational neuroscientists can capitalize on what behavioral theoreticians have learned since Pavlov, they could apply more effective strategies in their search of how biological entities compute learning.

As examples of this synergy between behaviorally and biologically oriented research, we can mention the detailed circuit for rabbit eyeblink conditioning in the cerebellum, which appears to computes the aggregated prediction as a function of the differences between the CS and the US pathways (Thompson, Thompson, Kim, Krupa & Shinkman, 1998; Christian & Thompson, 2003) and to produce timing as an emergent property of the collective activity of Golgi cells in the cerebellar cortex (e.g., Mauk, Medina, Nores, & Ohyama, 2000); the role of the hippocampus in configural and temporal learning (Sanderson, Pearce, Kyd & Aggleton, 2006), the dissociation between sensory an emotional conditioning in the cerebellum (Nixon, 2003) and the amygdala (Fanselow & LeDoux, 1999; Lanuza, Moncho-Bogani & LeDoux, 2008); and the involvement of recurrent inhibition circuits in classical conditioning and habituation of the siphon withdrawal reflex of Aplysia (e.g., Bristol & Carew, 2005). It can be expected that the interaction between these disciplines would lead to significantly more comprehensive models of conditioning, embracing not only behavioral regularities bust also their possible instantiation in the nervous system.

ACKNOWLEDGMENT

The preparation of this article was supported by grants from Fondecyt (N° 1090640) to Edgar Vogel and from the University of Talca to the Program of Research on Quality of Life (Res. 387/2007).

REFERENCES

Atkinson, R. C., & Estes, W. K. (1963). Stimulus sampling theory. In Luce, R. D., Bush, R. R., & Galanter, E. (Eds.), *Handbook of mathematical psychology.* New York: Wiley.

Aydin, A., & Pearce, J. M. (1995). Summation in autoshaping with short- and long-duration stimuli. *Quarterly Journal of Experimental Psychology, 42,* 215–234.

Bitterman, M. E. (1964). Classical conditioning in goldfish as function of CS-US interval. *Journal of Comparative and Physiological Psychology, 58,* 359–366. doi:10.1037/h0046793

Blought, D. S. (1975). Steady state data and a quantitative model of operant generalization and discrimination. *Journal of Experimental Psychology. Animal Behavior Processes, 104,* 3–21. doi:10.1037/0097-7403.1.1.3

Boneau, C. A. (1958). The interstimulus interval and the latency of the conditioned eyelid response. *Journal of Experimental Psychology, 56,* 464–471. doi:10.1037/h0044940

Brandon, S. E., Bombace, J. C., Falls, W. T., & Wagner, A. R. (1991). Modulation of unconditioned defensive reflexes via an emotive Pavlovian conditioned stimulus. *Journal of Experimental Psychology. Animal Behavior Processes, 17,* 312–322. doi:10.1037/0097-7403.17.3.312

Brandon, S. E., Vogel, E. H., & Wagner, A. R. (2000). A componential view of configural cues in generalization and discrimination in Pavlovian conditioning. *Behavioural Brain Research, 110,* 67–72. doi:10.1016/S0166-4328(99)00185-0

Brandon, S. E., Vogel, E. H., & Wagner, A. R. (2003). Stimulus representation in SOP: I. Theoretical rationalization and some implications. *Behavioural Processes, 62,* 5–25. doi:10.1016/S0376-6357(03)00016-0

Brandon, S. E., & Wagner, A. R. (1991). Modulation of a discrete Pavlovian conditioning reflex by a putative emotive Pavlovian conditioned stimulus. *Journal of Experimental Psychology. Animal Behavior Processes, 17,* 299–311. doi:10.1037/0097-7403.17.3.299

Bristol, A. S., & Carew, T. J. (2005). Differential role of inhibition in habituation of two independent afferent pathways to a common motor output. *Learning & Memory (Cold Spring Harbor, N.Y.), 12,* 52–60. doi:10.1101/lm.83405

Brown, P. L., & Jenkins, H. M. (1968). Autoshaping the pigeons's key peck. *Journal of Experimental Psychology, 11,* 1–8.

Burkhardt, P. E., & Ayres, J. J. B. (1978). CS and US duration effects in one-trial simultaneous fear conditioning as assessed by conditioned suppression of licking in rats. *Animal Learning & Behavior, 6*, 225–230.

Bush, R. R., & Mosteller, F. (1955). *Stochastic models for learning.* New York: Wiley.

Christian, K. M., & Thompson, R. F. (2003). Neural substrates of eyeblink conditioning: Adquisition and retention. *Learning & Memory (Cold Spring Harbor, N.Y.), 10,* 427–455. doi:10.1101/lm.59603

Cole, R. P., Matter, L., & Miller, R. R. (1995). Attenuation of the relative validity effect by post-training extinction of the more valid cue. *Proceedings and Abstracts of the Annual Meeting of the Eastern Psychological Association,* Boston.

Coleman, S. R., & Gormezano, I. (1971). Classical conditioning of the rabbit's (orictolagus cuniculus) nictitating membrane response under symmetrical CS-US interval shifts. *Journal of Comparative and Physiological Psychology, 77,* 447–455. doi:10.1037/h0031879

Collins, D. J., & Shanks, D. R. (2006). Summation in causal learning: Elemental processing or configural generalization. *Quarterly Journal of Experimental Psychology, 59,* 1524–1534. doi:10.1080/17470210600639389

Davis, M. (1970). Effects of interstimulus interval length and variability on startle response habituation in the rat. *Journal of Comparative and Physiological Psychology, 72,* 177–192. doi:10.1037/h0029472

Davis, M., Schlesinger, L. S., & Sorenson, C. A. (1989). Temporal specificity of fear conditioning - effects of different conditioned-stimulus - unconditioned stimulus intervals on the fear-potentiated startle effect. *Journal of Experimental Psychology. Animal Behavior Processes, 15,* 295–310. doi:10.1037/0097-7403.15.4.295

Desmond, J. E. (1990). Temporally adaptive responses in neural models: The stimuli trace. In Gabriel, M., & Moore, J. (Eds.), *Learning and computational neuroscience: Foundations and adaptive networks.* Cambridge, MA: The MIT Press.

Donegan, N. H. (1981). Priming-produced facilitation or diminution of responding to a Pavlovian unconditioned stimulus. *Journal of Experimental Psychology. Animal Behavior Processes, 7,* 295–312. doi:10.1037/0097-7403.7.4.295

Ellison, G. D. (1964). Differential salivatory conditioning to traces. *Journal of Experimental Psychology, 57,* 373–380.

Estes, W. K. (1950). Toward a statistical theory of learning. *Psychological Review, 57,* 94–104. doi:10.1037/h0058559

Estes, W. K., & Skinner, B. F. (1941). Some quantitative properties of anxiety. *Journal of Experimental Psychology, 29,* 390–400. doi:10.1037/h0062283

Fanselow, M. S., & LeDoux, J. E. (1999). Why we think plasticity underlying Pavlovian fear conditioning occurs in the basolateral amygdala. *Neuron, 23,* 229–232. doi:10.1016/S0896-6273(00)80775-8

Gallistel, C. R., & Gibbon, J. (2000). Time, rate, and conditioning. *Psychological Review, 107,* 289–344. doi:10.1037/0033-295X.107.2.289

García, J., & Koelling, R. A. (1966). Relation of cue to consequence in avoidance learning. *Psychonomic Science, 4,* 123–124.

Gibbon, J., & Balsam, P. (1981). Spreading association in time. In Locurto, C. M., Terrace, H. S., & Gibbon, J. (Eds.), *Autoshaping and conditioning theory.* New York: Academic Press.

Gluck, M. A., & Myers, C. E. (2001). *Gateway to memory: An introduction to neural network modeling of the hippocampus and learning.* Cambridge, MA: The MIT Press.

Gormezano, I., Schneiderman, N., Deaux, E., & Fuentes, I. (1962). Nictitating Membrane: Classical Conditioning and Extinction in the Albino Rabbit. *Science. New Series, 136,* 33–34.

Grossberg, S. (1991). A neural network architecture for Pavlovian conditioning: Reinforcement, attention, forgetting, timing. In Commons, M. L., Grossberg, S., & Staddon, J. E. R. (Eds.), *Neural networks models of conditioning and action.* Hillsdale, NJ: Lawrence Erlbaum Associates.

Grossberg, S., & Schmajuk, N. A. (1989). Neural dynamics of adaptive timing and temporal discrimination during associative learning. *Neural Networks, 2,* 79–102. doi:10.1016/0893-6080(89)90026-9

Gulliksen, H. (1934). A rational equation of the learning curve based on Thorndike's law effect. *The Journal of General Psychology, 11,* 395–434. doi:10.1080/00221309.1934.9917847

Gulliksen, H., & Wolfe, D. L. (1938). A theory of learning and transfer: I. *Psychometrika, 3,* 127–149. doi:10.1007/BF02288482

Hall, G., & Channell, S. (1985). Differential-effects of contextual change on latent inhibition and on habituation of an orienting response. *Journal of Experimental Psychology. Animal Behavior Processes, 11,* 470–481. doi:10.1037/0097-7403.11.3.470

Hall, G., & Minor, H. (1984). A search for context-stimulus associations in latent inbihition. *Quarterly Journal of Experimental Psychology: Comparative and Physiological Psychology, 36,* 145–169.

Harris, J. A. (2006). Elemental Representations of Stimuli in Associative Learning. *Psychological Review, 113,* 584–605. doi:10.1037/0033-295X.113.3.584

mHarris, J. A. (2010). The arguments of associations. In Schmajuk, N. A. (Ed.), *Computational Models of Classical Conditioning.* Cambridge: Academic Press.

Harris, J. A., & Livesey, E. (2008). Comparing patterning and biconditional discriminations in humans. *Journal of Experimental Psychology. Animal Behavior Processes, 34,* 144–154. doi:10.1037/0097-7403.34.1.144

Harris, J. A., Livesey, E., Gharaei, S., & Westbrook, F. (2008). Negative patterning is easier than a biconditional discrimination. *Journal of Experimental Psychology. Animal Behavior Processes, 34,* 494–500. doi:10.1037/0097-7403.34.4.494

Hilgard, E. R., & Campbell, A. A. (1936). The course of acquisition and retention of conditioned eyelid responses in man. *Journal of Experimental Psychology, 19,* 227–247. doi:10.1037/h0055600

Hinson, R. E. (1982). Effects of UCS preexposure on excitatory and inhibitory rabbit eyelid conditioning: An associative effects of conditioned contextual stimuli. *Journal of Experimental Psychology. Animal Behavior Processes, 8,* 49–61. doi:10.1037/0097-7403.8.1.49

Hoehler, F. K., & Leonard, D. W. (1976). Double responding in classical nictitating membrane conditioning with single-CS, dual-ISI pairing. *The Pavlovian Journal of Biological Science, 11,* 180–190.

Honey, R. C., & Ward-Robinson, J. (2002). Acquired equivalence and distinctiveness of cues: I. Exploring a neural network approach. *Journal of Experimental Psychology. Animal Behavior Processes, 28,* 378–387. doi:10.1037/0097-7403.28.4.378

Hull, C. L. (1943). *Principles of behavior: An introduction to behavior theory.* New York: Appleton-Century-Crofts.

Jordan, W. P., Strasser, H. C., & McHale, L. (2000). Contextual control of long-term habituation in rats. *Journal of Experimental Psychology. Animal Behavior Processes, 26,* 323–339. doi:10.1037/0097-7403.26.3.323

Kalat, J. W., & Rozin, P. (1973). Learned-safety as a mechanism in long-delay taste-aversion learning in rats. *Journal of Comparative and Physiological Psychology, 83,* 198–207. doi:10.1037/h0034424

Kehoe, E. J. (1990). Classical conditioning: Fundamental issues for adaptative network models. In Gabriel, M., & Moore, J. W. (Eds.), *Learning and computational neuroscience: Foundations of adaptative networks.* Cambridge, MA: The MIT Press.

Kehoe, E. J., Graham-Clarke, P., & Schreurs, B. G. (1989). Temporal patterns of the rabbit's nictitating membrane response to compound and components stimuli under mixed CS-US intervals. *Behavioral Neuroscience, 103,* 283–295. doi:10.1037/0735-7044.103.2.283

Killeen, P. R., & Fetterman, J. G. (1988). A behavioral theory of timing. *Psychological Review, 95,* 274–285. doi:10.1037/0033-295X.95.2.274

Kimble, G. A., & Ost, J. W. P. (1961). A conditioned inhibitory process in eyelid conditioning. *Journal of Experimental Psychology, 61,* 150–156. doi:10.1037/h0044932

Kimmel, H. D. (1965). Instrumental inhibitory factors in classical conditioning. In Prokasy, W. F. (Ed.), *Classical conditioning: A symposium. New-York.* Appleton-Century-Crofts.

Kirkpatrick, K., & Church, R. M. (1998). Are separate theories of conditioning and timing necessary? *Behavioural Processes, 44,* 163–182. doi:10.1016/S0376-6357(98)00047-3

Konorski, J. (1948). *Conditioning reflexes and neuron organization.* Cambridge, UK: University Press.

Konorski, J. (1967). *Integrative activity of the brain: An interdisciplinary approach.* Chicago: Chicago University Press.

Kundey, S. M., & Wagner, A. R. (2004). *Further test of elemental versus configural models of Pavlovian conditioning.* Paper presented at the meetings of the Comparative Cognition Society, Melbourne Florida.

Lanuza, E., Moncho-Bogani, J., & LeDoux, J. E. (2008). Unconditioned stimulus pathways to the amygdala: Effects of lesions of the posterior intralaminar thalamus on foot-shock-induced c-Fos expression in the subdivisions of the later amygdala. *Neuroscience, 155,* 959–968. doi:10.1016/j.neuroscience.2008.06.028

Ludwig, I., & Lachnit, H. (2003). Asymmetric interference in patterning discriminations: A case of modulated attention. *Biological Psychology, 62,* 133–146. doi:10.1016/S0301-0511(02)00124-2

Machado, A. (1997). Learning the temporal dynamics of behavior. *Psychological Review, 104,* 241–265. doi:10.1037/0033-295X.104.2.241

Mackintosh, N. J. (1975). A theory of attention: Variations in the associability of stimuli with reinforcement. *Psychological Review, 82,* 276–298. doi:10.1037/h0076778

Mauk, M. D., Medina, J. F., Nores, W. L., & Ohyama, T. (2000). Cerebella function: coordination, learning or timing. *Current Biology, 10,* 522–525. doi:10.1016/S0960-9822(00)00584-4

Mauk, M. D., & Ruiz, B. P. (1992). Learning-dependent timing of Pavlovian eyelid responses: Differential conditioning using multiple interstimulus. *Behavioral Neuroscience, 106,* 666–681. doi:10.1037/0735-7044.106.4.666

McLaren, I. P. L., & Mackintosh, N. J. (2000). An elemental model of associative learning: I. Latent inhibition and perceptual learning. *Animal Learning & Behavior, 38,* 211–246.

McLaren, I. P. L., & Mackintosh, N. J. (2002). Associative learning and elemental representation: II. Generalization and discrimination. *Animal Learning & Behavior, 30,* 177–200.

Melchers, K. G., Lachnit, H., Üngör, M., & Shanks, D. R. (2005). Past experience can influence whether the whole is different from the sum of its parts. *Learning and Motivation, 36,* 20–41. doi:10.1016/j.lmot.2004.06.002

Millenson, J. R., Kehoe, E. J., & Gormezano, I. (1977). Classical-conditioning of rabbits nictitating-membrane response under fixed and mixed CS-US intervals. *Learning and Motivation, 8,* 351–366. doi:10.1016/0023-9690(77)90057-1

Miller, R. R., & Matzel, L. D. (1988). The comparator hypothesis: A response rule for the expression of associations. In Bower, G. H. (Ed.), *The psychology of learning and motivation.* San Diego: Academic Press.

Moore, J. W., Desmond, J. E., & Berthier, N. E. (1989). Adaptively timed conditioned-responses and the cerebellum: A neural network approach. *Biological Cybernetics, 62,* 17–28. doi:10.1007/BF00217657

Moore, J. W., & Stickney, K. J. (1980). Formation of attentional-associative networks in real-time - role of the hippocampus and implications for conditioning. *Physiological Psychology, 8,* 207–217.

Nixon, P. D. (2003). The role of the cerebellum in preparing responses to predictable sensory events. *Cerebellum (London, England), 2,* 114–122. doi:10.1080/14734220309410

Pavlov, I. P. (1927). *Conditioned reflexes.* London: Oxford University Press.

Pearce, J. M. (1987). A model for stimulus generalization in Pavlovian conditioning. *Psychological Review, 94,* 61–75. doi:10.1037/0033-295X.94.1.61

Pearce, J. M. (1994). Similarity and discrimination: A selective review and a connectionist model. *Psychological Review, 101,* 587–607. doi:10.1037/0033-295X.101.4.587

Pearce, J. M. (2002). Evaluation and development of a connectionist theory of configural learning. *Animal Learning & Behavior, 30,* 73–95.

Pearce, J. M., & Hall, G. (1980). A model for Pavlovian learning: Variations in the effectiveness of conditioned but not unconditioned stimuli. *Psychological Review, 87,* 532–552. doi:10.1037/0033-295X.87.6.532

Pearce, J. M., & Wilson, P. N. (1991). Failure of excitatory conditioning to extinguish the influence of a conditioned inhibitor. *Journal of Experimental Psychology. Animal Behavior Processes, 17,* 519–529. doi:10.1037/0097-7403.17.4.519

Pfautz, P. L., & Wagner, A. R. (1978). Sensory preconditioning versus protection from habituation. *Journal of Experimental Psychology. Animal Behavior Processes, 4,* 286–295. doi:10.1037/0097-7403.4.3.286

Prokasy, W. F., & Papsdorf, J. D. (1965). Effects of increasing the interstimulus interval during classical conditioning of the albino rabbit. *Journal of Comparative and Physiological Psychology, 60,* 249–252. doi:10.1037/h0022341

Rankin, C. H. (2000). Context conditioning in habituation in the nematode C. elegans. *Behavioral Neuroscience, 114,* 496–505. doi:10.1037/0735-7044.114.3.496

Reiss, S., & Wagner, A. R. (1972). CS habituation produces a "latent inhibition effect" but not active conditioned inhibition. *Learning and Motivation, 3,* 237–245. doi:10.1016/0023-9690(72)90020-3

Rescorla, R. A. (1967). Inhibition of delay in Pavlovian fear conditioning. *Journal of Comparative and Physiological Psychology, 64,* 114–120. doi:10.1037/h0024810

Rescorla, R. A. (1969). Pavlovian conditioned inhibition. *Psychological Bulletin, 72,* 77–94. doi:10.1037/h0027760

Rescorla, R. A. (1971). Summation and retardation test of latent inhibition. *Journal of Comparative and Physiological Psychology, 75,* 77–81. doi:10.1037/h0030694

Rescorla, R. A. (1972). Configural conditioning in discrete-trial bar pressing. *Journal of Comparative and Physiological Psychology, 79,* 307–317. doi:10.1037/h0032553

Rescorla, R. A. (1979). Aspects of the reinforcer learned in second-order pavlovian conditioning. *Journal of Experimental Psychology. Animal Behavior Processes, 5,* 79–95. doi:10.1037/0097-7403.5.1.79

Rescorla, R. A. (1997). Summation: Assessment of a configural theory. *Animal Learning & Behavior, 25,* 200–209.

Rescorla, R. A. (2000). Associative changes in excitors and inhibitors differ when they are conditioned in compound. *Journal of Experimental Psychology. Animal Behavior Processes, 26,* 428–438. doi:10.1037/0097-7403.26.4.428

Rescorla, R. A., & Wagner, A. R. (1972). A theory of Pavlovian conditioning: Variations in the effectiveness of reinforcement and non reinforcement. In Black, A. H., & Proasky, W. F. (Eds.), *Classical Conditioning II: Current Theory and Research.* New York: Appleton-Century-Crofts.

Ross, R. T., & Holland, P. C. (1981). Conditioning of simultaneous and serial feature-positive discriminations. *Animal Learning & Behavior, 9,* 292–303.

Rumelhart, D. E., Hinton, G. E., & Williams, G. E. (1986). Learning internal representations by error propagation. In Rumelhart, D. E., & McClelland, J. L. (Eds.), *Parallel Distributed Processing: Explorations in the Microstructure of Cognition. Cambridge, MA.* Bradford: MIT Press.

Saavedra, M. A. (1975). Pavlovian compound conditioning in the rabbit. *Learning and Motivation, 6,* 314–326. doi:10.1016/0023-9690(75)90012-0

Sanderson, D. J., Pearce, J. M., Kyd, R. J., & Aggleton, J. P. (2006). The importance of the rat hippocampus for learning the structure of visual arrays. *The European Journal of Neuroscience, 24,* 1781–1788. doi:10.1111/j.1460-9568.2006.05035.x

Schamjuk, N. A. (2009). Attentional and error-correcting associative mechanisms in classical conditioning. *Journal of Experimental Psychology. Animal Behavior Processes, 3,* 407–418. doi:10.1037/a0014737

Scheffield, F. D. (1965). Relation between classical conditioning and instrumental learning. In Prokasi, W. F. (Ed.), *Classical conditioning: A symposium. New-York.* Appleton-Century-Crofts.

Schmajuk, N. A. (1997). Stimulus configuration, long-term potentiation, and the hippocampus. *The Behavioral and Brain Sciences, 20,* 629–631. doi:10.1017/S0140525X97411597

Schmajuk, N. A., & Dicarlo, J. J. (1992). Stimulus configuration, classical conditioning, and hippocampal function. *Psychological Review, 99,* 268–305. doi:10.1037/0033-295X.99.2.268

Schmajuk, N. A., Lam, Y. W., & Gray, J. A. (1996). Latent inhibition: A neural network approach. *Journal of Experimental Psychology. Animal Behavior Processes, 22,* 321–349. doi:10.1037/0097-7403.22.3.321

Schmajuk, N. A., Lamoureux, J. A., & Holland, P. C. (1998). Occasion setting: A neural network approach. *Psychological Review*, *105*, 3–32. doi:10.1037/0033-295X.105.1.3

Schneiderman, N. (1972). Response system divergencies in aversive classical conditioning. In Black, A. H., & Proasky, W. F. (Eds.), *Classical conditioning II: Current theory and research*. New York: Appleton-Century-Crofts.

Schneidermann, N. (1966). Interstimulus interval function of nictitating membrane response of rabbit under delay versus trace conditioning. *Journal of Comparative and Physiological Psychology*, *62*, 397–402. doi:10.1037/h0023946

Schneidermann, N., & Gormezano, I. (1964). Conditioning of nictitating membrane of rabbit as function of CS-US interval. *Journal of Comparative and Physiological Psychology*, *57*, 188–195. doi:10.1037/h0043419

Siegel, S., & Domjan, M. (1971). Backward conditioning as an inhibitory procedure. *Learning and Motivation*, *2*, 1–11. doi:10.1016/0023-9690(71)90043-9

Smith, M. C. (1968). CS-US interval and US intensity in classical conditioning of the rabbit's nictitating membrane response. *Journal of Comparative and Physiological Psychology*, *66*, 679–687. doi:10.1037/h0026550

Smith, M. C., Coleman, S. R., & Gormezano, I. (1969). Classical conditioning of rabbits nictitating membrane response at backward, simultaneous, and forward CS-US intervals. *Journal of Comparative and Physiological Psychology*, *69*, 226–231. doi:10.1037/h0028212

Soto, F. A., Vogel, E. H., Castillo, R. D., & Wagner, A. R. (2009). Generality of the summation effect in causal learning. *Quarterly Journal of Experimental Psychology*, *62*, 877–889. doi:10.1080/17470210802373688

Spence, K. W., Farber, I. E., & McFann, H. H. (1956). The relation of anxiety (drive) level of performance in competitional and non-competitional paired associates. *Journal of Experimental Psychology*, *52*, 296–305. doi:10.1037/h0043507

Sutton, R. S., & Barto, A. G. (1981). Toward a modern theory of adaptive networks: Expectation and prediction. *Psychological Review*, *88*, 135–170. doi:10.1037/0033-295X.88.2.135

Tait, R. W., & Saladin, M. E. (1986). Concurrent development of excitatory and inhibitory associations during backward conditioning. *Animal Learning & Behavior*, *14*, 133–137.

Terry, W. S. (1976). Effects of priming unconditioned stimulus representation in short-term memory on Pavlovian conditioning. *Journal of Experimental Psychology. Animal Behavior Processes*, *2*, 354–369. doi:10.1037/0097-7403.2.4.354

Thompson, R. F., & Spencer, W. A. (1966). Habituation: A model phenomenon for the study of neuronal substrates of behavior. *Psychological Review*, *73*, 16–43. doi:10.1037/h0022681

Thompson, R. F., Thompson, J. K., Kim, J. J., Krupa, D. J., & Shinkman, P. G. (1998). The nature of reinforcement in cerebellar learning. *Neurobiology of Learning and Memory*, *70*, 150–176. doi:10.1006/nlme.1998.3845

Thurnstone, L. L. (1930). The learning function. *The Journal of General Psychology*, *3*, 469–493. doi:10.1080/00221309.1930.9918225

Tomsic, D., Pedreira, M. E., Romano, A., Hermitte, G., & Maldonado, H. (1998). Context- US association as a determinant of long-term habituation in the crab Chasmagnathus. *Animal Learning & Behavior*, *26*, 196–209.

Vogel, E. H., Brandon, S. E., & Wagner, A. R. (2003). Stimulus representation in SOP: II. An application to inhibition of delay. *Behavioural Processes*, *62*, 27–48. doi:10.1016/S0376-6357(03)00050-0

Vogel, E. H., Castro, M. E., & Saavedra, M. A. (2004). Quantitative models of Pavlovian conditioning. *Brain Research Bulletin*, *63*, 173–202. doi:10.1016/j.brainresbull.2004.01.005

Wagner, A. R. (1969). Stimulus validity and stimulus selection in associative learning. In Mackintosh, N. J., & Honig, W. K. (Eds.), *Fundamental issues in associative learning*. Halifax, Canada: Dalhousie University Press.

Wagner, A. R. (1976). Priming in STM: An information-processing mechanism for self-generated or retrieval-generated depression in performance. In Tighe, T. J., & Leaton, R. N. (Eds.), *Habituation: Perspectives from child development, animal behavior and neurophysiology*. Hillsdale, NJ: Elrbaum.

Wagner, A. R. (1978). Expectancies and the priming of STM. In Hulse, S. H., Fowler, W., & Honing, W. K. (Eds.), *Cognitive aspects of animal behavior*. Hillsdale, NJ: Erlbaum.

Wagner, A. R. (1979). Habituation and memory. In Dickinson, A., & Boakes, R. A. (Eds.), *Mechanisms of learning and motivation: A memorial volume for Jerzy Konorski*. Hillsdale, NJ: Erlbaum Associates.

Wagner, A. R. (1981). SOP: A model of automatic memory processing in animal behavior. In Spear, N. E., & Miller, R. R. (Eds.), *Information Processing in Animals: Memory Mechanisms*. Hillsdale, NJ: Erlbaum.

Wagner, A. R. (2003). Context-sensitive elemental theory. *Quarterly Journal of Experimental Psychology*, *56*, 7–29. doi:10.1080/02724990244000133

Wagner, A. R., & Brandon, S. E. (1989). Evolution of a structured connectionist model of Pavlovian conditioning (AESOP). In Klein, S. B., & Mowrer, R. R. (Eds.), *Contemporary learning theories: Pavlovian conditioning and the status of traditional learning theory*. Hillsdale, NJ: Erlbaum.

Wagner, A. R., & Brandon, S. E. (2001). A componential theory of Pavlovian conditioning. In Mower, R. R., & Klein, S. B. (Eds.), *Handbook of contemporary learning theories*. Mahwah, NJ: Lawrence Erlbaum Associates, Inc.

Wagner, A. R., Logan, F. A., Haberlandt, K., & Price, T. (1968). Stimulus selection in animal discrimination learning. *Journal of Experimental Psychology*, *76*, 171–180. doi:10.1037/h0025414

Wagner, A. R., & Rescorla, R. A. (1972). Inhibition in Pavlovian conditioning: Application of a theory. In Halliday, M. S., & Boakes, R. A. (Eds.), *Inhibition and learning*. San Diego, CA: Academic Press.

Wagner, A. R., Rudy, J. W., & Whitlow, J. W. (1973). Rehearsal in animal conditioning. *Journal of Experimental Psychology*, *97*, 407–426. doi:10.1037/h0034136

Wagner, A. R., & Vogel, E. H. (2009). New and current views in basic conditioning: Theories of conditioning. In Squirre, L. (Ed.), *The new encyclopedia of Neuroscience*. New York: Elsevier.

Whitlow, J. W. (1975). Short-term memory in habituation and dishabituation. *Journal of Experimental Psychology*, *104*, 189–206.

Whitlow, J. W., & Wagner, A. R. (1972). Negative patterning in classical conditioning: Summation of response tendencies to isolable and configural components. *Psychonomic Science*, *27*, 299–301.

Williams, B. A. (1996). Evidence that blocking is due to associative deficit: Blocking history affects the degree of subsequent associative competition. *Psychonomic Bulletin & Review*, *3*, 71–74.

Williams, D. A., & Braker, D. S. (1999). Influence of past experience on the coding of compound stimuli. *Journal of Experimental Psychology. Animal Behavior Processes*, *25*, 461–474. doi:10.1037/0097-7403.25.4.461

Williams, D. R. (1965). Classical conditioning and incentive motivation. In Prokasy, W. F. (Ed.), *Classical conditioning: A symposium. New-York*. Appleton-Century-Crofts.

KEY TERMS AND DEFINITIONS

Aggregated Prediction: The theoretical supposition that the amount of learning accrued to any CS depends on the summed associative strength of all CSs present in the trial.

Associative Strength: The strength of the association between the CS and the US.

Componential Stimulus Representation: The assumption that the CS is made up of a number of elements that develop separable associations with the US.

Context Sensitive Stimulus Representation: A variation in the representation of a nominal CS, A, when presented in different stimulation contexts (eg., AB versus AC).

Error Term: A theoretical value used to compute changes in associative strength.

Pavlovian Conditioning: An experimental procedure in which a target stimulus, designated as conditioned stimulus (CS) is repeatedly paired with a reflex-eliciting stimulus, designated as unconditioned stimulus (US), resulting in a progressive change in the response to the CS, designated as conditioned response (CR).

Recurrent Inhibition: A theoretical mechanism whereby activation of one stimulus reduces or inhibits its own likelihood of being re-activated.

Reinforced Trial: A trial in which the CS is paired with the US.

Saturation: The assumption that there is a limited amount of associative strength that can be acquired by each conditioned stimulus or by any of its representational components.

Time Varying Stimulus Representation: The supposition that the effective representation of the CS varies in intensity over time.

Chapter 6

A Primer on Reinforcement Learning in the Brain:
Psychological, Computational, and Neural Perspectives

Elliot A. Ludvig
University of Alberta, Canada

Marc G. Bellemare
University of Alberta, Canada

Keir G. Pearson
University of Alberta, Canada

ABSTRACT

In the last 15 years, there has been a flourishing of research into the neural basis of reinforcement learning, drawing together insights and findings from psychology, computer science, and neuroscience. This remarkable confluence of three fields has yielded a growing framework that begins to explain how animals and humans learn to make decisions in real time. Mastering the literature in this sub-field can be quite daunting as this task can require mastery of at least three different disciplines, each with its own jargon, perspectives, and shared background knowledge. In this chapter, the authors attempt to make this fascinating line of research more accessible to researchers in any of the constitutive sub-disciplines. To this end, the authors develop a primer for reinforcement learning in the brain that lays out in plain language many of the key ideas and concepts that underpin research in this area. This primer is embedded in a literature review that aims not to be comprehensive, but rather representative of the types of questions and answers that have arisen in the quest to understand reinforcement learning and its neural substrates. Drawing on the basic findings in this research enterprise, the authors conclude with some speculations about how these developments in computational neuroscience may influence future developments in Artificial Intelligence.

DOI: 10.4018/978-1-60960-021-1.ch006

INTRODUCTION

The last decade has seen a proliferation of research exploring the neural and psychological mechanisms of reinforcement learning (for some good reviews and perspectives, see Dayan & Daw, 2008; Doya, 2007; Maia, 2009; Niv, 2009; Rangel, Camerer, & Montague, 2008; Schultz, 2002, 2007). This flourishing area of computational neuroscience draws on the expertise and knowledge in many sub-disciplines, including psychology, neuroscience, computer science, philosophy, and economics, amongst others. This remarkable confluence of fields was catalyzed by the discovery of a close correspondence between the behaviour of dopamine neurons in classical conditioning tasks and the prediction error in the temporal-difference (TD) algorithm from reinforcement learning (Montague, Dayan & Sejnowski, 1996; Schultz, Dayan, & Montague, 1997; Sutton, 1988; Sutton & Barto, 1990; see Figure 5). The import of this finding has filtered outward from a strikingly successful model of the neural basis of a simple conditioning behavior in animals to theoretical models of human economic decision making and, in part, to an entire field of neuroeconomics (e.g., Glimcher et al., 2009; Platt & Huettel, 2008; Rangel et al., 2008; Schultz, 2009).

Our goal in this chapter is two-fold. First, we aim to provide a primer of basic introductory materials in three of the constitutive disciplines of this enterprise—psychology, computer science, and neuroscience—to facilitate access by Artificial Intelligence (AI) researchers and other computational neuroscientists into this exciting field. As our second goal, we will not directly re-tread the ground covered in detail by the many comprehensive recent reviews, but rather we use some selective examples of reinforcement-learning research and show how this multi-disciplinary enterprise has helped inform and been informed by these basic lines of inquiry.

In considering the relationship between observed behaviour, computational models, and neural mechanisms, Marr's (1982) three levels of analysis prove very instructive. Marr proposed that any information-processing system can be analyzed at three different levels: the computational or functional, the algorithmic or representational, and the implementational. At the computational level, one specifies the goals and objectives of the system. What does the system do? For example, the computational goal for classical conditioning might be the prediction of important biological events. Second, at the algorithmic level, one specifies the step-by-step procedure by which this function is accomplished. What algorithm or procedure does the system use to accomplish the computational goals? Again, for classical conditioning, this might be the Rescorla-Wagner rule (Rescorla & Wagner, 1972) or the TD algorithm (Sutton & Barto, 1990) or any other set of rules that describe how the computation happens. Finally, at the implementational level, the important details of how these different algorithms and representations can be instantiated in neural tissue or other mediums are laid out. How are these algorithms physically realized? One example would be the equating of the reward-prediction error from reinforcement learning with the burst firing of dopamine neurons (Schultz et al., 1997). A full explanation of any information-processing system would require adequate accounts at each of the three levels of analysis.

Our chapter follows Marr's proposal by dividing this introduction to neural reinforcement learning into three sections that roughly correspond to his three levels of analysis. Section 1 describes the computational problems facing creatures in simple learning and decision-making situations and summarizes some of the attempts within psychology to characterize the algorithms that may be used by animals to solve these problems. Section 2 introduces the core computational ideas of reinforcement learning (RL) and shows how ideas from RL are particularly well suited as potential algorithms for models of natural learning. Section 3 ties the first two sections together in the brain, by introducing the neurobiological evidence that different RL algorithms have strong neurophysiological correlates. Our general strategy in each of the three sections is to introduce some of the fundamental problems and terminology in the sub-field before detailing the role and contribution of RL.

1. THE PSYCHOLOGY OF LEARNING AND DECISION MAKING

The first step towards understanding the modern study of reinforcement learning in the brain is a basic grasp of the major behavioral phenomena within the realms of animal learning and behavioral economics. We start by discussing two simple forms of learning—classical and operant conditioning—before progressing to more complex value-based decision making in humans and animals. In each case, we attempt to illustrate the major empirical phenomena and the functional goals for these behaviors, in addition to touching on some of the explanations that have been proffered within psychology to deal with these data. Our goal in this section is to lay out the behavioral puzzles for which the RL algorithms discussed in Section 2 provide a potential computational mechanism.

1.1. Predicting the Future: Classical Conditioning

In a recent episode of the American TV show *The Office*, the protagonist Jim decides to play a prank on his co-worker Dwight. Repeatedly, each time Jim shuts down his computer (making a telltale beep), he offers Dwight a small candy. After several iterations, Dwight begins to stick his hand out for the candy immediately upon hearing the beep, even claiming a bad taste in his mouth on a "trial" when Jim fails to present the candy. This

little fictional snippet evokes (and was inspired by) the classic work of the Russian physiologist Ivan Pavlov, who spent many years studying the salivary reactions of dogs to various sounds that were reliably followed by food delivery (Pavlov, 1927). This simple form of associative learning, known as classical or Pavlovian conditioning, is widely exhibited in the natural world, spanning many species from insects to fish to dogs to humans (for some good reviews and perspectives, see Domjan, 2005; Pearce & Bouton, 2001; Rescorla, 1988).

More precisely, classical conditioning is said to occur whenever a previously neutral stimulus (the CS or conditioned stimulus), such as the beep, is paired with a rewarding stimulus (the US or unconditioned stimulus). This reward can either be positive, such as the candy in *The Office* episode, or aversive, such as an electric shock or puff of air to the eye. Initially, only the reward elicits a response, such as reaching out a hand or salivation, but after sufficient training, the CS will also elicit a conditioned response (CR).

Most early views of classical conditioning proposed that animals learn an association between the CS and reward solely due to temporal contiguity (e.g., Guthrie, 1930; Pavlov, 1927; but really back to Aristotle). This simple idea entailed that whenever the CS and reward occurred around the same time, an association formed between them—the simple co-occurrence of the beep and candy was sufficient for Dwight to learn a link between them. Three major empirical findings from the animal learning literature in the late 1960's helped upend this contiguity-centered point-of-view: blocking, contingency effects, and conditioned taste aversion.

The first finding, blocking, showed that stimuli that perfectly predict reward do not always elicit conditioning responding. Only if the reward is unpredicted or surprising does learning occur. In the blocking procedure, a CS is paired with reward until the association is well learned. At this point, a second CS is introduced, and both

CSs are now paired with the reward. Typically, the newly introduced CS, when presented alone, does not elicit conditioned responding, even after substantial training with both CSs and the reward. It is as though the pre-trained cue "blocks" any learning from happening to the newly introduced cue, despite the temporal contiguity of this cue and reward (Kamin, 1969; Waelti et al., 2001). As a real-life example, imagine your friend has a known peanut allergy, and she experiences an allergic reaction after eating shrimp satay with peanut sauce at a Thai restaurant. Your friend may also be allergic to the shellfish, but from the restaurant incident, you would not make this connection because the potential association between shellfish and the allergic reaction was "blocked" by the known allergy to peanuts.

Second, Rescorla (1968) found in a series of experiments that a contingency or predictive relationship is crucial for establishing an association between two stimuli. As opposed to contiguity, which only requires that two events occur at the same time, contingency requires that the predicted stimulus (US) be more probable during the CS than at other times. For example, Rescorla found that inserting extra rewards into the experiment when the CS was not present (i.e., during the inter-trial intervals) eliminated responding to that cue (but the temporal relations might matter; see Williams et al., 2008). Only when the CS predicted a reliably higher rate of reward than the background rate did conditioned responding emerge.

These two experiments—blocking and contingency effects—demonstrated how temporal contiguity by itself was insufficient for classical conditioning; some form of contingency or predictive relationship was needed for conditioning to occur. Finally, a third set of experiments firmly established that temporal contiguity was not even necessary for conditioning. In these *conditioned taste aversion* experiments, rats were presented with flavoured water and then made ill several hours later through a dose of radiation (e.g., Garcia & Koelling, 1966). Rats subsequently avoided drinking this flavoured water, even though there was no temporal contiguity between the cue and reward, as several hours intervened between the initial drinking session and the illness. The key ingredient for successful conditioning in this case was that a valid predictive relationship (contingency) existed between the water and the illness, even when there was no temporal contiguity whatsoever.

This perspective that surprise and contingency, rather than contiguity, are the most important factors for conditioning found its most succinct expression in what has become known as the Rescorla-Wagner (RW) model (Rescorla & Wagner, 1972). In the RW model, learning occurs whenever the reward exceeds expectations. Figure 1A depicts how learning occurs in the RW model for a negative shock reward. There is an initial reward prediction (read: associative strength) on a given trial, followed by the actual outcome. At the end of the trial, this outcome is compared with the prediction, and the difference between the two, the *reward-prediction error*, is used to improve the prediction for next time. This simple learning rule describes precisely how the associative strength or reward prediction V for each CS present in a trial changes as a result of experience:

$$V = V + \alpha\,[r - V_{\text{Sum}}] \tag{1}$$

where r is the reward on that trial, V_{Sum} is the net associative strength based on all available CSs, and α is a parameter that controls the speed of learning. According to the RW model, there is an increment (or decrement) in the strength of an association based on the discrepancy between the reward received and the expected reward on a given trial. The expected reward (i.e., the net associative strength) is derived from all CSs present on a given trial as a simple sum of their associative strengths with the reward in question. The reward-prediction error drives all learning, leading to the experimental prediction that associative learning should only occur when expectations

Figure 1. Learning rule schematics for an experiment with a negative shock reward. A. Learning in the Rescorla-Wagner rule is driven by the difference (two-sided arrow) between the reward prediction and the actual reward on a given trial. This reward-prediction error is used to create a new reward prediction (down arrow), which can be used on the next trial (curved arrow). B. Learning in the temporal-difference (TD) algorithm. The Old prediction is the reward prediction based on the stimuli that were around on the last time step. The Current prediction is the prediction based on the stimuli that are currently available. An error is generated by comparing these two predictions with the reward (two-sided arrow). This error is then used to change the way the algorithm makes its predictions (down arrow). As a result, a New prediction can be made based on the stimuli that are still currently available. In some sense, the learning process converts the Current prediction into the New prediction. On the next time step, this New prediction becomes the Old prediction, and the process begins all over again (curved arrow)

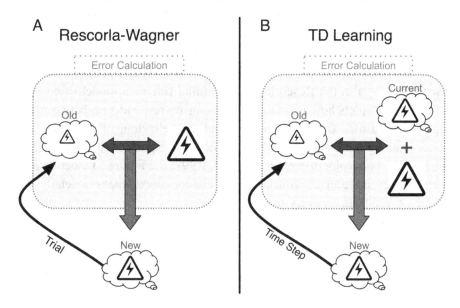

about rewards are violated. As a result, blocking is quite naturally explained. When the second cue is introduced, the first cue already perfectly predicts the reward, thus no reward-prediction error occurs on that trial, and no new learning occurs to the second cue.

The RW model has been remarkably successful in explaining and predicting many phenomena in animal and human conditioning (Rescorla & Wagner, 1972; Miller, 1996), but there are numerous empirical difficulties and theoretical alternatives (e.g., Gallistel & Gibbon, 2000; Pearce & Hall, 1980; Sutton & Barto, 1981, 1990; Wagner, 1981). Miller et al. (1996) compiled an extensive list of these empirical challenges to the RW model, and

many of these challenges also extend to newer extensions of this error-correcting learning rule, such as those from reinforcement learning (see below). Beyond these empirical concerns, one major conceptual problem that confronts the Rescorla-Wagner model is that the model is not real time and relies quite heavily on the concept of a trial, which is not immediately apparent in the experience of an animal (see Gallistel & Gibbon, 2000; Sutton & Barto, 1981; 1990). In fact, the relative times of the stimulus-reward and inter-trial intervals might be the most important determinants of the speed of learning, rather than trials themselves (e.g., Gottlieb, 2008). In addition, animals can learn to predict stimuli other than rewards (e.g., Brogden, 1939; Ludvig & Koop, 2008; Rescorla, 1980), perhaps even taking into account the causal structure of the environment (e.g., Blasidell et al., 2006; Dwyer, Starns, & Honey, 2009). These simple learning phenomena lie beyond the explanatory scope of the RW model.

The basic idea of error-driven learning has also been adopted into many of the learning rules that characterize modern RL (see Sutton & Barto, 1990, 1998). For example, in temporal-difference (TD) learning (see also Section 2.2), the discrepancy between prediction and outcome is also used to drive the value function or the prediction of future rewards on a moment-to-moment basis. This value function is roughly equivalent to the net associative strength (V_{Sum}) in the Rescorla-Wagner model. Figure 1B depicts how learning proceeds on a single time step in the TD algorithm. The learning proceeds along quite similar lines to the RW model, but with one major difference: Instead of comparing the reward received with the reward predicted on a given trial, on every time step t, the reward received is compared with *the change* in reward prediction to generate a reward-prediction error (δ):

$$\delta(t) = r(t) - [V(t-1) - V(t)]. \qquad (2)$$

With some easy algebra, this equation can be written to make it clear that the TD or reward-prediction error reflects how much better the world is at this time step (current reward plus newly predicted upcoming reward) versus what it was expected to be (the old prediction of reward):

$$\delta(t) = [r(t) + V(t)] - V(t-1). \qquad (3)$$

This error can then be used to update the old reward prediction to bring it more in line with what was experienced by adding a portion of the error to that old reward prediction:

$$V(t-1) = V(t-1) + \alpha \, \delta(t), \qquad (4)$$

where α is a parameter that controls the speed of learning. What the error does is change the value function or the way that predictions about rewards are made based on the stimuli. This updated value function can now be used to make a new prediction about the upcoming reward for the next time step.

As a result of this real-time updating, TD learning can make moment-to-moment predictions about reward and does not operate solely at the trial level, leading to improved correspondence with numerous conditioning behaviors in models based on this learning rule (e.g., Sutton & Barto, 1981, 1990; Ludvig et al., 2009). In addition to a better fit with some conditioning data, what is probably most compelling about this alternative learning rule as a model of conditioning is the strong correspondence between the error term and the behaviour of dopamine neurons in the midbrain (e.g., Montague et al., 1996; Schultz et al., 1997; see Figure 5). Section 3.3 will discuss these correspondences in detail.

1.2. Controlling the Future: Operant Conditioning

Classical conditioning is restricted in scope because most conditioned responses already exist as reflexive reactions to the rewarding or conditioned stimuli (but see Domjan, 2005). What classical conditioning does is tune when and how strongly animals perform these reactive responses. In contrast, novel responses that are shaped and reinforced by rewards from the environment are not possible within the classical conditioning framework. Indeed, the RW model of classical conditioning ignores responding altogether, providing a model for how associative strength changes over time, but leaving out the important issue of how this associative strength might get translated into behavior (see Stout & Miller, 2007; Ludvig et al., 2009). Operant or instrumental conditioning deals directly with how animals learn to make potentially novel responses that yield rewarding outcomes.

Figure 5. Dopamine neurons and reinforcement learning. A. Results from Schultz et al. (1997) of dopamine neuron activity in three situations. In the first case, an unpredicted reward (R) occurs, and a burst of dopamine firing follows. In the second case, a predicted reward occurs, and a burst follows the onset of the predictor (CS or conditioned stimulus), but there is no firing after the now-predicted reward. Finally, in the bottom case, a predicted reward is omitted, with a corresponding trough in dopamine responding. B. How the various elements of the TD learning algorithm—reward (r), value (V), and error (δ)—change during the time course of the different trials (adapted with permission from Doya, 2007)

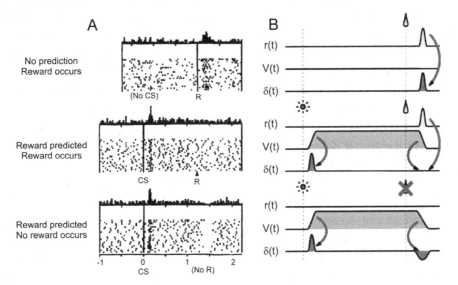

Perhaps the first example of operant conditioning in modern experimental psychology was Thorndike's puzzle box for cats (Thorndike, 1911). This experimental chamber was a small enclosure from which cats could escape given the right sequence of actions. In different permutations of the box, they could either pull a chain, or push a bar, or step on a latch to escape. After repeated exposure to this puzzle box, the cats gradually learned to perform the appropriate actions and escape more and more quickly. This gradual, trial-and-error learning of new actions typifies many of the procedures in the modern study of operant conditioning (see Staddon & Cerutti, 2003, for a review).

In classical conditioning, animals learn to predict the US on the basis of the CS, or, in more traditional psychological terms, the animals learn an association between the CS and the US. In operant conditioning, when a new response is performed, which predictive relationships animals learn are not nearly as obvious. At least two possibilities present themselves: Animals might learn a link between the stimulus and response (S-R association) or between a response and outcome (R-O association). In Thorndike's puzzle box, the cat may have learned (1) to step on the latch in the box or (2) that stepping on the latch leads to escape. This three-way connection between stimulus, response, and outcome is known as the *three-term contingency* (Skinner, 1938). Initial investigations of operant conditioning tended to focus most strongly on the S-R association. For example, on the basis of the cat puzzle boxes, Thorndike (1911) formulated his famous *Law of Effect:*

"Of several responses made to the same situation, those which are accompanied by or closely followed by satisfaction to the animal will, other

things being equal, be more firmly connected with the situation, so that, when it recurs, they will be more likely to recur..." (p. 244)

Here, he clearly pegs operant conditioning as learning a connection between a situation (stimulus) and response. RL has also mostly adopted this convention, wherein agents try to learn a policy—a mapping from stimuli to responses—on the basis of the previous reward history (see Section 2.3).

More recent work has drawn into question to what degree these simple stimulus-response associations drive behaviour in operant conditioning experiments (Balleine & Dickinson, 1998; Daw, Niv, & Dayan, 2005; Dickinson & Balleine, 1994; for a recent review, see Balleine & O'Doherty, 2009). An important distinction between habitual (S-R) and goal-directed (R-O) systems has been proposed, with separate neural substrates for each. One empirical example in support of this distinction comes from reinforcer devaluation experiments (e.g., Adams & Dickinson, 1981; Rescorla & Colwill, 1985). In these experiments, animals are trained to perform a particular response, say press a lever, for a food reward. After training, the food reward is devalued typically by either satiating the animal with the food or poisoning the animal following consumption of the food, but in a different context so as not to contaminate the previous training. When those animals are brought back to the original experimental set-up, they press the lever for the now-devalued food less than a comparable group of animals that had a different food reward devalued in the interim.

In loose terms, this decrease in responding indicates that animals know which food reward is upcoming and are not solely reacting reflexively to the stimulus. In more technical terms, these animals are sensitive to the association between response and outcome (R-O), and not only between stimulus and response (S-R). Responding, however, does not entirely disappear in these situations, suggesting that a S-R connection does

exist and persist. In addition, this decrease in responding following devaluation depends on the amount of training given to the animals: Highly overtrained animals become insensitive to the devaluation manipulation and continue to press the lever even afterward. Thus, there is evidence for both habitual (S-R) and goal-directed (R-O) responses. From these experiments, it would seem that Thorndike's cats may have learned both associations: to step on the latch in the box and that latch-stepping leads to escape.

For animals to turn this learning into the effective control of future outcomes requires a solution to two significant problems: how much and when to respond? These questions about the rate and timing of learned responding have dominated much of the literature on operant conditioning. The primary tactic for asking and answering these questions empirically has been through the two major schedules of reinforcement: ratio and interval schedules (Ferster & Skinner, 1957). In a ratio schedule, animals are rewarded after a certain number of responses are emitted; in an interval schedule, animals are rewarded for the first response after a certain amount of time has elapsed. Both ratio and interval schedules come in fixed or variable varieties; in a fixed schedule, the number of responses or time to reward is always the same, whereas in a variable schedule, only the average number or time is specified. Much of the theoretical work in this area has focused on steady-state behaviour—what the animal does after the course of learning is complete (e.g., Gibbon, 1977; Herrnstein, 1961). As with the Rescorla-Wagner model of classical conditioning, these real-time limitations to many models of operant conditioning suggest an opening for future theoretical contributions. Recent computational models based on RL have begun to make in-roads on both these problems with new models of both response vigor (Niv et al., 2005) and response timing (Daw, Courville, & Touretsky, 2006; Ludvig et al., 2008, 2009).

1.3. Evaluating the Future: Choice

Imagine that you are on the game show *Deal or No Deal* and faced with the choice of taking the offer from the banker for a guaranteed $100,000 and going home or continuing onward in the game and gambling for a 50/50 chance between two briefcases with either $1 or $250,000 in them. How would you decide what to do? You might be "rational" and figure out that the *expected value* of the second, risky option is ~$125,000 (50% of $250K), which is higher than the expected value of the safe option and decide to gamble. As it turns out, most people faced with this choice would take the less-"valuable" safe option, acting risk averse, and walk away with the guaranteed $100K (e.g., Kahneman & Tversky, 1979). This question of how people and animals value different outcomes and make decisions between them has been the purview of behavioral economics (Camerer & Loewenstein, 2003; see also Ariely, 2008) and, more recently, as questions about brain mechanisms have come to the fore, of neuroeconomics (e.g., Glimcher, 2009; Platt & Huettel, 2007; Trepel et al., 2005).

Why do people tend to undervalue the gamble and play it safe? One possible answer comes from *prospect theory* (Kahneman & Tversky, 1979; Tversky & Kahneman, 1981; but back to Bernoulli, 1738), which proposes that people make choices based on the *expected utility* of an outcome rather than the expected value. In this context, the utility can be thought of as the subjective value—how much the $250,000 is worth to the decision maker, rather than what its objective value is. Prospect theory contends that the relationship between objective value and subjective utility is sub-linear for gains: Winning $200 is less than twice as good as winning $100. As a result, people tend to choose the safer option as opposed to an objectively equivalent, but riskier option; they are *risk averse* for gains.

The converse result, however, is seen when the decision involves a sure small loss (losing $100)

vs. the chance of a big loss (50/50 chance of losing $200). In this instance, people tend to choose the gamble, making them *risk prone* or *risk seeking* for losses. Prospect theory proposes a similar non-linearity for the negative utility curve: Losing $200 is less than twice as bad as losing $100. As a result, someone trying to minimize their subjective loss would take the gamble. Within prospect theory, this asymmetry between risk sensitivity for decisions about gains and losses means that the way a question is framed or anchored can have a great influence on how people make choices about different potential economic outcomes (e.g., Tversky & Kahneman, 1981).

Animals, too, show varying risk sensitivity profiles based on the types of choices with which they are faced (e.g., Bateson & Kacelnik, 1995; Shafir, 2000). For example, Bateson and Kacelnik (1995) found that starlings, like humans, were risk averse when the reward was the amount of food. In contrast, when these birds were tested with delays to food, the starlings were risk seeking, preferring variable delays to food over fixed delays. In general, as might be imagined, shorter delays to reward are preferred to longer delays to reward, the result of a phenomenon known as *temporal discounting* (e.g., Green & Myerson, 2004). In this instance, the asymmetry between amounts and delays may be explained by the increase in variance that goes along with estimating larger magnitudes. Larger amounts are good, but larger delays are bad. As a result, the good amounts have more variance in their estimate, but the bad delays have more variance in their estimate. Simply sampling from this remembered distribution of amounts or delays produces this asymmetry in risk sensitivity (e.g., Marsh & Kacelnik, 2002). This risk sensitivity in birds also manifests itself in more naturalistic conditions. In one series of experiments, dark-eyed juncos, a small bird, chose the safe, small food option when the external temperature was warm, but in cold conditions, when they needed a larger meal to survive through the night, the juncos were risk seeking and sought the larger, more variable food source (Caraco, 1981; Caraco et al., 1990). Thus, though variations in risk sensitivity may reflect seemingly sub-optimal non-linearities in subjective utilities, these variations may still have strong adaptive value in an ecological context.

The preferences in the various choice situations described above are typically not pure preferences, but rather a tendency towards picking one option or another. In fact, when animals and humans are confronted with repeated options to which they can allocate varying portions of behaviors, they often show a distinct regularity known as *matching* behaviour (Herrnstein, 1961, 1970; Davison & McCarthy, 1988). In matching behaviour, the degree of preference for different options depends on the rates of reward for those options. So, if a monkey can press Button A and get on average 2 candies or press Button B and get on average 4 candies, the monkey will tend to press Button B twice as often. Numerous mechanisms have been proposed to explain how animals achieve this matching behaviour (e.g., Jozefowiez et al., 2009; McDowell, 2004; Simen & Cohen, 2009; Sugrue et al., 2005), but only recently have the potential connections to RL models begun to be evaluated (e.g., Lau & Glimcher, 2005; Loewenstein, Prelec, & Seung, 2009; Sakai & Futai, 2008).

In this section, we have reviewed some of the major findings in the psychology of learning and decision making in animals and humans. These represent many of the core behavioral phenomena that reinforcement-learning models attempt to explain. Most of the theoretical work has focused on the simpler learning phenomena of classical conditioning (e.g., Sutton & Barto, 1990; Schultz et al., 1997), but more recent work has made headway on operant conditioning and even more complex decision making (Gureckis & Love, 2009; Niv et al., 2005; Wunderlich, Rangel, & O'Doherty, 2009). One of the challenges for RL researchers in the future will be how to reconcile the simple learning rules that guide performance in classical- and operant-conditioning tasks with the more

complex decision making exhibited by humans and animals in behavioral-economics settings.

2. ALGORITHMS FOR REINFORCEMENT LEARNING

Reinforcement learning (RL) is a branch of AI that is concerned with the computational study of real-time decision making (Sutton & Barto, 1998). In RL, agents are assumed to interact with an environment while attempting to maximize a reward signal (see Figure 2A). In biological terms, these agents can be conceived as entire organisms or, occasionally, as control centers in the brain that receive filtered input from the external environment. For a rigorous and accessible introduction to RL, see the book by Sutton and Barto (1998). Here, we first introduce the formalisms and goals of RL in the context of broader work in machine learning and then step through some of the key concepts in the area, including value functions and the temporal-difference (TD) learning algorithm. We conclude with a discussion of some of the key issues in the design and use of RL algorithms, including strategies for action selection and efficient exploration.

2.1. Machine Predictions: Supervised Learning

Although the idea of learning is familiar to young children, the computational mechanisms that drive learning remain largely unknown. With the *Dartmouth Summer Research Conference on Artificial Intelligence*, held in 1956 and organized by the pioneers of the field, computer scientists began to consider how to describe intelligent concepts in machine terms. They conjectured that "every aspect of learning or any other feature of intelligence can in principle be so precisely described that a machine can be made to simulate it" (McCarthy et al., 1955/2006, p. 12). Thus the field of AI was born—in a quest to discover and understand

Figure 2. Reinforcement Learning and Markov Decision Processes. A. The world according to reinforcement learning. There is an agent that interacts with an environment by emitting actions, and receiving states (or observations) and rewards in return. B. A small maze in which the rat at the bottom can navigate and obtain various rewards. Signed values (+ or -) are the reward magnitudes at different end points. Probabilities (p) of previous actions at the final choice points are indicated. The states are numbered S1 through S4. C. Same maze problem, but abstracted to a series of connected states. Numbers in the circles indicate the values of various states, given the history

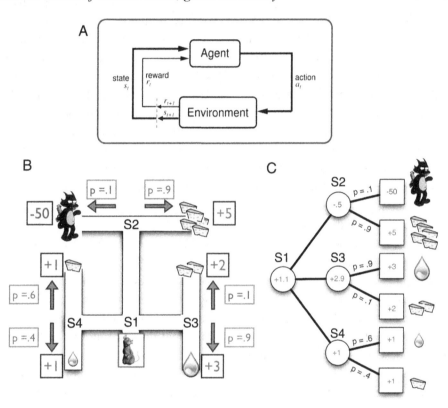

algorithms that exhibit intelligent behavior. Paramount to the study of AI is learning, which is often investigated in three guises: supervised learning, unsupervised learning, and reinforcement learning (Mitchell, 1997; Sutton & Barto, 1998). We first turn our attention to supervised learning—a framework for describing how machines can learn to predict the future from data—whose limitations will provide computational motivation for the techniques of reinforcement learning.

From a mathematical perspective, learning is about finding input-output mappings that are consistent with some dataset. In supervised learn-ing, this data is usually provided as a set of inputs and desired outputs; these desired outputs act as a supervisory signal, telling the algorithm what it should learn about the data. For example, a popular supervised-learning problem is handwritten-digit recognition (e.g., LeCun et al., 1998). In this problem, the inputs are grainy images of handwritten digits, and the desired outputs are corresponding labels between 0 and 9. The goal for supervised-learning algorithms is to learn a mapping from a set of already-labeled images, so that the algorithm can correctly identify the digits in novel images.

One popular technique for solving supervised-learning problems is the family of gradient-descent algorithms. These algorithms are highly analogous to the Rescorla-Wagner model (see Section 2.1), wherein learning occurs in response to prediction errors. These algorithms operate by examining a group of inputs (stimuli) and making a prediction about the corresponding output. The prediction is computed through a set of weights that act in a similar fashion to the associative strengths present in the Rescorla-Wagner model. A prediction error is calculated, which is simply the difference between the prediction and the output. If this error is positive, then the prediction gets adjusted upwards; if the error is negative, then the prediction gets adjusted downwards. In the digit-recognition example, the algorithm might learn the probability that an image corresponds with each digit. If the algorithm predicts the correct label with less than 100% probability, there would be a positive error, and the algorithm would predict the correct label for this image next time with a higher probability. If the algorithm predicts the wrong labels, there would be a negative error, and those predictions would be downgraded. These algorithms are known as gradient-descent algorithms because they adjust their prediction by looking at the gradient (slope and direction) of the error.

In this supervised-learning framework, it is generally assumed that the learning algorithms attempt to solve one-shot prediction problems. These ideas have proved enormously useful on a wide variety of problems, from bioinformatics to health care (e.g., Asgarian et al., 2010; Cooper et al., 2005). Animals and humans in the real world, however, face a constant stream of information, which can only be coarsely represented as a one-shot prediction problem. One major element is missing in the supervised-learning formulation of the prediction problem: time.

2.2. Temporal Predictions: Reinforcement Learning

A major limitation of supervised-learning methods is that they ignore the temporal aspects of decision-making problems. For a supervised learner, there is some data from which a prediction is made. The consequences of that prediction are limited to the congruence with the output; future success is not directly compromised by one bad prediction/decision. In contrast, in real-world systems, both natural and artificial, time plays a crucial role: Every decision made by an agent affects all possible future decisions. Consider the task of going out for lunch at work. Your first choice might involve selecting your lunch mates. The second choice determines the restaurant where you will eat. Pending which restaurant you choose, you would be faced with different menus and thus different options. After ordering, you may then decide whether to eat with your hands, utensils, or chopsticks. This inherent sequentiality of real-world decision making necessitates a different set of learning methods for predicting and behaving in a real-time setting. RL addresses exactly this set of questions.

Figure 2A shows how, in RL, the world is typically divided into an interacting agent and environment. The agent receives observations (stimuli) from the world and emits actions. In biological terms, the agent can be thought of as the whole animal, a small control center in the brain, or even an extended cognitive apparatus (e.g., Clark, 2008). A common assumption in most RL problems is that the environment or outside world consists of different states, and given that state, the future is entirely independent of the history before that state. This assumption, known as the Markov property, ensures that knowledge of the state is sufficient information for predicting anything (rewards or otherwise) that can be known about the future—no other information can help.

An entire RL problem can be fully described as a Markov Decision Process (MDP), which consists of the set of environmental states, the possible actions available to the agent, the reward function, and the transition function that details how the environment changes from state to state. For RL researchers, the usual task is to develop an algorithm for an agent that best picks actions so as to maximize future rewards in such an MDP. In doing so, useful sub-problems can include learning to predict the future rewards, exploring the environment successfully, inferring the state from given observations, or building a model of the environmental state transitions.

An illustrative example should help make these concepts clearer. Figure 2B shows a schematic of a rat in a fairly simple maze. There are multiple choice points for this rat, with the possibility of cheese or water rewards at some end points, while a big cat awaits in another corner. The reward values for each end point (i.e., the reward function) are presented in blue boxes, and some transition probabilities (p) are presented in the orange boxes. Each decision the rat makes influences possible future decisions. If the rat goes up from the start state S1, then it is faced with the prospect of possibly meeting the cat, getting a big hunk of cheese, or returning back to the start. Describing this problem as an MDP involves detailing the 4 states (the choice points), the 4 possible actions (up, down, left, right), the reward function (0, except where indicated), and the transition probabilities (the probability of each action succeeding). From the RL point-of-view, this abstract description captures the whole problem (see Figure 2C). The research question becomes: How do you learn to maximize rewards in this context?

Predicting Rewards: Value functions. A *value function* is the prediction of future rewards from the different states, and is a fundamental tool in RL for solving MDPs. The value of being in an environmental state (s) at a particular time (t) can be defined as the weighted sum of all future rewards:

$$V(s_t) = r_{t+1} + \gamma\, r_{t+2} + \gamma^2 r_{t+3} + \gamma^3 r_{t+4}\cdots, \tag{5}$$

where t denotes the current time step and t +1, t + 2... are future time steps, making r_{t+1} the reward following the current state, r_{t+2} the reward after the following state, and so on. The parameter γ is a discount factor that (when less than 1) causes distant rewards to matter less than immediate rewards in determining the value of a state. At the extreme, with a discount factor of 0, the value of a state is exactly equal to the immediately ensuing reward. The value is thus the sum of all future rewards from a given state, appropriately discounted. Of course, this "true" value is never directly available to the agent, but must somehow be estimated based on the agent's experience. Approximating this idealized value function can be thought of as the goal for all of RL.

One interesting relationship emerges if we compare the values at successive states. The values of two consecutive states (s_t and s_{t+1}) are respectively equal to:

$$V(s_t) = r_{t+1} + \gamma\, r_{t+2} + \gamma^2 r_{t+3} + \gamma^3 r_{t+4}\cdots$$

$$V(s_{t+1}) = r_{t+2} + \gamma\, r_{t+3} + \gamma^2 r_{t+4}\cdots \tag{6}$$

The right half of Equation 6 is intentionally shifted to the right to highlight the similarities between the two equations: the value of the second state (s_{t+1}) is almost the same as the value of the first state (s_t), save the first reward (r_{t+1}) and the degree of discounting. Combining the two equations, we get the following relationship between the value of a state, and the value of its successor:

$$V(s_t) = r_{t+1} + \gamma\, V(s_{t+1}). \tag{7}$$

Because of the Markov property, the value of a state can be fully expressed as the next reward plus the discounted value of the following state. This relationship will prove important in calculating value functions through the temporal-difference (TD) algorithm below.

Let us return to the example of the rat in the maze for a moment. Figure 2C provides an alternate view of the maze as a tree of possible paths. The circles represent the different states, and the squares represent the rewarding outcomes following different choices. For illustrative purposes, we assume that the rat has had some prior experience with the maze: Whenever the rat was in the top state (S2), the rat ended up meeting the cat with probability (p).1 (i.e., 10% of the time) and finding the big cheese with probability.9 (i.e., 90% of the time). As a result, the estimated value of that top state is -.5, which is equal to -5 (i.e.,.1 times the -50 reward for meeting the cat) plus +4.5 (i.e.,.9 times the +5 reward for getting the big cheese). Similar calculations can be conducted for the left (value = +1) and right states (value = +2.9), and the results are displayed inside the circles in Figure 2C, representing states. For the value of the start state (S1), the calculation is a little more interesting. There are no immediate rewards following any of the actions from this state. Instead, all actions take the rat to another state; however, the value of these potential future states is known. We can therefore calculate the value of S1 from the values of the three immediately succeeding states. If the agent went up, left, or right with equal probability from S1, the value of this state becomes $(1 + 2.9 - 0.5)/3 \approx 1.1$. Note that this example implicitly assumes a discount factor of 1.

Value functions are closely related to the associative strengths present in the Rescorla-Wagner model. Associative strengths can be thought of as the prediction of the upcoming US or reward. Value functions are similarly predictions of upcoming rewards, not only of the immediately ensuing reward, but a function of many future rewards. This subtle difference between associative strength and value functions has a distinct analogy to the difference between supervised learning for prediction and reinforcement learning. In one case, the target is a timeless entity, and in the latter case, the target is a time-embedded set of future outcomes.

Learning Values: The temporal-difference (TD) algorithm. Pending what information is available to the agent, there are many methods for estimating value functions. For example, if the agent has a model of the environment and therefore knows what the next state will be, then the value function can be computed directly through *dynamic programming* methods (Bertsekas & Tsitsiklis, 1996). When agents do not have such a model of the environment, they must somehow estimate the value function from their stream of experience. The temporal-difference (TD) learning algorithm is a procedure for learning these reward predictions in an efficient manner (Sutton, 1988). The key idea behind the TD algorithm is *bootstrapping*: learning a guess from a guess. The agent improves its estimate for the value of a state by learning from the value of the next state. This incremental improvement capitalizes on the key relationship between the values of successive states (see Equation 7 and Figure 2B): The value of a given state depends only on the immediate reward and the value of the next state.

The TD-learning algorithm provides a very simple and elegant way of learning to predict future rewards. The algorithm works in a similar fashion to the Rescorla-Wagner model (see Section 2.2) by learning through a reward-prediction error or TD error. In this case, the reward-prediction error (δ) is the discrepancy between what was expected (the old value) and what actually occurred (a reward plus the new value):

$$\delta_t = [r_t + \gamma \, V(s_t)] - V(s_{t-1}). \qquad (8)$$

TD learning then updates the estimate for the value of the last state based on the TD error and a parameter α that helps determine the speed of learning:

$$V(s_{t-1}) = V(s_{t-1}) + \alpha \, \delta_t. \qquad (9)$$

As a result, through the TD-learning algorithm, the estimated value of the new state directly influences the estimated value of the old state. Through this process, over repeated iterations, the reward prediction can percolate back to earlier and earlier states.

To step through these details of the TD learning algorithm more carefully, let us revisit the maze of Figure 2B. Suppose that the rat is completely naive, never having visited this maze before. For simplicity in calculation in this example, we set the step-size parameter α to .5 and the discount factor γ to 1. On the first trial, let us imagine that the rat goes up from the start state S1 to state S2. At this point, no rewards have been received, and the value of all states is 0, thus no learning occurs. Now, the rat goes to the right and receives a reward of +5. Because the value of S2 is 0, a large prediction error of +5 occurs, and the value of this state is updated to +2.5 (step size of .5 times a reward of +5). On the second trial, the rat again goes up from the start state S1 to state S2. This time, however, state S2 has a non-zero value. This change in estimated value induces a prediction error of +2.5 (value of state S2 minus the value of state S1), and the value of state S1 is now updated to +1.25 (.5 x +2.5), even though a reward has not been encountered yet. This propagation of value back through the states is the *bootstrapping* mechanism through which TD learning achieves efficient learning from the experienced rewards. Finally, imagine the rat again goes to the right and gets a reward of +5—the value of state S2 will again be updated, but this time by a smaller amount as there was already a reward prediction of +2.5 in state S2. The new value for state S2 will be +3.75, which is the original value of +2.5, plus .5 (the learning rate) times the difference between the reward received (+5) and the reward predicted (+2.5). The value of state S1 does not get updated again at this point, unless a memory mechanism known as *eligibility traces* are used—an RL technique we do not discuss here (see Sutton & Barto, 1998). Thus, after only two trials, the agent has gained new information about the value of these two states, propagating

information back through the states as they were encountered.

2.3. From Predictions to Actions

One limitation to TD learning, as discussed above, is that the algorithm does not provide a direct way of learning how to select actions. The TD algorithm only learns the value or predicted future rewards from different states, and thus could not be directly used by real agents that act upon their world and control the rewards they receive. Several solutions to this limitation suggest themselves. One idea would be to learn a separate value for each action leading out of a state, instead of for the state itself. We discuss a pair of such action-value methods—SARSA and Q-learning—below (Sutton & Barto, 1998; Watkins, 1989). Another idea would be to separately store a probability for taking each action in each state (known as a policy) and then adjust that policy based on the agent's experience, as in the actor-critic architecture that is popular in biological circles (e.g., Joel, Niv, & Ruppin, 2002; O'Doherty et al., 2004; Samejima & Doya, 2007). We evaluate the strengths and limitations of these major approaches for action selection in MDPs.

Action Values. We have discussed how a value function encodes the expected future reward from a given state. Value functions, however, cannot directly be used to decide which action to take, without knowledge of the transition function to the next state. The *action-value function* (Q), on the other hand, stores the value of taking a certain action from a state. In our maze example, the action-values in state S2 for the left and right actions are correspondingly -50 and 5. In mathematical notation, we would write that as Q(S2, left) = -50 and Q(S2, right) = +5. Similarly, the action-value for the up action in state S1 is -0.5, which corresponds to the expected reward if the rat moves up, based on past experience.

As with the value function for states, the action value for a state-action pair is the expected immediate reward (given that action) plus the sum of all future rewards. To make this clearer, let us denote the reward returned from the environment following action a_t as $r_{t+1}(a_t)$. The definition for the action-value function is quite similar to the equation for the value function of a state (compare Equation 5):

$$Q(s_t, a_t) = r_{t+1}(a_t) + \gamma r_{t+2} + \gamma^2 r_{t+3}..., \qquad (10)$$

with the key difference that the action value does not depend on all the possible immediate rewards, but only on the rewards that follows the action in question. As with the value function (see Equation 7), this action-value function can be expressed so that it also depends only on the next reward and the value of the next state:

$$Q(s_t, a_t) = r_{t+1}(a_t) + \gamma V(s_{t+1}). \qquad (11)$$

So, in the maze example, the value of going up from S1 (i.e., Q(S1, up)) depends solely on the immediate reward for going up (0) and the value of the next state S2 (-.5). This relationship between the action value and the value of the next state is critical for the performance of model-free learning algorithms, which do not rely on knowing the transition function to learn about the world, but rather learn solely from experienced samples.

Learning about actions. The first action-value algorithm we review, SARSA (State-Action-Reward-State-Action), can be thought of as the natural extension of TD Learning to the decision-making case. The goal of an agent taking actions in an MDP is to maximize the sum of future rewards. When the environmental model is unknown, the agent must learn, from experience, about the value of the actions in each state. A very simple extension of the TD algorithm is to consider bootstrapping (learning a guess from a guess) from the action values, rather than the state values. Once again, we calculate a TD error (see Equation 8), but this time based on the difference between the old ac-

tion value (what was expected) and the new action value plus the reward (what actually happened):

$$\delta_t = [r_t + \gamma Q(s_t, a_t)] - Q(s_{t-1}, a_{t-1}). \qquad (12)$$

This error can then be used to update the old action value with a similar step-size parameter α that controls the speed of learning:

$$Q(s_{t-1}, a_{t-1}) = Q(s_{t-1}, a_{t-1}) + \alpha \delta_t \qquad (13)$$

These two equations form the basis of the SARSA algorithm. Similar to what occurs in the TD algorithm, the action value of the next state-action pair percolates back to influence the estimate of the action value for the previous state-action pair.

To highlight the relationship between SARSA and TD learning, consider a naïve rat back in our example maze. For simplicity in calculation in this example, we again set the step-size parameter α to .5 and the discount factor γ to 1. As before, on the first trial, the rat goes up from state S1 to state S2; at this point, no rewards have been received, and no learning occurs. The rat then goes to the right and gets the large cheese reward (+5). Because the action value of going to the right in state S2 (Q(S2, right)) is 0, there is a large prediction error (+5), and this action value is updated to +2.5, which is equal to the old value of 0 plus the step size .5 times the prediction error of +5. On the next trial, imagine the rat again goes up from state S1 into state S2. At this point, unlike in TD learning, nothing happens yet. State S2 does not directly have a value of its own; another action needs to be taken before the state-action pair can be updated. When the action from state S2 is selected, then the learning occurs. The action value for going up in state S1 (Q(S1, up)) is updated based on the old action value (0), the reward received for going up (0), and the next action value (Q(S2, right) = +2.5), so that this action value is now +1.25 (consult Eqs. 12 and 13). Finally, the rat receives the large reward again (+5), and the action value for going right in state S2 is duly updated to +3.75, based on the difference between the action value or expected reward (+2.5) and the reward actually received. As with TD learning, through the SARSA algorithm, the action values back up to earlier and earlier state-action pairs.

Exploration vs. exploitation. A new wrinkle is introduced when action selection is incorporated into learning. The agent now controls what experiences it receives. To perform well in any environment, the agent needs to encounter the states and actions that yield high reward. Yet, sampling new actions and states can be fraught with risk, especially when rewarding actions are already available to the agent. This delicate balance between maximizing the reward from known actions and sampling new opportunities is known in RL as the exploration-exploitation dilemma.

This dilemma is perhaps best explained through the example of a slot machine (often known as a bandit problem: Robbins, 1952). In this problem, an agent is faced with a number of slot machines, each with unknown payout rates. For example, Machine 1 pays out 4 dollars 10% of the time, while Machine 2 pays out only 1 dollar, but 50% of the time. At every time step, the agent must repeatedly choose between one of the machines. Here, Machine 2 has the higher expected value for each pull than Machine 1 (50 cents versus 40 cents). An agent learning about these slot machines, however, only has access to samples of the payouts; it does not have access to this underlying distribution. Suppose that on the first trial, the agent plays the first machine and receives $4. An agent using a learning rule such as SARSA would then update the action value for selecting the first machine towards $4. If the initial estimates were $0 for both machines, the agent would treat Machine 1 as the better choice, and would never select Machine 2. The more general issue at stake is that relying exclusively on imperfect action-value estimates for action selection can lead to distinctly sub-par behavior. The dilemma is as follows: An agent must de-cide at each step whether to collect information to refine its estimates (explore) or take the best (greedy) action with respect to its action-value estimates (exploit).

To remedy this trade-off between exploiting current knowledge and sampling new options, a variety of algorithms to guide exploration have been developed in the RL literature (for overviews, see Kaelbling, Littman, & Moore, 1996; Sutton & Barto, 1998; for particulars, see Auer, 2003; Brafman & Tenneholz, 2003; Daw et al., 2006; Kolter & Ng, 2009). Perhaps the simplest exploration rule is the ε-greedy algorithm, which picks the best action (highest action value) most of the time, but for some small portion ε of actions, picks an action at random. Slightly more sophisticated is the Softmax rule, wherein actions are taken at a frequency proportional to their action values. In both these cases, some randomness is inserted into the action selection process to ensure adequate coverage of the potential state space. Newer algorithms tend to direct exploration through optimism in the face of uncertainty (e.g., Auer, 2003; Brafman & Tenneholz, 2003). These important computational issues about balancing reward and knowledge in action selection have only recently begun to be addressed in a biological context (e.g., Daw et al., 2006).

Q-Learning. In the SARSA algorithm described above, the agent computes the value of a state-action pair based on the immediate reward and the next observed state-action pair, independent of whether the second action was exploratory. There is thus an interaction between future action choices and the process for updating the current state-action pair. But, imagine that the next action was a particularly bad exploratory action: Updating from the action value for that state-action pair seems like a very poor idea. As a result of this limitation, SARSA does not learn the best possible policy in certain situations (see Sutton & Barto, 1998).

The Q-Learning algorithm (Watkins, 1989) remedies this problem by learning from what the agent could have done, rather than from what the agent actually did. To do so, Q-Learning uses a slightly different reward-prediction error for updating the action values (compare Equation 12):

$$\delta_t = [r_t + \gamma \max_a Q(s_t, a)] - Q(s_{t-1}, a_{t-1}). \qquad (14)$$

In Q-Learning, the agent learns from the difference between what was expected (the old action value) and the best possible outcome (maximum action value for that state ($\max_a Q(s_t, a)$), plus the reward). The action value is updated exactly as in SARSA (see Equation 13). The key difference between Q-learning and the SARSA algorithm is that the agent learns from the estimated best action that it could have taken (Q-Learning), rather than from the action that it actually chose (SARSA).

Let us return again to the naïve rat in our example maze (Figure 2A). Imagine that on the second trial, instead of going to the big cheese from the top state S2, the rat explored and found the cat (-50). With SARSA, learning is from the actual experience: The rat would compare the action value for going up in S1 ($Q(S1, up) = 0$) with the reward received for that action (0) and the action value for the next action ($Q(S2, left) = 0$, when it was taken), and no learning would occur. On future trials, selecting this exploratory action in state S2 would have even worse ramifications, as the action value would be negative, and the action value for going up in state S1 would be updated accordingly. With Q-Learning, however, the update is from the estimated best possible action out of state S2. As a result, the rat would compare the action value for going up in S1 ($Q(S1, up) = 0$) with the reward received for that action (0) and the action value for the *best possible action in the next state* ($Q(S2, right)$, which after the first trial was updated to +2.5; see above). The action value $Q(S1, up)$ would then be updated to +1.25, despite not taking the right action in state S2. By effectively ignoring the exploratory action, with this action sequence, Q-Learning learns more quickly than SARSA.

In our discussion of decision making, we suggested that a good agent should select actions to maximize the sum of future rewards. This action selection process, or policy, is optimal for a given MDP, if the policy maximizes the sum of future rewards from every state. Even with sufficient data, the SARSA algorithm does not learn the optimal policy unless strict conditions are enforced. In contrast, under specific technical conditions, Q-learning can be proven to converge to the value function that will yield the optimal policy (Watkins & Dayan, 1992). There are cases, however, when Q-learning is known to diverge (i.e., its prediction error grows without bounds)—for example, when the value function is only approximated because the state space is too large, as would be the case for most biologically relevant problems (Baird, 1995; for newer, related algorithms that do not diverge, see Maei et al., 2009; Sutton et al., 2009)—limiting the value of the algorithm in many computational settings. In addition, from a biological perspective, the maximization and counterfactual learning that drive Q-Learning may seem less plausible, but the evidence as to what type of action values may be used in the brain is mixed (Morris et al., 2005; Roesch, Calu, & Schoenbaum, 2007; Wunderlich, Rangel, & O'Doherty, 2009; see Section 3.3).

In the two action-selection algorithms discussed thus far (SARSA and Q-Learning), the behavior of the agent is driven by the action-value function. In those cases, modifying the action values immediately leads to changes in behavior. There is no separation between the evaluation system and decision-making system, which is perhaps not ideal for modeling decision making in animals. A more biologically plausible approach might be to explicitly separate the policy evaluation from the action-selection process (e.g., Joel et al., 2002; Samejima & Doya, 2007). The actor-critic algorithm is one such approach. This algorithm explicitly defines modules for each of the two mechanisms. The critic module plays the role of the evaluator, receiving the reward signal and estimating state values through an algorithm like TD learning. The critic also outputs an error signal to the actor, which selects actions based on a set of stored preferences. A positive error from the critic reinforces the actor into taking the same action again, whereas a negative error inhibits such behavior. To compare the actor-critic framework with SARSA and Q-Learning, one may think of the latter two algorithms as implicitly defining the actor module while explicitly representing the value function. The actor-critic framework, on the other hand, defines both modules explicitly.

In this section, we introduced some of the major ideas that characterize the modern study of RL. We started with the concept of prediction from supervised learning and then discussed how RL adds time and sequentiality to the prediction problem. The main RL algorithms reviewed, TD-learning, SARSA, and Q-Learning, all take advantage of this temporality by bootstrapping or learning a guess from a guess. These simple algorithms provide the base for a powerful framework that has had many computational successes and is now being used as a model for learning in animals (see Section 1.2) and the brain (see Section 3.3).

3. BRAIN MECHANISMS FOR REINFORCEMENT LEARNING

Learning in animals requires some modification of the neuronal networks within the brain. One challenge for contemporary neuroscience is to determine the mechanisms underlying these modifications and how these mechanisms function in different forms of learning (see Section 2 for a discussion of computational strategies for learning). Substantial progress has been made over the past decade in understanding some of the neuronal events associated with reinforcement learning and value-based decision making as well as linking the computational models with neurobiological findings. This progress has been summarized in many excellent reviews (Daw & Doya, 2006;

Dayan & Niv, 2008; Maia, 2009; Niv, 2009; Niv & Schoenbaum, 2008; Platt, 2002; Rangel et al., 2008; Rushworth & Behrens, 2008; Rushworth et al., 2009; Schultz, 2002, 2007; Schultz et al., 2008). Our goal in this section is not to go over the same ground as these reviews (some of which are quite advanced), but rather to describe some of the basic physiological processes underlying reinforcement learning in a manner that is accessible to investigators in the fields of machine learning and behavioral psychology wishing to become familiar with the relevant neurophysiology and brain anatomy.

3.1. Basic Concepts in Cellular Neurobiology

A fundamental requirement for understanding the neurobiology of reinforcement learning is some basic knowledge of the cellular properties of nerve cells, the mechanisms for the transmission of information between nerve cells, and the processes by which the properties of nerve cells, and the networks they form, are modified (an essential requirement for learning). Thus we begin this section by briefly summarizing the key concepts related to this requirement.

Action potentials in nerve cells. Information in the nervous system is transmitted from one region to another in the form of *action potentials*. Action potentials are brief changes in the voltage levels around the membrane of a nerve cell (a *neuron*). They are initiated at or near the cell body and propagate in an all-or-none manner along the axon of the neuron. The amplitude and duration of action potentials are about 100 mV and 1 ms, respectively, and the velocity of conduction along the axon ranges from about 1 to 100 m/s depending on axon diameter. Information about the internal state of the nervous system and external events are often represented by the timing and frequency of action potentials (e.g., Rieke et al., 1999).

Recording the activity of single neurons (i.e., the occurrence of action potentials) during a behavioral task is one of the most powerful methods for gaining an understanding of the neuronal mechanisms underlying the functioning of the nervous system. Indeed, most of what we know about the connection between reinforcement learning and the brain comes from these types of studies in monkeys and rats (e.g., Schultz et al., 1997). Figure 3A shows how this method involves positioning the tip of a fine microelectrode close to the cell body of a neuron to detect voltage changes generated by currents produced by action potentials in the space immediately outside the neuron. These *extracellularly* recorded potentials (spikes) are relatively small, typically having amplitudes in the range of .1 to .5 mV (Figure 3B and C). This method is often referred to as *single-unit recording*. Figure 3D shows the activity patterns of single neurons derived from single-unit recording displayed as a *raster plot* in which the occurrence of each spike during a trial is represented by a dot along a time axis; the data for multiple trials are aligned horizontally and separated vertically to form a raster of spike activity. An average pattern of activity across many trials is illustrated as a histogram (Figure 3D, bottom; see also Figure 5A), which is the sum of the spikes recorded during multiple trials relative to an event in the behavioral sequence, such as the time of reward delivery in a reinforcement-learning task.

Single-unit recordings have been made during a variety of reinforcement-learning paradigms in rodents and non-human primates (see Section 3.3). Because of its invasive nature, single-unit recording cannot be used routinely in humans. Currently, the study of the neurobiology of reinforcement learning in humans primarily utilizes *function magnetic resonance imaging* (fMRI) to identify brain regions in which changes in blood flow produced by neuronal activity in large numbers of neurons are correlated with specific parameters in reinforcement-learning tasks. The signal detected in fMRI studies is usually referred to as the BOLD signal (**B**lood-**O**xygen-**L**evel-**D**ependent) and is thought to originate in brain regions sending and receiving task-related information (e.g., Logothetis et al., 2001). A major advantage of fMRI is that multiple brain systems can be examined simultaneously, but two drawbacks are that it has poor spatial and temporal resolution and an inability to distinguish the activity between different classes of neurons.

Synaptic transmission. Most communication between neurons occurs at specialized junctions called *synapses* between the axon terminals of one neuron (the *presynaptic* neuron) and localized sites on the dendrites and/or cell body of another neuron (the *postsynaptic* neuron). Each action potential in the presynaptic neuron causes the release of a chemical transmitter, which binds to receptor molecules embedded in the membrane of the postsynaptic neuron. Depending on the transmitter and the type of postsynaptic receptor, the transmitter can act to either increase (excitatory transmission) or decrease (inhibitory transmission) the activity in the postsynaptic neuron. In the mammalian central nervous system, the most common excitatory and inhibitory transmitters are glutamate and gamma-amino-butyric-acid (GABA), respectively. Significant modification in the activity of a postsynaptic neuron by synaptic input requires the cooperative action of large numbers of synapses because the effect of transmitter release from a single synapse is very small. A single presynaptic neuron may make hundreds of synapses with a single postsynaptic neuron, and each postsynaptic neuron can receive inputs from hundreds of presynaptic neurons.

Neuromodulation. Closely related to synaptic transmission is the phenomenon of neuromodulation. Both neurotransmitters and neuromodulators are released in a similar manner from the axonal terminals, but they exert their actions on other neurons in different ways. Neurotransmitters bind to receptors associated with ion channels and briefly alter the ionic conductance of these channels, directly changing how molecules can get into and out of the neuron. On the other hand, neuromodulators usually exert their action much

Figure 3. Single unit recording. A. Schematic showing the placement of the tip of an electrode outside but close to the body of a nerve cell. B-C. Drawings of a single spike (action potential) (B) and train of spikes (C) recorded in the extracellular space. Note the small amplitude and the biphasic shape. The time of the occurrence of spikes in a spike train are usually illustrated by a small marker as shown above the spike train. D. Top. Raster display of spike trains recorded in response to multiple presentation of a stimulus. Each dash represents a single potential, and each row represents a separate trial, each aligned on the time of the stimulus. Bottom. Peri-stimulus time histogram showing the average activity across all trials

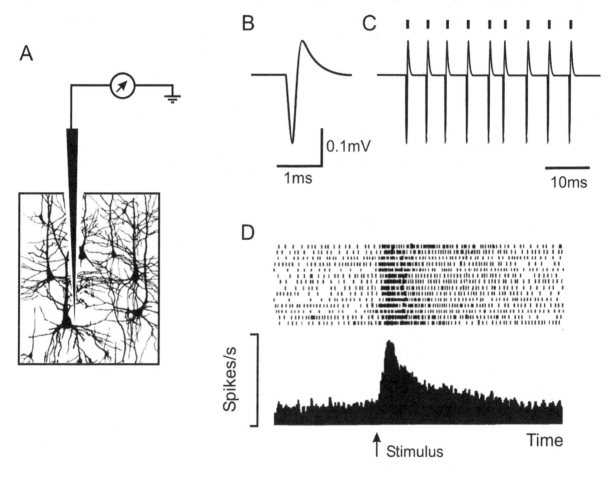

more slowly (but still in a sub-second range) via a relatively complex signaling pathway starting with the binding of the neuromodulator to specific receptors coupled to membrane proteins (*G-proteins*). The G-proteins then bind to other membrane molecules that, when activated, increase the level of molecules called *second messengers* inside the postsynaptic neurons and/or axonal terminals. Second messengers have a widespread influence in cells, one of which can be to modify the strength of the synaptic transmission for conventional

synapses. For example, a neuromodulator may increase the number of transmitter receptors in the postsynaptic membrane.

The most common neuromodulators are dopamine, noradrenaline, serotonin and acetylcholine. A striking characteristic of these four neuromodulatory systems in the mammalian brain is that they all originate from localized regions within the brain stem and all have diffuse and widespread projections to many regions of the brain. Thus these systems have the capacity to globally alter the functioning of the brain. For example, three of these systems (noradrenergic, serotonergic, and cholinergic) have important roles in regulating the sleep-wake cycle. Neuromodulatory systems can also have more specific actions, such as modification of the level of arousal (noradrenergic system) and the mediation of rewards (dopaminergic system). This global effect on brain function allows the dopamine reward system to potentially affect a wide array of behaviours.

Neuronal plasticity. All forms of learning, and the long-term storage of information in the brain (memory), are associated with long-term modification in the functioning of neuronal networks. The capacity of neuronal networks to be modified by experience (and in response to injury) is termed *neuronal plasticity*. Over the past 20 years, enormous advances have been made in our understanding of the cellular and molecular mechanisms associated with neuronal plasticity. We now know that experiential events can alter the properties of synaptic transmission, change the structure of synapses, and cause the growth of dendritic and axonal processes. Especially important is that the magnitude of these changes can be strongly influenced by neuromodulators. An example relevant for the neurobiology of reinforcement learning is that the long-terms effects of high-frequency stimulation on the pathways from the cerebral cortex to the striatum (see next section for anatomy) are highly dependent on the level of dopamine (Reynolds et al., 2001). When dopamine levels are low, the transmission in these pathways is depressed, whereas facilitation occurs when dopamine levels are high, providing a potential outlet for a dopamine error signal to modulate long-term changes in the brain (see Section 3.3).

3.2. Anatomy of the Brain

General organization. Another essential requirement for understanding the neurobiology of reinforcement learning is some knowledge of the anatomy of the brain. The brain consists of reasonably well-defined major structures that include the cerebral hemispheres, the brain stem, and the cerebellum. The hemispheres themselves are divided into four lobes: frontal, parietal, occipital, and temporal. Neurons in the cerebral hemispheres are primarily confined to a thin layer (the *cerebral cortex*) covering the entire outside surface of the hemispheres. Neurons located in the cerebral cortex make synaptic connections with neurons in other regions of the cortex and to neurons located in regions outside the cortex. Many of the latter are located in the brain stem. Distributed throughout the brain stem, and the junction between the brain stem and cerebral hemispheres are numerous clusters of neurons, called *nuclei*. Some major nuclei are illustrated in Figure 4A. These nuclei are the regions in which synaptic connections between neurons within the nuclei, and onto these neurons from other brain regions, are made. Two of the major structures in the forebrain are the thalamus and basal ganglia. The latter is known to be especially important for reinforcement learning in the brain, so it is necessary to consider the organization of the basal ganglia in detail.

The basal ganglia and dopaminergic neurons. The basal ganglia are situated on both sides of the upper brain stem and consist of an aggregation of anatomically distinct nuclei that are conventionally divided into two groups: the *striatum* consisting of the caudate nucleus, putamen, and nucleus accumbens, and the *globus pallidus* consisting of internal and external segments (Figure 4B). The basal ganglia are traditionally thought to be important in the control and initiation of movement and are the main area of the brain damaged in certain movement disorders, such as Parkinson's and Huntington's disease.

The striatum receives inputs from the cortex and from numerous nuclei in the brain stem. Cortical inputs terminate largely in dorsal (upper) regions of the striatum (caudate nucleus and putamen), whereas inputs from brain stem nuclei

Figure 4. Basic anatomy of brain regions involved in reinforcement learning. A. Drawing of sagittal (side) section through the brain showing the location of the basal ganglia (shaded grey) and some brain stem nuclei (filled black). B. Schematic diagram showing the anatomy of the basal ganglia in more detail (note the striatum is the combination of the caudate nucleus, putamen and nucleus accumbens) and some of the main connections to and from the basal ganglia. Dopaminergic pathways (DA, thick arrows) originate in the ventral tegmental area (VTA) and project densely to the nucleus accumbens in the ventral striatum and to the prefrontal cortex

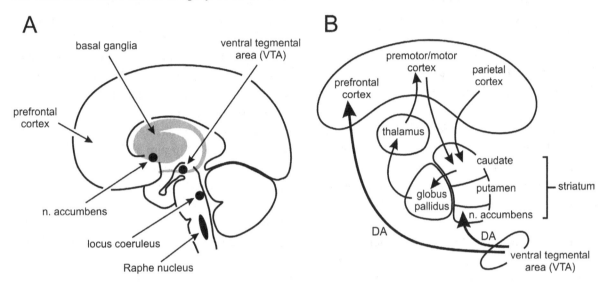

terminate in both the dorsal and ventral (lower) regions of the striatum (especially the nucleus accumbens). This division may be related to the fact that neuronal systems in the dorsal and ventral regions of the striatum are differentially recruited in different reinforcement-learning paradigms (e.g., O'Doherty et al., 2004). Prediction-learning tasks (classical conditioning) recruit neuronal systems in the ventral striatum, while more complex action-choice tasks (operant conditioning) recruit networks in both the dorsal and ventral regions. Output from the basal ganglia originates primarily from the globus pallidus, with feedback to the cerebral cortex going via the thalamus.

Although the neuronal circuitry formed by the basal ganglia with other brain regions is quite complex (see Figure 4B), a number of pathways important for mediating reinforcement learning have been well defined. By far the most intensively investigated are the input pathways to the striatum

from the *substantia nigra pars compacta* (SNc) and *ventral tegmental area* (VTA). Neurons in these pathways release the neuromodulator dopamine. Neurons releasing dopamine are termed *dopaminergic* neurons. One critical function of dopaminergic neurons is to provide information about rewards, which, in turn, modifies neuronal networks in the basal ganglia mediating behavioral actions (Schultz, 2002; Doya, 2007). Two observations provided initial evidence for the importance of dopaminergic neurons in behavioral modification: (1) electrical stimulation at sites close to the axons of dopaminergic neurons can function as the primary reward for instrumental conditioning, and (2) depletion of dopamine disrupts reward-based learning (see Schultz, 2007). Recently, a causal role for dopaminergic neurons in mediating reward has been demonstrated in genetically engineered mice (Tsai et al., 2009). Selective activation of dopaminergic neurons by light pulses in these animals can directly modify behavioral choice. We should also emphasize that the dopaminergic neurons originating in the VTA project in a diffuse manner to many other regions of the brain (not only the striatum) and thus have a role in other aspects of behavior apart from those involving reward, such as memory consolidation (e.g., Rossato et al., 2009) and mood (e.g., Yadid & Friedman, 2008).

3.3. The Neurobiology of Reinforcement Learning

A striking advance in the field of reinforcement learning has been the linking of the computational theory with the neurobiology of the brain. Numerous brain regions have been identified as being involved in different aspects of reinforcement learning and decision making, and strong correlations have been found between the activity of neurons in some of these regions with important variables from the computational models. In this section, we focus on the neuronal representation of only three of these variables: reward prediction error, reward value, and action value. Our goal is to illustrate, with a few examples, the neurobiological approach to reinforcement learning.

The general strategy used in neurobiological studies has been to record neuronal activity in different brain regions during a reinforcement-learning task designed to focus on a specific variable (or a set of variables) from a computational model. In animals (primarily rats and monkeys), this strategy usually involves recording the activity of single neurons (Figure 3), whereas, in humans, the most common technique is to image the brain using functional magnetic resonance imaging (fMRI).

Representing reward-prediction errors. Most algorithms for reinforcement learning use a reward-prediction error (δ) to either predict a reward (as in classical conditioning) or to modify the probability of choosing different actions (as in instrumental/operant conditioning). Earlier, we detailed one

computational use of a reward-prediction error in describing the temporal-difference (TD) algorithm (see Sections 1.1 and 2.2). A neuronal correlate to this TD error has been found in dopaminergic neurons through single-unit recording. Figure 5 illustrates the activity of a dopaminergic neuron at the beginning of a classical conditioning procedure and after conditioning has been established (Schultz et al., 1997; figure from Doya, 2007). This highly influential finding catalyzed the growing body of research looking at the correspondence between reward-based learning in the brain and the algorithms of RL.

We will now step through this important result in some detail (see Figure 5). In the Schultz et al. (1997) study, at the beginning of training, dopamine neurons discharge briefly to an unpredicted reward (top row in Figure 5A). After conditioning has been established, the neurons discharge only in response to the conditioned stimulus (CS), but not to the reward (middle row). This shift in the timing of the activity burst from the time of reward to the time of the CS is exactly what is expected if the activity is related to the reward-prediction error, as formalized in the TD algorithm. Prior to conditioning, an unpredicted reward leads to a large prediction error because the animal is not predicting any rewards. After conditioning, the CS produces a large prediction error because the animal is not predicting any reward prior to the CS, but the arrival of the CS leads to an increase in the predicted value of the upcoming reward and a corresponding reward-prediction error. During the interval between the CS and reward, the predicted value of the upcoming reward does not change (ignoring any temporal discounting), so there is no prediction error, corresponding to the low level of activity in dopaminergic neurons. Finally, when the predicted reward arrives, there is no difference between the predicted reward and the reward received, thus there is still no prediction error, which corresponds to the absence of activity in dopaminergic neurons. If, instead, the reward is reduced or omitted when predicted, then there is a negative prediction error because the animal received less reward than expected and, notably, there is a reduction in the activity of the dopaminergic neurons (bottom row in Figure 5). This real-time, moment-to-moment correspondence between the behaviour of dopamine neurons and the reward-prediction error in the TD algorithm is quite remarkable, and provides strong support for a real-time reinforcement-learning model, such as TD, over other trial-based, error-correcting algorithms, such as the Rescorla-Wagner model from psychology (see Sections 1.1 and 2.2).

This reward-prediction error can also serve as a crucial signal in modifying behaviour in instrumental learning tasks (see section 1.2), and the activity of dopaminergic neurons has been found to reflect this error in these tasks (Morris et al., 2005; O'Doherty et al., 2004; Roesch et al., 2007). Reward-prediction error signals in instrumental learning tasks have been postulated to change the probabilities of specific actions by modifying the strengths of pathways between the cortex and the striatum (see Samejima & Doya, 2007).

Representing reward value. Another component that plays a prominent role in many RL algorithms is the reward value (V) or expected reward (illustrated in Figure 5B; see Section 2.2). This value is the reward prediction from which the reward-prediction error (TD error) is generated. The reward value can be manipulated in decision-making tasks by varying the magnitude and probability of rewards associated with different choice options. For example, in behaving monkeys, Tobler et al. (2005) found that the phasic bursts of activity in dopaminergic neurons following the presentation of the choice options were related to the expected reward value of the choice made by the animal. Larger and more probable rewards produced larger bursts in dopaminergic firing, presumably reflecting a larger reward-prediction error, due to the larger expected reward values. It is important to note that the increased activity occurred before the onset of any overt behavior and was therefore related to the decision-making

process and not the motor action performed by the animal. This neuronal representation of expected reward value is not restricted to dopaminergic neurons. For example, single-unit recordings in behaving monkeys and rats have also revealed neuronal responses related to reward value in the striatum (Ito & Doya, 2009), orbitofrontal and prefrontal cortex (Duuren et al., 2009; Kennerley & Wallis, 2009; for a review, see Schoenbaum et al. 2009), and the posterior parietal cortex (Sugrue et al., 2004, 2005). Given the widespread projections of midbrain dopaminergic neurons, it is not surprising that expected reward value would be represented in widespread networks within the brain. This view receives support from fMRI studies in humans in which the magnitude of BOLD signals in the ventral striatum and regions of the prefrontal cortex, both of which receive strong input from dopaminergic neurons, are related to expected reward value (Knutson et al., 2005; Tobler et al., 2007).

Representing action value. During instrumental learning tasks, an action or a sequence of actions must be selected to maximize reward. A fundamental question, therefore, is how does an animal learn the best action to execute from each state? (see discussion in Section 2.3 on computational schemes for action selection). A number of RL algorithms utilize a variable termed the *action value* (or *Q-value*), where the action value represents the expected reward for a given action. A neurophysiological correlate of these action values has been found in the activity patterns of neurons in the striatum of monkeys (Samejima et al., 2005; see also Kim et al., 2009; Morris et al., 2006; Roesch et al., 2007, 2009). In their experiment, monkeys were trained to choose between two actions (a left or right movement of a handle) in a task in which the probabilities of receiving a large juice reward for each action was varied. The reward probabilities were arranged in blocks, so that each action was reinforced either 10%, 50%, or 90% of the time. From an RL perspective, this probability manipulation would result in different action values for the actions, pending the reward probability currently in place for that action. The main finding was that nearly 50% of the recorded neurons in the striatum (putamen and anterior caudate) significantly changed their activity based on the change in the reward probability of only one action (i.e., the action value). These action-value specific neurons did not change their activity when the reward probability for the other action changed, suggesting that they were not encoding a composite value across both actions. Instead, the response of these neurons is related to a combination of the reward value and action. The action-value algorithms in reinforcement learning (such as Q-learning or SARSA; see Section 2.3) propose that action values are directly involved in the selection of future actions. How the representation of action value in the activity of striatal neurons might be utilized to determine future actions is currently unknown, but the close association of these neurons with other neuronal networks in the basal ganglia involved in motor actions suggests that these neurons may also be elements in the action selection networks.

In this section, we started with a didactic overview of broad issues in neuroscience important for understanding the neural basis of reinforcement learning, specifically intended for a non-neuroscience audience. We then briefly introduced some of the main neuroscience findings providing evidence that certain areas of the brain may be understood as implementing algorithms from RL. We reviewed findings that some of the major constructs from these RL algorithms, such as predictions errors, reward values, and action values, have strong correlates in the dopaminergic system and related areas of the brain. Together, these ideas from RL are having a transformational effect on this area of neuroscience, providing a well-grounded, normative framework for detailing what these neurons are computing while animals are making value-based decisions.

4. IMPLICATIONS OF THE COMPUTATIONAL NEUROSCIENCE OF REINFORCEMENT LEARNING

Throughout this chapter, we have illustrated the remarkable synergy between neuroscience, computer science, and psychology that characterizes the modern multi-disciplinary study of reinforcement learning. Our purpose in this chapter has been two-fold. We primarily attempted to provide an introduction to the key ideas in these three fields that is accessible to those unfamiliar with this literature. In addition, we played out some examples of how reinforcement learning is studied within each of these disciplines—from classical conditioning in psychology to TD learning in computer science to the firing of dopamine neurons in the brain. Along the way, we tried to clarify some of the subtler aspects of the different theories to perhaps enhance understanding of each domain for researchers in the other disciplines. We hope that our readers are now better prepared to learn more about this exciting and rapidly growing field.

One interesting question is how these findings from the computational neuroscience of RL have resonated back into the constitutive disciplines. In neuroscience, the effects have been clearly transformative—the ideas from reinforcement learning are central to all discussions of neural valuation and decision making, and new papers on the subject are published weekly. The ideas have taken less of a hold in psychology, where a long tradition of theorizing in animal learning has yet to absorb the potential insights from RL, still preferring older formalisms such as the Rescorla-Wagner rule (see Section 1.1). More broadly in cognitive science, the associative mechanisms of RL as a potential account for human cognition face a significant uphill battle in an environment where information processing is often viewed as strictly symbolic (e.g., Gallistel & King, 2009). In the future, as these RL models come to explain more behavioural data, and as neuroscience ideas become more mainstream in psychology, we expect RL to gain a central place in psychology, as well.

Somewhat surprisingly, the least influenced home discipline seems to have been AI and computer science. The transfer of ideas here has been mostly a one-way street, with neuroscience using the formalisms of RL for modeling the brain and behavior, but with little direct feedback. A potential future avenue for this sort of reciprocating feedback may eventually come from more detailed knowledge of the psychological and neural mechanisms that drive reward-based learning and decision making than what exists today. Indeed, historically, the computational study of RL was originally inspired by exactly these sorts of psychological and neural considerations (see Sutton & Barto, 1981, 1998). For example, one of the very first RL algorithms, the associative search network (Barto, Sutton, & Brewer, 1981), drew on the fact that animals do not require target outputs, such as which motor command to execute at each moment, to learn about the world. This algorithm stood in contrast to the existing supervised-learning approaches of the time, and started setting the way for the full development of RL ideas within AI that has followed over the past 25 years (see Section 2.1).

Another angle for potential feedback from computational neuroscience to AI is suggested by the fact that many of the computational challenges currently facing RL stem from tasks that the brain seems to handle naturally. For instance, the action-selection mechanisms discussed here (Q-Learning, SARSA, actor-critic, see Section 2.3) all depend on the explicit enumeration of the actions in order to obtain their values—something not possible when many different actions are possible. By studying action selection in the brain more closely, we might gain insight into appropriate algorithms that may be applicable to large-scale problems, such as real-world robots.

Perhaps the most likely source for the transmission of ideas back to AI from this area of computational neuroscience, however, lies not in direct inspiration from the biological substrate, but rather from the new models that have grown up to explain the neuroscientific and psychological data. Though the initial RL models in neuroscience came from AI, newer models have grown from these roots and adapted as they attempt to accommodate more and more data. Variations on well-known RL ideas to deal with issues like temporal discounting (Kurth-Nelson & Redish, 2009), motivational effects (Niv et al., 2005), or response timing (Ludvig et al., 2008) could eventually provide a new source of inspiration for those researchers interested in creating artificial systems with human- or animal-like learning abilities.

REFERENCES

Adams, C. D., & Dickinson, A. (1981). Instrumental responding following reinforcer devaluation. *Quarterly Journal of Experimental Psychology, 33B*, 109–122.

Ariely, D. (2008). *Predictably Irrational: The Hidden Forces that Shape our Decisions*. New York: Harper.

Asgarian, N., Hu, X., Aktary, Z., Chapman, K. A., Lam, L., & Chibbar, R. (2010). Learning to predict relapse in invasive ductal carcinomas based on the subcellular localization of junctional proteins. *Breast Cancer Research and Treatment, 121*, 527–538. doi:10.1007/s10549-009-0557-0

Auer, P. (2003). Using confidence bounds for exploitation-exploration trade-offs. *Journal of Machine Learning Research, 3*, 397–422. doi:10.1162/153244303321897663

Baird, L. (1995). Residual algorithms: Reinforcement learning with function approximation. *International Conference on Machine Learning, 12*, 30-37.

Balleine, B. W., & Dickinson, A. (1998). Goal-directed instrumental action: Contingency and incentive learning and their cortical substrates. *Neuropharmacology, 37*, 407–419. doi:10.1016/S0028-3908(98)00033-1

Balleine, B. W., & O'Doherty, J. P. (2009). Human and rodent homologies in action control: Corticostriatal determinants of goal-directed and habitual action. *Neuropsychopharmacology, 35*, 48–69. doi:10.1038/npp.2009.131

Barto, A. G., Sutton, R. S., & Brouwer, P. (1981). Associative search network: A reinforcement learning associative memory. *Biological Cybernetics, 40*, 201–211. doi:10.1007/BF00453370

Bateson, M., & Kacelnik, A. (1995). Preferences for fixed and variable food sources: Variability in amount and delay. *Journal of the Experimental Analysis of Behavior, 63*, 313–329. doi:10.1901/jeab.1995.63-313

Bernoulli, D. (1738. (1954). Exposition of a new theory on the measurement of risk. *Econometrica, 22*, 23–36. doi:10.2307/1909829

Bertsekas, D. P., & Tsitsiklis, J. N. (1996). *Neurodynamic programming*. Belmont, MA: Athena Scientific.

Blaisdell, A. P., Sawa, K., Leising, K. J., & Waldmann, M. R. (2006). Causal reasoning in rats. *Science, 311*, 1020–1022. doi:10.1126/science.1121872

Brafman, R. I., & Tennenholtz, M. (2003). R-MAX—A general polynomial time algorithm for near-optimal reinforcement learning. *Journal of Machine Learning Research, 3*, 213–231. doi:10.1162/153244303765208377

Brogden, W. J. (1939). Sensory pre-conditioning. *Journal of Experimental Psychology, 25*, 323–332. doi:10.1037/h0058944

Camerer, C., & Loewenstein, G. (2003). Behavioral economics: Past, present, future. In Camerer, C., Loewenstein, G., & Rabin, M. (Eds.), *Advances in Behavioral Economics* (pp. 3–51). New York, Princeton: Russell Sage Foundation Press and Princeton University Press.

Caraco, T. (1981). Energy budgets, risk and foraging preferences in dark-eyed juncos (*Junco hyemalis*). *Behavioral Ecology and Sociobiology, 8*, 213–217. doi:10.1007/BF00299833

Caraco, T., Blanckenhorn, W. U., Gregory, G. M., Newman, J. A., Recer, G. M., & Zwicker, S. M. (1990). Risk-sensitivity: Ambient temperature affects foraging choice. *Animal Behaviour, 39*, 338–345. doi:10.1016/S0003-3472(05)80879-6

Clark, A. (2008). *Supersizing the Mind: Embodiment, Action, and Cognitive Extension*. New York, NY: Oxford University Press.

Colwill, R. C., & Rescorla, R. A. (1985). Postconditioning devaluation of a reinforcer affects instrumental responding. *Journal of Experimental Psychology. Animal Behavior Processes, 11*, 120–132. doi:10.1037/0097-7403.11.1.120

Cooper, G. F., Abraham, V., Aliferis, C. F., Aronis, J. M., Buchanan, B. G., & Caruana, R. (2005). Predicting dire outcomes of patients with community acquired pneumonia. *Journal of Biomedical Informatics, 38*, 347–366. doi:10.1016/j.jbi.2005.02.005

Davison, M., & McCarthy, D. (1988). *The Matching Law: A Research Review*. Hillsdale, NJ: Erlbaum.

Daw, N. D., Courville, A. C., & Touretzky, D. S. (2006). Representation and timing in theories of the dopamine system. *Neural Computation, 18*, 1637–1677. doi:10.1162/neco.2006.18.7.1637

Daw, N. D., & Doya, K. (2006). The computational neurobiology of learning and reward. *Current Opinion in Neurobiology, 16*, 199–204. doi:10.1016/j.conb.2006.03.006

Daw, N. D., Niv, Y., & Dayan, P. (2005). Uncertainty based competition between prefrontal and dorsolateral striatal systems for behavioral control. *Nature Neuroscience, 8*, 1704–1711. doi:10.1038/nn1560

Daw, N. D., O'Doherty, J. P., Dayan, P., Seymour, B., & Dolan, R. J. (2006). Cortical substrates for exploratory decisions in humans. *Nature, 441*, 876–879. doi:10.1038/nature04766

Dayan, P., & Daw, N. D. (2008). Decision theory, reinforcement learning, and the brain. *Cognitive, Affective & Behavioral Neuroscience, 8*, 429–453. doi:10.3758/CABN.8.4.429

Dayan, P., & Niv, Y. (2008). Reinforcement learning: The good, the bad and the ugly. *Current Opinion in Neurobiology, 18*, 185–196. doi:10.1016/j.conb.2008.08.003

Dickinson, A., & Balleine, B. (1994). Motivational control of goal-directed action. *Animal Learning & Behavior, 22*, 1–18.

Domjan, M. (2005). Pavlovian conditioning: A functional perspective. *Annual Review of Psychology, 56*, 179–206. doi:10.1146/annurev.psych.55.090902.141409

Doya, K. (2007). Reinforcement learning: Computational theory and biological mechanisms. *Human Frontiers Science Program Journal, 1*, 30–40.

Dwyer, D. M., Starns, J., & Honey, R. C. (2009). "Causal reasoning" in rats: A reappraisal. *Journal of Experimental Psychology. Animal Behavior Processes, 35*, 578–586. doi:10.1037/a0015007

Gallistel, C. R., & Gibbon, J. (2000). Time, rate, and conditioning. *Psychological Review, 107*, 289–344. doi:10.1037/0033-295X.107.2.289

Gallistel, C. R., & King, A. P. (2009). *Memory and the Computational Brain: Why Cognitive Science Will Transform Neuroscience*. Malden, MA: Wiley-Blackwell.

Garcia, J., & Koelling, R. A. (1966). Relation of cue to consequence in avoidance learning. *Psychonomic Science, 4*, 123–124.

Glimcher, P. W., Camerer, C. F., Fehr, E., & Poldrack, R. A. (Eds.). (2009). *Neuroeconomics: Decision making and the brain*. San Diego, CA: Academic Press.

Gottlieb, D. A. (2008). Is the number of trials a primary determinant of conditioned responding? *Journal of Experimental Psychology. Animal Behavior Processes, 34*, 185–201. doi:10.1037/0097-7403.34.2.185

Green, L., & Myerson, J. (2004). A discounting framework for choice with delayed and probabilistic rewards. *Psychological Bulletin, 130*, 769–792. doi:10.1037/0033-2909.130.5.769

Gureckis, T. M., & Love, B. C. (2009). Short-term gains, long-term pains: How cues about state aid learning in dynamic environments. *Cognition, 113*, 293–313. doi:10.1016/j.cognition.2009.03.013

Guthrie, E. R. (1930). Conditioning as a principle of learning. *Psychological Review, 37*, 412–428. doi:10.1037/h0072172

Herrnstein, R. J. (1961). Relative and absolute strength of response as a function of frequency of reinforcement. *Journal of the Experimental Analysis of Behavior, 4*, 267–272. doi:10.1901/jeab.1961.4-267

Herrnstein, R. J. (1970). On the law of effect. *Journal of the Experimental Analysis of Behavior, 13*, 243–266. doi:10.1901/jeab.1970.13-243

Ito, M., & Doya, K. (2009). Validation of decision-making models and analysis of decision variables in the rat basal ganglia. *The Journal of Neuroscience, 29*, 9861–9874. doi:10.1523/JNEUROSCI.6157-08.2009

Joel, D., Niv, Y., & Ruppin, E. (2002). Actor-critic models of the basal ganglia: New anatomical and computational perspectives. *Neural Networks, 15*, 535–547. doi:10.1016/S0893-6080(02)00047-3

Jozefowiez, J., Staddon, J. E., & Cerutti, D. T. (2009). The behavioral economics of choice and interval timing. *Psychological Review, 116*, 519–539. doi:10.1037/a0016171

Kaelbling, L. P., Littman, M. L., & Moore, A. W. (1996). Reinforcement learning: A survey. *Journal of Artificial Intelligence, 4*, 237–285.

Kahneman, D., & Tversky, A. (1979). Prospect theory: An analysis of decision under risk. *Econometrica, 47*, 263–292. doi:10.2307/1914185

Kamin, L. J. (1969). Predictability, surprise, attention and conditioning. In Campbell, B. A., & Church, R. M. (Eds.), *Punishment and aversive behavior* (pp. 279–296). New York: Appleton-Century-Crofts.

Kennerley, S. W., & Wallis, J. D. (2009). Evaluating choices by single neurons in the frontal lobe: Outcome value encoded across multiple decision variables. *The European Journal of Neuroscience, 29*, 2061–2073. doi:10.1111/j.1460-9568.2009.06743.x

Kim, H., Sul, J. H., Huh, N., Lee, D., & Jung, M. W. (2009). The role of striatum in updating values of chosen actions. *The Journal of Neuroscience, 29*, 14701–14712. doi:10.1523/JNEUROSCI.2728-09.2009

Knutson, B., Taylor, J., Kaufman, M., Peterson, R., & Glover, G. (2005). Distrubuted neural representation of expected value. *The Journal of Neuroscience, 25*, 4806–4812. doi:10.1523/JNEUROSCI.0642-05.2005

Kolter, J. Z., & Ng, A. Y. (2009). Near-bayesian exploration in polynomial time. *International Conference on Machine Learning, 26*, 513-520.

Kurth-Nelson, Z., & Redish, A. D. (2009). Temporal-difference reinforcement learning with distributed representations. *PLoS ONE, 4*, e7362. doi:10.1371/journal.pone.0007362

Lau, B., & Glimcher, P. W. (2005). Dynamic response-by-response models of matching behavior in rhesus monkeys. *Journal of the Experimental Analysis of Behavior, 84*, 555–579. doi:10.1901/jeab.2005.110-04

LeCun, Y., Bottou, L., Bengio, Y., & Haffner, P. (1998). Gradient-based learning applied to document recognition. *Proceedings of the IEEE, 86*, 2278–2324. doi:10.1109/5.726791

Loewenstein, Y., Prelec, D., & Seung, H. S. (2009). Operant matching as a Nash equilibrium of an intertemporal game. *Neural Computation, 21*, 2755–2773. doi:10.1162/neco.2009.09-08-854

Logothetis, N. K., Pauls, J., Augath, M., Trinath, T., & Oeltermann, A. (2001). Neurophysiological investigation of the basis of the fMRI signal. *Nature, 412*, 150–157. doi:10.1038/35084005

Ludvig, E. A., & Koop, A. (2008). Learning to generalize through predictive representations: A computational model of mediated conditioning. In *From Animals to Animats. Proceedings of Simulation of Adaptive Behavior, 10*, 342–351.

Ludvig, E. A., Sutton, R. S., & Kehoe, E. J. (2008). Stimulus representation and the timing of reward-prediction errors in models of the dopamine system. *Neural Computation, 20*, 3034–3054. doi:10.1162/neco.2008.11-07-654

Ludvig, E. A., Sutton, R. S., Verbeek, E. L., & Kehoe, E. J. (2009). A computational model of hippocampal function in trace conditioning. *Advances in Neural Information Processing Systems, 21*, 993–1000.

Maei, H. R., Szepesvari, C., Bhatnagar, S., Precup, D., Silver, D., & Sutton, R. S. (2009). Convergent temporal-difference learning with arbitrary smooth function approximation. *Advances in Neural Information Processing Systems, 21,* 1609–1616.

Maia, T. V. (2009). Reinforcement learning, conditioning, and the brain: Successes and challenges. *Cognitive, Affective & Behavioral Neuroscience, 9,* 343–364. doi:10.3758/CABN.9.4.343

Marr, D. C. (1982). *Vision: A Computational Investigation into the Human Representation and Processing of Visual Information.* New York: Freeman.

Marsh, B., & Kacelnik, A. (2002). Framing effects and risky decisions in starlings. *Proceedings of the National Academy of Sciences of the United States of America, 99,* 3352–3355. doi:10.1073/pnas.042491999

McCarthy, J., Minsky, M. L., Rochester, N., & Shannon, C. E. (1955. (2006). A proposal for the Dartmouth summer research project on artificial intelligence. *AI Magazine, 27,* 12–14.

McDowell, J. J. (2004). A computational model of selection by consequences. *Journal of the Experimental Analysis of Behavior, 81,* 297–317. doi:10.1901/jeab.2004.81-297

Miller, R. R., Barnet, R. C., & Grahame, N. J. (1995). Assessment of the Rescorla-Wagner Model. *Psychological Bulletin, 117,* 363–386. doi:10.1037/0033-2909.117.3.363

Mitchell, T. (1997). *Machine learning.* Burr Ridge, IL: McGraw Hill.

Montague, P. R., Dayan, P., & Sejnowski, T. J. (1996). A framework for mesencephalic dopamine systems based on predictive Hebbian learning. *The Journal of Neuroscience, 16,* 1936–1947.

Morris, G., Nevet, A., Arkadir, D., Vaadia, E., & Bergman, H. (2006). Midbrain dopamine neurons encode decisions for future action. *Nature Neuroscience, 9,* 1057–1063. doi:10.1038/nn1743

Niv, Y. (2009). Reinforcement learning in the brain. *Journal of Mathematical Psychology, 53,* 139–154. doi:10.1016/j.jmp.2008.12.005

Niv, Y., Daw, N. D., & Dayan, P. (2005). How fast to work: Response vigor, motivation and tonic dopamine. *Advances in Neural Information Processing Systems, 18,* 1019–1026.

Niv, Y., & Schoenbaum, G. (2008). Dialogues on prediction errors. *Trends in Cognitive Sciences, 12,* 265–272. doi:10.1016/j.tics.2008.03.006

O'Doherty, J., Dayan, P., Schultz, J., Deichmann, R., Friston, K., & Dolan, R. J. (2004). Dissociable roles of ventral and dorsal striatum in instrumental conditioning. *Science, 304,* 452–454. doi:10.1126/science.1094285

Pavlov, I. P. (1927). *Conditioned Reflexes: An Investigation of the Physiological Activity of the Cerberal Cortex (G. V. Anrep Trans.).* London: Oxford University Press.

Pearce, J. M., & Bouton, M. E. (2001). Theories of associative learning in animals. *Annual Review of Psychology, 52,* 111–139. doi:10.1146/annurev.psych.52.1.111

Pearce, J. M., & Hall, G. (1980). A model for Pavlovian learning: Variations in the effectiveness of conditioned but not of unconditioned stimuli. *Psychological Review, 87,* 532–552. doi:10.1037/0033-295X.87.6.532

Platt, M. L. (2002). Neural correlates of decisions. *Current Opinion in Neurobiology, 12,* 141–148. doi:10.1016/S0959-4388(02)00302-1

Platt, M. L., & Huettel, S. A. (2008). Risky business: The neuroeconomics of decision making under uncertainty. *Nature Neuroscience, 11,* 398–403. doi:10.1038/nn2062

Rangel, A., Camerer, C., & Montague, P. R. (2008). A framework for studying the neurobiology of value-based decision making. *Nature Reviews. Neuroscience, 9*, 545–556. doi:10.1038/nrn2357

Rescorla, R. A. (1968). Probability of shock in the presence and absence of CS in fear conditioning. *Journal of Comparative and Physiological Psychology, 66*, 1–5. doi:10.1037/h0025984

Rescorla, R. A. (1980). Simultaneous and successive associations in sensory preconditioning. *Journal of Experimental Psychology. Animal Behavior Processes, 6*, 207–216. doi:10.1037/0097-7403.6.3.207

Rescorla, R. A. (1988). Pavlovian conditioning: It's not what you think it is. *The American Psychologist, 43*, 151–160. doi:10.1037/0003-066X.43.3.151

Rescorla, R. A., & Wagner, A. R. (1972). A theory of Pavlovian conditioning: Variations in the effectiveness of reinforcement and nonreinforcement. In Black, A. H., & Prokasy, W. F. (Eds.), *Classical conditioning II* (pp. 64–99). New York: Appleton-Century-Crofts.

Reynolds, J. N., Hyland, B. I., & Wickens, J. R. (2001). A cellular mechanism of reward-related learning. *Nature, 413*, 67–70. doi:10.1038/35092560

Rieke, F., Warland, D., van Steveninch, R. R., & Bialek, W. (1999). *Spikes: Exploring the Neural Code*. Cambridge, MA: MIT Press.

Robbins, H. (1952). Some aspects of the sequential design of experiments. *Bulletin of the American Mathematical Society, 58*, 527–535. doi:10.1090/S0002-9904-1952-09620-8

Roesch, M. R., Calu, D. J., & Schoenbaum, G. (2007). Dopamine neurons encode the better option in rats deciding between differently delayed or sized rewards. *Nature Neuroscience, 10*, 1615–1624. doi:10.1038/nn2013

Roesch, M. R., Singh, T., Brown, P. L., Mullins, S. E., & Schoenbaum, G. (2009). Ventral striatal neurons encode the value of the chosen action in rats deciding between differently delayed or sized rewards. *The Journal of Neuroscience, 29*, 13365–13376. doi:10.1523/JNEUROSCI.2572-09.2009

Rossato, J. I., Bevilaqua, L. R. M., Izquierdo, I., Medina, J. H., & Cammarota, M. (2009). Dopamine control persistence of long-term memory storage. *Science, 325*, 1017–1020. doi:10.1126/science.1172545

Rushworth, M. F. S., & Behrens, T. E. J. (2008). Choice, uncertainty and value in prefrontal and cingulate cortex. *Nature Neuroscience, 11*, 389–397. doi:10.1038/nn2066

Rushworth, M. F. S., Mars, R. B., & Summerfield, C. (2009). General mechanisms for making decisions? *Current Opinion in Neurobiology, 19*, 75–83. doi:10.1016/j.conb.2009.02.005

Sakai, Y., & Fukai, T. (2008). The actor-critic learning is behind the matching law: Matching versus optimal behaviors. *Neural Computation, 20*, 227–251. doi:10.1162/neco.2008.20.1.227

Samejima, K., & Doya, K. (2007). Multiple representations of belief states and action values in corticobasal ganglia loops. *Annals of the New York Academy of Sciences, 1104*, 213–228. doi:10.1196/annals.1390.024

Samejima, K., Ueda, Y., Doya, K., & Kimura, M. (2005). Representation of action-specific reward values in the striatum. *Science, 310*, 1337–1340. doi:10.1126/science.1115270

Schoenbaum, G., Roesch, M. R., Stalnaker, T. A., & Takahashi, Y. K. (2009). A new perspective on the role of the orbitofrontal cortex in adaptive behaviour. *Nature Reviews. Neuroscience, 12*, 885–892.

Schultz, W. (2002). Getting formal with dopamine and reward. *Neuron, 36*, 241–263. doi:10.1016/S0896-6273(02)00967-4

Schultz, W. (2007). Multiple dopamine functions at different time courses. *Annual Review of Neuroscience, 30,* 259–288. doi:10.1146/annurev. neuro.28.061604.135722

Schultz, W. (2009). Neuroeconomics: The promise and the profit. *Philosophical Transactions of the Royal Society of London. Series B, Biological Sciences, 363,* 3767–3769. doi:10.1098/rstb.2008.0153

Schultz, W., Dayan, P., & Montague, P. R. (1997). A neural substrate of prediction and reward. *Science, 275,* 1593–1599. doi:10.1126/science.275.5306.1593

Shafir, S. (2000). Risk-sensitive foraging: The effect of relative variability. *Oikos, 88,* 663–669. doi:10.1034/j.1600-0706.2000.880323.x

Simen, P., & Cohen, J. D. (2009). Explicit melioration by a neural diffusion model. *Brain Research, 1299,* 95–117. doi:10.1016/j.brainres.2009.07.017

Skinner, B. F. (1938). *The behavior of organisms: An experimental analysis.* New York: Appleton-Century-Crofts.

Staddon, J. E. R., & Cerutti, D. T. (2003). Operant conditioning. *Annual Review of Psychology, 54,* 115–144. doi:10.1146/annurev. psych.54.101601.145124

Stout, S. C., & Miller, R. R. (2007). Sometimes-competing retrieval (SOCR): A formalization of the comparator hypothesis. *Psychological Review, 114,* 759–783. doi:10.1037/0033-295X.114.3.759

Sugrue, L. P., Corrado, G. S., & Newsome, W. T. (2004). Matching behavior and the representation of value in the parietal cortex. *Science, 304,* 1782–1790. doi:10.1126/science.1094765

Sugrue, L. P., Corrado, G. S., & Newsome, W. T. (2005). Choosing the greater of two goods: Neural currencies for valuation and decision making. *Nature Reviews. Neuroscience, 6,* 363–375. doi:10.1038/nrn1666

Sutton, R. S. (1988). Learning to predict by the methods of temporal differences. *Machine Learning, 3,* 9–44. doi:10.1007/BF00115009

Sutton, R. S., & Barto, A. G. (1981). Toward a modern theory of adaptive networks: Expectation and prediction. *Psychological Review, 88,* 135–171. doi:10.1037/0033-295X.88.2.135

Sutton, R. S., & Barto, A. G. (1990). Time-derivative models of Pavlovian reinforcement. In Gabriel, M., & Moore, J. W. (Eds.), *Learning and computational neuroscience* (pp. 497–537). Cambridge, MA: MIT Press.

Sutton, R. S., & Barto, A. G. (1998). *Reinforcement Learning: An Introduction.* Cambridge, MA: MIT Press.

Sutton, R. S., Maei, H. R., Precup, D., Bhatnagar, S., Silver, D., Szepesvari, C., & Wiewiora, E. (2009). Fast gradient-descent methods for temporal-difference learning with linear function approximation. *International Conference on Machine Learning, 26,* 993-1000.

Thorndike, E. L. (1911). *Animal Intelligence.* New York: Macmillan.

Tobler, P. N., Fiorillo, C. D., & Schultz, W. (2005). Adaptive coding of reward value by dopamine neurons. *Science, 307,* 1642–1645. doi:10.1126/science.1105370

Tobler, P. N., O'Doherty, J. P., Dolan, R. J., & Schultz, W. (2007). Reward value coding distinct from risk attitude-related uncertainty coding in human reward systems. *Journal of Neurophysiology, 97,* 1621–1632. doi:10.1152/jn.00745.2006

Trepel, C., Fox, C. R., & Poldrack, R. A. (2005). Prospect theory on the brain? Toward a cognitive neuroscience of decision under risk. *Brain Research. Cognitive Brain Research, 23,* 34–50. doi:10.1016/j.cogbrainres.2005.01.016

Tsai, H.-C., Zhang, F., Adamantidis, A., Stuber, G. D., Bonci, A., de Lecea, L., & Deisseroth, K. (2009). Phasic firing of dopaminergic neurons is sufficient for behavioral conditioning. *Science*, *324*, 1080–1084. doi:10.1126/science.1168878

Tversky, A., & Kahneman, D. (1981). The framing of decisions and the psychology of choice. *Science*, *211*, 453–458. doi:10.1126/science.7455683

van Duuren, E., van der Plasse, G., Lankelma, J., Joosten, R. N. J. M. A., Feenstra, M. G. P., & Pennartz, C. M. A. (2009). Single-cell and population coding of expected reward probability in the orbitofrontal cortex of the rat. *The Journal of Neuroscience*, *29*, 8965–8976. doi:10.1523/JNEUROSCI.0005-09.2009

Waelti, P., Dickinson, A., & Schultz, W. (2001). Dopamine responses comply with basic assumptions of formal learning theory. *Nature*, *412*, 43–48. doi:10.1038/35083500

Wagner, A. R. (1981). SOP: a model of automatic memory processing in animal behavior. In Spear, N. E., & Miller, R. R. (Eds.), *Information Processing in Animals: Memory Mechanisms* (pp. 5–47). Hillsdale, NJ: Erlbaum.

Watkins, C. J. C. H. (1989). *Learning from delayed rewards*. Ph.D. Thesis. University of Cambridge, England.

Watkins, C. J. C. H., & Dayan, P. (1992). Q-Learning. *Machine Learning*, *8*, 279–292. doi:10.1007/BF00992698

Williams, D. A., Lawson, C., Cook, R., Mather, A. A., & Johns, K. W. (2008). Timed excitatory conditioning under zero and negative contingencies. *Journal of Experimental Psychology. Animal Behavior Processes*, *34*, 94–105. doi:10.1037/0097-7403.34.1.94

Wunderlich, K., Rangel, A., & O'Doherty, J. P. (2009). Neural computations underlying action-based decision making in the human brain. *Proceedings of the National Academy of Sciences of the United States of America*, *106*, 17199–17204. doi:10.1073/pnas.0901077106

Yadid, G., & Friedman, A. (2008). Dynamics of the dopaminergic system as a key component in the understanding of depression. *Progress in Brain Research*, *172*, 265–286. doi:10.1016/S0079-6123(08)00913-8

KEY TERMS AND DEFINITIONS

Reinforcement Learning (RL): Branch of Artificial Intelligence (AI) that focuses on learning from interactive experience. Also used to describe the collection of processes whereby humans and animals learn through rewards.

Classical Conditioning: Simple learning process whereby humans and animals learn predictive relationships between stimuli and rewards.

Operant Conditioning: Simple learning process whereby humans and animals learn to perform actions based on rewarding experience.

Dopamine: Small molecule that is used in the brain as a neurotransmitter to communicate between neurons. Thought to encode the error in reward predictions.

Temporal-Difference (TD) Algorithm: Reinforcement-learning technique that learns to predict rewards based on the error between predicted outcomes and actual outcomes.

Striatum: Brain area that receives heavy input from dopamine neurons. Thought to be important for reward valuation and action selection.

Reward: An important outcome, which can be positive or negative. Maximization of reward serves as the goal for reinforcement-learning agents.

Neuroeconomics: New multi-disciplinary enterprise that attempts to explain how value-based decisions are made in the brain.

Chapter 7
APECS:
An Adaptively Parameterised Model of Associative Learning and Memory

I.P.L. McLaren
University of Exeter, UK

ABSTRACT

In this chapter the author will first give an overview of the ideas behind Adaptively Parameterised Error Correcting Learning (APECS) as introduced in McLaren (1993). It will take a somewhat historical perspective, tracing the development of this approach from its origins as a solution to the sequential learning problem identified by McCloskey and Cohen (1989) in the context of paired associate learning, to its more recent application as a model of human contingency learning.

BACKGROUND: THE SEQUENTIAL LEARNING PROBLEM

The development of novel connectionist algorithms (Rumelhart, Hinton, and Williams, 1986; Ackley, Hinton, and Sejnowski, 1985) capable of driving learning in multi-layer networks can be seen as one of the major developments in cognitive science in the nineteen-eighties. One of these algorithms, Back Propagation (Rumelhart, Hinton, and Williams, 1986) used gradient descent to learn input / output relationships, and was typically instantiated in feed-forward architectures. This otherwise successful approach, however, came up against the sequential learning problem identified by McCloskey and Cohen (1989) and further analysed by Ratcliff (1990). A general statement of this problem is that if a network employing Back Propagation is first taught one set of input / output relations, and then some other mapping is learnt whose input terms are similar to those first used in training, then a near complete loss of performance on the first mapping is observed on test. We can say that the new learning wipes out the old. This is not a necessary characteristic of the feed-forward architecture, because, if training alternates between the two mappings, repeatedly teaching first one and then the other, eventually a solution is reached that captures both sets of input / output relationships. Thus, this "catastrophic

DOI: 10.4018/978-1-60960-021-1.ch007

interference", when new learning erases old, is only seen if the two mappings are learnt in sequence. This does not mean that this property of the learning algorithm can be ignored, however, as learning (in humans and networks) often takes place within a sequential format (eg see Ratcliff, 1990; Hinton and Plaut, 1987; Sejnowski and Rosenberg, 1987).

As a simple example of this general type of problem, consider modelling a paired-associate experiment (based on Barnes and Underwood, 1959) in which human subjects are required to learn a list (list 1) of eight nonsense syllable - adjective pairs to a criterion of 100%. That is, after some number of training trials, the subject is able to provide the correct adjectival response to each nonsense syllable stimulus. After learning list 1, the subjects learn list 2, which employs the same nonsense syllables as the first, but new adjectives paired with them. Training continues until subjects are near perfect on this list (>90%). They are then asked to recall the original list 1 adjectival responses for each nonsense syllable. Performance drops to around 50% for this list, which is taken to be an instance of retroactive interference (control groups suggest that it is not simply the passage of time that is responsible for this decline in performance).

As McCloskey and Cohen (1989) showed, this task can be modelled in a feed-forward two layer network running Back Propagation. The list 'context' and the nonsense syllables (eg dax, teg) are the input, and the adjectives (e.g. regal, sleek) are the output (see Figure 1 which shows both the network in question and the experimental design).

After cycling through the list several times, activation of the input nodes representing list context in conjunction with a nonsense syllable results in the activation of the output nodes corresponding to the correct adjective via the set of connection strengths or weights developed by the network. During learning of the second list, nodes standing for the List 2 context are used in conjunction with the old nonsense syllable nodes, to-

gether with extra output nodes representing the new adjectives (keen, swift). Training proceeds until activation of nodes representing List 2 + dax (for example) results in activation of the 'keen' node. Now, List 1 recall can be tested by presenting List 1 + dax as input. The result produced by the network is – 'keen'. There is no sign of previously having learnt 'regal' to this input. McCloskey and Cohen were able to show that even minimal training on List 2 resulted in (at best!) nearly complete loss of List 1 on test, rather than the 50% loss shown in humans (at worst). This result does not depend on the local coding scheme employed here, as they obtained the same outcome using distributed representations of contexts, stimuli and responses.

Figure 2 gives simulation results for this sequential learning task employing a two item list and employing a modified version of Back Propagation that is used throughout this paper. Despite these minor differences, the results are the same as those reported by McCloskey and Cohen.

After training on List 1 until performance meets their "within 0.1" criterion on test, i.e. activation of an input pattern produces the correct response to within 0.1 of each node's target activation level, learning the List 2 items to the same criterion powerfully degrades List 1 performance. In fact, testing on List 1 now fails to meet a "best match" criterion which requires that the output be more similar to the target response than to any of the other possible responses in the lists. Analysis of these simulation results indicates that the difficulty facing the network is that the initial List 1 solution (i.e. the weights) is not one that can survive learning of List 2, because the List 1 responses to the nonsense syllables have to be suppressed in some fashion, and once this is done they cannot be recovered. Only when the lists are alternated during training can a List 1 solution that is protected from the effects of List 2 learning be developed (an example is shown in Figure 3). In fact, if the network was alternated on the two

Figure 1. Top panel: The design of Barnes and Underwood's (1959) experiment reduced to a two item list for simulation purposes. Bottom panel: A feed-forward architecture running back propagation used to simulate performance on the task outlined in the top panel

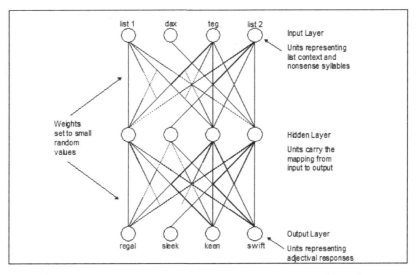

This network is an adaptation of one of the networks used by McCloskey and Cohen (1989) and uses two item-pair lists. Each node in the input and output layers stands for some stimulus, list context, or response; signalling its presence or absence via its activity. Learning proceeds by changing the values of the connection strengths between nodes (called 'weights') so that the input nodes can transmit activation, via the hidden units, to the output nodes

lists, then it was found that it could achieve 100% performance on each list on test.

The route to a solution of the sequential learning problem would hence seem relatively straightforward. Simply modify Back Propagation so that List 1 learning takes a form which survives List 2 learning by ensuring that List 1 responses do not pose problems during the learning of the second list. Inspection of the rightmost set of weights in Figure 2 (and some analysis) indicates a number of possible List 1 solutions that might work. All of these candidate solutions share certain properties, in that none of them will produce much in the way of a response to a nonsense syllable input on its own. They each require the conjunction of nonsense syllable and list context

Figure 2. The pattern of weights developed by the network after learning list 1 (left panel), then after learning list 2 (right panel)

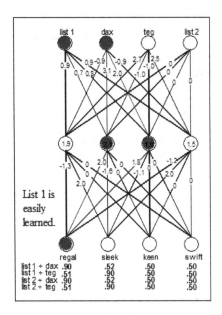 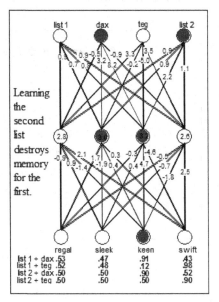

Weights for a typical simulation are shown next to the appropriate link, those shown as zero have an absolute magnitude less than 0.1, and hidden unit bias (best interpreted as a weight from a unit that is always on) is given inside the icon representing each unit. The average activation values obtained on test are shown underneath the output nodes and alongside the input pattern applied. A somewhat modified version of standard Back Propagation was used; no bias was allowed for the output units, and their target activation level when 'off' was taken as 0.5, corresponding to zero net input. Each list was cycled through 250 times with 100 weight changes per learning episode involving a given list pair. Target values for the simulations were 0.5 (off) and 0.9 (on). Performance on List 1 is good, for example dax presented in the context of List 1 (both units shown as grey=active) activates the unit for regal to 0.9 and leaves the others at 0.5 (left panel). The List 1 learning is lost, however, after learning List 2 (right panel)

to produce the appropriate adjectival response, and thus should not be susceptible to unlearning of List 1 during acquisition of List 2. It is difficult to see how solutions of the type that require negative weights from the input layer to the hidden layer, and then negative weights from the hidden layer to output would develop, however, and a stricter version of the sequential learning problem poses difficulties for them. If learning on each list is in strict sequence, i.e. a pair is learnt and then the next pair and so on until the list is learnt without ever returning to a pair, then it would seem that those solutions which <u>depend</u> on cycling through a given list could not develop. This is the case for solutions using negative weights to hidden units that themselves possess negative

weights to output units. They require the prior development of positive weights from input to output (first pairing), followed by negative weights from the hidden units to the output units (suppression of the response when inappropriate), and only then can negative weights to the hidden unit(s) possessing negative weights to the output units develop (on a second pairing). It could be argued that learning each pair involves alternating between context + stimulus - response and context - no response, which will enable this type of solution, but note that acquisition of pairs by sequentially learning context plus stimulus - response and context - no response (rather than alternating between them) will not suffice to arrive at this type of solution, and that this is a plausible

Figure 3. Results for a simulation in which learning of the two lists was alternated (left panel)

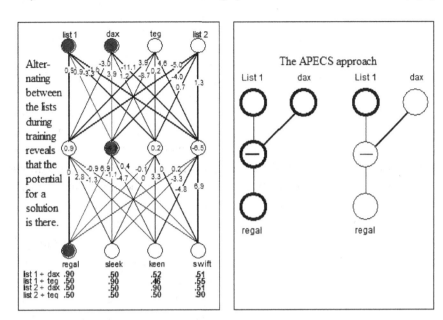

The network would be trained on List 1, then List 2, before returning to List 1 etc. This process was repeated 500 times, 250 times per list, with 100 weight changes per learning episode involving a list pair as before. Performance on both lists after training is very good, the example of dax in List 1 activating regal is shown (active units in grey). The right panel shows one of the possible solutions to learning a list 1 item that would survive the learning of list 2, and this is the one implemented in APECS. Solid lines denote positive weights, and this solution requires a negative bias on the hidden unit. Only if both input nodes are activated (outlines in bold) is there activation of the output node, a single input activation is ineffective because of the bias

model for human performance when learning a list in strict sequence (and the one used in the simulation reported later). In any case it would seem unwise to adopt solutions that suffered from this restriction.

Hence, the solution given in the right panel of Figure 3, which can be characterised as an "AND" solution capturing the need for both List 1 context and dax to be input to give regal as an output, seems worthy of investigation. It is a promising candidate, as experience of a list context plus nonsense syllable input paired with an adjectival response should set up positive weights between them (via hidden units), and then experience of the context alone could be used to set the bias so that both inputs were needed to overcome the bias (which in effect acts as a threshold) to generate an output. Given this, the problem becomes one of how to modify Back Propagation so as to

achieve such a solution in the normal course of events without losing the desirable characteristics of this algorithm: namely that it performs error correcting learning in multi-layer networks so as to solve problems such as Exclusive-OR (EOR, but often called XOR). The answer adopted here is to proceed by allowing some of the parameters of the Back Propagation learning algorithm to vary in an adaptive fashion, an idea borrowed from animal learning theory (eg Mackintosh, 1975; Pearce and Hall, 1980; McLaren and Dickinson, 1990). In particular, the learning rate parameters applicable to a given hidden unit in making changes in the weights from it to any of the output units, and to it from any of the input units is brought under adaptive control. The next section formalises this notion.

APECS

Consider a hidden unit i which has links to output unit j of strength wij. The standard error correcting rule prescribing the change in a weight, ∂w_{ij}, is:

$$\partial w_{ij} = S \Delta_j a_i \qquad (1)$$

where S is the learning rate parameter, Δ_j is an error signal given by the difference between the output units target activation and current activation multiplied by the derivative of the activation function with respect to input evaluated at the current value of the input to that output unit, and a_i is the hidden unit's activation. The proposed change is simply to set:

$$\partial w_{ij} = S_i \Delta_j a_i \qquad (2)$$

so that each hidden unit has its own variable learning rate parameter. To achieve the desired solution, we need presentation of an input / output pair to result in one (or a few) hidden units being selected to mediate the positive weights from input to output nodes. For arbitrary mappings such as those modelled in the example that follows there is little point in dedicating more than one hidden unit to bind input to output, and it simplifies the next stage, which is to protect the mapping once it is established (the case of non-arbitrary mappings possessing statistical structure will be considered later). Protection is needed when only a part of the input (e.g. context or stimulus alone) is applied without concomitant application of the output previously paired with it (which will be termed "extinction" here), the weights formed in the previous learning episode(s) should not change much, rather the hidden unit's bias should increase so as to inactivate it. This means that the results of previous learning episodes are not so much frozen as taken out of circulation. This can be achieved if determination of the S_i is made competitive, so that the hidden unit whose connections best meet the demands imposed by current output activa-

tion is selected by having its S set high and the other S_i set near zero. The same mechanism can ensure that the S of this hidden unit is near zero during extinction.

To promote shifts in bias, the parameters controlling changes in bias for the hidden units should be high when the error term is negative (i.e. during extinction), and low otherwise. The parameters controlling weight changes in the input to hidden layer should be high when the hidden unit error is positive, but low when negative, so that the mechanisms for raising and damping hidden unit activity are equal in strength. These parameters will take the values 1 (high) and 0.02 (low) in the simulations to follow.

This gives us three guiding principles to follow in modifying Back Propagation. The first one is selection: the process of picking out one (or a few) hidden unit(s) to mediate a mapping. This facilitates implementation of the second, protection: preventing unlearning in the hidden to output layer by reducing the learning rate parameter for that hidden unit to near zero. The third is the asymmetric parametrisation of learning in the input to hidden layer and for the hidden unit thresholds, so that extinction is mainly accomplished by bias changes rather than weight reduction in the input to hidden layer. Exactly how these principles are implemented is probably not of crucial significance, and different methods may well be appropriate for different systems. An example of the algorithm determining the S_i used in the simulations reported here is given in outline form in Figure 4. This Adaptively Parameterised Error Correcting System (APECS) can now be run on the sequential learning problem as defined by McCloskey and Cohen, using exactly the same procedures employed in the Back Propagation simulations reported earlier. The results are shown in Figure 5.

After learning both lists, performance on test is perfect by the best match criterion in the two pair list simulation, and not far from meeting the .1 criterion (left panel of figure). The units shown

Figure 4. An example of the algorithm for the adaptive parametrisation of an error correcting system (APECS)

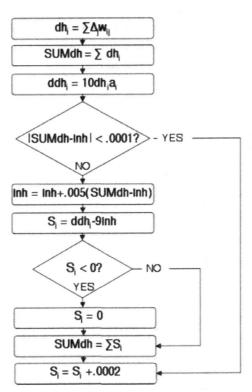

The aim of this algorithm is to give those hidden units with the highest error scores high parameters for changing the weights (apart from the bias where the converse applies). Start by setting $dh_i = \sum \Delta_j w_{ij}$, where w is a weight from hidden to output units, so that dh_i is the raw error for hidden unit i, i.e. before multiplying by the derivative of the activation function for that unit. Now $ddh_i = 10dh_ia_i$, where a_i is the activation of hidden unit i; and $SUMdh = \sum dh_i$, where the sum is over all hidden units (this initialises SUMdh). Now the ddh_i compete to determine the S_i in an algorithm which is based on the idea of all the ddh_i inputting to a system which then provides inhibitory feedback. Only the largest ddh_i will result in a non-zero f_i. The competition is done by setting a variable, Inh, to gradually converge to within .0001 of sumdh which itself is updated to equal $\sum S_i$. This negative feedback system can then be used to select the largest of the ddh_i by updating the S_i to equal $ddh_i - 9Inh$. Any S_i that drops below zero is set to zero during this procedure. The system settles down to stable values for sumdh and Inh and only the largest ddh_i gives rise to a positive S_i. This is a convenient algorithm to use, but no doubt there are many other methods of arriving at the same end result. Finally, all the S_i are incremented by .0002 to allow some learning for the hidden units that have been selected against and limited to a maximum value of 1. This permits the system to escape from situations in which all the dh_i are negative. Typical settings for the parameters controlling learning would then be input layer to hidden layer; $10S_i$, hidden layer to output layer; S_i, bias $10(1- S_i)$

in lighter grey are those responsible for one of the List 1 mappings, and those shown in the darker grey carry one of the List 2 mappings involving the same stimulus (dax). Though not shown in the figure, performance is even better in the eight pair list simulation, meeting the stringent .1 criterion in all cases. The reason for this seems to be that the longer list allows more complete extinction via bias becoming increasingly negative, minimising the contribution from other sources (e.g. unlearning of input to hidden weights, development of negative input to hidden unit weights). In the two pair lists, the presence of a given stimulus whenever the other is not present introduces a strong negative contingency that the system exploits, and negative weights of some

Figure 5. Left: The pattern of weights and results on test after learning List 1 then List 2 (50 cycles through the list with 200 weight changes per learning episode involving a given list pair.) using APECS. Performance on both lists is good, the example of dax in List 1 (lighter grey) and List 2 (darker grey) is shown in the figure. Right: are the results for strictly sequential learning of both lists; in which each list pair, once learned, is never returned to until test, the simulation simply moves onto the next list pair until all items in List 1 and then List 2 have been acquired

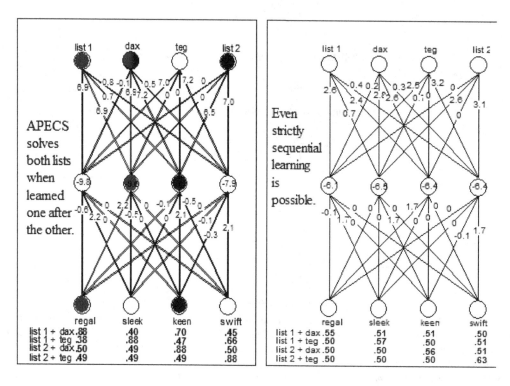

The test results show performance on these list pairs at the end of this process. As can be seen, learning is weak, but still meets a best match criterion for success

strength develop. In the eight pair lists this contingency is much weaker and no longer a significant factor. Performance in the two pair list condition can be improved by allowing presentations of the context for each list alone, which also degrades this negative contingency.

Having had some success with the sequential learning problem as defined by McCloskey and Cohen (1989), the next simulation tackles the strictly sequential version in which each input / output pair is learnt in one episode and never returned to. The results are shown in the right panel of Figure 5. Note that the weights have developed appropriately but that the performance on test is now rather

weak, though it still meets the best match criterion. The output activations are attenuated because the thresholds have shifted so as to almost completely suppress hidden unit activity, even when optimal input patterns of activation are applied. This is a property of the activation function employed here, which requires a substantial change in bias during extinction, outweighing the influence of the positive weights developed during list pair learning. It cannot be avoided by some choice of parameters, though adopting a different activation function could help. This route will not be explored here, as the problem is one of performance rather than learning. The weights are appropriate, allowing a retrieval strategy, such as increasing input activation (trying harder!), to enhance performance.

I offer one more example to illustrate the generality of the sequential learning problem and the associated catastrophic interference, and to show how APECS can deal with this issue. It is possible to construct a model that translates orthography into phonology using a feed-forward back propagation network. Seidenberg and Mc-Clelland (1989) give an extended example of this approach, the simulation offered here is somewhat simpler and involves using the network to code for the words HE, ART and HEART orthographically at input and phonologically at output. If the pronunciations of the words HE and ART are first learned by the network (Phase 1), and then the word HEART is learned without returning to either HE or ART (Phase 2), the results obtained are shown in the top panel of Figure 6. In Phase 1 the standard feed-forward network running back Propagation learns both HE and ART rather well as shown by the low mean square error (MSE) for both words. This means that, when presented with input corresponding to the orthography of HE or ART, the network is able to respond with the correct output denoting the appropriate phonology for the corresponding word. The MSE for HEART is much higher in Phase 1 as this word has not been trained, and so has not been learned by the network. Then, in Phase 2, HEART is learned (and learned well as its MSE is low when tested after Phase 2) and subsequently the networks response to HE and ART is tested. The result is a much higher MSE for both words after Phase 2 than after Phase 1, suggesting that considerable interference has occurred. In the case of ART, the MSE is now as high after Phase 2 as it was for HEART after Phase 1, when it had not been trained. Hence, the effect is for learning HEART to have resulted in complete unlearning of ART in this version of the sequential learning problem.

The lower panel of Figure 6 shows the APECS networks performance on an identical problem. It can be simply summarised by saying that it learns HE and ART in Phase 1, HEART in Phase 2, and suffers relatively little interference to HE and ART as a consequence. There is certainly no sign of the catastrophic interference seen with the standard back propagation network.

BEYOND THE SEQUENTIAL LEARNING PROBLEM

The modified algorithm seems to handle sequential learning well, certainly a lot better than standard Back Propagation. But at what cost? Can APECS still solve problems that Back Propagation solved well? As one example the results for EOR (XOR) will be given here. This is a suitable test case, as it is a standard problem requiring a multi-layer net that might be expected to pose difficulties for an algorithm that generates "AND" type solutions to problems. In fact, APECS solves EOR very well as is shown in Figure 7 (left), where the solution produced by Back Propagation (right) is also shown. It can be seen, however, that the nature of the solution arrived at is different in the two cases. Whilst there is some variation in the particular solution to the EOR problem adopted by standard back propagation which depends on the networks initial conditions, the solution adopted by APECS is predominantly the one shown. It exploits the algorithm's ability to construct configural representations requiring conjoint input to activate a unit at the hidden level. This makes the solution quite easy to interpret. In this case the rightmost hidden unit simply activates if either input is on, which consequently activates the output unit. The leftmost hidden unit detects conjoint activation of both inputs, and turns off the output unit in these circumstances. As we shall see in a moment, this tendency towards a form of representation development which produces very particular solutions to problems will have important consequences for modelling behaviour.

One might conjecture that, even if APECS could solve all the problems that Back Propaga-

Figure 6. Graphs for a feed-forward network running back propagation (top) and APECS (bottom) which has been trained to translate orthography into phonology for the words HE and ART in Phase 1, and HEART in Phase 2

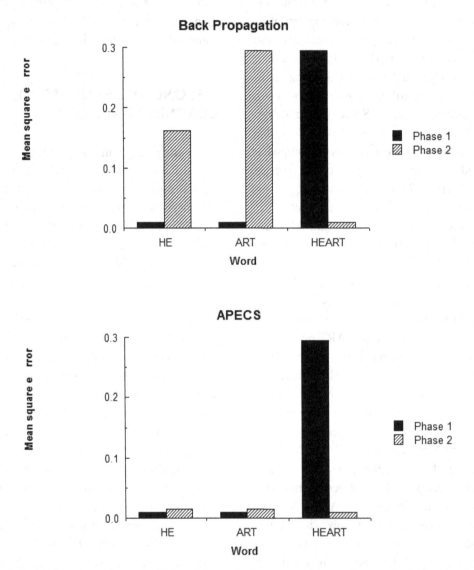

The top graph shows clear signs of catastrophic interference, the bottom one does not. See text for further details

tion can, one possible difficulty is that it might solve them in a way that is undesirable, i.e. by developing local representations at the hidden unit level. This is not a drawback in the case of arbitrary associations between input and output, APECS copes with arbitrary associations efficiently and well, but what of the case when there is statistical structure to be extracted from the input / output relationships and distributed representation at the level of the hidden units might be considered appropriate? In fact, APECS will develop distributed representations in these circumstances, though the results will not be given here. Imagine that if node A is active as input then node B is active as output, but this relation is embedded in noise, hence the input / output pair-

Figure 7. On the left is the solution to EOR developed by APECS in 60 cycles through the problem, with 200 weight changes per learning episode involving a given list pair. On the right is the solution produced by modified Back Propagation in 100 cycles, with 200 weight changes per learning episode involving a given list pair

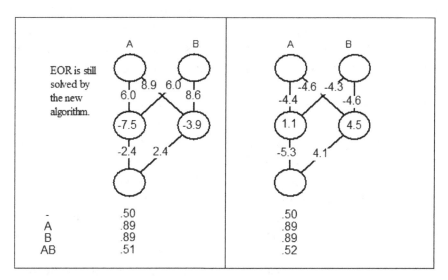

In interpreting this solution recall that a unit has an activation of 0.5 given zero input, and thus an activation of 0.5 denotes a unit that is turned 'off'. The bottom left shows which input nodes were active on test along with the output node's response beneath the relevant solution. The "-" denotes no applied input. Both networks solve the task, but tend to adopt quite different solutions in doing so

ings are X_1A-Y_1B, X_2A-Y_2B and so on, where the Xs and Ys denote other nodes that are active. This models trying to learn a reliable relation in a variety of different contexts. Simulations show that the network develops a local representation (at the hidden unit level) for each learning episode in a different context, and as the learning episodes increase and are distributed across contexts, so the number of hidden units mapping this relation increases so that it is distributed across them. Each hidden unit contributes weakly to this relation, as each has been extinguished, and eventually the A-B relation becomes context independent.

Hence, a fundamental property of the APECS algorithm is an increase in what might be termed the distributedness of representation when comparing associations formed by a single context and 'episode' and associations accumulated over many such episodes, each somewhat different. This property may hold the key to understanding

how one network may learn and represent both "episodic" and "semantic" knowledge (Tulving, 1972; 1983), and why the former is more vulnerable both to interference from other knowledge, and to neurological damage. It may also be possible to explain differences in the treatment of "rules" and "exceptions" in these terms (eg in modelling word recognition, Seidenberg and McClelland, 1989). We can return here to our simulation of the mapping between orthography and phonology in naming which I used earlier to illustrate catastrophic interference and show how APECS deals with the classic problem of learning the *INT cohort of words (e.g. MINT, TINT etc) and dealing with the exception word within this cohort, PINT.

Patterson, Seidenberg and McClelland (1989) report that when a standard back propagation network is trained on this cohort (and others) and then lesioned by deleting some of the hidden units, it shows a degradation in performance (which is the correct result if simulating neural damage), but that some aspects of the detailed changes in performance do not match those observed in any acquired dyslexia. Whilst the model was able to make a novel prediction, that the frequency of errors (in pronunciation) should be a function of phonetic distance (number of features changed) between correct and incorrect phonologies with smaller distances leading to the more frequent incorrect pronunciations (and this prediction was confirmed by a re-analysis of existing data), the major finding was that the damaged model did not preferentially regularise in the way that surface dyslexics do. Instead of there being a strong bias in favour of regularising when the model gave an incorrect pronunciation, there was a bias in favour of changing only one or a few phonetic features which did not selectively favour changes that would lead to a more regular phonology. Thus PINT (normally pronounced /pynt/) was not preferentially pronounced /pint/ as in /mint/ after damage to the network.

Figure 8 illustrates the type of solution generated by APECS when trained on this type of input – output mapping. The exact nature of the coding schemes used for input and output are of little consequence for the main point illustrated here, which is that when trained on a cohort of words with a regular pronunciation APECS will develop a distributed representation over many hidden units that captures this regularity. The input – output mapping for an exception word, PINT in this case, will be represented by relatively few hidden units that respond specifically to the conjunction of orthographic features that represent PINT. If these units are damaged, then the exceptional mapping for this word is lost, and generalisation via the common orthographic features (INT) will weakly activate many of the units for the other words in the cohort. This leads to a preference in the network for the regular pronunciation of an exception word if an error is made (and simulation confirms this). Hence the APECS solution does produce a pattern of performance that is more reminiscent of that found in a surface dyslexic. The requirement that the network adopt a certain solution to carrying a mapping so as to avoid the possibility of catastrophic interference has had far reaching consequences here which allows the network to capture a behavioural effect that eludes conventional back propagation models. And this result is not limited to the case of brain damage / degraded networks. Monsell, Patterson, Tallon and Hill (1989) have shown that undergraduates can be encouraged to voluntarily regularise exception words, and can learn to do this rapidly and efficiently in at least some cases. The issue here is how a conventional feed-forward network running back propagation could be controlled in such a fashion as to enable this option. The APECS solution makes this possible by simply increasing the gain applied to input – so that the inputs to the hidden layer are increased across the board. The ability of PINT to command an exceptional pronunciation is brought about by the hidden units representing it's particular combination of input features counteracting any generalisation from those units that carry the regular mapping, although there will be many more of the latter they will not be very active, whereas the former will tend to be near asymptote. If the input to all units is increased it has relatively little impact on the few units carrying the exceptional mapping (as they are near asymptote already), but increases the activity of the many units carrying the regular mapping substantially. If this is taken far enough, then the effect on the many will outweigh the contribution from the few, and the regular mapping will come to dominate, swamping the exceptional pronunciation, and a regular pronunciation of PINT will be the result (again, confirmed by simulation).

Figure 8. Representations formed by APECS at the hidden unit level when a feed-forward network translating orthography to phonology is trained on the "MINT" cohort

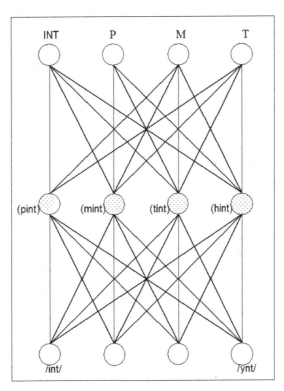

Localist representations of input and output are shown for simplicity, the argument remains the same when fully distributed representations are used. The mapping between orthography and phonology for PINT is carried by relatively few hidden units (only one shown), whereas the mappings for MINT, TINT etc can all generalise one to the other as they agree on the pronunciation of INT. There will be many such mappings, as there are many more regular than exception words, and hence the regular pronunciation becomes more distributed at the hidden unit level than the irregular version

CONTINGENCY LEARNING IN APECS

I have already shown that the APECS algorithm is quite capable of solving problems such as EOR, and it will come as no surprise that it is also capable of solving many of the problems inherent in the designs that are run under the aegis of causal or contingency learning with human participants. Perhaps more worthy of note, however, is the fact that the solutions arrived at by APECS also allow it to demonstrate the phenomenon of retrospective revaluation without any changes to the fundamentally error correcting nature of the learning algorithm. It's use of configural representations

is such that it can produce the standard difference between backward blocking, AB+|A+ and unovershadowing, CD+|C-, whereby responding to (or the rating given to) B in the first case is lower than that given to D in the second, without needing to invoke the idea that associatively retrieved representations should engage in learning with a "negative alpha" (Van Hamme & Wasserman, 1994) or with the opposite sign to perceptually activated representations in some other way (Dickinson & Burke, 1996). This has the advantage of allowing the retention of the idea that an associatively retrieved representation can be conceptualised as being similar to a perceptually activated one, but somewhat weaker. The implication of this is that associatively activated representations should act in the same way as perceptually activated ones, so that seeing a stimulus and being reminded of it should have similar consequences for behaviour. Surely this is desirable. If we are reminded of a stimulus, A, and then experience a painful shock it makes sense that we should be more wary of A when next encountered, not less so. And this simple idea makes it natural that the response to being reminded of A will be similar to that which occurs when A is presented; the change in sign for learning without any corresponding change in sign for performance has always seemed a somewhat forced and inelegant solution to the challenge posed by retrospective revaluation.

APECS encourages us to see retrospective revaluation as more an effect of associative memory than of associative learning. The basic idea is that it is not so much the learning on trials when the stimuli are presented that produces retrospective revaluation, but rather that it is more a consequence of subsequent adaptation by the network after these trials. This idea was first put forward by Le Pelley and McLaren (2001) and can also be found in the work of Ghirlanda (2005), though in the latter case the model offered has difficulties with the typical within-subject designs that contrast backward blocking and unovershadowing in the same subject. Le Pelley and Mclaren (2001; see also Le Pelley, Cutler and McLaren, 2000) were able to empirically demonstrate reliable differences in the ratings given to cues in backward blocking and unovershadowing conditions, and went on to show that a model running APECS was able to account for these results. A brief reprise of this explanation will be given here, before going on to consider the APECS account of retrospective revaluation more carefully in an attempt to tease apart explanations that appeal to associative memory and those that require modification of associative learning. The point here is that showing that APECS can produce retrospective revaluation only establishes its status as a candidate explanation for this phenomenon. What is needed

is some empirical reason (in addition to the arguments already given in this chapter) to prefer this account over others that involve modification of learning as it applies to associatively retrieved representations.

Consider first an unovershadowing design, AB+ | A-. The first phase of this design will set up one or more hidden units that code for the mapping between the inputs A and B, and the output +, called the AB+ hidden units in what follows. There will also be periods when no inputs are presented to the network and these will result in these AB+ hidden units acquiring a negative bias, and other hidden units forming negative connections to the output unit. Now we train on A-, and new hidden units are recruited to carry this mapping, and specifically to counteract the generalisation from activation of the hidden units that carried the AB+ mapping. The bias on these AB+ hidden units will become somewhat more negative on A- trials, but this will change when the network goes through a period of experiencing no input. If we assume that, prior to A- training, the network was in a kind of equilibrium, so that when no input was presented no output was predicted, but when A and B were presented the unit representing + was activated, then the experience of A- will have disturbed this equilibrium. The increased negative input to the + unit needed to counteract the positive generalisation from the AB+ hidden units will no longer be needed when that generalisation disappears once the inputs are off. The activation of the + output unit will be depressed below 0.5 (the baseline "off" value in these simulations) and changes in the network will occur to remedy this. One of these changes will be that the bias on the AB+ hidden units will increase, i.e. become less negative. The consequence of this is that as a consequence of A- traning, B will now be better able to activate the hidden units that carry the AB+ mapping, and so unovershadowing will have occurred. A similar analysis applies to backward blocking, though this effect tends to be weaker in our simulations to date (see Le Pelley and McLaren, 2001, for details).

Retrospective revaluation effects, then, can be seen as a consequence of the network's trying to maintain equilibrium in the face of new input that affects old. The effect for first order retrospective revaluation, as in the unovershadowing design just discussed is very much in line with the effects that might be expected by modified associative learning algorithms such as those of Van Hamme and Wasserman, and Dickinson and Burke. If we extrapolate to second order retrospective revaluation, however, then they both agree that the result will be the same as for first order, but disagree on its relative size. Models and theories that posit that associatively retrieved representations engage in learning in a similar fashion but with the opposite sign to perceptually activated representations make another prediction as well. Associative activation in these theories is generally weaker than perceptual activation, especially if it is the perceptual activation that produced the learning that allows associative activation in the first place. Only at asymptote can associative activation be as strong as perceptual activation. In general, then, if perceptual activation leads to some value, a, then associative activation will lead to a value pa, where p<1. In a second order retrospective revaluation design this effect is magnified. Second order unovershadowing will take the form: BC+| AB+| A-, and the second order effect will be on C. Presenting A will associatively retrieve B (one factor of p), and this in turn can result in associative retrieval of C (another factor of p, giving p^2). Hence, if this retrieval is a necessary part of generating any retrospective revaluation effect, it can be expected to be weaker for second order retrospective revaluation than first order retrospective revaluation. This is a general prediction that follows from one of the core assumptions of this type of model. It does not, however, apply to the APECS account.

In fact, there is something of a bias in APECS in favour of the retrospective revaluation effect being larger for second order than first order designs. The reason is as follows. In a BC+| AB+| A- design APECS will form hidden unit representations for the BC+ and AB+ mappings. When A- occurs this will activate the AB+ hidden units which will allow some small decrements in the weights from the input to these units and from these units to the output, and the fact that the units are active will facilitate changes in the bias as well. These effects have to be overcome by the rebalancing effect that takes place post-A- trials, when the bias is increased to offset the residual negative input from these hidden units when no input units are on. There will be nothing to overcome for the BC+ hidden units, however, and they are just as eligible for bias increase as the AB+ hidden units. All other things being equal then, the second order retrospective revaluation effect (rating or responding to C) may be expected to be somewhat greater than the first order one (rating or responding to B).

McLaren and McLaren (paper presented at the 50th Annual Meeting of the Psychonomic Society, 2009) have performed an experiment that looks at first and second order unovershadowing and backward blocking. They found, first of all, that in conditions which make cognitive inference difficult (many cues over a period of time making it difficult to work out what contingencies are in play explicitly), both first and second order retrospective revaluation effects are in the same direction as all associative models considered so far in this chapter would predict. An inferential account would expect the second order effect to be in the opposite direction to the first because the logic for unovershadowing would be "If A (will be given a low rating) does not cause the outcome then B (given a high rating relative to controls) must have, and so there is no strong reason to attribute causal power to C (given a low rating relative to controls). Both B and C received higher ratings than control cues in the unovershadowing condition, however, supporting the associative accounts. The crucial analysis for current purposes, however, concerns the size of the effects. In both experiments (there were two replications) the second order effect was numerically larger than the first order effect, and taken in combination the two experiments give an average effect size 0.52 larger for the second order cue relative to the first order cue (these are ratings on a scale of 0 to 10 in the first experiment and 1 to 9 in the second). The effect is not reliable in either experiment, but it surely allows us to say this. The evidence for the second order effect being weaker than the first order effect in these experiments is simply not there, and it should be if the modified associative learning models are correct. Note that the prediction that APECS makes is not unequivocal. Whilst in many circumstances it predicts that the second order effect will be larger, it is possible to find circumstances where the effects are equal in magnitude and it may be possible (I have not been able to discover a suitable set of circumstances as yet) to find some where first order effects are larger. Given this, the contribution from APECS here is simply to acknowledge the possibility that second order effects can be larger, a possibility denied by negative alpha or modified SOP type models of associative learning.

CONCLUSION

One possible criticism of the APECS approach would be to say that it is just another member of the class of configural models that are exemplified by the work of John Pearce (1987, 1994) and more recently Rob Honey (e.g. Honey, 2000; Honey and Ward-Robinson, 2002). These models have their strengths when it comes to modelling human and infra-human associative learning, but neither of them offers the full range of capabilites inherent in the APECS approach. The main difference is that APECS is adaptive in the way that it varies it's threshold (i.e. the bias), and this allows it to function as a model of both associative learning and associative memory. It can adaptively vary it's

ability to generalise from one stimulus combination to another, which gives it a flexibility that goes beyond what other configural models can offer. I've tried to illustrate the power of this approach by means of the sheer diversity of examples I've offered in this chapter, but one more will serve to bring out this point.

My final case study is one considered in McLaren (1994), Bouton and King's demonstration that generalisation between contexts can vary as a function of experience with those contexts. In their experiments rats were conditioned to a CS in Context 1, and then split into two groups. One group was extinguished in Context 1, the other in a different Context 2. Early on, both sets of animals showed comparable responding to the CS in either context, hence we can say that generalisation of responding to the CS between contexts was essentially perfect. Once responding was extinguished, however, both groups were tested for the CS in the original context. The group extinguished in that context showed little by way of conditioning as expected. But the group extinguished in the other context when returned to the original context showed considerable recovery of responding to the CS, i.e. they displayed considerable conditioning. The implication is that now the learning that has taken place in one context (extinction in Context 2) is not generalising to the other (Context 1), whereas previously it did. APECS can successfully model this pattern of results (see McLaren, 1994 for details) because it's ability to adaptively vary the parameters governing learning allows it to start with representations that permit near perfect generalisation between contexts and then change them so that there is instead near perfect context-specificity after extinction. Essentially the model develops configural units that map the CS and Context 1 representations to the outcome (fear), and then during extinction in Context 2 the bias on these units becomes increasingly negative so that CS presentation on its own is relatively ineffective. What excitation from the CS remains is completely cancelled by the inhibition from the new (inhibitory) mapping between the CS and Context 2 to the outcome also produced as a result of extinction. Then when transferred back to Context 1, the combination of context and CS can still activate the old mapping, and the new inhibitory mapping is now relatively weakly activated as only the CS is relevant to it. The net effect is one of powerful recovery that is entirely context dependent. Bouton (e.g. Bouton, 2004) has returned to this issue a number of times and has argued persuasively for more memory-based explanations of these phenomena.

I believe that APECS has the potential to provide just such an explanation. In doing so, it promises to move away from associative learning considered in isolation towards a more unified approach to associative learning and memory. As such, it may prove able to accommodate a wider range of phenomena, captured under a greater variety of conditions. It is a robust approach to learning and memory that can cope with real world constraints, learning rapidly and varying the accessibility of what has been learned so as to avoid catastrophic interference. The next step will be to explore other applications of APECS, and to evaluate the extent to which it can integrate with more elemental approaches to stimulus representation and learning (e.g. McLaren, Kaye and Mackintosh, 1989; McLaren and Mackintosh, 2000, 2002) and attention and learning (Le Pelley and McLaren, 2003; Le Pelley, Oakeshott, Wills and McLaren, 2005; Le Pelley, Oakeshott and McLaren, 2005). If these different approaches can be reconciled and harmoniously combined, we may find ourselves with a model of associative learning and memory that has some claim to be truly comprehensive in scope.

ACKNOWLEDGMENT

I would like to thank Eduardo Alonso for his patience, encouragement and many helpful comments in the course of writing this chapter.

REFERENCES

Ackley, D. H., Hinton, G. E., & Sejnowski, T. J. (1986). A learning algorithm for Boltzmann machines. *Cognitive Science*, *9*, 147–169. doi:10.1207/s15516709cog0901_7

Barnes, J. M., & Underwood, B. J. (1959). "Fate" of first-list associations in transfer theory. *Journal of Experimental Psychology*, *58*, 97–105. doi:10.1037/h0047507

Bouton, M. E., & King, D. A. (1983). Contextual control of the extinction of conditioned fear: test for the associative value of the context. *Journal of Experimental Psychology. Animal Behavior Processes*, *9*, 248–265. doi:10.1037/0097-7403.9.3.248

Bouton (2004). Context and behavioral processes in extinction. *Learning & Memory, 11*, 485-494.

Dickinson, A., & Burke, J. (1996). Within-compound associations mediate the retrospective revaluation of causality judgements. *Quarterly Journal of Experimental Psychology, 49B*, 60–80.

Ghirlanda, S. (2005). Retrospective revaluation as simple associative learning. *Journal of Experimental Psychology. Animal Behavior Processes*, *31*, 107–111. doi:10.1037/0097-7403.31.1.107

Hillsdale. NJ. Erlbaum.

Hinton, G. E., & Plaut, D. C. (1987). Using fast weights to deblur old memories. In *Program of the Ninth Annual Conference of the Cognitive Science Society* (pp. 177-86).

Honey, R. C. (2000). The Experimental Psychology Society Prize Lecture: Associative priming in Pavlovian conditioning. *Quarterly Journal of Experimental Psychology, 53B*, 1–23.

Honey, R. C., & Ward-Robinson, J. (2002). Acquired equivalence and distinctiveness of cues: I. Exploring a neural network approach. *Journal of Experimental Psychology. Animal Behavior Processes*, *28*, 378–387. doi:10.1037/0097-7403.28.4.378

Le Pelley, M. E., Cutler, D. L., & McLaren, I. P. L. (2000). Retrospective effects in human causality judgment. In *Proceedings of the Twenty-second Annual Conference of the Cognitive Science Society* (pp. 782–787). Hillsdale, NJ: Lawrence Erlbaum Associates, Inc.

Le Pelley, M. E., & McLaren, I. P. L. (2001). Retrospective revaluation in humans: Learning or memory? *Quarterly Journal of Experimental Psychology*, *54B*, 311–352.

Le Pelley, M. E., & McLaren, I. P. L. (2003). Learned associability and associative change in human causal learning. *Quarterly Journal of Experimental Psychology*, *56B*, 56–67.

Le Pelley, M. E., Oakeshott, S. M., & McLaren, I. P. L. (2005). Blocking and unblocking in humans. *Journal of Experimental Psychology. Animal Behavior Processes*, *31*, 56–70. doi:10.1037/0097-7403.31.1.56

Le Pelley, M. E., Oakeshott, S. M., Wills, A. J., & McLaren, I. P. L. (2005). The outcome-specificity of learned predictiveness effects: Parallels between human causal learning and animal conditioning. *Journal of Experimental Psychology. Animal Behavior Processes*, *31*, 226–236. doi:10.1037/0097-7403.31.2.226

Mackintosh, N. J. (1975). A theory of attention: Variations in the associability of stimuli with reinforcement. *Psychological Review*, *82*, 276–298. doi:10.1037/h0076778

McCloskey, M., & Cohen, N. J. (1989). Catastrophic interference in connectionist networks: The sequential learning problem. *Psychology of Learning and Motivation*, *24*, 109–166. doi:10.1016/S0079-7421(08)60536-8

McLaren, I. P. L. (1993). APECS: A solution to the sequential learning problem. In *Proceedings of the XVth Annual Convention of the Cognitive Science Society*, (pp. 717–722).

McLaren, I. P. L. (1994). Representation development in associative systems. In Hogan, J. A., & Bolhuis, J. J. (Eds.), *Causal mechanisms of behavioural development* (pp. 377–402). Cambridge, UK: Cambridge University Press. doi:10.1017/CBO9780511565120.018

McLaren, I. P. L., & Dickinson, A. (1990). The conditioning connection. *Philosophical Transactions of the Royal Society of London. Series B, Biological Sciences*, *329*, 179–186. doi:10.1098/rstb.1990.0163

Monsell, S., Patterson, K. E., Tallon, J., & Hill, J. (1989). *Voluntary surface dyslexia: A new argument for two processes in reading?* Paper presented at the January meeting of the Experimental Psychology Society, London.

Patterson, K., Seidenberg, M. S., & McClelland, J. L. (1989). Connections and disconnections: acquired dyslexia in a computational model of reading processes. In Morris, R. G. M. (Ed.), *Parallel Distributed Processing - Implications for Psychology and Neurobiology*. Oxford: OUP.

Pearce, J. M. (1987). A model for stimulus generalization in Pavlovian conditioning. *Psychological Review*, *94*, 61–73. doi:10.1037/0033-295X.94.1.61

Pearce, J. M. (1994). Similarity and discrimination: A selective review and a connectionist model. *Psychological Review*, *101*, 587–607. doi:10.1037/0033-295X.101.4.587

Pearce, J. M., & Hall, G. (1980). A model for Pavlovian conditioning: Variations in the effectiveness of conditioned but not of unconditioned stimuli. *Psychological Review*, *87*, 532–552. doi:10.1037/0033-295X.87.6.532

Ratcliff, R. (1990). Connectionist models of memory: constraints imposed by learning and forgetting functions. *Psychological Review, 97*, 285–308. doi:10.1037/0033-295X.97.2.285

Rescorla, R. A., & Wagner, A. R. (1972). A theory of Pavlovian conditioning: Variations in the effectiveness of reinforcement and non-reinforcement. In Black, A. H., & Prokasy, W. F. (Eds.), *Classical conditioning II: Current research and theory* (pp. 64–99). New York: Applet on-Century-Crofts.

Rumelhart, D. E., Hinton, G. E., & Williams, R. J. (1986). Learning internal representations by error propagation. In Rumelhart, D. E., & McClelland, J. L. (Eds.), *Parallel Distributed Processing* (*Vol. 1*). Cambridge, Mass.: Bradford Books.

Seidenberg, M. S., & McClelland, J. L. (1989). A distributed developmental model of word recognition and naming. *Psychological Review, 96*, 523–568. doi:10.1037/0033-295X.96.4.523

Sejnowski, T. J., & Rosenberg, C. R. (1987). Learning and representation in connectionist models. In Gazzaniga, M. S. (Ed.), *Perspectives in memory research and training* (pp. 532–552). Cambridge, MA: MIT Press.

Tulving, E. (1972). Episodic and semantic memory. In Tulving, E. and Donaldson, W. (Eds.), *Organisation of memory.* New York: AP.

Tulving, E. (1983). *Elements of episodic memory.* New York: OUP.

Van Hamme, L. J., & Wasserman, E. A. (1994). Cue competition in causality judgements: The role of nonpresentation of compound stimulus elements. *Learning and Motivation, 25*, 127–151. doi:10.1006/lmot.1994.1008

Wagner, A. R. (1981). SOP: A model of automatic memory processing in animal behaviour. In Spear, N. E., & Miller, R. R. (Eds.), *Information processing in animals: Memory mechanisms* (pp. 5–47). Hillsdale, NJ: Lawrence Erlbaum Associates, Inc.

KEY TERMS AND DEFINITIONS

APECS: Adaptively Parameterised Error Correcting System

Error Correction: Using a mismatch between a desired state and the actual state to control learning.

Catastrophic Interference: Later learning that completely erases old learning.

Sequential Learning Problem: learning items in sequence without returning to old items.

Local Representation: use of a single unit to stand for an input or output.

Distributed Representation: using a set of overlapping units to stand for different inputs or outputs.

Blocking: Earlier learning that one cue signals an outcome prevents learning that another cue now paired with the first cue also signals the outcome.

Backward Blocking: Same as blocking, but you train both cues first then the blocking cue on its own second.

Unovershadowing: two cues are paired with an outcome then one is revealed not to predict that outcome.

Retrospective Revaluation: a procedure in which two cues are paired with an outcome then information after that event causes a change in their association with the outcome.

Section 3
From Neuroscience to Robotics and AI

Chapter 8
Using Myoelectric Signals to Manipulate Assisting Robots and Rehabilitation Devices

Mohammadreza Asghari-Oskoei
University of Essex, UK

Huosheng Hu
University of Essex, UK

ABSTRACT

Myoelectric signal is known as an alternative human-machine interface (HMI) for people with motor disability in dealing with assisting robots and rehabilitation devices. This chapter examines a myoelectric HMI in real-time application and compares its performance with traditional tools. It also studies the manifestation of fatigue in long-term muscular activities and its impact on ultimate performance. The core of applied HMI is built on the support vector machine as a classifier. The experiments confirm that the myoelectric HMI is a reliable alternative to traditional HMI. Meanwhile, they show a significant decline in the dominant frequency of myoelectric signals during long-term applications.

INTRODUCTION

Since most disabled people have problems manipulating current assistive robots and rehabilitation devices that employ traditional user interfaces, such as a joystick and/or keyboard, they need more advanced hands-free human-machine interfaces (HMIs). Surface myoelectric signal (MES) is a biological signal collected non-invasively from surface of the skin covering the muscles, and contains rich information to identify neuromuscular activities. A myoelectric HMI uses MES as

an input signal to recognize various patterns of muscular activities and employs them to produce the effect of user's intention on its output. It eases the interaction with electric devices, assisting robots, or rehabilitating devices to the minimum level of movements for the disabled.

A pattern recognition-based myoelectric HMI recognizes input patterns by classifying the signal features, and outputs their corresponding commands, hence, the selection of effective features and a classifier that provide accurate as well as fast reactions are crucial issue (Asghari-Oskoei & Hu, 2007). The application of pattern recognition to myoelectric HMI was first introduced in the

DOI: 10.4018/978-1-60960-021-1.ch008

1960-70s (Englehart et al., 2001b); however, due to limited acquisition instruments and computing capacity at that time, real time control was not feasible. (Hudgins et al., 1993) were pioneers in developing a real time pattern-recognition-based myoelectric HMI. Using time domain (TD) features and a multilayer perceptron (MLP) neural network, they succeeded in classifying four types of upper limb motion, with an accuracy of approximately 90%. This work was continued over the last fifteen years, by employing various classifiers, such as LDA, MLP/RBF neural networks, time-delayed ANN, Fuzzy, NEURO-Fuzzy, Fuzzy ARTMAP networks, Fuzzy-MINMAX networks, Gaussian mixture models (GMM), and hidden Markov models (HMM). (Vuskovic & Du, 2002) introduced a modified version of a fuzzy ART-MAP network to classify prehensile myoelectric signals. (Englehart et al., 2001a) showed that linear discriminant analysis (LDA) outperforms MLP on time-scale features which are dimensionally reduced by PCA.

In addition, significant results were achieved using probabilistic approaches. (Chan & Englehart, 2005) applied a hidden Markov model (HMM) to discriminate six classes of limb movement based on a four-channel MES. It resulted in an average accuracy of 94.63%, which exceeded an MLP based classifier used in (Englehart et al., 2003) (93.27%). Furthermore, (Huang et al., 2005) and (Fukuda et al., 2003) developed a Gaussian mixture model (GMM) as a classifier; the former showed an accuracy of approximately 97%. (Englehart et al., 2003) introduced a continuous classification scheme that provided more robust results for a shortened segment length of signal, and high speed controllers.

In (Asghari-Oskoei & Hu, 2008), the authors have conducted a research to deploy support vector machine (SVM) as a classifier for myoelectric HMI. It proposes and evaluates the application of SVM to classify upper limb muscle activities using surface myoelectric signals. The optimum configuration for a SVM-based myoelectric HMI is explored by suggesting an advantageous data segmentation technique, feature set, model selection approach for SVM, and post-processing method. Meanwhile, it presents a method to adjust SVM parameters before classification. It is shown that SVM offers classification performance that matches or exceeds other classifiers (i.e. LDA and MLP). A TD multi-feature set consisting mean absolute value (MAV), waveform length (WL), and zero-crossing (ZC), outperforms other features, because of its relatively high rate of accuracy, stability against changes in segment (window) length, low discrepancy over several sessions, and computational simplicity. WL outperforms single-features, because of its high rate of accuracy and stability to changes in segmentation methods. A disjoint segmentation with a length of 200 ms provides high performance during MES classification, and a reasonable response time to allow real-time application. Overlapped segmentation with a length of 200ms and an increment of 50 ms shortens the response time without a noticeable degradation in accuracy. Majority voting (MV), as a post-processing method, provides stable output. It is also shown that the entropies of correct and non-correct outputs are significantly distinct.

However, the performance of myoelectric HMI in real-time applications is still an open question. This Book Chapter makes an effort to examine myoelectric HMI in real applications and evaluate its performance in dynamic aspects. This study employs the HMI developed in (Asghari-Oskoei & Hu, 2008) and applies it to an assisting robot and a rehabilitation device. In real-time applications, visual feedback provides interactive interface that improves the quality of control. Users can adjust the level of muscles contraction using visual feedback and improve their controlling ability during operation. This affects the HMI performance and urges independent investigation.

Accuracy, intuitiveness and response time are the three aspects of HMI performance in real-time applications, which are either hardly measurable or entirely immeasurable. Moreover, they don't demonstrate directly the user's actual satisfaction. Consideration of HMI's success in providing the qualified service can be a good measure of performance, but it thoroughly depends on the type of application and the desired functions that should be fulfilled.

To evaluate the performance of real-time myoelectric HMI, we examined it in two applications: wheelchair and video game. Manipulating a wheelchair provides an interactive real-time environment, in which the user comes across with obstacles or routes that should be managed on time. It reveals the level of dexterity and intuitiveness of HMI along with its accuracy and response time. Travel time or average speed and number of failures show the level of success in wheelchair manipulation and represent indirectly the rate of accuracy, intuitiveness and response time of the applied HMI.

Beside its advantages, due to practical problems wheelchair manipulation was not endured for a long period, in which we could study the effect of long-term applications. Video game being controlled by a myoelectric HMI could provide a setup for a long-term interactive application. It made the user react fast and properly during the game and this required an HMI with high level of performance. Its performance was evaluated using the level of success in accomplishment of the game functions in a long lasting test.

This chapter studies a myoelectric HMI in two real time applications. Section 2 evaluates the performance of a myoelectric HMI applied to a wheelchair and compares it with a traditional HMI. Section 3 studies the long-term application of a myoelectric HMI applied to a video game, and investigates the manifestation of fatigue in the muscles. Summary and conclusion have been presented in Section 4.

MYOELECTRIC HMI APPLIED TO WHEELCHAIR

This section evaluates a myoelectric HMI applied to manipulate a powered wheelchair and compares it with its traditional HMI (i.e. joystick). Obviously, the manipulation of a powered wheelchair depends on many factors, such as the hardware of wheelchair, the user's skill, the route complexity, and the applied control strategy via HMI. The last one is in the scope of our study, and to avoid any dependency to other factors, we compare the performance of HMIs obtained from identical wheelchair, users, and routes. Firstly let us have a quick look at the recent works which have suggested myoelectric HMI for wheelchair navigation.

(Moon et al., 2005) presented a non-pattern recognition based myoelectric HMI, in which a subject with motor disabilities can generate navigating commands to a wheelchair using shoulder elevation gesture. The core of the controller is a threshold-based method applied on the mean absolute value (MAV) of MES. It uses two thresholds as primary and auxiliary to cope with time differences of muscle activation. This method, namely double threshold, considers the time difference of muscle activation caused by fatigue or training level. The performance was evaluated in two experiments: the first was to navigate a wheelchair to a goal in a virtual environment with six random obstacles and the second was in a real environment, to pass a maze type corridor whose width was twice of the wheelchair width. The elapsed time for the navigation from start point to the goal was compared in both traditional keypad and myoelectric interface. The results showed similar average time for the first and about 50% overload (i.e. time) for the second experiment.

(Felzer & Freisleben, 2002) applied a finite state machine to drive a wheelchair using myoelectric signals collected from forehead skin. In order to

Figure 1. Schematic diagram of applied myoelectric HMI to manipulate a powered wheelchair

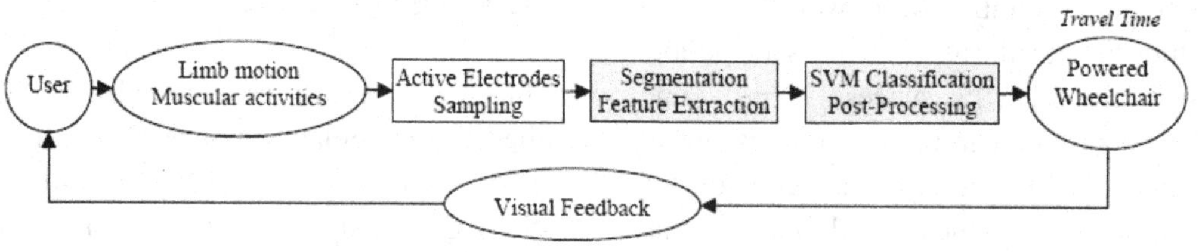

evaluate the performance of the proposed system, they recoded and compared the times needed to drive a wheelchair at an identical speeds, routes, and distances for both myoelectric and joystick-based HMIs. As expected, the myoelectric HMI was slower but the exceeded time was not more than the 50%. (Han et al., 2003) also applied fuzzy min-max neural networks to classify MES collected from the neck to drive a wheelchair using head movements and showed that the average speed of the wheelchair was declining remarkably.

Myoelectric Joystick

A SVM-based myoelectric HMI was applied to manipulate a wheelchair. It recognizes hand gestures using collected MES from forearm and then applies them to drive a wheelchair. Because of similarity in function, we called it "myoelectric joystick", and compared it with real joystick. The proposed myoelectric joystick works based on MES generated by muscular activities rather than the mechanical handle. The desired commands of subject, who may have hand but not with full control, are detected from MES patterns during five touch-less limb motions comprised of hand flexion/extension, abduction/adduction, and keeping straight. In subjects with amputation or deficient limb, the command was being recognized using muscle contraction patterns depending on their ability and convenience. The motion commands applied to the wheelchair were: Go-Forward, Go-Backward, Turn Left, Turn Right, and Stop.

The structure of applied myoelectric HMI was adopted from (Asghari-Oskoei & Hu, 2008). A 4-channel surface MES was collected from forearm, using wearable bipolar active electrodes located on biarticulate wrist flexor and triarticulate and biarticulate wrist extensor muscles. A C++ based software running on a Laptop with CPU Pentium IV 2.3GHz and platform Windows XP was developed to grab the collected MES data, implement a real-time myoelectric HMI, and finally send the manipulating command to either a powered wheelchair connected through a USB port or a simulated wheelchair (Pioneer Inc. RSim) through a TCP/IP socket. The developed software was using standard C++, Biometrics Ltd., Pioneer Inc., and LIBSVM libraries.

Three time domain features (i.e. MAV, WL, and ZC) extracted from disjoint segments with length 100 ms were applied to a SVM classifier with kernel RBF. As it was shown in (Asghari-Oskoei & Hu, 2008), reducing segment length of time domain features into 100 ms increases the HMI response time without noticeable decline in accuracy. The parameters of SVM (i.e. C and γ) were adjusted for each subject using grid search method, and majority voting was employed as the post-processing. Figure 1 demonstrates a schematic diagram of the proposed myoelectric HMI with visual feedback. To evaluate the performance of the applied HMI, we recorded the travel time between two points with a particular segment of corridors or obstacles. We also considered the number of failures, in which the travels have not been finished properly.

According to machine learning scheme, the SVM initially has to be trained using MES data. This is called offline training. Hence, before using myoelectric joystick, subjects were asked to do repeatable hand gestures or muscle contractions (depending onto their body's physical situation) corresponding to the wheelchair's motion commands, and labeled MES data (5 seconds for each command) were concurrently recorded for offline training. Training SVM constructs the boundaries between classes using support vectors.

Experiments and Results

The experiments were conducted in both virtual and real environments. In the first experiment, a simulated wheelchair should be passed through a maze type corridor whose width was less than twice of the wheelchair width (Figure 2). The area was 20×20m, the length of path was about 88m, and the transition and rotation speed of wheelchair was 40% and 10% of its maximum speed, respectively. In order to evaluate the performance of the proposed system, subjects were asked to navigate the wheelchair in two sessions: using a real joystick and using a myoelectric joystick.

In the second experiment, the proposed HMI was evaluated over a real powered wheelchair. In this experiment, users should drive the wheelchair through a path between obstacles in a circular area with diameters 15m, using both real and myoelectric joysticks. The powered wheelchair has two wheels powered by two independent DC motors, a motor driver board with speed and position feedback control, six ultrasonic sensors for obstacle avoidance (disabled in this experiment), a joystick, a DSP controller TMS320LF2407, and batteries for power supply. The DSP controller offers excellent processing capabilities (30MIPS) for both low level motor control functions and high level control functions coming from either a joystick or a laptop connected through its serial port. The laptop (Pentium IV 2.3GHz, Windows XP) runs myoelectric HMI that collects

Figure 2. Rout map of the wheelchair driven in a virtual environment

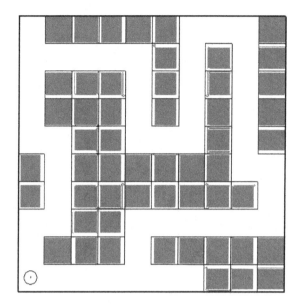

MES data and generates corresponding motion commands in every 100 ms (Figure 5).

Five (three male and two female) healthy subjects aged between 18 and 28 and without any motor disability on their upper limb participated in the experiments. The subjects were first briefed on experiments and then filled the Ethics Consent Forms. Each session, in the first experiment, was repeated two times for real joystick and three times for myoelectric joystick and their averages were compared together. The subjects were asked to drive as fast as possible, and there was no penalty for probable hitting to borders.

Statistical analysis (i.e. Wilcoxon rank-sum) was applied to interpret the experimental results. The purpose of applying the statistical analysis was to find statistically meaningful differences with certain significance over the observations (DeGroot & Schervish, 2002). The critical p-value, which determines whether a result is judged "statistically significant", was chosen as 0.05.

Results of the experiment conducted in virtual environment have been shown in Table 1. It indicates that the average travel time of wheelchair

Figure 3. Trajectory of wheelchair manipulated by conventional and myoelectric HMIs in virtual environment

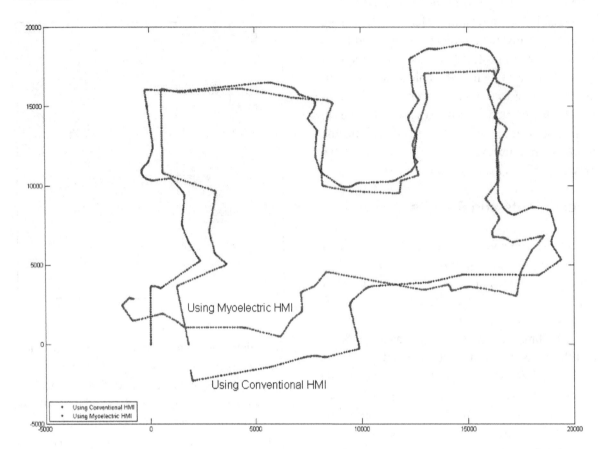

using virtual and real joystick was about 500s and 475s, respectively. For an instant, the trajectory of simulated wheelchair in a virtual environment is shown in Figure 3.

Table 2 shows the travel time of each subject (once only) in a real environment. It points out that the travel time of wheelchair using a myoelectric joystick instead of a real joystick raised from 140s to 165s. Figure 4 demonstrates a subject driving the powered wheelchair by a myoelectric HMI.

Figure 6 compares the performance of a real joystick with a myoelectric joystick in virtual environment. As seen, there is no significant difference between performance of real and myoelectric joysticks in manipulating a wheelchair in a virtual environment. Discrepancy of observations in real joystick is much less than of myoelectric joystick.

Statistical analysis applied to the results of the real wheelchair is demonstrated in Figure 7. It

Table 1. Average travel times (sec) recorded in virtual environment

Subject	Real Joystick	Myoelectric Joystick
#1	528	347
#2	430	402
#3	550	600
#4	480	493
#5	503	540

Figure 4. A subject driving powered wheelchair using myoelectric HMI

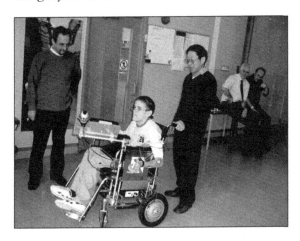

shows that using the myoelectric joystick significantly increases the travel time by about 20%. This shows remarkable improvement in HMI performance with regard to (Felzer & Freisleben, 2002) and (Moon et al., 2005) that were indicating 50% of overload. Furthermore, the results confirm that the myoelectric HMI can be an alternative to traditional HMIs for people with motor disabilities.

MYOELECTRIC HMI APPLIED TO VIDEO GAME

The video game industry is growing rapidly and diversified digital games have entered thousands of homes worldwide and welcomed by people of different ages, gender and capabilities. Majority of users use control panels to enjoy game playing. However, disabled people have huge difficulty using such conventional control panels. It becomes necessary to design and build novel HMIs suited for people with motor disability or deficiency. Myoelectric HMI can be an alternative to the conventional game control panels, and help the disabled people to play. Meanwhile, the application of myoelectric HMI to a game enables us to study HMI performance during long lasting operations. A video game is reasonably attractive such that a user sits to play with it for a long period, and it can enforce the user to react quickly and precisely in safe, secure, and traceable circumstances. This helps us to evaluate the proposed HMI in a novel real-time application, study manifestation of fatigue in MES, and examine myoelectric HMI reliability and robustness during long-term applications. The rest of this Chapter evaluates myoelectric HMI applied to a video game, and examines manifestation of muscles fatigue in myoelectric signals collected whilst playing game.

Table 2. Recorded travel times (sec) in real environment

Subject	Real Joystick	Myoelectric Joystick
#1	150	170
#2	125	190
#3	145	157
#4	130	135
#5	150	175

Figure 5. Real powered wheelchair utilized in the second experiment

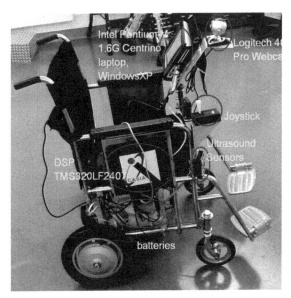

Figure 6. there is no significant difference between travel time of simulated powered wheelchair manipulated by real and myoelectric joysticks

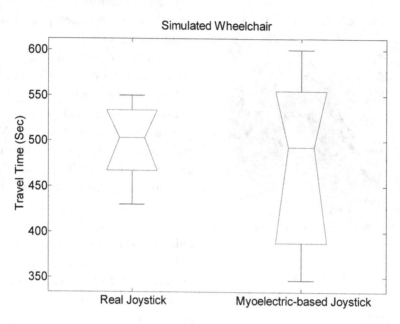

Figure 7. Using myoelectric joystick increases the travel time of real wheelchair about 20%

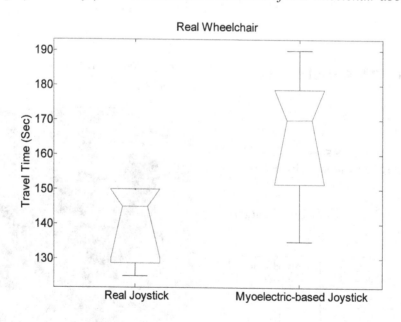

Computer-Based Video Game

The game was developed under Java Applet using the C++ cores previously developed for the wheelchair, and run in two parallel threads (a thread to collect MES data and a thread to process myoelectric HMI and refresh game graphics) on a PC (Pentium IV 2.3GHz with Windows XP platform). The game was graphically making a virtual driving environment, and enforcing the user to drive a car in a route with randomly appearing obstacles, having five ordinary manipulating commands: Go Forward, Backward, Right, Left, and Stop. The commands were being produced by a myoelectric HMI using MES corresponding to five hand motions: hand flexion, extension, abduction, adduction, and keeping straight. For subjects with amputation or deficient limb, the commands were being recognized through the muscular contractions depending to their ability and convenience.

Comparison of the achieved scores by a subject who had got matured training and exercises, during several sessions of playing game could be a measurable index to evaluate the HMI performance. The game scoring policy was oriented towards a safe and quick driving. Every forward step was gaining a positive score and every wrong step, in which car hit to an obstacle or a border, was gaining ten negative scores. This policy highlights inappropriate commands produced by the HMI for a game-skilled user. To study the developing of the fatigue during the experiments, the subjects were encouraged to achieve the highest score as far as possible, and carry on with the game until they feel fatigue in their muscles. The random generator applied to produce obstacles was such that the distribution of activities was identical in the whole session.

Myoelectric HMI classified MES data and generated manipulating commands to drive the car in the game. The applied HMI was similar to the one that had applied to the powered wheelchair, described in the last Section. Four-channel MES collected from forearm muscles (same locations adopted for the wheelchair) was applied to HMI. Its time domain features, including MAV, WL, and ZC, and extracted from disjoint segments with length of 100 ms, was classified by a SVM-based classifier with RBF kernel that its parameters had been adjusted by a grid search method applied on training data set. The output stream of the classifier was post-processed by majority voting (MV) to reduce the error of the transient states and provide a smooth stream of commands. MV was designed to output the most prevalent commands in the last three segments, otherwise STOP. Meanwhile, the post-processing module had an accelerating option that made acceleration by doubling the output command when the last three recent HMI outputs were identical. Figure 8 shows a user whilst playing game using myoelectric HMI.

The proposed myoelectric HMI had been developed to override some control functions of XBOX 360 (Microsoft) control pad that result in driving a car in standard XBOX games, but due to its untraceable outputs and scoring system, it was not considered in our experiments.

Figure 8. A user, with wearable MES electrodes on his forearm, drives a car in a video game using myoelectric HMI

Manifestation of Fatigue in MES

Muscle fatigue is a subjective feeling whose quantitative assessment is very complex, not unique and sometimes controversial. It influences muscle activity and has a direct impact on MES particularly on long-term activities. This phenomenon plays an important rule when myoelectric is being used for HMI, because MES patterns are gradually changing and HMI has to adapt itself based on the changes.

Fatigue is a concept determined by two dimensions: psychological and physiological (Zwarts et al., 2008). In physiology, fatigue is usually defined as the loss of voluntary force-producing capacity during exercise, and is not necessarily accompanied by self-perceived fatigue, which is known as psychological concept. An important problem in interpreting changes during fatiguing contraction is that it is not always clear whether a change is a direct result of the exhaustion or whether it is an adaptation. Meanwhile, frequent distractions and re-attentions, which can be named as a type of psychological fatigue, make it more complex. Fatigue has mostly been studied at peripheral level (i.e. muscles) rather than central level (i.e. central nervous system) and MES provides useful information about peripheral fatigue. Manifestation of fatigue can be studied by means of signal amplitude, signal frequency and muscle conduction velocity (CV) (Zwarts et al., 2008).

Fatigue has mostly been studied in sustained contraction, while the muscle length and tension are hold constant. During non-maximal voluntary sustained contraction, signal amplitude usually increases considerably due to the recruitment of extra motor units and increasing in firing rate of motor units. Both are mechanisms to cope with the declining force output. In contrast, during high and maximal voluntary sustained contractions, the amplitude usually declines. Furthermore, in sustained contractions, the muscle conduction velocity (CV) decreases with fatigue due to the change in the metabolic of cellular environment,

and this phenomenon is reflected as a shift to the lower frequencies of signal spectrum. Hence, signal frequency is known as the main manifestation of fatigue in MES under static conditions (MacIsaac et al., 2006a), and spectral features are well-suited quantitative index to indicate it.

During unconstrained contractions, however, when the muscle length and/or tension are free to vary, the frequency characteristics of MES are influenced by many factors rather than fatigue. Geometrical factors, which indicate the relative position of active and detectable motor units, significantly change the signal frequency spectrum that may incorrectly attributed to physiological factors. High degree of non-stationarity of signal is another major problem in dealing with unconstrained contractions. Therefore, powerful methods rather than classical spectral techniques are required to investigate frequency shift during unconstrained contractions. Time-scale methods, particularly Wavelets are introduced to cope with signal's non-stationarity and sudden changes. Furthermore, direct measurement of conduction velocity (CV) is difficult to attain accurately during unconstrained contractions, possibly because of muscle innervations zone migration and/or end-effects (Zwarts et al., 2008), (MacIsaac et al., 2006b).

Regarding to its inherent complexity and significance, many articles have been studying manifestation of fatigue in MES during unconstrained contractions, and this is still an open issue to model the MES changes during fatigue. (Karlsson et al., 2000) applied different time-scale methods to analysis MES during dynamic contractions, and found that continuous wavelet transform (CWT) provides more accurate estimation comparing with short-time Fourier transform (STFT), Wigner-Ville distribution, and Choi-Williams distribution. (Farina et al., 2004) proposed a technique for detection and processing of muscles CV during dynamic contraction, and showed that its decline is reflecting muscle fatigue. (Bonato et al., 2001) applied Cohen class time-scale transform for assessing muscle fatigue during cyclic dynamic contractions. It was assumed that non-physiological factors contributing MES non-stationarity could be constrained and isolated for cyclic contractions.

(Georgakis et al., 2003) showed that average instantaneous frequency (AIF), obtained through time-scale methods, outperforms the conventional mean and median spectrum frequency in fatigue analysis of sustained contraction. Recently, (MacIsaac et al., 2006a) presented a mapping function that maps MES time domain features for fatigue estimation during dynamic contractions. This function was tuned by artificial neural networks (ANN), and was capable to utilize in real time applications, but need to be trained before application. Now, simultaneous with evaluation of myoelectric HMI, we are going to study MES frequency shift, as a manifestation of fatigue, during unconstrained muscular activities conducted to play a computer based game. For this purpose, we have considered both the spectral and time-scale features for comparison.

Spectral Features

Mean and median frequencies are the most commonly used spectral features in MES analysis. The mean frequency (MNF) is the average frequency of the power spectrum density (PSD) and is defined using its first-order moment.

$$MNF = \frac{\int_0^\infty \omega P(\omega)d\omega}{\int_0^\infty P(\omega)d\omega} \tag{1}$$

The median frequency (MDF) is a frequency at which PSD is divided into two equal areas. Involving zero-order moment of PSD, it mathematically is defined by:

$$\int_0^{MDF} P(\omega)d\omega = \int_{MDF}^\infty P(\omega)d\omega = \frac{1}{2}\int_0^\infty P(\omega)d\omega \tag{2}$$

These two features are mostly applicable in sustained contraction, where the signal is quasi-stationary, and provide basic information about how the power spectrum changes with time. To calculate spectral features, recorded signals were segmented into consecutive disjoint segments with a certain length (e.g. 200 ms) and then PSD estimation took place for each segment. Thus, a time course of signal spectral features, as shown in Figure 9, was formed.

Features trend, particularly its linear slope, can be considered as a manifestation of fatigue in MES (Zwarts et al., 2008), (Merletti et al., 2004). Least-square linear regression was applied to estimate features linear slope, and their shift after a certain time was considered as a quantitative index for the fatigue. Regarding to result of preliminary experiments, we employed only MNF to compare with other features.

Time-Scale Features

As it mentioned before, time-scale methods (e.g. wavelets transform) are an alternative to classical spectral techniques to analyze MES in dynamic conditions, in which the muscle's length and force are varying. A wavelet is a mathematical function used to divide a signal into different frequency components and study each component with a resolution that matches its scale. Wavelet transform represents a signal using wavelet functions.

Continuous wavelet transform (CWT) represents a signal over every possible scale (i.e. linearly proportional to inverse of frequency) and translation (i.e. time shifting) and offers both time and frequency localized analysis. It reveals data aspects that other techniques miss, such as signal trends, breakdown points, discontinuities in higher derivatives, and self-similarity. Given s as a scale

Figure 9. Spectral features (MNF) of a 4-channel MES during repeating hand states (50 seconds holding at flexion and 5 seconds rest)

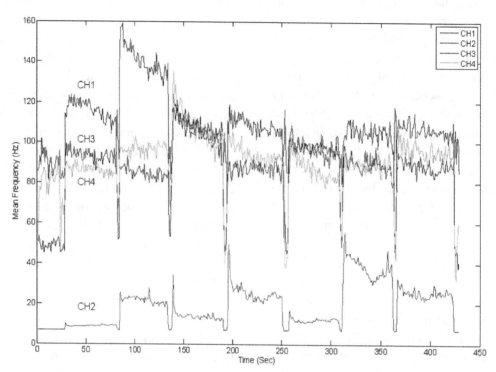

parameter, and τ as a translation (time shifting) parameter, CWT of signal $x(t)$ is defined as

$$CWT(s,\tau) = \int x(t)\Psi^{*}_{s,\tau}(t)dt \qquad (3)$$

Basic function $\Psi_{s,\tau}$ is obtained by scaling the mother wavelet Ψ at time τ and scale s:

$$\Psi_{s,\tau}(t) = \frac{1}{\sqrt{s}}\Psi(\frac{t-\tau}{s}) \qquad (4)$$

The scalogram (corresponding to periodogram in spectral analysis) of a signal is defined as the square of CWT and then the mean scale (corresponding to mean frequency) of signal in CWT is obtained by

$$MNS = \frac{\int_{0}^{\tau 1}\int_{0}^{s1} s\left|CWT(s,\tau)\right|^{2} dsd\tau}{\int_{0}^{\tau 1}\int_{0}^{s1}\left|CWT(s,\tau)\right|^{2} dsd\tau} \qquad (5)$$

The inverse of mean scale (MNS), known as instantaneous mean frequency (IMNF) (Bonato et al., 2001) and (Georgakis et al., 2003), is proportional to the signal frequency and used in this work as a time-scale feature to analyze manifestation of fatigue in dynamic contractions. We compared three well-known wavelet families, including Duabechies (db), Symlet (sym), and Coiflet (coif) in various orders and found out that they behave identically in generating IMNF (as depicted in Figure 10), to this end we applied just one of them (i.e. db5) in this work. Linear regression, as described in spectral features, was applied to this feature to evaluate the signal trend in time-scale domain (Figure 11).

Figure 10. Spectral (MNF) and time-scale (IMNF) features using db5, sym5 and coif3 during repeating 'Hand Extension' motion

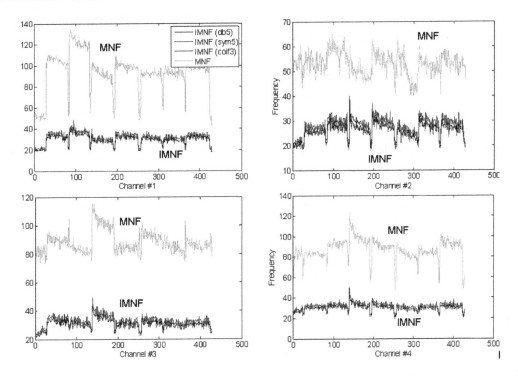

Figure 11. IMNF of MES and its linear slope during a session of playing game

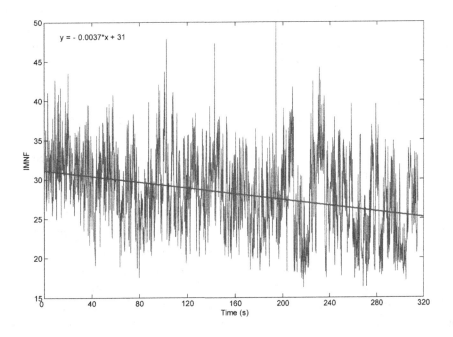

Experiments and Results

Ten subjects with average age 20, four (two male and two female) without motor disability on their upper limb, and six (five male and one female) with motor disability or lack of full control on their upper limb, took part in our experiments and conducted totally 26 sessions. Each session was comprised of playing game, and subjects after about 10 minutes briefing and pre-training, were asked to play the game and encouraged to gain as high a score as possible until they felt fatigued. The recorded times of the 26 sessions, depicted in Table 3, reveal the relative success of myoelectric HMI adopted as an alternative for keypad or joystick to play a game. Particularly, the unhealthy participants indicated either satisfaction or high satisfaction in their brief questionnaire after the experiment.

To study the manifestation of fatigue during playing game, we examined the trend of frequency of the recorded myoelectric signals. The recorded signals were segmented into consecutive disjoint segments (with the length of 200 ms), and then spectral and time-scale features calculated. The features represent dominant frequency in each segment, and their trends stand for frequency shift in each session. As expected for dynamic muscular activities, the dominant frequency in the course of time was greatly fluctuating (Figure 10 and Figure 11). Despite unpredictable fluctuations, the trend of frequency worked out by linear regression declines significantly in most of channels and sessions. This trend has been illustrated by the negative slope of linear regression applied to the frequencies.

To have a comparable estimation of frequency changes in a signal, we estimated the percentage of frequency shift after 15 minutes for all channels and sessions. The estimation was conducted using parameters obtained through the regression. We also calculated the confidence interval of estimation that generates 95% prediction intervals for new observations at the estimated point. It accom-

Table 3. Elapsed time to play the game using myoelectric HMI in each session

Healthy Subjects		Unhealthy Subjects	
Subject	Time (min)	Subject	Time (min)
#1	10	#5	4
#1	7	#5	7
#1	11	#6	10
#1	22	#6	15
#2	8	#7	9
#2	7	#7	7
#2	6	#8	15
#2	8	#8	5
#3	15	#9	24
#3	7	#10	14
#3	6	#10	17
#3	6		
#4	9		
#4	10		
#4	7		
Average	10±4	Average	12±6

modates all observations with the probability 95% around the estimated point. Kruskal-Wallis was applied to find meaningful difference or similarity over observations with certain significance (0.05).

The results are illustrated in box-plots. On each box, the central mark is the median, the edges of the box are the 25th and 75th percentiles, the whiskers (dashed lines) extend to the most extreme data points not considered outliers, and outliers are plotted individually (marked by red plus sign). The assumption of observations is that all come from populations having the same continuous distribution and are mutually independent. Basically, the median approaches the mean if they had a normal distribution.

Figure 12 and Figure 13 illustrate the shift of frequency in 4-channel MES after 15 minutes operation yielded by spectral (MNF) and time-scale (IMNF) features, respectively. They include all hand states corresponding to five motion commands in playing game. As it can be

Figure 12. Frequency shift (%) after 15min operation yielded by spectral features

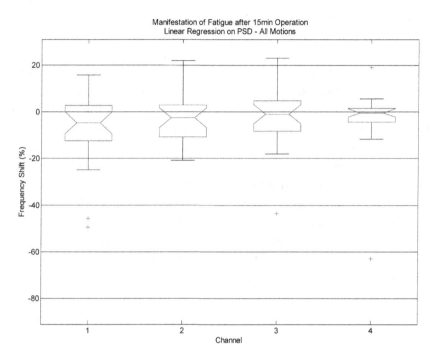

Figure 13. Frequency shift (%) after 15min operation yielded by time-scale features

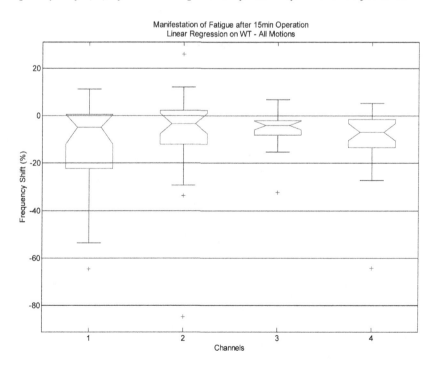

seen, the shift of frequency was mainly negative. The results suggest that the dominant frequency of myoelectric signals declines about 5% in all channels. For instance, the dominant frequency of channel #1 yielded by MNF had a shift between -15 and +2%, meanwhile, IMNF points out a decline between zero and -21%.

The hand motions make jumps in frequency. This is clearly perceivable in Figure 9 and Figure 10. The jumps make positive impact on the trend of frequency in sessions. To this end, focusing on a particular hand state and eliminating of MES data corresponding to other states might make the trend of frequency remarkably more negative. Figure 14 approves this idea, and shows that the overall decline is about 10% (rather than 5%) when we consider the frequencies of a particular hand state corresponding to a particular command (e.g. Go Forward). Although this can't remove completely the impact of switch between hand states, it reduces the effect of dynamic contractions and makes the frequency decline corresponding to fatigue more visible.

Physiologically, as we best know, there is no time limit for developing fatigue in muscles, and the time that it becomes perceivable is entirely dependent to conditions of the subjects and types of the activities. The sessions were ended due to fatigue in either psychological or physiological aspects. For example, subjects were giving up wheelchair manipulation after a short period but were lasting much longer during the game though they had to do same physical activities in both. In long-term sessions, there is more chance to detect manifestation of fatigue in MES because of enough time to develop physiological fatigue by more muscular activities. Hence, rationally it

Figure 14. Estimated frequency shift (%) of four-channel MES, computed based on time-scale features, for Go Forward motions

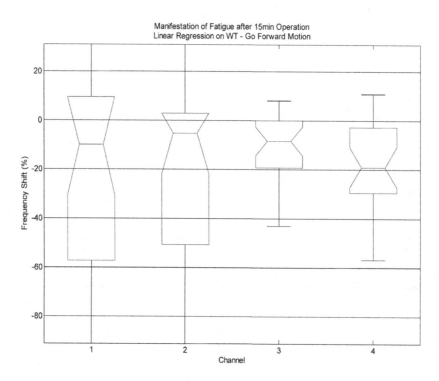

is expected to observe a difference in frequency shift between short and long-term sessions.

The experimental results we employed to estimate meaningful difference in the rate of frequency shift between short and long term sessions. Statistical analysis showed that there was a meaningful difference in trend of frequency between sessions longer than 7 minutes and other sessions. Figure 15 depicts that the frequency shift in long-term sessions are significantly more than the short-term sessions. This is because manifestation of fatigue (i.e. physiological fatigue) is more perceivable during long-term activities.

Statistically, there is no meaningful difference between the declines of frequency resulted by spectral and time-scale features, but their range of observations differ. Figure 16 depicts that the discrepancy of the observations by time-scale feature is much less than the spectral feature. This means that the time-scale feature depicts the frequency decline clearer than the spectral feature. This can be justified by the fact that the time-scale

features perform better on non-stationary signal analysis.

Figure 17 shows that the confidence interval of estimation of linear regressions applied on two types of features (i.e. spectral and time-scale features) were statistically same, but they had different range. The error of estimations was located between 29 and 32% for time scale feature, while it was between 26 and 36% for spectral features. The recent two figures point out that the time-scale features are more reliable to be used as a manifestation of fatigue in dynamic muscular activities.

CONCLUSION

The first part of this Chapter proposes a myoelectric-based virtual joystick to manipulate a powered wheelchair. Its core is a SVM-based myoelectric HMI. The experimental results confirm that the myoelectric joystick is a reliable alternative to real joysticks and its performance is acceptable. The

Figure 15. Frequency shift in long-term sessions are more than the short-term sessions

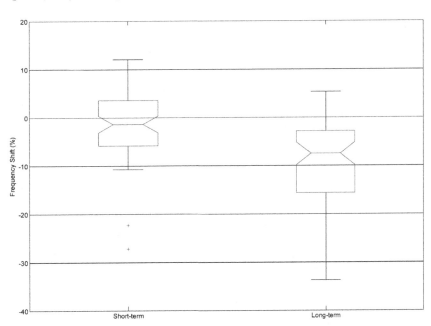

Figure 16. Time-scale features represent the frequency decline much better than the spectral features

Figure 17. Confidence interval (%) of estimation by linear regression applied on time-scale and spectral features

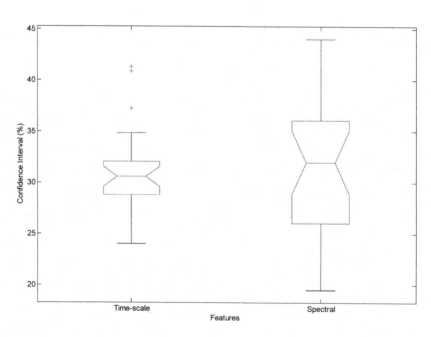

proposed myoelectric HMI imposes an overload about 20% comparing with real joystick in wheelchair manipulation. This is a notable improvement regarding to the latest works showing overload about 50%.

MES patterns gradually change in long-term muscle activities, due to developing fatigue in muscles. The second part of this Chapter studies the trend of frequency as a manifestation of fatigue in myoelectric signals. It examines MES data of dynamic muscular activities conducted during playing a video game. The game was being manipulated by the proposed myoelectric HMI. The experimental results indicate the success of a myoelectric HMI as being used as an alternative to conventional game pads, for the disabled people. Meanwhile, they show a significant decline in the dominant frequency of myoelectric signals during a session of game. Statistical analysis figures out a meaningful difference in frequency shift between short and long-term sessions, and reveals that the long-term sessions accommodate more frequency decline. This means that the manifestation of fatigue in myoelectric signals is perceivable in long-term muscular activities. Comparing the spectral and time-scale features reveals that the former represent the frequency decline clearer than the latter.

REFERENCES

Asghari-Oskoei, M., & Hu, H. (2007). Myoelectric control systems-A survey. *Journal of Biomedical Signal Processing and Control, 2*(4), 275–294.. doi:10.1016/j.bspc.2007.07.009

Asghari-Oskoei, M., & Hu, H. (2008). Support Vector Machine-Based Classification Scheme for Myoelectric Control Applied to Upper Limb. *IEEE Transactions on Bio-Medical Engineering, 55*(8), 1956–1965. Retrieved from http://ieeexplore.ieee.org/stamp/stamp.jsp?arnumber=04463647. doi:10.1109/TBME.2008.919734

Bonato, P., Roy, S. H., Knaflitz, M., & Luca, C. (2001). Time-frequency parameters of the surface myoelectric signal for assessing muscle fatigue during cyclic dynamic contractions. *IEEE Transactions on Bio-Medical Engineering, 48*(7), 745–753. Retrieved from http://ieeexplore.ieee.org/stamp/stamp.jsp?tp=&arnumber=930899&userType=inst. doi:10.1109/10.930899

Chan, A. D. C., & Englehart, K. (2005). Continuous Myoelectric Control for Powered Prostheses Using Hidden Markov Models. *IEEE Transactions on Bio-Medical Engineering, 52*(1), 121–124. Retrieved from http://ieeexplore.ieee.org/stamp/stamp.jsp?arnumber=01369595. doi:10.1109/TBME.2004.836492

DeGroot, M. H., & Schervish, M. J. (2002). *Probability and statistics*. New York: Addison Wesley.

Englehart, K., & Hudgins, B. (2003). A robust, real-time control scheme for multifunction myoelectric control. *IEEE Transactions on Bio-Medical Engineering, 50*(7), 848–854. Retrieved from http://ieeexplore.ieee.org/stamp/stamp.jsp?tp=&arnumber=1206493&userType=inst. doi:10.1109/TBME.2003.813539

Englehart, K., Hudgins, B., & Parker, P. (2001). A wavelet-based continuous classification scheme for multifunction myoelectric control. *IEEE Transactions on Bio-Medical Engineering, 48*(3), 302–310. Retrieved from http://ieeexplore.ieee.org/stamp/stamp.jsp?arnumber=00914793. doi:10.1109/10.914793

Englehart, K., Hudgins, B., & Parker, P. (2001). Intelligent systems and technologies in rehabilitation engineering. In Teodorrescu, H. L., & Jain, L. C. (Eds.), *Intelligent systems and technologies in rehabilitation engineering*. Boca Raton, FL: CRC Press.

Farina, D., Pozzo, M., Merlo, E., Bottin, A., & Merletti, R. (2004). Assessment of average muscle fibber conduction velocity from surface EMG signals during fatiguing dynamic contractions. *IEEE Transactions on Bio-Medical Engineering, 51*(8), 1383–1393. Retrieved from http://ieeexplore. ieee.org/xpls/abs_all.jsp?arnumber=1315860. doi:10.1109/TBME.2004.827556

Felzer, T., & Freisleben, B. (2002). HaWCoS: the hands-free wheelchair control system. *ACM Conference on Assistive Technologies*, Scotland, (pp. 127-134). New York: ACM Press Retrieved from http://portal.acm.org/citation.cfm?id=638249.638273

Fukuda, O., Tsuji, T., Kaneko, M., & Otsuka, A. (2003). A human-assisting manipulator teleoperated by emg signals and arm motions. *IEEE Transactions on Robotics and Automation, 19*(2), 210–222. Retrieved from http://ieeexplore.ieee.org/stamp/stamp.jsp?arnumber=01192150. doi:10.1109/TRA.2003.808873

Georgakis, A., Stergioulas, L. K., & Giakas, G. (2003). Fatigue analysis of the surface EMG signal in isometric constant force contractions using the averaged instantaneous frequency. *IEEE Transactions on Bio-Medical Engineering, 50*(2), 262–265. Retrieved from http://ieeexplore.ieee.org/stamp/stamp.jsp?tp=&arnumber=1185153&userType=inst. doi:10.1109/TBME.2002.807641

Han, J. S., Bien, Z. Z., Kim, D. J., Lee, H. E., & Kim, J. S. (2003). Human-machine interface for wheelchair control with emg and its evaluation. In *Proceedings of IEEE International Conference on Engineering in Medicine and Biology Society*, (pp. 1602-1605). doi: 10.1109/IEMBS.2003.1279672

Huang, Y., Englehart, K., Hudgins, B., & Chan, A. D. C. (2005). A gaussian mixture model based classification scheme for myoelectric control of powered upper limb prostheses. *IEEE Transactions on Bio-Medical Engineering, 52*(11), 1801–1811. Retrieved from http://ieeexplore.ieee.org/stamp/stamp.jsp?tp=&arnumber=1519588. doi:10.1109/TBME.2005.856295

Hudgins, B., Parker, P., & Scott, R. (1993). A new strategy for multifunction myoelectric control. *IEEE Transactions on Bio-Medical Engineering, 40*(1), 82–94..doi:10.1109/10.204774

Hudgins, B., Parker, P., & Scott, R. (1994). Control of artificial limbs using myoelectric pattern recognition. *Medical & Life Science Engineering, 13*, 21–38. doi:.doi:10.1016/S1350-4533(99)00066-1

Karlsson, S., Yu, J., & Akay, M. (2000). Time-frequency analysis of myoelectric signals during dynamic contractions: a comparative study. *IEEE Transactions on Bio-Medical Engineering, 47*(2), 228–238. Retrieved from http://ieeexplore.ieee.org/stamp/stamp.jsp?tp=&arnumber=821766. doi:10.1109/10.821766

MacIsaac, D., & Englehart, K. (2006). The science in science fiction artificial men. *Journal of Defence Software Engineering, 19*(10), 4–8. Retrieved from http://handle.dtic.mil/100.2/ADA487418.

MacIsaac, D. T., Parker, P., Englehart, K., & Rogers, D. R. (2006). Fatigue estimation with a multivariable myoelectric mapping function. *IEEE Transactions on Bio-Medical Engineering, 53*(4), 694–700. Retrieved from http://ieeexplore.ieee.org/stamp/stamp.jsp?arnumber=01608519. doi:10.1109/TBME.2006.870220

Merletti, R., Farina, D., & Rainoldi, A. (2004). Myoelectric manifestations of muscle fatigue. In Kumar, S. (Ed.), *Muscle Strength*. Boca Raton, FL: CRC Press.

Moon, I., Lee, M., Chu, J., & Mun, M. (2005). Wearable emg-based hci for electric-powered wheelchair users with motor disabilities. In *Proceedings of IEEE International Conference on Robotics and Automation*, (pp. 2649-2654). Retrieved from http://ieeexplore.ieee.org/xpl/mostRecentIssue.jsp?punumber=10495

Vuskovic, M., & Du, S. J. (2002). Classification of prehensile EMG patterns with simplified fuzzy ARTMAP networks. *Proceedings of International Joint Conference on Neural Networks, 3,* 2539–2544. Retrieved from http://medusa.sdsu. edu/Robotics/Neuromuscular/Our_publications/ Hawaii/Paper.pdf.

Zwarts, M. J., Bleijenberg, G., & Engelen, B. G. M. (2008). Clinical neurophysiology of fatigue. *Clinical Neurophysiology, 119*(1), 2–10.. doi:10.1016/j.clinph.2007.09.126

KEY TERMS AND DEFINITIONS

Surface Myoelectric Signal (MES): Surface myoelectric signal (MES) is a biological signal collected non-invasively from surface of the skin covering the muscles, and contains rich information to identify neuromuscular activities.

Myoelectric Human-Machine Interface (HMI): A myoelectric human-machine interface (HMI) uses MES as an input signal to recognize various patterns of muscular activities and employs them to interact with electric devices, assisting robots, or rehabilitating devices.

Support Vector Machine (SVM): Support Vector Machine (SVM) is a kernel-based approach for machine learning tasks involving classification and regression. It constructs an optimal separating hyperplane between classes of training data. Because of using nonlinear kernel function, it is in effect of a nonlinear classifier.

Signal Features: Myoelectric signal features signify the key differences between the desired classes of muscular activities for the classification. They fall into three categories: time domain, frequency (spectral) domain, and time-scale (time-frequency) domain.

Feature Selection/Extraction: Feature selection plays a crucial role in improving the performance of myoelectric HMI. Mapping the raw data into a set of features (feature vector) is called feature extraction.

Myoelectric Joystick: Myoelectric Joystick is a SVM-based myoelectric HMI that has been applied to manipulate a wheelchair or video game.

Fatigue: Fatigue is a subjective feeling that influences muscle activity and has a direct impact on MES. It should be seen when myoelectric is being used for HMI, particularly on long-term activities.

Chapter 9
Modelling and Analysis of Agent Behaviour

Ulrich Nehmzow
University of Ulster, UK

ABSTRACT

Mobile robotics can be a useful tool for the life scientist in that they combine perception, computation and action, and are therefore comparable to living beings. They have, however, the distinct advantage that their behaviour can be manipulated by changing their programs and/or their hardware. In this chapter, quantitative measurements of mobile robot behaviour and a theory of robot-environment interaction that can easily be applied to the analysis of behaviour of mobile robots and animals is presented. Interestingly such an analysis is based on chaos theory.

1 INTRODUCTION

1.1 Life Sciences and Robotics

One major aspect of the life sciences, psychology and ethology is the description and analysis of behaviour, for instance the behaviour of a foraging mammal or insect, following a specific trajectory, the navigating behaviour of migrant birds, or the search behaviour of desert ants.

For principled experimentation it would be of great interest to describe the observed behaviour quantitatively, i.e. to measure it. Qualitative de-

scriptions are only of limited use if the relationship between an independent variable, such as room temperature, is to be set in relation to a dependent variable, such as shape of trajectory taken. But how can behaviour be measured, how can it be described quantitatively?

It is also often of interest to predict behaviour, and to form and test hypotheses. If a set of experimental parameters is given, how is the agent going to respond to them? Faithful models of animal behaviour would give an answer to this question, but how could one obtain these models? Faithful models would not only answer this question, but due to their abstraction and reduction to relevant factors would also allow us to make

DOI: 10.4018/978-1-60960-021-1.ch009

further statements about the observed animal behaviour, perhaps to discover new factors that govern a particular behaviour.

Often it is interesting in ethology and related disciplines to compare the behaviours of individual animals. Is there a difference in the navigation behaviour between young and older, more experienced carrier pigeons? Is a particular observed behaviour typical for all animals of the same kind, or an individual deviation? Again, "measuring" behaviour could give an answer, but the "behaviour meter" has to be obtained first!

And finally, it is sometimes interesting to design behaviour, not only for machines like robots, but also in animals. If a certain animal behaviour is desired, which environmental parameters would lead to that behaviour? If a certain robot behaviour is the goal, which environmental parameters, as well as which sensors are required? Again, faithful modelling could provide an answer here.

At this point mobile robotics can be a useful tool for the life scientist. Mobile robots combine perception, computation and action, and are therefore in some aspects comparable to living beings. They have, however, the distinct advantage that their behaviour can be manipulated not only by changing environmental parameters, as in animals, but also by changing their control code or their morphology (e.g. placement of sensors).

In experiments at the University of Essex and the University of Ulster we have developed quantitative descriptions of mobile robot behaviour that can easily be applied to the analysis of animal behaviour. The same can be said for the modelling methods we have developed to form testable hypotheses about mobile robot behaviour, and model analysis methods. This work is described in detail in (Nehmzow, 2009).

1.2 Objectives of the Work Described in this Chapter

The overall objective of the work described in this chapter is to develop a theory of robot-

Figure 1. The behaviour of a mobile robot emerges from the interaction between the robot's control program (task), the morphology of the robot and the environment

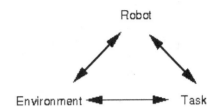

environment interaction, i.e. a description of all aspects that govern the behaviour of a mobile robot and their relationship to each other. Such a theory would allow to form testable hypotheses about a robot's behaviour, make predictions about the robot's behaviour and allow the principled design of robot behaviour, off-line and without using a real robot. This idea is discussed further in the following section 1.2.1.

A further objective of this chapter is to show in practical examples how such a theory and the tools it provides can be applied to the analysis of behaviour of mobile robots and animals. This is presented in section 2.

1.2.1 A Theory of Robot-Environment Interaction

The behaviour of a mobile robot is not only a result of the control program that is running on the robot, but emerges from the interaction between three components: the robot's morphology, i.e. placement and type of sensors, centre of gravity, aspects of the drive system *etc.*, the robot's control program, and the environment the robot is operating in. Figure 1 shows this relationship.

This fact can easily be visualised by the following thought experiment. Suppose a wall-following robot is not performing the wall-following action correctly. We can change the robot's behaviour by changing the control program – the

Figure 2. Behaviour as the result of an analog computation process

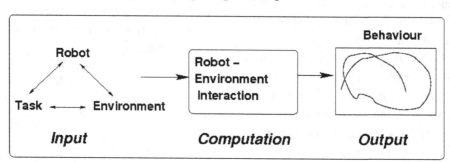

most frequently used approach in mobile robotics. But we could also change the environment, and achieve success that way. Placing reflective strips at crucial locations along the robot's path, or changing the position of some wall components slightly, might result in correct wall-following behaviour. Third, we can change the robot itself. Relocating the sensors, for example making them face the wall at a slightly different angle, or higher up or lower down, might result in correct wall-following. In fact, the robot is acting like an analog computer: behaviour (the output of the analog computation process) is computed as a function of the three inputs robot, task and environment (Figure 2).

It is the purpose of the theory of robot-environment interaction to determine what kind of computation is happening here, and to describe this computation quantitatively.

2 PART 1: TOOLS FOR BEHAVIOUR ANALYSIS AND THEIR APPLICATION

2.1 The "Behaviour Meter"

When we talk, rather colloquially, about a "behaviour meter", we mean a quantitative measurement that describes the robot's behaviour. In this section we will discuss how phase space analysis and chaos theory can supply such a quantitative description, and therefore serve as part of our desired theory of robot-environment interaction.

2.1.1 Description of Dynamical Systems in Physical and in Phase Space

Every dynamical system, i.e. every physical system that is time-dependent, can be described either in physical space, through differential equations, or in the so-called phase space, which is the space defined by the system's velocity and position along each degree of freedom it has. We will illustrate the concept of phase space by a simple example, the ideal pendulum.

The Phase Space of the Ideal Pendulum

An ideal pendulum, for instance, has one degree of freedom—the arc along which it is swinging, and the knowledge of the pendulum's position $\phi(t)$ and its velocity $\dot{\phi}(t)$ describes the motion of the pendulum fully, for all times t. The phase space of the ideal pendulum, therefore, is the two-dimensional space defined by $\phi(t)$ and $\dot{\phi}(t)$ and the physical motion of the pendulum can be fully described by the motion through that phase space.

It turns out that the phase space of the ideal pendulum is an ellipse (see Figure 3). As the pendulum swings backward and forward in physical space, its $(\phi, \dot{\phi})$ coordinates in phase space move from $(\phi_{max}, 0)$ through $(0, -\phi_{max})$, $(-\phi_{max}, 0)$ and $(0, \phi_{max})$ back to $(\phi_{max}, 0)$.

The trajectory ("orbit") through phase space - in the ideal pendulum's case the ellipse shown in Figure 3 - is referred to as the "attractor", because the dynamical system will follow that

Figure 3. Physical movement and phase space of an ideal pendulum. Arrows indicate how physical space and phase space relate to each other

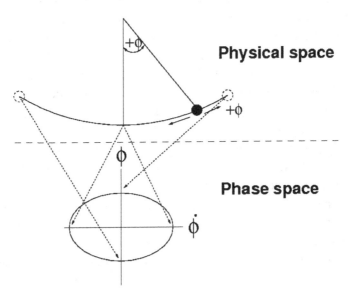

particular orbit, irrespective of initial conditions - it is "attracted" to that orbit through phase space.

2.1.2 Quantitative Descriptions of Phase Space

Why should we be interested in a system's phase space when looking to describe that system's behaviour quantitatively? The phase space of a system is a canonical description of any physical system's behaviour, meaning that *any* phase space can be analysed using the same methods. This is very useful in practice. Furthermore, there are various quantitative descriptors of a phase space, such as Lyapunov exponent, prediction horizon and correlation dimension: essentially the behaviour meters we are looking for.

2.1.3 Reconstruction of the Attractor

Our first step towards analysis of a dynamical system, then, is to reconstruct its phase space. Using theoretical considerations, this is not always as easy as it was in the case of the ideal pendulum. Fortunately, however, phase space can

be directly reconstructed from a time series $x(t)$ of observations of the physical system, through a method called time-lag embedding (Peitgen, Jürgens, & Saupe, 1992; Kantz & Schreiber, 1997; Abarbanel, 1996).

Suppose we measure some descriptive element of the agent's behaviour over time, e.g., the movement of the agent in $<x, y>$ space, obtaining two time series $x(t)$ and $y(t)$ The attractor $\mathbf{D}(t_n)$— the trajectory taken through phase space — can then be reconstructed through time-lag embedding as given in Eq. 1:

$$\mathbf{D}(t_n) = \left(x\left(t_n - (p-1)\tau\right), x\left(t_n - (p-2)\tau\right)..., x\left(t_n - \tau\right), x\left(t_n\right)\right),$$
(1)

with $x(t)$ being a sequential set of measurements (the time series), p being the embedding dimension, and τ being the embedding lag. In order to reconstruct the system's phase space through time lag embedding from an observed time series, therefore, two parameters need to be chosen: the embedding dimension p and the embedding lag τ.

Choosing the Embedding Dimension

There are three possible scenarios: (i) the embedding dimension chosen is too small to reconstruct the attractor, (ii) it is "just right", or (iii) it is too large. Only the first case will result in errors, because an attractor whose dimension is larger than the chosen embedding dimension cannot be fully unfolded, which means that points that are distant in time end up as close neighbours in phase space (because these neighbours in space are distant in time they are referred to as "false nearest neighbours"). If the embedding dimension is the same or just slightly larger than the dimension of the attractor, reconstruction is obviously no problem. If the embedding dimension chosen is much larger than the attractor's dimension, there is theoretically no problem—the attractor can be reconstructed perfectly—but there are practical (computational and accuracy) reasons why this case is undesirable. It is therefore preferable to select the minimum required embedding dimension.

An established method to determine a suitable embedding dimension is to use the false nearest neighbours method discussed in (M. B. Kennel, Brown, & Abarbanel, 1992). This method determines the number of false nearest neighbours (close in the reconstructed phase space, but far apart in time) in the reconstructed phase space – when this number is near zero, the attractor is properly unfolded and contains no self-intersections.

Choosing the Embedding Lag

The second variable to be chosen for the time lag embedding method is the embedding lag τ. The right choice of τ means determining that point at which the sample $x(t + \tau)$ of the observed time series contains new information, compared with $x(t)$. For example, if a slow-moving system is sampled at a high sampling frequency, the required τ is going to be large, because it will take many samples before $x(t + \tau)$ actually contains new information. On the other hand, if the sampling rate

is low with respect to the motion of the system, the required τ is going to be small.

First of all, there is a qualitative method to see the influence of increasing τ. For a small τ, $x(t)$, and $x(t+\tau)$ are essentially identical. If they are plotted against one another, therefore, all points would lie on the diagonal identity line. As τ increases, the reconstructed attractor will expand away from the identity line. This expansion gives us an indication about a suitable choice of τ (Rosenstein, Collins, & De Luca, 1994).

There are other ways to determine the point in time at which $x(t)$ and $x(t + \tau)$ contain different information. For example, (Kaplan & Glass, 1995) suggest a suitable τ is found when the autocorrelation between $x(t)$ and $x(t + \tau)$ has fallen below $e^{-1} = 0.37$.

2.1.4 Deterministic, Stochastic and Chaotic Systems

When asked to predict the motion of a model train, moving at a constant velocity on a circular track, one will have little difficulty and make only a very small prediction error. When asked to predict the outcome of a throw of a die, one can only resort to a random guess, or always predict the mean of all numbers on the die. The former system is deterministic and fully predictable; the latter is stochastic and not predictable. There is a third kind of system: it is deterministic rather than random, and yet not predictable, unless predictions concern the immediate, short-term future.

The weather falls into this category, so does the motion of a billiard ball, or the motion of a mobile robot in some cases. This kind of system is said to exhibit deterministic chaos. "Deterministic", because the system's behaviour is governed by deterministic laws such as the laws of motion, rather than randomness. "Chaotic", because it appears to behave like a stochastic system, and cannot be predicted for all times.

If it turns out that the observed robot behaviour is chaotic, then chaos theory can supply us with quantitative descriptions of robot behaviour, i.e. be used as the behaviour meter we need.

2.2 How to Determine if a System is Chaotic

Specifically, deterministic chaos is said to be present if the system under investigation exhibits these four properties:

1. The system's behaviour is (predominantly) deterministic.
2. The system's behaviour is bounded and stationary.
3. The system's behaviour is sensitive to slight changes in initial conditions.
4. The system's behaviour is aperiodic.

We are now going to discuss these four points in turn.

2.2.1 Testing for Determinism

All considerations presented in this chapter refer to deterministic systems, i.e., systems that are not mainly governed by stochastic (random) behaviour. We therefore need to establish first whether the time series $x(t)$ is deterministic, i.e., causally dependent on past events, or not. To do this, we use the following method, described by Kaplan and Glass (Kaplan & Glass, 1995, p. 324) (see also (M. Kennel & Isabelle, 1992)).

The underlying assumption in determining whether the signal is deterministic or not is that in a deterministic signal D of length $2T$ the first half of the signal should be usable as a "good" predictor for the second half—in a purely stochastic (random) system this assumption would not hold. In other words: if a model-based prediction of the system is perfect (zero prediction error), the system is purely deterministic. If there is some small prediction error, the system has a deterministic component, and if the model-based

prediction is only as good as a random guess, the system is not deterministic at all.

To find out whether the first half of D is a good predictor of the second half, we split the time series D into two halves of length T each, and construct an embedding $\boldsymbol{D}$ as given in Eq. 2:

$$\mathbf{D}(T+i) = \big[D(T+i), D(t+i-1), D(T+i-2)\big], \forall i = 3 \dots T. \tag{2}$$

In other words, we construct an embedding for the second half of the time series, using an time lag τ of 1 and an embedding dimension p of 3 (of course, one could use other values for τ and p).

To make a prediction of $D(t_k + 1)(T < t_k \le 2T)$, we determine the closest point $\mathbf{D}_c(t_c)(0 < t_c \le T)$ to $\mathbf{D}(t_k)$ in Euclidean distance, and select $D(t_c + 1)$ as the prediction of $D(t_k + 1)$. In this fashion all points of the second half are predicted (we always only predict one-step ahead). Figure 4 shows this.

We then compute the mean squared prediction error ϵ. In order to decide whether this error is "large" or "small", we set it in relation to the error ϵ_b of a baseline prediction of simply using the average of the first half of the signal as a prediction of the second. In a purely stochastic signal the ratio ϵ / ϵ_b 1 or larger than 1, indicating that the mean would have been the best prediction possible, and therefore that the system is nondeterministic. If, on the other hand, the ϵ / ϵ_b is smaller than 1, this indicates that the first half of the time series indeed is a good predictor of the second, and that therefore the time series has a deterministic component.

There is a second way of establishing whether the time series is deterministic (i.e., signal values are dependent of signal values in the past) or stochastic (i.e., signal values are independent from those of the past). By simply plotting $x(t)$ *vs.* $x(t-\tau)$ one sees visually whether there is a causal rela-

Figure 4. Prediction of the robot's movement along the x-axis, performing obstacle-avoidance behaviour

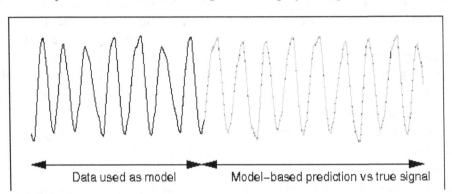

Figure 5. Return plots for random noise (left), wall-following behaviour (middle), and obstacle-avoidance behaviour (right). Wall-following and obstacle-avoidance both clearly have a deterministic element

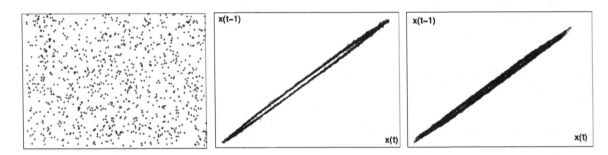

tionship between past and present signal values, or not. These plots are called return plots, and Figure 5 shows three examples.

2.2.2 Testing for Boundedness and Stationarity

The analysis of a dynamical system such as a mobile robot, interacting with its environment, is the attempt to identify and to quantify the statistical characterisations of that interaction. This means that if the statistical characterisations are not constant in time – non-stationarity – the methods for time series analysis presented in this chapter cannot be applied. Before analysing a signal using the methods outlined in this chapter, therefore, it is necessary to establish that the signal in question is stationary.

A signal is defined as stationary if it shows similar behaviour throughout its duration. "Similar behaviour" here is defined as having similar mean, standard deviation and autocorrelation structure throughout the time series (Kaplan & Glass, 1995, p.314) (Peña, Tiao, & Tsay, 2001, p. 29). In practice, real world signals often show constant mean and autocorrelation structure, but different variance throughout the time series. Such signals are sometimes referred to as "weakly stationary", but considered near enough the ideal of stationarity to be treated as stationary signals. The concept of stationarity is clearly relative to the highest frequency component in the data, meaning that a meaningful analysis can only be conducted if data is used that contains the longest period inherent in the data.

To test for stationarity, therefore, entails testing whether mean and standard deviation (we do not consider the autocorrelation function for the following tests) of different parts of the data differ significantly from one another or not.

A simple test to investigate this is to divide the time series into a number of sections, and to test whether the distributions underlying each section differ from one another or not. Because it is unknown whether the underlying distributions are normal or not (this can be tested, however, using the method described in (Nehmzow, 2009, p.42), a non-parametric test such as the non-parametric ANOVA (Kruskal Wallis test) discussed in (Nehmzow, 2009, p.63) is suitable.

2.2.3 Testing for Sensitivity to Initial Conditions

Consider the following thought experiment: you observe the motion of a physical system, a pendulum, say, in physical space. That motion corresponds to a motion in phase space, the "orbit." In the ideal pendulum's case, the orbit has the shape of an ellipse.

If you imagine starting the pendulum off at some location ϕ, and at the same time (it is a thought experiment!) at a point $\phi + \Delta$, where Δ is a small distance, we then have two motions through physical space and phase space that have started very close to each other. For some systems, such as the pendulum, these two motions will neither get further apart nor closer together over time; for other systems the two orbits will converge into one orbit; and for yet other systems the two orbits will diverge and very quickly be far apart from each other (this would happen, e.g., in the case of a billiard ball). The rate of divergence or convergence of two orbits that started infinitesimally close to each other describes one property of the attractor—it is known as the Lyapunov exponent.

Lyapunov Exponent and Chaos
One of the most distinctive characteristics of a chaotic system is its sensitivity to a variation in the system's variables: two trajectories in phase space that started close to each other will diverge from one another as time progresses; the more chaotic the system, the greater the divergence.

Consider some state S_0 of a deterministic dynamical system and its corresponding location in phase space. As time progresses the state of the system follows a deterministic trajectory in phase space. Let another state S_1 of the system lie arbitrarily close to S_0, and follow a different trajectory, again fully deterministic. If d_0 is the initial separation of these two states in phase space at time $t = 0$, then their separation d_t after t seconds can be expressed by Eq. 3:

$$d_t = d_0 e^{\lambda t}. \tag{3}$$

Or, stated differently, consider the average logarithmic growth of an initial error E_0 (the distance $|x_0 - (x_0 + \epsilon)|$, where ϵ is some arbitrarily small value and x_0 a point in phase space) (Peitgen et al., 1992, p. 709). If E_k is the error at time step k and E_{k-1} the error at the previous time step, then the average logarithmic error growth can be expressed by Eq. 4:

$$\lambda = \lim_{n \to \infty} \lim_{E_0 \to 0} \frac{1}{n} \sum_{k=1}^{n} \log \left| \frac{E_k}{E_{k-1}} \right| \tag{4}$$

λ (which is measured in s^{-1} or in bits/s, depending on whether the natural logarithm or a logarithm to base 2 is used) is known as the Lyapunov exponent.

For an m-dimensional phase space, there are $m\lambda$ values, one for each dimension. If any one or more of those components are positive, then the trajectories of nearby states diverge exponentially from each other in phase space and the system is deemed chaotic. Because any system's variables of state are subject to uncertainty, a knowledge of what state the system is in can quickly become unknown if chaos is present. The larger the positive Lyapunov exponent, the quicker knowledge about the system is lost. One only knows that the state of the system lies somewhere on one of the trajectories traced out in phase space, i.e., somewhere on the attractor.

The Lyapunov exponent is one of the most useful quantitative measures of chaos, because it will reflect directly whether the system is indeed chaotic, and will quantify the degree of that chaos. It therefore can serve as the "behaviour meter" we mentioned earlier. Also, knowledge of the Lyapunov exponents becomes imperative for any analysis on prediction of future states.

The question at this point, of course, is: how can the Lyapunov exponent be computed?

Estimation of the Lyapunov Exponent of a Time Series

One method to determine the Lyapunov of an attractor describing the behaviour of a physical system is to estimate it from an observed time series of the system's motion (Peitgen et al., 1992). However, the estimation of a Lyapunov exponent from a time series is not trivial, and often strongly dependent upon parameter settings. It is therefore not sufficient to simply take an existing software package, select parameter settings that seem appropriate, and compute the exponent. Instead, computations have to be performed for ranges of settings. There will usually be ranges of settings for which the computed Lyapunov exponent does not change—so-called scaling regions. These scaling regions indicate good parameter settings and reliable results.

There are a number of software packages available for the computation of Lyapunov exponents from a time series, e.g., (Kantz & Schreiber, 2003), discussed in (Kantz & Schreiber, 1997), (ANS, 2003) (discussed in (Abarbanel, 1996)) and (Wolf, 2003), based on (Wolf, Swift, Swinney, & Vastano, 1985).

The Prediction Horizon

The Lyapunov exponent, whose unit is bits/s, indicates the loss of information due to the chaotic nature of the signal as one predicts the signal for longer and longer times ahead. A perfectly noise-free and non-chaotic signal, with a Lyapunov exponent of zero, can be predicted for any length of time, without suffering from a prediction error. On the other hand, a chaotic signal cannot be predicted for arbitrary lengths of time, because with each prediction step uncertainty increases, until finally the prediction is no longer better than an educated guess. At this point "complete loss of predictability' has occurred, and all one is able to predict is that the system state is going to be somewhere on the attractor.

If, for example, you are asked to predict the temperature in your home town 10 minutes from now and to give an uncertainty indication of your prediction, you can make a fairly good prediction with a small uncertainty interval, by simply saying the temperature is going to be the same as it is at the moment. To predict 2 h ahead, you will be a little less certain, even more so for 12 h ahead, and eventually your prediction will on average be no better than an educated guess (e.g., looking up the mean temperature in a tourist guide).

The Lyapunov exponent can be used to compute when this complete loss of predictability will occur, i.e., when any model of your data is going to perform no better than an educated guess (we refer to this point in time as the "prediction horizon"). Bear in mind that the Lyapunov exponent is an averaged measure—there may well be situations in which predictions are better than educated guesses well beyond the estimated prediction horizon, but on average the prediction horizon estimated by the Lyapunov exponent is when complete loss of predictability occurs.

By way of illustration, let's assume you are measuring the pressure in some industrial plant, and you would like to predict what the pressure is going to be at some time in the future. Having logged a sufficiently long time series of pressure measurements in the past, you estimate the Lyapunov exponent to be 0.5 bit/s. The pressure sensor you are using has a resolution of 256 different pressure values, i.e., log(256)/log(2) = 8bit. This means that on average total loss of predictability will happen after 16 s. In other words: on average even a "gold standard" model of the pressure profile will do no better than an educated guess of the pressure after 16 s.

"Educated guess" here means a prediction of a value that is not based on specific past values, but that exploits global properties of the signal. It is the baseline against which we compare the prediction performance of our model (which does take past values into account). A simple baseline to use would be for each point $x(t_p)$ whose development over time we would like to predict to pick some other point $x(t_m)$ randomly from the time series, and to use the successors of $x(t_m)$ as predictions of the successors of $x(t_p)$.

As the Lyapunov exponent can be used to estimate that point in time at which an educated guess will produce as small a prediction error (on average) as a "gold standard" model, we should be able to do the reverse as well: determine that point in time at which we might as well make random guesses about the signal, and deduce the Lyapunov exponent from this.

The "gold standard" model we will use is the data itself. Splitting the data into two equal halves of length T each, we will use the first half of the data as a model of the second. This is a sensible procedure, because we only deal with deterministic data here, meaning that past data points are to some degree predictive of future data points.

In order to predict future data points $D(t_2), t_2 = T + 1 \ldots 2T$ of the second half of our data, we construct a three-dimensional embedding $\mathbf{D}(t_2)$ as given in Eq. 5, and search through the rst half of the data for the vector $\mathbf{D}(t_1), 1 \leq t_1 \leq T$ that is closest to $\mathbf{D}(t_2)$ (Euclidean distance):

$$\mathbf{D}(t_2) = \left[D(t_2), D(t_2 - \tau), D(t_2 - 2\tau) \right],$$

$$(5)$$

with τ the embedding lag, as described on page 5. This is a three-dimensional reconstruction of phase space, by now familiar to us.

We then predict the next k data points $D_m(t_2 + 1) \ldots D_m(t_2 + k)$ as given in Eq. 6:

$$D_m(t_2 + i) = D(t_1 + i), i = 1 \ldots k, 1 < t_1 < T, T < t_2 < 2T.$$

$$(6)$$

This prediction we will compare against our baseline, which states that we select a point $D_B(t_r), 1 < t_r < T$ at random, and predict $D_B(t_2 + i)$ as given in Eq. 7:

$$D_B(t_2 + i) = D_B(t_r + i), i = 1 \ldots k, 1 < t_r < T, T < t_2 < 2T.$$

$$(7)$$

The point at which the average model error $\overline{D_M - D}$ is the same as the average baseline error $\overline{D_B - D}$ is the prediction horizon.

2.2.4 Testing for Aperiodicity

Another main characteristic of a dynamical system exhibiting deterministic chaos is that the state variables never return to their exact previous values, i.e., the system's behaviour is not periodic. The trajectory in phase space lies on an attractor with a fractal dimension, a "strange" attractor. There is, however, variation from system to system in how close state variables return to previous values, and it is therefore desirable to quantify this degree of "proximity."

The measure to quantify the degree of aperiodicity is the correlation dimension d of the attractor. The correlation dimension indicates whether data is aperiodic or not, and to what degree: Periodic data has a correlation dimension of zero; increasingly more chaotic attractors have increasingly larger non-integer correlation dimensions (Kaplan & Glass, 1995, p. 321).

Determining the Correlation Dimension

The dimensionality of an attractor is related to its aperiodicity: the more aperiodic the dynamics, the greater the dimension of the attractor. In order to measure how periodic a trajectory through phase space is, one uses the following idea.

Suppose you take an arbitrary point on the attractor, draw a hypersphere of radius r—the so-called "correlation distance"—around that point, and count how many points of the attractor lie within that hypersphere. This number of points is referred to as the "correlation integral" $C(r)$, given by Eq. 8:

$$C(r) = \frac{\theta}{N(N-1)}, \qquad (8)$$

where θ is the number of times that $|\mathbf{D}(t_i) - \mathbf{D}(t_j)| < r$. i and j are two different times at which an embedding $\mathbf{D}$ is taken (Eq. 1), and r is the "correlation distance." $N(N-1)$ is obviously the maximum number of cases where $|\mathbf{D}(t_i) - \mathbf{D}(t_j)| < r$ is theoretically possible (the trivial case $i = j$ is excluded).

In a perfectly periodic attractor, e.g., in the case of the ideal pendulum, the correlation integral is not going to increase with increasing r. The slope $C(r)$ vs r is zero. In other cases, $C(r)$ is going to increase as one increases r. It is the slope of $C(r)$ vs r that is defined as the "correlation dimension" of the attractor.

In practical computations, this slope is often estimated using Eq. 9 (Kaplan & Glass, 1995, p. 354):

$$d = \frac{\log C(r_1) - \log C(r_2)}{\log r_1 - \log r_2}, \qquad (9)$$

where r_1 is chosen such that r_1 is roughly $\sigma/4$ (σ being the standard deviation of the time series),

and $C(r_1)/C(r_2) \approx 5$ (Theiler & Lookman, 1993).

Clearly, the computation of the correlation dimension is dependent upon the chosen embedding dimension p and the correlation distance r. To compute both p and d from the same process is an ill-defined problem, and the goal is to find a range of parameters p and r for which d is computed virtually identically (a so-called "scaling region"). In other words, one aims to find a region where the computation of the correlation dimension d, using Eq. 9, is not critically dependent upon the choice of embedding dimension p and correlation distance r.

To find such a scaling region, one can plot the correlation dimension d as a function of correlation distance r for all embedding dimensions p between, say, 1 and 10 (Kaplan & Glass, 1995, p. 323), and check whether there are regions for which the choice of r and p does not alter the computed correlation dimension d. That d is then our estimate of the dimension of the attractor.

2.3 Robotics Example

We now have all elements in place to describe the behaviour of a dynamical system, such as a robot or an animal performing a task in its environment:

1. Establish if the system is chaotic or not, as discussed in section 2.2. If it is chaotic, continue. If it is not, seek to find other quantitative descriptions of behaviour.
2. Reconstruct the system's phase space through time-lag embedding, as discussed in section 2.1.3.
3. Describe the system's phase space, and therefore its dynamical behaviour, through Lyapunov exponent (see section 2.2.3, page 9), prediction horizon (section 2.2.3, page 11) or correlation dimension (section 2.2.4, page 12).

Figure 6. The three different data sets (robot trajectories) used in this section for illustration of the use of chaos theory for behaviour analysis: set 1406 (wall-following), set 2406 (billiard ball obstacle-avoidance), and set 0507 (billiard ball obstacle-avoidance with off-centre obstruction). From set 1406 to 2406 robot and environment remained the same, but the task changed. Between set 1406 and 0507 robot and task remained the same, but the environment changed.

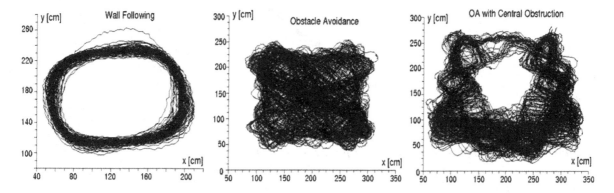

In the following, we will analyse the behaviour of three different robots. Between any two of these behaviours just one aspect of robot-task-environment (Figure 1) has changed, so that one can easily see how our three behaviour meters—Lyapunov exponent, prediction horizon and correlation dimension—can describe quantitatively how the behaviour changes if one element of the behaviour-governing components is changed.

The three behaviours we will investigate are the wall-following behaviour (data set 1406) shown in Figure 6 (left), the obstacle-avoidance behaviour (data set 2406) shown in Figure 6 (middle) and the obstacle-avoidance behaviour in a different environment (data set 0507), shown in Figure 6 (right).

2.3.1 Testing for Chaotic Properties

We will first discuss if these three signals are amenable to analysis using chaos theory, as discussed in section 2.2.

The return plots for the three behaviours (Figure 7) indicate clearly that all three behaviours have a strong deterministic component.

Furthermore, using the method outlined in section 2.2.2 and discussed in detail in (Nehmzow,

2009), we establish that our signals are bounded, meaning that chaos theory can be applied to their analysis: if they turn out to be sensitive to initial conditions and aperiodic, they are chaotic.

Phase Space Reconstruction

Figure 8 shows the reconstructed phase space of our three behaviours. Just looking at these reconstructions, one would say that the wall following behaviour is the most predictable, while the obstacle avoidance behaviour in the environment containing an off-centre obstruction is the least predictable and most complex behaviour. We will now check whether these conjectures can be supported by "hard numbers".

2.3.2 Estimating Both Lyapunov Exponent and Prediction Horizon

Figure 9 shows the data-based prediction error vs. the baseline prediction error (random guess) for predicting the robot's x-coordinate, executing the wall-following behaviour (data set 1406).

We can see that even for times exceeding 6 minutes (360 seconds) the databased prediction error remains smaller than an educated guess, giving a prediction horizon very close to infinity,

Figure 7. Return plots for wall-following behaviour (left), obstacle-avoidance behaviour (middle) and obstacle avoidance in an altered environment (right). All three clearly have a deterministic element, in that the x-position at time t is clearly a function of the x-position at time t – 1

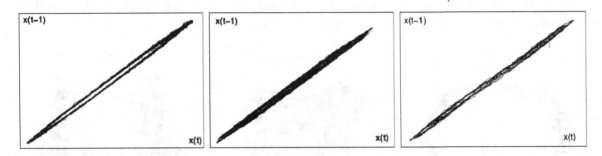

Figure 8. Phase space reconstruction of wall-following behaviour (left), obstacle avoidance behaviour in the open arena (middle) and obstacle avoidance behaviour in the environment containing an off-centre obstruction (right)

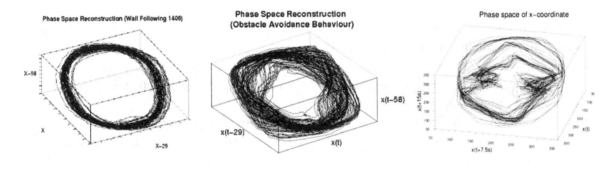

Figure 9. Prediction error and information loss for the wall-following behaviour (data set 1406)

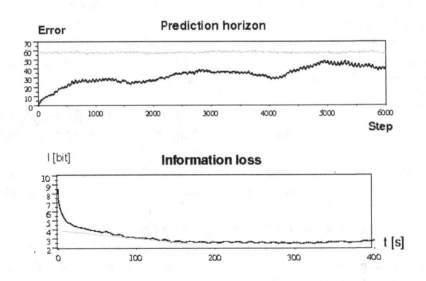

Figure 10. The prediction horizon of the x-coordinate of the obstacle-avoidance behaviour (set 2406) is around 72 s. As there are 7.9 bits of information available initially, this means the Lyapunov exponent is around 0.1 bits/s

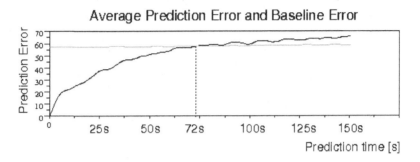

Figure 11. The prediction horizon of the x-coordinate of the obstacle-avoidance behaviour (set 0507) is around 80s. As there are 8.1 bits of information available initially, this means the Lyapunov exponent is around 0.1 bits/s

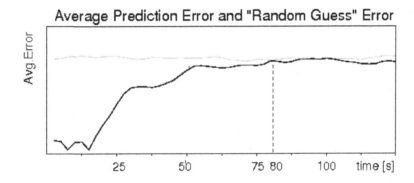

and a Lyapunov exponent close to zero. The wall-following behaviour is indeed very predictable, and not chaotic.

Figure 10 shows the data-based prediction error vs. the baseline prediction error (random guess) for predicting the robot's x-coordinate, executing the obstacle avoidance behaviour in the open arena.

It turns out that the robot's *x*-coordinate can be predicted better than random guessing up to around 72 s ahead, beyond that a random guess based on "where the robot usually is" is just as good. As the logging system is able to pinpoint the robot's *x*-position to one out of 239 different locations, we have $\frac{\ln 239}{\ln 2} = 7.9$ bits/s of infor-

mation initially, yielding a Lyapunov exponent of about 0.1 bit/s.

Adding an obstacle to the environment does not influence the Lyapunov exponent very much. For the obstacle avoidance behaviour in the environment containing an off-centre obstacle, the prediction horizon turns out to be around 80 seconds (figure 11), with an initial information of 8.1 bits this results in $\lambda \approx 0.1$ bits/s

2.3.3 Estimating the Correlation Dimension

Looking at the reconstructed attractors of the three behaviours (figure 8), we can intuitively say that the data set 1406 (wall following) has

Figure 12. Estimate of the correlation dimension of the wall-following behaviour. The dimension is between 1.2 and 1.6

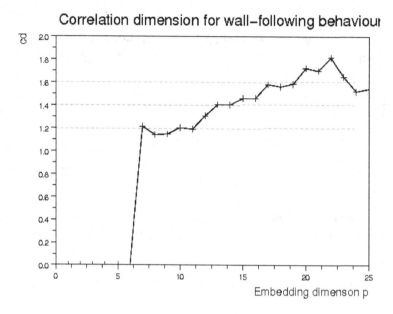

the "crispest" attractor, and should therefore have the lowest correlation dimension, while the attractor of behaviour 0507 (obstacle avoidance in an environment containing an obstacle) is the "fuzziest", and should therefore have the highest correlation dimension.

Indeed, wall following has a correlation dimension of about 1.4 (figure 12), while obstacle avoidance in an environment containing an obstacle has the highest correlation dimension (cd ≈ 2.9, figure 14) Obstacle avoidance in an empty environment lies in the middle, with a correlation dimension of about 2.5 (figure 13).

2.3.4 Summary and Conclusion of Part 1

Summary

As stated in section 1.2 the objective of the work described in this chapter is to develop a theory of robot-environment interaction, i.e. a quantitative, measurable and testable description of a robot's interaction with its environment.

The first step towards such a theory, we argued in section 2, is a quantitative description of the robot's behaviour, something we colloquially termed a "behaviour meter". We showed that chaos theory can provide such quantitative descriptions (section 2.1, (Nehmzow & Walker, 2005)), the process consists of the following steps:

1. Establish that the robot's behaviour is deterministic and bounded (section 2.2.2).
2. Reconstruct the phase space (the "attractor") of the robot's behaviour, using time-lag embedding of the robot's behaviour in physical space (section 2.1.3).
3. Compute the attractor's Lyapunov exponent (section 2.2.3), which is the first quantitative description of the robot's behaviour, and measures how sensitive the behaviour is to initial conditions.
4. Compute the prediction horizon (section 2.2.3), the second quantitative descriptor that states how predictable the robot's behaviour is, and
5. compute the correlation dimension (section 2.2.4), the third quantitative descriptor that

Figure 13. Estimate of the correlation dimension of the obstacle-avoidance behaviour in the empty environment. The scaling region around r/0.433 = 64indicates that the dimension is between 2.2 and 2.8

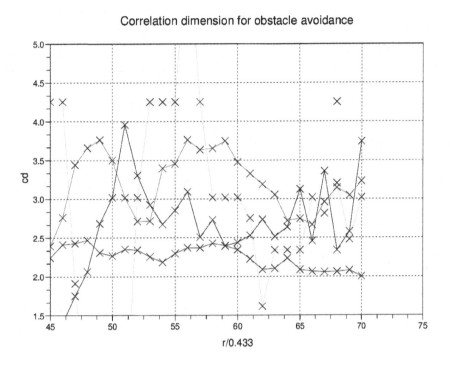

Figure 14. Estimate of the correlation dimension of the obstacle avoidance behaviour in the environment that contains an object. The scaling region in the centre of the image (r=0:537 = 38, indicated by the ellipse) shows the dimension is between 2.5 and 3.2

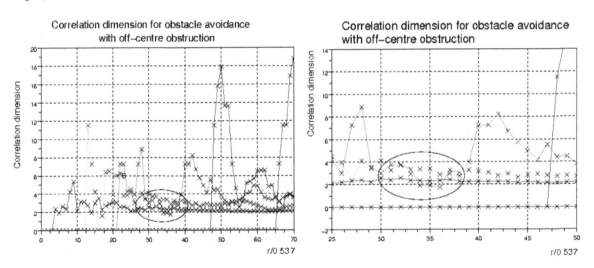

indicates how repeatable the robot's behaviour is.

Once we have these quantitative descriptors, we can carry out principled experiments. For instance, we said that the robot's behaviour emerges from the interaction between the robot's control program, its morphology and the environment it is operating in (figure 1). We can now measure the effect of changing *one* of the three components upon the robot's behaviour. Example: we measure Lyapunov exponent, prediction horizon and correlation dimension for a simple wall-following behaviour (figure 6, left), then change the behaviour to a "jumping billiard ball behaviour", leaving the robot and its environment unchanged (figure 6, middle), and measure the three again. We find that the latter behaviour is much less predictable, and revisits previously visited states far less frequently (Table 1).

Conclusion
Table 1 gives the results of the analyses of the three robot behaviours shown in figure 6. We can see that the wall-following behaviour is very predictable (prediction horizon near infinity, Lyapunov exponent near zero), and fairly periodic (low correlation dimension). This behaviour is not chaotic.

If we leave environment and robot unchanged, but change the control program to obstacle avoidance, the behaviour changes drastically: it becomes much less predictable (higher Lyapunov exponent, lower prediction horizon) and more aperiodic (higher correlation dimension).

If we now leave robot and program unchanged, but add an obstacle to the robot's environment, the behaviour's predictability remains largely unchanged, and the behaviour becomes a little less periodic. But basically, adding the obstacle does not change the behaviour of the robot much.

Applications
There are some useful applications of these behaviour measurements. For instance, if one wants to describe the robot's environment precisely in a publication—and of course here it does not matter whether the walls were red or green, but how the properties of the environment influenced the dynamical behaviour of the robot—one can take a simple, agreed standard program and a commonly used robot platform and run it in the environment. Lyapunov exponent, prediction horizon and correlation dimension then describe the environment. In this way one can therefore establish whether two laboratories use the same type of environment, from the robot's point of view.

3 PART 2: MODELLING BEHAVIOUR

In the second part of this chapter we will look at a second component of a theory of robot-environment interaction: modelling the behaviour under investigation, and analysing the *model*, rather than the original behaviour.

A robot's interaction with its environment is a highly complex, usually non-linear and often chaotic function of robot, task and environment (Nehmzow & Walker, 2003a, 2003b). To analyse

Table 1. Quantitative comparison ("measurement") of the three behaviours shown in figure 6

	Wall following	Obstacle avoidance (open environment)	Obstacle avoidance (env. with obstacle)
Lyapunov exp	*0.02 – 0.03 bit/s*	*0.1 – 0.13 bit/s*	*0.1 bits/s*
Prediction horiz.	*> 25 min*	*70 – 80 s*	*80 s*
Correlation dim.	*d ≈ 1.4 – 1.6*	*d ≈ 2.2 – 2.8*	*d ≈ 2.5 – 3.2*

such behaviour directly is difficult, often impossible.

However, if one had a faithful, yet transparent and analysable model of that behaviour, one could analyse the model instead. This is the motivation behind the work described in this section.

The most important aspect of the modelling process to support a theory is that the model must be transparent and analysable. Many popular modelling methods (e.g. artificial neural networks) are opaque, meaning that the analysis of the model is as hard as analysing the modeled behaviour. Instead of using opaque modelling methods, we therefore need to use transparent methods, such as for instance system identification (Pearson, 1999).

3.1 Transparent Modelling, Using System Identification

Figure 15 shows the fundamental modelling scenario: a system—for example a wall-following robot—receives certain input signals $\vec{u}$ (e.g. sensor readings) and responds to these signals with an output signal y (e.g. a turning speed).

The purpose of the system identication process is to find a transparent function $y(t) = f\left\{\vec{u}(t-k), y(t-l)\right\}, k = 0, 1, \ldots, l = 1, 2, \ldots$ The Armax (Auto-Regressive Moving-Average modelling with eXogeneous inputs) (Pearson, 1999) or Narmax (Non-linear Armax) (Chen & Billings, 1989) system identification processes can find such models.

3.1.1 The Armax Process

ARMAX (Auto-Regressive, Moving Average models with eXogenous inputs) is a discrete time series model, commonly used in system identification, that models the relationship between the independent input variable $\vec{u}(t)$ and the dependent output variable $y(t)$ as the linear polynomial given in Eq. 10:

$$
\begin{aligned}
y_t = & -a_1 y_{t-1} - a_2 y_{t-2} \ldots - a_i y_{t-i} \\
& + b_1 u_{t-1} + b_2 u_{t-2} \ldots + b_i u_{t-i} \\
& + d_1 e_{t-1} + d_2 e_{t-2} \ldots + d_i e_{t-i} + e_t,
\end{aligned}
\tag{10}
$$

with $\vec{u}$ being the input, y being the output e being the noise model and a_k, b_k and d_k being the model parameters that have to be determined. This process is shown in Figure 16.

The ARMAX model has been widely studied for system identification, detailed information can be found for instance in (Pearson, 1999; Box, Jenkins, & Reinsel, 1994).

The ARMAX model is limited, in that it is a linear model. However, as we will see, for many robotics modelling tasks a linear model is sufficient, and it is often possible to model input-output relationships such as sensory-perception-motor response.

The ARMAX system identification process is available in scientific programs such as Matlab (The MathWorks, 2009; Attaway, 2009) or Scilab (Scilab Consortium, 1989{2004; Gomez, 1999).

Figure 16. ARMAX system identification process

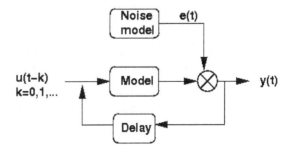

Figure 15. The fundamental simulation/computer modelling scenario

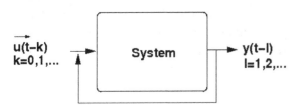

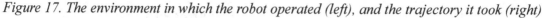

Figure 17. The environment in which the robot operated (left), and the trajectory it took (right)

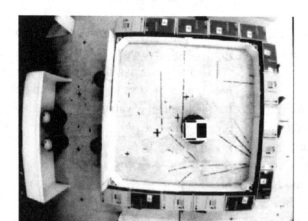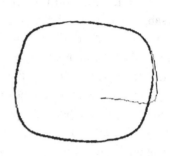

3.2 Modelling Robot Behaviour: Example

In this section we will show how the transparent Narmax system identification process can be applied to mobile robotics. The system under investigation is a *Magellan Pro* mobile robot, carrying out wall-following behaviour in the environment shown in figure 17.

Our goal here is to obtain a model $\omega(t) = f(\omega(t-1), \vec{L})$, where $\omega(t)$ is the robot's turning speed at time t, and $\vec{L}$ is a vector containing (some of) the robot's laser perception.

3.2.1 Basic Model (model 1)

As stated, our goal here is to obtain a model $\omega(t) = f(\omega(t-1), \vec{L})$. Without further analysis we do not exactly know which laser perceptions we will need to model this relationship we, so we choose $\vec{L} = \left[L_0, L_{30}, L_{60}, L_{90}, L_{120}, L_{150}, L_{180} \right]$, i.e. the robot's laser perception for angles $0°...180°$ which gives us a sparse coverage of the entire semicircle in front of the robot. Figure 18 shows these input and output signals.

The model obtained through the Narmax process is given in equation 11. (see Box 1)

To see whether or not this model represents the relationship between laser perception and robot turning speed accurately, we plot true turning speed vs. model-predicted turning speed (Figure 19).

Indeed, the model is faithful, and we will now aim to improve the model by analysing it.

3.2.2 Model Analysis Using Sensitivity Analysis Based on Entropy

The analysis of a linear model is relatively easy, and discussed in many textbooks. (Nehmzow, 2009, p.172) also contains a discussion of this.

For non-linear models, the analysis is harder, but can still be achieved by using for instance Sobol's Monte-Carlo method, who showed how the sensitivity of a function with respect to arbitrary groups of variables could be estimated (Sobol, 1993).

Here, we will estimate the importance (sensitivity) of model inputs using information-theoretic measures (entropy), by computing how much information about y is conveyed if given input u_i alone. This is the mutual information, which is computed as follows.

Figure 18. The seven laser input signals (left) and the robot's turning speed (right), used as output in the modelling example

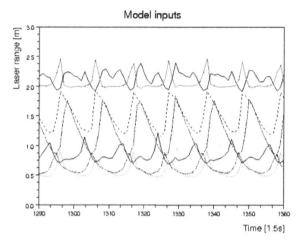
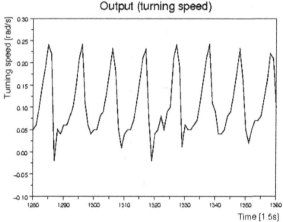

Computing the Mutual Information between Two Variables

The principle is this. We want to know how much information about output y (figure 15) is given if only input u_3, say, is given. To do this, we construct a contingency table such as the one shown in figure 2, by generating a random input vector $\vec{u}$, computing y, and incrementing a counter in field (a, b) of the contingency table, where a is the bin into which u_3 falls and b the bin into which y falls. The contingency table contains n × n bins ($n = 60$, say) to cover the entire range of values u_3 and

y span. Table 2 shows such a contingency table for $n = 5$.

For contingency table analysis the row totals N_r for each output bin, column totals N_{rc} for each input bin and the table total N are calculated according to Eqs. 12, 13 and 14 respectively. N_{rc} is the number of data points contained in the cell at row r and column c:

$$N_{r\cdot} = \sum_c N_{rc} \tag{12}$$

Box 1.

$$
\begin{aligned}
\omega(t) = {} & -1.2 + 1.70 * u(n,1) + 1.02 * u(n-1,1) + 0.33 * u(n,2) \\
& -0.04 * u(n-1,2) - 0.32 * u(n-1,3) - 0.05 * u(n,4) - .020 * u(n-1,4) \\
& -0.03 * u(n,5) + 0.38 * u(n,6) + 0.69 * u(n,7) - 0.34 * u(n-1,7) \\
& +0.004 * u(n,1)^2 - 0.001 * u(n-1,1)^2 + 0.003 * u(n,2)^2 + 0.083 * u(n,3)^2 \\
& +0.060 * u(n,4)^2 + 0.049 * u(n-1,4)^2 - 0.089 * u(n,7)^2 + 0.070 * u(n-1,7)^2 \\
& +0.14 * y(n-1) - 0.50 * u(n,1) * u(n-1,1) - 0.58 * u(n,1) * u(n,2) \\
& +0.05 * u(n,1) * u(n-1,2) - 0.57 * u(n,1) * (n,3) - 0.27 * u(n,1) * u(n,7) \\
& -0.30 * u(n-1,1) * u(n,6) + 0.35 * u(n-1,3) * u(n,4) - 0.21 * u(n,4) * u(n,6)
\end{aligned} \tag{11}
$$

Figure 19. True vs. model-predicted turning speed (model 1)

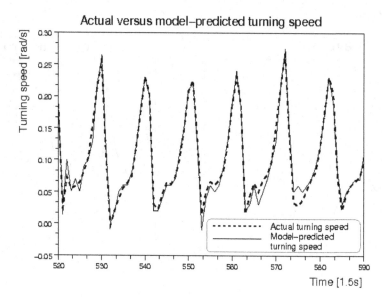

Table 2. *Example contingency table. The columns are the bins for the model input under analysis, the rows the bins for the model output*

Model input under analysis					
0	2	15	0	1	18
10	10	0	0	0	20
0	2	1	0	19	22
5	7	3	1	1	17
0	0	0	23	0	23
15	21	19	24	21	100

$$N_{.l} = \sum_{r} N_{rc} \qquad (13)$$

$$N = \sum_{r,c} N_{rc} \qquad (14)$$

The row probability $p_{r.}$, column probability $p_{.c}$ and cell probability p_{rc} can then be calculated according to Eqs. 15, 16 and 17:

$$p_{r.} = \frac{N_{r.}}{N} \qquad (15)$$

$$p_{.c} = \frac{N_{.c}}{N} \qquad (16)$$

$$p_{rc} = \frac{N_{rc}}{N} \qquad (17)$$

Computing Sensitivity

The sensitivity of y with respect to u_i is the mutual information $M(u_i, y)$, defined in Eq. 18. The higher $M(u_i, y)$, the more information about y is conveyed by stating u_i—in other words, the more sensitive is y with respect to u_i.

$$MI = H\left(u_i\right) + H\left(y\right) - H(u_i, y), \qquad (18)$$

with $H(u_i)$, $H(y)$ and $H(u_i, y)$ as defined in Eqs. 19 and 21.

$$H\left(u_i\right) = -\sum_{c} p_{.c} \ln p_{.c} \qquad (19)$$

$$H\left(y\right) = -\sum_{r} p_{r.} \ln p_{r.} \qquad (20)$$

Figure 20. Sensitivity analysis of model 1

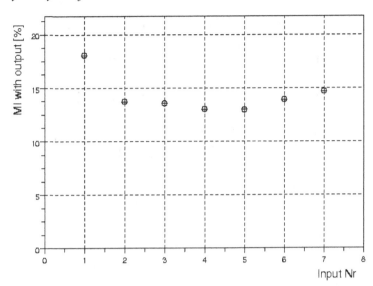

$$H\left(u_i, y\right) = -\sum_{r,c} p_{rc} \ln p_{rc} \qquad (21)$$

3.2.3 Sensitivity Analysis of Model 1

The result of a sensitivity analysis of model 1, as discussed in section 3.2.2, is shown in figure 20.

It shows that input 1 (laser 0 to the extreme right of the robot) is the most important input, but that all inputs are about equal in importance. However, guided by figure 20 we can postulate that inputs 1, 2, 7 and 8 should suffice to model the relationship between the robot's turning speed and sensory perception. We will investigate this hypothesis now.

3.2.4 Hypothesis-Led Improvement to Model 1 (Model 2)

For the second model, therefore, we use a 4-dimensional input $u = [L_0, L_{30}, L_{150}, L_{180}]$, and obtain the model given in equation 22 through the Narmax process.

$$
\begin{aligned}
\omega(n) = &+7.27 + 2.70 * u(n,1) - 7.00 * u(n,2) \\
&-4.56 * u(n,3) - 1.64 * u(n,4) - 0.03 * u(n,2)^2 \\
&+0.029 * u(n,3)^2 - 0.38 * u(n,4)^2 + 0.44 * u(n,1) * u(n,2) \\
&-1.25 * u(n,1) * u(n,3) - 0.21 * u(n,1) * u(n,4) \\
&+2.81 * u(n,2) * u(n,3) + 0.66 * u(n,2) * u(n,4) + 1.67 * u(n,3) * u(n,4)
\end{aligned}
$$

$$(22)$$

This model is indeed a lot simpler, and nevertheless a faithful representation of the robot's turning speed as a function of robot perception, as figure 21 shows.

The sensitivity analysis (figure 22) shows that all four sensors have about equal sensitivity, with sensor L_{30}, the second input component, being the most important.

Looking at figure 22, we can see that the laser sensors to the left and right of the robot suffice to model the robot's turning speed for wall-following, lasers that look forward are not needed.

3.3 Summary and Conclusion of Part 2

Summary

We argued in part 1 that in order to describe the behaviour of a mobile robot, interacting with its

Figure 21. True turning speed vs. turning speed predicted by model 2

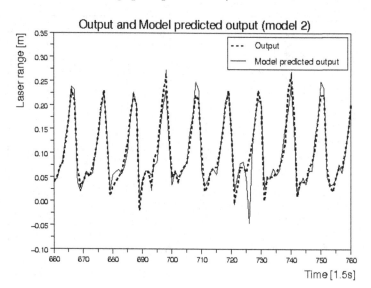

Figure 22. Sensitivity analysis of model 2

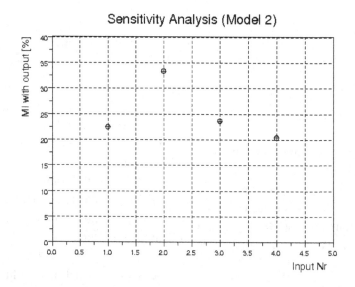

environment, one needs a precise and, most importantly, quantitative measurement of the robot's behaviour. We showed that chaos theory could be used for that purpose.

The argument in the second part of this chapter is that a feasible way of analysing and understanding robot behaviour would be to obtain a faithful mathematical model of the robot's behaviour, and then to analyse that model. For obvious reasons

the modelling method used has to be transparent, and we showed how a Narmax model such as the model for wall-following given in equation 11 can be used for the purpose.

In that model, we expressed the robot's turning speed $\omega(t)$ as a function of the robot's sensory perception $\vec{L}$, where $\vec{L}$ is constructed from the robot's laser range finder. We were able to show qualitatively that the model is faithful (figure 19).

Because the model is a mathematical equation, it is amenable to various analysis methods, and through sensitivity analysis (see section 3.2.2) we could show that it is possible to construct an even more parsimonious model (given in equation 22), which also represented $\omega\left(t\right) = f(\vec{L})$ faithfully (figure 21).

Conclusion

Even at this early stage of our research we have two very powerful tools at our disposal in transparent Narmax modelling and sensitivity analysis. These methods allow us, for instance, to program robots very efficiently – equation 22 can be used as a control program for a wall-following robot – or to analyse how the robot actually achieves a given task—the sensitivity analysis revealed that the wall-following robot in our example only uses side-looking sensors to perform its task (figure 20), and that the right-looking sensors are more important than the left-looking ones in this case of right-hand wall-following.

For the future more analysis tools will be needed to deepen our insight into robot-environment interaction. Ultimately, these methods will lead to very compact robot control programs, to faithful robot simulators, and to a theory of robot-environment interaction that will make testable and falsifiable hypotheses about robot behaviour.

4 SUMMARY AND CONCLUSION

4.1 Summary

The ultimate aim of the research presented in this chapter is to develop a theory of robot-environment interaction. By "theory" we mean a consistent framework of laws and quantitative descriptions that allows us to

- Describe the behaviour under investigation quantitatively, so that the descriptions can be evaluated and verified against the behaviour of the actual physical system,
- Form testable and falsifiable hypotheses,
- Describe robot-environment interaction in such a way that the behaviour can be described in simple terms, expressed in a "most compact" and common form, irrespective of which behaviour is being investigated,
- Analyse and predict the stability and reliability of the robot's behaviour.

In some sciences such theories are well developed. Control theory, for instance, fulfills the points mentioned above, and therefore allows off-line design of controllers that can be described through control theory.

Unfortunately, there is no theory yet in mobile robotics yet that fulfills all points mentioned above, and designing robot control code is still large achieved through initial "educated guesses" and subsequent refinement through trial-and-error. In the next section we discuss how a theory of robot-environment interaction might be established, and which future research is needed at this point.

4.2 Conclusion

4.2.1 Towards a Theory of Robot-Environment Interaction

We argue that a theory of robot-environment interaction requires at least these two fundamental components: i) *quantitative* descriptions of the behaviour, to allow quantitative comparisons between behaviours, and ii) *transparent* models of robot behaviour, to allow a canonical and simplified representation of the behaviour, in order to compare like with like.

Quantitative Descriptions of Robot Behaviour

We have shown in section 2.1 how chaos theory can be used to describe the behaviour of dynamical systems quantitatively:

1. Reconstruct the phase space, i.e. the attractor of the system under investigation (see section 2.1.3). This will allow the computation of three quantitative descriptors of this attractor, and therefore the behaviour underlying this attractor:

2. Lyapunov exponent (see section 2.2.3), which expresses in bits/s how much information about the system is lost over time. In other words, the Lyapunov exponent describes the predictability of the system, a large Lyapunov exponent means the system is very unpredictable and probably chaotic.

3. Prediction horizon (see section 2.2.3), which is that point in time at which any model-based prediction of the system's state is as accurate as an intelligent random guess. In other words, if at $t = 0$ we know everything about the system (position and speed of the robot), and the prediction horizon is 80 seconds, then after 80 seconds we cannot predict the robot's speed and position any more accurately than making an educated guess.

4. Correlation dimension (see section 2.2.4), which describes the aperiodicity of the attractor, or the periodicity of the behaviour. A high correlation dimension means that the robot hardly ever re-visits previously visited states (i.e. its behaviour is quite unpredictable), whereas a low correlation dimension means that the robot's behaviour repeats itself regularly.

The three measurements of robot behaviour—Lyapunov exponent, prediction horizon and correlation dimension—therefore form the first fundamental element of our theory of robot-environment interaction. Section 2.3.4 shows how these measurements are obtained in practice, using real robot data.

Transparent Models of Robot Behaviour

A second fundamental component of a theory of robot-environment interaction is, we argue, the ability to obtain canonical, precise, transparent and parsimonious models of robot behaviour, which simplify the description and analysis of the behaviour under investigation.

In section 3 we show how non-linear, autoregressive moving average modelling using exogeneous inputs (Narmax, (Chen & Billings, 1989)) can be used to obtain such models. Narmax models are polynomial functions that express the output variable y (for instance the turning speed of a robot) in terms of an input vector $\vec{P}$ (for instance, the perception of the laser scanner of the robot). They are transparent, hence analysable, canonical (the Narmax process produces under identical situations identical models), and they are parsimonious.

Analysis of Models of Robot Behaviour

One way of analysing non-linear input-output mappings is to determine how much an individual input influences the output. This is referred to as sensitivity analysis (Sobol, 1993) (Saltelli, Tarantola, & Campolongo, 2000; Saltelli, Campolongo, & Ratto, 2004; Saltelli, 2005), and discussed briefly in section 3.2.2 of this chapter, as well as in more detail in (Nehmzow, 2009).

4.2.2 Future Work

The work presented here raises some questions that will have to be addressed by future research. Here we give a brief indication of what this work entails.

Model Verification

In general, work has to be done to demonstrate that model and modelled behaviour do not differ from each other significantly. For instance, if a navigation behaviour is being investigated, in which the shape of a trajectory is relevant, methods of trajectory comparison from biology (Kohler & Wehner, 2005), (Nehmzow, 2009, p. 226-228) can be used very effectively.

Also, a closer connection between quantitative behaviour measures and Narmax behaviour modelling will ascertain that indeed model and original behaviour do not differ significantly from each other, with respect to predictability and periodicity.

Increasingly, statistical methods need to be used in mobile robotics research to establish *significant* differences between descriptors of robot behaviour, such as distributions of turning speeds or distances to a wall, say.

Advanced Analysis of Models of Robot Behaviour

Sensitivity analysis is but one way of analysing Narmax models, and other methods need to be developed. Methods investigating the stability and reliability (repeatability) of the robot's behaviour are of particular interest here.

ACKNOWLEDGMENT

I thank Esther Mondragón, for the valuable support and help in converting this document from Latex to.doc.

REFERENCES

Abarbanel, H. (1996). *Analysis of observed chaotic data*. New York: Springer Verlag.

Applied Nonlinear Sciences. (2003). *Tools for dynamics*. Retrieved from http://www.zweb.com/apnonlin: Applied Nonlinear Sciences.

Attaway, S. (2009). *Matlab: A practical introduction*. Burlington, Oxford: Butterworth Heinemann.

Box, G., Jenkins, G., & Reinsel, G. (1994). *Time series analysis*. Old Tappan, NT: Prentice-Hall.

Chen, S., & Billings, S. A. (1989). Representations of non-linear systems: The Narmax model. *International Journal of Control, 49*, 1013–1032.

Gomez, C. (1999). *Engineering and scientific computing with scilab*. Boston, MA: Birkhäuser.

Kantz, H., & Schreiber, T. (1997). *Nonlinear time series analysis*. Cambridge, UK: Cambridge University Press.

Kantz, H., & Schreiber, T. (2003). Tisean—nonlinear time series analysis. Retrieved from http://www.mpipkd-dresden.mpg.de/tisean.

Kaplan, D., & Glass, D. (1995). *Understanding nonlinear dynamics*. New York, NY: Springer Verlag.

Kennel, M., & Isabelle, S. (1992). Method to distinguish possible chaos from colored noise and to determine embedding parameters. *Physical Review A., 46*, 3111–3118. doi:10.1103/PhysRevA.46.3111

Kennel, M. B., Brown, R., & Abarbanel, H. D. I. (1992). Determining embedding dimension for phase-space reconstruction using a geometrical construction. *Physical Review A., 45*, 3403–3411. doi:10.1103/PhysRevA.45.3403

Kohler, M., & Wehner, R. (2005). Idiosyncratic route-based memories in desert ants, melophorus bagoti: How do they interact with path-integration vectors? *Neurobiology of Learning and Memory, 83*, 1–12. doi:10.1016/j.nlm.2004.05.011

Nehmzow, U. (2009). *Robot behaviour: Design, description, analysis and modelling*. London, UK: Springer Verlag.

Nehmzow, U., & Walker, K. (2003a). The behaviour of a mobile robot is chaotic. *AISB Journal, 1*, 373–388.

Nehmzow, U., & Walker, K. (2003b). Is the behaviour of a mobile robot chaotic? In Gregor Schöner and Ulrich Nehmzow (Eds.), *AISB Convention proceedings*. Aberystwyth, UK: AISB convention.

Nehmzow, U., & Walker, K. (2005). Quantitative description of robot-environment interaction using chaos theory. *Robotics and Autonomous Systems*, *53*, 177–193. doi:10.1016/j.robot.2005.09.009

Pearson, R. (1999). *Discrete-time dynamic models*. Oxford, UK: Oxford University Press.

Peitgen, H., Jürgens, H., & Saupe, D. (1992). *Chaos and fractals—new frontiers of science*. New York, Berlin, Heidelberg, London: Springer Verlag.

Peña, D., Tiao, G., & Tsay, R. (Eds.). (2001). *A course in time series analysis*. New York, NY: Wiley.

Rosenstein, M. T., Collins, J. J., & De Luca, C. J. (1994). Reconstruction expansion as a geometry-based framework for choosing proper delay times. *Physica D. Nonlinear Phenomena*, *73*, 82–98. doi:10.1016/0167-2789(94)90226-7

Saltelli, A. (2005). Global sensitivity analysis: an introduction. In Hanson, K. M., & Hemez, F. M. (Eds.), *Sensitivity analysis of model output*. Los Álamos, NM: Los Álamos National Laboratory.

Saltelli, A., Campolongo, F., & Ratto, M. (2004). *Sensitivity analysis in practice*. New York, NY: Wiley.

Saltelli, A., Tarantola, S., & Campolongo, F. (2000). Sensitivity analysis as an ingredient of modeling. *Statistical Science*, *15*(4), 377–395. doi:10.1214/ss/1009213004

Scilab Consortium. (1989-2004). *The Scilab programming language*. Retrieved from http://www.scilab.org.

Sobol, I. (1993). Sensitivity estimates for nonlinear mathematical models. *Mathematical Modelling and Computational Experiment*, *1*, 407–414.

The MathWorks. (2009). *Commercial Matlab website*. Retrieved from http://www.mathworks.co.uk/.

Theiler, J., & Lookman, T. (1993). Statistical error in a chord estimator of the correlation dimension: the rule of `five'. *Bifurcation and Chaos*, *3*, 765–771. doi:10.1142/S0218127493000672

Wolf, A. (2003). *Chaos analysis software*. Retrieved from http://www.cooper.edu/wolf/-chaos/chaos.htm.

Wolf, A., Swift, J., Swinney, H., & Vastano, J. (1985). Determining Lyapunov exponents from a time series. *Physica*, *16D*(3), 285–317.

KEY TERMS AND DEFINITIONS

Robot-Environment Interaction: The behaviour of a mobile robot is not only a function of the robot's control programme, but emerges through the interaction between the three components Robot-Task (program)-Environment. A change in any of these three will result in a change of robot behaviour. The term "Robot-environment interaction" is used to refer to this relationship.

Robotics as Science: A coherent body of hypothetical, conceptual and pragmatic generalisations and principles that form the general frame of reference within which mobile robotics research is conducted.

Robotics Theory: A coherent body of hypothetical, conceptual and pragmatic generalisations and principles that form the general frame of reference within which mobile robotics research is conducted.

Chaos Theory: A theory that describes dynamical physical systems, which are deterministic, stationary and bounded, sensitive to initial conditions, and aperiodic.

System Identification in Robotics: System identification is a general term to describe mathematical tools and algorithms that build dynamical models from measured data (Wikipaedia).

Quantitative Analysis of Robot Behaviour: The description of robot behaviour using measurements, rather than qualitative descriptions.

Chapter 10
Artificial Neural Systems for Robots

Phil Husbands
University of Sussex, UK

Andy Philippides
University of Sussex, UK

Anil K. Seth
University of Sussex, UK

ABSTRACT

This chapter reviews the use of neural systems in robotics, with particular emphasis on strongly biologically inspired neural networks and methods. As well as describing work at the research frontiers, the paper provides some historical background in order to clarify the motivations and scope of work in this field. There are two major sections that make up the bulk of the chapter: one surveying the application of artificial neural systems to robot control, and one describing the use of robots as tools in neuroscience. The former concentrates on biologically derived neural architectures and methods used to drive robot behaviours, and the latter introduces a closely related area of research where robotic models are used as tools to study neural mechanisms underlying the generation of adaptive behaviour in animals and humans.

INTRODUCTION

The idea of robots is rooted in the dreams and myths of old Europe and Ancient Greece in which mechanical men acted as either slaves or oppressors. Indeed the modern word 'robot' was introduced in Karel Čapek's 1921 play *R.U.R.* (Rossum's Universal Robots) which told of artificial men manufactured as a source of cheap labour on an isolated island. This often dark and dystopian play was a world-wide smash hit capturing the popular imagination as well as sparking much intellectual debate (Horáková and Kelemen 2007). In the process it helped forge the predominant image of robots that now permeates our culture – that of life-like artificial creatures.

In fact this image refers to what we now call autonomous robots. In contrast to machines that perform precise repetitive tasks ad nauseam (e.g. robots used in manufacturing production lines),

DOI: 10.4018/978-1-60960-021-1.ch010

autonomous robots are required to behave in an appropriate way in a very broad range of circumstances. Like biological creatures, their behaviour must be self-generated, making use of sensory information to moderate their responses to the world. With these animal connotations, it is no surprise that when simple autonomous robots became a reality in the mid 20th century, researchers looked to natural nervous systems for inspiration as they developed their early control systems.

The huge advances in our understanding of real neural networks over the past few decades, coupled with our development of increasingly sophisticated artificial varieties, has led to significant growth in research on artificial neural systems in robotics. This chapter concentrates on the use of explicitly biologically inspired artificial neural networks in autonomous robotics, reviewing key applications and forms of neural system used. There are a variety of drives underlying such work, ranging from straightforward engineering motivations – the desire to build better, smarter machines – to purely scientific ones, particularly in the use of robots as tools to study mechanisms underlying the generation of adaptive behaviour in animals and humans. Often varying degrees of both these motivations are present in any particular project. This chapter will highlight work that falls at the two extremes of this spectrum, as well as much that rests in between.

The next section gives some historical background to the area in order to motivate the remainder of the chapter. Following that, there are two major sections that make up the bulk of the paper: one on the application of artificial neural systems to robot control, and one on the use of robots as tools in neuroscience. The chapter closes with a general discussion of prospects for such research. There is not enough space to give a comprehensive review of all major work in the area, instead we have concentrated on a few important topics that give a good overall flavour of research in the field. For more detailed coverage see e.g. Siciliano and Khatib (2008), Webb and Consi (2001), Ayers et al.

(2002), Bekey (2005), Bekey and Goldberg (1993) and Floreano and Mattiussi (2008).

HISTORY

Despite the construction of many ingenious mechanical automata over the centuries (including chess playing Turks and flatulent ducks (Wood 2003)), it was not until the 1930s that devices recognizable as robots (in the present day sense of the term) appeared. Early mobile robots, such as Thomas Ross's 'robot rat', completed in 1935, were designed for narrowly focused single behaviours (often maze running) and employed highly specific mechanisms to achieve their intended task (Cordeschi, 2002). These 'artificial animals' inspired what were probably the very first examples of more general mobile autonomous robots – W. Grey Walter's tortoises (Walter, 1950). These robots were also the first to employ an early form of neural network as their artificial nervous system. They were born out of the cybernetics movement, a highly interdisciplinary endeavour – drawing together pioneers of computing and modern neuroscience – which was the forerunner of much of contemporary AI and robotics, and the origin of artificial neural networks and evolutionary computing, as well as control and information theory (Boden, 2006; Husbands et al., 2008).

In 1949, Walter, a neurologist and cyberneticist based at the Burden Institute in Bristol, UK, who was also a world leader in EEG research, completed a pair of revolutionary machines he called 'tortoises'. The devices were three-wheeled and sported a protective 'shell' (see Figure 1). They had a light sensor, touch sensor, propulsion motor, steering motor, and an electronic valve (vacuum tube) based analogue 'nervous system'. Whereas earlier machines such as Ross's were constrained to run on rails, the tortoises could roam freely around their environment. Walter's intention was to show that, contrary to the prevailing opinion at the time, even a very simple nervous system (the tortoises had two artificial neurons) could generate complex behaviour as long as there was a sufficiently large number of possible interaction patterns between the neurons (Walter, 1950). By studying whole embodied sensorimotor systems acting in the real world, he was pioneering a style of research that was to become very prominent in AI many years later, and remains so today (Brooks, 1999; Holland, 2003). Between Easter 1948 and Christmas 1949, he built the first tortoises, Elmer and Elsie. They were rather unreliable and required frequent attention. In 1951, his technician, Mr. W.J. 'Bunny' Warren, designed and built six new tortoises to a much higher standard. Three of these tortoises were exhibited at the Festival of Britain in 1951; others were regularly demonstrated in public throughout the 1950s. The robots were capable of phototaxis (steering towards a light source), by which means they could find their way to a recharging station when they ran low on battery power. He referred to the devices as *Machina speculatrix* after their apparent tendency to speculatively explore their environment.

Walter was able to demonstrate a variety of interesting behaviours as the robots interacted with their environment and each other. In one experiment he placed a light on the 'nose' of a tortoise and watched as the robot observed itself in a mirror. "It began flickering," he wrote. "Twittering, and jigging like a clumsy Narcissus." Walter argued that if this behaviour was observed in an animal it "might be accepted as evidence of some degree of self-awareness." (Walter, 1953). The behavioural complexity was partly due to the fact that the neural circuitry exploited the non-linear properties of the electronic valves and photoreceptors such that very bright lights were repellent when the battery charge was high and attractive when it was low, thus allowing the tortoise to return to its hutch (marked by a bright light) when it needed to recharge. Interactions with obstacles and gradients produced oscillatory signals that powered alternating pushing and

Figure 1. Grey Walter watches one of his tortoises push aside some wooden blocks on its way back to its recharging hutch. Circa 1952

withdrawal movements that resulted in small objects being pushed out of the way while large obstacles and gradients were avoided. Walter developed a later generation of robots that were equipped with extended, although still relatively simple, artificial nervous systems capable of exhibiting learning behaviour: a conditioned reflex (Walter, 1951). With this work Walter demonstrated, for the first time, an artificial neural mechanism that generated interesting learning behaviour in an embodied autonomous sensorimotor system. While Walter's motivations were primarily scientific – he used the robots to investigate ideas about neural processing in brains – potential practical applications of such technology were not lost on him and his cybernetics colleagues. For instance, Thomas Gold recalled discussion of possible future uses at a meeting of the Ratio Club, a London-based cybernetics dining club (Husbands and Holland, 2008), including grass cutting and house cleaning – robot applications that have both come to pass.

Walter's robots became very famous, featuring in newsreels, television broadcasts and numerous newspaper articles, and did much to generate interest in robotics and artificial neural systems. They have been acknowledged as a major early influence by many leading robotics and neural network researchers of later generations.

The appearance of Walter's (1950; 1951) *Scientific American* articles on his tortoises generated a global wave of interest in building artificial animals. Prominent examples include Angyan's *Machina reproducatrix*, built in Hungary in 1955. This descendent of the tortoises used more sophisticated neural circuitry and, responding to visual and acoustic stimuli, demonstrated a range of more complex conditioning and habituation learning behaviours (Angyan, 1959).

From these biologically inspired, and rather exploratory, beginnings, the focus of robotics began to turn to more immediately practical applications towards the end of the 1950s. The main emphasis was on the development of robot arms, particularly for use on production lines. Hence developers of robot control systems started to focus on methods based on solutions to equations describing the inverse-kinematics problem (finding the angle through which the joints should be rotated to achieve a specific position of the arm's end effector). These solutions usually rely on precise knowledge of the robot's mechanics and its environment. Industrial robots are programmed to repeat precise manipulations, such as welding or paint spraying, over and over again. Although they make use of sensors to help control their movements, their behaviour cannot be said to be in any way intelligent – if the car on the production line is misaligned or is not the expected shape, generally the robot cannot react to the new set of circumstances, it can only repeat its pre-programmed movements. While these limitations are manageable in the highly controlled environment of a production line, they become

problematic if a robot is to be used in less structured and predictable environments – for instance in exploration applications. In such scenarios, the robot, usually a mobile free-roaming device, must interact with its environment in a much more intelligent and adaptive way in order to cope with a noisy, dynamic world. The control methods used for industrial arms are no longer sufficient.

The next phase in robot evolution, which attempted to address this issue by developing control methods for autonomous systems, ran from the mid 1960s to the mid 1980s. It is typified by pioneering work at the Artificial Intelligence Center at SRI International (then Stanford Research Institute) on a mobile robot system nicknamed 'Shakey'. The robot had a vision system which gave it the ability to perceive and model its environment in a limited way. Shakey could perform tasks that required planning, route-finding, and the rearrangement of simple objects. It became a paradigm case for early AI driven robotics. The robot accepted goals from the user, planned how to achieve them and then executed those plans (Nilsson 1984). The overall processing loop had at its heart the sequence of operations shown in Figure 2. Here robot intelligence is functionally decomposed into a strict pipeline of operations. Central to this view of intelligence is a single explicit internal model of the world which must be extended, maintained and constantly referred to in order to decide what to do next. In Shakey's case, as in much of AI at the time, the world model was defined in terms of formal logic. The robot was provided with an initial set of axioms and then perceptual routines were used to build up and modify the world model based on sensory information, particularly from the robot's vision system.

Even though Shakey and robots like it were controlled by computers the size of a room, the demands of the sequential processing model they employed (Figure 2) were such that they could not operate in real-time. They would often take tens of minutes or even hours to complete a single task such as navigating across a room avoiding

Figure 2. Pipeline of functionally decomposed processing used in most classical AI robotics (after Brooks 1986)

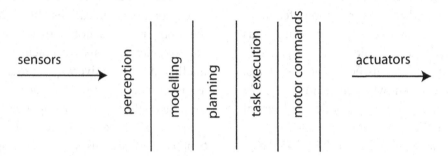

obstacles. By the mid 1980s a number of leading researchers from the main AI robotics centres were becoming more and more disillusioned with the approach.

Hans Moravec, an influential roboticist who had carried out important work on the Stanford Cart, a project similar in spirit and approach to SRI's Shakey and which ran at about the same time, summed up such feelings:

"For the last fifteen years I have worked with and around mobile robots controlled by large programs that take in a certain amount of data and mull it over for seconds, minutes or even hours. Although their accomplishments are sometimes impressive, they are brittle - if any of many key steps do not work as planned, the entire process is likely to fail beyond recovery." (Moravec 1987, p.1)

Moravec goes on to point out how this is in strange contrast to the pioneering work of Grey Walter and the projects that his tortoises inspired; such early robots' simple sensors were connected to their motors via fairly modest circuits and yet they were able to behave very competently and 'managed to extricate themselves out of many very difficult and confusing situations' without wasting inordinate amounts of time 'thinking'.

The limitations of traditional AI had become evident in many other areas as well as in robotics. The major problem was brittleness – an inability to deal with circumstances even slightly outside the boundaries of the programmed-in knowledge of the system, leading to poor performance in the face of noise and uncertainty. This was largely a consequence of traditional AI ignoring work on learning and adaptation (Husbands et al., 2008). Hence biologically inspired areas, with their roots in cybernetics, such as neural networks, adaptive systems, artificial evolution, behaviour-based robotics, artificial life, and the related field of probabilistic robotics, swept to the fore in the mid 1980s and have remained dominant ever since (Floreano and Mattiussi, 2008).

Artificial neural networks became particularly popular in robotics because of a number of key properties, listed below, that had potential to overcome the weaknesses of traditional AI methods.

- They could generalise and deal with incomplete data.
- They could handle noisy data.
- They could, at least in theory, adapt to new circumstances.
- By employing parallel distributed processing they offered a potentially more robust and efficient alternative to the sequential pipeline model of traditional AI.

The closely related area of computational neuroscience also came out of the shadows at about this time. Work in this field, particular the modelling of behaviour generating circuits in the nervous system, also became a rich seam of inspiration

Figure 3. Left: Genghis, one of the robots produced by Brooks' group at MIT to demonstrate the efficacy of the subsumption architecture. Right: schematic of the control network. Each box represents an AFSM, those without bands on top are repeated six times, those with solid bands are not repeated and represent 'central' control units, those with striped bands are repeated twice and are specific to particular legs. Reproduced with permission

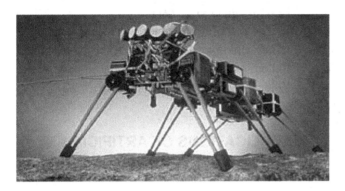
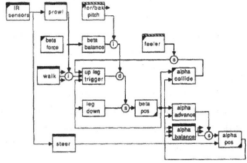

to roboticists for similar reasons: animals can do all the things traditional AI could not.

Key early successes from this era include various applications of supervised learning techniques to develop neural network controllers for a variety of robots, from industrial arms (Lewis et al., 1999) to Pomerleau's famous autonomous van that drove around the campus of Carnegie Melon University in the late 1980s (Pomerleau, 1991). In the latter case a feedforward network was trained using a backpropagation algorithm to drive the van. The system, known as ALVINN, using input from a camera, was able to learn in under 5 minutes to autonomously control the vehicle by watching the reactions of a human driver. ALVINN was successfully trained to drive in a variety of circumstances including single-lane paved and unpaved roads, and multilane lined and unlined roads, at speeds of up to 20 miles per hour. Although the system used a standard backpropagation scheme, results were impressive – in no small part due to the clever on-the-fly training scheme employed, which involved 'additional' scenarios generated by deliberately shifting the input images to simulate poor driving. Such a scheme produced robust, general controllers that were far superior to those previously achieved using traditional methods.

This work also highlighted the fact that, given its inherently noisy nature, robotics applications required carefully thought-out input and output representations and training regimes.

A more biologically inspired, and highly influential, example from the mid 1980s is Brook's development of the hexapod robot Ghengis (Brooks, 1989). The body and control system for the robot, shown in Figure 3, were directly inspired by insect neuroethology. A network of 57 augmented finite state machines (AFSMs), including six repeated sub-networks (one for each leg), enabled the robot to walk over rough terrain and follow a person located by its infrared sensors. The networks can be thought of as a variety of hardwired dynamical neural network. They provided highly distributed efficient control and coordination of multiple parallel behaviours.

At the heart of Brooks' approach was the idea of behavioural decomposition as opposed to traditional functional decomposition. The overall control architecture involves the coordination of several loosely coupled behaviour generating systems all acting in parallel. Each has access to sensors and actuators and can act as a standalone control system, and usually involved tightly coupled sensorimotor feedback loops going through the environment. Each such layer was thought of as a *level of competence*, with the simpler competences at the bottom of a vertical decomposition and the more complex ones at the top. Brooks' called his concrete implementation of this idea the subsumption architecture (Brooks, 1986), of which Ghengis's control system is an example. Higher level layers are able to subsume the role of lower levels by taking over control of their motor outputs. The architecture can be partitioned at any level with the layers below always forming a complete control system. The idea was to allow overall competence to be increased by adding new behaviour generating layers without having to change lower levels. Brooks' team at MIT developed a wide variety of robots using these principles (Brooks, 1999), demonstrating an efficient and robust alternative to the monolithic representation and reasoning hungry approaches of traditional AI. They are the ancestors of the highly successful commercial robots, such as the Roomba vacuum cleaner, produced by iRobot, the company Brooks and colleagues set up to exploit their work.

As well as being an important example of neural-like control in robotics, the philosophy underlying Brooks work was crucial in pushing biologically inspired robotics back to centre stage for the first time since the heyday of cybernetics. Echoing the earlier sentiments of Grey Walter, he pointed out that the major part of natural intelligence is closely bound up with the generation of adaptive behaviour in the harsh unforgiving environments most animals inhabit. Hence he proposed that just as real creatures should be the focus of inspiration for autonomous robotics, the investigation of complete autonomous sensorimotor systems – 'artificial creatures' – was the most fruitful way forward in developing theories of intelligence. This triggered a movement, still strong today, involving collaborations between computer scientists, neuroscientists and roboticists in developing both robotic applications and embodied models of neural mechanisms underly-

ing behaviour. Another notable early example of such work was Arkin's behaviour-based robotics (Arkin, 1998) which built on Arbib's schema theory, developed as a high-level top-down way of modelling brain function and architecture (Arbib 1972, Arbib et al., 1997).

The rest of this chapter will review a number of key examples of work from the bio-inspired and bio-modelling robotics that originated in the 1980s movement outlined above.

APPLICATIONS OF ARTIFICIAL NEURAL SYSTEMS IN ROBOTICS

There is now a large body of work in building neural control systems for robots that takes explicit inspiration from biology. Examples range from complex motor coordination to visually guided navigation in large scale environments. This section highlights some important examples from this range but of course cannot cover the whole field. For further reading in this area see for instance chapters 56-64 of Sciliano and Khatib (2008), Bekey (2005) and Ayers et al. (2002).

Locomotion

Locomotion in legged robots, which involves the coordination of multiple actuators, is a non-trivial matter. Traditional methods, often employing finite state machine based central control systems using parameterised rules governing the relative timing of individual leg movements (e.g. Laszlo et al. 1996), usually result in rather unresponsive, 'clunky' motion involving limited gait patterns. Insects, with their wide range of gaits and robust locomotion behaviours, generated despite rather limited neural resources, have thus become an important source of inspiration for roboticists interested in walking machines. Brooks' distributed dynamical network controller for Ghengis, described in the previous section, was an early example of an insect- inspired walking controller.

Figure 4. LEFT: schematic diagram of a distributed neural network for the control of locomotion as used by Beer et al. (1989). Excitatory connections are denoted by open triangles and inhibitory connections are denoted by filled circles. C, command neuron; P, pacemaker neuron; FT, foot motor neuron; FS and BS, forward swing and backward swing motor neurons; FAS and BAS, forward and backward angle sensors. Reproduced with permission. RIGHT: generalised architecture using a fully connected dynamical network controller for each leg (A), cross coupled as shown (B). Solid lines are cross body connections, dashed lines are intersegmental connections

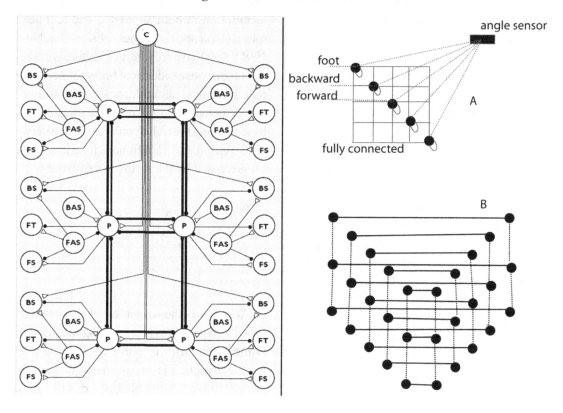

Figure 4 illustrates another very influential strand of work originating in the late 1980s: the neural architecture introduced by Beer et al. (1989) to control walking in a hexapod robot.

This architecture was based on prior studies of the neural basis of locomotion in cockroaches (Pearson, 1976) and generalisations and extensions of it have been much used ever since. As with Ghengis, a key lesson taken from insect locomotion was that of distribution of control.

"Rather than concentrating responsibility for locomotion in one centralized system, animals distribute this responsibility across the physical

characteristics of the legs themselves, endogenous and reflexive circuitry local to each leg, and additional circuitry that interconnects these local leg controllers. Rather than having a single module directing the movements of the legs in a master/slave fashion, in a distributed locomotion controller stable gaits arise from the cooperative interactions between many different components." (Beer et al., 1997 p.33)

As shown in Figure 4(left), each leg has a local control circuit consisting of a pacemaker neuron (P), two sensory neurons that signal when the leg has reached an extreme forward (FAS) or backward

(BAS) angle, and three motor neurons responsible for controlling the state of the foot (FT), and the rate with which the leg swings forward (FS) and backward (BS). Each of these leg controllers receives identical excitation from a command neuron (C). The model neurons were all implemented as leaky integrators with a linear activation function. Each pacemaker neuron produced a rhythmical bursting output whose frequency depended on its overall level of excitation. In legged locomotion, the movement of each leg can be divided into a stance phase, in which the leg is providing support and propelling the body, and swing phases, in which the leg is lifted from the ground and swinging through the air in order to begin another stance phase. With this architecture the basic generation of leg movement works as follows. The foot motor neuron is active by default and excitation from the command neuron activates the backward swing motor neuron, producing a stance phase. Periodic bursts of activity from the pacemaker neuron, partly controlled by sensory feedback from leg angle sensors, inhibit the foot and backward swing motor neurons and excite the forward swing motor neuron, thus producing a swing phase. The command neuron sets the overall speed of locomotion by controlling both the frequency of pacemaker bursts and the rate at which the leg swings backward during the stance phase. To produce locomotion the individual leg movements must be properly coordinated. This was accomplished by two mechanisms. First, mutually inhibitory connections between the pacemaker neurons of adjacent leg controllers prevent adjacent legs from stepping at the same time. This mechanism was sufficient to producing a stable tripod gait at relatively high walking speeds. At lower speeds, a mechanism based on slightly lowering the natural frequency of the rear legs, so that the rear pacemakers entrain the middle and front pacemakers in a metachronal sequence, was also needed (Beer et al., 1997). This latter mechanism is a good example of how interplay

between neural control and embodied physical processes can give rise to the overall behaviour (Pfeifer and Bongard, 2007). This architecture was successfully used to generate locomotion in simulations and on a real robot (Beer et al., 1997).

A generalised version of the architecture, as shown in Figure 4 (right), was also used to produce locomotion in both simulated and real hexapod robots (Beer and Gallagher, 1992; Gallagher et al., 1996). This version of the architecture is interesting because it uses an identical fully-connected recurrent dynamical network for local control of each leg, dispensing with explicit pacemaker neurons by exploiting the rich dynamics of such networks. Each neuron was a continuous time leaky integrator governed by the following equations.

$$\tau_i \frac{dy_i}{dt} = -\gamma_i + \sum_{j=1}^{N} \omega_{ji}\sigma(y_j) + I_i(t)$$

$$\sigma(y_j) = \frac{1}{1 + e^{-(y_j + \theta_j)}}$$

Where y is the activation of a neuron (sometimes interpreted as representing the mean membrane potential), τ is a time constant, ω is a connection weight, I is an external input (e.g. from a sensor), θ is a neuron bias, and σ is of course the sigmoid function. Each leg was controlled by a fully-connected network of five such neurons, each receiving a weighted sensory input from that leg's angle sensor as shown in Figure 4. The parameters of the symmetrically coupled architecture were set using an evolutionary robotics methodology (Nolfi and Floreano, 2000; Floreano et al., 2008) such that the connection weights and neuron time constants and biases were under the control of a genetic algorithm. Networks were produced that successfully generated a range of efficient tripod gaits for walking on flat surfaces.

The work of Beer and colleagues inspired a great deal of other evolutionary robotics research on walking machines using similar networks and architectures. For instance, Jakobi (1998) evolved modular controllers based on Beer's recurrent network architecture to control an eight-legged robot as it engaged in walking about its environment, avoiding obstacles and seeking out goals. The robot could smoothly change gait, move backward and forward, and even turn on the spot. Kodjabachian and Meyer (1998) extended Beer's architecture by incrementally adding other behaviour generating networks, through an evolutionary process, developing more sophisticated locomotion behaviours that incorporated target seeking and obstacle avoidance. More recently, related approaches have been successfully used to evolve controllers for more mechanically sophisticated robots such as the Sony Aibo (Tllez et al. 2006). In the last few years there has also been successful work on evolving neural controllers for the highly unstable dynamic problem of bipedal walking (Reil and Husbands 2002, Vaughan et al. 2004).

Holk Cruse and colleagues have also made important contributions to biologically influenced neural systems for robotic locomotion. Using detailed data from behavioural experiments on arthropods, particularly stick insects, they have developed a series of kinematic models of hexapod walking that have been used to control real and simulated robots. Initially the models were built from state based algorithms for controlling and coordinating the various phases of leg motion. This approach was replaced by a distributed neural network model, WALKNET, that has been refined over the years (Cruse et al., 1995; Durr et al., 2004; Schilling et al., 2007). The overall architecture, which has commonalities with those of Beer and Brooks, is shown in Figure 5. Each leg controller contains a number of different subnetworks for controlling stance and swing phases. The various subnets are usually implemented as small recurrent or feedforward networks of simple artificial neurons. The system is able to generate adaptive gaits capable of dealing with irregular surfaces at a range of walking speeds, as well as being able to cope with leg disruptions and even amputations.

Ijspeert and colleagues have produced a number of interesting robots based on studies of animal locomotion. A good example is their impressive salamander robot that combines three modes of locomotion - swimming, serpentine crawling and walking (Ijspeert et al. 2007). The controller is based on central pattern generator (CPG) circuits in the salamander spinal cord that underly locomotion. It is implemented as a system of coupled nonlinear oscillators and runs on a microcontroller on-board the amphibious robot.

As these examples show, locomotion, involving complex motor coordination, is an area of robotic control where neural systems excel. The distributed nature of such systems, coupled with the subtle, adaptive dynamics they can generate, give them many advantages over traditional control methods including efficiency, robustness and plasticity. The smooth dynamics generated by the kinds of neural systems outlined result in much more fluid, 'natural' gaits and motions than with the traditional control systems mentioned at the start of this section. All of the examples discussed also exploit mechanisms which highlight a general lesson from animal locomotion studies: the importance of subtle interactions between nervous system, body and environment in the overall generation of behaviour.

Navigation

Efficient and robust navigation through complex terrain using visual cues is an important capability for many animals as well as autonomous robots. Insects demonstrate remarkable navigational ability despite small brains and low resolution vision which has made them a topic of special interest for both engineers and biologists. A simple strategy used by insects and mimicked by roboticists is view-based homing or snapshot guidance (Cartwright and Collett, 1983; Wehner et al., 1996). In these strategies, insects navigate back to a location by remembering a retinotopic view of the world, or snapshot, from the goal position. Subsequent

Figure 5. Representation of the WALKNET architecture. A: Individual leg controllers are coupled to allow coordination. Global signals from a higher control level (dashed lines) model descending signals from the brain. B: each single-leg controller consists of a number of ANN modules. Their outputs set the angular velocities of the leg joints (TC,CT,FT). The selector net gates the stance and swing nets in a mutually exclusive manner. Half circles indicate sensory input. v, y and w are global commands controlling body velocity, yaw and forward walking respectively. The height net controls body clearance and the PEP net encodes the 'posterior extreme position' of leg movement. Sensory information is encoded into a target posture by the target net. Reproduced with permission

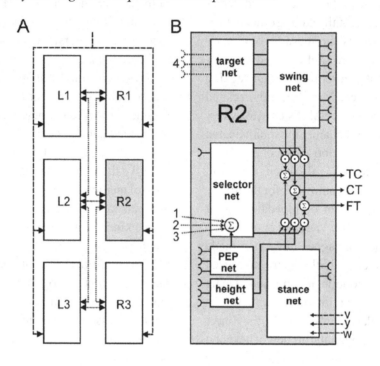

navigation is then achieved by moving so as to make the current view of the world more closely match the remembered goal view. In general, algorithmic instantiations of this process work by iteratively comparing a (parameterised) view of the world from the agent's current position with a view stored at the goal location, with differences between current and goal views transformed into an approximate direction to the goal (for reviews see: Franz and Mallot, 2000; Vardy and Möller, 2005).

One of the simplest and most elegant implementations of snapshsot homing for robotic navigation is the Average Landmark Vector (ALV) model (Lambrinos et al., 2000). The ALV model works by first identifying recognisable visual features, or *landmarks*, from a 360° panoramic view of the environment. The view of the world from that position is then represented as the average of the unit vectors pointing from the agent to each landmark – the ALV, a two-dimensional vector. The algorithm works since the vector difference between the current ALV and an ALV stored at the goal position points approximately back to the goal (Lambrinos et al., 2000). Although this direction is approximate, using an iterative process with a sufficiently small step-size achieves robust navigation provided the majority of landmarks can be reliably identified in both current and goal views. In the simplest form of the algorithm, the heading vector at iteration i, V_i, is calculated as $A_i - G$, where A_i is the current ALV and G is the stored ALV taken at the goal location. A useful refinement, which smoothes out noise by using a 'momentum' term, works as follows (Smith et al., 2007). The heading direction at step i, θ_i, is calculated as a weighted average of the direction of V_i, ϕ_i, and the previous heading, θ_{i-1}, with the weight, ω_i, of the previous heading increasing with the value of $|\theta_{i-1}-\phi_i|$, as described by the following equations. This method prevents large jumps in direction, ignoring ϕ_i altogether when $|\theta_{i-1} - \phi_i| \geq \dfrac{\pi}{2}$.

$$\theta_i = \omega_i \theta_{i-1} + (1 - \omega_i)\phi_i, \quad \text{where } \omega_i = min(\frac{|\theta_{i-1} - \phi_i|}{0.5\pi}, 1)$$

The ALV thus provides a sparse representation of the current visual scene by processing it into a single vector which essentially represents the 'visual centre-of-mass' of the surrounding landmarks. Despite minimal computation and memory requirements, the ALV model has been shown to be effective for visual navigation in both computer simulation (Lambrinos et al., 2000) and using autonomous mobile robots (Möller, 2000; Hafner and Möller 2001). While the method appears fragile, the idea of encoding a visual scene as the visual centre-of-mass of objects, or visual features, or even simply pixel intensities, is surprisingly robust and is a general purpose method for retinotopic encoding of a visual scene. Although the standard ALV model requires object extraction, Möller (2001) presented a method which functions on natural images while the work of Hafner and Möller (2001) has shown that the model can work quite reliably in the real world where every pixel of the image is considered a feature which is weighted by its intensity. The latter piece of work is of particular interest because the ALV model was not pre-specified but was generated as the optimal solution in a simple feedforward

ANN model trained with either backpropagation or unsupervised learning.

Many variants of this class of view-based homing algorithm exist (Möller and Vardy, 2006) which can be implemented in terms of ANNs or as higher-level algorithms, or a mixture of both. However, as with the ALV, successful navigation requires the current view to be similar to the goal view (Cartwright & Collett, 1987) and so the region in which they can function is local to the goal.

Another insect-inspired solution which increases the scale over which visually guided robots can navigate is route-following. It has long been known that insects demonstrate robust navigation using visually guided routes *without recourse to map-like representations* (e.g. Rosengren, 1971; Collett et al., 1992; Wehner et al., 2006) and navigation algorithms in autonomous robotics have used this idea in various forms (Nehmzow, 2000; Smith, et al., 2007, 2008; Argyros et al., 2005; Vardy, 2006; Giovannangeli et al., 2006). In such approaches, the agent learns routes consisting of multiple goal locations, or waypoints, with navigation between waypoints achieved using a local homing method. The main problems to be solved in such approaches is to determine at which point a waypoint should be set during route construction, and deciding when a waypoint has been reached during navigation. Successful schemes therefore require robust solutions to a number of general visual problems, such as place recognition and the detection of change (Smith et al., 2007). In conjunction with environmental noise, these problems make robust route navigation a non-trivial aim; particularly as we do not yet properly understand how it is achieved by insects. While robotic models have been successful in particular environments, some extra mechanism to reliably determine where along the route an agent is, that is, a sense of place, is needed for more robust and general navigation (Smith et al., 2008).

Equipping a robot with a sense of place, however, allows for a more complex approach, specifically the use of a map-based strategy. Thus, while essentially the same as route-following in that local homing was used between waypoints, Franz et al. (1998) linked waypoints together into a view graph rather than a route. This map-like organisation allows more sophisticated navigation behaviour, particularly with respect to dealing with changes to the environment and recognizing when a wrong turn has been taken.

Rats provide the most studied example of map-like navigation in nature. They are capable of navigation through complex changing worlds over hundreds of metres with memories that persist for several years. This navigational ability is underpinned by hippocampal place cells which reliably fire when the animal is in a specific location in the world. Experiments have shown that rats use these cells for navigation and they have therefore been thought of as a form of cognitive map. Interestingly, while visual cues (as well as odometric and vestibular information) have been shown to be necessary to generate reliable place cells, once established, the cells fire accurately even if the rat navigates in the dark. The more recent discovery of other cells which fire when the rat's head is at certain angle (head-direction cells) (Taube et al, 1990a,1990b) or which fire periodically as the rat crosses an environment (grid-cells) (Hafting et al., 2005) have led to a deeper understanding of how the rat integrates vestibular and odometric information to create and utilise the map.

Inspired by the organisation of spatial memories in the mammalian hippocampus, a number of algorithms for the autonomous construction of place graphs representing the structure of the environment have been developed (Mataric, 1992; Franz et al., 1998). In the engineering sciences, state-of-the-art robot navigation is dominated by probabilistic algorithms which also maintain a sense of place while simultaneously mapping the environment (Thrun et al., 2005). An approach which combines both these methodologies is RatSLAM, an autonomous navigation system modelled on the organisation and structures of the

rodent brain (Milford et al., 2004). Specifically, it uses a three-dimensional continuous attractor network as a layer of 'Pose cells' which ape the function of grid and head direction cells by integrating odometric information into a map-like representation (Figure 6). Visual information feeds into local view cells which encode the visual scene as a vector, and feed into both the pose-cells and the experience map, a third network of neurons analogous to place cells. The RatSLAM system navigates reliably on real robots operating continuously in both indoor and outdoor environments, producing impressively accurate maps over regions covering tens of kilometres (Milford and Wyeth, 2008).

While aspects of the RatSLAM system can give insights into the workings of the brain, the project's main goal was robust navigation rather than biological modelling. Similarly, the 'Psikharpax' project (Meyer et al., 2005) is another interesting example of robotics research making use of simulations of hippocampal place-cell mechanisms for navigation, this time integrating learning (based on dopamine reinforcement mechanisms). In contrast, see the later section on Darwin X for an example of a biological modelling approach aimed at understanding how hippocampal-cortical interactions could underlie spatial navigation.

Visually Guided Behaviours

One area in which neuro-inspired robotics has been particularly successful is in unmanned air vehicle (UAV) guidance, especially for mini- or micro- air vehicles.

This work has drawn on observations of the unparalleled abilities of insects – often bees, fruit-flies and dragonflies – to maintain stability and perform complex flight manoeuvres whilst operating in complicated cluttered environments. Aping these abilities, engineers have developed algorithms capable of stabilising and controlling flying robots, based on measurements of optic

Figure 6. The RatSLAM architecture. Each local view cell is associated with a distinct visual scene in the environment and becomes active when the robot sees that scene. The pose cells comprise a 3-D continuous attractor network, where active pose cells encode the estimate of the robot's pose. Each pose cell is connected to proximal cells by excitatory and inhibitory connections with wrapping across all six faces of the network. Active local view and pose cells drive the creation of experience nodes in the experience map, a semi-metric graphical representation of places in the environment and their interconnectivity. From Wyeth and Milford (2009), (© 2009 IEEE), used with permission

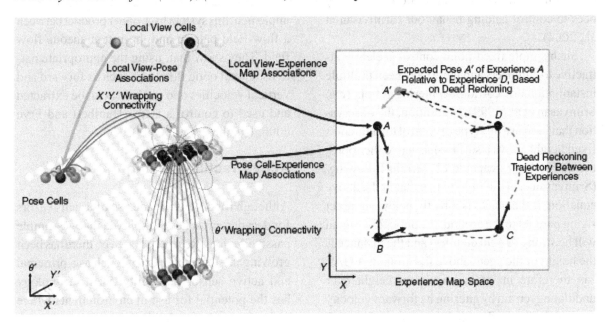

flow. The methodology often followed has been dubbed 'Gibsonian robotics', after the psychologist J. J. Gibson, as the work starts with observation of a target behaviour and proceeds by trying to understand what variable(s) should be controlled to achieve such a behaviour.

This approach is exemplified by the work of Srinivasan and colleagues. They have used the behaviour of honeybees as inspiration to develop controllers for a number of UAVs (Srinivasan, 2002). Many of these algorithms have come from observations of experiments in which bees were trained to fly through a tunnel with stripes on the walls (and occasionally, the floor). Experiments in which one of the walls was moved showed that bees maintained a central position in the tunnel by balancing the image motion, or optic flow, perceived by each eye. The optic flow, *F*, gener-

ated by a simple object at a distance *d* from an observer moving with an instantaneous velocity *v* can be calculated as:

$$F = -\omega + \frac{v}{d}\sin\theta$$

where ω is the optic flow generated by self-rotation and θ is the angle of the object relative to the direction of travel. In the absence of self-rotation (often assumed to be subtracted out through measurement by gyroscopic sensors) it can be seen that balancing the optic flow on each side of the bee (i.e. at +/- θ) would mean that *d* would be the same for both sides (as *v* is constant for both eyes). Similarly, maintaining constant optic flow requires that if the tunnel narrows, the bee must lower its speed. This means that in more cluttered environments, the bee automatically responds appropriately. Thus this simple and elegant solution of balancing optic flow results in a bee being able to chart a safe path through a cluttered environment *without* knowing its own speed or measuring the distance to nearby objects. A similar solution of monitoring and matching optic flow is used by bees to control landing behaviour (Srinivisan et al., 2004).

Such simple fixed-point control is clearly attractive to engineers and there have been multiple instantiations of corridor–centering robots (e.g. Srinivasan et al., 1999). In addition, the observation that bees use this type of control to maintain a fixed height above a surface has led to the robust control of UAVs capable of 'terrain following' (Srinivasan et al., 2006). Notice that in the above equation, if the object is directly below an insect flying parallel to the ground, the optic flow signal will be strong ($\theta = 90$ degrees) and the distance is the height of the agent above the ground. A UAV can therefore maintain a constant height over undulating terrain by altering its forward velocity so that the optic flow measured from a downward facing camera remains constant. This type of control has been implemented on free-flying helicopters and fixed wing aircraft (Srinivasan, 2006; Franceschini et al., 2007).

Crucial to the success of these systems is the extraction of reliable optic flow signals. In general, these rely on models of neural circuitry implementing insect elementary motion detectors, or EMDs (Reichardt, 1961). Many neural and neural-like models of EMDs have been developed (Horn and Schunck, 1981; Higgins 2004; Riabinina and Philippides, 2009) and, particularly interesting from a robotics perspective, they are often suitable for implementation in parallel hardware leading to extremely lightweight and fast sensor arrays (Aubepart and Franceschini, 2007).

A different approach is that of Humbert and Frye (2006) who have achieved robust control by going a stage further down the visual pathway and modelling the wide-field integration of the

Lobula Plate Tangential cells (LPTCs). These cells take input from across the retina and electrophysiological studies indicate that they respond preferentially to particular global patterns of optic flow, such as an expanding flow-field caused by pure forward-motion (Krapp and Hengstenberg, 1996; Borst and Haag, 2002). Humbert and Frye implement this system by an inner product between a flow-field pattern and the instantaneous flow field. They show that, using the appropriate patterns, global optic flow cues such as forward and vertical velocities and pitch rate can be extracted and used to control a UAV (Humbert and Frye 2006, Humbert at al., 2009).

Active Tactile Sensing

Although robots have made use of touch sensors for decades, most have employed them as simple passive devices. Recently, however, there has been growing interest in the use of touch as a principal and active sensory modality. Such technology has the potential for use in environments where vision and other modalities are severely limited, such as underground, in the sea, or in rescue applications in smoke-filled burning buildings. Most examples of such research take inspiration from rodent whisker sensor systems.

For instance, Scratchbot – developed in a collaboration between Sheffield University and the Bristol Robotics Lab, is a biologically inspired robotic implementation of the rat whisker sensory system. It mimics the sweeping motion of rodent whiskers to determine the size and shape of objects in front of it. The system embodies neural control algorithms capable of generating contact-mediated adaptation of a whisking pattern displayed by rats – active touch (Pearson et al., 2007). Sensory information derived from the artificial whiskers has also been used to enact orientation behaviour in the robot. This involved the integration of neural models of the superior colliculus, basal ganglia and the trigeminal sensory complex at different levels of abstraction. Real-time performance was achieved by implementing the neural systems in a mix of hardware (FPGAs) and software.

An alternative approach to tactile perception via whiskers was explored by Seth et al. (2004b). In this study, a neurorobotic 'brain-based device' (Darwin IX) learned to discriminate among textures by categorizing the spatiotemporal patterns evoked by whisker deflections. Darwin IX was controlled by a simulated nervous system capturing detailed properties of the rodent somatosensory system, and its analysis made predictions about the existence of so-called 'lag cells' which would respond to presynaptic input with varying delays. The brain-based device approach is described in more detail in the later section on robotics tools in neuroscience.

GasNets

This section concentrates on the use of a novel form of biologically inspired neural system in robot control. It describes experiments with robot nervous systems employing a style of artificial neural network strongly inspired by those parts of contemporary neuroscience that emphasize the complex electrochemical nature of biological brains. In particular, they make use of an analogue of *volume signalling*, whereby neurotransmitters freely diffuse into a relatively large volume around a nerve cell, potentially affecting many other neurons irrespective of whether or not they are electrically connected (Gally et al., 1990; Wood and Garthwaite, 1994). This exotic form of neural signalling does not sit easily with classical connectionist (point-to-point) pictures of brain mechanisms and is forcing a radical re-think of existing theory (Dawson and Snyder, 1994; Philippides et al., 2000; Philippides et al., 2005a; Bullock et al., 2005; Katz, 1999). These systems have been used in a range of robot applications related to some of those described in the preceding sections.

The class of artificial neural networks developed to explore artificial volume signalling are known as GasNets (Husbands et al., 1998) which take particular inspiration from nitric oxide (NO) signalling (Gally et al., 1990). They comprise a fairly standard artificial neural network augmented by a chemical signalling system based on a diffusing *virtual* gas which can modulate the response of other neurons. A number of GasNet variants, inspired by different aspects of real nervous systems, have been explored in an evolutionary robotics (Floreano et al., 2008) context as artificial nervous systems for mobile autonomous robots. They were introduced to explore their potential as robust 'minimal' systems for controlling behaviour in very noisy environments. They have been shown to be significantly more evolvable, in terms of speed to a good solution, than other forms of neural networks for a variety of robot tasks and behaviours (Husbands et al., 1998; Smith et al., 2003; McHale and Husbands, 2004; Philippides et al., 2005b; Vargas et al., 2008; Husbands et al., in press). They are being investigated as potentially useful engineering tools, including as modules in complex robot control systems (Vargas et al., 2009), while a related strand of more detailed modelling work is aimed at gaining helpful insights into biological systems (Philippides et al., 2000, 2003, 2005a).

By analogy with biological neuronal networks, GasNets incorporate two distinct signalling mechanisms, one 'electrical' and one 'chemical'. The underlying 'electrical' network is a discrete time step, recurrent neural network with a variable number of nodes. These nodes are connected by either excitatory or inhibitory links with the output, O_i^t, of node i at time step t determined by the following equation.

$$O_i^t = \tanh\left[k_i^t\left(\sum_{j \in \Gamma_i} w_{ji} O_j^{t-1} + I_i^t\right) + b_i\right]$$

where Γ_i is the set of nodes with connections to node i and $w_{ji} = \pm 1$ is a connection weight. I_i^t is the external (sensory) input to node i at time t, and b_i is a genetically set bias. Each node has a genetically set default transfer function gain parameter, k_i^0, which can be altered at each time-step according to the concentration of diffusing 'gas' at node i to give k_i^t (as described later).

In addition to this underlying network in which positive and negative 'signals' flow between units, an abstract process loosely analogous to the diffusion of gaseous modulators is at play. Some units can emit virtual 'gases' which diffuse and are capable of modulating the behaviour of other units by changing their transfer functions. The networks occupy a 2D space; the diffusion processes mean that the relative positioning of nodes is crucial to the functioning of the network. Spatially, the gas concentration varies as an inverse exponential of the distance from the emitting node with spread governed by a parameter, r, genetically set for each node, which governs the radius of influence of the virtual gas from the node as described by the equations below and illustrated in Figure 7. The maximum concentration at the emitting node is 1.0 and the concentration builds up and decay linearly as dictated by the time course function, $T(t)$, defined below.

$$C(d,t) = \begin{cases} e^{-2d/r} \times T(t) & d < r \\ 0 & \text{else} \end{cases}$$

$$T(t) = \begin{cases} 0 & t = 0 \\ min(1,(T(t-1)+\frac{1}{s})) & \text{emitting} \\ max(0,(T(t-1)-\frac{1}{s})) & \text{not emitting} \end{cases}$$

where $C(d,t)$ is the concentration at a distance d from the emitting node at time t and s (controlling the slope of the function T) is genetically determined for each node. The range of s is such that the gas diffusion timescale can vary from 0.5 to

Figure 7. A basic GasNet showing excitatory (solid) and inhibitory (dashed) 'electrical' connections and a diffusing virtual gas creating a 'chemical' gradient

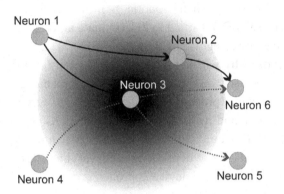

A GasNet. Neuron 3 is emitting gas, and modulating neuron 2 despite there being no synaptic connection.

0.09 of the timescale of 'electrical' transmission (i.e. a little slower to much slower). The total concentration at a node is then determined by summing the contributions from all other emitting nodes (nodes are not affected by their own emitted gases to avoid runaway positive feedback). The diffusion process is modelled in this simple way to provide extreme computational efficiency, allowing arbitrarily large networks to be run very fast.

For mathematical convenience, in the original basic GasNet there are two 'gases', one whose modulatory effect is to increase the transfer function gain parameter (k_i^t) and one whose effect is to decrease it. It is genetically determined whether or not any given node will emit one of these two gases (gas 1 and gas 2), and under what circumstances emission will occur (either when the 'electrical' activation of the node exceeds a threshold, or the concentration of a genetically determined gas in the vicinity of the node exceeds a threshold; note these emission processes provide a coupling between the electrical and chemical mechanisms). The concentration-dependent modulation is described by the following equation, with transfer function parameters updated on every time step as the network runs:

$$k_i^t = k_i^0 + \alpha C_1^t - \beta C_2^t$$

where k_i^0 is the genetically set default value for k_i (the transfer function gain), C_1^t and C_2^t are the concentrations of gas 1 and gas 2 respectively at node i on time step t, and α and β are constants such that $k_i^t \in [-4, 4]$. Thus the gas does not alter the electrical activity in the network directly but rather acts by continuously changing the mapping between input and output for individual nodes, either directly or by stimulating the production of further virtual gas. The general form of diffusion is based on the properties of a (real) single source neuron as modelled in detail in Philippides et al. (2000; 2003). The modulation chosen is motivated by what is known of NO modulatory effects at synapses (Baranano et al., 2001). For further details see (Husbands et al., 1998; Phillippides et al., 2005, Husbands et al., in press).

When they were first introduced, GasNets were demonstrated to be significantly more evolvable than a variety of standard ANNs on some noisy visually guided evolutionary robotics tasks (Husbands, 1998; Husbands et al., 1998). Typically the increase in evolvability, in terms of number of fitness evaluations to a reliable good solution, was an order of magnitude or more. The solutions found were often very lean with few nodes and connections, typically far fewer than were needed for other forms of ANN (Husbands et al., 1998). But the action of the modulatory gases imbued such networks with intricate dynamics: they could not be described as simple. Oscillatory sub-networks based on interacting 'electrical' and 'gas' feedback mechanisms acting on different timescales were found to be very easy to evolve and cropped up in many forms, from CPG circuits for locomotion (McHale and Husbands, 2004) to noise filters and timing mechanisms for visual

processing (Husbands et al., 1998, Smith et al., 2002). GasNets appeared to be particularly suited to noisy sensorimotor behaviours which could not be solved by simple reactive feedforward systems, and to rhythmical behaviours.

Two recent extensions of the basic GasNet, the receptor and the plexus models, incorporated further influence from neuroscience (Philippides et al., 2005b). In the receptor model modulation of a node is now a function of gas concentration and the quantity and type of receptors (if any) at the node. This allows a range of site specific modulations within the same network. In the plexus model, inspired by a type of NO signalling seen in the mammalian cerebral cortex (Philippides et al, 2005a), the emitted gas 'cloud', which now has a flat concentration, is no longer centred on the node controlling it but at a distance from it. Both these extended forms proved to be significantly more evolvable again than the basic GasNet. Other varieties include non-spatial GasNets where the diffusion process is replaced by explicit gas connections with complex dynamics (Vargas et al., 2008, 2009) and version with other forms of modulation and diffusion (Husbands et al., in press). In order to gain insight into the enhanced evolvability of GasNets, detailed comparative studies of these variants with each other, and with other forms of ANN, were performed using the robot task illustrated in Figure 8 (Philippides et al., 2005b;Husbands et al., in press).

Starting from an arbitrary position and orientation in a black-walled arena, a robot equipped with a forward facing camera must navigate under extremely variable lighting conditions to one shape (a white triangle) while ignoring the second shape (a white rectangle). The robot must successfully complete the task over a series of trials in which the relative position and size of the shapes varies. Both the robot control network and the robot sensor input morphology, i.e. the number and positions of the camera pixels used as input and how they were connected into the network, were under evolutionary control as illustrated in

Figure 8. LEFT: The gantry robot. A CCD camera head moves at the end of a gantry arm allowing full 3D movement. In the study referred to in the text 2D movement was used, equivalent to a wheeled robot with a fixed forward pointing camera. A validated simulation was used: controllers developed in the simulation work at least as well on the real robot. RIGHT: The simulated arena and robot. The bottom right view shows the robot position in the arena with the triangle and rectangle. Fitness is evaluated on how close the robot approaches the triangle. The top right view shows what the robot 'sees', along with the pixel positions selected by evolution for visual input. The bottom left view shows how the genetically set pixels are connected into the control network whose gas levels are illustrated. The top left view shows current activity of nodes in the GasNet

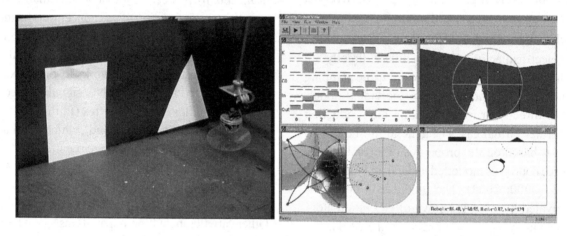

Figure 8. The network architecture (including number of nodes) and all properties of the nodes and connections and gas diffusion parameters were set by an evolutionary search algorithm. Because of the noise and variation, and limited sensory capabilities (only very few pixels are used), this task is challenging, requiring robust, general solutions. The gantry robot shown in the figure was used. Evolution took place in a special validated simulation of the robot and its environment.

The comparative studies revealed that the rich dynamics and additional timescales introduced by the gas played an important part in enhanced evolvability, but were not the whole story (Philippides et al., 2005; Husbands et al., in press). The particular form of modulation was also important – multiplicative or exponential modulation (in the form of changes to the transfer function) were found to be effective, but additive modulations were not. The former kind of modulations may well confer evolutionary advantages by allowing nodes to be sensitive to different ranges of input (internal and sensory) in different contexts. The spatial embedding of the networks also appears to play a role in producing the most effective coupling between the two distinct signalling processes ('electrical' and 'chemical'). By exploiting a loose, flexible coupling between the two processes, it is possible to significantly reduce destructive interference between them, allowing one to be 'tuned' against the other while searching for good solutions. It has been suggested that similar forces may be at play in spiking networks, where sub-threshold and spiking dynamics interact with each other, which have been evolved to drive vision-based robot behaviours (Floreano and Mattiussi, 2006; Floreano et al., 2008). In the most successful varieties of GasNet, dynamics, modulation and spatial embedding act in concert to produce highly evolvable degenerate (Tononi et al., 1999) networks.

ROBOTICS TOOLS IN NEUROSCIENCE

Natural adaptive and intelligent behaviour is the result of complex interactions between nervous system, body and environment. Biological neural systems are embodied and embedded. Because of this there has been a growing interest in using robots, employing on-board neural circuitry, to model aspects of animal behaviour. Such a methodology, the argument goes, can give deeper insights into behaviour generating neural mechanisms than disembodied models (Webb, 2001), as well as fresh perspectives on what it means to be a cognitive agent (Wheeler, 2005). Like any modelling enterprise, there are many issues surrounding how to make robotic models, with their inevitably different implementation constraints, properly relevant to biological enquiry. For a discussion of such matters see Webb (2001,2009) and AB (2009).

A prominent example of such research is Barbara Webb's programme of work on robotic models of cricket behaviour. Webb and colleagues have used a series of robot models to investigate the phonotaxis behaviour of crickets whereby female crickets can recognise and locate the calling songs of male crickets. The robots have an analogue electronic auditory system to represent the physical auditory receptor mechanism of the cricket. The auditory input is translated into spike trains that are fed into a simulation of the neural circuitry under investigation, the output of which is used to drive the wheels of the robot. Cricket neural systems are modelled using spiking leaky integrate-and-fire model neurons with suitable internal dynamics. Synaptic dynamics are also modelled. The models have been used to test existing hypotheses about behavioural mechanisms as well as to propose new ones (Webb and Scutt, 2000; Reeve et al., 2005).

As well as being a good example of a neural architecture for motor control, Ijspeert and colleagues' work on the salamander robot, mentioned

earlier in the section on locomotion, also has important biological modelling aspects. Their novel salamander-like robot, *Salamandra robotica,* is driven by a computational (neural) model of the salamander's spinal cord. This implementation allowed the team to address three fundamental issues related to vertebrate locomotion: (i) the modifications undergone by the spinal locomotor circuits during the evolutionary transition from aquatic to terrestrial locomotion, (ii) the mechanisms necessary for coordination of limb and axial movements, and (iii) the mechanisms that underlie gait transitions induced by simple electrical stimulation of the brain stem (Ijspeert et al., 2007).

The concept of action selection is well known in studies of animal behaviour and has also been used in robotic and computational models of adaptive behaviour (Prescott et al., 1999, 2007). A selection problem arises whenever an animal has two or more behavioural alternatives which require the same mechanism for execution. It has been proposed that the basal ganglia, a group of interconnected sub-cortical brain structures, play a crucial role in vertebrates in resolving such conflicts. An extended computational model of the basal ganglia, based on current neurophysiological data, was developed and embedded in a robot control architecture (Prescott et al., 2006). The robot engaged in a variety of behaviours, including food-seeking and wall-following, which are analogous to rat behaviours. (Rats are the main animal model for basal ganglia studies). These behaviours were successfully selected and switched between by the embedded basal ganglia model and coherent sequences of behaviour were formed. It was claimed that this is the strongest evidence yet that the basal ganglia are directly involved in action selection.

Recently techniques and ideas from probabilistic robotics (Thrun et al., 2005) have been imported into studies of insect behaviour in order to shed new light on the behavioural strategies employed by visually navigating animals (Baddeley et al.,

2009). The ultimate aim of such work is to help unravel the neural mechanisms underlying the observed behaviour. An approach derived from probabilistic simultaneous localisation and mapping (SLAM) was used to analyse bee orientation flights in order to investigate whether they are structured to efficiently learn the positions of the landmarks that are available in a given terrain. It was shown that the flights are not optimised to learn about the position of a prominent landmark, but are more suited to learn about objects near the nest.

There is not enough space to review in detail each of the examples mentioned above; instead the remainder of this section will focus on the pioneering and unique research associated with Edelman's brain-based devices, which involve much larger numbers of simulated neurons than all the work mentioned to this point.

Brain-Based Devices

Brain-based devices (BBDs) are neurorobotic devices whose development is most closely associated with Edelman and colleagues at the Neurosciences Institute in San Diego. Edelman's 'Darwin' series of BBDs has an extensive history dating back to 1990 (Reeke et al., 1990) and continuing to the present day (Fleischer et al., 2007; McKinstry et al., 2008). BBDs are constructed according to the methodology of 'synthetic neural modelling', which has four key components (Krichmar and Edelman, 2005). First, a BBD needs to engage in a behavioural task. Second, its behaviour must be controlled by a simulated nervous system having a design that reflects the brain's architecture and dynamics. Third, it needs to be situated in the real world. And fourth, its behaviour and the activity of its simulated nervous system must allow comparison with empirical data. Of these components, the emphasis on fidelity to systems-level neuroanatomy and neurophysiology, and on the comparison with empirical data, together provide the strongest contrast with other

neurorobotic approaches (Edelman, 2007). For example, unlike most other neurorobots, BBDs typically involve simulated nervous systems having tens of thousands of simulated 'neuronal units', where each unit reflects the mean spiking activity of a group (~1000) of biological neurons.

Although BBDs can be analysed in terms of Edelman's 'theory of neuronal group selection' (TNGS, also known as 'neural Darwinism' (Edelman, 1993)), they should not be seen as implementations or models of this theory per se. Rather, and in common with other neurorobotic approaches, BBDs play a dual role. They have scientific value as heuristics for unravelling complex multi-level brain-body-environment interactions, and they have technological value as examples of practically useful robotic devices. Here we focus on the scientific role of BBDs. Over the last ten years, BBDs have been constructed to explore neural mechanisms underlying conditioning to visual stimuli (Darwin VII,(Krichmar and Edelman, 2002)), visual binding (Darwin VIII, (Seth et al., 2004a)), texture discrimination using artificial whiskers (Darwin IX,(Seth et al., 2004b)), spatial navigation and episodic memory (Darwin X,(Krichmar et al., 2005a;Krichmar et al.,2005b)), and predictive motor control (Darwin XI,(McKinstry et al., 2006)). We will give brief details of two of these BBDs, Darwin VIII and Darwin X.

Darwin VIII

Effective visual object recognition requires mechanisms to bind object features (e.g., colour, shape, motion) while distinguishing distinct objects. Darwin VIII was constructed to test the idea that such a mechanism could be provided by synchronously active neuronal circuits among re-entrantly connected cortical areas. Its simulated nervous system, schematized in Figure 9, has two key features. First, visual areas are massively interconnected via re-entrant projections, where re-entry refers to parallel reciprocal connectivity

Figure 9. A. Darwin VIII in its environment, together with 'screen shots' depicting activity in selected neural areas. Each pixel represents a single neuronal unit with brightness reflecting activity and colour indicating phase. B. Darwin VIII's simulated nervous system, which contains 28 neural areas, 53,450 neuronal units, and ~1.7 million synaptic connections. Topographic visual areas are labelled V1-V4 (interareal connections are not shown); IT (inferotemporal) is a non-topographic visual area; S is the value system; A-left/right are auditory input areas, and the BBDs behaviour is driven by activity in area C. Unlike voltage independent connections, voltage dependent connections require above-threshold post-synaptic activity to have an effect. Plastic connections are modulated according to the Bienenstock-Cooper-Munro (BCM) rule; value-dependent plastic connections are additionally modulated by activity in area S

A.

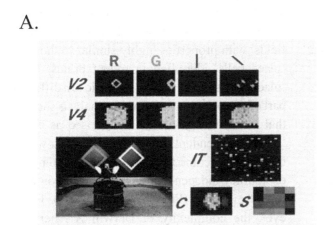

B.

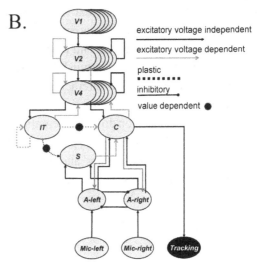

without connotations of 'error signals' (Edelman, 1993). Second, neuronal units in any given area had a 'phase' value such that units at the same phase could be considered to be synchronized in their activity.

Darwin VIII was placed in an environment containing visual objects with overlapping features, namely red and green diamonds and squares. It was trained to approach one 'target' object (e.g., a red diamond), and to ignore potentially confusing distracters (red squares, green diamonds), by association of the target stimulus with an auditory tone which would activate the value system (area S), inducing plasticity in the nervous system (Figure 9). Darwin VIII was able to perform the task, showing discriminatory orienting behaviour

after about 10 experimental 'trials', even in the absence of the tone (the conditioning stimulus). As shown in the figure, Darwin VIII's nervous system exhibited the dynamic formation of distinct synchronous neural circuits corresponding to objects in its visual field. In this example, area S is firing strongly in phase with the target object (the red diamond), reflecting a conditioned response.

A major feature of BBDs is that their neural dynamics can be analyzed at all levels of description in arbitrary detail during behaviour, unlike in corresponding animal experiments. In the case of Darwin VIII, Seth et al. were able to track the phase distributions of all neuronal units in all neural areas both during normal behaviour and in a 'lesion' condition in which inter-areal re-entrant connections were removed. A key observation was that the dynamically formed object-specific synchronous circuits broke down in the lesion condition, leaving only locally (intra-areal) synchronized responses to object features. Discriminatory orienting behaviour also disappeared in this condition. Thus, intact re-entrant connections may be a key condition for successful visual binding. The neurorobotic implementation of Darwin VIII also showed that such binding is feasible in a real-world environment where objects are constantly changing size and position. More generally, the operation of Darwin VIII could best be understood in terms of interacting local and global processes, as opposed to standard concepts of 'bottom up' versus 'top down' information flow Finally, the implementation of a phase parameter showed how 'temporal coding' and 'rate coding' could be combined in a single network model in a synergetic way.

Darwin X

Darwin X was constructed to explore how hippocampal-cortical interactions could underlie spatial navigation and episodic memory (Kritchmar et al., 2005a;Kritchmar et al., 2005b). Darwin X's simulated nervous system contained 50 neural areas, ~90,000 neuronal units and ~1.4 million simulated synapses (Figure 10). The simulated areas included visual and head-direction input streams, a detailed model of the two primary pathways through the hippocampus ('trisynaptic' and 'perforant') and, as with Darwin VIII, a value system that modulated synaptic plasticity. Darwin X was tested in an environment resembling the 'water maze' experiments introduced by Morris (1984). A 'hidden platform' was placed in a rectangular arena, detectable only when directly underneath the robot, and the arena was decorated with visual landmarks consisting of stripes of various colours. In a given trial, Darwin X was placed at one of four different starting points and allowed

to explore the environment. Darwin X learned to navigate directly to the hidden platform after ~10 trials. Moreover, in a 'probe' trial in which the hidden platform was removed, Darwin X spent substantial time in the part of the environment where the platform would have been located. These observations strongly resemble the learning patterns exhibited by rodents in the original Morris water maze studies.

Analysis of Darwin X's nervous system revealed several interesting features. First, it was found that units in area CA1 developed 'place fields' with properties highly similar to those of 'place cells' identified in rodent brains: Each 'place unit' showed activity specific to a different part of the environment. Further analysis showed that place units could be categorised as either 'journey dependent' (activity depends on where the BBD has come from, or where it is going to) or 'journey independent', again in common with rodent evidence (Fleischer et al., 2007). However, the complexity of Darwin X's nervous system made it difficult to expose the neural pathways driving the activity of these place units. To address this challenge, a new analysis based on 'Granger causality' (G-causality) was developed. The basic idea of G-causality is that one time series can be called 'causal' to another if it contains information that helps predict the other, where prediction is standardly operationalized using vector autoregression (Kritchmar et al., 2005a; Seth and Edelman, 2007). Application of this analysis to Darwin X showed that, as learning progressed, the proportion of CA1 units driven by the 'direct' (perforant) pathway increased, while the proportion driven by the 'indirect' (trisynaptic) pathway decreased. This observation generated the interesting hypothesis that trisynaptic interactions may be more important in unfamiliar environments due to their ability to integrate more widely across different input modalities and across time. By contrast, the perforant pathway may be more efficient for transforming familiar cues into actions.

Figure 10. Darwin X's simulated nervous system, consisting of visual input streams (IT, Pr) and odometric (head-direction) input (ATN). These inputs were reciprocally connected with the hippocampus which included entorhinal cortical areas (ECin, ECout), dentate gyrus (DG), and the CA1 and CA3 hippocampal subfields. The size each area is indicated by the adjacent number. Area S is a value system initially activated only by the hidden platform

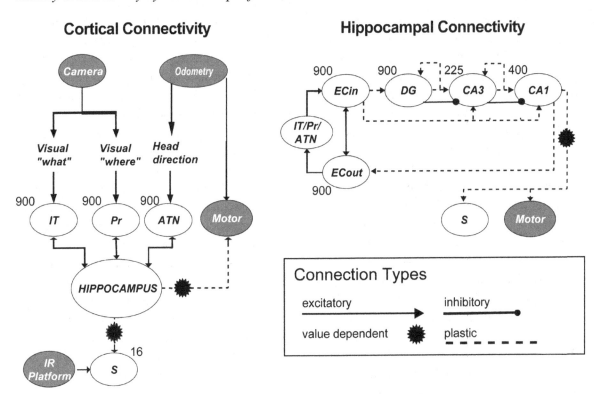

A second G-causality analysis of Darwin X developed the novel concept of a 'causal core', with potentially important implications for general neural theories of learning (Seth and Edelman, 2007). In this analysis, a first step was to identify the 'context' network associated with a particular CA1 unit active at a particular time (the 'neural reference', NR). This network consisted of all interactions that could have potentially contributed to the NR and was found by recursively identifying pre-synaptically active neuronal units over a few time-steps (Kritchmar et al., 2005a). The corresponding causal core was then identified by preserving only those parts of the context network that were (i) causally significant as assessed by G-causality, and (ii) resided within chains of

other G-causal connections leading to the NR. Causal cores therefore reflect the set of neuronal interactions that are significant for a given output. Remarkably, it turned out that causal cores were much smaller as compared to context networks (mean sizes of 29 and 723 units respectively), suggesting that even in large neural populations only comparatively small subsets may be causally recruited at a given time for a given function. Even more interesting was the observation that causal cores for a given NR tended to diminish in size during learning, suggesting that synaptic plasticity underlies learning in Darwin X via modulation of causal networks at the population level, and not by strengthening of weakening of associative links between neural representations of objects and actions.

BBDs in Context

Why are BBDs so complex? A simple response is that the BBD methodology reflects the underlying belief that the secrets of the brain will only be revealed by a detailed consideration of neuroanatomy. Brains are large in scale, complex in dynamics, and have multiple levels of control. According to the BBD approach, useful models need to reflect aspects of this multi-level complexity. For example, the concept of the 'causal core' could not have been identified given a neurorobotic model with only tens of simulated neurons. BBDs are also designed at a level of complexity that encourages direct comparison with empirical data. For example, various statistics relating to place fields of units in CA1 of Darwin X invites direct comparison with rodent data, given that the ratios of the relevant neuroanatomical variables are comparable across both systems.

Because BBDs are complex they often require the development of novel analysis methods. There is a potential virtuous circularity involved in this dialogue. The application of novel analyses to BBDs can expand theoretical and conceptual horizons, and can serve to integrate existing empirical data into broader frameworks. At the same time, BBDs can serve as a 'test bed' anticipating future biological data. For example, the rapid development of high-resolution neural imaging via voltage-sensitive dyes is giving rise to an avalanche of data which will require novel population-based analysis methods. The causal core analysis is an example of one such method.

PROSPECTS

This chapter has concentrated on strands of autonomous robotics that employ neural systems, focusing particularly on strongly biologically-inspired approaches. Although great progress has been made, and techniques similar to those discussed earlier are used in many of the ever-proliferating mobile robots we now see in the home (e.g. autonomous vacuum cleaners and toys), or in areas such as planetary exploration, security or military applications, many challenges remain.

It is now possible to produce autonomous robots that behave in a robust and reliable way in real environments, engaging in real tasks in real-time. However, the behaviours involved are still relatively simple. Progress has been slow towards more sophisticated tasks such as learning what to focus attention on in a complex environment, coordinating many conflicting goals and drives, interacting with other robots in complex group behaviours, learning to communicate in a sophisticated way about the task at hand, and so on. Perhaps this should not be at all surprising. One lesson that most neuroscientists have understood for many decades, but which has often been overlooked in AI, is that the generation of intelligent embodied behaviour is an extremely complicated problem. However, progress *is* being made and there are many promising lines of research. It is likely that directions involving artificial neural systems and other biologically inspired methods will become even more important as attempts to tackle these hard problems gather momentum. One direction, briefly mentioned earlier, that is likely to become increasingly important is the continued dismantling of the line between brain and body that has traditionally been present in studies of both natural and artificial intelligence.

The topics highlighted in this chapter have, appropriately enough, been fairly mature areas of research. However, there are a number of potentially important emerging fields that may have a radical impact in the decades to come. These include developments in interfacing digital electronics to neural tissue. The most frequent motivation for such work is to allow improved prosthetics to be directly controlled by the nervous system. This points to the possibility of an increased merging of robotic technology with human bodies –something that a number of people have reflected on recently (e.g. Brooks 2002) and which the work of Stelarc, the radical performance artist, has long explored. A related area involves attempting to harness the sophisticated non-linear adaptive properties of cultured (real) neural networks to create hybrid machines (DeMarse et al. 2001), pointing towards the possibility of robots that include biological matter in their control systems – a development that would echo the imagined landscapes of dozens of sci-fi books and movies. It is possible that in the long-run that kind of approach may prove more powerful than attempting to understand biological systems in sufficient detail to be able to abstract general mechanisms underlying the generation of intelligent behaviour. However, such research is at an extremely early stage, so we cannot yet properly assess its potential.

Another possible long-range goal for neurorobotics is the construction of a conscious artifact. Justification for this point of view – which can be called 'strong artificial consciousness' – derives from the idea that biological consciousness comes from (complex) brain-body-environment interactions, and that there is no reason in principle why such interactions cannot be instantiated in synthetically constructed systems. However, there are as yet no credible instances of strong artificial consciousness, nor any on the horizon (Seth, 2009a). A more modest goal is described by 'weak artificial consciousness' according to which neurorobotic devices are treated as models of their target phenomenon, in much the same way that a computational model of a hurricane can shed light on meteorology without itself being windy. According to the weak approach, neurorobots can be used to derive and explore the consequences of hypotheses linking phenomenal aspects of conscious experience to underlying mechanisms. For example, it has been suggested that a subjective first-person perspective could be engendered by predictive forward modelling of sensorimotor interactions. Neurorobotic models may develop this suggestion by specifying necessary and sufficient neural requirements for such predictive modelling, and by analyzing the model behavior for patterns that resemble the functional architecture of the corresponding phenomenology (in this case, interactions between egocentric and allocentric reference frames) (Seth, 2009b). Owen Holland's 'CRONOS' neurorobot is in fact an example of exactly this approach (Holland, 2007).

The field of robotics has massively expanded since the days when it was dominated by cumbersome industrial arms; it is now quite possible that in the not too distant future robots will become as widespread and as common as computers are now. If such a technological revolution comes to pass, it is highly likely that artificial neural systems will play an important part as there will be greater demands for robust, reliable adaptation and learning, as well as sophisticated pattern recognition and sensory processing – all areas in which neural systems have great potential.

REFERENCES

A.B. (2009)... *Adaptive Behavior, 17*(4).

Angyan, A. J. (1959). Machina Reproducatrix. In D. V. Blake and A. M. Uttley (Eds.), *The Mechanization of Thought Processes*: *Proceedings of a Symposium held at the National Physical Laboratory on 24-27 November 1958*, (vol. 2, pp. 933-944). London: Her Majesty's Stationery Office.

Arbib, M. A. (1972). *The Metaphorical Brain: An Introduction to Cybernetics as Artificial Intelligence and Brain Theory*. New York: Wiley-Interscience.

Arbib, M. A., Érdi, P., & Szentágothai, J. (1997). *Neural Organization: Structure, Function, and Dynamics*. Cambridge, MA: MIT Press.

Argyros, A., Bekris, K., Orphanoudakis, S., & Kavraki, L. (2005). Robot homing by exploiting panoramic vision. *Autonomous Robots, 19*, 7–25. doi:10.1007/s10514-005-0603-7

Arkin, R. (1998). *Behavior-based robotics*. Cambridge, MA: MIT Press.

Aubepart, F., & Franceschini, N. (2007). Bio-inspired optic flow sensors based on FPGA: application to micro-air-vehicles. *Microprocessors and Microsystems, 31*, 408–419. doi:10.1016/j.micpro.2007.02.004

Ayers, J., Davis, J., & Rudolph, A. (2002). *Neurotechnology for Biomimetic Robots*. Cambridge, MA: MIT Press.

Baddeley, B., Graham, P., Philippides, A., Hempel de Ibarra, N., Collett, T., & Husbands, P. (2009). What can be learnt from analysing insect orientation flights using probabilistic SLAM? *Biological Cybernetics, 101*(3), 169–182. doi:10.1007/s00422-009-0327-4

Baranano, D., Ferris, C., & Snyder, S. (2001). Atypical neural messengers. *Trends in Neurosciences, 24*(2), 99–106. doi:10.1016/S0166-2236(00)01716-1

Beer, R. D., & Gallagher, J. C. (1992). Evolving dynamical neural networks for adaptive behavior. *Adaptive Behavior, 1*, 94–110. doi:10.1177/105971239200100105

Beer, R. D., Quinn, R. D., Chiel, H. J., & Ritzmann, R. E. (1997). Biologically-inspired approaches to robotics. *Communications of the ACM, 40*(3), 30–38. doi:10.1145/245108.245118

Bekey, G. (2005). *Autonomous Robots: From Biological Inspiration to Implementation and Control*. Cambridge, MA: MIT Press.

Bekey, G., & Goldberg, K. (Eds.). (1993). *Neural Networks in Robotics*, (Springer International Series in Engineering and Computer Science, Vol. 202). Berlin: Springer.

Boden, M. (2006). *Mind as Machine: A History of Cognitive Science*. Oxford, UK: OUP.

Borst, A., & Haag, J. (2002). Neural networks in the cockpit of the fly. *Journal of Comparative Physiology. A, Neuroethology, Sensory, Neural, and Behavioral Physiology, 188*, 419–437. doi:10.1007/s00359-002-0316-8

Brooks, R. A. (1986). A Robust Layered Control System for a Mobile Robot. *IEEE Journal on Robotics and Automation, 2*(1), 14–23.

Brooks, R. A. (1989). A Robot that Walks; Emergent Behaviors from a Carefully Evolved Network. *Neural Computation, 1*(2), 253–262. doi:10.1162/neco.1989.1.2.253

Brooks, R. A. (1999). *Cambrian Intelligence: The Early History of the New AI*. Cambridge, MA: MIT Press.

Brooks, R. A. (2002). *Flesh and Machines: How Robots Will Change Us*. New York: Pantheon Books.

Bullock, T., Bennett, M., Johnston, D., Josephson, R., Marder, E., & Fields, R. (2005). The neuron doctrine, redux. *Science, 310*(5749), 791. doi:10.1126/science.1114394

Cartwright, B., & Collett, T. (1983). Landmark learning in bees. *Journal of Comparative Physiology. A, Neuroethology, Sensory, Neural, and Behavioral Physiology, 151*, 521–543. doi:10.1007/BF00605469

Cartwright, B., & Collett, T. (1987). Landmark maps for honeybees. *Biological Cybernetics, 57*(1-2), 85–93. doi:10.1007/BF00318718

Collett, T., Dillmann, E., Giger, A., & Wehner, R. (1992). Visual landmarks and route following in desert ants. *Journal of Comparative Physiology. A, Neuroethology, Sensory, Neural, and Behavioral Physiology, 170*, 435–442. doi:10.1007/BF00191460

Cordeschi, R. (2002). *The Discovery of the Artificial: Behavior, Mind and Machines Before and Beyond Cybernetics*. Dordrecht: Kluwer Academic Publishers.

Cruse, H., Bartling, C., Cymbalyuk, G., Dean, J., & Dreifert, M. (1995). A modular artificial neural net for controlling a six-legged walking system. *Biological Cybernetics, 72*(5), 421–430. doi:10.1007/BF00201417

Dawson, T., & Snyder, S. (1994). Gases as biological messengers: nitric oxide and carbon monoxide in the brain. *The Journal of Neuroscience, 14*(9), 5147–5159.

DeMarse, T., Wagenaar, D., Blau, A., & Potter, S. (2001). The Neurally Controlled Animat: Biological Brains Acting with Simulated Bodies. *Autonomous Robots, 11*, 305–310. doi:10.1023/A:1012407611130

Durr, V., Schmitz, J., & Cruse, H. (2004). Behaviour-based modelling of hexapod locomotion: linking biology and technical application. *Arthropod Structure & Development, 33*, 237–250. doi:10.1016/j.asd.2004.05.004

Edelman, G. M. (1993). Neural Darwinism: selection and reentrant signaling in higher brain function. *Neuron, 10*(2), 115–125. doi:10.1016/0896-6273(93)90304-A

Edelman, G. M. (2007). Learning in and from brain-based devices. *Science, 318*(5853), 1103–1105. doi:10.1126/science.1148677

Fleischer, J. G. (2007). Retrospective and prospective responses arising in a modeled hippocampus during maze navigation by a brain-based device. *Proceedings of the National Academy of Sciences of the United States of America, 104*(9), 3556–3561. doi:10.1073/pnas.0611571104

Floreano, D., Husbands, P., & Nolfi, S. (2008). Evolutionary Robotics. In Siciliano, B., & Khatib, O. (Eds.), *Springer Handbook of Robotics* (pp. 1423–1451). Berlin: Springer. doi:10.1007/978-3-540-30301-5_62

Floreano, D., & Mattiussi, C. (2001). Evolution of Spiking Neural Controllers for Autonomous Vision-Based Robots. In Gomi, T. (Ed.), *Evolutionary Robotic: From Intelligent Robotics to Artificial Life*. Tokyo: Springer Verlag. doi:10.1007/3-540-45502-7_2

Floreano, D., & Mattiussi, C. (2008). *Bio-Inspired Artificial Intelligence*. Cambridge, MA: MIT Press.

Franceschini, N., Ruffier, F., & Serres, J. (2007). A bio-inspired flying robot sheds light on insect piloting abilities. *Current Biology, 17*, 329–335. doi:10.1016/j.cub.2006.12.032

Franz, M., & Mallot, H. (2000). Biomimetic robot navigation. *Robotics and Autonomous Systems, 30*, 133–153. doi:10.1016/S0921-8890(99)00069-X

Franz, M., Schölkopf, B., Mallot, H., & Bülthoff, H. (1998). Learning View Graphs for Robot Navigation. *Autonomous Robots, 5*, 111–125. doi:10.1023/A:1008821210922

Gallagher, J., Beer, R., Espenschiel, M., & Quinn, R. (1996). Application of evolved locomotion controllers to a hexapod robot. *Robotics and Autonomous Systems, 19*(1), 95–103. doi:10.1016/S0921-8890(96)00036-X

Gally, J., Montague, P., Reeke, G., & Edelman, G. (1990). The NO hypothesis: possible effects of a short-lived, rapidly diffusible signal in the development and function of the nervous system. *Proceedings of the National Academy of Sciences of the United States of America, 87*, 3547–3551. doi:10.1073/pnas.87.9.3547

Giovannangeli, C., Gaussier, P., & Désilles, G. (2006). Robust Mapless Outdoor Vision-Based Navigation. In *Intelligent Robots and Systems, 2006 IEEE/RSJ International Conference*, (pp. 3293-3300).

Hafner, V., & Moller, R. (2001). Learning of Visual Navigation Strategies. In Quoy, M. & Gaussier, P. & Wyatt, J. (Eds.), *Proceedings of the European Workshop on Learning Robots*, 1, (pp. 47-56).

Hafting, T., Fyhn, M., Molden, S., Moser, M. B., & Moser, E. I. (2005). Microstructure of a spatial map in the entorhinal cortex. [REMOVED HYPERLINK FIELD]. *Nature*, *436*, 801–806. doi:10.1038/nature03721

Higgins, C. (2004). Nondirectional motion may underlie insect behavioral dependence on image speed. *Biological Cybernetics*, *91*, 326–332. doi:10.1007/s00422-004-0519-x

Holland, O. (2003). Exploration and High Adventure: The Legacy of Grey Walter. *Philosophical Transactions of the Royal Society of London. Series A: Mathematical and Physical Sciences*, *361*, 2085–2121. doi:10.1098/rsta.2003.1260

Holland, O. (2007). Strongly embodied approach to machine consciousness. *Journal of Consciousness Studies*, *14*(7), 97–110.

Horáková, J., & Kelemen, J. (2008). The Robot Story: Why Robots Were Born and How They Grew Up. In Husbands, P., Holland, O., & Wheeler, M. (Eds.), *The Mechanical Mind in History* (pp. 283–306). Cambridge, MA: MIT Press.

Horn, B., & Schunck, B. (1981). Determining optical flow. *Artificial Intelligence*, *17*, 185–203. doi:10.1016/0004-3702(81)90024-2

Humbert, J., Conroy, J., Neely, C., & Barrows, G. (2009). Wide-Field Integration Methods for Visuomotor Control. In Floreano, D., & Zufferey, J.-C. (Eds.), *Flying Insects and Robots* (pp. 63–72). Berlin: Springer Verlag. doi:10.1007/978-3-540-89393-6_5

Husbands, P., & Holland, O. (2008). The Ratio Club: A Hub of British Cybernetics. In P. Husbands, O. Holland & M. Wheeler, *2008*, (pp. 91-148).

Husbands, P., Holland, O., & Wheeler, M. (Eds.). (2008). *The Mechanical Mind in History*. Cambridge, MA: MIT Press.

Husbands, P., Philippides, A., Vargas, P., Buckley, C., Fine, P., Di Paolo, E., & O'Shea, M. (in press). Spatial, temporal and modulatory factors affecting GasNet evolvability in a visually guided robotics task. *Complexity*.

Husbands, P., Smith, T., Jakobi, N., & O'Shea, M. (1998). Better Living through Chemistry: Evolving GasNets for Robot Control. *Connection Science*, *10*(3&4), 185–210. doi:10.1080/095400998116404

Ijspeert, A., Crespi, A., Ryczko, D., & Cabelguen, J.-M. (2007). From Swimming to Walking with a Salamander Robot Driven by a Spinal Cord Model. *Science*, *315*(5817), 1416–1420. doi:10.1126/science.1138353

Jakobi, N. (1998). Running across the reality gap: Octopod locomotion evolved in a minimal simulation. In P. Husbands & J.-A. Meyer, (Eds), *Evolutionary Robotics: First European Workshop, EvoRobot98* (pp. 39–58). Berlin: Springer.

Katz, P. (Ed.). (1999). *Beyond Neurotransmission: Neuromodulation and its Importance for Information Processing*. Oxford, UK: Oxford University Press.

Kodjabachian, J., & Meyer, J.-A. (1998). Evolution and development of neural networks controlling locomotion, gradient following and obstacle avoidance in artificial insects. *IEEE Transactions on Neural Networks*, *9*, 796–812. doi:10.1109/72.712153

Kohler, M., & Wehner, R. (2005). Idiosyncratic route-based memories in desert ants, Melophorus bagoti: How do they interact with path-integration vectors? *Neurobiology of Learning and Memory, 83*, 1–12. doi:10.1016/j.nlm.2004.05.011

Krapp, H., & Hengstenberg, R. (1996). Estimation of self-motion by optic flow processing in a single visual interneuron. *Nature, 384*, 463–466. doi:10.1038/384463a0

Krichmar, J. L., & Edelman, G. M. (2002). Machine psychology: autonomous behavior, perceptual categorization and conditioning in a brain-based device. *Cereb Cortex, 12*(8), 818–830. doi:10.1093/cercor/12.8.818

Krichmar, J. L., & Edelman, G. M. (2005). Brain-based devices for the study of nervous systems and the development of intelligent machines. *Artificial Life, 11*(1-2), 63–77. doi:10.1162/1064546053278946

Krichmar, J. L., Nitz, D. A., Gally, J. A., & Edelman, G. M. (2005a). Characterizing functional hippocampal pathways in a brain-based device as it solves a spatial memory task. *Proceedings of the National Academy of Sciences of the United States of America, 102*(6), 2111–2116. doi:10.1073/pnas.0409792102

Krichmar, J. L., Seth, A. K., Nitz, D. A., Fleischer, J. G., & Edelman, G. M. (2005b). Spatial navigation and causal analysis in a brain-based device modeling cortical-hippocampal interactions. *Neuroinformatics, 3*(3), 197–222. doi:10.1385/NI:3:3:197

Lambrinos, D., Möller, R., Pfeifer, R., Wehner, R., & Labhart, T. (2000). A Mobile Robot Employing Insect Strategies for Navigation. *Robotics and Autonomous Systems, 30*, 39–64. doi:10.1016/S0921-8890(99)00064-0

Lehrer, M., & Bianco, G. (2000). The turn-back-and-look behaviour: bee versus robot. *Biological Cybernetics, 83*(3), 211–229. doi:10.1007/s004220000165

Lewis, F., Jagannathan, S., & Yesildirek, A. (1999). *Neural Network Control of Robot manipulators and Nonlinear Systems*. London: Taylor & Francis.

Matarić, M. (1992). Integration of Representation Into Goal-Driven Behavior-Based Robots. *IEEE Transactions on Robotics and Automation, 8*(3), 304–312. doi:10.1109/70.143349

McHale, G., & Husbands, P. (2004). GasNets and other evovalble neural networks applied to bipedal locomotion. In S. Schaal et al. (Eds), *From Animals to Animats 8: Proceedings of the Eigth International Conference on Simulation of Adaptive Behaviour (SAB'2004)* (pp. 163-172). Cambridge, MA: MIT Press.

McKinstry, J. L. (2008). Embodied models of delayed neural responses: spatiotemporal categorization and predictive motor control in brain based devices. *Neural Networks, 21*(4), 553–561. doi:10.1016/j.neunet.2008.01.004

McKinstry, J. L., Edelman, G. M., & Krichmar, J. L. (2006). A cerebellar model for predictive motor control tested in a brain-based device. *Proceedings of the National Academy of Sciences of the United States of America, 103*(9), 3387–3392. doi:10.1073/pnas.0511281103

Meyer, J. A., Guillot, A., Girard, B., Khamassi, M., Pirim, P., & Berthoz, A. (2005). The Psikharpax project: Towards building an artificial rat. *Robotics and Autonomous Systems, 50*(4), 211–223. doi:10.1016/j.robot.2004.09.018

Milford, M., & Wyeth, G. (2008). Mapping a Suburb with a Single Camera using a Biologically Inspired SLAM System. *IEEE Transactions on Robotics, 24*(5), 1038–1053. doi:10.1109/TRO.2008.2004520

Milford, M., Wyeth, G., & Prasser, D. (2004). Rat-SLAM: A Hippocampal Model for Simultaneous Localization and Mapping. *Proc. IEEE International Conference on Robotics and Automation* (pp. 403-408). Pasadena, CA: IEEE Press.

Möller, R. (2000). Modelling the Landmark Navigation Behavior of the Desert Ant *Cataglyphis*. Technical Report IFI-AI-00.24, Artificial Intelligence Lab, Dept. Computer Science, University of Zurich. Zurich.

Möller, R. (2001). Do Insects Use Templates or Parameters for Landmark Navigation. *Journal of Theoretical Biology, 210*(1), 33–45. doi:10.1006/jtbi.2001.2295

Möller, R., & Vardy, A. (2006). Local visual homing by matched-filter descent in image distances. *Biological Cybernetics, 95*(5), 413–430. doi:10.1007/s00422-006-0095-3

Morris, R. (1984). Developments of a water-maze procedure for studying spatial learning in the rat. *Journal of Neuroscience Methods, 11*(1), 47–60. doi:10.1016/0165-0270(84)90007-4

Nehmzow, U., & Owen, C. (2000). Robot Navigation in the Real World: Experiments with Manchester's *FortyTwo* in Unmodified, Large Environments. *Robotics and Autonomous Systems, 33*, 223–242. doi:10.1016/S0921-8890(00)00098-1

Nilsson, N. J. (Ed.). (1984). *Shakey The Robot, Technical Note 323. AI Center, SRI International, Menlo Park CA., Nolfi, S., & Floreano, D. (2000) Evolutionary Robotics: The Biology, Intelligence, and Technology of Self-Organizing Machines.* Cambridge, MA: MIT Press.

Pearson, K. G. (1976). The control of walking. *Scientific American, 235*, 72–86. doi:10.1038/scientificamerican1276-72

Pearson, M., Pipe, A., Melhuish, C., Mitchinson, B., & Prescott, T. (2007). Whiskerbot: A Robotic Active Touch System Modeled on the Rat Whisker Sensory System. *Adaptive Behavior, 15*(3), 223–240. doi:10.1177/1059712307082089

Pfeifer, R., & Bongard, J. (2007). *How the body shapes the way we think: a new view of intelligence.* Cambridge, MA: MIT Press.

Philippides, A., Husbands, P., & O'Shea, M. (2000). Four Dimensional Neuronal Signaling by Nitric Oxide: A Computational Analysis. *The Journal of Neuroscience, 20*(3), 1199–1207.

Philippides, A., Husbands, P., Smith, T., & O'Shea, M. (2003). Structure based models of NO diffusion in the nervous system. In Feng, J. (Ed.), *Computational Neuroscience: a comprehensive approach* (pp. 97–130). London: Chapman and Hall/CRC Press. doi:10.1201/9780203494462.ch4

Philippides, A., Husbands, P., Smith, T., & O'Shea, M. (2005b). Flexible couplings: diffusing neuromodulators and adaptive robotics. *Artificial Life, 11*(1&2), 139–160. doi:10.1162/1064546053279044

Philippides, A., Ott, S., Husbands, P., Lovick, T., & O'Shea, M. (2005a). Modeling co-operative volume signaling in a plexus of nitric oxide synthase-expressing neurons. *The Journal of Neuroscience, 25*(28), 6520–6532. doi:10.1523/JNEUROSCI.1264-05.2005

Pomerleau, D. (1991). Efficient Training of Artificial Neural Networks for Autonomous Navigation. *Neural Computation, 3*, 88–97. doi:10.1162/neco.1991.3.1.88

Prescott, T. J., Bryson, J. J., & Seth, A. K. (2007). Modelling natural action selection: Introduction to the theme issue. *Philosophical Transactions of the Royal Society of London. Series B, Biological Sciences, 362*(1485), 1521–1529. doi:10.1098/rstb.2007.2050

Prescott, T. J., Montes-Gonzalez, F., Gurney, K., Humphries, M. D., & Redgrave, P. (2006). A robot model of the basal ganglia: Behavior and intrinsic processing. *Neural Networks, 19*, 31–61. doi:10.1016/j.neunet.2005.06.049

Prescott, T. J., Redgrave, P., & Gurney, K. N. (1999). Layered control architectures in robots and vertebrates. *Adaptive Behavior, 7*, 99–127. doi:10.1177/105971239900700105

Reeke, G. N., Sporns, O., & Edelman, G. M. (1990). Synthetic neural modeling: The "Darwin" series of recognition automata. *Proceedings of the IEEE, 78*(9), 1498–1530. doi:10.1109/5.58327

Reeve, R., Webb, B., Indiveri, G., Horchler, A., & Quinn, R. (2005). New technologies for testing a model of cricket phonotaxis on an outdoor robot. *Robotics and Autonomous Systems, 51*(1), 41–54. doi:10.1016/j.robot.2004.08.010

Reichardt, W. (1961). Autocorrelation, a principle for the evaluation of sensory information by the central nervous system. In Rosenblith, W. (Ed.), *Principles of sensory communication* (pp. 303–317). New York: Wiley.

Reil, T., & Husbands, P. (2002). Evolution of central pattern generators for bipedal walking in real-time physics environments. *IEEE Transactions on Evolutionary Computation, 6*(2), 10–21. doi:10.1109/4235.996015

Riabinina, O., & Philippides, A. (2009). A model of visual detection of angular speed for bees. *Journal of Theoretical Biology, 257*(1), 61–72. doi:10.1016/j.jtbi.2008.11.002

Rosengren, R. (1971). Route Fidelity, Visual Memory and Recruitment Behaviour in Foraging Wood Ants of the *Genus Formica* (Hymenopteran Formicidae). *Acta Zoologica Fennica, 133*, 1–150.

Schilling, M., Cruse, H., & Arena, P. (2007). Hexapod Walking: an expansion to Walknet dealing with leg amputations and force oscillations. *Biological Cybernetics, 96*, 323–340. doi:10.1007/s00422-006-0117-1

Seth, A. K. (2009a). The strength of weak artificial consciousness. *International Journal of Machine Consciousness, 1*(1), 71–82. doi:10.1142/S1793843009000086

Seth, A. K. (2009b). Explanatory correlates of consciousness: Theoretical and computational challenges. *Cognitive Computation, 1*(1), 50–63. doi:10.1007/s12559-009-9007-x

Seth, A. K., & Edelman, G. M. (2007). Distinguishing causal interactions in neural populations. *Neural Computation, 19*(4), 910–933. doi:10.1162/neco.2007.19.4.910

Seth, A. K., McKinstry, J. L., Edelman, G. M., & Krichmar, J. L. (2004a). Visual binding through reentrant connectivity and dynamic synchronization in a brain-based device. *Cerebral Cortex, 14*(11), 1185–1199. doi:10.1093/cercor/bhh079

Seth, A. K., McKinstry, J. L., Edelman, G. M., & Krichmar, J. L. (2004b). Active sensing of visual and tactile stimuli by brain-based devices. *International Journal of Robotics and Automation, 19*(4), 222–238. doi:10.2316/Journal.206.2004.4.206-2802

Siciliano, B., & Khatib, O. (Eds.). (2008). *Springer Handbook of Robotics*. Berlin: Springer. doi:10.1007/978-3-540-30301-5

Smith, L., Philippides, A., Graham, P., Baddeley, B., & Husbands, P. (2007). Linked local navigation for visual route guidance. *Adaptive Behavior, 15*(3), 257–271. doi:10.1177/1059712307082091

Smith, L., Philippides, A., Graham, P., & Husbands, P. (2008). Linked Local Visual Navigation and Robustness to Motor Noise and Route Displacement. In M.Asada et al. (Eds.), *Proc. SAB'08: Animals to Animats X* (LNCS 5040, pp. 179-188). Berlin: Springer.

Smith, T. M. C., Husbands, P., & O'Shea, M. (2003). Local evolvability of statistically neutral GasNet robot controllers. *Bio Systems, 69*, 223–243. doi:10.1016/S0303-2647(02)00139-9

Smith, T. M. C., Husbands, P., Philippides, A., & O'Shea, M. (2002). Neuronal plasticity and temporal adaptivity: GasNet robot control networks. *Adaptive Behavior, 10*(3/4), 161–184.

Srinivasan, M. (2006). Small brains, smart computations: Vision and navigation in honeybees, and applications to robotics. *International Congress Series, 1291*, 30–37. doi:10.1016/j.ics.2006.01.055

Srinivasan, M., Chahl, J., Weber, K., Venkatesh, S., Nagle, M., & Zhang, S. (1999). Robot navigation inspired by principles of insect vision. *Robotics and Autonomous Systems, 26*(2-3), 203–216. doi:10.1016/S0921-8890(98)00069-4

Srinivasan, M., Thurrowgood, S., & Soccol, D. (2006). An optical system for guidance of terrain following in UAVs. *Proc IEEE International Conference on Advanced Video and Signal Based Surveillance* (AVSS '06), Sydney (pp. 51-56). Pasadena, CA: IEEE Press.

Srinivasan, M., Zhang, S., Chahl, J., Stange, G., & Garratt, M. (2004). An overview of insect inspired guidance for application in ground and airborne platforms. *Proceedings of the Institution of Mechanical Engineers. Part G, Journal of Aerospace Engineering, 218*, 375–388. doi:10.1243/0954410042794966

Srinivasan, M. V. (2002). Visual Flight Control and Navigation in Honeybees, and Applications to Robotics. In Ayers, J., Davis, J. L., & Rudolph, A. (Eds.), *Neurotechnology for Biomimetic Robots* (pp. 593–610). Cambridge, MA: MIT Press.

Taube, J. S., Muller, R. U., & Ranck, J. B. (1990a). Head-direction cells recorded from the postsubiculum in freely moving rats, I: Description and quantitative analysis. *The Journal of Neuroscience, 10*(2), 420–435.

Taube, J. S., Muller, R. U., & Ranck, J. B. (1990b). Head-direction cells recorded from the postsubiculum in freely moving rats, II: Effects of environmental manipulations. *The Journal of Neuroscience, 10*(2), 436–447.

Thrun, T., Burgard, W., & Fox, D. (2005). *Probabilistic Robotics*. Cambridge, MA: MIT Press.

Tononi, G., Sporns, O., & Edelman, G. (1999). Measures of degeneracy and redundancy in biological networks. *Proceedings of the National Academy of Sciences of the United States of America, 96*, 3257. doi:10.1073/pnas.96.6.3257

Vardy, A. (2006). Long-Range Visual Homing. In *Proceedings of the 2006 IEEE International Conference on Robotics and Biomimetics* (pp. 220-226).

Vardy, A., & Moller, R. (2005). Biologically plausible visual homing methods based on optical flow techniques. *Connection Science, 17*(1), 47–90. doi:10.1080/09540090500140958

Vargas, P., Di Paolo, E., & Husbands, P. (2008). Exploring non-spatial GasNets in a delayed response robot task. In Bullock, S. (Eds.), *Proc. Artificial Life XI* (pp. 640–647). Cambridge, MA: MIT Press.

Vargas, P., Moioli, R., Von Zuben, F., & Husbands, P. (2009). Homeostasis and Evolution Together Dealing with Novelties and Managing Disruptions. *International Journal of Intelligent Computing and Cybernetics*, *2*(3), 435–454. doi:10.1108/17563780910982680

Vaughan, E., Di Paolo, E., & Harvey, I. (2004) The evolution of control and adaptation in a 3D powered passive dynamic walker. In J. Pollack, M. Bedau, P. Husbands, T. Ikegami, & R. Watson, (Eds), *Proceedings of the Ninth International Conference on the Simulation and Synthesis of Living Systems, Artificial Life IX* (pp. 139–145). Cambridge, MA: MIT Press.

Walter, W. G. (1950). An imitation of life. *Scientific American*, *182*(5), 42–45. doi:10.1038/scientificamerican0550-42

Walter, W. G. (1951). A machine that learns. *Scientific American*, *185*(2), 60–63.

Walter, W. G. (1953). *The Living Brain*. London: Duckworth.

Webb, B. (2001). Can robots make good models of biological behaviour? *The Behavioral and Brain Sciences*, *24*(6), 1033–1050. doi:10.1017/S0140525X01000127

Webb, B. (2009). Animals versus animats: or why not model the real iguana? *Adaptive Behavior*, *17*(4), 269–286. doi:10.1177/1059712309339867

Webb, B., & Consi, T. (Eds.). (2001). *Biorobotics*. Cambridge, MA: MIT Press.

Webb, B., & Scutt, T. (2000). A simple latency dependent spiking neuron model of cricket phonotaxis. *Biological Cybernetics*, *82*(3), 247–269. doi:10.1007/s004220050024

Wehner, R., Boyer, M., Loertscher, F., Sommer, S., & Menzi, U. (2006). Ant Navigation: One-Way Routes Rather Than Maps. *Current Biology*, *16*, 75–79. doi:10.1016/j.cub.2005.11.035

Wehner, R., Michel, B., & Antonsen, P. (1996). Visual Navigation in Insects: Coupling of Egocentric and Geocentric Information. *The Journal of Experimental Biology*, *199*, 129–140.

Wheeler, M. (2005). *Reconstructing the Cognitive World*. Cambridge, MA: MIT Press.

Wood, G. (2003). *Living Dolls: A Magical History of the Quest for Mechanical Life*. London: Faber and Faber.

Wood, J., & Garthwaite, J. (1994). Model of the diffusional spread of nitric oxide - implications for neural nitric oxide signaling and its pharmacological properties. *Neuropharmacology*, *33*, 1235–1244. doi:10.1016/0028-3908(94)90022-1

Wyeth, G., & Milford, M. (2009). Spatial Cognition for Robots: Robot Navigation from Biological Inspiration. *IEEE Robotics & Automation Magazine*, *16*(3), 24–32. doi:10.1109/MRA.2009.933620

KEY TERMS AND DEFINITIONS

Autonomous Robot: a device that interacts with the world via sensors and actuators in an autonomous way. Such robots are usually mobile and exhibit sensorimotor behaviours such as navigation.

Biologically-Inspired Artificial Neural Systems: an artificial neural system, usually organised as one or more networks of artificial neurons, inspired by neural architectures and mechanisms found in biology. Such systems are often used as artificial nervous systems for robots.

Brain-Based Device: neurorobotic (see below) devices whose development is most closely associated with Edelman and colleagues at the Neurosciences Institute in San Diego.

Evolutionary Robotics: an approach to robotics in which some or all aspects of a robot's design (control system, body morphology etc) is achieved using evolutionary search.

GasNet: a form of artificial neural network incorporating an analogue of volume signalling whereby gaseous neurotransmitters diffuse from a neural site so to as affect other neurons in the vicinity, even if they are not electrically connected to the source neuron.

Insect-Inspired Robotics: a branch of autonomous robotics inspired by studies of insect behaviours, neural mechanisms and biomechanics.

Neural Systems for Navigation: neural circuits involved in generating navigation be-haviours, including route learning and landmark detection.

Neurorobotics: an area of research in which autonomous robots are used to study embodied situated models of biological neural systems. A form of biological modelling using robots.

View-Based Homing: local visual navigation methods and algorithm for returning 'home' based on information gleaned from the current view of the world. Often the current view of the world is compared with a stored view taken from 'home' in order to calculate which direction to move in.

Section 4
Neuroscience and Business

Chapter 11
Designing Useful Robots:
Is Neural Computation the Answer?

David Bisset
iTechnic Ltd, UK

ABSTRACT

This chapter explores the challenges presented by the introduction of robots into our everyday lives, examining technical and design issues as well as ethical and business issues. It also examines the process of designing and specifying useful robots and highlights the practical difficulties in testing and guaranteeing behaviour and function in adaptive systems. The chapter also briefly reviews the current state of robotics in Europe and the global robotic marketplace. It argues that it is essential, for the generation of a viable industry, for the Academic and Business sectors to work together to solve the fundamental technical and ethical problems that can potentially impede the development and deployment of autonomous robotic systems. It details the reality and expectations in healthcare robotics examining the demographics and deployment difficulties this domain will face. Finally it challenges the assumption that Neural Computation is the technology of choice for building autonomous cognitive systems and points out the difficulties inherent in using adaptive "holistic" systems within the performance oriented ethos of the product design engineer.

INTRODUCTION

The purpose of this chapter is not to describe new technologies or explore the state of the art, instead its aim is to highlight the challenges of designing useful robots. It will review some of the challenges that designers of useful robots will face in trying to make systems that can carry out real tasks in everyday environments. Its intention is to stimulate, with the hope that researchers will engage in exploring the means by which some of the fundamental issues in robotics might be addressed, not as bench top experiments in robotics but through the development of technologies that can be integrated into deployed, functional robotic systems.

DOI: 10.4018/978-1-60960-021-1.ch011

It is widely acknowledged that Robotics will be the next major electro-technical revolution. Unlike the computer revolution and the communications revolution, which we are still in the middle of, it is likely to take longer to establish itself. Firstly because the technologies are more complex and currently less well understood, and secondly because the pervasiveness of the technology will be much greater. The computer revolution has always been bounded by our ability to create faster processors and larger memories as characterised by Moore's Law (Moore, 1965) (Moore, 1975), the communications revolution is driven by standards and the creation of infrastructure, where technology has not limited its expansion in the same way it has limited the computer revolution. As might be expected Robotics has different constraints and drivers. In addition to technology and cost limitations, legal, societal and ethical issues will play a major role in the delivery and approval of many potential applications of robotics. There is no doubt that the robotics revolution has already started, but there is a long way to go before we will notice its impact and it will take several decades for the full impact to be felt. It will develop at a considerable pace but only once the technology is established and the service and delivery models have been refined. It is possible that Robotics will be the last great electro-technical revolution, and that its conclusion will mark the end of the era of electro-technical revolutions, at the conclusion of which the machine will be able to replicate the thoughts and intentional actions of humans. For this reason building useful robots is the ultimate engineering challenge.

This chapter will explore the design of robots and the potential for applications. It will also explore how they will impact on our daily lives possibly to a greater extent than any other technology ever has. Their pervasiveness in 50 years will surprise us but the Armageddon so loved by science fiction will not happen. They will alter our home and work lives, our transport and our healthcare. They will enrage, delight and the ethical, legal and societal issues will be a major cause of concern for government, parents and the children of the elderly.

There is also a sub-text to this chapter; it is to attempt to bring closer together the industrial and the academic, thus connecting the means of production with the research base. Only by working towards a mutual understanding of issues and by joining to solve common problems will the best outcome be achieved. In many cases across Europe there is a good working relationship between industry and academia, but what is required is a greater common understanding of how to effectively work together in a more open community that allows a greater transfer of technology to mutual benefit. The EU has recognised that this joining is particularly important in the field of robotics and is working to bring both groups together. This was no more clearly stated than at the launch of the Strategic Research Agenda for Robotics in Europe where Dr Rudolf Strohmeier (Head of Cabinet EU Commission for Information Society and Media) stated "Europe cannot afford the fragmentation of its research resource". Some of the larger manufacturing organisations within Europe are beginning to offer more open routes to design and to offer support for a freer flow of knowledge and resources and the move to Open Innovation practices will help.

EUROPEAN ROBOTICS

Europe has an extremely strong robotics industry founded on car manufacture and process automation. This has created global companies at the heart of Europe's robotics industry. While the industrial robotics community and the autonomous robotics community sometimes only see themselves as linked by the word robot, there is in fact a much deeper synergy that is possible. The development of the robotics market will take place across a broad spectrum of very different market sectors, and in many of these sectors real world sensing, object handling and locomotion are critical technologies for the creation of viable products. For example in construction, food processing, transport, space and a number of defence applications' potential solutions involve a synthesis of the industrial robot arm with intelligent autonomous systems providing adaptation and flexibility of operation. Add to this mix the fact that most of Europe's industrial robotics manufacturers will seek to diversify in order to expand their business it makes sense for them to invest in autonomous systems technology in order to enter and advance in these market sectors, which at the same time will impact on the general level of funding and investment. This closer coupling may well need to be matched by a deeper embrace of open standards and open design processes.

Research goals and directions have been successfully channelled by "Grand Challenges" and by competitions. These activities showcase development teams and force the integration of technologies and a pragmatic approach to design and implementation issues. Of course these challenges carry the danger that they can focus too tightly on solving specific problems, which is of course very often what the sponsors of the competitions want. While these competitions have their place it is also important that generalisations of architecture and sensor processing mechanisms are properly explored, and access to open solutions created so that resulting technologies can be exploited to the full.

The high profile challenges have an additional benefit in that they stimulate technology and knowledge transfer. The funding of technology transfer and its management is just as important as funding the research that generated the IP in the first place. Within Europe there are many SME spin-outs from Universities that are using "seed corn" investment to create products and systems components. However the market will fail to grow without larger scale enterprises investing in this crop of ideas so that the SMEs can flourish. The transfer of IP between organisations of unequal

size is a particularly difficult task and will need support.

In addition to the sectors mentioned, Europe also has strong domestic appliance, medical equipment and automotive industries, in each case robotics will have a significant impact on almost every aspect of their markets.

Thus Europe has the pre-requisites for the creation of a strong global advanced robotics industry by coupling its existing industrial base to the expertise of its academic community and its strong history of innovation. So to do Korea and Japan. This will be a global race just as every other electro-technical revolution has been.

The global market for advanced service robotics is growing year on year. According to the most recent IFR report (International Federation of Robotics, 2009) the value of all professional service robots sold to the end of 2008 was $11.2 Billion, on a total of 63,000 units with 30% of this value in the military and defence area. Projections place the sale of professional service robots at 49,000 robots for the period 2009-2012. For personal use some 7.2 Million units were sold to the end of 2009, and it is projected that some 4.8 Million units will be sold into the domestic market and 6.8 Million into the entertainment sector in the period 2009-2012. While these figures include relatively low level functions they indicate that the market is growing and while this is nowhere near the levels of sale of computers or phones it indicates that there is a growing potential for revenue generation.

Today's robot technology is not sufficiently advanced to achieve the wide spread use of robots in everyday human environments, but many of the elements are in place. If these technologies are to mature and novel ones emerge, then it is important that the funding for research is well managed and targeted at areas of importance. Clearly in a European context this must focus on areas in which Europe needs to enhance its capability, while at the same time support the continuation of existing world-class research and development. Key to the development of a viable robotics industry is the underpinning of all aspects of the industrial community, both small and large, because without this community the opportunity to exploit key advances and the resulting technology will not exist. Given the extended timescales between innovation and realisation and the investments being made by Europe's industrial competitors it is important that research and development funds are invested now to ensure that Europe has access to the right technical and personnel resources to exploit the emerging robotics market. However it is not easy to predict where the weaknesses lie. The recently published Strategic Research Agenda for Robotics in Europe 2009 (EUROP, 2009) (The SRA) has used a defined methodology to explore the opportunity and technology that is likely to be required over the coming 10-20 years.

It is impossible to predict exactly how markets will develop and what "killer applications" might emerge. However it is important to identify common ground where technology is weak, and to ensure an effective and flexible support structure is in place that allows appropriate realisation and can react to emerging technologies and markets. The time scales of 10 years or more before the market fully develops mean Europe cannot afford to wait and see what emerges, it needs to act on the best evidence to date and invest to strengthen its technology base. The process that created the SRA involved a broad range of robotics experts from both academic and industrial communities from across Europe in an examination of what they think the key issues and technologies will be and so must be considered as a fairly representative current view of the state of robotics development in Europe. The document provides a clear insight into the future requirements of robotics design in terms of the analysis of the likely application areas and an overview of the capabilities of current technologies, although it is inevitable that the stated viewpoint will shift over time. As the conclusion of the SRA states "this report should not be judged on the accuracy of its visions but on

its ability to stimulate collaboration and investment in the technology and infrastructure required to achieve a viable robotics industry in Europe by 2020" (EUROP, 2009 pp35)

ANALYSING ROBOT TECHNOLOGY

Having argued the need to identify how to support the emerging industry as well as enhance European research capability it is therefore important to try and predict how the robotics market might unfold, and in particular what types of technical capability might be needed in order to create a viable market.

In considering what robots might achieve it is important to try and approach the problem from both ends, to both extrapolate what can currently be achieved with existing technology or at least what might realistically be achieved within the next 10 to 20 years and to attempt to see how these developments might lead to product capabilities, and from the other end to examine what users might want or need in each application domain and to gauge the level of technological capability required to achieve it. Obviously there will be unpredicted leaps in capability and when these happen they will cause product development to focus on markets that can exploit those leaps, but these will simply modulate the way that applications are addressed rather than alter the basic domains where robots are likely to be applied or alter the capability levels required of each technology. It is important to focus on the capability levels that need to be achieved for any given application rather than on specific technologies or on timescales. In analysing these capabilities it is important to distinguish between functional requirements and the technology that might fulfil the requirement. By concentrating on the requirements needed to create a given application, or class of application, it is possible to assess how capable each technology is and by examining the requirements of each application, the fit between technical capability and application requirement can be assessed.

This double ended analysis underpins the way that the SRA has attempted to analyse the technology required to create a viable market. Firstly defining application domains that loosely align with existing industrial sectors, and brainstorming areas of application within each domain. Then identifying generic application scenarios that encapsulate the key aspects of a domain that might be applicable to robotics. Finally assessing the specific technical requirements (Application Requirements) for each scenario and comparing these to the current technology capability in each area of requirement.

During the production of the SRA a further step (cross fertilisation) was taken that accumulated all of the application requirements from across the domains and created a set of generic Application Requirements for robotics. Such an approach requires extensive ground work. Firstly to define the scope of "Application Scenarios" so that the scenario descriptions are generic enough to encompass the area of application without pre-judging which technologies will be required. Secondly the Application Requirements must be written in a common language so that cross domain analysis can be carried out, and finally definitions for technologies need to be created so that capability can be assessed across domains. Great care must be taken at this stage to ensure that Requirements are phrased in technology independent language. The net result is a clear distinction between Application Requirements, such as sensing and locomotion, and technologies such as computer vision or neural networks.

APPLICATIONS

There are a large number of potential applications for robotics, these can be categorised by the market place and by the specific functional applications within those markets. While it is not possible to predict which specific applications might appear in each market it is possible to analyse each market in terms of the requirements the market places on the technology. In turn by examining the current status of each technology it is possible to build a picture of the match between technical capability and application requirements.

So while one application might demand a certain level of capability from a given technology another application may demand a lower level of capability and thus represent a more immediately viable opportunity.

The main application areas are:

- Space
- Security
- Military
- Logistics, transport and storage.
- Domestic
- Entertainment
- Agriculture and food
- Medical
- Health care
- Manufacturing

One thing that is clear when examining this list is the fact that almost every aspect of our daily lives might eventually be impacted by robotics. In each of the above application areas there are either examples of deployed robots or feasibility studies and prototypes testing the opportunity. Of course in only a very small number of cases are these robots being manufactured in volume however the fact of their existence marks the start of the market exploration and development process.

The important step change in requirements in these areas is the push for closer interaction between people and robots, closer than it has ever been in the past. The nature of the interaction is also changing from being between a trained operator, or programmer working in a constrained environment, to an interaction with untrained people in everyday environments. This step change in the nature of the interaction has a correspond-

Figure 1. The robot interaction matrix with example applications

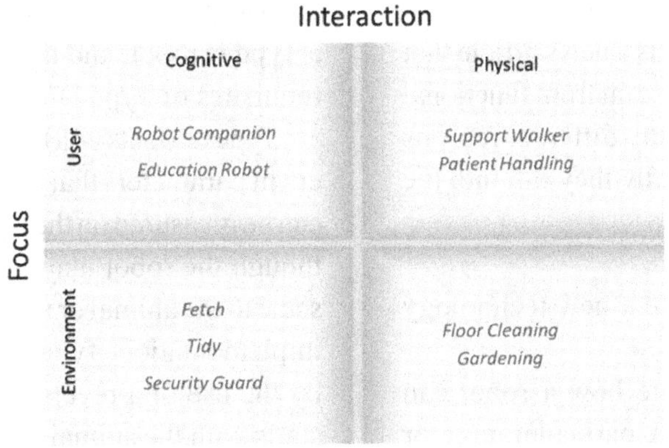

ing impact on the technologies used within the robots, both in terms of sensing and sense data processing as well as control, planning, safety and user interface technology.

The nature of this interaction between robot, environment and user can be captured in a simple matrix.

The applications that have been tackled to date are characterised by low levels of cognitive interaction, and by low levels of autonomy.

Why is the above discussion important to academics focused on a paradigm such as neural computation? The answer is that if research is to be relevant and in context, focusing on the challenges of a particular field of application such as robotics is best carried out with a full understanding of the context of its application. It is often that the use of a particular technology, that might appear at first sight to be relevant to a particular area of application, can be eliminated on the grounds of cost, poor dependability or performance once the area of application and its requirements are well understood. Such an understanding may increase the efficiency of research by appropriately applying technology. This is not to say that the only use for neural computation is robotics but it is likely to be a significant one, not only because of the interesting challenges it presents but also because of the eventual funding it might provide.

WHY BUILD A ROBOT?

If we are to discuss the problems that surround the design and deployment of robots in everyday human environments then it is important to examine both the design processes as well as the technologies that are required.

It is important to build robots to demonstrate function, but this is an expensive and time consuming task that should only be undertaken after there has been a full analysis of the requirements and objectives of the system. This applies equally to the design and construction of experimental robots in an academic environment as it does to the development of robotic products. Industrial design processes are geared to reducing time to market and optimising resources by challenging design choices and assumptions early in the design process. It is cheaper and quicker to alter a design while it is a concept, or model, than after it has been made even in prototype form. The waste of resource inevitable in building the wrong robot, or using the wrong technology is too great to ignore. In addition the essential synergy between the different components of the robot and the cross disciplinary skills required to design and build robots at the cutting edge of technology require the coordination of a team of people and resources that is not easily gathered in one place.

(The Willow Garage project seems to have found a working model for this process).

Almost every week there is a news article that highlights a new robot, most are far from functional in a real sense. There are many different reasons for building a robot but broadly they fall into the following categories:

- *Type A*: To demonstrate a new technology applicable to robots.
- *Type B*: To demonstrate how a robot can be made to perform a particular task or interaction.
- *Type C*: To prove a theory about the function or construction of animals.
- *Type D*: To carry out a specific functional task, or tasks.

Examples of Type A robots are likely to involve novel software or hardware and the function the robot performs will most likely have been chosen to allow investigation of the parameters of the design in comparison with other different techniques or methods. Type A robots are likely to work only with careful handling as they need only perform a small number of times in order for results to be captured and an assessment made of the effectiveness of the technology. It is likely that the robot has been designed from modular components that can be easily adapted to allow experimentation on different technologies and that it will be relatively easy to re-design and reconstruct to achieve a new goal.

Type B robots will most likely perform the particular task in a sub-optimal way but with new or different technology with the expectation that it will demonstrate the viability of performing this particular task with a robot. The implication is that the design is either scalable or can be made more efficient such that it might eventually provide a useful function. Type B robots are likely to be specially constructed, while software may use a common core the mechanics may be specific to the task and considerable effort may have been invested in finding solutions to specific problems. Considerable thought is likely to have gone into a Type B robot, and they are likely to be the prerequisites of Type D robots.

Type C robots will be constructed so that the relevant parameters that are known about the animal can be measured on the robot for comparison even though the robot may be on a different physical scale to the animal or use different mechanisms of implementation. Type C robots are characterised by the use of a reverse engineering process that starts with the animal and finishes with the robot. Like Type A robots the number of times it must run is limited and once the results are gathered, attention is likely to switch to modification or abandonment. Here the assumption is that there is an equivalence in the processing or design and that ultimately there will be a parity of function.

It is most likely that Type D robots will be designed to carry out a very specific and well defined task but more importantly their success is measured by the effectiveness in performing the specified task rather than the elegance of the design or design process or the nature of the technology used. The design will be focused on the task or set of tasks and the system will be engineered to specifically achieve those tasks. These robots are most likely to make extensive use of standardised parts but it is likely that there will be a significant custom element to the design involving high cost and effort. These robots are likely to be required to carry out their task repeatedly and in real environments as well as adhere to safety criteria and survive unskilled operation. Clearly this type of robot must be carefully designed and constructed to meet its requirements.

Robots are the result of a synthesis of a very broad range of technologies encompassing a wide range of technical disciplines. Making the right robot requires a sympathetic understanding of how these different domains interact. How mechanical problems may be better solved in software or electronics and how software problems may be better solved with improved sensors or a different mechanical configuration. The skill of robot design is in the fine understanding of the integration of its different technologies and the exploitation of their synergies.

This chapter will now concentrate on Type D robots, because in the long term these will be the most prevalent; robots that provide a useful function. Later sections will explore the likely end uses and forms of these Type D robots and examine many of the real problems that will face those who set out to design, build and deliver them to end users. Examining these problems uncovers significant technical challenges that will need to be solved if robots are to perform the types of functions that we expect of them.

It is important when designing a robot, or indeed any product, to ensure that unnecessary preconceptions about the right form or method required to fulfil a design requirement are eliminated. Any product designed with a form that is inappropriate or the result of a "it must have wheels" design requirement will most likely result in a sub-optimal system, unless of course wheels are the right solution. Rather like the currently growing misconception that all robots that are going to work in cooperation with people will have to be bipedal.

APPLICATION REQUIREMENTS

The design of robots is intimately bound with the discipline of systems engineering. The fundamental design methodology of systems engineering is to divide the system into parts and layers and to attempt to isolate these into manageable units that can be designed with well defined interfaces then constructed and tested independently. This has the advantage that the resulting components and modules have the potential to be reusable and thus speed the construction of future systems. All major manufacturing industries are based on collections of common components, or on the use of common design processes or processing techniques, be it a

means of applying a plastic surface to a metal substrate or an algorithm for extracting faces from an image. These modules or processes encapsulate IP and allow enterprises to profit from narrow advantages in technology that scale to distinct advantages in end products. The encapsulation and distribution of IP also allows smaller enterprises to sell to larger ones and thus represents an important part of the interchange and growth within an industry. As a consequence of this decomposition and the desire to encapsulate IP the specification of systems is also typically broken down along the boundaries that divide distinct IP segments as well as along functional dividing lines.

In addition to compartmentalising key functional elements, this approach to decomposition also has the advantage that it allows independent and parallel development to take place across a project and allows bought in and designed modules to be incorporated alongside each other within a design. In particular modules for specific functional elements that provide the encapsulation of IP also provide an economy of scale across multiple domains requiring the same function.

When analysing the likely functions that robots could perform in each of the different application areas a number of core application requirement groups can be identified. These requirement groups represent all the different aspects of robotics that might need to be captured by requirements. The SRA identifies them as follows:

- Sustainability
- Configuration
- Adaptation
- Autonomy
- Positioning
- Manipulation and Grasping
- Robot-Robot interaction
- Human-Robot interaction
- Process Quality
- Dependability
- Physical attributes
- Standardisation

Each of these groups of requirements covers a specific aspect of the operation of a robot and is therefore the basis for the division of design effort and modularisation. For any particular application there will be detailed requirements that fall into each of these categories. For each of these detailed requirements there will be a technology or more likely a range of possible technologies that could fulfil the requirements. The exact technology that fulfils the requirement for a given product will vary from domain to domain and task to task. Any company that seeks to design, build or deploy advanced robots will need access to each of these technology areas, either through its own development capabilities or through buying in services and modules. Within a European context it is important that each of these areas of technology are accessible and that there is a good research resource base on which to draw.

The robotics industry, just like the automotive industry, is likely to be built on layers of organisations providing compartmentalised IP as modules and services. Consequently the specification and design methodologies used are likely to be formulated to match the systems engineering approach to development and design. So by using a hierarchical deconstruction of the whole task into requirements and then into technologies and finally to components complex systems can be efficiently designed, constructed and tested. Note that this hierarchical deconstruction should not be confused with the flow of the design process, just because the design can be compartmentalised does not mean that the development process proceeds by building each module then trying to fit them together. The most successful development processes follow an "end to end" approach where the whole system is designed with all major building blocks in place and blocks are then refined to achieve the desired level of performance. Because the robotics industry is at an early stage of development the right way to deconstruct designs is still being worked out, as are the best technologies and the right means of

specifying functions. This means that (except for industrial robot arm manufacture) robotics is still a high risk industry. All industries, and investors, seek risk reduction, both by adopting well founded techniques and technologies and by gaining the experience of applying them over many products. This reduces the risk in developing new products to a level that encourages the large investment needed to build volume manufacturing capability. The robotics industry is in the early stages of this process and the technologies and their limitations are not yet well understood and so the risk of picking the wrong combination of technologies is high. However to balance this the competition in the market place is minimal and there is a consequently lower level of user expectation.

The automotive industry provides a close parallel example both in terms of the development of the industry and its supporting technology and the format of its infrastructure. There are many fundamental design decisions that have become standardised in the design of a car, the placement of the pedals, the operation of the steering wheel the way that doors open etc... To change any of these fundamental features might be described as "radical" and is likely to confuse the everyday car driver. Making changes that do not significantly affect the driver's operation of the vehicle such as changing from petrol to hydrogen fuel will require an extensive infrastructural change that might take a decade or more to introduce. The lesson for robotics is that once technologies are established and the infrastructure is built, design changes that might be technically desirable become difficult. (The 4 year switch over to digital TV in the UK being another example of the length of time it takes to make a relatively simple technical change). Often outdated technical solutions survive far longer than expected because of the investment and refinement that has gone into reducing the impact of their deficiencies.

Without design ground rules it is difficult to find the right combination of technologies. This is true in other areas of design but in robotics there is the added problem that the technologies are not well understood in a design context. For each problem there may be a selection of competing technologies, but there is little or no consensus as to the most optimal. The industry is yet to set benchmarks and standards, outside of the industrial application area, and the knowledge of how to effectively design robots to work over extended periods in everyday environments, and the wider infrastructure of maintenance and installation is essentially non-existent. After 100 years the automotive industry has well defined standards, a legal framework, a good understanding of the capabilities of users, well defined technology and established service and delivery systems. In 100 years from now the robot industry will be in the same state, but just as the "ultimate driving machine" does not exist, neither will the "perfect robot".

ADAPTATION

Despite these similarities in terms of industrial infrastructure and design integration there are a number of requirement groups that are unique to robotic applications and will present their own engineering challenges, in particular adaptability and dependability stand out. Building machines that will be dependable in everyday environments and which have the capability of carrying out useful tasks with either minimal or no direct human command is a significant challenge. Dependability where there is close human interaction will require novel means of system analysis, design methodologies and testing strategies. With respect to adaptation there are more fundamental problems. In the simplest of applications, robots will need to adapt to their environments, and to their users and the systems around them. Their autonomy and the adaptation of that autonomy particularly in applications that rely on a significant level of adaptation could present a challenge to the conventional design and development approach. If a robot must adapt its actions according to the circumstances it finds, then testing and verifying that the robot complies with functional requirements and safety criteria may become difficult. The testing and verification of modules typically relies on a fixed sequence of events stimulating a module in a repeatable and consistent way. Deviation from the expected output is usually interpreted as failure of the unit. If the unit adapts is output over time by learning from the user or the environment then the output of the system to a fixed sequence of stimuli will also change over time. This means that testing must examine both the long term performance after learning (which may need to take place in a real environment) as well as the performance on a trial by trial basis. So for example testing a non-adapting robot vacuum cleaner might measure the speed with which it cleans a standard room, containing known difficulties and hazards and compare times and performance against different starting points in order to assess if it is operating correctly. If the robot adapts to the room as it cleans it and that adaptation is useful and significant then this testing cycle would have to be repeated many times in order to establish that the learning algorithm firstly works correctly and secondly has a measurable effect. In a research environment it may be enough to do this once to prove the point but in a product development environment each time changes are made to the system and software these tests would need to be carried out again to ensure performance is maintained. This will slow development.

It is easy to extrapolate this testing problem to a more complex task and operating environment, such as one that needs to interact with people where the real variation in response might be far greater. There is the added problem that it may be unethical to test robots on real users, particularly if they are elderly or vulnerable. The only way to solve this problem might be to use either actors, or humanoid robots trained or programmed to mimic people to test the adaptive responses of the functional robots. However the fundamental problem remains; while product verification is based on empirical test, as it always has been, the development cycle for a complex adaptive machine could be a prohibitive part of the development cycle.

If adaptation, or even cognitive capability, is best provided through a more homogeneous or "holistic" architecture that learns or adapts, a possibility that has been at the heart of the AI debate for decades, then the current deconstructive approach to system design and specification may not suit the types of computational structures that are required. Homogeneous systems such as neural networks might present a problem in terms of the conventional product engineering methods used to build testable, dependable and safe machines.

Although it might be attractive from a product testing point of view to ignore adaptation it is clear that any robot that needs to cognitively interact with either the environment or the user will have to be capable of adaptation to the environment of the user, in other words adaptation in their everyday environment will need to take place. The success of this adaptation to the user's environment will be fundamental to the success of the robot and thus its acceptability as a useful functional device.

Ultimately most robot applications that rely on interaction with people will require significant cognitive compatibility between the user and the robot which almost inevitably involves adaptation.

Using the example of a robot vacuum cleaner, where the primary interaction is a physical one with the environment. Robot cleaners will over time become more complex. They will have interactions with the user and these interactions will become more significant to the function of the machine. Eventually the interaction will require greater cognitive compatibility, at this point the success of adaptation to the user's environment will become a key feature of the robot. So that when the users says "Please clean the mess in front of the sofa" the cleaner will know which

room "the sofa" is in, it will know how to reach that room, how to locate the sofa, even if it has been moved, it will be able to identify "mess" and will know how to clean it. Clearly this requires considerable cognitive compatibility between the robot's understanding of the environment and the user's descriptions of that environment. Such compatibility of descriptions is only possible through adaptation to the user's environment which by necessity will have taken place in the environment of the user. If the user lends the robot to their neighbour it will not perform as well and may even perform less well on its return having started to adapt to the neighbour's house. This example firstly points out the dependence on adaptation but also shows that any particular application scenario occupies a trajectory in the Robot Interaction Matrix over time where primarily physical robot applications will tend to become more cognitive and primarily cognitive interactions will tend to become more physical. Secondly this shows that although initially there will be distinct areas of interaction, eventually the combination of the physical interaction technologies and the cognitive interaction technologies will converge as products progress from simple to complex functions. In this example it is likely that the adaptation features will only be added to robot vacuum cleaners once they become a well established technology, and the initial market for robot cleaners is unlikely to depend on adaptation. However it is likely that a robot that adapts poorly will fail in the market place even if it cleans well.

From this discussion it can be concluded that testing adaptation, guaranteeing its effect and designing it to be dependable will be important and challenging aspects of robot design.

NEURAL COMPUTATION

How does this discussion fit into the context of exploiting neural computation? Will neural computation offer technologies that fit into this design process, or does it require a re-examination of the structure of robots and the ways in which we design and construct them? Can what neural computation provides be achieved in other ways and what are its limitations?

It is interesting that the current wave of robotic development started with Brooks' Subsumption Architecture (Brooks, 1985) which in its original form has little hierarchy. With this architecture it is also difficult to exactly pinpoint why the network of Finite State Machines results in a particular external behaviour. Indeed it was common for simulations of the network not to match the observed behaviour of a robot, not in minor ways but in major and unpredictable ways (Bisset & Vandenburgh, 1997). This structure fundamentally jump started the current wave of robotics. What is interesting is that subsumption went out of favour exactly because of its unpredictability and the difficulty of performing post-hoc analysis on the reasons for a particular behaviour. In other words because subsumption did not fit the modular well defined compartments that systems engineering demands in order to build large complex systems, its benefits have been provided by alternative implementation mechanisms that can be compartmentalised and managed. Neural computation has a similar problem. It is not that functions cannot be guaranteed, it is that adaptation and the integration of adaptive systems has the potential to make the testing and development of large systems difficult and time consuming.

WHAT WILL ROBOTS DO?

Firstly let's take an example based on their most traditional area of application, factory assembly work. Traditionally robots in this environment are fixed and carry out well defined repetitive tasks in an environment engineered for success. The precision of motion is such that quality and repeatability are guaranteed. This will always be a cost effective approach to the mass production

of high volume items with low levels of variation such as cars, or white goods. The use of robots on small production lines is increasing, but it is still on the basis of fixed physical location and pre-defined action, for example picking and packing chocolate bars.

There are various factors that drive the use of robotics on smaller volume production lines. In the food industry the requirements for hygiene and standardised quality mean that the manipulation of soft items such as raw meat or sandwich fillings is beginning to become a viable market for robotic manipulation, but functions are typically pre-determined and repetitive, much as they are in the car industry, with little or no requirement for adaptation.

One vision of the future is that people and robots will work in adaptable cooperation on production lines where there is more product variation, or where a high level of adaptive skill is required, for example working with unprocessed raw materials (e.g. making jewellery). For robots to be cost effective in these work scenarios they would have to represent an advantage over the use of people. This advantage is typically either in terms of speed or accuracy and repeatability. Such close cooperation brings its own problems, safe operation, compliant manipulation, the need to have systems to train the robot without the use of specialist programmers, so that it can be adapted quickly to new tasks.

As with almost all areas of robot application this work scenario also raises ethical and societal issues, concerning work place displacement and workplace practice. For example Scheutz and Crowell (2007) have shown that a robot can be used to pressurise a human co-worker into working harder. In the example investigated the robot spoke to the co-worker complaining that its battery needed recharging and that they should speed up so that the task could be completed before it ran out of power. It is easy to see how speeding up the robot by just a few percent might in turn speed up the human co-worker. This clearly represents cause for concern.

There are also similar issues about robots that learn by observing a person perform a repetitive task. The robot may not be able to figure out exactly how to do the task for itself or the most efficient means of work organisation, these are things that people are good at. With good manipulators and body position monitors it is possible for the robot to observe and replicate the actions of a co-worker. Of course the robot may well be able to move 10% or 100% faster than the person, it won't tire even working 24 hours per day; so what happens to the person once the robot can do the job faster and more efficiently? While these are potential issues, the main one is: Will such a system ever be cost effective? For the price of the minimum wage a person is a remarkably adaptable worker, and it is quite likely that with the exception of hazardous environments people will always be more cost effective than robots.

A similar situation exists with cleaning robots. It is still not cost effective to make office cleaning robots. People are still cheaper and more effective and it may always be so. There will be a minimum level of dexterity and cognitive awareness that is required to carry out all the functions of an office cleaner, emptying bins, cleaning desks, polishing glass and telephones etc. Despite our expectation that technology will continue to get ever cheaper, there is in fact a lower limit on minimum price that any particular technical item can be made for. This will depend on the cost of raw materials and the complexity of the device being constructed. Although that price may fall year on year it is asymptotic to a level determined by the fundamental complexity of the item in question. The cost of making a car will never fall below a certain level because the cost of steel and aluminium, the machining and welding of steel, the cost of making seats and engine blocks, the cost of transport and the cost of design and test will never fall to zero. Similarly a mobile phone will always cost more than a certain amount to make

no matter how they might be offered to us in the market place. By the same argument robots with human levels of dexterity and cognition that can do some things humans can do may well always cost more to build and deploy than the hourly minimum wage; taking into account lifecycle costs, the cost of the capital needed to purchase them, the inevitable unreliability made worse by the fact they will have been engineered for minimal cost/function. People oriented service providers will always adapt their systems and services to beat them and provide a viable service.

So where will advanced robots find real applications?

They will be used where there is a real advantage to the people who own them. If using a robot buys time or adds function at a cost that is acceptable then there will be a market. People will buy robots when they can effectively replace themselves doing things they don't want to do, cleaning, tidying, sorting, maintaining. If a robot vacuum cleaner can keep your house clean, remove stains from the carpet, clean every room in the house while you are out, acts as a security guard at the same time, feed the cat, and water the pot plants, then for a few thousand pounds many will be happy to buy that time back for themselves. But only if it is reliable.

For the elderly and disabled these devices will give a level of independence that is currently impossible except with permanent care which for most will either be unacceptable, or unavailable, both in terms of cost and the intrusion into the private life of the individual. It is possible that a robot will be much more effective and even acceptable as a companion and able to adapt to the user without imposing. But only if it is reliable.

The use of robots to care for the elderly raises many ethical and societal problems (RAE, 2009), problems that will require an engineering and design process solution to ensure the dependability and function guarantees that will be expected. There is a tendency to imagine that the ethical issues in robotics can be debated independently of the technology but this is not the case, it is the technology and the design processes that will deliver the ethical performance, not simply in terms of the ethics of patient confidentiality but in terms of the ethics of reliability. It is unethical to deploy a product that will fail, and is known to fail, into a market where the consequences of failure could be death or serious injury. As a consequence the design, development and test cycle must be able to deliver, and must be certifiably able to deliver, the high standard of performance that manufacturers and insurers will require. The ethical issues are more obvious and clear in military robots, but the danger posed to a growing elderly population by poorly designed robots has the potential for a much larger scale of failure than any military conflict. A recent Royal Academy of Engineering report observed "It is important that ethical issues are not left for programmers to decide – either implicitly or explicitly" (RAE, 2009 p13). Design and development processes will need to be constructed that can establish and guarantee ethical robots.

Taking a more detailed example imagine a robot that cares for an elderly person who is suffering from mild dementia. The robot has been bought by her children so that they can be sure she is well cared for and in case there is an emergency, she falls or the kitchen tap is left running the robot will be able to alert them or the emergency services. Is this scenario realistic? The robot will be expensive, but is likely to be cheaper than full care. Robotic care will not necessarily be chosen because it is better but because it may be the only choice. One way of analysing the importance of alternative forms of care, such as robotic helpers, is by examining the Potential Support Ratio (PSR) (UN, 1999). This is the ratio of the number of people in a given population aged 15-64 available to support a single person over 65. In the developed world in the year 2000 this ratio was 9:1 already a decline from 12:1 in 1950, but by 2050 the ratio will be 2:1 which means that potentially a very high proportion of the labour force would need

to be involved in elderly care just to provide the level of care our elderly population currently get. As a consequence of the shortfall in the number of carers it is inevitable that the cost of carers will rise disproportionately unless alternative solutions are found. It is currently thought that the best option is to keep people at home for as long as possible. While robots will not be the only solution to this problem it is conceivable that they may be a reasonably cost effective option, they are likely to carry residual value (just as a car does) and they may provide a more adaptable solution allowing them to be used for longer as the person's condition changes or deteriorates. This robot will be able to move around the house with the person, it may take a zoomorphic form (Paro, 2009), or be inconspicuous in some way. It will be able to monitor the environment and detect abnormal events, it will know where a few hundred key objects are, glasses case, walking stick, scissors etc and be able to locate them or even fetch them. It will be able to interpret sounds, running water, the kettle boiling, the front door bell, and it will understand spoken commands and speak back. It will be capable of basic health assessment either remotely assessing daily patterns of behaviour, by direct contact, or by body attached remote sensing. It may be able to help the person rise from a chair or in getting dressed. It may even be able to prepare simple microwave meals. In order to be effective it will have to be reliable and safe.

The basic elements of much of this technology exist in laboratory prototype form today (Fraunhofer IPA, 2009), much of the refinement that would make it a viable product and the support and infrastructure is missing but the core technical elements are in place.

This is a highly complex machine, it will go wrong. It will make mistakes. It will not be perfect. But despite this in 2050 it may be the best option.

There are inevitably many issues with this scenario. How will the person adapt to living with a robot, will they have a choice? Will they understand that choice? (In fact if you are over the age of 35 it may be you that will need this robot carer). How will we prevent the robot from disseminating data it has gathered about that person, their habits and environment, how will we stop inappropriate access to the command structure in the robot. There are clear personal privacy issues. If the robot has a camera how will we ensure that the design of the robot is such that these images can never be viewed, either by service personnel or remotely via the inevitable communication link? There is already a requirement for organisations that store and keep images of people in public and private locations such as shops and workplaces to place public notices warning them that video surveillance is taking place. There is considerable sensitivity to the use of video monitoring of elderly people in both care homes and their own homes. Clearly the design of the robot and the legislative infrastructure will need to address all of these issues and more.

Who will be liable when it makes a mistake? Will you have to pay higher house insurance premiums if you have a robot at home? Where will responsibility lie between the designer, the manufacturer, the installation company and the maintenance service or even the user?

TECHNOLOGIES

It is important to define what is meant by the term "technology" as distinct from methodology or paradigm. Computational neuroscience and biological inspiration are, from a designer's perspective, unconventional paradigms. They characterise a particular approach to discovering technology or explaining function. They do not provide technology per-se that can be used to build better robots. As paradigms outside of the designer's conventional toolbox they may not be accepted as "useful". If a paradigm is to be useful it must produce technology with a functional benefit in comparison to other paradigms or at least over and above established methodologies. Designers need

to be agnostic about where technologies originate and concentrate on the capabilities they provide.

Robot designers will always focus on technologies that fulfil the application requirements that are thrown up by the task or problem at hand. If technologies can be likened to memes then designers are meme arbiters acting as selectors in the evolution of product technologies. They are not the only meme arbiters, on the broader scale users are also testers and selectors of good technology.

So for a technical paradigm to survive it must be of utility in the production of technology, or in the production of explanations. In order to understand the significance of this it is necessary to examine the process of designing and developing a robot. This process has a series of distinct stages.

For most product development the process follows a similar path. An initial idea or observation about a market opportunity or an existing product, or the novel application of a technology will spark the process. This is followed by exploration of both market and technologies in order to provide a clearer identification of form, function and opportunity. Eventually a set of requirements will be written and the technologies required to fulfil those requirements identified. The most important step in the development of a product is the selection and assessment of technologies. It is the mix and integration of technologies that determine product function and more critically the limitations of those technologies that determine the limitations of the final product. Finally production prototypes will be built tested and approved ready for sale. In this sense robot design will be no different.

Once the functional goals have been elucidated then it is possible to write out the requirements. These requirements are a series of statements. Typically they are broken down so that each statement encapsulates a single aspect of function, this is important as it can then be related to a particular technology within the product and it can be tested to see if the requirement has been fulfilled. The statements also need to be composed so that they are technology neutral, (unless the system being designed has a requirement to use a particular technology). This technology neutrality must be strongly defended during the specification process as it provides the space in which novel solutions emerge, just as the removal of pre-conceived solutions and limitations are important at the ideas stage.

For each requirement it must be possible to identify technologies that might fulfil that requirement. According to the SRA these core technologies can be categorised into the following major groups:

- System Architecture
- System Engineering Tools
- Cooperation and Ambient Intelligence
- Communication
- Human Machine Interface
- Safety
- Actuation
- End Effectors
- Locomotion
- Materials
- Navigation
- Planning
- Power Management
- Control
- Learning
- Modelling
- Sensors
- Sensing and Perception

In each case the technology group might fulfil a number of the different requirement groups. So for example planning technologies might be employed to fulfil requirements in both the Positioning, and in Manipulation groups. The distinction between requirement and technology is an important one.

Although this chapter is only considering Type D robots those of other types also need to be specified in this way with a clear distinction between requirement and technology descriptions. The specification of support systems, data capture process etc. will also benefit from a similar approach.

Why is this level of specification important? The answer lies in the cost of correcting mistakes and the cost of making the wrong machine. It is estimated that if the unit cost of changing a design at the ideas stage is taken to be 1 then the cost of changing an idea at the testing stage before mass production is 1000, with a similar scaling in terms of the time taken to implement the change. For this reason the most important part of the development of a product is the ideas stage, here is where significant time should be spent trying ideas and technologies to understand how they fit the requirements. A missed opportunity or an unchallenged assumption at this stage may prove very costly later in the process.

Product design options are sometimes restricted by backward compatibility and constrained by what users understand. New technology can allow the radical alteration of form and function thereby driving new generations of a product. Indeed step changes in product function are always driven by step changes in technical capability. So from CD to DVD to Blue-Ray rides on the back of incremental advances in laser diode manufacture. The shift from vinyl discs to CD to MP3 player similarly follows step changes in storage and coding technology.

For this reason designers are always seeking out new technology that might provide better solutions to existing problems. In robotics there are few existing solutions and the sea of technology that can be used is limited in terms of the maturity of the technologies and the understanding of the fit between technology and function.

EXPLOITING NEURAL COMPUTATION AS A TECHNOLOGY

The neural approach to computation is typically applied as a "holistic" solution. It is common in experimental systems for every aspect of the experimental system to be governed by neural computational mechanisms. While this might show off the abilities of NC in isolation it should be clear from the above discussion it is unlikely that NC will impact on design in this way. It is important to examine how realistic the NC approach is and how NC technology might end up in products and to examine the difficulties posed and identify if it can be accommodated within the modularised structures of systems engineering and product design.

To use a single computational mechanism across all aspects of a system makes little sense in current engineering methodologies where the "divide and conquer" system engineering methodology is applied and each piece of the system is crafted to function both in isolation and in conjunction with the other neighbouring pieces. While at the same time the design of the whole system is developed to meet the product requirements, approvals and safety specifications. In this process individual modules are either bought in as pre-defined units and the system wrapped around them, or they are designed to integrate into the whole. Modules are specified to ensure that the system is testable and that the impact of design changes can be minimised and isolated simply because that is what minimises cost and time to market. System design techniques such as extreme programming and object oriented design have altered the methodologies adopted to develop systems but are characterised by their ability to enhance the compartmentalisation and testability of software and hardware systems.

To adopt a system of product construction that uses a holistic solution and one that is often grown or adapted from an almost blank sheet seems like a difficult step to take. Throwing away the longstanding certainty of the modular developmental processes is likely to be a step too far for most designers and engineers developing products and systems.

There are two solutions to this problem. The first is to compartmentalise the neural computation such that it can be modularised and parameterised and then built into the existing systems that compose the robot. The second is to try and build a design framework around the neural computation approach that is able to ensure the functional guarantees inherent in the modular development process while allowing it to integrate with the existing support systems on the robot. Each approach has its difficulties.

If neural computation is compartmentalised then there are a number of potential problems:

- If the power of the NC system comes from its pervasive spread throughout the system and its ability to adapt or learn from direct access to sensor data and actuators it may loose its power if it is only feed data as a module and its outputs are scrutinised before being applied to actuators, or modulated by a conventional control system.
- There is a possibility that many NC systems can be reduced to a more conventional algorithmic computation that is essentially equivalent. While the NC may be able to adapt or learn how to achieve a given level of control it is likely that a more conventional engineering approach will also lead to an acceptable solution. There is an implication that NC systems will be more likely to scale their performance in the presence of novel data, or provide better responses to novel circumstances, however these benefits are difficult to assess and difficult to guarantee. So for example if an adaptive system is used to plan the motion of a vacuum cleaner around a room and the adaptive system gives a 10% advantage over a more conventional planning approach the testing overhead required to gain a 10% advantage may simply not be worth the effort.

Natural selection and product engineering have very different driving forces. What is at issue is the combining of the advantages of neural computation, artificial evolution and other biologically inspired paradigms with the focused requirement driven approach to product design. The issues are clearly highlighted in considering how to design adaptive robots for everyday environments where the adaptation is complex and unpredictable and the testing problem is significant.

Biology has engineered adaptation into the structure of its systems at every level to the extent that most of the system is adaptive, engineering does not yet have the technologies to provide this level of adaptation. Natural selection is a continuous self sustaining "product" development process. In some senses the development and deployment of complex engineered systems is similar; particularly in software systems where the cost of alteration is relatively low and new revisions can be quickly spread to a significant fraction of the user base. The engineering design approach is able to create very robust machines that can with stand the natural environment far better than natural creations because of its wider access to materials. Biological systems compensate for this by being adaptive.

When a knee joint is damaged it protects itself and if it can it repairs itself, it increases calluses to cushion the parts if the joint that are being impacted the most. An engineered solution will examine wear rates and peak forces, and often measure them under extreme loads, and then choose a design and materials to provide the desired wear and durability demanded by the application. The advantage of the natural approach is that the system adapts to failure and at peak load safety systems kick in to protect the joint, and eventually modify it or repair it. In the engineering solution the worst case has to be assessed and designed for and a choice is made between over engineering or a higher failure rate. With engineered systems we can simply replace the worn or broken part, in the natural world the organism may not survive long enough for a repair to take effect. The design goals are very different as are the end results but both provide a useful system.

SUMMARY

This chapter has provided an overview of the issues that surround the design testing and deployment of useful robots. It has described the development process and the potential market, while highlighting a diverse range of challenges. There are many unknowns, however in the context of neural computation and a natural engineering approach it is important to stimulate the development of systems that are compatible with neural computation on the assumption that they can be proven to provide significant end product benefit for "in task" adaptation. If they cannot then maybe they can provide the benchmarks used to prove engineered systems. If the integration of NC systems is too complex or too fraught then they will fail to deliver any advantage over engineered solutions. The natural inbuilt caution of the product engineer, and the scepticism of the buying public mean that it is important to be able to show how a new technology performs and offers a product benefit. Deploying NC systems will require either modules that can be readily integrated by designers and system builders, or a system design methodology that can yield the benefits of NC coupled to the benefits of engineering product design. Without this design guarantee the risk of in-field product failure will be high. When building one system in the research lab failure is inevitable abut manageable, when building 10 system prototypes it is undesirable but manageable for short periods of time, when building 1000 in production it can bring down the project or company. When building a million it is cheaper to wait for the reliability and dependability to improve before launching the product. Product engineering is based on building in appropriate levels of reliability and controlling cost and time to market, to achieve this in a new industry takes time and resource to understand the best processes and technologies for each area of requirement. This is the expertise of the manufacturer, often hidden in the detail of a design, the sizes of parts, safety margins, tooling, materials choice, algorithms etc. It is the reason it takes 20 years for ideas to propagate from the research lab to the market place. But for NC to do so it must either be able to fit into the existing design methodology or it must define its own such that it can be understood and made useful.

REFERENCES

Bisset, D. L., & Vandenburgh, R. C. (1997). The dynamics of photo-taxis: Applying the agent environment interaction system to a simple Braitenburg robot. In P. Husbands and I. Harvey (Eds.), *Proceedings of the fourth European conference on artificial life* (pp. 327-336). Cambridge, MA: The MIT press.

Brooks, R. A. (1985). A robust layered control system for a mobile robot. *IEEE Journal on Robotics and Automation, 2*(1), 14–23.

EUROP. (2009). *The strategic research agenda for robotics in Europe*. Retrieved from http://www.robotics-platform.eu/

Fraunhofer, I. P. A. (2009). *Care-O-Bot*. Retrieved from http://www.care-o-bot.de/english/

International Federation of Robotics. (2009). *World Robotics: Service Robots 2009*. Retrieved from http://www.worldrobotics.org/

Moore, G. E. (1965, April 19). Cramming more components onto integrated circuits. *Electronics Magazine, 38*(8), 4.

Moore, G. E. (1975). Progress in digital integrated electronics. *International Electron Devices Meeting, 21*, 11-13.

Paro. (2009). Retrieved from http://www.paro-robots.com/

RAE. (2009). *Autonomous systems: Social, legal and ethical issues*. The Royal Academy of Engineering No.

Scheutz, M., & Crowell, C. R. (2007). *The burden of embodied autonomy: Some reflections on the social and ethical implications of autonomous robots.*, Dept Computer Science and Engineering, University of Notre Dame. Retrieved from http://hri.cogs.indiana.edu/publications/ethicsworkshoprevised.pdf

UN. (1999). *The world at six billion.* Population division of the Department of Economic and Social Affairs of the United Nations Secretariat. Retrieved from http://web.ukonline.co.uk/thursday.handleigh/demography/united-nations/19-supportratio.htm

KEY TERMS AND DEFINTIONS

Service Robot: A robot that performs tasks that provide services to people or organisations. This covers a wide range of different tasks from security through healthcare to transport and cleaning. The label "Service Robot" is often used as a generic collective for all non-industrial robots.

Industrial Robot: The term used to describe all factory automation robots. These robots typically carry out a repetitive fixed function with little or no adaptation. Their operation is often characterised by high levels of task repeatability and positional accuracy. Car manufacture is the most iconic usage example for an Industrial Robot.

Domestic Robot: A robot that operates in the home environment, this includes applications both inside and outside of the house. They are characterised by relatively low cost, high levels of user interaction and simple user interfaces. They must conform to domestic product safety standards and provide a good cost function trade-off.

Robot Ethics: Robot Ethics refers to the ethical issues that surround robots. In the main this refers to the ethics of using robots in close cooperation with people, particularly in the work place and when interacting with vulnerable user groups. It also covers the active use of military robots on the battlefield, and the issues surrounding the deployment of invasive autonomous medical robots. In the extreme it touches on the potential rights of robots in the event that one day they develop more human like cognitive attributes.

Healthcare Robot: A robot that interacts with people in the context of health but in only in non-invasive ways. For example a rehabilitation robot, an elderly care robot, or a patient handling robot. This type of robot is often designed for a specific task and the design may well have safety critical elements because of the close interaction with people.

Medical Robotics: The term is typically used to describe body invasive robotics. These can be passive diagnostic robots that assess different medical conditions by passing into or through the body, or active robots able to perform surgical procedures, either by tele-operation or with varying degrees of autonomy.

Robot Technology: Technology that is specifically applied to the design or construction of robots. Such technology may only be applicable to robots, such as navigation, object manipulation etc.

SME: Small and Medium Enterprise is defined by the EU as being a company or organisation employing less than 250 people and having a turn over of less than €50M.

SRA: Strategic Research Agenda. The document produced summarising the directions research should take over a long time scale.

EUROP: European Robotics Platform. A European Technology Platform set up to promote robotics in Europe and set the task of coordinating the robotics industry within the European Community. Also tasked with production and dissemination of the SRA.

Chapter 12

Neural–Symbolic Processing in Business Applications:
Credit Card Fraud Detection

Nick F. Ryman-Tubb
City University London, UK

1. ABSTRACT

Neural networks are mathematical models, inspired by biological processes in the human brain and are able to give computers more "human-like" abilities. Perhaps by examining the way in which the biological brain operates, at both the large-scale and the lower level anatomical level, approaches can be devised that can embody some of these remarkable abilities for use in real-world business applications. One criticism of the neural network approach by business is that they are "black boxes"; they cannot be easily understood. To open this black box an outline of neural-symbolic rule extraction is described and its application to fraud-detection is given. Current practice is to build a Fraud Management System (FMS) based on rules created by fraud experts which is an expensive and time-consuming task and fails to address the problem where the data and relationships change over time. By using a neural network to learn to detect fraud and then extracting its' knowledge, a new approach is presented.

2. INTRODUCTION

Given the high stakes and intense competition in almost all industries, making intelligent business decisions is more important than ever - few disagree that information is a powerful business asset. The ability to harness that power to drive the decision-making processes that are central to a business's success is fundamental. Over the last three decades, businesses have been faced with growing quantities of transaction data, in terms of the number of records and fields; typically, millions of records and hundreds of fields. Their unenviable task is to extract suitable information from this raw data. As well as summaries of current or past performance, they need to study the complex inter-relationships between various factors. Given a thorough understanding, predictions can be made and decisions determined. When faced with this task, the traditional ap-

DOI: 10.4018/978-1-60960-021-1.ch012

Figure 1. Left: biological neurons. Right: artificial neuron

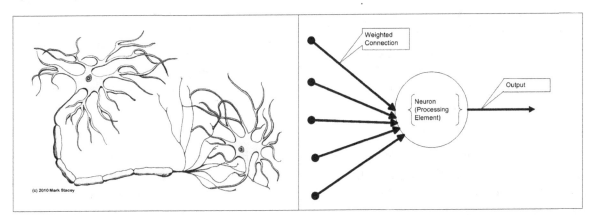

proach has been to use analytical or AI methods. These methods produce a hypothesis based on *a priori* knowledge – typically in the form of rules (a knowledge-base) or a model induced from labeled examples (for which a classification is already known). However, there are many areas where such an analytical approach fails to provide the information needed. Business, like nature, is often chaotic and an approach is needed to tame this chaos, to be able to provide information even when the task is subjective, when it is not possible to have an example of every pattern in order to make a decision. Giving computers more "human-like" abilities, for example allowing them to make judgments, requires a different approach. Humans learn by example and do not need to see every example to make a guess, a judgment based upon what has been taught.

Neural networks are mathematical models, inspired by biological processes in the human brain. They are constructed from a number of simple processing elements (neurons) interconnected by weighted pathways to form networks. Each element computes its output as a non-linear function of its weighted inputs. Figure 1 compares a biological neuron with an artificial neuron. When combined into networks, these processing elements can implement complex non-linear functions that are used to solve classification, prediction or optimization problems. Knowledge

is encoded and distributed throughout the neural network architecture using an iterative learning algorithm. The neural network is therefore poly-thetic – all inputs are simultaneously considered to produce an output. Unlike conventional systems, neural networks are not programmed to perform a particular task using rules. Instead, they are trained on historical data, using a learning algorithm. The learning algorithm changes the functionality of the network to suit the problem by modifying the values of the connection weights between processing elements. Once trained, the network interprets new data in a way that is consistent with the experience gathered during training.

Neural networks can provide highly accurate and robust solutions for complex non-linear tasks such as fraud detection (N. Ryman-Tubb, 1998), business lapse/churn analysis, credit and risk analysis and data mining. One of their main benefits is that the method for performing a task need not be known in advance; instead, it is automatically inferred from the data. Once learned, the method can be quickly and easily adjusted to track changes in the business environment. A further advantage of neural networks over conventional rule-based systems and fuzzy systems is that, once trained, they are far more efficient in their storage requirements and operation. A single mathematical function can replace a large number of rules. An added benefit of this more compact mathe-

Table 1. Payment card fraud types

1. Inner		This is the collusion between a merchant and a cardholder using false transactions.
2. External	Offline fraud	Committed using the physical payment card where the Cardholder is assumed to be Present (CP) – such as the interception of new credit cards in the mail, stolen/lost cards or the copying of card information onto counterfeit physical cards, employee fraud at the issuing bank, etc.
	Online fraud	Committed through the use of the internet or telephone, where the Cardholder is Not Present at the point of transaction (CNP). Here only the basic card information is normally required.

matical representation is that it introduces a natural form of regularization or generalization. This makes neural systems robust to noisy, imprecise, or incomplete data.

However, one criticism of the neural network approach by business is that they are "black boxes"; they cannot be easily understood. Neural networks are essentially a large number of real-valued parameters with no obvious method to determine their function. The knowledge learnt is represented by the distributed weights between neuron connections, threshold values and the activation function. This makes them normally impenetrable to human understanding. Over the last decade, the focus in neural network research has been in the symbolic interpretation of a neural network through the extraction of knowledge or symbolic rules.

The detection of fraud in credit card transactions is presented as an important business application that benefit from the use of a combined neural and symbolic approach. Fraud is a serious and long term threat to a peaceful and democratic society; the total cost of all fraud to the UK alone was estimated by Association of Chief Police Officers to be at least £14bn a year (*Fraud in the UK*, 2007). One such fraud is payment card fraud[1] – to detect this fraud, businesses use a range of methods, with the majority employing some form of automated rules-based Fraud Management System (FMS). These rules are normally produced by experts and it is often an expensive and time-consuming task, requiring a high degree of skill. This approach fails to address the fraud problem where the data and relationships change

over time. Criminals soon learn the fixed rules and adapt their strategy to overcome these. An alternative is the use of neural networks that learn relationships in the data based purely on learning from examples of transactions. However, the function of the neural network is hidden from the user – making business managers weary of their use in such critical part of their business. The ability to then induce a set of generalizing rules that are human comprehensible and accurate and can be rapidly deployed into an existing FMS is therefore important.

There are two types of fraud (see Table 1).

In a number of cases, businesses process and authorize payment card transactions to later find out that the money must be refunded because the genuine cardholder was not responsible for the payment. The business receives a charge-back and has to take the financial loss as the goods that were purchased are unrecoverable. Businesses are facing a serious challenge fighting against this well organized and determined criminal group. Fraudulent orders are in significant proportions, but a business interprets these orders as good business to generate profits until they receive a charge back some time later. Businesses sometimes find themselves using their credit facilities to fulfill some of these fraudulent orders. This puts a significant stress on the business and can jeopardize sustainability, as it uses all its available credit to fulfill the orders. Fraud comes in many forms, and regardless of the form it always leads to financial loss. In addition, fraud can have significant non-financial impacts to a business. It can damage the trust between the business and its most important stakeholders, which can seriously damage its reputation. For a business that is dependent on a limited number of customers or suppliers this can lead to loss in a significant revenue stream, especially when the business is operating in a severe competitive environment. When fraud is constantly reoccurring within a business, an atmosphere of distrust is created and it can leave a demoralizing effect on the employees and would inevitably impact their performance and customer service. It can also lead to fines and even withdrawal of card facilities (which can even lead to business failure). On a wider scale, fraud can have a serious effect on competitiveness and in the end it can damage the economy of the region and the market in which it occurs. The history of the uptake of payment cards runs in parallel to that of computing and financial fraud; each fed a revolution in fiscal, technological and social developments that continue to shape the world today.

An outline of neural networks and symbolic rule extraction and their application to fraud-detection is given in a historical context – especially in relation to the growth of the use of payment cards and that of computing itself. A survey of research into neural fraud detection and rule extraction from neural networks is then given. A new method for the detection fraud using neural-symbolic processing will be described in detail as an example business case study. The last section of this chapter includes a discussion for future directions.

3. BACKGROUND

The first general payment card was launched in 1950. The Diners Club issued the card in New York, which was first used in a restaurant – an event known in the industry as "*the first supper*" (Grossman, 1987). By the end of that year, 20,000 cards had been issued in five cities which grew to 200,000 over the following 5-years (Chakra-

vorti, 2000). In 1958, Visa was formed, originally named *BankAmericard* by the Bank of America (Wolters, 2000). The Bank of America were the first bank to use computers in card transaction processing – they started processing data in 1956 using the Electronic Recording Method of Accounting (ERMA) – based on the then new solid-state transistors and a magnetic core memory (Stanford-Research-Institute, 2008). These early computers continued in use until the 1970's. At the same time as Visa, American Express started its credit card operations after seeing their successor's growth (Grossman, 1987). Over the next five years American Express gained more than 1m cardholders that were in use at 85,000 establishments.

3.1. Computers and Crime

In 1958, criminals began to take notice especially when the newly formed payment card firms began posting credit cards to 60,000 random individuals, regardless of their credit status or if the card had been requested or not, in a rush to gain market share (Stein, 2004). The earliest fraud was the simple theft of the physical card from the post. Since individuals had not asked for the card, it was not until they were presented a bill, that the crime came to light. In 1966, a new US national credit card system was formed by a group of credit-issuing banks who together created the InterBank Card Association[2] (ICA) – known as MasterCard Worldwide. That same year, the UK and Europe joined this "plastic money" economy when Barclaycard was launched (Consoli, 2003). It took just 30-years from the creation of the first[3] binary digital computer (Zuse, 1993) to the first computer crime. In 1966, Mr. Milo Arthur Bennett was the first criminal to be brought to justice (Carroll, 1996; Parker, 1972) for a computer related crime. Bennett was a programmer for the National City Bank of Minneapolis and programmed the computer to clear all his cheques and ignore his overdraft flag. 1966 was the start of another booming "industry" – that of computer crime. The establishment of standards for the magnetic stripe in 1970[4] (Field & Agnew, 1996) along with the development of the first microprocessor at Intel (Jackson, 1997) initiated the wide use of computers for processing credit card transactions. In 1973, Visa implemented the first computerized authorization system, followed a year later by a computerized clearing and settlement system. Intel launched the first home computer, the MITS Altair kit based on their 8080 microprocessor with 4,500 transistors. This was the starting point for both Microsoft and Apple Computers - The 1970's computing boom had started. (Laing, 2004).

The 1980's saw a dramatic upwards trend of consumer consumption as a share of personal income in the US (Johnson, 2005). This boom in expenditure led to the growing use of credit cards and their revolving-debt. At the same time, the US national savings rate was rapidly declining; by 1989, 70% of the US population had a payment card – with 40% having a "balance" after each month. Approaches to detect credit card fraud were based upon a manual periodic report review, e.g., a report listing all cardholders who exceeded a fixed number of transactions in a day, or a sum of purchase values. Simple statistical and database reports were used, with cut-off values chosen based on human analysis of past fraudulent behavior. This was a period in computing history when a new home computer was launched almost monthly – there was unprecedented variety, innovation and passion in computing (Laing, 2004); the first IBM PC was launched, Dell Computers were formed, Apple launched the Apple MAC and was the first computer company to hit $1bn in sales, Microsoft launched Windows and in the UK Sinclair launched the first computer under £100.

3.2. Neural Computing Emerges

This availability of cost-effective computing power led to the start of a new growth period for research in AI and neural computing. The 1982 John Hopfield paper on emergent neural networks (Hopfield, 1982) combined with his style of lecturing, that became known as "neural-evangelism", started the interest in the practical application of neural computers to real-world problems. A number of the early neural computing pioneers, such as Robert Hect-Nielsen, Stephen Grossberg and others, in interviews in 1998 stated they were "*irritated*" (Anderson & Rosenfeld, 2000) by Hopfield. They felt Hopfield had stolen their limelight and made the field his own – some even suggested that one of his published papers was obviously based upon other work that he had not cited. This attitude from the academic researchers towards those who tried to promote the use of neural computing in practical business applications was to continue for many years. It was a type of academic "snobbery" that did nothing but hamper the uptake of the new technology in business. At the Neural Networks for Defense meeting, Bernard Widrow, an early neural pioneer, told the audience that, "*they were engaged in World War IV, World War III never happened…where the battlefields are world trade and manufacturing*"(Attoh-Okine & Ayyub, 2005). In other words, neural computers needed to move out of academia and into the business world. The 1990's were set to become the start of applied AI and Neural Computing – solving real-world business problems. At this time, there was an almost saturated payment card market in the US and UK and the payment card companies started to change their underwriting standards to allow more individuals to qualify for a card (Edelberg, 2003). Most of their business growth now came from accepting riskier individuals – cards were issued to those who would not have qualified in the previous decade. The use of credit scoring was introduced, not to stop the issue of cards, but to alter the interest rates on certain cards to compensate for this risk. Not surprisingly, bad-debt and charge-offs were now substantial, with a growing portion of this due to fraud. By 1992, credit card charge-offs accounted for US$8.5bn, out of which 10% was recognized

Figure 2. The cost of fraud

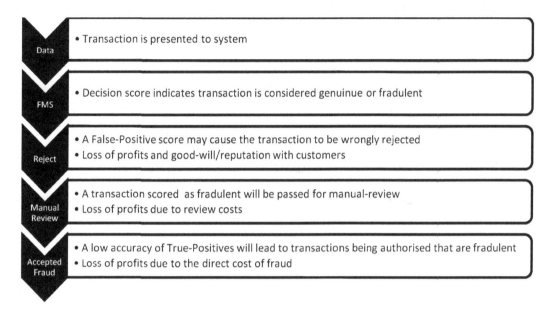

as fraud, a 10% increase on the previous year (Nilson-Report, 1993).

In the USA total card fraud losses cost banks and merchants $8.6 billion per year (Crosman, 2010), where in Europe this figure was €1 billion in losses, made up of 10 million fraudulent transactions in the Single Euro Payments Area (SEPA), affecting 500,000 merchants (*EPC Card Fraud Prevention Task Force* 2006). A more recent European figure estimates this at €1.5 billion in losses per annum ("Report on fraud regarding non cash means of payments in the EU: the implementation of the 2004-2007 EU Action Plan," 2008). The typical *a priory* probability of fraud for Card Holder Not Present (CNP) transactions is in the order 1:500 to 1:1,500 and for Cardholder Present (CP) transactions 1:20,000 to 1:150,000. In both cases, the impact of fraud clearly remains substantial. While new laws fighting cyber crimes have been passed by many EU members, it still remains a dangerous place for businesses, according to the report. A separate study (EC, 2005) has found that almost a third of payment card fraud victims are never reimbursed for their loss by their card provider, despite claims

to the contrary by banks. Although chip and PIN has resulted in a fall in some types of card fraud, there has been a corresponding rise in the level of CNP fraud mainly committed on the Internet. There is a need for a robust and adaptable FMS that evolves dynamically and stays ahead of a majority of fraud activities in the digital economy.

Automating the detection of fraud, through the use of a Fraud Management System (FMS) based on learning technologies is of strategic business importance. The impact of fraud is substantial to the digital economy, society and the state – with the proceeds paying for organized crime, drug smuggling and terrorism. Fraud is prevalent in many high-volume areas, such as on-line shopping, telecommunications, banking, social security claims, where manual review of all transactions is not possible and decisions must be made quickly to prevent crime. Fraud is increasing with the expansion of computing technology and globalization, with criminals devising new frauds to overcome the strategies already in place to stop them. The Fourth Annual UK Online Fraud Report (CyberSource, 2008) identifies that existing approaches are not keeping pace with the growing

Figure 3. Moore's law.vs. payment card usage. Both show an almost straight line on a log-scale, showing exponential growth. The thin-line plots show a forecast exponential trend (Sources: Intel, 2008 & Evans & Schmalensee, 2005)

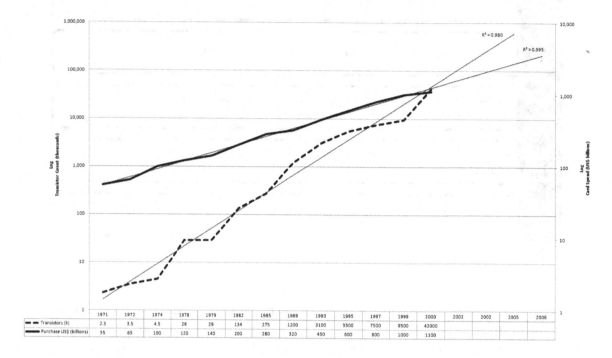

	1971	1972	1974	1978	1979	1982	1985	1989	1993	1995	1997	1999	2000	2002	2002	2005	2006
Transistors (k)	2.3	3.5	4.5	29	29	134	275	1200	3100	5500	7500	9500	42000				
Purchase US$ (billions)	55	65	100	120	140	200	280	320	450	600	800	1000	1100				

levels of fraud. This failure is perhaps part of the reason why just 30% of UK firms use FMS tools with the majority relying on manual review as their primary line of defense. These same firms rated online payment fraud as the most critical threat to their business; *"...as long as criminals believe they can get away with committing fraud, the problem will continue to grow to a point where it may challenge the competitiveness of the [UK] online model"* (CyberSource, 2008). If anti-fraud technologies do not keep pace many of these business models will fail.

Computer systems, using pattern recognition based on supervised neural networks were developed first in the US as an automated method of fraud detection, the earliest being called Falcon from HNC Inc., (Arend, 1993) and Prism from Nestor Inc., ('Applied AI News', 1993). Other US firms were soon to follow as the payment card crime wave continued to grow. The growth

of the computer through the microprocessor that was started in the 1970's, approximately doubling every 18-months, a prediction made by Gordon Moore (Moore, 1965) in his famous article that was to become known as "Moore's Law".[5] The growth of payment card usage also followed an exponential growth (Evans & Schmalensee, 2005). The use (and misuse) of payment cards has been facilitated by the growth and use of computers – with home banking and more recently on-line payments creating a new surge of use.

4. FRAUD DETECTION METHODS

Current practice is to build a static FMS based on detecting known patterns of fraud. Neural computers and expert systems in the form of rules are the main technologies used in FMS. Criminals are growing more sophisticated and are testing defenses in pursuit of high value rewards; new methods of fraud are being created that this static FMS approach is unable to detect. It therefore becomes a battle between the criminals and how rapidly the FMS can be updated and then deployed again. Fraud is dynamic – both the transactions and relationships change over time. Transactional data is noisy, incomplete, highly dimensional, has an uneven distribution; the fields cannot be assumed independent and contain a mixture of symbolic and continuous variables. A FMS needs to adapt to reflect the changing environment and recognize the temporal nature of transactions. It needs to identify fraud at the time of the transaction and provide clear reasons for its decision. An alternative to the existing approach is needed where prior, possibly outdated knowledge can be revised dynamically. Fraud needs to be detected on the fly from unlabeled data where a classification (e.g. fraud or genuine) is not available. In problems such as fraud detection, where the examples contain noise, current approaches generate a large number of rules, where each rule has many conditions that are then difficult to understand. A lengthy process is undertaken where human experts create the rules/models that are tested and validated using labeled examples before being deployed. While it was found that such systems provide an initial level of success in automating decision making, often their accuracy worsened over time. To try to improve the accuracy, more rules are added or models updated, but the system then becomes increasingly complex, slower to process and harder to maintain and understand. This approach fails to address problems in real-world applications that are *dynamic* – where the data and relationships change in real time and therefore are unlabeled.

Key research into fraud detection methods breakdown into three main approaches:

1. AI
2. Neural Networks (or connectionist approach)
3. Eclectic and Hybrid

Each of which is described in the following sections.

4.1. AI

Expert systems are probably the most established form of AI technique. They attempt to embody human knowledge in a computer program through the creation of a set of "rules" that describe the behavior and thought processes of the human expert concerned. This capture of human knowledge is achieved by interviewing or monitoring human experts and then representing this information in the form of a set of rules. The main strength of expert systems is that they store and use knowledge in a transparent way that is easy for an expert to modify or an operator to interpret. This is only true for small rule-bases, with many rules the system becomes difficult to maintain or understand. The main disadvantage of expert systems is that human experts often find it hard to explain clearly the processes they use when performing a task. This makes making the generation of clear, logical rules difficult. Even when it is possible to devise rules, it is often an expensive and time-consuming task, requiring a high degree of skill, both in terms of the developers and the experts concerned. The performance of the system is dependent upon the skill of the human expert and how this is interpreted into the rule set. Experts are often subjective and can only deal with a limited number of variables. The precise, inflexible nature of the rules themselves, leads to poor performance when the data contains errors, contradictions, or missing values. Finally, most expert systems lack any form of automated learning and cannot adapt to follow changes in the business environment – changes have to be implemented manually and are typically expensive to perform. As the rule-base grows it becomes hard to maintain and requires considerable computing power to run.

4.1.1. Rule Based Fraud Detection

The rule based approach is based upon building a knowledge-base created by experts in fraud, where each of these rules typically defines a membership to a fraud/not-fraud class detection (Chan, Fan, & Prodromidis, 1999; Chiu & Tsai, 2004; Kokkinaki, 1997; Stolfo, Fan, Lee, Prodromidis, & Chan, 1997). Current practice is to build a FMS using rules where rule sets are created by fraud experts manually, based on their experience and a review of past fraud cases. Once the rules are built, it is deployed to make an approval or referral decision. Detecting fraud using a system based on rules will recognize previously known types of fraud but once it is deployed, the criminals can devise new methods of frauds to overcome the system. Criminals are growing more sophisticated and are testing defenses in pursuit of high value rewards; new methods of fraud are being created that this static FMS approach is unable to detect. It therefore becomes a battle between the criminals and how rapidly the FMS can be updated and then deployed again.

An alternative is the use of inductive learning methods. These methods do not require explicit *a priori* knowledge – they learn relationships in the data based purely on learning from examples. This has the advantage in not imposing arbitrary assumptions on the problem. Based on this learning, the system forms a model that can then be used to process new input data and produce an output. The ability of any model to generalize is vital – it must be able to produce a reasonable output on previously unseen data.

4.1.2. Case Based Reasoning

Rather than formulate specific rules to describe the processes used to detect payment card fraud, historical data is accumulated. When a new transaction is tested, the most similar previous historical cases are used to determine a possible match – the decision is typically determined by a majority vote of the historical responses. If the current transaction is determined to be actual fraud then it is then added to the historical cases. The advantages of case-based reasoning systems over rule-based expert systems are that fraud experts are not needed to create the rule-base. This means, as in all inductive learning methods, that knowledge is embodied in the historical data and the processes that make use of this data. This feature makes it easy to automate these systems and allows them to adapt to changes in the environment. The main disadvantage to case based reasoning is that it is not efficient in operation. A large number of historic examples are typically needed to replace a single rule in a rule-based system. As the complexity of the problem grows, the number of historical examples increases dramatically. This leads to large computational and storage overheads in operational use. Furthermore, while they are more robust to noisy or imprecise data than the expert systems, their performance is significantly degraded when there is only a limited amount of data (which is typically the case with fraud) or the responses are contradictory.

4.1.3. Decision Tree

One common approach to learning from historical data is the Decision Tree (DT). Here a tree-structured set of rules are created where each of these rules typically defines a membership to a class. The decision tree performs a comparison at each node of the tree and then branches to either the left or the right based on the result (Quinlan, 1986). For example, consider a GENUINE/FRAUD classification (e.g. payment transaction) which depends on just two factors A and B (e.g. amount and number of past transactions) that are each either "HIGH" or "LOW". If both factors take the same value, the classification is "GENUINE," otherwise it is "FRAUD", see Table 2.

The above example can be summarized as a decision tree, as shown in Figure 4.

A decision tree consists of:

Table 2. Simple example data for decision tree

	LOW	*HIGH*
LOW	GENUINE	FRAUD
HIGH	FRAUD	GENUINE

Figure 4. Simple example decision tree

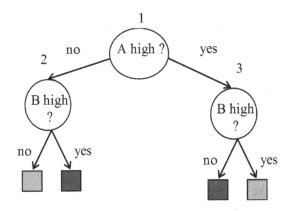

- A set of nodes, which are either non-terminal (internal) or terminal (leaf). The tree starts with a single root node (node #1 in Figure 4), and every possible path eventually leads to a leaf node.
- A set of decision functions, one associated with each internal node. Each decision function is expressed in terms of a subset of the attributes (which correspond to neural network inputs) of the learning set. The attributes may be ordered or symbolic (categorical) variables and the decision function may be a linear or Boolean combination of these.
- Each internal node generates child nodes, according to the decision. For example, node #1 in Figure 4 generates two children; #2 and #3.
- The number of branches (or children) generated by an internal node may be fixed (e.g. to two for a binary tree) or variable. Typically the degree of splitting is binary for numeric attributes and variable

for symbolic attributes: an optimum split (in terms of information gain) is chosen at each internal node, regardless of how many branches this gives.

- Every leaf node has an associated class label which classifies any data example which traverses a path from the top of the tree to that leaf node. More generally, each leaf node has a propensity for each output class, based on the class distribution of the training subset associated with that node.
- Every internal node can be treated as a leaf node, if required. Hence every node in the decision tree may have associated class labels and propensities.
- Most widely-available decision tree implementations only handle binary outputs.

A key benefit of this approach is that the English-like symbolic rules generated are explicable. Every classification is easily understood by a rule generated by the path from the root node to the leaf. The general form of the rule is:

IF (decision1) AND (decision2) AND... THEN (class label)

For example, the leaves in Figure 4 correspond to the following rules:

IF (A low) AND (B low) THEN GENUINE IF (A low) AND (B high) THEN FRAUD IF (A high) AND (B low) THEN FRAUD IF (A high) AND (B high) THEN GENUINE

Clearly, for long root-leaf paths ("deeper" trees), the rules become more complicated to understand, since they contain many conditions which must all be true simultaneously. The tree size needs to be limited in a way that achieves good explainability as well as generalization ability. Since comparisons are made at each node based upon constant thresholds. In applications such as fraud detection, where the data may contain "noise",

Table 3. Format of confusion matrix

		PREDICTED BY THE MODEL		
		Genuine (p')	Fraud (n')	
ACTUAL VALUE	Genuine (p)	TRUE POSITIVE (TP)	FALSE POSITIVE (FP)	p
	Fraud (n)	FALSE NEGATIVE (FN)	TRUE NEGATIVE (TN)	n
		p'	n'	

decision trees generate a large number of rules. Again, a large number of rules, where each rule has many conditions, are unfortunately difficult to understand. The monothetic algorithms typically used contribute to a lack of accuracy especially when generalizing. Previous work has compared this approach to a connectionist approach (Fisher & McKusick, 1989; Geoffrey G. Towell, Shavlik, & Noordewier, 1990) and found that in almost all cases, neural networks outperform in terms of accuracy with generalization.

With millions of transactions a day, the FMS cannot wait for confirmation as to whether a transaction is fraudulent or not. Fraud is dynamic – both the transactions and relationships change over time. Transactional data is noisy, incomplete, highly dimensional, has an uneven distribution; the fields cannot be assumed independent and contain a mixture of symbolic and continuous variables. A FMS needs to adapt to reflect the changing environment and recognize the temporal nature of transactions. It needs to identify fraud at the time of the transaction and provide clear reasons for its decision. An alternative to the existing AI approaches are needed where prior, possibly outdated knowledge can be revised dynamically. Fraud needs to be detected on the fly from unlabeled data where a classification (e.g. fraud or genuine) is not available. It is clear that the pattern of frauds continues to change over time and adapt to the anti-fraud systems put in place to stop them, hence an alternative approach that allows for a robust and adaptable FMS that evolves dynamically and stays ahead of a majority of fraud activities, is needed. All these features are

"human-like" in their requirements, perhaps by understanding some of the biological processes that ability can be captured by a computer?

4.2. Neural Networks

A neural network is deployed into an FMS as software to analyze transaction and other data available at the time of a transaction and to then make an approval or referral decision. Current practice is for a human expert to first build a neural decision model using transaction data to produce a "fraud score". This can be a lengthy process, where the model is first tested and validated before being deployed into the real-time environment. There are two main approaches to the neural model building:

1. Supervised: uses data that includes examples of both fraud and non-fraud
2. Unsupervised: uses just the data to detect anomalous events

Once a neural network is trained, a confusion matrix is used to evaluate its performance; the confusion matrix format is given in Table 3.

The FMS tries to maximize the number of transactions correctly identified as genuine (TP) and the number correctly identified as suspicious (TN), the FMS must minimize the number of transactions wrongly identified as suspicious (FP) and the number wrongly identified as genuine (FN). An FMS that generates too many false-alerts is susceptible to the "base-rate fallacy" (Bar-Hillel, 1977) – where human reviewers have a tendency to start ignoring the information produced.

4.2.1. Supervised Neural Networks

Supervised neural networks are trained using data examples, where there is a set of input values with a corresponding output value (often called a *vector*). It is with the background of exponential growth in both computing power and computer fraud as context, that the earliest credit card fraud detection paper was published by Nestor Inc. (Ghosh & Reilly, 1994). Their product, PRISM® continues to use the algorithms in this seminal paper and it is for this reason that a detail analysis of their approach has been undertaken herein – to provide a useful benchmark[6]. The paper details a feasibility study undertaken for Mellon Bank in the USA to detect payment card fraud.

4.2.2. Restricted Coulomb Energy (RCE) and Probabilistic-RCE (P-RCE)

Nestor, Inc. was founded by Leon N Cooper and Charles Elbaum. Copper is a physicist who was a Research Associate (1955-57) at University of Illinois, close to where Metropolis and Teller were based when they produced their seminal paper (Metropolis, Rosenbluth, N., Teller, & Teller, 1953) on electrostatic principals in physics at University of Illinois at Chicago. Cooper went on to be awarded a Nobel Prize in Physics in 1972 on the theory of superconductivity (Lundqvist, 1992). When he later formed Nestor, Inc., he created a supervised neural network called "Restricted Coulomb Energy" architecture (RCE), clearly motivated by electrostatic principals from his earlier physics work. In this context, it is of little surprise that the neural network chosen for the Mellon Bank feasibility study in the paper is motivated by physics rather than from a more usual biological or AI perspective. The neural network used is a modification of the RCE, called the Probabilistic-RCE (P-RCE) that Cooper

patented in the US (Cooper, Elbaum, & Reilly, 1980). Although the P-RCE does not typically store all training vectors, if the number of items per vector is large and the data set disparate, then this algorithm will create a large number of hidden neurons, requiring substantial storage and processing power – in fact, it could store the entire training set. If this were the case, then it would be acting exactly as the Probabilistic Neural Network in (Specht, 1988). With a large set of fraud data the approach would be impractical. In order to be effective, the data used to train the P-RCE will need to be pre-processed such that there are only a small number of "prototypes" representing the differing fraud types. The intended use of this algorithm appears to have originally been created for Optical Character Recognition (Scofield & Reilly, 1991) which was one of the first "paying applications" for Nestor, Inc. Given the low processing power at the time, this simple algorithm was developed into a single Integrated Circuit (IC) by Nestor, Inc., in collaboration with Intel (Holler, et al., 1992). In the OCR application, the width of the training vector is fixed and small (being the number of pixels, typically an 8x8 grid of pixels for each character) – quite different than the more varied environment of data mining and fraud detection. The approach used labeled data – with both good transactions and known frauds. The data set was extracted from the banks authorization settlement file and consisted of 50 data fields that were combined to produce just 20 input features that were grouped into four categories (see Table 4).

Table 4. Fraud data set categories

1.	Current transaction	E.g. Amount, date, SIC code of merchant,
2.	History of transaction	Values calculated over the previous 8-10 weeks of transactions
3.	History of payment	Values calculated over the previous 8-10 weeks of payments
4.	Other	Date of issue, etc.

The data was pre-processed so that the ratio of good to fraudulent was 30:1 – with a total of 450,000 transactions and some verification was carried out[7]. The data was also split into a training set and a blind set. The blind set was taken from a period after that of the training set that was used to validate the model once it was trained. The P-RCE was used with a single output neuron that produced a "fraud score" as a continuous numerical value – although it was noted that this value is not strictly a probability indication of fraud. The results showed that if a score cut-off point was selected such that 50 accounts would be marked for review, 40% of these would contain the fraudulent transactions. This was compared with the current approach taken by the bank that required the review of 750 accounts a day, yielding just one detected fraud per week. They measured the "earliest" point of fraud detection – the earlier the detection the greater economic benefit to the bank in stopping a series of fraudulent transactions on a single payment card. It was found that the system could detect fraud on either the first or second day with an accuracy of 60%.

4.2.3. Radial Basis Function (RBF)

Similar to the P-RCE, a data mining approach can be taken using a neural network called the Radial Basis Function (RBF). Two separate models are created; (1) the symbolic data fields are analyzed using rule-induction and (2) continuous data fields are modeled using an RBF. A single RBF is created for each feature group in the continuous data fields and a voting system used for the final classification. The results show that the approach worked well on real-world fraud data; the claim of 99.955% accuracy may seem high but when the system processes 400,000 transactions a day, this is equivalent of 180 transactions being flagged wrongly (false-positives) for human review per day (Brause, Langsdorf, & Hepp, 1999).

4.2.4. Multi-Layer Perceptron (MLP) using Back-Propagation

The MLP using the back-propagation learning approach, is a common neural network used in the detection of known patterns of fraud. A three-layer neural network structure is capable of approximating any *Borel measurable*[8] function from one finite topological space to another to any degree of accuracy provided that there is sufficient number of hidden neurons (See Figure 5). Most supervised neural networks used in practice therefore have a three-layer, feed-forward structure, where neurons in one layer are connected to the neurons in the preceding layer. There are a number of different algorithms that can be used to train such a neural network; one of the most common is back-propagation. This is an iterative process which measures the error between the outputs generated and the outputs required, this error is then back-propagated to the previous layer, where the weights between the layers are adjusted in proportion to the error. Over a number of iterations the neural network will converge upon a set of weights that minimizes the overall error.

Typical FMS practice is to use a supervised neural network model based on *a priori* knowledge created from labeled data of past fraudulent and genuine transactions in the FMS. Here, a project is first undertaken off-line, where human experts train a neural model from previously stored transaction data. The neural model is then tested and validated before being deployed on-line. Once deployed, the neural model is used to generate an output that indicates if the transaction is considered suspicious or genuine. Results were an impressive 85% of fraudulent transactions correctly identified with 100% of genuine transactions passed (Aleskerov, Freisleben, & Rao, 1997). A modified MLP approach based on a novel training algorithm based upon Fisher's discriminant analysis has also been used. This approach does not seek to minimize the overall error during training as back-propagation, but to minimize the ratio of the

Figure 5. Example MLP

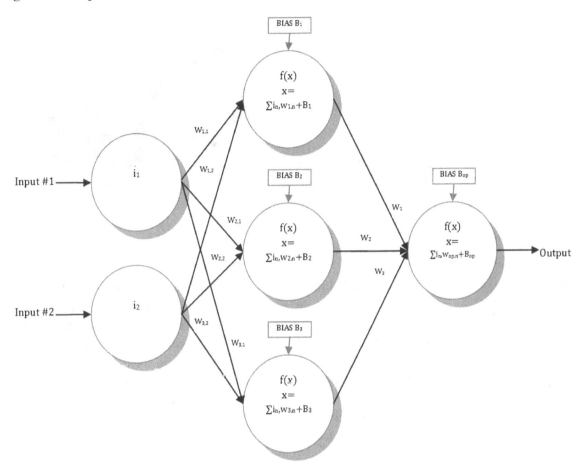

determinants of in-class and outside-class variances with respect to linear projections of the targets. The results have been tabulated against a "cut-off", with 84% of fraud being detected with an 11% false-positive rate (Dorronsoro, Ginel, & Sgnchez, 1997).

4.3. Unsupervised Neural Networks

This type of neural network only requires input data and typically organises itself as clusters that represent the high-dimensional input data into a lower dimensional space. The training algorithm uses competitive learning; this is an iterative process that adjusts the weights so as to cause different parts of the network to respond similarly to

certain input patterns – therefore creating clusters. The most common unsupervised network is called a Self-Organising Map SOM (Kohonen, 1984) created as a biological model of sensory neurons creating cognitive maps – see Figure 6. The SOM organizes itself into clusters that represent high-dimensional input data as a two-dimensional map while maintaining the topological properties of the input space. The two-dimensional map can be thought of as a regular array of neurons that are updated using a repeated heuristic learning algorithm, so that a single neuron is more likely to "fire" for specific patterns of data. However, it is not straightforward to assess convergence of a SOM, there is no guarantee of self-organization and it is dependent upon the initialization and

Figure 6. Left: Biological neurons from the neocortex in the brain. Right: Artificial SOM

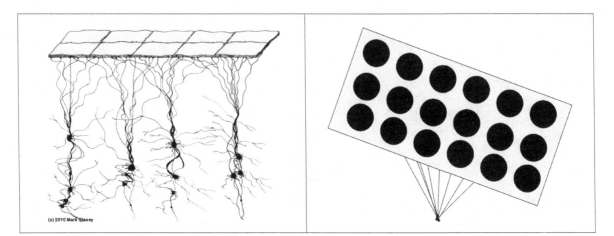

setting of parameters making it unsuitable in this application.

With an unsupervised network, a cardholder behavioural profile can be learnt for each cardholder. This profile represents the generalised pattern of prior transactions for that cardholder. The approach is to create profiles using a Self-Organizing Map (SOM) on individual cardholders to detect when a transaction is unusual. Most humans develop habitual behaviors – this is true of their financial transactions, where reoccurring patterns of expenditure on certain goods/shops/time/brands/amounts can be observed over time. It can therefore be argued that any (sudden) change in such a cardholder's behavior from what is typical could indicate a fraudulent event (or at least an interesting event). The SOM is used as an anomaly detector that can identify atypical transactions. Research has concentrated on creating profiles where temporal data is encoded by creating derived variables – such as the total number of transactions on the card that day/over 5-days, the average transaction amount in the same day/over 5-days, etc. For a new transaction, the deviation "score" from this profile is calculated (using a distance measure) and compared to a threshold set for that profile. If the threshold is exceeded the transaction is considered suspi-

cious and flagged as potential fraud. As with the supervised methodology, this approach trains the unsupervised network using collected transactional data off-line. Once the unsupervised models are built they are fixed and then updated at certain intervals as part of an off-line project. The unsupervised approach has a number of potential benefits: it does not require labelled data to train; it can model each cardholder's behaviour; it is a computationally light algorithm (Jungwon, Ong, & Overill, 2003; Quah & Sriganesh, 2007; Rong-Chang, Shu-Ting, & Xun, 2005; Zaslavsky & Strizhak, 2006).

The SOM is not the only type of unsupervised neural network; counter propagation (Hect-Nielsen, 1987) is an approach that uses competitive learning and was created to map one set of patterns to another. It is a multi-layer network, with the middle layer implementing completive learning. Adaptive Resonance Theory (ART) is a network that features automatic clustering and feedback (Hartigan, 1975). The Generative Topographic Mapping (GTM) has been developed to provide a statistically principled alternative to SOM that represents the mathematical probability density of data in a space of several dimensions (Bishop, Svensen & Williams, 1998).

4.4. Eclectic and Hybrid

There are a range of more exotic approaches to detecting patterns of fraud. For example, an interesting approach is to consider that perpetrating fraud is a type of "game", with two conflicting parties – one the criminal and the other the rest of society (or at very least, the merchant or bank where the liability rests). The first layer of the system used conventional rules to perform a type of pre-processing. The second layer consisted of the game-theory component. This component had feedback, since it can be assumed that the game is made up of a number of repeated "moves", with the criminal trying a number of approaches to avoid detection. The new FMS must therefore update its strategy to counter this. This has the advantage that the system is not a fixed rule base (where the criminals can quickly learn the limited) but adapts to the opponent. The system used a Markov Chain[9] to make a prediction on the likely "next move" of the fraudster. Simulated data was used with interesting results – specifically relating to the inability of humans to learn the strategy of the FMS (Vatsa, Sural, & Majumdar, 2005).

The addition of sequence information would appear to be an obvious improvement in any fraud management system. Using gray incidence analysis and Depster-Shafer theory, the fields from a transactional database can be ranked. Only those with a high ranking can then used as inputs to a neural network model. The gray incidence analysis transforms a sequence of transactions into single-dimensional space. Here various different grey sequences can be generated and the Depster-Shafer theory then used to fuse these together. The results are a subset of input features that can then be used to train a neural network. In general the fewer input features the neural network was more accurate (Tsung-Nan, 2007).

From the seminal paper to date, there are approximately 25 payment card fraud-application papers published in journals of note – the scarcity of research papers many in part be put down to the difficulty of obtaining real-world data to test the

algorithms, although some authors resort to creating their own data sets. It may also be due to the commercial sensitivity of fraud and the difficulty in obtaining real-world data from businesses and the security issues that surround this data.

5. NEURAL SYMBOLIC SYSTEMS

A key objective of an FMS is the easy comprehensibility of the neural model used for detecting fraud while maintaining an acceptable level of accuracy. In fact, the fewer rules generated the better – as a "global" view of the key fraud factors is preferred over actual accuracy. As discussed, with a neural network knowledge is encoded and distributed throughout its architecture using an iterative learning algorithm. Typical real-world applications use hundreds of neurons and thousands of connections – the knowledge is encoded into the connection weights, neurons bias, as well as the choice of architecture. The problem of extracting rules or symbolic knowledge from a supervised neural network has attracted much interest; in part as it provides a method to combine the knowledge-intensive deductive learning and the knowledge-free approach of inductive learning into a hybrid system. Any approach that aims to extract this encoded knowledge into rules can be assessed according to seven key criteria (d'Avila Garcez, Broda, & Gabbay, 2001; Taha & Ghosh, 1997; Geoffrey G. Towell & Shavlik, 1993).

There are two key approaches to opening the black-box of the neural network:

1. Decompositional
2. Pedagogical

These are discussed below:

5.1. Decompositional (Local) Approach

The decompositional method works by decomposing the neural network architecture itself and are

Table 5. Key rule extraction algorithm criteria

	Criteria	Details
1.	Comprehensibility	The ability to inspect the learnt knowledge – this is normally presented in the form of written English-like rules (such as "if x is true then output is fraud"). The ease of discovery of key relationships and features is important. Too many rules may be of a high quality, but do not aid the explainability of the neural network. The more expressive the rules and compact the better.
2.	Translucency	How easy the rules are to understand in terms of relating the inputs to the outputs? Are the rules related to individual neurons in the network or do they express the relationships only in terms of the inputs and outputs?
3.	Quality	This measures the accuracy of the extracted rules when compared to the original neural network and the consistency of the extracted rule-set.
4.	Soundness and completeness	Are the rules provably equivalent to the neural network?
5.	Generality	How general is the approach – is it independent of the neural network architecture and data sets?
6.	Algorithmic complexity	How complex is the approach?
7.	Applicability	Can the rules be applied to a specific application domain?

therefore are only applicable to specific neural network architecture and training algorithms. A SUBSET method can be used as a decomposition approach by imposing limits on the depth of search since it assumes that neurons tend to be either highly active or inactive – the algorithm searches for minimal sets of antecedent neurons that when maximally active cause the connected neuron to also become maximally active to a fix number of combinations of inputs (Saito & Nakano, 1988). The extracted rules are then written as in Table 6.

Obviously, by arbitrarily limiting the combinations that are searched, important rules can be easily ignored – leading to a lack of soundness in the approach. One of the other early decompositional approaches for the extraction of rules from a feed forward neural network was the *KT* algorithm (Fu, 1991). This simply mapped the hidden and output neurons into a Boolean function, shown in Table 7.

Following the earlier SUBSET approach, it was noticed that many of the rules generated could be expressed in the general form[10], in Table 8.

An approach called the MofN algorithm that was developed to extract concise and accurate rules from a MLP network (G. G. Towell, 1991). The key to this approach is the creation of groups

of input connections on a neuron that are found by clustering the weight values. This allows the group to be considered as a whole, rather than having to process all the combinations of the individual links. Once groups are found, any that can never affect the connected neuron or have no effect for the training data examples are removed. This considerably reduces the search space. Although the effectiveness of pruning after training is limited – a better approach would be to carry out the process during training, so that the remaining weights can adjust to the removal of the weak weights. The MofN rule extraction method assumes that the hidden and output neurons can be approximated using a step function so that they can be described as being either "on" (activation is 1) or "off" (activation is 0). Given this assumption, each individual hidden and output neuron can be described in a set of rules based on their weighted connections. If a group of input connections summed weight exceeds the bias, regard-

Table 6. SUBSET Rules

IF a and NOT b THEN CLASS1 [or]
IF c and NOT a THEN CLASS2 [or ...]
...

Table 7. KT Rules

IF output $<=threshold_1$ THEN NO IF $threshold_2 <=output$ THEN YES where $threshold_1 < threshold_2$ ...

Table 8. MofN Rules

If (M of the following N antecedents are true) then [or]
If (M of the following N antecedents are true) then [or...]
...

less of the activation carried by other connections, then a rule can be created from that group. The individual rules can then be combined into a single rule-set that describe the network model as a whole. When the activations of each neuron are limited to [0, 1] – then the relationship between any input connection and the output of the neuron is monotonic. This considerably simplifies the search space – if the sign of an input connection is positive it can only move the neuron's output towards 1. Conversely, if the sign of an input connection is negative it can only move the neuron's output away from 1.

Therefore, to extract a rule to explain when the neuron has an activation of 1:

- only positive literals (antecedents) for input connections that are positive need be considered,
- only negative literals (antecedents) for input connections that are negative need be considered.

The MofN approach represents each hidden neuron as a set of rules. This means that an assumption is made about how each hidden neuron represents a single concept – rather than this being encoded across many neurons. If this is not the case, then the generated rules will not be easy to understand. This may be a limitation that needs further work. The MofN algorithm was developed in the thesis to extract rules from a specialized MLP neural network. The neural network, known as a knowledge-based network (KBANN), had its weights initially specified by inducing them from a set of symbolic rules (i.e. inserting symbolic rules into a neural network first). A more general MLP

network starts from a set of randomized weights and is trained from examples. The reliance of the MofN algorithm on the initial setting of weights means that it may not perform well on the more general MLP network. Although the author later notes that experimental results with a standard neural network trained using back-propagation did appear to cluster. However, there is no reason why this should be so. The author even states that the assumptions made are "not particularly restrictive". The approach can be modified to properly overcome the requirement for the weights to be set by rule insertion. This approach allows a standard neural network to be trained using back-propagation and the MofN algorithm then applied (Craven & Shavlik, 1993a, 1993b). The approach modifies the training algorithm such that the weights are encouraged to form natural clusters during training using a form of Soft Weight Sharing (Nowlan & Hinton, 1992) to help with generalization. In fact, the approach encourages local clustering, rather than global. The results were first class and demonstrated that small sets of concise rules can be automatically extracted from ordinary trained neural networks. Interestingly later results (Craven, 1996) present an empirical evaluation of the use of this modification, which shows that the method made little effect on the accuracy of the extracted rules. It did, however, make a significant impact on the number of literals in the rules. The MofN approach has been applied to a real-world problem of predicting carcinogenicity of chemical compounds (Bahler, Stone, & Wellington, 2000) where it yielded a tractable sized set of rules that had substantial explanatory power. These were compared with decision trees and a newer Bayesian Classifier and still found to be reasonable.

One method to reduce the number of rules extracted is to first prune the neural network connections (Ridella, Speroni, & Trebino, 1993), pruning removes connections (and whole neurons if all connections to it are removed), so as to create a "slimmer" neural network that still models the training data with the same accuracy. Typically the pruning process often requires a re-training of the slimmer network. The resulting smaller network should then help with rule extraction. There is a possible reduction of generalization that pruning can cause - which is an important aspect when applied to data-sets such as fraud, which will not hold all the possible patterns, but still a "prediction" on unseen data is required. The rule extraction approach requires the original training data set that is fed into the slimmer network where groups are formed that are associated with a class. The algorithm is recursive and stops when the composition of each group satisfies a condition. Clearly such an approach is dependent upon the training data set and may therefore fail to represent the generalization within the neural network. The idea of pruning during learning is to simplify the representation of the learnt knowledge prior to rule extraction – in the hope of generating a smaller, more understandable set of rules. This concept was expanded upon using a modified back-propagation algorithm, so that bigger weights represent more important connections using a weight-decay method (Setiono & Liu, 1995). The lower weights can then be pruned while maintaining accuracy and finally the rules extracted by discretising the hidden neuron activation values using clustering. The rule extraction algorithm extracts rules from the hidden-layer to the output-layer and from the input-layer to the hidden-layer and then merges the rules from these two steps. The approach again relies on the training data set for the rule extraction. There is no test for the generalization of the network post pruning and the extracted rules can be difficult to understand in networks

Table 9. NeuroLinear Rules

If type-of-terminal=POS and institution-id>K and Type=01, then Transaction = FRAUD
If type-of-terminal=POS and amount>£500 and institution-id>K and Type=01, then Transaction = FRAUD
If type-of-terminal=POS and CVV=NO and amount>£500 and institution-id>K and Type=01, then Transaction = FRAUD
If institution-id<=K and Type>01 and Amount <£55, then Transaction = GOOD
else if institution-id<=K and Type>01 and Institution-id=G-K and Type=04 and CVV=YES, then Transaction = GOOD
else if institution-id<=K and Type>01 and Institution-id=G-K and Type=04 and CVV=NO, then Transaction = FRAUD
…

with more than a small number of connections. This work was extended and created an algorithm called NeuroRule (Setiono & Liu, 1996). However, this still relies upon a large number of constants that needed to be manually set for the weight decay and cross entropy functions within the back-propagation algorithm. These constants are often referred to as "fiddle-factors" as they are manually set, often by trial-and-error.

NeuroLinear was then developed that deals with both discrete and continuous data – an important factor when dealing with real-world data sets (Setiono & Liu, 1997). This is essentially the same as previously discussed except that the hidden-layer activation values are discretised using the Chi2 (Liu & Setiono, 1995; Liu & Teck Tan, 1995) algorithm. The algorithm makes no assumption on the weights or type of activation functions used in each neuron – see Table 9 for an example of the rules generated. NeuroLinear may produce more compact rules than the *MofN* approach but this clearly depends upon the number of decision boundaries within the fraud data set but the algorithm is computationally expensive compared to other approaches. As before, pruning was again considered, this time pruning larger networks such that new sub-networks are created (Setiono, 1997). It is argued that the rules found in smaller sub-networks are easier to understand and that the training is faster, as unneeded inputs in each sub-network can be removed and trained independently; the approach is recursive, more sub-networks are automatically created. Again, the same approach as before is used, this time rules are extracted from each sub-network and then the original network, so that hierarchical rules are generated. A sound and complete pedagogical approach using sub-networks was subsequently proved (d'Avila Garcez, et al., 2001).

A case study using NeuroLinear was for the a real-world problem of identifying businesses adopting IT (Setiono, Thong, & Yap, 1998). The rules extracted were shown to achieve higher predictive accuracy than the conventional analysis of the same data. This is encouraging that such techniques from academic research can be translated into useful tools for business. This work also proposed a method of extracting decision trees into neural networks – so that their inherent intolerance to noise could be overcome (Setiono & Leow, 1999). This is interesting as it combines the traditional AI approach with that of neural networks. The work demonstrated that decision trees extracted from the neural network are often smaller and simpler.

Although to date only rule extraction from standard MLP neural networks has been discussed, local function networks, such as the RBF can be directly "decompiled" into rules. As in the P-RCE previously discussed, local function networks typically work by mapping an output to a single area of the input space represented by a single hidden neuron in the middle layer (these can be thought of as representing "prototypes" of similar data). To extract rules, a minimum and maximum value can be determined that cause a hidden layer to be active. These values can then be simply expressed as a Boolean rule. The extraction of rules is trivial, since each hidden neuron represents one rule described by its parameters. Unfortunately, a standard RBF uses a sigmoid as its function, that are combined to cover a radial area and once combined they create secondary ridges that extend to infinity that must be cut off. An alternative to the radial area is a rectangular area that is simpler

Table 10. RBF Fuzzy Rules

If type-of-terminal=POS and CVV=NO and amount is LARGE and institution-id is SMALL and Type QUITE NORMAL, then Transaction = FRAUD
If institution-id<=K and Type NORMAL and Amount QUITE SMALL, then Transaction = GOOD
...

in terms of implementation and circumvents the previous problem. The Rectangular Basis Function (RecBFN) is one alternative, here a hyper rectangle is formed in the feature space (Huber & Berthold, 1995). Although a promising approach, in terms of simplicity of rule extraction, the network had some problems in classifying data sets with a large number of input parameters. The training algorithm has a dependency on the order of these parameters that may make it inappropriate for large real-world problems. Local function networks using the radial (combined sigmoidal) functions (for the first time) can also be used (K. McGarry, Wermter, & MacIntyre, 2001; K. J. McGarry & MacIntyre, 1999; K.J. McGarry, Tait, & Wermter, 1999). LREX (Local Rule Extraction) was subsequently devised; this approach uses two rule extraction algorithms; mREX extracts IF... THEN rules as previously described, where it is assumed that a hidden neuron uniquely represents a specific output class. However, the hidden units of an RBF tend to be shared across output classes or may not contribute at all on non-linear or complex data. In this case a new approach, hREX is proposed. This approach first quantizes the weights and then the hidden neuron activation levels – so that any below a defined cut-off value do not participate in the rule extraction. A rule can then be created that consists of one or more hidden neuron which must all be active for the class to be active. There is an upper limit on the rules extracted for each class – which enables a trade-off between comprehensibility and soundness. The local functions suffer from poor accuracy with certain types of data – they are especially sensitive to inputs that are non-discriminatory, which typically leads to substantial overlap of the hidden neurons. Further work is required on this overlap – perhaps by using other Gaussian like radial functions. At this stage, however, the approach does not look to be sufficiently robust for real-world fraud type data. The RBF approach suffers from the same drawbacks on real-world data as previously discussed. RBF Fuzzy (Jin, Seelen, & Sendho, 2000) uses a standard RBF network with a weight sharing (similar in concept to the Soft Weight Sharing discussed as part of the MofN extensions) regularization term to learn classifications and then extracts rules in the form of a set of fuzzy rules. Depending upon the membership functions, the extracted rules have the potential to have high comprehensibility as shown in Table 10.

However, the approach is somewhat academic in nature and has not been tested on real-world data sets. It fails to address the previously discussed limitations of local functions and RBF, but concentrates on the generation of fuzzy rules as more an academic exercise. However, the idea looks promising, as a small set of rules with good comprehensibility and translucency (See Table 5) are highly desirable in the fraud detection application.

Rough set theory (Pawlak, 1991) is based upon finite (crisp) sets and was created to help classify uncertain or imprecise (or even fuzzy) data. A method based on this theory and that uses a standard neural network, again (as with MofN and others) with the assumption that neurons are either active or inactive was proposed (Lazar & Sethi, 2000). A neural network is trained and then used to extract a complete decision table. Such a decision table can become large for networks that have a large number of connections. The decision table is then reduced using rough logic to remove superfluous entries associated with the same class. Finally, the reduced table is converted into rules. Although there are some interesting concepts, it appears to be only practical for "toy problems", where the size of the initial decision table can be

kept manageable – it grows exponentially. Continuing the theme of fuzzy data, the C-MLP2LN model starts with a standard MLP using a sigmoidal function and gradually reduces the slope during training (Duch, Adamczak, & Grabczewski, 2000). There is a considerable problem of training a neural network with a sharp-slope required by these algorithms. A steep sigmoidal-function only has non-zero gradients in small regions of the feature space – it is therefore possible that the number of input examples contributing to the learning process goes to zero! This approach may be applicable to the earlier MofN work. A "regularization" is proposed for the error function in the back-propagation algorithm. The approach allows for both discrete and continuous valued inputs. Back-propagation is applied to a single neuron at a time for a single class using regularization, if the error rate stalls, then an additional neuron is added. The weights and bias can then be analyzed by checking the combinations of features that activate the first neuron(s). Once these rules are extracted, a complex optimization procedure is carried out on the rules (independent of the neural network), that allows rules to produce probabilities of class membership rather than "YES/NO". This optimization may be slow for large sets of rules as it is based upon a gradient method.

An interesting approach uses multiple networks called "ensembles of neural networks". These have been shown to outperform a single neural network in terms of accuracy (Wall & Cunningham, 2000). The key research question is how to combine he rule-sets from individual neural networks – especially when some of the rules may conflict. This may be an area for future research consideration.

Finally, an unusual four layer MLP is used in the DIMLP (Discretised Interpretable MLP) approach (Bologna, 2001). Each neuron in the input layer is connected to just one equivalent neuron in the first hidden layer that uses a "staircase" activation function, with the rest of the layers connected as a standard sigmoid MLP. The idea is that hyper rectangles are better defined (which easily define normal symbolic rules) – as the staircase function provides precise localization of discriminant hyper-planes. Here the number of stairs corresponds to the number of hyper-planes. To extract rules, the algorithm checks where a hyper-plane is effective or not for a given region of input space. This gives the "relevance" of each and a decision tree is then built starting at the highest number of points is added to the tree (i.e. the hyper-plane transition to another class). This has the potential to generate a large tree and therefore a pruning approach is applied. When the approach is compared to C4.5 decision tree induction (see Section 4.1.3), in general the neural model is more accurate (which is not a surprise) but the number of rules generated is equal to or considerably larger in many cases. The work shows promise – when the pruning approaches previously discussed are applied it may outperform. It would be interesting to see the performance if the weight decay and cross entropy functions within the back-propagation algorithm were implemented as per the earlier NeuroRule.

5.2. Pedagogical (Global) Approach

A *pedagogical* approach can be taken to the problem of rule extraction where a set of global rules are extracted to describe each individual input and output neuron in terms of their relationships. The rules for the individual neurons are then combined into a set of rules that describes the network as a whole. The problem with this approach is that the size of the rule space is large; there are three possible conditions for a conjunctive rule:

1. Feature is absent from the antecedent
2. Feature is a positive literal in the antecedent
3. Feature is a negative literal in the antecedent

With n binary features, the complexity is therefore $o(3^n)$. Clearly, a simple *pedagogical*

approach is not practical in real-world problems, where even a small number of input neurons mean an unrealistic level of computing power required – in the previously discussed example in Section 4.2.2, with just 20 input neurons, this would give a search of 3,486,784,401 permutations per hidden layer neuron! Even with a small problem the number of rules generated is large.

One of the earliest rule extraction methods analyses the weights on each connection on each neuron in the neural network – called the SUBSET method (Saito & Nakano, 1988). It looks at every possible combination of positive input weights that will cause that neuron to become active (or not) – i.e. it exceeds the bias of that neuron. With each of these "subsets" of positively weighted connections, a search is then undertaken for combinations within the sub-set and negatively weighted links that still cause the neuron to be active. It can then produce a rule for each of these combinations, e.g.

If p and NOT n then class…

Clearly there is a major combinatorial problem as the number of connections to each neuron grows – as previously discussed.

An approach to extract rules based on SUBSET called RuleNeg was developed – that allows a classification to be made using stepwise negation (Hayward, Ho-Stuart, & Diederich, 1996). Validity Interval Analysis (VIA) was then developed that tests rules by propagating neuron activation intervals through the network, after input and output neurons are constrained (fixed). The method assumes that the hidden layer neurons act independently – and so the rule-set may not represent the network as intended. The key to this algorithm is the setting of initial intervals for the neuron activations – this requires a linear programming method such as the simplex algorithm. Here, intervals are refined by propagating them through the neural network and then making sure that the initial interval constraints set can be satisfied by the data – inconsistent constraints are removed (Thrun, 1995). However, VIA does have the advantage of working with continuous valued inputs, rather than the requirement for discreet values as in the other approaches. An extraction algorithm that is provably both sound and complete was developed by applying an ordering on the input data. This method is not dependent upon the architecture of the neural network (although it does assume only one hidden layer), nor does it have any (re-)training requirements (d'Avila Garcez, et al., 2001).

A framework for data mining using neural networks and rule extraction is a more recent development, called STARE, again considers the neural network as a black box (Z.-H. Zhou, Chen, & Chen, 2000; Z. H. Zhou, Jiang, & Chen, 2000). A sample-set of data is created for rule extraction, by "slowly sliding" the input neurons through instance space i.e. across its value range. Again, a modified Chi2 algorithm, called Chi-Merge (Kerber, 1992) is first used on the data set where there are continuous values. The rule creation approach is similar to the *KT* algorithm (Fu, 1991), where a subset of inputs is found and a rule then created. Here a single input is randomly selected and then a value searched for where it falls into a specific class. If it does then a rule can be created. If it does not, then the next single input is selected and the process continues. If no rule has been created after processing all the single inputs, two input are chosen and the process repeats (here the rule would have two conjunctive antecedents, i.e. a AND b). The number of possible antecedents is limited to three (for obvious combinatorial reasons). While there is little new in terms of rule extraction, the "slowly sliding" method may have some applicability in the generation prototype rules.

A pedagogical approach to extracting rules from a Support Vector Machine (SVM)[11] was devised where a labeled dataset was used to train a SVM as a classifier to satisfactory accuracy. Once trained, a synthetic dataset was derived from the support vectors from the trained SVM, with the target class being generated by the SVM then using K-means clustering to reduce the number of "synthetic" examples. Rules were then extracted from the synthetic dataset by mapping to if-then rules (Barakat & Diederich, 2004). The SVM is used as an "Oracle" to produce synthetic datasets. However, the approach was found not to scale well. By omitting the clustering step and replacing it with the C5[12] decision tree algorithm this was somewhat improved (Barakat & Diederich, 2005). In large scale problems such as fraud detection, decision trees generate a large number of rules and are affected by "noise". A large number of rules, where each rule has many conditions are unfortunately difficult to understand. Therefore this approach would fail to create comprehensible rule sets that adequately capture the generalization of the classifier. The extraction step above was then replaced with an approach called GSVMORC[13] based on locating the points on the SVM classification boundary by constructing hypercubes using a search based on the distance between each class point and the hyperplane (Ren & d'Avila Garcez, 2009). Decision Boundary Analysis (DBA) in neural networks has generated much research literature, with a number of researchers using sensitivity analysis as the search method, where (Engelbrecht & Cloete, 1998; Engelbrecht & Viktor, 1999; Goh, 1993; Viktor, Engelbrecht, & Cloete, 1995) are all based on using an MLP as the classifier. The work in (Zhang & Liu, 2005) is based on an SVM and is most closely related to GSVMORC. Synthetic examples are first created using kernel density estimates that are the same as described for TREPAN (Craven, 1996). In fact, many 100,000's of synthetic examples may be needed to be generated to locate one that would be subsequently classified as fraud. Once a ruleset is extracted, it is optimized by combining or removing discretised field elements (where they may have overlapping real-ranges) and removing those rules that are duplicated.

Figure 7. SOAR rule extraction

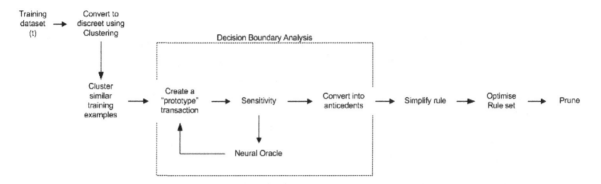

6. NEURAL SYMBOLIC PROCESSING IN FRAUD DETECTION

A fraud detection framework has the key requirements:

- Process a large quantity of heterogeneous, noisy data.
- Make fast decisions.
- Adapt to changing patterns and identify interesting new relationships dynamically.
- Add new transactions without the previous knowledge being damaged.
- Detect and explain anomalous behavior based on unlabeled data.
- Recognize and reason about transactions.

These requirements are difficult and lead to complex research questions; disparate research from AI, symbolic and connectionist approaches is at a point where it can be united to make fraud detection more effective.

6.1. A New Approach

The research into symbolic rule extraction discussed is largely based on small-scale datasets. There is no reason to assume that these techniques will produce a small set of comprehensible rules when applied to real-world business applications

such as fraud detection. Therefore, a new algorithm has been devised based on a pedagogical approach for the use in credit card fraud detection *(N. Ryman-Tubb, 2010b)*. The key to this new algorithm, called SOAR (Sparse Oracle-based Adaptive Rule) extraction is the use of sensitivity analysis that avoids the exhaustive decision boundary searches of the other rule extraction algorithms. The SOAR algorithm (N. Ryman-Tubb, 2010a), shown in Figure 7 uses a standard MLP as a Neural "Oracle", which was chosen to produce good generalization and noise-tolerance.

In the SOAR extraction algorithm, sparse training examples are used as the initial search space "seeds" – since locating null hypothesis[14] points on the decision boundary in a large search space would be otherwise inefficient. The SOAR extraction algorithm is independent of the neural structure and has the following key steps:

1. Continuous valued fields are converted into discreet literals using a well known clustering algorithm called ART2 (Carpenter & Grossberg, 1987) that is applied to group together similar fraud examples. A step-by-step description of the algorithm used here is given by (Pao, 1989). The algorithm creates a new cluster when the input does not belong to the cluster that was determined as most probable, based on a user defined parameter. The Euclidean distance measure

293

Figure 8. Existing rule-based FMS

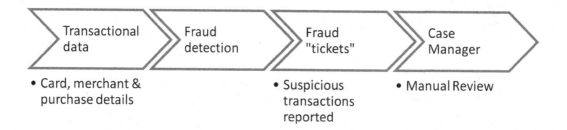

is used for measuring similarities between the input pattern and the exemplars in each cluster.

2. The trained MLP neural system is used as an "Oracle", to interrogate

3. Prototypes are formed by grouping similar examples from the fraud dataset class to reduce complexity

4. Each "prototype" is expanded using sensitivity analysis (based on the output of the neural Oracle) to search for points on the decision boundary and forming a hyper-polytope that contains only one class – the aim is to capture the generalization of the neural model while covering as much of the space contiguously as is possible. This is then used to create a rule as a list of antecedents as a combination of the expanded input fields.

5. The rules are optimized to avoid overlap, etc. This step includes rule pruning to remove rules that have a large estimated error and those which never "fire" (have zero coverage) for the training set.

6. A false-positive ratio is calculated for each rule using the training dataset, those rules that have a large ratio (i.e. produce a large number of false-positives compared to the correct number of frauds detected) are removed.

Since the fraud data examples are sparse, the above procedure is computationally efficient. This approach will approximate the classification of

the neural system by creating a set of rules. The optimization steps 5 and 6 above aim to improve comprehensibility by reducing the number of rules and approximation errors.

6.2. Case Study: International Credit Card Fraud Detection

A large international company processes a high volume of CP transactions a day. It uses a FMS based on rules created by experts, which generate a number of fraud alerts that must be reviewed each day.

The type and patterns of fraud continued to change over time, so the effectiveness of their FMS reduced. This case study uses the SOAR Extraction approach to automatically create a set of rules overnight to accurately detect the most current fraud patterns.

There are three main stages to project, shown in Figure 9:

1. Data pre-processing
2. Neural model learning
3. Symbolic rule extraction

Pre-processing of the transactional data is a key part of creating a successful neural approach. This normalizes the data and converts it to a suitable numerical representation for the model. The data available for the detection of fraud has some unique properties:

Figure 9. Case study overview

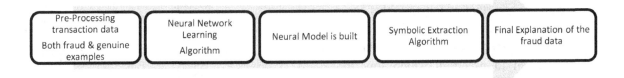

- Sparse examples of fraud
- Large number of input fields
- Non-normal distributions
- Made up of a sequence of events over time

These attributes make it a difficult real-world problem to model the data in order to aid in the detection of fraud. The transaction data is highly dimensional, with 30-100 fields defining each transaction that are made up of both continuous and discreet values and is not normally distributed[15]. The intrinsic dimensionality is high and indicates that an unrealistic number of examples would be required, (Bishop & Ryman-Tubb, 1994)[16] to comprehensibly build a model. Therefore, pre-processing is an important part of developing a more accurate model. Given the highly dimensional nature of the data and the lack of null hypothesis examples a method is needed to reduce the dimensionality (Maaten, Postma, & Herik, 2008) and to group similar examples prior to class classification. Principal Component Analysis (PCA) (Pearson, 1901) is a powerful technique for reducing the dimensionality of data by projecting it onto a lower dimensional linear subspace. PCA is based on the data being continuously valued and made up of linear-Gaussian distributions. However, it was found that real-world fraud data is both nonlinear and non-Gaussian, so that PCA would not be an optimal approach. One method to model this non-linear data is to use a combination of linear PCA models so that an approximation is made piecewise (Hinton, Revow, & Dayan, 1995).

A further technique such as K-means clustering (MacQueen, 1967) can be used to first cluster the data into separate groups and to then apply PCA to each of these groups. However this approach is not computationally efficient for large datasets and is based on arbitrary heuristics. A variant of PCA, called Probabilistic-PCA (PPCA) (Roweis, 1998; Tipping & Bishop, 1999), represents data as mixtures of PCA in the constrained form of a Gaussian distribution where the dimensionality of the subspace is found automatically from the data. This creates a linear generative model of the data – i.e. a model of the data based on a probability density function. Here, the approach tries to model the density function, constrained to a low intrinsic dimensionality, which is assumed to have generated the data.

In this case study the pre-processing was designed to enhance the modeling characteristics of the data by:

- All records checked for incomplete or missing data. These records are ignored if found.
- Roll-up fields are calculated and added to each transaction record.
- Attempts are made to identify outliers in the data and to make a decision if these records should be included in the modeling process.
- Assessing the relevance of each field (to ensure *maximum entropy).*
- Identifying redundancy in the data.

- Relevance Determination.
- Redundancy Removal.
- Frequency histograms of numeric data are created to ascertain which variables could benefit from transformation.
- Frequency analysis of symbolic data is undertaken to ascertain which low frequency variables could benefit from being grouped.
- Re-weighting and Splitting.

The pre-processing split the transaction data into two datasets. (see Table 11)

A sampled dataset was created from a natural population of transactions over a fixed time period so as to be representative of the natural population containing 100% of the marked (known) fraud, shown in Table 12.

A three layer MLP architecture was selected as being the common choice in the previous research discussed and noted as exhibiting good generalization ability. In this case study the MLP had 60 inputs, 10 hidden and 1 output neuron that were chosen through experimentation. All neuron values were in the range 0 to 1 using a standard sigmoidal activation function. The training of the neural network is an iterative process that requires considerable processing power to complete, where the more transactions presented the longer the algorithm will take. For this reason a Modeling dataset was created as a sub-sample shown in Table 13. The Modeling Dataset used a small sub-sample of 40,000 transaction records with 2,800 example fraud transactions. The remaining 1,200 marked fraud transactions were reserved as "unseen" in a Validation Dataset to produce performance metrics. The MLP was then trained using this Modeling dataset by interleaving and repeating the fraud examples with the genuine examples so that they were balanced, using the Conjugate Gradient Descent (CGD) (Fletcher & Powell, 1963) training algorithm.

Table 11. Datasets

1	Modelling Dataset	Consists of a randomly selected proportion of the transaction data where the outcome is known. This information is fed into the neural modelling system, to train it to learn the relationships within the data and build the model.
2	Validation Dataset	Consists of a sample of data where the outcome is known and is fed through the system only once the model has been completed, to validate the accuracy of the model.

Table 12. Case study dataset

Natural Population: Transactions	60m
Natural Population: Cards	8m
Natural Population: Number of Fraud Transactions	4,000
Natural Population: Value of Fraud Transactions	€1m
A priory transaction fraud	1:15,000
Sample %	0.3%

Once the neural network was trained, the SOAR extraction algorithm was applied to the trained neural network. The rule set created consisted of 47 rules; the top five are given in Table 14.

The values enclosed in brackets are a list of symbols automatically grouped together by the pre-processing step, such as a specific list of countries. Fraud analysts were able to look at each rule and quickly understand the key relationships discovered. The rules therefore have a high level of comprehensibility, one of the key criteria in Table 5. Each rule, if true, indicates fraud and therefore the rules are also translucent in terms of directly relating the output (fraud) to the inputs (transactional details).

A confusion matrix is used to evaluate the performance of both the trained neural network and the extracted rule set on the Validation dataset. The confusion matrix format is given in Table 3. Performance metrics were also produced on the Validation dataset calculating accuracy given in (1) and precision (2)(3).

Table 13. Data distribution

	TOTAL	Modelling Dataset		Validation Dataset	
Total Transaction Records	1,100,000	40,000	4%	1,060,000	96%
Containing Fraud Records	4,000	2,800	70%	1,200	30%
Euro Value of Fraud Records	€1m	€703,000		€297,000	

Table 14. Top five rules

#	Rule	%
1.	RECORDTYPE=(A) AND COUNTRY=(L1) AND CODE=(CODE1) AND PRDCODE=(10) AND NETW=(ID1) AND TRANSTYPE=(5) AND IND=(1)	30
2.	RECORDTYPE=(A) AND COUNTRY=(COUNTRY3) AND CODE=(CODE1) AND DISS=(DISS1) AND PRD-CODE=(30) AND NETW=(NETW1) AND TRANSTYPE=(1) AND IND=(1)	7
3.	RECORDTYPE=(A) AND COUNTRY=(COUNTRY1) AND CODE=(CODE1) AND DISS=(DISS1) AND PRDCODE=(PRDCODE1) AND NETW=(NETW1) AND TRANSTYPE=(1) AND IND=(1) AND NOT AVERAGE_SPEND=[$0-$1569] OR AVERAGE_SPEND=[$0-$5] OR AVERAGE_SPEND=[$100-$604] AND NOT AMOUNT=[$0-$1331] OR AMOUNT=[$0-$200] OR AMOUNT=[$467-$2000]	5
4.	RECORDTYPE=(A) AND COUNTRY=(COUNTRY2) AND CODE=(CODE2) AND DISS=(DISS1) AND PRD-CODE=(37)+(12) AND NETW=(E)+(S) AND TRANSTYPE=(1) AND IND=(0) AND AVERAGE_SPEND=[$0-$504]	6
5.	RECORDTYPE=(A) AND COUNTRY=(COUNTRY1) AND CODE=(CODE1) AND DISS=(DISS1) AND PRDCODE=(PRDCODE2) AND NETW=(NETW1) AND TRANSTYPE=(1) AND IND=(1)	5

$$accuracy = \frac{TP + TN}{TP + FN + FP + TN} \qquad (1)$$

$$precision_{genuine} = \frac{TP}{TP + FP} \qquad (2)$$

$$precision_{fraud} = \frac{FP}{TP + FP} \qquad (3)$$

Table 15 details the results for the case study. The extracted rules have a high accuracy and a low false positive rate. Counterintuitively, the rules outperform the neural model in terms of accuracy. It is suggested that the rules are able to outperform as the boundaries located are crisp boundaries so that the (inaccurate) generalization of the neural model is not captured in the extraction. This tends to create rules that do not cover the decision boundary correctly (as evidenced by the reduced precision), which also tends to reduce the false-positive rate suffered by the neural network. The false-positive rate is further reduced by pruning those rules that exhibit a high rate, no doubt reducing precision, but contributing to improved accuracy. There is no such equivalent process for the neural network. The company fraud analysts found that the rules identified both

Table 15. Evaluation of neural network.vs. extracted rules

		PREDICTED BY NEURAL		PREDICTED BY RULES	
		Genuine	Fraud	Genuine	Fraud
ACTUAL VALUE	Genuine	667,800	391,000	964,600	94,200
	Fraud	139	1,061	157	1,043

Table 16. Evaluation of accuracy and precision

	PREDICTED BY NEURAL	PREDICTED BY RULES
Accuracy (1)	63%	91%
Precision$_{genuine}$ (2)	63%	91%
Precision$_{fraud}$ (3)	88%	87%
False Positive Rate	1:468	1:112

Figure 10. Performance of extracted rules for detecting fraud

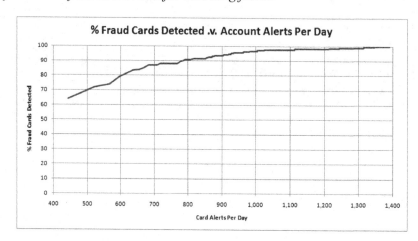

already known patterns as well as previously unknown patterns of fraud. The graph below shows that if the fraud team at the international company review the 1,000 alerts generated by the extracted rules each day, 97.5% of credit card frauds are correctly identified.

The ROC chart shows how well the neural network is able to be specific (catch only "frauds") and sensitive (catch all "frauds") simultaneously. Sensitivity (y) and 1-Specificity (x) are displayed for various cut-off values. The more the chart bends to the top left, the better. The best possible predictive model would be closest to the upper left corner - known as a perfect classification (i.e. 100% sensitivity or no false negatives) and 100% specificity (no false positives). A completely random guess would give a point along a diagonal line (the line of no-discrimination). Points above this line indicate a good prediction, points below indicate an error. The chart in Figure 11 was cre-

ated using the Validation dataset and shows that the neural network is a good classifier.

To provide a measure of rule comprehensibility the following two measures were used:

- Total number of rules to classify unseen transactions
- Average number of antecedents per rule in the rule set

The rules are processed one at a time by the FMS, if a rule "fires", that is it is true, then fraud is indicated and no further rules are processed for that transaction. Therefore, the rule-depth has a direct influence on the performance of the classifier. Figure 12 details the depth of rules in the rule set and calculates both the accuracy for fraud detection and genuine recognition (on a per transaction basis). As can be seen, while the full 47 rules are needed to achieve 87% fraud detection

Figure 11. Receiver operating characteristic

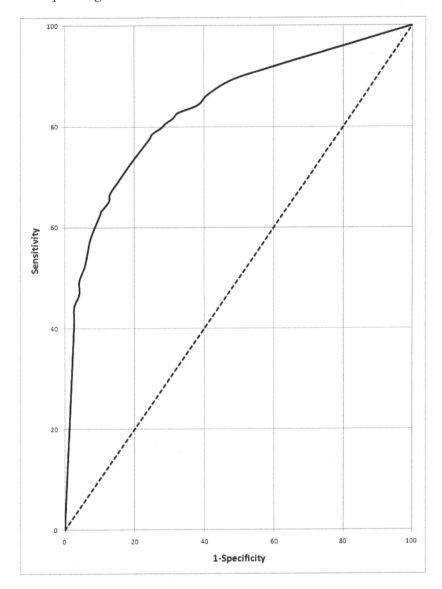

precision given in Table 15, selecting 25 rules, detects 82% frauds, a 5% reduction of accuracy, with a 46% reduction in the number of rules.

The number of antecedents in each rule is a good measure on human comprehensibility; shorter and simpler rules are more straightforward to understand than complex rules. (see Table 17)

The SOAR Extraction algorithm has been shown to be an effective approach in the battle against credit card fraud. It produced a small set of accurate rules, with a low false positive rate

and a manageable number of alerts per day. Used on a regular basis, it has the promise of enabling a more dynamic FMS that can **respond** to the changing patterns of fraud.

7. FUTURE RESEARCH DIRECTIONS

The case study has shown how neural networks can be combined with other techniques to help solve a difficult real world problem. To try to

Figure 12. Rule comprehensibility: Depth of rules vs. accuracy

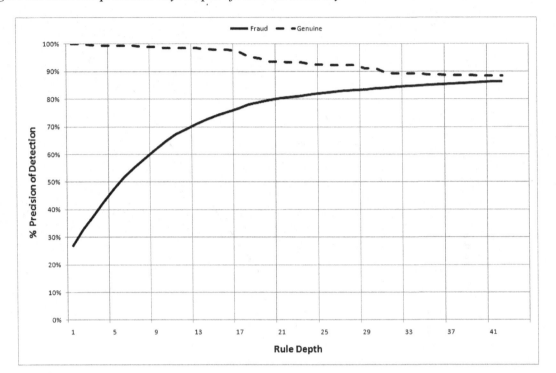

cope with the temporal and sequential dimension of the problem, the approach has been to use "global features" by producing derived variables. However, information is clearly lost *inter alia* by "flattening" the sequence and related temporal data. From Figure 13, an example sequence of credit card transactions has been be clustered; the resulting sequence of transactions by cluster is "222323323231".

This sequence of transactions can be plotted over the time of the transactions (e.g. normalized into one-hour slots over the month), see Figure 14, where a single element of that sequence cannot be predicted based simply on the previous element.

It is the recognition of this sequence that identifies the individual cardholder – and conversely if a transaction does not conform to the expected sequence then it may be fraudulent. The timing of each transaction within the sequence contains critical information for recognizing a behavioral profile, e.g. shopping is normally carried out at 11am on Saturdays. Therefore, both the time between transactions and actual normalized time-of-day are essential. To improve model accuracy, clearly this information needs to be encoded. Research needs to be carried out on a new neural classifier that can identify an atypical sequence of transactions for a specific account or group of accounts to improve the accuracy of fraud detection. An improved neural approach is

Table 17.

	Average per rule	Smallest Number	Largest Number
Antecedents	9.4	7	17

Figure 13. Sequence of transactions in a single account

Observation	Cluster #	Date Day	Type	Merchant	Amount
1	2	15	1	1	£24.98
2	2	16	1	2	£15.70
3	2	19	2	3	£33.04
4	3	19	1	1	£20.00
5	2	20	2	3	£31.47
6	3	20	3	4	£21.60
7	3	20	1	2	£10.35
8	2	22	1	2	£10.35
9	3	23	2	3	£13.91
10	2	27	1	2	£15.70
11	3	28	4	5	£6.00
12	1	29	1	1	£10.35

therefore needed that is able to make use of sequential information. While a sequence of transactions is indicative of the behavior of a cardholder, a more subtle approach may be to view the sequence as a series of spending *cycles* (or oscillations), e.g. petrol is purchased every 3-days, shopping once a week, etc. In this case, the sequence over time can be transposed from that in Figure 14 into a continuous-time signal composed of a number of oscillating components. Digital Signal Processing (DSP) techniques, such as the Fast Fourier Transform (FFT) or wavelet analysis (Vetterli & Duhamel, 1990) can be used to convert such a signal to the frequency domain. The fundamental frequency components can then be analyzed. Figure 15 shows this signal converted into frequency components.

By expressing the time series in the frequency domain, a considerable noise reduction in the data can be achieved. The most closely related research on payment fraud detection using event features is based on Hidden Markov Models (HMM) to model transaction sequences (Srivastava, Kundu, & Sural, 2008). A Hidden Markov Model (HMM) is used to predict temporal sequences based on cardhodler transactions. An HMM is a statistical model based on the parametric probability distribution of "observable" features. HMMs are commonly used in temporal pattern recognition such as speech recognition where time related sequences are important.[17] HMMs are trained by

Figure 14. Transactions over time. X-Axis is time over one month and Y-Axis the cluster-id

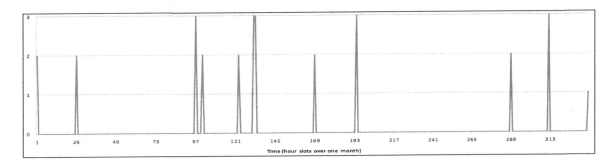

Figure 15. Frequency analysis

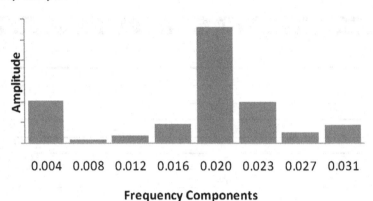

statistical estimation algorithms that calculate parameters based on the probability of observing a sequence. Statistical independence of observations and mutually independent outputs are assumed. HMMs do not account for correlation between adjacent feature vectors give a state sequence. The research does not address the requirement of adding a subsequent new transaction into the HMM sequence and it takes an empirical approach to setting the sequence length and the number of states within the HMM. This makes it not practical in the real-world. In the research, observations (i.e. transaction data) are first quantized into a limit set of symbols that are determined using a K-means clustering algorithm, for example, just three symbols, low, medium, high, are used for the amount spent per transaction. This research is based on artificial data but was successful is showing good TP while maintaining a low FP. The results are encouraging as the research successfully demonstrates the power of using temporal sequences for fraud detection for the first time. Both the training phase of the HMM, performed offline and the detection phase were performed online and computation increases linearly against the number of transaction sequences. The HMM algorithm is computationally complex and may not be sufficiently scalable to a deployable solution where a model is trained

for each cardholder (typically 2m-3m cardholders per bank).

An approach to aligning transaction sequences has been researched where it is argued that a fraudster is unlikely to be able to replicate the spending behavior of the cardholder – especially as the criminals tend to try to maximize their possible gain within a limited time period that they believe they have before detection (compare this to the earlier game-theoretic approach where the FMS player minimizes its loss by detecting fraud at an early stage and the criminal player modifies their behavior based upon their own belief on detection according to a Nash Equilibrium (Rosenthal, 1973) such that he can play no better given the strategy of the other player). A two stage approach is taken; (1) current transaction is aligned with the cardholders sequence (2) mismatches are then aligned with known sequences of fraud. The first stage performs an anomaly type detection looking for unusual cardholder behavior. However, this tends to produce a significant level of false-positives as the cardholders behavior changes. The second stage therefore provides a filter to help reduce these false alarms. Again synthesized data is used to perform empirical experiments – the results show good true-positives, but the false-positives still remain at an unacceptable level for a real-world solution (Kundu, Sural, & Majumdar, 2008). The research is well motivated and it appears that more researchers are turning their attention to the issue of recognizing sequences. It is the recognition of a sequence that identifies the individual cardholder – and conversely if a transaction does not conform to the expected sequence then it may be fraudulent. The timing of each transaction within the sequence contains critical information for recognizing a behavioral profile, e.g. shopping is normally carried out at 11am on Saturdays. Therefore, both the time between transactions and actual normalized time-of-day are essential. Perhaps a better approach would be to view the sequence as a series of spending cycles (or oscillations) – and use digital signal processing techniques to extract these cycles, that are then part of a sequence of such oscillations.

The Restricted Boltzmann Machine (RBM) (Smolensky, 1986) is a probabilistic generative approach, which uses an unsupervised learning algorithm on a two-layer network made up of binary stochastic neurons connected as a visible and hidden layer. Rather than the EM algorithm, the Contrastive Divergence algorithm (Ackley, Hinton, & Sejnowski, 1985) is used to train the RBM. A single RBM has a Boltzmann-distributed joint probability and effectively learns the correlations between the inputs where each hidden unit creates a linearly separated 2-region division of the input space[18]. However, the standard binary RBM is not suited to modeling continuous valued inputs (these must be first encoded into discrete values). A continuous adaptation (Chen & Murray, 2003) also has a computationally inexpensive training algorithm. RBM appears to be an interesting approach for further research. RBMs are interesting as there are a number of extensions for sequence recognition, such a Temporal RBM (TRBM) (Bengio, 2007; Hinton, 2002; Sutskever, Hinton, & Taylor, 2009) that is able to model high dimensional sequences by using a separate RBM for each time step (see Figure 16). The Temporal Convolution Machine (TCM) generalizes the TRBM by allowing a time-varying bias to be a convolution of prior states with any function, instead of a particular fixed

linear function (Lockett & Miikkulainen, 2009). Here a deep three-layer TCM model proved to be significantly more accurate in reconstructing artificially generated spatiotemporal sequences than dynamic Bayesian networks. The TCM was robust with long sequences: in one experiment it was able to reconstruct a sequence of 491 notes in Scarlatti's Piano Sonata No. 1. By clamping the right-hand notes, TCM was able to reproduce the left-hand harmony, thereby performing a sequence mapping task, even with Gaussian noise added to the input signal. This preliminary research shows TCM as a promising starting point for sequence processing and therefore event feature recognition in the structured, noisy, long sequences of real-world fraud account transactions.

By considering transactions as event features, research into computational music also offers some key insights. For example, a sparse data problem is examined where prior knowledge of music is encoded into a statistical model (Conklin, 2003). A similar approach could be applied to fraud, where background expert knowledge, in the form of rules, could be inserted into the neural network. Importantly, (Hillewaere, Manderick, & Conklin, 2009) demonstrates that event models are considerably more powerful than the "encoded" global feature models, when used for music classification. With this result and that of the HMM research, it would appear that considerable accuracy uplift could be obtained by using sequence based classification for fraud detection.

There is much research on the use of the SOM in sequence and temporal processing the principals of which could be applied to the GTM previously described. Early work (Chappell & Taylor, 1993) was biologically inspired – the Temporal Kohonen Map (TKM) – practical for only a small number of contexts. This was followed by the Recurrent SOM (RSOM) (Koskela, Varsta, Heikkonen, & Kaski, 1998), which significantly improved the TKM with a better but constant depth of representation. RSOM was enhanced by a Contextual SOM (CSOM) (Voegtlin, 2000) that shows promise

Figure 16. A stacked TCM

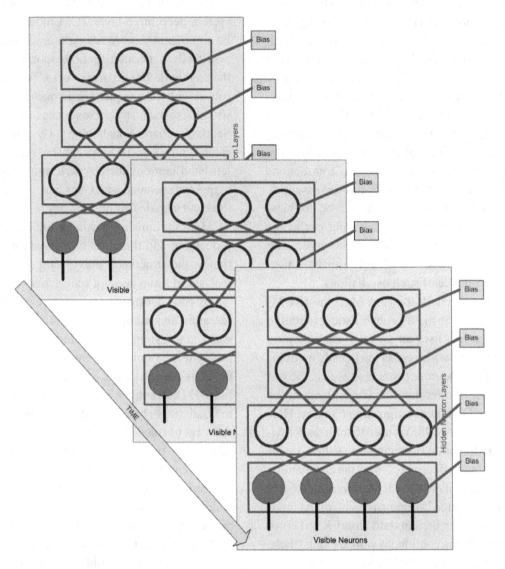

producing an optimal representation of temporal context. None of these approaches was tested on real-world problems and all require a fixed network structure. The Recurrent-Energy Competitions SOM (R-ECSO) more recently used in the field of robotics[19] (Shimozaki & Kuniyoshi, 2003) demonstrates real-world event feature detection abilities – coping with noisy image data. In this research, the SOM must be able to handle time-sensitive patterns – the temporal ordering of the input sequence, the time between transactions (cycles) and the actual normalized time-of-day.

However, the reliance on the SOM means that these approaches all suffer from the lack of a principled framework with problems such as convergence, initialization, tuning of learning parameters, [20]etc.

8. CONCLUSION

It can be seen that the growth of computing power has led to a growth in the research and the abilities of neural networks, originally inspired by biological processes, implemented on a computer. At the same time, this growth has fuelled another "industry" – that of fraud through the use of computers. The ability of a neural network to recognize complex patterns and to make a "guess" based on past experience gives computers more "human-like" qualities. These qualities can be used by businesses for a range of real-world applications; in particular, helping to cut crime by detecting patterns of fraud in credit card transactions. While businesses have criticized neural networks as being "black boxes", it has been shown that the emerging field of neural-symbolic research is now able to provide explanations for what has been learnt and generalized by the neural network. The case study demonstrates how the combination of two technologies, using a newly proposed algorithm, work together to provide first class results, helping to discover new patterns of fraud in a changing environment and allowing the rules to be deployed rapidly into an online FMS system without the fear of a "black box" approach.

9. REFERENCES

Ackley, D. H., Hinton, G. E., & Sejnowski, T. J. (1985). A learning algorithm for Boltzmann machines. *Cognitive Science*, *9*, 147–169. doi:10.1207/s15516709cog0901_7

Aleskerov, E., Freisleben, B., & Rao, B. (1997, 25/03/1997). *CARDWATCH: a neural network based database mining system for credit card fraud detection*. Paper presented at the Computational Intelligence for Financial Engineering (CIFEr).

Anderson, J. A., & Rosenfeld, E. (2000). *Talking nets - an oral history of neural networks*. MIT Press.

Attoh-Okine, N. O., & Ayyub, B. M. (2005). Neural networks for residential infrastructure management. *Applied Research in Uncertainty Modeling and Analysis*, *20*, 215–217. doi:10.1007/0-387-23550-7_10

Bahler, D., Stone, B., & Wellington, C. (2000). Symbolic, neural, and Bayesian machine learning models for predicting carcinogenicity of chemical compounds. *Journal of Chemical Information and Computer Sciences*, *40*(4), 906–914. doi:10.1021/ci990116i

Bar-Hillel, M. (1977). *The base-rate fallacy in probability judgments*. Decisions and Designs.

Barakat, N., & Diederich, J. (2004). *Learning-based rule-extraction from support vector machines*. Paper presented at the 12th International Conference on Computer Theory and Applications.

Barakat, N., & Diederich, J. (2005). Eclectic rule-extraction from support vector machines. *International Journal Computational Intelligence*, *2*(1), 59–62.

Bengio, Y. (2007). Learning deep architectures for AI *Technical Report 1312*: Université de Montréal.

Bishop, C., & Ryman-Tubb, N. (1994). *Best practice guidelines for developing neural computing applications*. London: Department for Business Innovation and Skills.

Bologna, G. (2001). A study on rule extraction from neural networks applied to medical databases. [IJNS]. *International Journal of Neural Systems*, *11*(3), 247–255. doi:10.1016/S0129-0657(01)00068-0

Brause, R., Langsdorf, T., & Hepp, M. (1999, 01/01/1999). *Neural data mining for credit card fraud detection*. Paper presented at the 11th International Conference on Tools with Artificial Intelligence.

Carpenter, G. A., & Grossberg, S. (1987). ART2: Self-organization of stable catagory recognition codes for analog input patterns. *Applied Optics*, *26*, 4919–4930. doi:10.1364/AO.26.004919

Carroll, J. M. (1996). Unathororized modification of software *Computer Security* (3 ed., pp. 54): Butterworth-Heinemann.

Chakravorti, S. (2000). Why has stored value not caught on? *Federal Reserve Bank of Chicago Policy Studies*(6), 1-36.

Chan, P. K., Fan, W., & Prodromidis, A. L. (1999). Distributed data mining in credit card fraud detection. *Intelligent Systems and Their Applications*, *14*(6), 67–74. doi:10.1109/5254.809570

Chappell, G. J., & Taylor, G. J. (1993). The temporal Kohonen map. *Neural Networks*, 441–445. doi:10.1016/0893-6080(93)90011-K

Chen, H., & Murray, A. F. (2003). *Continuous restricted Boltzmann machine with an implementable training algorithm*. Paper presented at the Vision, Image and Signal Processing.

Chiu, C.-C., & Tsai, C.-Y. (2004). A web services-based collaborative scheme for credit card fraud detection. *e-Technology, e-Commerce and e-Service*, 177-181.

Conklin, D. (2003). *Music generation from statistical models*. Paper presented at the AISB 2003 Symposium on Artificial Intelligence and Creativity in the Arts and Sciences, Aberystwyth, Wales.

Consoli, D. (2003). The evolution of retail banking services in United Kingdom: a retrospective analysis. *Centre for Research on Innovation & Competition*, *13*, 1–28.

Cooper, L. N., Elbaum, C., & Reilly, D. L. (1980). USA Patent No. 4326259. U. S. Patent.

Craven, M. (1996). *Extracting comprehensible models from trained neural models*. Madison, USA: University of Wisconsin.

Craven, M., & Shavlik, J. W. (1993a). Learning symbolic rules using artificial neural networks. *Proceedings of the 10th International Conference on Machine Learning*.

Craven, M., & Shavlik, J. W. (1993b). *Understanding neural networks via rule extraction and pruning*. Lawerence Erlbaum Associates.

Crosman, P. (2010). *Card fraud costs U.S. payment providers $8.6 billion per year*. New York: Bank Systems & Technology.

CyberSource. (2008). *Fourth Annual UK Online Fraud Report*. Reading, UK.

d'Avila Garcez, A. S., Broda, K., & Gabbay, D. M. (2001). Symbolic knowledge extraction from trained neural networks: A sound approach. *Artificial Intelligence*, (125): 155–207. doi:10.1016/S0004-3702(00)00077-1

Dorronsoro, J. R., Ginel, F., & Sgnchez, C. (1997). Neural fraud detection in credit card operations. *IEEE Transactions on Neural Networks*, *8*(4), 827–834. doi:10.1109/72.595879

Duch, W., Adamczak, R., & Grabczewski, K. (2000). *Neural methods of knowledge Extraction*. Control and Cybernetics.

EC. (2005). *EuroBarometer Research* (Vol. 63).

Edelberg, W. (2003). *Risk-based pricing of interest rates in household loan markets*. Washington, DC: U.S. Board of Governors of the Federal Reserve System.

Engelbrecht, A. P., & Cloete, I. (1998, 22 - 24 September, 1998). *Feature extraction from feedforward neural networks using sensitivity analysis*. Paper presented at the International Conference on Systems, Signals, Control, Computer, Durban, South Africa.

Engelbrecht, A. P., & Viktor, H. L. (1999). *Rule improvement through decision boundary detection using sensitivity analysis* (Vol. 1607). Berlin: Springer.

EPC Card Fraud Prevention Task Force*(2006)*.

Evans, D. S., & Schmalensee, R. (2005). *Market performance Paying with Plastic - The Digital Revolution in Buying and Borrowing* (2nd ed.). Cambridge, MA: MIT.

Field, D. L., & Agnew, N. P. (1996). *London Underground's ticketing, past, present and future.* Paper presented at the Public Transport Electronic Systems, 1996., International Conference on (Conf. Publ. No. 425).

Fisher, D. H., & McKusick, K. B. (1989, 01/01/1989). *An empirical comparison of ID3 and back-propagation.* Paper presented at the International Joint Conference on Artificial Intelligence (IJCAI).

Fletcher, R., & Powell, M. J. D. (1963). A rapidly convergent descent method for minimization. *The Computer Journal, 6,* 163–168.

Fraud in the UK, Association of Chief Police Officers (2007).

Fu, L. (1991, 19/07/1991). *Rule learning by searching on adapted nets.* Paper presented at the Ninth National Conference on Artificial Intelligence (AAAI-91), Anaheim, California.

Ghosh, S., & Reilly, D. L. (1994). *Credit card fraud detection with a neural network.* Paper presented at the International Conference on System Sciences, Hawaii

Goh, T. H. (1993). Semantic extraction using neural network modelling and sensitivity analysis. *IJCNN '93-Nagoya. Proceedings of 1993 International Joint Conference on Neural Networks, 1,* 1031-1034.

Grossman, P. Z. (1987). *American Express: The unofficial history of the people who built the great financial empire.* New York: Random House Value Publishing.

Hayward, R., Ho-Stuart, C., & Diederich, J. (1996). *RULENEG: extracting rules from a trained ANN by stepwise negation. Queensland University of Technology.* QUT.

Hillewaere, R., Manderick, B., & Conklin, D. (2009). *Global feature versus event models for folk song classification.* Paper presented at the 10th International Society for Music Information Retrieval Kobe, Japan.

Hinton, G. E. (2002). Training products of experts by minimising contrastive divergence. *Neural Computation, 14*(8), 1527–1554. doi:10.1162/089976602760128018

Hinton, G. E., Osindero, S., & Yee-Whye, T. (2006). A fast learning algorithm for deep belief nets. *Neural Computation, 18*(7), 1527–1554. doi:10.1162/neco.2006.18.7.1527

Hinton, G. E., Revow, M., & Dayan, P. (1995). *Recognising handwritten digits using mixtures of linear models. Advances in neural information processing systems, 7.* Cambridge, MA: MIT Press.

Holler, M., Park, C., Diamond, J., Santoni, U., The, S. C., Glier, M., et al. (1992, November). *A high performance sdaptive classifier ssing radial basis functions.* Paper presented at the Government Microcircuit Applications, Las Vegas, Nevada.

Hopfield, J. J. (1982). *Neural networks and physical systems with emergent collective computational abilities.* Paper presented at the National Academy Science.

Huber, K. P., & Berthold, M. R. (1995). Building precise classifiers with automatic rule extraction. *IEEE International Conference on Neural Networks, 3,* 1263-1268.

Intel. (2008). *The revolution continues The revolution begins.* Retrieved 26th May, 2008, from ftp:// download.intel.com/pressroom/kits/IntelProcessorHistory.pdf

Jackson, T. (1997). *Inside Intel: Andrew Grove and the rise of the world's most powerful chip company. Berlin*. New York: Dutton Books.

Jin, Y., Seelen, W. v., & Sendho, B. (2000). *Extracting interpretable fuzzy rules from RBF neural networks*. Internal Report Institut fur Neuroinformatik, Ruhr-Universitat.

Johnson, K. W. (2005). *Recent developments in the credit card market and the financial obligations ratio* (pp. 473–486). Washington, USA.

Jungwon, K., Ong, A., & Overill, R. E. (2003). Design of an artificial immune system as a novel anomaly detector for combating financial fraud in the retail sector. *The 2003 Congress on Evolutionary Computation, 2003. CEC '03., 1*, 405-412.

Kerber, K. (1992). *Chi-Merge: discretization of numeric attributes*. Paper presented at the National Conference on Artificial Intelligence, San Jose, California, USA.

Kokkinaki, A. I. (1997). On atypical database transactions: identification of probable frauds using machine learning for user profiling. In *Knowledge and Data Engineering Exchange Workshop, 1997*, (pp. 107-113).

Koskela, T., Varsta, M., Heikkonen, J., & Kaski, K. (1998). *Temporal sequence processing using recurrent SOM*. Paper presented at the Second International Conference on Knowledge-Based Intelligent Electronic Systems, Australia

Kundu, A., Sural, S., & Majumdar, A. K. (2008). *Two-stage card fraud detection using sequence alignment*. Kharagpur, India: Indian Institute of Technology.

Laing, G. (2004). *Digital retro: The evolution and design of the personal computer*. SyBex.

Lazar, A., & Sethi, I. K. (2000). *Decision rule extraction from trained neural networks using rough sets*. Vision and Neural Networks Laboratory.

Liu, H., & Setiono, R. (1995). *Chi2: Feature selection and discretization of numeric attributes*. Paper presented at the Seventh International Conference on Tools with Artificial Intelligence

Liu, H., & Teck Tan, S. (1995, 25/10/1995). *X2R: a fast rule generator*. Paper presented at the 'Intelligent Systems for the 21st Century'.

Lockett, A. J., & Miikkulainen, R. (2009). *Temporal convolution machines for sequence learning*. Neural Networks Research Group, University of Texas at Austin.

Lundqvist, S. (Ed.). (1992). *Nobel lectures - physics 1971-1980*. Singapore: World Scientific Publishing.

Maaten, L. J. P. d., Postma, E. O., & Herik, H. J. d. (2008). *Dimensionality reduction: A comparative review*. Paper presented at the Pattern Analysis and Machine Intelligence

MacQueen, J. B. (1967). *Some Methods for classification and analysis of multivariate observations*. Paper presented at the 5th Berkeley Symposium on Mathematical Statistics and Probability.

McGarry, K., Wermter, S., & MacIntyre, J. (2001). The extraction and comparison of knowledge from local function networks. *International Journal of Computational Intelligence and Applications, 1*(4), 369–382. doi:10.1142/S1469026801000305

McGarry, K. J., & MacIntyre, J. (1999). Knowledge extraction and insertion from radial basis function networks. *IEE Colloquium on Applied Statistical Pattern Recognition (Ref. No. 1999/063)*(15), 1-6.

McGarry, K. J., Tait, J., & Wermter, S. (1999). Rule-extraction from radial basis function networks. *Ninth International Conference on Artificial Neural Networks, 1999. ICANN 99., 2*, 613-618.

Metropolis, N. A., & Rosenbluth, A. W., N., R. M., Teller, A. H., & Teller, E. (1953). Equation of state calculations by fast computation machines. *The Journal of Chemical Physics, 21,* 1087–1091. doi:10.1063/1.1699114

Moore, G. (1965). The experts look ahead: cramming more components onto integrated circuits. *Electronics, 38*(8).

Nilson-Report. (1993). *Credit card fraud* (Robertson, D., Ed.). *Vol. 540).* Carpinteria, California, USA.

Nowlan, S. J., & Hinton, G. E. (1992). Simplifying neural networks by soft-weight sharing. *Neural Computation, 4,* 473–493. doi:10.1162/neco.1992.4.4.473

Pao, Y.-H. (1989). Nets for discovering cluster structure. In *Adaptive pattern recognition and neural networks* (pp. 178–181). Reading, MA: Addison-Wesley.

Parker, D. B. (1972, 25 December). Key-punch crooks. *Time Magazine.*

Pawlak, Z. (1991). *Rough sets: Theoretical aspects of reasoning about data.* Amsterdam: Kluwer Academic Publishing.

Pearson, K. (1901). On lines and planes of closest fit to systems of points in space. *Philosophical Magazine, 2*(6), 559–572.

Quah, J. T. S., & Sriganesh, M. (2007). Real time credit card fraud detection using computational intelligence. *International Joint Conference on Neural Networks,* 863-868.

Quinlan, J. R. (1986). Induction of decision trees. *Machine Learning, 1,* 81–106. doi:10.1007/BF00116251

Quinlan, J. R. (1993). *C4.5: Programs for machine learning.* Morgan Kaufmann.

Ren, L., & d'Avila Garcez, A. S. (2009). Symbolic knowledge extraction from support vector machines: A geometric approach. *Lecture Notes in Computer Science, 5507,* 335–343. doi:10.1007/978-3-642-03040-6_41

Report on fraud regarding non cash means of payments in the EU: the implementation of the 2004-2007 EU Action Plan. (2008) *Commission Staff Working Document* (pp. 34). Brussels: Commission of the European Communities.

Ridella, S., Speroni, G., & Trebino, P. (1993, 01/01/1993). *Pruning and rule extraction using class entropy.* Paper presented at the International Conference on Neural Networks.

Rong-Chang, C., Shu-Ting, L., & Xun, L. (2005). Personalized Approach Based on SVM and ANN for detecting credit card fraud. *International Conference on Neural Networks and Brain, 2005. ICNN&B '05., 2,* 810-815.

Rosenthal, R. W. (1973). A class of games possessing pure-strategy Nash equilibria. *International Journal of Game Theory, 2*(1), 65–67. doi:10.1007/BF01737559

Roweis, S. (1998). EM algorithms for PCA and SPCA. [Cambridge, MA: MIT Press.]. *Advances in Neural Information Processing Systems, 10,* 626–632.

Ryman-Tubb, N. (1998). Combating application fraud. *Credit Control, 19*(11/12), 15–20.

Ryman-Tubb, N. (2010a). USA Patent No. 61326452 (provisional).

Ryman-Tubb, N. (2010b). *SOAR - Sparse Oracle-based Adaptive Rule extraction: knowledge extraction from large-scale datasets to detect credit card fraud.* Paper presented at the World Congress on Computational Intelligence, Barcelona, Spain.

Saito, K., & Nakano, R. (1988). *Medical diagnostic expert system based on PDP model*. Paper presented at the International Conference on Neural Networks.

Scofield, C. L., & Reilly, D. L. (1991, 8-14 July). *Into silicon: real time learning in a high density RBF neural network*. Paper presented at the International Joint Conference on Neural Networks, Seattle, WA, USA.

Setiono, R. (1997). Extracting rules from neural networks by pruning and hidden-unit splitting. *Neural Computation, 9*(1), 205–225. doi:10.1162/neco.1997.9.1.205

Setiono, R., & Leow, W. K. (1999). On mapping decision trees and neural networks. *Knowledge-Based Systems, 12*(3), 85–99. doi:10.1016/S0950-7051(99)00009-X

Setiono, R., & Liu, H. (1995). Understanding neural networks via rule extraction. *Proceedings of the 14th International Joint Conference on Artificial Intelligence*, 480-485.

Setiono, R., & Liu, H. (1996). Symbolic representation of neural networks. *Computer, 29*(3), 71–77. doi:10.1109/2.485895

Setiono, R., & Liu, H. (1997, 01/04/1997). *NeuroLinear: A system for extracting oblique decision rules from neural networks*. Paper presented at the 9th European Conference on Machine Learning.

Setiono, R., Thong, J. Y. L., & Yap, C. (1998). Symbolic rule extraction from neural networks: An application to identifying organizations adopting IT. *Information & Management, 34*(2), 91–101. doi:10.1016/S0378-7206(98)00048-2

Shawe-Taylor, J., & Cristianini, N. (2000). *Support Vector Machines and other kernel-based learning methods*. Cambridge University Press.

Shimozaki, M., & Kuniyoshi, Y. (2003, 27-31 October). *Integration of spatial and temporal contexts for action recognition by self organizing neural networks*. Paper presented at the International Conference Intelligent Robots and Systems.

Smolensky, P. (1986). *Information processing in dynamical systems: Foundations of harmony theory (Vol. 1)*. MIT Press.

Specht, D. F. (1988, July). *Probabilistic neural networks for classification, mapping, or associative memory*. Paper presented at the International Conference on Neural Networks, San Diego, CA, USA.

Srivastava, A., Kundu, A., & Sural, S. (2008). Credit Card Fraud Detection Using Hidden Markov Model. *Dependable and Secure Computing, 5*(1), 37–48. doi:10.1109/TDSC.2007.70228

Stanford-Research-Institute. (2008). *Timeline of SRI International Innovations: 1940s - 1950s*. Retrieved 19 May, 2008, from http://www.sri.com/about/timeline

Stein, R. (2004). The Ascendancy of the Credit Card Industry. *Secret History of the Credit Card* Retrieved 19 May, 2008, from http://www.pbs.org/wgbh/pages/frontline/shows/credit/more/rise.html

Stolfo, S., Fan, W., Lee, W., Prodromidis, A., & Chan, P. (1997). Credit card fraud detection using meta-learning. *Working notes of AAAI Workshop on AI Approaches to Fraud Detection and Risk Management*.

Sutskever, I., Hinton, G. E., & Taylor, G. (2009). The Recurrent Temporal Restricted Boltzmann Machine. *Advances in Neural Information Processing Systems, 21*.

Taha, I., & Ghosh, J. (1997). Evaluation and ordering of rules extracted from feed forward networks. *IEEE International Conference on Neural Networks, 1*, 408-413.

Thrun, S. (1995). *Extracting rules from artificial neural networks with distributed representations* (*Vol. 7*). Cambridge, MA: MIT Press.

Tipping, M. E., & Bishop, C. M. (1999). Probabilistic Principal Component Analysis. *Journal of the Royal Statistical Society. Series B. Methodological*, *21*(3), 611–622. doi:10.1111/1467-9868.00196

Towell, G. G. (1991). *Symbolic Knowledge and Neural Networks: Insertion, Refinement and Extraction*. Madison, USA: PhD, University of Wisconsin.

Towell, G. G., & Shavlik, J. W. (1993). Extracting refined rules from knowledge-based neural networks. *Machine Learning*, *13*(1), 71–101. doi:10.1007/BF00993103

Towell, G. G., Shavlik, J. W., & Noordewier, M. O. (1990, July/August). *Refinement of Approximate Domain Theories by Knowledge-Based Neural Networks*. Paper presented at the The Eighth National Conference on Artificial Intelligence (AAAI-90), Boston, Massachusetts.

Tsung-Nan, C. (2007). *A Novel Prediction Model for Credit Card Risk Management*. Paper presented at the Innovative Computing, Information and Control, 2007. ICICIC '07. Second International Conference on.

Vatsa, V., Sural, S., & Majumdar, A. K. (2005). A Game-Theoretic Approach to Credit Card Fraud Detection. *Lecture Notes in Computer Science*, *3803*, 263–276. doi:10.1007/11593980_20

Vetterli, M., & Duhamel, P. (1990). Fast Fourier transforms: a tutorial review and a state of the art. *Signal Processing*, *19*, 259–299. doi:10.1016/0165-1684(90)90158-U

Viktor, H. L., Engelbrecht, A. P., & Cloete, I. (1995). Reduction of symbolic rules from artificial neural networks using sensitivity analysis. *IEEE International Conference on Neural Networks*, *4*, 1788-1794.

Voegtlin, T. (2000). *Context quantization and contextual self-organizing maps*. Paper presented at the International Joint Conference on Neural Networks.

Wall, R., & Cunningham, P. (2000). Exploring the Potential for Rule Extraction from Ensembles of Neural Networks. *11th Irish Conference on Artificial Intelligence & Cognitive Science*, 52-68.

Wolters, T. (2000). Carry your credit in your pocket: the early history of the credit card at Bank of America and Chase Manhattan. *Enterprise & Society: The International Journal of Business History*, *1*(2), 315–354.

Zaslavsky, V., & Strizhak, A. (2006). Credit Card Fraud Detection Using Self-Organizing Maps. *Cybercrime and Cybersecurity*, 48-63.

Zhang, J., & Liu, Y. (2005). SVM decision boundary based discriminative subspace induction. *Pattern Recognition*, *38*(10), 1746–1758. doi:10.1016/j.patcog.2005.01.016

Zhou, Z.-H., Chen, S.-F., & Chen, Z.-Q. (2000). A Statistics Based Approach for Extracting Priority Rules from Trained Neural Networks. *International Joint Conference on Neural Networks (IJCNN'00), 3*.

Zhou, Z. H., Jiang, Y., & Chen, S. F. (2000). A General Neural Framework for Classification Rule Mining. *International Journal of Computers. Systems and Signals*, *1*(2), 154–168.

Zuse, K. (1993). *The Computer – My Life*. Berlin: Springer-Verlag.

ADDITIONAL READING

Calvin, W. H. (1996). *The Cerebral Code*. Bradford Books.

d'Avila Garcez, A. S., Broda, K. B., & Gabbay, D. M. (2002). *Neural-symbolic learning Systems*. Springer.

d'Avila Garcez, A. S., Lamb, L. C., & Gabbay, D. M. (2009). *Neural-symbolic cognative reasoning*. Springer-Verlag.

Diederich, J. (Ed.). (2008). *Rule extraction from support vector machines*. Springer.

Evans, D. S., & Schmalensee, R. (2005). *Paying with plastic* (2nd ed.). MIT Press.

Hendrickson, R. (1972). The Cashless Society: Dodd Mead & Company.

Houk, J. C., & Davis, J. L. (Eds.). (1995). *Models of Information Processing in the Basal Ganglia*. MIT Press.

Jain, L. C., & Vemuri, V. R. (Eds.). (1999). *Industrial Applications of Neural Networks*. CRC Press.

Koch, C., & Davis, J. L. (Eds.). (1994). Large-scale neuronal theories of the brain: MIT Press. Lisboa, P. J. G., Edisbury, B., & Vellido, A. (Eds.). (2000). Business Applications of Neural Networks: World Scientific Publishing.

Mann, R. J. (2006). *Charging ahead: the growth and regulation of payment card markets*. Cambridge University Press. doi:10.1017/CBO9780511754227

McNelis, P. D. (2005). *Neural networks in finance: gaining predictive edge in the market*. Elsevier.

Palmer-Brown, D., Draganova, C., Pimenidis, E., & Mouratidis, H. (Eds.). (2009). Engineering Applications of Neural Networks. London.

Ryman-Tubb, N. (1994). Implementation - the only sensible route to wealth creating success: a range of applications. Paper presented at the EPSRC: Information Technology Awareness in Engineering, London.

Sun, R. (Ed.). (1997). *Connectionist-Symbolic Integration*. Lawrence Erlbaum Associates.

KEY TERMS AND DEFINITIONS

Black Box: A process or device that can only be viewed in terms of its inputs and outputs – without any obvious means of its internal workings. *Fraud Management System:* A computer system that is designed to detect Payment Card Fraud. *AI:* Artificial Intelligence aims to make computers intelligent. AI typically uses rules based on examining human experts as they solve a problem step-by-step. *Processing element:* Typically a single simple mathematical equation that takes a range of inputs as weighted connections and generates an output, possibly simulating the function of a biological neuron.

Weighted connections: A real world input value, typically set by the learning algorithm, possibly simulating the function of a biological synapse/axon.

Learning algorithm: The algorithm used to set the values of the weighted connections so that the neural network acquires knowledge based on inputs (and possibly outputs).

Generalization: The ability of the neural network to produce a reasonable output when presented with input data that was not used to train it; this is normally known as interpolation if the data lies in the same range as the training data.

Regularization: See generalization.

Card Not Present Fraud: Payment Card Fraud typically committed through the use of the internet or telephone, where the Cardholder is Not Present at the point of transaction (CNP).

Card Present Fraud: Payment Card Fraud committed using the physical payment card – such as the interception of new credit cards in the mail, stolen/lost cards or the copying of card information onto counterfeit physical cards, employee fraud at the issuing bank, etc.

Payment Card Fraud: The criminal act of deception through the use of a physical plastic card or card information without the knowledge of the cardholder.

Neural Computing: See Connectionist.

Connectionist: An approach that creates models in terms of a network of interconnected Processing Elements where information is distributed throughout this network as weighted connections and activations levels, possibly simulating the function of a biological neural network in the brain.

Supervised: A learning algorithm where each input vector is associated with an output vector (labeled). The difference between the output of the neural network for a given input vector and the expected output vector is calculated and used to update the Weighted connections.

Unsupervised: A learning algorithm where the input vector is unlabelled and the algorithm seeks to determine how the data is structured – typically forming clusters of associated data.

Decompositional: A neural-rule extraction method that works by decomposing the neural network architecture itself, so that rules are created that describes each neuron in terms of its individual input and outputs.

Pedagogical: A neural-rule extraction method that works by creating a single set of rules that describe the function of the neural network, assuming that the neural network is a black box.

Neuron: See Processing element

ENDNOTES

[1] Includes credit and debit cards, gift cards, top-up cards, fuel cards, pre-paid cards, etc.

[2] "MasterCard" was named in 1979; initially it was called the InterBank Card Association (ICA).

[3] The use of the word "first" is evocative; however, there is some agreement among historians that in 1936, Konrad Zuse in Germany created the Z1, one of the first binary digital computers and a machine that could be controlled through a punch tape.

[4] The first use of magnetic stripes on cards was in the UK, in 1966, when the London Transit Authority installed a magnetic stripe system for tickets in the London Underground.

[5] The original prediction was for a doubling every year.

[6] PRISM® is a registered trademark of Retail Decisions, Inc. (www.redplc.com)

[7] No details of this process are given. Given the limitations of the P-RCE algorithm (in common with all local function neural networks), the data pre-processing is vital for correct classification performance.

[8] The Borel measurable is the measure on σ-algebra which gives to the interval [a, b] the measure b−a, where a < b.

[9] A Markov chain is a sequence of values whose probabilities at a time interval depend upon the value of the number at the previous time.

[10] If N=M, then the rule is conjunctive, that is all the antecedents must be true, or if M=1 then the rule is considered disjunctive, that any of them can be true to activate the rule.

[11] See (Shawe-Taylor & Cristianini, 2000).

[12] This is a commercial successor of the C4.5 algorithm, (Quinlan, 1993).

[13] GSVMORC was latterly renamed to GOSE (Geometric and Oracle-based Support vector machines rule Extraction).

[14] I.e. *a priory* probability of fraud.

[15] A Gaussian distribution.

[16] See discussion, "Intrinsic Dimensionality", p.109.

[17] E.g. To recognize a word through a sequence of specific phonemes, where each phoneme recognised statistically determines the set of most likely phonemes to follow.

[18] i.e. a cluster where each cluster is similar to a 2-leaf decision tree.

[19] A range of different application areas has been reviewed where the proposed approach is equally applicable, including robotics, speech recognition, gesture-analysis, computer-gaming, medicine, weather and image analysis.

[20]   In (Hinton, Osindero, & Yee-Whye, 2006) a toy OCR problem was reported to take several hours per layer. Over 8 hours for their experiment.

Epilogue

Chapter 13

Computational Models of Learning and Beyond:
Symmetries of Associative Learning

Eduardo Alonso
City University London, UK

Esther Mondragón
Centre for Computational and Animal Learning Research, UK

ABSTRACT

The authors propose in this chapter to use abstract algebra to unify different models of theories of associative learning -- as complementary to current psychological, mathematical and computational models of associative learning phenomena and data. The idea is to compare recent research in associative learning to identify the symmetries of behaviour. This approach, a common practice in Physics and Biology, would help us understand the structure of conditioning as opposed to the study of specific linguistic (either natural or formal) expressions that are inherently incomplete and often contradictory.

1. INTRODUCTION

The ability of animals to recognize and link different patterns of stimuli to adapt to dynamic environments is essential for their survival. Associative learning studies how animals *learn* by connecting the relevant events in their environment (that is, how they acquire causal information) and *behave* (that is, how what has been learned is expressed in their behavior) and is, therefore, of paramount importance in Psychology. Indeed, models of associative learning have proved to be relevant to human learning both theoretically (judgment of

causality and categorization, *e.g.*, Shanks, 1995) and in practice (in such diverse areas as behavioral therapy, drug addiction rehabilitation, or anticipatory nausea in cancer treatment to name just a few).

Of course, associative learning is not the only type of learning. There are learning phenomena such as habituation or sensitization that are traditionally considered as non-associative. Others such as spatial learning, perceptual learning and some forms of social learning seem to admit an associative account but such an interpretation is debatable. Besides, behavior – not even adaptive behavior – cannot be reduced to learned behavior. Some reflexes such sucking in babes or sexual

DOI: 10.4018/978-1-60960-021-1.ch013

patterns of behavior are indeed adaptive but not learned (although this is also controversial, see, *e.g.*, Dickinson & Balleine, 2002). Finally, it must be stressed the difference between learning, the hypothetical psychological and physical changes in the brain (memory), and performance, the manifestation of such change in behavior (see, *e.g.*, Bouton & Moody, 2004).

All this taken into account, it is commonly accepted that *associative learning is at the basis of most learning phenomena and behavior*.

2. PSYCHOLOGICAL MODELS OF ASSOCIATIVE LEARNING

The study of associative learning in Psychology has specialized in two sub-fields: Classical (Pavlovian) conditioning focuses on how "mental" representations of stimuli are linked whereas instrumental conditioning deals with response-outcome associations. It is agreed though that, at the most general level, their *associative structures* are isomorphic (Hall, 2002). In both procedures, changes in behavior are considered the result of an association between two concurrent events and explained in terms of operations of a (conceptual) system that consists of nodes among which links can be formed. Since research in associative learning has predominantly focused on classical conditioning, we will use it as our leading example.

At the risk of over-simplification, we can identify the main trends in classical conditioning according to two dimensions, namely, the mechanisms of the learning process and the way in which the stimuli are represented by the learning system. The former fuels the debate between stimulus-processing theories *vs.* connectionist models, exemplified in the competitive model of (Rescorla & Wagner, 1972) and the Standard Operating Procedures (SOP) theory (Wagner, 1981) respectively; the latter illustrates the distinction between elemental models (for instance, both

Rescorla and Wagner's and SOP) and configural approaches (*e.g.*, Pearce, 1987).

Rescorla and Wagner's model rests on a sum error term. The idea that all stimuli present in a trial compete for associative strength is at the heart of the model. It is precisely this characterizing feature that differentiates it from earlier models such as Hull's (Hull, 1943). This assumption allows the model to explain phenomena such as blocking and conditioned inhibition, that is, phenomena that result from the interaction among different stimuli. Other assumptions of the model are path-independence (*i.e.*, that the associative strength of a stimulus does not depend on its previous learning history), monotonicity (*i.e.*, that learning and behavior are one and the same thing), that acquisition and extinction are opposite processes, and that the associability of the conditioned stimulus (CS) is fixed.

It has been argued, quite rightly, that Rescorla and Wagner made such assumptions not to reflect strong psychological principles but, rather, to express their main discovery (competitiveness among stimuli) in a general, abstract model. It should not come as a surprise, therefore, that many phenomena cannot be accounted for by their model (latent inhibition being, perhaps, the most paradigmatic) and that myriads of extensions and truly innovative variants regarding the underlying psychological processes involved have been proposed (*e.g.*, attentional approaches like Mackintosh, 1975 and Pearce & Hall, 1980). It remains the case however, that Rescorla and Wagner's model is still the most influential theory of associative learning.

SOP, on the other hand, is a broader theoretical framework of stimulus processing and memory. Unlike Rescorla and Wagner's model, SOP is not based on familiar theories of conditioning (although stochastic approaches used in SOP can be traced back to Estes, 1950) but instead borrows ideas from both information-processing theories and connectionism. It is beyond this proposal to give a detailed account of SOP. Suffice it to say that, in SOP stimuli activate memory nodes for which transitional probabilities are dictated by decay functions (traces); that learning rules separately account for excitatory and inhibitory links depending on the particular level of activation of the stimulus traces; and that behavior is explicitly dealt with through weighted response-generation rules. Regardless of its merits, it is difficult to assess the explanatory and predictive power of SOP due to its representational and algorithmic complexity.

Both Rescorla and Wagner's model and SOP share the assumption that when two or more stimuli are presented at the same time of conditioning, each element may enter into an association with the reinforcer that follows (an unconditioned stimulus, US). In general, such elemental theories further assume that responding in the presence of the compound is determined by the sum of the associative strengths of the constituents. As an alternative, configural theories are based on the assumption that conditioning with a compound results in a unitary representation of the compound entering into a single association with the reinforcer. Responding in the presence of the compound is then determined by its own associative strength, together with any associative strength that generalizes to it from similar compounds that have also taken part in conditioning. Configural models have proved to be particularly useful when studying conditional associations where a stimulus comes to control responding to a CS in a manner that is independent of its direct association with the US (Honey and Watt, 1998) or forming a configural cue that becomes associated with the US (Wilson and Pearce, 1989, 1990). Contrarily, elemental accounts tend to focus on the modulatory properties of the conditional cue over the CS-US association (Holland, 1983, Bonardi, 1991) or over the US representation (Rescorla, 1985).

Regardless of the individual merits of each model, research in associative learning suffers from various fundamental problems, namely:

1. **Incomplete theories:** There is no model that satisfactorily accounts for all the phenomena under study. Each theory explains a set of particular phenomena. Latent inhibition, that the Pearce-Hall model predicts, cannot be explained in Rescorla and Wagner's whereas over-expectation, on the other hand, can be explained by the latter but not by the former. Similarly, configural theories can account for feature discrimination effects but cannot predict summation effects, exactly the opposite of what elemental theories are able to account for;

2. **Inconsistent theories:** Different models make contradictory predictions under the same conditions. Mackintosh's and Pearce and Hall's models predict opposite changes in the associability of a stimulus as a consequence of the very same procedure. Likewise, elemental models predict that when two compounds (AB, CD) are trained their associative strength will be the same that the one observed when novel compounds (AC, BD) are tested. Contrarily, configural theories predict that the associative strengths of trained and novel compounds will differ. The problem is that evidence is not conclusive in neither of these cases;

3. **Excluding paradigms:** Certain theories are based on *a priori* excluding assumptions. For instance, although all stimulus processing models are cue competition models, Rescorla and Wagner's refers to competition for US processing whereas Mackintosh's model invokes competition between conditioned stimuli for a limited CS processing capacity. As another example, in configural theories like Pearce's a compound AB is viewed as a unique configuration, distinct from its component parts and from other stimuli. Each configuration develops associative strength through its own pairing with an US and also receives generalized associative strength from other configurations based on its simi-

larity. Elemental theories, on the other hand, simply assume that the associative strength of an AB compound can be viewed as the sum of the strengths of the elements;

4. **Unaccounted phenomena:** There are phenomena that are still waiting for a model to be dealt with. For example, it is not obvious (at least not without making use of *ad hoc* arguments) how to explain spontaneous recovery.

3. MATHEMATICAL MODELS OF ASSOCIATIVE LEARNING

Associative theories of associative learning have been mathematically expressed as quantitative models in the form of (sets of) equations. In the traditional syntactic view of mathematical models, equations are taken as formal models in which variables and their relations explicitly denote the phenomena under study.

In particular, Rescorla and Wagner use a simple difference equation (the well-known delta rule) to express the change in associative strength across discrete trials. On the other hand, continuous (a.k.a. real-time) models like SOP are, at least in theory, useful when it comes to making accurate predictions about inter-stimulus intervals effects. Finally, Pearce's model just adds a similarity function specified in terms of the proportion of elements that the stimuli share.

All in all, mathematical models of associative learning have so far been used as a means to make calculations through elementary algebra or differential analysis. The problem with adopting this narrow version of mathematical model is that it does not provide us with tools to address the above-mentioned limitations. For example, if the meaning of a mathematical model is in the linguistic expression it takes (that is, if there is a unique isomorphism between phenomena and algorithms) then either (a) we cannot explain how a theory can be expressed in different sets of equations or (b)

we will not be sure about the effect the addition or the removal of a simple parameter may have. Paraphrasing (Chakravartty, 2001), theories and models can be given linguistic formulations but theories and models should not be identified with such formulations.

4. COMPUTATIONAL MODELS OF ASSOCIATIVE LEARNING[1]

The use of computational models of associative learning has followed the connectionist trend and borrowed from computer science several techniques, mainly Artificial Neural Networks (ANNs, for a review, Volge *et al.*, 2004, and Balkenius & Morén, 1998). It is claimed that such models are adequate models of associative phenomena for four main reasons:

Firstly, computational models are considered material and/or formal analogue models of associative learning. The underlying reasoning is that (a) ANNs model by analogy natural neural networks and that (b) psychological processes, including associative learning, are ultimately embedded in natural neural networks; hence, indirectly, ANNs model associative learning.

However appealing this line of argumentation may be, it is widely acknowledged that ANNs do not resemble natural neural networks in any fundamental way (Enquist & Ghirlanda, 2005); besides, there is no strong evidence suggesting that electrical or chemical neural activity and associative learning are related (Morris, 1994) –or for that matter, that psychological processes can be localized in specific brain regions as recently exposed in (Vul *et al.*, 2009), but already advanced in (Uttal, 2001). That a version of Dirac's rule can be taken as a model of both neural plasticity and long-term potentiation effects –the Hebbian rule (Hebb, 1949) – and association formation –for example, Rescorla and Wagner's rule– cannot be considered as proof of any common underlying structure and should not be used as an argument to reduce psychological phenomena to their alleged neural substratum[2]. Likewise, that Rescorla and Wagner's rule is essentially identical to the Widrow-Hoff rule (Widrow & Hoff, 1960) for training *Adeline* units and that, in turn, such a rule can be seen as a primitive form of the generalized delta rule for backpropagation only tells us that, computationally speaking, associative learning follows an error-correction algorithm. What a computational model does not tell us, however, is which underlying psychological processes (attention, motivation, etc.) intervene in associative learning or how the physical characteristics of the units involved (*e.g.*, the salience of the stimuli) affect such processes.

Clearly, sharing a common mathematical expression does not imply that the phenomena it describes are of the same nature: For instance, power functions can be used to express the relationship between (1) the magnitude of a stimulus and its perceived intensity (Stevens' law), (2) the metabolic rate of a species and their body mass (Kleiber's law), and (3) the orbital period of a planet and its orbital semi-major axis (Kepler's third law).

Secondly, ANNs are connectionist models according to which information is not stored explicitly in symbols and rules but rather in the weights (strengths) of the connections; learning would consist of changes in such weights. It is claimed, rightly, that these are precisely the assumptions associative learning models are based upon and hence, wrongly, that ANNs are an ideal candidate to model associative learning. This quite straightforward argument is, in fact, a fallacy: As connectionists (at least implementational connectionists) themselves concede the way we represent learning, either as continuous changes of weighted connections or as the result of discrete symbolic processing, is *a matter of convenience* and therefore irrelevant to the study of the structures involved.

This brings us to the third argument. ANNs can be used, of course, not as models of phenomena but to solve problems that cannot be solved analytically –or when *in silico* experiments are needed. After all, ANNs are powerful statistical tools (with a misleading name) implemented in architectures that take advantage of massive computational parallelism – not surprisingly, Rumelhart's et al. *new connectionism* landmark paper introduced the Parallel Distributed Processing paradigm in cognition (Rumelhart *et al.*, 1986). Although they are certainly not the simplest, fastest or most efficient data mining techniques (see, *e.g.*, Mitchie *et al.*, 1994), ANNs have proved useful when analytical methods fail and a bottom-up, data-driven approach is needed. Indeed, it is a common practice to use sheer computational power to simulate the dynamics of non-linear (chaotic or not) systems such as population growth or the weather. The point is, however, that associative learning does not seem to be one of such systems. In fact, the analytical solution of Rescorla and Wagner's equation represents a linear discrete dynamical system of the 1st order; besides, associative learning is not so data intensive as other areas like genetics where there is an obvious need for statistical tools (see, for example, Hastings & Palmer, 2003). Of course, we could study associative learning from a behavioral regulation approach according to which animals adjust their long-term behavior so as to reach an optimal (bliss or equilibrium) point (Timberlake, 1980). However interesting this point of view may be, it does not by itself oblige us to adopt numerical tools as (Dank, 2003) and (Yamaguchi, 2006) have proved.

Relatedly, ANNs typically approximate solutions by iteratively minimizing an error function. This can be understood as a type of learning that resembles learning by "trial and error" of which associative learning (and reinforcement learning) is an example. However, it is worth emphasizing that ANNs implement numerical *methods* whereas associative learning models such as Rescorla and Wagner's express dynamic *laws*. Against public opinion, animals do not make predictions and iteratively update an associative value through error minimization towards an optimal one. The associative value at a given time is the right associative value –that exactly describes to which extend the CS has become associated to the US. Let's put it another way: There is nothing to indicate that the system is compelled to gain a maximum value. That the system described by Rescorla and Wagner's rule is limited by an asymptote (λ, the reinforcing value of the US) does not confer any special status to such value –rather it just defines a constraint (limited capacity) of the system.

A final more general reason to explain the appeal of computational models in psychology rests on the idea that both computers and the brain are information processing systems, instantiations of a universal Turing machine or any other model of computation. But this alone does not justify the support the "computer metaphor" enjoys. After all, any phenomena can be expressed in terms of some sort of computation[3]. If this is such a powerful metaphor is because it is deeply rooted in Western philosophy and the mechanization of (formal) reasoning, reformulated in the twentieth century in terms of computation. That computation has been effectively embedded in computers has reinforced the idea that so it is in the brain, that the study of the former will help understand the latter and, in a *tour the force*, that computers may be capable of displaying intelligence. Indeed, every scientific theory is shaped in the context of its age's achievements and prejudices: Like Newton's laws of mechanics strengthened the view of the Universe as a deterministic machine that worked as the sophisticated clocks so popular at the time our conception of the mind as an information processing machine has certainly been influenced by the development of computing technology.

To sum it up, although the need to get influx from 'outsiders' is recognized within the psychology community (see Townsend, 2008) computational models of associative learning should be taken with caution. Computational models may provide us with complementary idealized models of psychological phenomena and with

powerful statistical tools to construct models of psychological data but they alone are not the appropriate instruments to answer psychological questions. This is an obvious, hardly original, conclusion –and yet more often than not we read flamboyant news about robots that learn, think and experience emotions or ANNs that can do anything psychological models do only better.

Our contention is that what we are lacking in the field of associative learning and behavior is the identification of invariant structures that underlie specific (psychological, mathematical and computational) models. That is, we need to study psychological symmetries. Crucially, symmetries can be formalized mathematically as operations satisfying the conditions for forming various algebraic structures –typically groups. We propose to employ abstract algebra to explore models of psychological theories from a non-syntactical view (as Physics and Biology have done).

5. SYMMETRIES

Generally speaking, symmetries define *invariance*, that is, impunity to possible alterations. They refer to the fact that parts of a whole are equivalent (interchangeable) under a group of operations. Interestingly, the fact that the parts that are related by means of an equivalence relation corresponds to the fact that the family of operations transforming the parts into each other while leaving the whole invariant satisfies the conditions for constituting a group (*i.e.*, the existence of the identity and inverse operations, associativity and the closure of the product). Consequently, it has traditionally been assumed that *group theory is the language of symmetries*.

What is more important, in group theory the objects do not need to be mathematical objects or physical, biological or psychological objects. Objects and their elements can be any abstraction (shapes, phrases, laws, mathematical equations and even theories). And the transformations or operations under which the whole remains invariant can be any operation (from a rotation over an axis to a specific conditioning procedure). This is because groups act on operations not on elements or objects. This feature makes groups a powerful tool to study symmetries independently of a particular theory or expression.

The study of symmetries flourished in the XIX century, originally as an instrument to solve algebraic equations: It was the young E. Galois who first understood that groups opened a new general way of finding the (invariant) structures that underlie the number and form of the solutions for equations of arbitrary degrees. This had an immediate effect in Physics: C. G. Jacobi developed a procedure for transforming step by step the Hamiltonian formulation of the dynamical equations of mechanics into new ones that are simpler but perfectly equivalent. In geometry, F. Klein (Klein, 1872) proposed the *Erlangen Program* to classify various geometries (Euclidean, affine, and projective) with respect to geometrical properties that are left invariant under rotations and reflections. It was also in Göttingen where E. Noether proved the connection between symmetries and conservation laws (Noether, 1918).

In fact, we can view the history of the theories of modern Physics in terms of their symmetries and groups. Newtonian classical mechanics was based on Galilei transformations formalized in the Galilei group; the special theory of relativity unified seemingly contradictory mechanical and electromagnetic phenomena of the hand of Lorentz transformations and their corresponding Lorentz groups; and the general theory of relativity explained gravity, the most symmetrical of field theories so far, under the group of all diffeomorphisms of a space-time.

It has been, however, with quantum mechanics when symmetry groups have become an indispensable tool in Physics (see Weyl, 1928, for a starter). Internal symmetries (*i.e.*, those which act on fields while at the nuclear level and cannot be reduced to "classical" spatiotemporal symmetries), both global and gauge, can only be fully understood when studied through the groups their representations form. In particular, the Standard Model classifies all elementary particles and their interactions according to their flavor, charge and color symmetries (the $SU(3) \otimes SU(2) \otimes U(1)$ group), and, in so doing, unifies electromagnetism, QED and QCD and explains electroweak interactions through spontaneous symmetry breaking.

Why is it that symmetries take such a prominent part in Natural Sciences? As argued in (Brading & Castellani, 2003):

1. First, we attribute symmetry properties to *theories and laws* (symmetry principles). It is natural to derive the laws of nature and to test their validity by means of the laws of invariance, rather than to derive the laws of invariance from what we believe to be the laws of nature;

2. At the same time, we may derive specific consequences with regard to particular *phenomena* on the basis of their symmetry properties (symmetry arguments). Pierre Curie (Curie, 1894) postulated a necessary condition for a given phenomenon to happen, namely, that it is compatible with the symmetry conditions established by a principle.

More specifically, symmetries play several inter-related roles that we illustrate with an example of the use of (point) groups in molecular biology (see *e.g.*, Atkins & Friedman, 2005):

- *Normative role:* One the one hand, symmetries furnish a kind of selection rule. Given an initial situation with a specified symmetry, only certain phenomena are allowed to happen; on the other side, it offers a falsification criterion for (physical) theories: A violation of Curie's principle may indicate that something is wrong with the (physical) description. That is, symmetries can be viewed as normative tools, as constraints on theories –the requirement of invariance with respect to a transformation group imposes several restrictions on the form the theory may take, limiting the types of quantities that may appear in the theory as well as the form of its fundamental equations. For instance, the rule that determines whether or not two atomic orbitals can form a chemical bond (*i.e.*, a molecule) is that they must belong to the same symmetry species within the point group of the molecule. The same applies to bonding in polyatomics;

- *Unification role:* Symmetries can be used as a heuristic to compare and unify theories, resulting from the possibility of unifying different types of symmetries by means of a unification of the corresponding transformation groups. Likewise, we can use symmetries to analyze whether or not different theories are, in fact, equivalent; and even if theories turn out to be incomparable (it seems, after all, that Rescorla and Wagner's model and SOP correspond to different algebraic structures –Rescorla and Wagner's model to groups, SOP to Lie groups) we will at least have a tool to formally show that they are so. Following our example in molecular biology, the analysis of symmetries and their corresponding groups provides us with a unifying approach to complex molecular behaviour such as molecular vibrations and vibrational spectroscopy;

- *Classificatory role:* Classifications can be used to identify gaps in the theories but also to predict the existence of new phenomena. This applies when new phenomena can be predicted exclusively in terms of symmetry and when the predictions so postulated are coherent with those of existing models. All possible molecules can be classified according to symmetry operations on five symmetry elements: the

identity operation (doing nothing) on the identity element (the entire molecule); rotation on the proper rotation axis; rotation on the improper rotation axis; reflection in the plane of symmetry; and inversion on the centre of symmetry. We can group together molecules that posses the same symmetry elements and classify molecules according to their symmetry: For example, water belongs to the C_{2v} group which contains the identity, a 2-fold axis of rotation and 2 vertical mirror planes. Interestingly, Dymethyl ether also belongs to such group no matter how different its composition and that of water's may look – $O(CH_3)_2$ and H_2O respectively;

- *Explanatory role:* Symmetries are also explanatory in that phenomena can be explained as consequences of symmetry arguments. We know that the symmetry elements of the causes must be found in their effects and that the converse is not true. That is, the effects can be (and often are) more symmetric than their causes. In group-theoretic terms this means that the initial symmetry conditions are lowered into (more constrained) sub-groups: The symmetry has been broken. In biology, we know that for a molecule to have a permanent dipole moment it must have an asymmetric charge distribution. The point group of the molecule not only determines whether a molecule may have a dipole moment but also in which direction(s) it may point. The only groups compatible with a dipole moment are C_n, C_{nv} and C_s. Besides, in molecules belonging to C_n or C_{nv} the dipole must lie along the axis of rotation. Now, we can explain and predict, at least partially, how a molecule of water behaves;

Of course, organizing our knowledge using symmetries does not prove anything. Symmetries (and group theory) provide us with very powerful abstract tools to analyze the structure of psychological models. But they are just abstract tools after all. In any empirical science, the ultimate proof rests on experimental evidence. Nonetheless, perhaps paradoxically, here it is precisely where the full strength of symmetries shows: Not from the models of theories built on symmetry principles but from the intimate connection (through symmetry arguments) between such models and observed phenomena.

If we look back to the problems faced by psychological models of associative learning as listed in section 2, we find that they relate to deficiencies that symmetry could be used to resolve. The first shortcoming, that no model accounts for all associative learning phenomena, refers to a lack of explanatory power in such models; the second one, that contradictory rules explain the same phenomena, claims for a normative approach; the third one, that models are partial, relates to the need for unifying principles where different theories that cover disjoint phenomena find common grounds and are made compatible; and the fourth one, that some phenomena remain unaccounted for, identifies a classification problem. It seems, therefore, that symmetries may be useful in solving such problems. First we must find the psychological symmetries. This is the purpose of our research.

6. IN SEARCH OF PSYCHOLOGICAL SYMMETRIES

Although there is not a universally accepted 'law of learning', all psychological models coincide in assuming that learning takes place when a (relatively permanent) change in behavior happens as a consequence of some experience. Now, we need to know whether such law establishes *sufficient* symmetry conditions for the occurrence of the observed phenomena –or, in other words, we have to investigate whether the observed phenomena describe *necessary* conditions for the law to hold

(invariantly) true. Unfortunately, a glimpse at the literature suggests it does not:

1. That the sensory and motivational features of the stimuli as well as their novelty and relevance affect learning are well documented facts (Kamin and Schaub, 1963; Pavlov, 1927; Jenkins and Moore, 1973; Randich and LoLordo, 1979; Lubow, 1989; Garcia and Koelling, 1966);

2. Procedurally, the idea that learning is context-specific is also gaining ground (Bouton, 1993; Bouton and Swartzentruber, 1986; Hall and Mondragón, 1998); also, different results emerge depending on the order in which stimuli are presented during training and on the number (single or compound) and representation (elemental or configural) of the cues themselves (see, *e.g.*, Pearce and Bouton, 2001 for a survey).

This first setback may not challenge our search for psychological symmetries though. It could we argued that, after all, we should expect that the parameters in (a) affected the pace of learning (accelerating or decelerating the learning process, *i.e.*, strengthening or weakening the links between nodes/stimuli as time goes), defining, in the extreme, explicit symmetry breaks. Unfortunately, the study of complex phenomena in (b) does not only tell us that the learning rate changes in different experimental conditions. What these results tell us is that the *rules* of learning themselves fluctuate depending on such factors and, consequently, that they do not reflect any genuine object of invariance.

Not surprisingly, a mathematical analysis of the above-mentioned issues reveals that each of them violates one of the conditions for group formation: Associativity. This is rather worrying since associativity is *the* key condition for symmetry. It tells us that the concatenation of two different operations gives the same result, and *that* gives us much more information and reflects much more structure than commutativity[4].

Let us illustrate this point with an example: Both elemental models and configural models of stimulus encoding anticipate that after conditioning is given to two compounds (say, AB and CD) responding to them will be greater than responding to the constituent elements. However, they differ in their expectations for responding to different compounds formed with the same elements (for example, AD and BC); elemental theories expect it to be as large as that to the trained compounds whereas Pearce's configural theory expects some generalization decrement and, as a consequence, responding should be as small as that to the elements. That is, elemental theories assume associative invariance under different compounds; Pearce's theory, on the other hand, assumes invariance under elements *per se* and new configurations. Unfortunately, evidence suggests (see, *e.g.*, Rescorla, 2003) that neither interpretation is complete: In agreement to Pearce's theory, novel compounds perform less than original compounds but, in agreement to elemental theories, novel compounds perform better than their separate elements. Symmetries, therefore, are elusive.

Should we conclude, on this basis, that there are no symmetries in associative learning? Perhaps we can try a different approach and investigate this issue through a representative case study, a model that embodies the fundamental laws of associative learning. Few would disagree that Rescorla and Wagner's model is such a model. Now, Rescorla and Wagner's model is based on five basic assumptions (see Miller *et al.*, 1995), namely:

1. The associative strength of a stimulus depends on the summed associative value of all the CSs present on a given trial;

2. Excitation and inhibition are represented by opposite signs on a single dimension of associative strength and, consequently, are assumed to be mutually exclusive;

3. Associability of a given stimulus (α) is constant, that is, associability is not subject to changes as function of experience;

4. New learning is invariant to any prior associative history (path independence). Past associative status of a cue, *per se*, is assumed to influence neither behavior nor future changes in associative status;

5. Differences in behavior reflect differences in associative strength, that is, there is a monotonically positive relationship between associative value and a relevant response.

A simple analysis of these five premises tells us that only the first one is *a*symmetric. It states that the associative strength of each CS present on a specific trial does not independently gravitate toward the asymptotic value of the US (λ). If it were so, then the associative strength of each CS would be invariant to the presence of other stimuli. This assumption (that is at the heart of cue competition) has proven to be the most innovative feature of Rescorla and Wagner's model.

The rest of assumptions are, in fact, symmetry postulates: Symmetry between excitation and inhibition (2), invariance of associativity to experience (3) and to learning history (4), and symmetry between learning and performance (5). Sadly, countless observations refute in a consistent manner such assumptions[5]. The important point is that such failures do not come from Rescorla and Wagner's disregard for parametric features. The disproving phenomena do not refer to specific values that the context, time/schedule or stimulus characteristics may take but rather are the result of fundamental assumptions on the structure of conditioning.

We can attribute this unsuccessful search for symmetries in associative learning to alternative causes:

- Is it that the laws of associative learning are simply wrong? This does not seem to be the case. Despite the problems referred to in section 2, psychological models of associative learning have been confirmed experimentally so as not to doubt their general validity. As stated by S. Spreat and S.R. Spreat *"much like the law of gravity, the laws of learning are always in effect"* (from Bouton, 2006, pp. 3);
- Or is it that associative learning phenomena (and the theories in which they are modeled) do not show any underlying structure, at least not in the form of symmetries? Again, this is dubious. As we have seen in the previous section, symmetry has proved to be just too powerful a principle in the study of Nature as not to be found in Psychology;
- Or is it that the formalization of symmetries in the notion of group is too constraining and that associative learning shows, to some extent, symmetries that should be expressed with a subtler concept? Is there any notion in abstract algebra that provides us with the required flexibility to represent associative learning phenomena and theories, and, at the same time, preserves the properties that have made groups so popular in Physics, Chemistry and Biology? Yes, there is: The notion of groupoid.

Indeed, it seems that groups do not provide us with the right ontology to deal with the type of symmetries that associative learning may show. Each associative learning theory could perhaps be modeled as a unidimensional single-object category, in other words, as a group. Yet, the problem is that groups (and the theories so modeled) are not expressive or flexible enough and, consequently, are prompt to generate inherently limited classifications and contradictory explanations. Besides, as groups are independent from each other and do not form more general structures

there seems to be no need for a meta-syntax that would regulate the relations between different theories and, potentially, unify them.

7. CONCLUSION: GROUPOIDS?

We have seen that mathematicians (and physicists) tend to think of the notion of symmetry as being virtually synonymous with the theory of groups (symmetry groups). In fact, though groups are indeed sufficient to characterize homogeneous structures, there are plenty of objects which exhibit what we clearly recognize as symmetry, but which admit few or no nontrivial automorphisms. It turns out that the symmetry, and hence much of the structure, of such objects can be characterized algebraically (and categorically) if we use groupoids and not just groups (see Brown, 1987, and Weinstein, 1996, for two formal introductions to groupoids).

Intuitively, a groupoid should be thought of as a group with many objects, or with many identities. A groupoid with an object is essentially just a group. So, the notion of groupoid is an extension of that of group. This apparently innocuous distinction between one-object structures (groups) and many-objects structures (groupoids) is actually crucial. The homomorphisms defined in groups are always automorphisms (homomorphisms of the object to itself). In other words, as groups are one-object categories, *all* morphisms can be composed with all other morphisms. From this, the algebraic conditions for the formation of groups (closure, unique identity, unique total inverse, and *total* associativity) follow directly. On the other hand, groupoids, can only compose morphisms (isomorphisms in their case) with the appropriate domains and co-domains. Algebraically, a groupoid is a set with a *partially* defined binary operation (that *is* associative *where* defined) and a total inverse function.

What is important to get from this mathematical mumbo-jumbo is (a) that in groupoids associativity is partially defined, allowing us to investigate *variable symmetries* (symmetry groupoids) and (b) that in groupoids isomorphisms are defined over sets of base points (fundamental groupoids), permitting us to study *more symmetries*. Indeed, groupoids show new structures that do not show at a group level –more specifically, in groupoids, the inverse relation, although total, is defined over paths; besides, groupoids lead to higher dimensional algebras and help us move between n-categories through natural transformations, limits and co-limits.

Summarizing, groupoids present three very useful properties: (1) Partial associativity, (2) path reversibility, and (3) hierarchism. How does this relate to our study of symmetries in associative learning?

1.   To start with, the very idea of associative learning can be nicely expressed as morphisms (associations) defined over objects (stimuli or nodes), that is, as categories;

2.   Building iteratively up categories may allow us to gain knowledge about hierarchical processes –associative processes between associative processes (Bonardi, 2001; Mondragón, Bonardi and Hall, 2003), in particular, about the role of context and occasion setters (Bouton, 1994);

3.   Also, the isomorphisms that define groupoids (unlike all or nothing equivalence relations that define groups) permit us to introduce partial symmetries that may explain results where novel compounds seem to elicit less response than the original trained compounds but more than each separate element;

4.   Finally, the ability to look at intermediate processes may be very useful in determining the causes for non-responding: Failure to express or failure to acquire (or to retrieve) information?

More generally, the theory of groupoids does not differ widely in spirit and aims from the theory of groups. The recognition of the utility of groupoids gives gains over the corresponding groups without any consequent loss. Our contention is that the above-described characteristics make groupoids an ideal candidate to fill in the symmetry roles that, we have argued, would help solve the problems outlined in section 2: Groupoids provide us with a multi-object language defined over paths along with rules of variance and rules of transformation with which to study both internal and external symmetries. In other words, the language of groupoids gives us the required expressiveness and flexibility to attack classification and explanation problems; and its syntax would allow us to solve normative and unification problems.

Admittedly, the debate over whether groupoids are useful or unmotivated abstractions is still going on (Corfield, 2003). Nevertheless, since they were introduced by H. Brandt in 1926 groupoids have been used in a wide area of mathematics as well as in theoretical physics, neurosciences, biodynamics and networks, and logic and computer science (see, *e.g.*, Ramsay & Renault, 1999).

REFERENCES

Atkins, P., & Friedman, R. (2005). *Molecular Quantum Mechanics*. Oxford, UK: Oxford University Press.

Balkenius, C., & Morén, J. (1998). Computational models of classical conditioning: a comparative study. In Mayer, J.-A., Roitblat, H. L., Wilson, S. W., & Blumberg, B. (Eds.), *From Animals to Animats 5*. Cambridge, MA: MIT Press.

Bonardi, C. (1991). Blocking of occasion setting in feature-positive discriminations. *The Quarterly Journal of Experimental Psychology. B, Comparative and Physiological Psychology, 43*, 431–448.

Bonardi, C., & Ward-Robinson, J. (2001). Occasion Setters: Specificity to the US and the CS-US Association. *Learning and Motivation, 32,* 349–366. doi:10.1006/lmot.2001.1089

Bouton, M. E. (1993). Context, time, and memory retrieval in the interference paradigms of Pavlovian learning. *Psychological Bulletin, 114,* 80–99. doi:10.1037/0033-2909.114.1.80

Bouton, M. E. (1994). Context, Ambiguity, and Classical Conditioning. *Current Directions in Psychological Science, 3,* 49–53. doi:10.1111/1467-8721.ep10769943

Bouton, M. E. (2006). *Learning and Behavior. A Contemporary Synthesis.* Sunderland, MA: Sinauer Associates.

Bouton, M. E., & Moody, E. W. (2004). Memory processes in classical conditioning. *Neuroscience and Biobehavioral Reviews, 28,* 663–674. doi:10.1016/j.neubiorev.2004.09.001

Bouton, M. E., & Swartzentruber, D. (1986). Analysis of the associative and occasion-setting properties of contexts participating in a Pavlovian discrimination. *Journal of Experimental Psychology. Animal Behavior Processes, 12,* 333–350. doi:10.1037/0097-7403.12.4.333

Brading, K., & Castellani, E. (Eds.). (2003). *Symmetries in Physics: Philosophical Reflections.* Cambridge, UK: Cambridge University Press. doi:10.1017/CBO9780511535369

Brown, R. (1987). From groups to groupies: a brief survey. *Bulletin of the London Mathematical Society, 19,* 113–134. doi:10.1112/blms/19.2.113

Chakravartty, A. (2001). The semantic or model-theoretic view of theories and scientific realism. *Synthese, 127,* 325–345. doi:10.1023/A:1010359521312

Corfield, D. (2003). *Towards a Philosophy of Real Mathematics.* Cambridge, UK: Cambridge University Press. doi:10.1017/CBO9780511487576

Curie, P. (1894). Sur la symétrie dans les phénomènes physiques. Symétrie d'un champ électrique et d'un champ magnétique. *Journal de Physique, 3rd series, 3,* 393-417.

Danks, D. (2003). Equilibria of the Rescorla-Wagner model. *Journal of Mathematical Psychology, 47,* 109–121. doi:10.1016/S0022-2496(02)00016-0

Dawkins, R. (1986). *The Blind Watchmaker.* New York: W. W. Norton & Company.

Dickinson, A., & Balleine, B. (2002). The role of learning in the operation of motivational systems. In H. Pashler & R. Gallistel (Eds.), *Stevens' Handbook of Experimental Psychology* (Third ed., Vol. 3: Learning, motivation, and emotion, pp. 497-533). New York: John Wiley & Sons.

Enquist, M., & Ghirlanda, S. (2005). *Neural Networks & Animal Behavior.* Princeton, NJ: Princeton University Press.

Estes, W. K. (1950). Toward a statistical theory of learning. *Psychological Review, 57,* 94–104. doi:10.1037/h0058559

Garcia, J., & Koelling, R. A. (1966). Relation of cue to consequence in avoidance learning. *Psychonomic Science, 4,* 123–124.

Hall, G. (2002). Associative structures in Pavlovian and instrumental conditioning. In Pashler, H., Yantis, S., Medin, D., Gallistel, R., & Wixted, J. (Eds.), *Stevens' Handbook of Experimental Psychology* (Vol. 3, pp. 1–45). Hoboken, NJ: John Wiley and Sons.

Hall, G., & Mondragón, E. (1998). Contextual control as occasion setting. In Schmajuk, N. A., & Holland, P. C. (Eds.), *Occasion Setting: Associative Learning and Cognition in Animals.* Washington, DC: American Psychological Association. doi:10.1037/10298-007

Hastings, A., & Palmer, M. A. (2003). A bright future for biologists and mathematicians? *Science, 299*(5615), 2003–2004. doi:10.1126/science.1081522

Hebb, D. O. (1949). *The Organization of Behavior: A Neuropsychological Theory.* New York: Wiley.

Hey, T., & Allen, R. W. (Eds.). (2000). *Feynman Lectures on Computation.* Boulder, CO: Westview Press.

Holland, P. C. (1983). Occasion-Setting in Pavlovian Feature Positive Discriminations. In M.L. Commons, R.J. Herrnstein, & A. R. Wagner (Eds.), *Quantitative Analyses of Behavior* (4 ed., pp. 183-206). New York: Ballinger.

Honey, R. C., & Watt, A. (1998). Acquired relational equivalence: implications for the nature of associative structures. *Journal of Experimental Psychology. Animal Behavior Processes, 24,* 325–334. doi:10.1037/0097-7403.24.3.325

Hull, C. L. (1943). *Principles of Behavior: An Introduction to Behavior Theory.* New York: Appleton-Century-Crofts.

Jenkins, H. M., & Moore, B. R. (1973). The form of autoshaped response with food or water reinforcers. *Journal of the Experimental Analysis of Behavior, 20,* 163–181. doi:10.1901/jeab.1973.20-163

Kamin, L. J., & Schaub, R. E. (1963). Effects of conditioned stimulus intensity on the conditioned emotional response. *Journal of Comparative and Physiological Psychology, 56,* 502–507. doi:10.1037/h0046616

Klein, F. (1872). Vergleichende Betrachtungen über neuere geometrische Forschungen, *Mathematische Annalen, 43* (1893) pp. 63-100 (Also: Gesammelte Abh. Vol. 1, Springer, 1921, pp. 460-497). An English translation by Mellen Haskell appeared in *Bull. N. Y. Math. Soc, 2*(1892-1893), 215–249.

Lubow, R. E. (1989). *Latent Inhibition and Conditioned Attention Theory.* Cambridge, UK: Cambridge University Press. doi:10.1017/CBO9780511529849

Mackintosh, N. J. (1975). A theory of attention: Variations in the associability of stimulus with reinforcement. *Psychological Review, 82,* 276–298. doi:10.1037/h0076778

Marr, D. (1982). *Vision: a Computational Investigation into the Human Representation and Processing of Visual Information.* San Francisco, CA: W.H. Freeman.

Miller, R. R., Barnet, R. C., & Grahame, N. J. (1995). Assessment of the Rescorla-Wagner model. *Psychological Bulletin, 117,* 363–386. doi:10.1037/0033-2909.117.3.363

Mitchie, D., Spiegelhalter, D. J., & Taylor, C. C. (Eds.). Elder, J.F., IV. (Rev) (1994). Machine Learning, Neural, and Statistical Classification. *Journal of the American Statistical Association, 91,* 436-438.

Mondragón, E., Bonardi, C., & Hall, G. (2003). Negative priming and occasion setting in an appetitive Pavlovian procedure. *Learning & Behavior, 31,* 281–291.

Morris, R. G. M. (1994). The neural Basis of Learning with particular Reference to the Role of Synaptic Plasticity: Where Are We a Century after Cajal's Speculations? In Mackintosh, N. J. (Ed.), *Animal Learning and Cognition* (pp. 135–183). San Diego, CA: Academic Press.

Noether, E.A. (1918). Invariante variationsprobleme, *Nachr. v. d. Ges. d. Wiss. zu Götingen* 1918, 235-257. English translation: M.A. Tavel, Reprinted from "Transport Theory and Statistical Mechanics" 1(3), 183-207 (1971).

Pavlov, I. P. (1927). *Conditioned reflexes* (Anrep, G. V., Trans.). London: Oxford University Press.

Pearce, J. M. (1987). A model for stimulus generalization in Pavlovian conditioning. *Psychological Review*, *94*, 61–67. doi:10.1037/0033-295X.94.1.61

Pearce, J. M., & Bouton, M. E. (2001). Theories of associative learning in animals. *Annual Review of Psychology*, *52*, 111–139. doi:10.1146/annurev.psych.52.1.111

Pearce, J. M., & Hall, G. (1980). A model for Pavlovian conditioning: Variations in the effectiveness of conditioned but not of unconditioned stimuli. *Psychological Review*, *87*, 532–552. doi:10.1037/0033-295X.87.6.532

Ramsay, A., & Renault, J. (Eds.). (1999). *Groupoids in Analysis, Geometry, and Physics. Contemporary Mathematics 282*. Providence, RI: American Mathematical Society.

Randich, A., & LoLordo, V. M. (1979). Associative and non-associative theories of the UCS preexposure phenomenon: Implications for Pavlovian conditioning. *Psychological Bulletin*, *86*, 523–548. doi:10.1037/0033-2909.86.3.523

Rescorla, R. A. (1985). Conditioned inhibition and facilitation. In Miller, R. R., & Spear, N. E. (Eds.), *Information processing in animals: Conditioned inhibition* (pp. 299–326). Hillsdale, NJ: Erlbaum.

Rescorla, R. A. (2003). Elemental and configural encoding of the conditioned stimulus. *The Quarterly Journal of Experimental Psychology*, *56B*(2), 161–176.

Rescorla, R. A., & Wagner, A. R. (1972). A theory of Pavlovian conditioning: The effectiveness of reinforcement and non-reinforcement. In Black, A. H., & Prokasy, W. F. (Eds.), *Classical Conditioning II: Current Research and Theory* (pp. 64–99). New York: Appleton-Century-Crofts.

Schmajuk, N. A., & DiCarlo, J. J. (1992). Stimulus configuration, occasion setting, and the hippocampus. *Psychological Review*, *99*, 268–305. doi:10.1037/0033-295X.99.2.268

Shanks, D. R. (1995). *The Psychology of Associative Learning*. Cambridge, UK: Cambridge University Press. doi:10.1017/CBO9780511623288

Skinner, B. F. (1989). The Origins of Cognitive Thought. *The American Psychologist*, *44*(1), 13–18. doi:10.1037/0003-066X.44.1.13

Timberlake, W. (1980). A molar equilibrium theory of learned performance. In Bower, G. H. (Ed.), *The psychology of learning and motivation* (*Vol. 14*, pp. 1–58). New York: Academic Press.

Townsend, J. T. (2008). Mathematical psychology: Prospects for the 21st century: A guest editorial. *Journal of Mathematical Psychology*, *52*, 269–280. doi:10.1016/j.jmp.2008.05.001

Uttal, W. R. (2001). *The New Phrenology: The Limits of Localizing Cognitive Processes in the Brain*. Cambridge, MA: The MIT Press.

Vedral, V. (2006). *Introduction to Quantum Information Science*. Oxford, UK: Oxford University Press. doi:10.1093/acprof:oso/9780199215706.001.0001

Vogel, E. H., Castro, M. E., & Saavedra, M. A. (2004). Quantitative models of Pavlovian conditioning. *Brain Research Bulletin*, *63*, 173–202. doi:10.1016/j.brainresbull.2004.01.005

Vul, E., Harris, C., Winkielman, P., & Pashler, H. (2009). Puzzlingly High Correlations in fRMI Studies of Emotion, Personality, and Social Sciences. *Perspectives on Psychological Science*, *4*(3), 274–290. doi:10.1111/j.1745-6924.2009.01125.x

Wagner, A. R. (1981). SOP: a model of automatic memory processing in animal behaviour. In Spear, N. E., & Miller, R. R. (Eds.), *Information Processing in Animals: Memory Mechanisms* (pp. 5–47). Hillsdale, NJ: Erlbaum.

Wasserman, E. A., & Miller, R. R. (1997). What's elementary about associative learning? *Annual Review of Psychology, 48,* 573–607. doi:10.1146/annurev.psych.48.1.573

Weinstein, A. (1996). Groupoids: Unifying internal and external symmetry (a tour through some examples). *Notices of the American Mathematical Society, 43*(7), 744–752.

Weyl, H. (1928). *Gruppentheorie und Quantenmechanik. Leipzig: S. Hirzel Verlag. English translation: The Theory of Groups and Quantum Mechanics.* New York: Dover Publications.

Wheeler, J. A. (1990). Information, physics, quantum: The search for links. In Zurek, W. (Ed.), *Complexity, Entropy, and the Physics of Information.* Redwood City, CA: Addison-Wesley.

Widrow, G., & Hoff, M.E. (1960). *Adaptive switching circuits.* Institute of radio engineers, Western Electronic show & convention, Convention record, Part 4, 96-104.

Wilson, P. N., & Pearce, J. M. (1989). A role for stimulus generalization in conditional discrimination learning. *The Quarterly Journal of Experimental Psychology. B, Comparative and Physiological Psychology, 41,* 243–273.

Wilson, P. N., & Pearce, J. M. (1990). Selective transfer of responding in conditional discriminations. *The Quarterly Journal of Experimental Psychology. B, Comparative and Physiological Psychology, 42,* 41–58.

Yamaguchi, M. (2006). Complete solution of the Rescorla-Wagner model for relative validity. *Behavioural Processes, 71,* 70–73. doi:10.1016/j.beproc.2005.10.001

Zuse, K. (1969). *Rechnender Raum.* Braunschweig, Germany: Friedrich Vieweg & Sohn.

KEY TERMS AND DEFINITIONS

Associative Learning: An account of learning and the process by which animals learn by associating or linking experienced events: stimuli and/or responses, and adjust their behavior accordingly.

Symmetries: Symmetries define invariance: that is, impunity to transformations. They refer to the fact that parts of a whole are equivalent (interchangeable) under a group of operations.

Groups: An algebraic structure consisting of a set together with an operation that satisfy the existence of the identity and inverse operations: associativity and the closure of the product. Groups have been traditionally used to represent symmetries.

Groupoids: A groupoid should be thought of as a group with many objects: or with many identities. A groupoid with an object is essentially just a group. So the notion of groupoid is an extension of that of group. Algebraically, a groupoid is a set with a partially defined binary operation (that is associative where defined) and a total inverse function.

ENDNOTES

[1] The very concept of computational model is controversial. If we refer to David Marr's levels of analysis of information processing systems (Marr, 1982) then models such as Rescorla and Wagner's are both computational and algorithmic --but allegedly not implementational, in that they analyse what the system does and how it does it. What we refer to as a computational model of (associative) learning however is the more mundane exercise of taking architectures

and techniques from machine learning and applying them to the modelling of psychological phenomena and data.

2   Even if it did, a neural analysis would not necessarily be the right level to study associative learning phenomena. In the words of Burruhs F. Skinner "The analysis of behaviour need not wait until brain science has done its part. The behavioural facts will not be changed (…). Brain science may discover other kinds of variables affecting behaviour, but it will turn to a behavioural analysis for the clearest account of their effects" (Skinner, 1989, emphasis ours). Regardless of the antipathy that Skinner's radical behaviorism provokes among neuroscientists such an statement does not contradict a version of reductionism that most of them would endorse, namely, Richard Dawkin's hierarchical reductionism (Dawkins, 1986).

3   And precisely because of its generality the information processing model is not necessary or sufficient: Working physicists do not model electrons, atoms or galaxies as information processing entities –be it in the form of a cellular automaton as envisaged in (Zuse, 1969) or as a participatory universe (Wheeler, 1990); on the other hand, neither (computational) physicists nor the public would presume that the simulation of a nuclear reaction generates real energy or that a flight simulator really flies. Of course, this does not preclude physicists from theorizing about what type of information is contained in a physical system (see, for example, literature on quantum entanglement or black holes) or about exploring the physical limits of computers (pioneered by Richard Feynman (Hey & Allen, 2000) and followed up to contemporary theories of quantum computing (e.g., Vedral, 2006)).

4   Incidentally, associative learning has shown to be stubbornly non-Abelian: 'Associative symmetry' phenomena and the basic distinction between latent inhibition and extinction are just two examples of non-commutativity.

5   In defence of Rescorla and Wagner, it must be said that they themselves expressed their doubts about these four assumptions. For instance, it is hard to believe that Rescorla and Wagner really mistook extinction for unlearning or that they were ignorant of silent learning phenomena. It should also be noted that alternative models based on contingencies do not seem to improve the landscape. Although it has been proved that the non-pairings of CS and US influence behaviour as do pairing of CS and US we know that the four inter-event combinations do not contribute equally to the acquired behaviour (*i.e.*, they have equal normative weights but not equal psychological weights, Wasserman & Miller, 1997).

Compilation of References

Abarbanel, H. (1996). *Analysis of observed chaotic data*. New York: Springer Verlag.

Ackley, D. H., Hinton, G. E., & Sejnowski, T. J. (1986). A learning algorithm for Boltzmann machines. *Cognitive Science, 9*, 147–169. doi:10.1207/s15516709cog0901_7

Adams, C. D., & Dickinson, A. (1981). Instrumental responding following reinforcer devaluation. *Quarterly Journal of Experimental Psychology, 33B*, 109–122.

Allman, M. J., Ward-Robinson, J., & Honey, R. C. (2004). Associative change in the representations acquired during conditional discriminations: Further analysis of the nature of conditional learning. *Journal of Experimental Psychology. Animal Behavior Processes, 30*, 118–128. doi:10.1037/0097-7403.30.2.118

Angyan, A. J. (1959). Machina Reproducatrix. In D. V. Blake and A. M. Uttley (Eds.), *The Mechanization of Thought Processes: Proceedings of a Symposium held at the National Physical Laboratory on 24-27 November 1958*, (vol. 2, pp. 933-944). London: Her Majesty's Stationery Office.

Applied Nonlinear Sciences. (2003). *Tools for dynamics*. Retrieved from http://www.zweb.com/apnonlin: Applied Nonlinear Sciences.

Arbib, M. A. (1972). *The Metaphorical Brain: An Introduction to Cybernetics as Artificial Intelligence and Brain Theory*. New York: Wiley-Interscience.

Arbib, M. A., Érdi, P., & Szentágothai, J. (1997). *Neural Organization: Structure, Function, and Dynamics*. Cambridge, MA: MIT Press.

Argyros, A., Bekris, K., Orphanoudakis, S., & Kavraki, L. (2005). Robot homing by exploiting panoramic vision. *Autonomous Robots, 19*, 7–25. doi:10.1007/s10514-005-0603-7

Ariely, D. (2008). *Predictably Irrational: The Hidden Forces that Shape our Decisions*. New York: Harper.

Arkin, R. (1998). *Behavior-based robotics*. Cambridge, MA: MIT Press.

Asgarian, N., Hu, X., Aktary, Z., Chapman, K. A., Lam, L., & Chibbar, R. (2010). Learning to predict relapse in invasive ductal carcinomas based on the subcellular localization of junctional proteins. *Breast Cancer Research and Treatment, 121*, 527–538. doi:10.1007/s10549-009-0557-0

Asghari-Oskoei, M., & Hu, H. (2007). Myoelectric control systems-A survey. *Journal of Biomedical Signal Processing and Control, 2*(4), 275–294..doi:10.1016/j.bspc.2007.07.009

Asghari-Oskoei, M., & Hu, H. (2008). Support Vector Machine-Based Classification Scheme for Myoelectric Control Applied to Upper Limb. *IEEE Transactions on Bio-Medical Engineering, 55*(8), 1956–1965. Retrieved from http://ieeexplore.ieee.org/stamp/stamp.jsp?arnumber=04463647. doi:10.1109/TBME.2008.919734

Atkins, P., & Friedman, R. (2005). *Molecular Quantum Mechanics*. Oxford, UK: Oxford University Press.

Atkinson, R. C., & Estes, W. K. (1963). Stimulus sampling theory. In Luce, R. D., Bush, R. R., & Galanter, E. (Eds.), *Handbook of mathematical psychology*. New York: Wiley.

Attaway, S. (2009). *Matlab: A practical introduction.* Burlington, Oxford: Butterworth Heinemann.

Aubepart, F., & Franceschini, N. (2007). Bio-inspired optic flow sensors based on FPGA: application to micro-air-vehicles. *Microprocessors and Microsystems, 31,* 408–419. doi:10.1016/j.micpro.2007.02.004

Auer, P. (2003). Using confidence bounds for exploitation-exploration trade-offs. *Journal of Machine Learning Research, 3,* 397–422. doi:10.1162/153244303321897663

Aydin, A., & Pearce, J. M. (1995). Summation in autoshaping with short- and long-duration stimuli. *Quarterly Journal of Experimental Psychology, 42,* 215–234.

Ayers, J., Davis, J., & Rudolph, A. (2002). *Neurotechnology for Biomimetic Robots.* Cambridge, MA: MIT Press.

Baddeley, B., Graham, P., Philippides, A., Hempel de Ibarra, N., Collett, T., & Husbands, P. (2009). What can be learnt from analysing insect orientation flights using probabilistic SLAM? *Biological Cybernetics, 101*(3), 169–182. doi:10.1007/s00422-009-0327-4

Baird, L. (1995). Residual algorithms: Reinforcement learning with function approximation. *International Conference on Machine Learning, 12,* 30-37.

Baker, C. I., Behrmann, M., & Olson, C. R. (2002). Impact of learning on representation of parts and wholes in monkey inferotemporal cortex. *Nature Neuroscience, 5,* 1210–1216. doi:10.1038/nn960

Balkenius, C., & Morén, J. (1998). Computational models of classical conditioning: a comparative study. In Mayer, J.-A., Roitblat, H. L., Wilson, S. W., & Blumberg, B. (Eds.), *From Animals to Animats 5.* Cambridge, MA: MIT Press.

Balleine, B. W., & Dickinson, A. (1998). Goal-directed instrumental action: Contingency and incentive learning and their cortical substrates. *Neuropharmacology, 37,* 407–419. doi:10.1016/S0028-3908(98)00033-1

Balleine, B. W., & O'Doherty, J. P. (2009). Human and rodent homologies in action control: Corticostriatal determinants of goal-directed and habitual action. *Neuropsychopharmacology, 35,* 48–69. doi:10.1038/npp.2009.131

Baranano, D., Ferris, C., & Snyder, S. (2001). Atypical neural messengers. *Trends in Neurosciences, 24*(2), 99–106. doi:10.1016/S0166-2236(00)01716-1

Barense, M. D., Bussey, T. J., Lee, A. C., Rogers, T. T., Davies, R. R., & Saksida, L. M. (2005). Functional specialization in the human medial temporal lobe. *The Journal of Neuroscience, 25*(44), 10239–10246. doi:10.1523/JNEUROSCI.2704-05.2005

Barense, M. D., Gaffan, D., & Graham, K. S. (2007). The human medial temporal lobe processes online representations of complex objects. *Neuropsychologia, 45*(13), 2963–2974. doi:10.1016/j.neuropsychologia.2007.05.023

Barnes, J. M., & Underwood, B. J. (1959). "Fate" of first-list associations in transfer theory. *Journal of Experimental Psychology, 58,* 97–105. doi:10.1037/h0047507

Barnet, R. C., Grahame, N. J., & Miller, R. R. (1993). Temporal encoding as a determinant of blocking. *Journal of Experimental Psychology. Animal Behavior Processes, 19,* 327–341. doi:10.1037/0097-7403.19.4.327

Barto, A. G., Sutton, R. S., & Brouwer, P. (1981). Associative search network: A reinforcement learning associative memory. *Biological Cybernetics, 40,* 201–211. doi:10.1007/BF00453370

Bateson, M., & Kacelnik, A. (1995). Preferences for fixed and variable food sources: Variability in amount and delay. *Journal of the Experimental Analysis of Behavior, 63,* 313–329. doi:10.1901/jeab.1995.63-313

Baxter, M. G. (2009). Involvement of medial temporal lobe structures in memory and perception. *Neuron, 61*(5), 667–677. doi:10.1016/j.neuron.2009.02.007

Beckers, T., De Houwer, J., Pineno, O., & Miller, R. R. (2005). Outcome additivity and outcome maximality influence cue competition in human causal learning. *Journal of Experimental Psychology. Learning, Memory, and Cognition, 31,* 238–249. doi:10.1037/0278-7393.31.2.238

Beckers, T., Miller, R. R., De Houwer, J., & Urushihara, K. (2006). Reasoning rats: forward blocking in Pavlovian animal conditioning is sensitive to constraints of causal inference. *Journal of Experimental Psychology. General, 135,* 92–102. doi:10.1037/0096-3445.135.1.92

Beer, R. D., & Gallagher, J. C. (1992). Evolving dynamical neural networks for adaptive behavior. *Adaptive Behavior*, *1*, 94–110. doi:10.1177/105971239200100105

Beer, R. D., Quinn, R. D., Chiel, H. J., & Ritzmann, R. E. (1997). Biologically-inspired approaches to robotics. *Communications of the ACM*, *40*(3), 30–38. doi:10.1145/245108.245118

Bekey, G. (2005). *Autonomous Robots: From Biological Inspiration to Implementation and Control*. Cambridge, MA: MIT Press.

Bekey, G., & Goldberg, K. (Eds.). (1993). *Neural Networks in Robotics*, (Springer International Series in Engineering and Computer Science, Vol. 202). Berlin: Springer.

Bernoulli, D. (1738. (1954). Exposition of a new theory on the measurement of risk. *Econometrica*, *22*, 23–36. doi:10.2307/1909829

Bertsekas, D. P., & Tsitsiklis, J. N. (1996). *Neuro-dynamic programming*. Belmont, MA: Athena Scientific.

Bisset, D. L., & Vandenburgh, R. C. (1997). The dynamics of photo-taxis: Applying the agent environment interaction system to a simple Braitenburg robot. In P. Husbands and I. Harvey (Eds.), *Proceedings of the fourth European conference on artificial life* (pp. 327-336). Cambridge, MA: The MIT press.

Bitterman, M. E. (1964). Classical conditioning in goldfish as function of CS-US interval. *Journal of Comparative and Physiological Psychology*, *58*, 359–366. doi:10.1037/h0046793

Blaisdell, A. P., Denniston, J. C., & Miller, R. R. (1998). Temporal encoding as a determinant of overshadowing. *Journal of Experimental Psychology. Animal Behavior Processes*, *24*, 72–83. doi:10.1037/0097-7403.24.1.72

Blaisdell, A. P., Sawa, K., Leising, K. J., & Waldmann, M. R. (2006). Causal reasoning in rats. *Science*, *311*, 1020–1022. doi:10.1126/science.1121872

Blake, L., Jarvis, C. D., & Mishkin, M. (1977). Pattern discrimination thresholds after partial inferior temporal of lateral striate lesions in monkeys. *Brain Research*, *120*, 209–220. doi:10.1016/0006-8993(77)90901-5

Blought, D. S. (1975). Steady state data and a quantitative model of operant generalization and discrimination. *Journal of Experimental Psychology. Animal Behavior Processes*, *104*, 3–21. doi:10.1037/0097-7403.1.1.3

Boden, M. (2006). *Mind as Machine: A History of Cognitive Science*. Oxford, UK: OUP.

Bonardi, C. (1991). Blocking of occasion setting in feature-positive discriminations. *The Quarterly Journal of Experimental Psychology. B, Comparative and Physiological Psychology*, *43*, 431–448.

Bonardi, C., & Ward-Robinson, J. (2001). Occasion Setters: Specificity to the US and the CS-US Association. *Learning and Motivation*, *32*, 349–366. doi:10.1006/lmot.2001.1089

Bonato, P., Roy, S. H., Knaflitz, M., & Luca, C. (2001). Time-frequency parameters of the surface myoelectric signal for assessing muscle fatigue during cyclic dynamic contractions. *IEEE Transactions on Bio-Medical Engineering*, *48*(7), 745–753. Retrieved from http://ieeexplore.ieee.org/stamp/stamp.jsp?tp=&arnumber=930899&userType=inst. doi:10.1109/10.930899

Boneau, C. A. (1958). The interstimulus interval and the latency of the conditioned eyelid response. *Journal of Experimental Psychology*, *56*, 464–471. doi:10.1037/h0044940

Borst, A., & Haag, J. (2002). Neural networks in the cockpit of the fly. *Journal of Comparative Physiology. A, Neuroethology, Sensory, Neural, and Behavioral Physiology*, *188*, 419–437. doi:10.1007/s00359-002-0316-8

Bouton, M. E., & King, D. A. (1983). Contextual control of the extinction of conditioned fear: test for the associative value of the context. *Journal of Experimental Psychology. Animal Behavior Processes*, *9*, 248–265. doi:10.1037/0097-7403.9.3.248

Bouton, M. E. (1993). Context, time, and memory retrieval in the interference paradigms of Pavlovian learning. *Psychological Bulletin*, *114*, 80–99. doi:10.1037/0033-2909.114.1.80

Bouton, M. E. (1994). Context, Ambiguity, and Classical Conditioning. *Current Directions in Psychological Science*, 3, 49–53. doi:10.1111/1467-8721.ep10769943

Bouton, M. E. (2006). *Learning and Behavior. A Contemporary Synthesis*. Sunderland, MA: Sinauer Associates.

Bouton, M. E., & Moody, E. W. (2004). Memory processes in classical conditioning. *Neuroscience and Biobehavioral Reviews*, 28, 663–674. doi:10.1016/j.neubiorev.2004.09.001

Bouton, M. E., & Swartzentruber, D. (1986). Analysis of the associative and occasion-setting properties of contexts participating in a Pavlovian discrimination. *Journal of Experimental Psychology. Animal Behavior Processes*, 12, 333–350. doi:10.1037/0097-7403.12.4.333

Bouton (2004). Context and behavioral processes in extinction. *Learning & Memory*, 11, 485-494.

Box, G., Jenkins, G., & Reinsel, G. (1994). *Time series analysis*. Old Tappan, NT: Prentice-Hall.

Brading, K., & Castellani, E. (Eds.). (2003). *Symmetries in Physics: Philosophical Reflections*. Cambridge, UK: Cambridge University Press. doi:10.1017/CBO9780511535369

Brafman, R. I., & Tennenholtz, M. (2003). R-MAX—A general polynomial time algorithm for near-optimal reinforcement learning. *Journal of Machine Learning Research*, 3, 213–231. doi:10.1162/153244303765208377

Brandon, S. E., Bombace, J. C., Falls, W. T., & Wagner, A. R. (1991). Modulation of unconditioned defensive reflexes via an emotive Pavlovian conditioned stimulus. *Journal of Experimental Psychology. Animal Behavior Processes*, 17, 312–322. doi:10.1037/0097-7403.17.3.312

Brandon, S. E., Vogel, E. H., & Wagner, A. R. (2000). A componential view of configural cues in generalization and discrimination in Pavlovian conditioning. *Behavioural Brain Research*, 110, 67–72. doi:10.1016/S0166-4328(99)00185-0

Brandon, S. E., Vogel, E. H., & Wagner, A. R. (2003). Stimulus representation in SOP: I. Theoretical rationalization and some implications. *Behavioural Processes*, 62, 5–25. doi:10.1016/S0376-6357(03)00016-0

Brandon, S. E., & Wagner, A. R. (1991). Modulation of a discrete Pavlovian conditioning reflex by a putative emotive Pavlovian conditioned stimulus. *Journal of Experimental Psychology. Animal Behavior Processes*, 17, 299–311. doi:10.1037/0097-7403.17.3.299

Bristol, A. S., & Carew, T. J. (2005). Differential role of inhibition in habituation of two independent afferent pathways to a common motor output. *Learning & Memory (Cold Spring Harbor, N.Y.)*, 12, 52–60. doi:10.1101/lm.83405

Brogden, W. J. (1939). Sensory pre-conditioning. *Journal of Experimental Psychology*, 25, 323–332. doi:10.1037/h0058944

Brooks, R. A. (1986). A Robust Layered Control System for a Mobile Robot. *IEEE Journal on Robotics and Automation*, 2(1), 14–23.

Brooks, R. A. (1989). A Robot that Walks; Emergent Behaviors from a Carefully Evolved Network. *Neural Computation*, 1(2), 253–262. doi:10.1162/neco.1989.1.2.253

Brooks, R. A. (1999). *Cambrian Intelligence: The Early History of the New AI*. Cambridge, MA: MIT Press.

Brooks, R. A. (2002). *Flesh and Machines: How Robots Will Change Us*. New York: Pantheon Books.

Brooks, R. A. (1985). A robust layered control system for a mobile robot. *IEEE Journal on Robotics and Automation*, 2(1), 14–23.

Brown, P. L., & Jenkins, H. M. (1968). Auto-shaping the pigeons's key peck. *Journal of Experimental Psychology*, 11, 1–8.

Brown, R. (1987). From groups to groupies: a brief survey. *Bulletin of the London Mathematical Society*, 19, 113–134. doi:10.1112/blms/19.2.113

Buckley, M. J. (2005). The role of the medial temporal lobe in memory and perception: evidence from rats, nonhuman primates and humans. *Quarterly Journal of Experimental Psychology, 58B*, 246–268.

Buckley, M. J., & Gaffan, D. (1997). Impairment of visual object-discrimination learning after perirhinal cortex ablation. *Behavioral Neuroscience, 111*, 467–475. doi:10.1037/0735-7044.111.3.467

Buffalo, E. A., Ramus, S. J., Clark, R. E., Teng, E., Squire, L. R., & Zola, S. M. (1999). Dissociation between the effects of damage to perirhinal cortex and area TE. *Learning & Memory (Cold Spring Harbor, N.Y.), 6*, 572–599. doi:10.1101/lm.6.6.572

Buffalo, E. A., Ramus, S. J., Squire, L. R., & Zola, S. M. (2000). Perception and recognition memory in monkeys following lesions of area TE and perirhinal cortex. *Learning & Memory (Cold Spring Harbor, N.Y.), 7*(6), 375–382.doi:10.1101/lm.32100

Buffalo, E. A., Reber, P. J., & Squire, L. R. (1998). The human perirhinal cortex and recognition memory. *Hippocampus, 8*, 330–339.doi:10.1002/(SICI)1098-1063(1998)8:4<330::AID-HIPO3>3.0.CO;2-L

Bullock, T., Bennett, M., Johnston, D., Josephson, R., Marder, E., & Fields, R. (2005). The neuron doctrine, redux. *Science, 310*(5749), 791. doi:10.1126/science.1114394

Burkhardt, P. E., & Ayres, J. J. B. (1978). CS and US duration effects in one-trial simultaneous fear conditioning as assessed by conditioned suppression of licking in rats. *Animal Learning & Behavior, 6*, 225–230.

Bush, R. R., & Mosteller, F. (1955). *Stochastic models for learning*. New York: Wiley.

Bussey, T. J. (2004). Multiple memory systems: Fact or fiction? *Quarterly Journal of Experimental Psychology, 57*, 89–94.

Bussey, T. J., & Saksida, L. M. (2002). The organization of visual object representations: a connectionist model of effects of lesions in perirhinal cortex. *The European Journal of Neuroscience, 15*(2), 355–364.doi:10.1046/j.0953-816x.2001.01850.x

Bussey, T. J., & Saksida, L. M. (2005). Object memory and perception in the medial temporal lobe:An alternative approach. *Current Opinion in Neurobiology, 15*, 730–737. doi:10.1016/j.conb.2005.10.014

Bussey, T. J., & Saksida, L. M. (2007). Memory, perception, and the ventral visual-perirhinal-hippocampal stream: thinking outside of the boxes. *Hippocampus, 17*(9), 898–908.doi:10.1002/hipo.20320

Bussey, T. J., Saksida, L. M., & Murray, E. A. (2002). Perirhinal cortex resolves feature ambiguity in complex visual discriminations. *The European Journal of Neuroscience, 15*, 365–374.doi:10.1046/j.0953-816x.2001.01851.x

Bussey, T. J., Saksida, L. M., & Murray, E. A. (2003). Impairments in visual discrimination after perirhinal cortex lesions: Testing 'declarative' versus 'perceptual-mnemonic' views of perirhinal cortex function. *The European Journal of Neuroscience, 17*, 649–660. doi:10.1046/j.1460-9568.2003.02475.x

Bussey, T. J., Saksida, L. M., & Murray, E. A. (2005). The PMFC model of perirhinal cortex function. *Quarterly Journal of Experimental Psychology, 58B*, 269–282.

Butter, C. M. (1972). Detection of Masked Patterns in Monkeys with Inferotemporal, Striate or Dorsolateral Frontal Lesions. *Neuropsychologia, 10*, 241–243. doi:10.1016/0028-3932(72)90066-8

Camerer, C., & Loewenstein, G. (2003). Behavioral economics: Past, present, future. In Camerer, C., Loewenstein, G., & Rabin, M. (Eds.), *Advances in Behavioral Economics* (pp. 3–51). New York, Princeton: Russell Sage Foundation Press and Princeton University Press.

Caraco, T. (1981). Energy budgets, risk and foraging preferences in dark-eyed juncos (*Junco hyemalis*). *Behavioral Ecology and Sociobiology, 8*, 213–217. doi:10.1007/BF00299833

Caraco, T., Blanckenhorn, W. U., Gregory, G. M., Newman, J. A., Recer, G. M., & Zwicker, S. M. (1990). Risk-sensitivity: Ambient temperature affects foraging choice. *Animal Behaviour, 39*, 338–345. doi:10.1016/S0003-3472(05)80879-6

Cartwright, B., & Collett, T. (1983). Landmark learning in bees. *Journal of Comparative Physiology. A, Neuroethology, Sensory, Neural, and Behavioral Physiology, 151,* 521–543. doi:10.1007/BF00605469

Cartwright, B., & Collett, T. (1987). Landmark maps for honeybees. *Biological Cybernetics, 57*(1-2), 85–93. doi:10.1007/BF00318718

Chakravartty, A. (2001). The semantic or model-theoretic view of theories and scientific realism. *Synthese, 127,* 325–345. doi:10.1023/A:1010359521312

Chan, A. D. C., & Englehart, K. (2005). Continuous Myoelectric Control for Powered Prostheses Using Hidden Markov Models. *IEEE Transactions on Bio-Medical Engineering, 52*(1), 121–124. Retrieved from http://ieeexplore.ieee.org/stamp/stamp.jsp?arnumber=01369595. doi:10.1109/TBME.2004.836492

Chen, S., & Billings, S. A. (1989). Representations of non-linear systems: The Narmax model. *International Journal of Control, 49,* 1013–1032.

Christian, K. M., & Thompson, R. F. (2003). Neural substrates of eyeblink conditioning: Adquisition and retention. *Learning & Memory (Cold Spring Harbor, N.Y.), 10,* 427–455. doi:10.1101/lm.59603

Churchland, P. S., & Sejnowski, T. J. (1988). Perspectives on Cognitive Neuroscience. *Science, 242*(4879), 741–745. doi:10.1126/science.3055294

Churchland, P. S., & Sejnowski, T. J. (1992). *The Computational Brain*. Cambridge: MIT Press.

Clark, A. (2008). *Supersizing the Mind: Embodiment, Action, and Cognitive Extension*. New York, NY: Oxford University Press.

Close, J., Hahn, U., & Honey, R. C. (2009). Contextual modulation of similarity in the rat. *Journal of Experimental Psychology. Animal Behavior Processes, 35,* 509–515. doi:10.1037/a0015489

Cole, R. P., Matter, L., & Miller, R. R. (1995). Attenuation of the relative validity effect by post-training extinction of the more valid cue. *Proceedings and Abstracts of the Annual Meeting of the Eastern Psychological Association,* Boston.

Coleman, S. R., & Gormezano, I. (1971). Classical conditioning of the rabbit's (orictolagus cuniculus) nictitating membrane response under symmetrical CS-US interval shifts. *Journal of Comparative and Physiological Psychology, 77,* 447–455. doi:10.1037/h0031879

Collett, T., Dillmann, E., Giger, A., & Wehner, R. (1992). Visual landmarks and route following in desert ants. *Journal of Comparative Physiology. A, Neuroethology, Sensory, Neural, and Behavioral Physiology, 170,* 435–442. doi:10.1007/BF00191460

Collins, D. J., & Shanks, D. R. (2006). Summation in causal learning: Elemental processing or configural generalization. *Quarterly Journal of Experimental Psychology, 59,* 1524–1534. doi:10.1080/17470210600639389

Colwill, R. C., & Rescorla, R. A. (1985). Postconditioning devaluation of a reinforcer affects instrumental responding. *Journal of Experimental Psychology. Animal Behavior Processes, 11,* 120–132. doi:10.1037/0097-7403.11.1.120

Cooper, G. F., Abraham, V., Aliferis, C. F., Aronis, J. M., Buchanan, B. G., & Caruana, R. (2005). Predicting dire outcomes of patients with community acquired pneumonia. *Journal of Biomedical Informatics, 38,* 347–366. doi:10.1016/j.jbi.2005.02.005

Cordeschi, R. (2002). *The Discovery of the Artificial: Behavior, Mind and Machines Before and Beyond Cybernetics*. Dordrecht: Kluwer Academic Publishers.

Corfield, D. (2003). *Towards a Philosophy of Real Mathematics*. Cambridge, UK: Cambridge University Press. doi:10.1017/CBO9780511487576

Coutureau, E., Killcross, A. S., Good, M., Marshall, V. J., Ward-Robinson, J., & Honey, R. C. (2002). Acquired equivalence and distinctiveness of cues: II. Neural manipulations and their implications. *Journal of Experimental Psychology. Animal Behavior Processes, 28,* 388–396. doi:10.1037/0097-7403.28.4.388

Cowell, R. A., Bussey, T. J., & Saksida, L. M. (2006). Why does brain damage impair memory? A connectionist model of object recognition memory in perirhinal cortex. *The Journal of Neuroscience, 26*(47), 12186–12197. doi:10.1523/JNEUROSCI.2818-06.2006

Cowell, R. A., Bussey, T. J., & Saksida, L. M. (2010). Functional dissociations within the ventral object processing pathway: cognitive modules or a hierarchical continuum? *Journal of Cognitive Neuroscience, 22*(11), 2460–2479. doi:10.1162/jocn.2009.21373

Cowell, R. A. (2006). *Modelling the effects of damage to perirhinal cortex and ventral visual stream on visual cognition.* Unpublished dissertation, University of Oxford, UK.

Cowey, A., & Gross, C. G. (1970). Effects of foveal prestriate and inferotemporal lesions on visual discrimination by rhesus monkeys. *Experimental Brain Research, 11*(2), 128–144. doi:10.1007/BF00234318

Cruse, H., Bartling, C., Cymbalyuk, G., Dean, J., & Dreifert, M. (1995). A modular artificial neural net for controlling a six-legged walking system. *Biological Cybernetics, 72*(5), 421–430. doi:10.1007/BF00201417

Curie, P. (1894). Sur la symétrie dans les phénomènes physiques. Symétrie d'un champ électrique et d'un champ magnétique. *Journal de Physique, 3rd series, 3,* 393-417.

Danks, D. (2003). Equilibria of the Rescorla-Wagner model. *Journal of Mathematical Psychology, 47,* 109–121. doi:10.1016/S0022-2496(02)00016-0

Davis, M. (1970). Effects of interstimulus interval length and variability on startle response habituation in the rat. *Journal of Comparative and Physiological Psychology, 72,* 177–192. doi:10.1037/h0029472

Davis, M., Schlesinger, L. S., & Sorenson, C. A. (1989). Temporal specificity of fear conditioning - effects of different conditioned-stimulus - unconditioned stimulus intervals on the fear-potentiated startle effect. *Journal of Experimental Psychology. Animal Behavior Processes, 15,* 295–310. doi:10.1037/0097-7403.15.4.295

Davison, M., & McCarthy, D. (1988). *The Matching Law: A Research Review.* Hillsdale, NJ: Erlbaum.

Daw, N. D., Courville, A. C., & Touretzky, D. S. (2006). Representation and timing in theories of the dopamine system. *Neural Computation, 18,* 1637–1677. doi:10.1162/neco.2006.18.7.1637

Daw, N. D., & Doya, K. (2006). The computational neurobiology of learning and reward. *Current Opinion in Neurobiology, 16,* 199–204. doi:10.1016/j.conb.2006.03.006

Daw, N. D., Niv, Y., & Dayan, P. (2005). Uncertainty based competition between prefrontal and dorsolateral striatal systems for behavioral control. *Nature Neuroscience, 8,* 1704–1711. doi:10.1038/nn1560

Daw, N. D., O'Doherty, J. P., Dayan, P., Seymour, B., & Dolan, R. J. (2006). Cortical substrates for exploratory decisions in humans. *Nature, 441,* 876–879. doi:10.1038/nature04766

Dawson, T., & Snyder, S. (1994). Gases as biological messengers: nitric oxide and carbon monoxide in the brain. *The Journal of Neuroscience, 14*(9), 5147–5159.

Dayan, P., & Daw, N. D. (2008). Decision theory, reinforcement learning, and the brain. *Cognitive, Affective & Behavioral Neuroscience, 8,* 429–453. doi:10.3758/CABN.8.4.429

Dayan, P., & Niv, Y. (2008). Reinforcement learning: The good, the bad and the ugly. *Current Opinion in Neurobiology, 18,* 185–196. doi:10.1016/j.conb.2008.08.003

De Houwer, J., & Beckers, T. (2002). Higher-order retrospective revaluation in human causal learning. *The Quarterly Journal of Experimental Psychology, 55B,* 137–151. doi:10.1080/02724990143000216

Dean, P. (1974). Choice reaction times for pattern discriminations in monkeys with inferotemporal lesions. *Neuropsychologia, 12,* 465–476. doi:10.1016/0028-3932(74)90076-1

DeGroot, M. H., & Schervish, M. J. (2002). *Probability and statistics.* New York: Addison Wesley.

Delamater, A. R. (1998). Associative mediational processes in the acquired equivalence and distinctiveness of cues. *Journal of Experimental Psychology. Animal Behavior Processes*, *24*, 467–482.doi:10.1037/0097-7403.24.4.467

DeMarse, T., Wagenaar, D., Blau, A., & Potter, S. (2001). The Neurally Controlled Animat: Biological Brains Acting with Simulated Bodies. *Autonomous Robots*, *11*, 305–310. doi:10.1023/A:1012407611130

Desmond, J. E. (1990). Temporally adaptative responses in neural models: The stimuli trace. In Gabriel, M., & Moore, J. (Eds.), *Learning and computational neuroscience: Foundations and adaptive networks*. Cambridge, MA: The MIT Press.

Devlin, J. T., & C.J., P. (2007). Perirhinal contributions to human visual perception. *Current Biology*, *17*(17), 1484–1488.doi:10.1016/j.cub.2007.07.066

Dickinson, A. (1980). *Contemporary animal learning theory* (1st ed.). Cambridge: Cambridge University Press.

Dickinson, A., & Burke, J. (1996). Within-compound associations mediate the retrospective revaluation of causality judgments. *Quarterly Journal of Experimental Psychology*, *49B*, 60–80.

Dickinson, A., & Balleine, B. (1994). Motivational control of goal-directed action. *Animal Learning & Behavior*, *22*, 1–18.

Dickinson, A., & Balleine, B. (2002). The role of learning in the operation of motivational systems. In H. Pashler & R. Gallistel (Eds.), *Stevens' Handbook of Experimental Psychology* (Third ed., Vol. 3: Learning, motivation, and emotion, pp. 497-533). New York: John Wiley & Sons.

Domjan, M. (2005). Pavlovian conditioning: A functional perspective. *Annual Review of Psychology*, *56*, 179–206. doi:10.1146/annurev.psych.55.090902.141409

Donegan, N. H. (1981). Priming-produced facilitation or diminution of responding to a Pavlovian unconditioned stimulus. *Journal of Experimental Psychology. Animal Behavior Processes*, *7*, 295–312. doi:10.1037/0097-7403.7.4.295

Doya, K. (2007). Reinforcement learning: Computational theory and biological mechanisms. *Human Frontiers Science Program Journal*, *1*, 30–40.

Dunsmoor, J., & Schmajuk, N. A. (2009). Interpreting patterns of brain activation in human fear conditioning with an attentional-associative learning model. *Behavioral Neuroscience*, *123*, 851–855.doi:10.1037/a0016334

Durr, V., Schmitz, J., & Cruse, H. (2004). Behaviour-based modelling of hexapod locomotion: linking biology and technical application. *Arthropod Structure & Development*, *33*, 237–250. doi:10.1016/j.asd.2004.05.004

Dwyer, D. M., Starns, J., & Honey, R. C. (2009). "Causal reasoning" in rats: A reappraisal. *Journal of Experimental Psychology. Animal Behavior Processes*, *35*, 578–586. doi:10.1037/a0015007

Eacott, M. J., Gaffan, D., & Murray, E. A. (1994). Preserved recognition memory for small sets, and impaired stimulus identification for large sets, following rhinal cortex ablations in monkeys. *The European Journal of Neuroscience*, *6*, 1466–1478.doi:10.1111/j.1460-9568.1994.tb01008.x

Eacott, M. J., & Gaffan, E. A. (2005). The roles of the perirhinal cortex, postrhinal cortex, and the fornix in memory for objects, contexts, and events in the rat. *Qaurterly Journal of Experimental Psychology*, *58B*, 202–217.doi:10.1080/02724990444000203

Edelman, G. M. (1993). Neural Darwinism: selection and reentrant signaling in higher brain function. *Neuron*, *10*(2), 115–125. doi:10.1016/0896-6273(93)90304-A

Edelman, G. M. (2007). Learning in and from brain-based devices. *Science*, *318*(5853), 1103–1105. doi:10.1126/science.1148677

Egger, M. D., & Miller, N. E. (1962). Secondary reinforcement in rats as a function of information value and reliability of the stimulus. *Journal of Experimental Psychology*, *64*, 97–104.doi:10.1037/h0040364

Ellison, G. D. (1964). Differential salivatory conditioning to traces. *Journal of Experimental Psychology*, *57*, 373–380.

Englehart, K., & Hudgins, B. (2003). A robust, real-time control scheme for multifunction myoelectric control. *IEEE Transactions on Bio-Medical Engineering, 50*(7), 848–854. Retrieved from http://ieeexplore.ieee.org/stamp/stamp.jsp?tp=&arnumber=1206493&userType=inst. doi:10.1109/TBME.2003.813539

Englehart, K., Hudgins, B., & Parker, P. (2001). A wavelet-based continuous classification scheme for multifunction myoelectric control. *IEEE Transactions on Bio-Medical Engineering, 48*(3), 302–310. Retrieved from http://ieeexplore.ieee.org/stamp/stamp.jsp?arnumber=00914793. doi:10.1109/10.914793

Englehart, K., Hudgins, B., & Parker, P. (2001). Intelligent systems and technologies in rehabilitation engineering. In Teodorrescu, H. L., & Jain, L. C. (Eds.), *Intelligent systems and technologies in rehabilitation engineering*. Boca Raton, FL: CRC Press.

Enquist, M., & Ghirlanda, S. (2005). *Neural Networks & Animal Behavior*. Princeton, NJ: Princeton University Press.

Estes, W. K. (1950). Toward a statistical theory of learning. *Psychological Review, 57*, 94–104. doi:10.1037/h0058559

Estes, W. K., & Skinner, B. F. (1941). Some quantitative properties of anxiety. *Journal of Experimental Psychology, 29*, 390–400. doi:10.1037/h0062283

EUROP. (2009). *The strategic research agenda for robotics in Europe*. Retrieved from http://www.robotics-platform.eu/

Evans, M., Hastings, N., & Peacock, B. (1993). *Statistical Distributions*. New York: Wiley.

Fanselow, M. S., & LeDoux, J. E. (1999). Why we think plasticity underlying Pavlovian fear conditioning occurs in the basolateral amygdala. *Neuron, 23*, 229–232. doi:10.1016/S0896-6273(00)80775-8

Farina, D., Pozzo, M., Merlo, E., Bottin, A., & Merletti, R. (2004). Assessment of average muscle fibber conduction velocity from surface EMG signals during fatiguing dynamic contractions. *IEEE Transactions on Bio-Medical Engineering, 51*(8), 1383–1393. Retrieved from http://ieeexplore.ieee.org/xpls/abs_all.jsp?arnumber=1315860. doi:10.1109/TBME.2004.827556

Felzer, T., & Freisleben, B. (2002). HaWCoS: the hands-free wheelchair control system. *ACM Conference on Assistive Technologies*, Scotland, (pp. 127-134). New York: ACM Press Retrieved from http://portal.acm.org/citation.cfm?id=638249.638273

Fleischer, J. G. (2007). Retrospective and prospective responses arising in a modeled hippocampus during maze navigation by a brain-based device. *Proceedings of the National Academy of Sciences of the United States of America, 104*(9), 3556–3561. doi:10.1073/pnas.0611571104

Floreano, D., & Mattiussi, C. (2008). *Bio-Inspired Artificial Intelligence*. Cambridge, MA: MIT Press.

Floreano, D., & Mattiussi, C. (2001). Evolution of Spiking Neural Controllers for Autonomous Vision-Based Robots. In Gomi, T. (Ed.), *Evolutionary Robotic: From Intelligent Robotics to Artificial Life*. Tokyo: Springer Verlag. doi:10.1007/3-540-45502-7_2

Floreano, D., Husbands, P., & Nolfi, S. (2008). Evolutionary Robotics. In Siciliano, B., & Khatib, O. (Eds.), *Springer Handbook of Robotics* (pp. 1423–1451). Berlin: Springer. doi:10.1007/978-3-540-30301-5_62

Forwood, S. E., Winters, B. D., & Bussey, T. J. (2005). Hippocampal lesions that abolish spatial maze performance spare object recognition memory at delays of up to 48 hours. *Hippocampus, 15*, 347–355. doi:10.1002/hipo.20059

Franceschini, N., Ruffier, F., & Serres, J. (2007). A bio-inspired flying robot sheds light on insect piloting abilities. *Current Biology, 17*, 329–335. doi:10.1016/j.cub.2006.12.032

Franz, M., & Mallot, H. (2000). Biomimetic robot navigation. *Robotics and Autonomous Systems, 30*, 133–153. doi:10.1016/S0921-8890(99)00069-X

Franz, M., Schölkopf, B., Mallot, H., & Bülthoff, H. (1998). Learning View Graphs for Robot Navigation. *Autonomous Robots, 5*, 111–125. doi:10.1023/A:1008821210922

Fraunhofer, I. P. A. (2009). *Care-O-Bot*. Retrieved from http://www.care-o-bot.de/english/

Fukuda, O., Tsuji, T., Kaneko, M., & Otsuka, A. (2003). A human-assisting manipulator teleoperated by emg signals and arm motions. *IEEE Transactions on Robotics and Automation, 19*(2), 210–222. Retrieved from http://ieeexplore.ieee.org/stamp/stamp.jsp?arnumber=01192150. doi:10.1109/TRA.2003.808873

Fuster, J. (2003). *Cortex and Mind*. Oxford: Oxford university Press.

Gaffan, D. (2002). Against memory systems. *Philosophical Transactions of the Royal Society of London. Series B, Biological Sciences, 357,* 1111–1121.doi:10.1098/rstb.2002.1110

Gaffan, D., & Murray, E. A. (1992). Monkeys (*Macaca fascicularis*) with rhinal cortex ablations succeed in object discrimination learning despite 24-hr intertrial intervals and fail at matching to sample despite double sample presentations. *Behavioral Neuroscience, 106,* 30–38. doi:10.1037/0735-7044.106.1.30

Gaioni, S. J. (1982). Blocking and nonsimultaneous compounds: Comparison of responding during compound conditioning and testing. *The Pavlovian Journal of Biological Science,* (January-March): 16–29.

Gallagher, J., Beer, R., Espenschiel, M., & Quinn, R. (1996). Application of evolved locomotion controllers to a hexapod robot. *Robotics and Autonomous Systems, 19*(1), 95–103. doi:10.1016/S0921-8890(96)00036-X

Gallistel, C. R., & Gibbon, J. (2000). Time, rate and conditioning. *Psychological Review, 107,* 289–344. doi:10.1037/0033-295X.107.2.289

Gallistel, C. R., & Gibbon, J. (2002). *The symbolic foundations of conditioned behavior.* Mahwah, NJ: Erlbaum Associates.

Gallistel, C. R., & Gibbon, J. (2000). Time, rate, and conditioning. *Psychological Review, 107,* 289–344. doi:10.1037/0033-295X.107.2.289

Gallistel, C. R., & King, A. P. (2009). *Memory and the Computational Brain: Why Cognitive Science Will Transform Neuroscience.* Malden, MA: Wiley-Blackwell.

Gally, J., Montague, P., Reeke, G., & Edelman, G. (1990). The NO hypothesis: possible effects of a short-lived, rapidly diffusible signal in the development and function of the nervous system. *Proceedings of the National Academy of Sciences of the United States of America, 87,* 3547–3551. doi:10.1073/pnas.87.9.3547

Garcia, J., & Koelling, R. A. (1966). Relation of cue to consequence in avoidance learning. *Psychonomic Science, 4,* 123–124.

Georgakis, A., Stergioulas, L. K., & Giakas, G. (2003). Fatigue analysis of the surface EMG signal in isometric constant force contractions using the averaged instantaneous frequency. *IEEE Transactions on Bio-Medical Engineering, 50*(2), 262–265. Retrieved from http://ieeexplore.ieee.org/stamp/stamp.jsp?tp=&arnumber=1185153&userType=inst. doi:10.1109/TBME.2002.807641

Ghirlanda, S. (2005). Retrospective revaluation as simple associative learning. *Journal of Experimental Psychology. Animal Behavior Processes, 31,* 107–111. doi:10.1037/0097-7403.31.1.107

Gibbon, J. (1977). Scalar expectancy theory and Weber's law in animal timing. *Psychological Review, 84,* 279–325. doi:10.1037/0033-295X.84.3.279

Gibbon, J., & Balsam, P. (1981). Spreading association in time. In Locurto, C. M., Terrace, H. S., & Gibbon, J. (Eds.), *Autoshaping and conditioning theory.* New York: Academic Press.

Gibson, J. J., & Gibson, E. J. (1955). Perceptual learning – differentiation or enrichment? *Psychological Review, 62,* 32–41.doi:10.1037/h0048826

Gilbert, P. E., & Kesner, R. P. (2003). Recognition memory for complex visual discriminations is influenced by stimulus interference in rodents with perirhinal cortex damage. *Learning & Memory (Cold Spring Harbor, N.Y.), 10*(6), 525–530.doi:10.1101/lm.64503

Giovannangeli, C., Gaussier, P., & Désilles, G. (2006). Robust Mapless Outdoor Vision-Based Navigation. In *Intelligent Robots and Systems, 2006 IEEE/RSJ International Conference,* (pp. 3293-3300).

Glimcher, P. W., Camerer, C. F., Fehr, E., & Poldrack, R. A. (Eds.). (2009). *Neuroeconomics: Decision making and the brain*. San Diego, CA: Academic Press.

Gluck, M. A., & Myers, C. E. (2001). *Gateway to memory: An introduction to neural network modeling of the hippocampus and learning*. Cambridge, MA: The MIT Press.

Gomez, C. (1999). *Engineering and scientific computing with scilab*. Boston, MA: Birkhäuser.

Gormezano, I., Schneiderman, N., Deaux, E., & Fuentes, I. (1962). Nictitating Membrane: Classical Conditioning and Extinction in the Albino Rabbit. *Science. New Series*, *136*, 33–34.

Gottlieb, D. A. (2008). Is the number of trials a primary determinant of conditioned responding? *Journal of Experimental Psychology. Animal Behavior Processes*, *34*, 185–201. doi:10.1037/0097-7403.34.2.185

Goulet, S., & Murray, E. A. (2001). Neural substrates of crossmodal association memory in monkeys: the amygdala versus the anterior rhinal cortex. *Behavioral Neuroscience*, *115*(2), 271–284. doi:10.1037/0735-7044.115.2.271

Grand, C., Close, J., Hale, J., & Honey, R. C. (2007). The role of similarity in human associative learning. *Journal of Experimental Psychology. Animal Behavior Processes*, *33*, 64–71. doi:10.1037/0097-7403.33.1.64

Grand, C. S., & Honey, R. C. (2008). Solving XOR. *Journal of Experimental Psychology. Animal Behavior Processes*, *34*, 486–493. doi:10.1037/0097-7403.34.4.486

Green, L., & Myerson, J. (2004). A discounting framework for choice with delayed and probabilistic rewards. *Psychological Bulletin*, *130*, 769–792. doi:10.1037/0033-2909.130.5.769

Gross, C. G., Cowey, A., & Manning, F. J. (1971). Further analysis of visual discrimination deficits following foveal prestriate and inferotemporal lesions in rhesus monkeys. *Journal of Comparative and Physiological Psychology*, *76*(1), 1–7. doi:10.1037/h0031039

Grossberg, S., & Schmajuk, N. A. (1989). Neural dynamics of adaptive timing and temporal discrimination during associative learning. *Neural Networks*, *2*, 79–102. doi:10.1016/0893-6080(89)90026-9

Grossberg, S. (1991). A neural network architecture for Pavlovian conditioning: Reinforcement, attention, forgetting, timing. In Commons, M. L., Grossberg, S., & Staddon, J. E. R. (Eds.), *Neural networks models of conditioning and action*. Hillsdale, NJ: Lawrence Erlbaum Associates.

Gulliksen, H. (1934). A rational equation of the learning curve based on Thorndike's law effect. *The Journal of General Psychology*, *11*, 395–434. doi:10.1080/00221309.1934.9917847

Gulliksen, H., & Wolfe, D. L. (1938). A theory of learning and transfer: I. *Psychometrika*, *3*, 127–149. doi:10.1007/BF02288482

Gureckis, T. M., & Love, B. C. (2009). Short-term gains, long-term pains: How cues about state aid learning in dynamic environments. *Cognition*, *113*, 293–313. doi:10.1016/j.cognition.2009.03.013

Guthrie, E. R. (1930). Conditioning as a principle of learning. *Psychological Review*, *37*, 412–428. doi:10.1037/h0072172

Hafner, V., & Moller, R. (2001). Learning of Visual Navigation Strategies. In Quoy, M. & Gaussier, P. & Wyatt, J. (Eds.), *Proceedings of the European Workshop on Learning Robots*, 1, (pp. 47-56).

Hafting, T., Fyhn, M., Molden, S., Moser, M. B., & Moser, E. I. (2005). Microstructure of a spatial map in the entorhinal cortex. [REMOVED HYPERLINK FIELD]. *Nature*, *436*, 801–806. doi:10.1038/nature03721

Hall, G. (1991). *Perceptual and associative learning*. Oxford, England: Clarendon.

Hall, G., Blair, C. A., & Artigas, A. A. (2006). Associative activation of stimulus representations restores lost salience: Implications for perceptual learning. *Journal of Experimental Psychology. Animal Behavior Processes*, *32*, 145–155. doi:10.1037/0097-7403.32.2.145

Hall, G., & Channell, S. (1985). Differential-effects of contextual change on latent inhibition and on habituation of an orienting response. *Journal of Experimental Psychology. Animal Behavior Processes, 11*, 470–481. doi:10.1037/0097-7403.11.3.470

Hall, G., & Minor, H. (1984). A search for context-stimulus associations in latent inbihition. *Quarterly Journal of Experimental Psychology: Comparative and Physiological Psychology, 36*, 145–169.

Hall, G. (2002). Associative structures in Pavlovian and instrumental conditioning. In Pashler, H., Yantis, S., Medin, D., Gallistel, R., & Wixted, J. (Eds.), *Stevens' Handbook of Experimental Psychology* (*Vol. 3*, pp. 1–45). Hoboken, NJ: John Wiley and Sons.

Hall, G., & Mondragón, E. (1998). Contextual control as occasion setting. In Schmajuk, N. A., & Holland, P. C. (Eds.), *Occasion Setting: Associative Learning and Cognition in Animals*. Washington, DC: American Psychological Association. doi:10.1037/10298-007

Hall, G. (1994). Pavlovian condition: Laws of association. In N. J. Mackintosh (Ed.) *Handbook of perception and cognition. Vol 9: Animal learning and cognition* (pp. 13-43). San Diego, CA: Academic Press.

Hampton, R. R. (2005). Monkey perirhinal cortex is critical for visual memory, but not for visual perception: Re-examination of the behavioural evidence from monkeys. *Quarterly Journal of Experimental Psychology, 58B*, 283–299.

Han, J. S., Bien, Z. Z., Kim, D. J., Lee, H. E., & Kim, J. S. (2003). Human-machine interface for wheelchair control with emg and its evaluation. In *Proceedings of IEEE International Conference on Engineering in Medicine and Biology Society*, (pp. 1602-1605). doi: 10.1109/IEMBS.2003.1279672

Harris, J. A. (2006). Elemental Representations of Stimuli in Associative Learning. *Psychological Review, 113*, 584–605. doi:10.1037/0033-295X.113.3.584

Harris, J. A., & Livesey, E. (2008). Comparing patterning and biconditional discriminations in humans. *Journal of Experimental Psychology. Animal Behavior Processes, 34*, 144–154. doi:10.1037/0097-7403.34.1.144

Harris, J. A., Livesey, E., Gharaei, S., & Westbrook, F. (2008). Negative patterning is easier than a biconditional discrimination. *Journal of Experimental Psychology. Animal Behavior Processes, 34*, 494–500. doi:10.1037/0097-7403.34.4.494

mHarris, J. A. (2010). The arguments of associations. In Schmajuk, N. A. (Ed.), *Computational Models of Classical Conditioning*. Cambridge: Academic Press.

Hartley, T., Bird, C. M., Chan, D., Cipolotti, L., Husain, M., & Vargha-Khadem, F. (2007). The hippocampus is required for short-term topographical memory in humans. *Hippocampus, 17*(1), 34–48. doi:10.1002/hipo.20240

Haselgrove, M. (2010). Reasoning Rats or Associative Animals? A Common-Element Analysis of the Effects of Additive and Subadditive Pretraining on Blocking. *Journal of Experimental Psychology. Animal Behavior Processes, 36*, 296–306. doi:10.1037/a0016603

Hastings, A., & Palmer, M. A. (2003). A bright future for biologists and mathematicians? *Science, 299*(5615), 2003–2004. doi:10.1126/science.1081522

Hebb, D. O. (1949). *The organization of behavior*. New York: Wiley & Sons.

Herrnstein, R. J. (1961). Relative and absolute strength of response as a function of frequency of reinforcement. *Journal of the Experimental Analysis of Behavior, 4*, 267–272. doi:10.1901/jeab.1961.4-267

Herrnstein, R. J. (1970). On the law of effect. *Journal of the Experimental Analysis of Behavior, 13*, 243–266. doi:10.1901/jeab.1970.13-243

Hey, T., & Allen, R. W. (Eds.). (2000). *Feynman Lectures on Computation*. Boulder, CO: Westview Press.

Higgins, C. (2004). Nondirectional motion may underlie insect behavioral dependence on image speed. *Biological Cybernetics*, *91*, 326–332. doi:10.1007/s00422-004-0519-x

Hilgard, E. R., & Campbell, A. A. (1936). The course of acquisition and retention of conditioned eyelid responses in man. *Journal of Experimental Psychology*, *19*, 227–247. doi:10.1037/h0055600

Hinson, R. E. (1982). Effects of UCS preexposure on excitatory and inhibitory rabbit eyelid conditioning: An associative effects of conditioned contextual stimuli. *Journal of Experimental Psychology. Animal Behavior Processes*, *8*, 49–61. doi:10.1037/0097-7403.8.1.49

Hinton, G. E., & Plaut, D. C. (1987). Using fast weights to deblur old memories. In *Program of the Ninth Annual Conference of the Cognitive Science Society* (pp. 177-86).

Hoehler, F. K., & Leonard, D. W. (1976). Double responding in classical nictitating membrane conditioning with single-CS, dual-ISI pairing. *The Pavlovian Journal of Biological Science*, *11*, 180–190.

Holdstock, J. S., Shaw, C., & Aggleton, J. P. (1995). The performance of amnesic subjects on tests of delayed matching-to-sample and delayed matching-to-position. *Neuropsychologia*, *33*(12), 1583–1596. doi:10.1016/0028-3932(95)00145-X

Holland, O. (2003). Exploration and High Adventure: The Legacy of Grey Walter. *Philosophical Transactions of the Royal Society of London. Series A: Mathematical and Physical Sciences*, *361*, 2085–2121. doi:10.1098/rsta.2003.1260

Holland, O. (2007). Strongly embodied approach to machine consciousness. *Journal of Consciousness Studies*, *14*(7), 97–110.

Holland, P. C. (1983). Occasion-Setting in Pavlovian Feature Positive Discriminations. In M.L. Commons, R.J. Herrnstein, & A. R. Wagner (Eds.), *Quantitative Analyses of Behavior* (4 ed., pp. 183-206). New York: Ballinger.

Honey, R. C., & Hall, G. (1989). Acquired equivalence and distinctiveness of cues. *Journal of Experimental Psychology. Animal Behavior Processes*, *16*, 178–184. doi:10.1037/0097-7403.16.2.178

Honey, R. C., & Ward-Robinson, J. (2002). Acquired equivalence and distinctiveness of cues: I. Exploring a neural network approach. *Journal of Experimental Psychology. Animal Behavior Processes*, *28*, 378–387. doi:10.1037/0097-7403.28.4.378

Honey, R. C., & Watt, A. (1998). Acquired relational equivalence: Implications for the nature of associative structures. *Journal of Experimental Psychology. Animal Behavior Processes*, *24*, 325–334. doi:10.1037/0097-7403.24.3.325

Honey, R. C., & Ward-Robinson, J. (2002). Acquired equivalence and distinctiveness of cues: I. Exploring a neural network approach. *Journal of Experimental Psychology. Animal Behavior Processes*, *28*, 378–387. doi:10.1037/0097-7403.28.4.378

Honey, R. C. (2000). The Experimental Psychology Society Prize Lecture: Associative priming in Pavlovian conditioning. *Quarterly Journal of Experimental Psychology*, *53B*, 1–23.

Honey, R. C., & Ward-Robinson, J. (2002). Acquired equivalence and distinctiveness of cues: I. Exploring a neural network approach. *Journal of Experimental Psychology. Animal Behavior Processes*, *28*, 378–387. doi:10.1037/0097-7403.28.4.378

Honey, R. C., & Watt, A. (1998). Acquired relational equivalence: implications for the nature of associative structures. *Journal of Experimental Psychology. Animal Behavior Processes*, *24*, 325–334. doi:10.1037/0097-7403.24.3.325

Honey, R. C., Close, J., & Lin, T. E. (2010). Acquired distinctiveness and equivalence: A synthesis. In Mitchell, C. J., & Le Pelley, M. E. (Eds.), *Attention and associative learning: From brain to behaviour* (pp. 159–186). Oxford: Oxford University Press.

Horáková, J., & Kelemen, J. (2008). The Robot Story: Why Robots Were Born and How They Grew Up. In Husbands, P., Holland, O., & Wheeler, M. (Eds.), *The Mechanical Mind in History* (pp. 283–306). Cambridge, MA: MIT Press.

Horn, B., & Schunck, B. (1981). Determining optical flow. *Artificial Intelligence*, *17*, 185–203. doi:10.1016/0004-3702(81)90024-2

Huang, Y., Englehart, K., Hudgins, B., & Chan, A. D. C. (2005). A gaussian mixture model based classification scheme for myoelectric control of powered upper limb prostheses. *IEEE Transactions on Bio-Medical Engineering*, *52*(11), 1801–1811. Retrieved from http://ieeexplore.ieee.org/stamp/stamp.jsp?tp=&arnumber=1519588. doi:10.1109/TBME.2005.856295

Hudgins, B., Parker, P., & Scott, R. (1993). A new strategy for multifunction myoelectric control. *IEEE Transactions on Bio-Medical Engineering*, *40*(1), 82–94.. doi:10.1109/10.204774

Hudgins, B., Parker, P., & Scott, R. (1994). Control of artificial limbs using myoelectric pattern recognition. *Medical & Life Science Engineering*, *13*, 21–38. doi:. doi:10.1016/S1350-4533(99)00066-1

Hull, C. L. (1939). The problem of stimulus equivalence in behavior theory. *Psychological Review*, *46*, 9–30. doi:10.1037/h0054032

Hull, C. L. (1943). *Principles of behavior: An introduction to behavior theory*. New York: Appleton-Century-Crofts.

Humbert, J., Conroy, J., Neely, C., & Barrows, G. (2009). Wide-Field Integration Methods for Visuomotor Control. In Floreano, D., & Zufferey, J.-C. (Eds.), *Flying Insects and Robots* (pp. 63–72). Berlin: Springer Verlag. doi:10.1007/978-3-540-89393-6_5

Husbands, P., Holland, O., & Wheeler, M. (Eds.). (2008). *The Mechanical Mind in History*. Cambridge, MA: MIT Press.

Husbands, P., Philippides, A., Vargas, P., Buckley, C., Fine, P., Di Paolo, E., & O'Shea, M. (in press). Spatial, temporal and modulatory factors affecting GasNet evolvability in a visually guided robotics task. *Complexity*.

Husbands, P., Smith, T., Jakobi, N., & O'Shea, M. (1998). Better Living through Chemistry: Evolving GasNets for Robot Control. *Connection Science*, *10*(3&4), 185–210. doi:10.1080/095400998116404

Husbands, P., & Holland, O. (2008). The Ratio Club: A Hub of British Cybernetics. In P. Husbands, O. Holland & M. Wheeler, *2008*, (pp. 91-148).

Ijspeert, A., Crespi, A., Ryczko, D., & Cabelguen, J.-M. (2007). From Swimming to Walking with a Salamander Robot Driven by a Spinal Cord Model. *Science*, *315*(5817), 1416–1420. doi:10.1126/science.1138353

International Federation of Robotics. (2009). *World Robotics: Service Robots 2009*. Retrieved from http://www.worldrobotics.org/

Ito, M., & Doya, K. (2009). Validation of decision-making models and analysis of decision variables in the rat basal ganglia. *The Journal of Neuroscience*, *29*, 9861–9874. doi:10.1523/JNEUROSCI.6157-08.2009

Iversen, S. D., & Humphrey, N. K. (1971). Ventral temporal lobe lesions and visual oddity performance. *Brain Research*, *30*(2), 253–263. doi:10.1016/0006-8993(71)90077-1

Iwai, E., & Mishkin, M. (1968). Two visual foci in the temporal lobe of monkeys. In Yoshii, N., & Buchwald, N. (Eds.), *Neurophysiological basis of learning and behavior* (pp. 1–11). Japan: Osaka University Press.

Jakobi, N. (1998). Running across the reality gap: Octopod locomotion evolved in a minimal simulation. In P. Husbands & J.-A. Meyer, (Eds), *Evolutionary Robotics: First European Workshop, EvoRobot98* (pp. 39–58). Berlin: Springer.

James, W. (1890). *The principles of psychology*. New York: Holt.

Jenkins, H. M., & Moore, B. R. (1973). The form of autoshaped response with food or water reinforcers. *Journal of the Experimental Analysis of Behavior, 20*, 163–181. doi:10.1901/jeab.1973.20-163

Jennings, D. J., Bonardi, C., & Kirkpatrick, K. (2007). Overshadowing and stimulus duration. *Journal of Experimental Psychology. Animal Behavior Processes, 33*, 464–475. doi:10.1037/0097-7403.33.4.464

Jennings, D. J., & Kirkpatrick, K. (2006). Interval duration effects on blocking in appetitive conditioning. *Behavioural Processes, 71*, 318–329. doi:10.1016/j.beproc.2005.11.007

Joel, D., Niv, Y., & Ruppin, E. (2002). Actor-critic models of the basal ganglia: New anatomical and computational perspectives. *Neural Networks, 15*, 535–547. doi:10.1016/S0893-6080(02)00047-3

Jordan, W. P., Strasser, H. C., & McHale, L. (2000). Contextual control of long-term habituation in rats. *Journal of Experimental Psychology. Animal Behavior Processes, 26*, 323–339. doi:10.1037/0097-7403.26.3.323

Jozefowiez, J., Staddon, J. E., & Cerutti, D. T. (2009). The behavioral economics of choice and interval timing. *Psychological Review, 116*, 519–539. doi:10.1037/a0016171

Kaelbling, L. P., Littman, M. L., & Moore, A. W. (1996). Reinforcement learning: A survey. *Journal of Artificial Intelligence, 4*, 237–285.

Kahneman, D., & Tversky, A. (1979). Prospect theory: An analysis of decision under risk. *Econometrica, 47*, 263–292. doi:10.2307/1914185

Kalat, J. W., & Rozin, P. (1973). Learned-safety as a mechanism in long-delay taste-aversion learning in rats. *Journal of Comparative and Physiological Psychology, 83*, 198–207. doi:10.1037/h0034424

Kamin, L. J., & Schaub, R. E. (1963). Effects of conditioned stimulus intensity on the conditioned emotional response. *Journal of Comparative and Physiological Psychology, 56*, 502–507. doi:10.1037/h0046616

Kamin, L. J. (1969). Predictability, surprise, attention and conditioning. In Campbell, B. A., & Church, R. M. (Eds.), *Punishment and aversive behavior* (pp. 279–296). New York: Appleton-Century-Crofts.

Kamin, L. J. (1968). "Attention-like" processes in classical conditioning. In M. R. Jones (Ed.), *Miami Symposium on the Prediction of Behavior: Aversive Stimulation* (pp. 9-33). Miami, FL: University of Miami Press.

Kantz, H., & Schreiber, T. (1997). *Nonlinear time series analysis*. Cambridge, UK: Cambridge University Press.

Kantz, H., & Schreiber, T. (2003). Tisean—nonlinear time series analysis. Retrieved from http://www.mpipkd-dresden.mpg.de/tisean.

Kaplan, D., & Glass, D. (1995). *Understanding nonlinear dynamics*. New York, NY: Springer Verlag.

Karlsson, S., Yu, J., & Akay, M. (2000). Time-frequency analysis of myoelectric signals during dynamic contractions: a comparative study. *IEEE Transactions on Bio-Medical Engineering, 47*(2), 228–238. Retrieved from http://ieeexplore.ieee.org/stamp/stamp.jsp?tp=&arnumber=821766. doi:10.1109/10.821766

Katz, P. (Ed.). (1999). *Beyond Neurotransmission: Neuromodulation and its Importance for Information Processing*. Oxford, UK: Oxford University Press.

Kehoe, E. J., Graham-Clarke, P., & Schreurs, B. G. (1989). Temporal patterns of the rabbit's nictitating membrane response to compound and components stimuli under mixed CS-US intervals. *Behavioral Neuroscience, 103*, 283–295. doi:10.1037/0735-7044.103.2.283

Kehoe, E. J. (1990). Classical conditioning: Fundamental issues for adaptative network models. In Gabriel, M., & Moore, J. W. (Eds.), *Learning and computational neuroscience: Foundations of adaptative networks*. Cambridge, MA: The MIT Press.

Kennel, M., & Isabelle, S. (1992). Method to distinguish possible chaos from colored noise and to determine embedding parameters. *Physical Review A., 46*, 3111–3118. doi:10.1103/PhysRevA.46.3111

Kennel, M. B., Brown, R., & Abarbanel, H. D. I. (1992). Determining embedding dimension for phase-space reconstruction using a geometrical construction. *Physical Review A.*, *45*, 3403–3411. doi:10.1103/PhysRevA.45.3403

Kennerley, S. W., & Wallis, J. D. (2009). Evaluating choices by single neurons in the frontal lobe: Outcome value encoded across multiple decision variables. *The European Journal of Neuroscience*, *29*, 2061–2073. doi:10.1111/j.1460-9568.2009.06743.x

Kikuchi, R., & Iwai, E. (1980). The locus of the posterior subdivision of the inferotemporal visual learning area in the monkey. *Brain Research*, *198*(2), 347–360. doi:10.1016/0006-8993(80)90749-0

Killeen, P. R., & Fetterman, J. G. (1988). A behavioral theory of timing. *Psychological Review*, *95*, 274–285. doi:10.1037/0033-295X.95.2.274

Kim, H., Sul, J. H., Huh, N., Lee, D., & Jung, M. W. (2009). The role of striatum in updating values of chosen actions. *The Journal of Neuroscience*, *29*, 14701–14712. doi:10.1523/JNEUROSCI.2728-09.2009

Kimble, G. A., & Ost, J. W. P. (1961). A conditioned inhibitory process in eyelid conditioning. *Journal of Experimental Psychology*, *61*, 150–156. doi:10.1037/h0044932

Kimmel, H. D. (1965). Instrumental inhibitory factors in classical conditioning. In Prokasy, W. F. (Ed.), *Classical conditioning: A symposium. New-York*. Appleton-Century-Crofts.

Kirkpatrick, K., & Church, R. M. (1998). Are separate theories of conditioning and timing necessary? *Behavioural Processes*, *44*, 163–182. doi:10.1016/S0376-6357(98)00047-3

Kirkpatrick, K., & Church, R. M. (2000). Stimulus and temporal cues in classical conditioning. *Journal of Experimental Psychology. Animal Behavior Processes*, *26*, 206–219. doi:10.1037/0097-7403.26.2.206

Kirkpatrick, K., & Church, R. M. (2003). Tracking of the expected time to reinforcement in temporal conditioning procedures. *Learning & Behavior*, *31*, 3–21.

Kirkpatrick, K., & Church, R. M. (1998). Are separate theories of conditioning and timing necessary? *Behavioural Processes*, *44*, 163–182. doi:10.1016/S0376-6357(98)00047-3

Knutson, B., Taylor, J., Kaufman, M., Peterson, R., & Glover, G. (2005). Distributed neural representation of expected value. *The Journal of Neuroscience*, *25*, 4806–4812. doi:10.1523/JNEUROSCI.0642-05.2005

Kodjabachian, J., & Meyer, J.-A. (1998). Evolution and development of neural networks controlling locomotion, gradient following and obstacle avoidance in artificial insects. *IEEE Transactions on Neural Networks*, *9*, 796–812. doi:10.1109/72.712153

Kohler, W. (1947). *Gestalt psychology*. New York: Liverright.

Kohler, E. A., & Ayres, J. J. B. (1982). Blocking with serial and simultaneous compounds in a trace conditioning procedure. *Animal Learning & Behavior*, *10*, 277–287.

Kohler, M., & Wehner, R. (2005). Idiosyncratic route-based memories in desert ants, melophorus bagoti: How do they interact with path-integration vectors? *Neurobiology of Learning and Memory*, *83*, 1–12. doi:10.1016/j.nlm.2004.05.011

Kolter, J. Z., & Ng, A. Y. (2009). Near-bayesian exploration in polynomial time. *International Conference on Machine Learning*, *26*, 513–520.

Konorski, J. (1948). *Conditioning reflexes and neuron organization*. Cambridge, UK: University Press.

Konorski, J. (1967). *Integrative activity of the brain: An interdisciplinary approach*. Chicago: Chicago University Press.

Krapp, H., & Hengstenberg, R. (1996). Estimation of self-motion by optic flow processing in a single visual interneuron. *Nature*, *384*, 463–466. doi:10.1038/384463a0

Krichmar, J. L., & Edelman, G. M. (2002). Machine psychology: autonomous behavior, perceptual categorization and conditioning in a brain-based device. *Cereb Cortex*, *12*(8), 818–830. doi:10.1093/cercor/12.8.818

Krichmar, J. L., & Edelman, G. M. (2005). Brain-based devices for the study of nervous systems and the development of intelligent machines. *Artificial Life*, *11*(1-2), 63–77. doi:10.1162/1064546053278946

Kruschke, J. K., & Blair, N. J. (2000). Blocking and backward blocking involve learned inattention. *Psychonomic Bulletin & Review*, *7*, 636–645.

Kundey, S. M., & Wagner, A. R. (2004). *Further test of elemental versus configural models of Pavlovian conditioning*. Paper presented at the meetings of the Comparative Cognition Society, Melbourne Florida.

Kurth-Nelson, Z., & Redish, A. D. (2009). Temporal-difference reinforcement learning with distributed representations. *PLoS ONE*, *4*, e7362. doi:10.1371/journal.pone.0007362

Lambrinos, D., Möller, R., Pfeifer, R., Wehner, R., & Labhart, T. (2000). A Mobile Robot Employing Insect Strategies for Navigation. *Robotics and Autonomous Systems*, *30*, 39–64. doi:10.1016/S0921-8890(99)00064-0

Lanuza, E., Moncho-Bogani, J., & LeDoux, J. E. (2008). Unconditioned stimulus pathways to the amygdala: Effects of lesions of the posterior intralaminar thalamus on foot-shock-induced c-Fos expression in the subdivisions of the later amygdala. *Neuroscience*, *155*, 959–968. doi:10.1016/j.neuroscience.2008.06.028

Larrauri, J. A., & Schmajuk, N. A. (2008). Attentional, associative, and configural mechanisms in extinction. *Psychological Review*, *115*, 640–676. doi:10.1037/0033-295X.115.3.640

Lau, B., & Glimcher, P. W. (2005). Dynamic response-by-response models of matching behavior in rhesus monkeys. *Journal of the Experimental Analysis of Behavior*, *84*, 555–579. doi:10.1901/jeab.2005.110-04

Le Pelley, M. E., & McLaren, I. P. L. (2001). Retrospective revaluation in humans: Learning or memory? *Quarterly Journal of Experimental Psychology*, *54B*, 311–352.

Le Pelley, M. E., & McLaren, I. P. L. (2003). Learned associability and associative change in human causal learning. *Quarterly Journal of Experimental Psychology*, *56B*, 56–67.

Le Pelley, M. E., Oakeshott, S. M., & McLaren, I. P. L. (2005). Blocking and unblocking in humans. *Journal of Experimental Psychology. Animal Behavior Processes*, *31*, 56–70. doi:10.1037/0097-7403.31.1.56

Le Pelley, M. E., Oakeshott, S. M., Wills, A. J., & McLaren, I. P. L. (2005). The outcome-specificity of learned predictiveness effects: Parallels between human causal learning and animal conditioning. *Journal of Experimental Psychology. Animal Behavior Processes*, *31*, 226–236. doi:10.1037/0097-7403.31.2.226

Le Pelley, M. E., Cutler, D. L., & McLaren, I. P. L. (2000). Retrospective effects in human causality judgment. In *Proceedings of the Twenty-second Annual Conference of the Cognitive Science Society* (pp. 782–787). Hillsdale, NJ: Lawrence Erlbaum Associates, Inc.

LeCun, Y., Bottou, L., Bengio, Y., & Haffner, P. (1998). Gradient-based learning applied to document recognition. *Proceedings of the IEEE*, *86*, 2278–2324. doi:10.1109/5.726791

Lee, A. C., Bandelow, S., Schwarzbauer, C., Henson, R. N., & Graham, K. S. (2006). Perirhinal cortex activity during visual object discrimination: an event-related fMRI study. *NeuroImage*, *33*(1), 362–373. doi:10.1016/j.neuroimage.2006.06.021

Lee, A. C., Buckley, M. J., Gaffan, D., Emery, T., Hodges, J. R., & Graham, K. S. (2006). Differentiating the roles of the hippocampus and perirhinal cortex in processes beyond long-term declarative memory: a double dissociation in dementia. *The Journal of Neuroscience*, *26*(19), 5198–5203. doi:10.1523/JNEUROSCI.3157-05.2006

Lee, A. C., Buckley, M. J., Pegman, S. J., Spiers, H., Scahill, V. L., & Gaffan, D. (2005). Specialization in the medial temporal lobe for processing of objects and scenes. *Hippocampus*, *15*(6), 782–797. doi:10.1002/hipo.20101

Lee, A. C., Levi, N., Davies, R. R., Hodges, J. R., & Graham, K. S. (2007). Differing profiles of face and scene discrimination deficits in semantic dementia and Alzheimer's disease. *Neuropsychologia*, *45*(9), 2135–2146. doi:10.1016/j.neuropsychologia.2007.01.010

Lee, A. C., Scahill, V. L., & Graham, K. S. (2008). Activating the medial temporal lobe during oddity judgment for faces and scenes. *Cerebral Cortex*, *18*(3), 683–696. doi:10.1093/cercor/bhm104

Lehrer, M., & Bianco, G. (2000). The turn-back-and-look behaviour: bee versus robot. *Biological Cybernetics*, *83*(3), 211–229. doi:10.1007/s004220000165

Levy, D. A., Shrager, Y., & Squire, L. R. (2005). Intact visual discrimination of complex and feature-ambiguous stimuli in the absence of perirhinal cortex. *Learning & Memory (Cold Spring Harbor, N.Y.)*, *12*(1), 61–66. doi:10.1101/lm.84405

Lewis, F., Jagannathan, S., & Yesildirek, A. (1999). *Neural Network Control of Robot manipulators and Nonlinear Systems*. London: Taylor & Francis.

Livesey, E. J., & Boakes, R. A. (2004). Outcome additivity, elemental processing and blocking in human causality judgments. *The Quarterly Journal of Experimental Psychology. B, Comparative and Physiological Psychology*, *57*, 361–379.doi:10.1080/02724990444000005

Loewenstein, Y., Prelec, D., & Seung, H. S. (2009). Operant matching as a Nash equilibrium of an intertemporal game. *Neural Computation*, *21*, 2755–2773. doi:10.1162/neco.2009.09-08-854

Logothetis, N. K., Pauls, J., Augath, M., Trinath, T., & Oeltermann, A. (2001). Neurophysiological investigation of the basis of the fMRI signal. *Nature*, *412*, 150–157. doi:10.1038/35084005

Lovibond, P. E., Been, S. L., Mitchell, C. J., Bouton, M. E., & Frohardt, R. (2003). Forward and backward blocking of causal judgment is enhanced by additivity of effect magnitude. *Memory & Cognition*, *31*, 133–142.

Lubow, R. E., & Moore, A. U. (1959). Latent inhibition: The effect of non-reinforced preexposure to the conditional stimulus. *Journal of Comparative and Physiological Psychology*, *52*, 415–419.doi:10.1037/h0046700

Lubow, R. E. (1989). *Latent Inhibition and Conditioned Attention Theory*. Cambridge, UK: Cambridge University Press. doi:10.1017/CBO9780511529849

Ludvig, E. A., & Koop, A. (2008). Learning to generalize through predictive representations: A computational model of mediated conditioning. In *From Animals to Animats. Proceedings of Simulation of Adaptive Behavior*, *10*, 342–351.

Ludvig, E. A., Sutton, R. S., & Kehoe, E. J. (2008). Stimulus representation and the timing of reward-prediction errors in models of the dopamine system. *Neural Computation*, *20*, 3034–3054. doi:10.1162/neco.2008.11-07-654

Ludvig, E. A., Sutton, R. S., Verbeek, E. L., & Kehoe, E. J. (2009). A computational model of hippocampal function in trace conditioning. *Advances in Neural Information Processing Systems*, *21*, 993–1000.

Ludwig, I., & Lachnit, H. (2003). Asymmetric interference in patterning discriminations: A case of modulated attention. *Biological Psychology*, *62*, 133–146. doi:10.1016/S0301-0511(02)00124-2

Machado, A. (1997). Learning the temporal dynamics of behavior. *Psychological Review*, *104*, 241–265. doi:10.1037/0033-295X.104.2.241

MacIsaac, D., & Englehart, K. (2006). The science in science fiction artificial men. *Journal of Defence Software Engineering*, *19*(10), 4–8. Retrieved from http://handle.dtic.mil/100.2/ADA487418.

MacIsaac, D. T., Parker, P., Englehart, K., & Rogers, D. R. (2006). Fatigue estimation with a multivariable myoelectric mapping function. *IEEE Transactions on Bio-Medical Engineering*, *53*(4), 694–700. Retrieved from http://ieeexplore.ieee.org/stamp/stamp.jsp?arnumber=01608519. doi:10.1109/TBME.2006.870220

Mackintosh, N. J. (1974). *The psychology of animal learning*. London: Academic Press.

Mackintosh, N. J. (1975). A theory of attention: Variations in the associability of stimuli with reinforcement. *Psychological Review*, *82*, 276–298.doi:10.1037/h0076778

Mackintosh, N. J. (1976). Overshadowing and stimulus intensity. *Animal Learning & Behavior*, *4*, 186–192.

Mackintosh, N. J., & Turner, C. (1971). Blocking as a function of novelty of CS and predictability of UCS. *The Quarterly Journal of Experimental Psychology, 23,* 359–366.doi:10.1080/14640747108400245

Mackintosh, N. J. (1975). A theory of attention: Variations in the associability of stimuli with reinforcement. *Psychological Review, 82,* 276–298. doi:10.1037/h0076778

Maei, H. R., Szepesvari, C., Bhatnagar, S., Precup, D., Silver, D., & Sutton, R. S. (2009). Convergent temporal-difference learning with arbitrary smooth function approximation. *Advances in Neural Information Processing Systems, 21,* 1609–1616.

Mahoney, W. J., & Ayres, J. J. B. (1976). One-trial simultaneous and backward fear conditioning as reflected in conditioned suppression of licking in rats. *Animal Learning & Behavior, 4,* 357–362.

Maia, T. V. (2009). Reinforcement learning, conditioning, and the brain: Successes and challenges. *Cognitive, Affective & Behavioral Neuroscience, 9,* 343–364. doi:10.3758/CABN.9.4.343

Maki, W. S., & Abunawass, A. M. (1991). A connectionist approach to conditional discriminations: Learning, short-term memory, and attention. In Commons, M. L., Grossberg, S., & Staddon, J. E. R. (Eds.), *Quantitative analysis of behavior: Neural network models of conditioning and action* (pp. 241–278). Hillsdale, NJ: Erlbaum.

Maki, W. S. (1993). From elementary associations to animal cognition: Connectionist models of discrimination learning. In Zentall, T. R. (Ed.), *Animal Cognition: A tribute to Donald A. Riley* (pp. 293–312). Hillsdale, NJ: Erlbaum.

Manns, J. R., Stark, C. E., & Squire, L. R. (2000). The visual paired-comparison task as a measure of declarative memory. *Proceedings of the National Academy of Sciences of the United States of America, 97*(22), 12375–12379. doi:10.1073/pnas.220398097

Marr, D., & Poggio, T. (1977). From understanding computation to understanding neural circuitry. *Neurosciences Research Program Bulletin, 15,* 470–488.

Marr, D. C. (1982). *Vision: A Computational Investigation into the Human Representation and Processing of Visual Information.* New York: Freeman.

Marsh, B., & Kacelnik, A. (2002). Framing effects and risky decisions in starlings. *Proceedings of the National Academy of Sciences of the United States of America, 99,* 3352–3355. doi:10.1073/pnas.042491999

Matarić, M. (1992). Integration of Representation Into Goal-Driven Behavior-Based Robots. *IEEE Transactions on Robotics and Automation, 8*(3), 304–312. doi:10.1109/70.143349

Mauk, M. D., Medina, J. F., Nores, W. L., & Ohyama, T. (2000). Cerebella function: coordination, learning or timing. *Current Biology, 10,* 522–525. doi:10.1016/S0960-9822(00)00584-4

Mauk, M. D., & Ruiz, B. P. (1992). Learning-dependent timing of Pavlovian eyelid responses: Differential conditioning using multiple interstimulus. *Behavioral Neuroscience, 106,* 666–681. doi:10.1037/0735-7044.106.4.666

McCall, R. B. (1970). *Fundamentals of statistics for psychology.* New York: Harcourt Brace Jovanovich.

McCarthy, J., Minsky, M. L., Rochester, N., & Shannon, C. E. (1955). (2006). A proposal for the Dartmouth summer research project on artificial intelligence. *AI Magazine, 27,* 12–14.

McClelland, J. L., & Rumelhart, D. E. (Eds.). (1986). *Parallel Distributed Processing: Explorations in the Microstructure of Cognition* (*Vol. 2*). Cambridge, MA: MIT Press.

McCloskey, M., & Cohen, N. J. (1989). Catastrophic interference in connectionist networks: The sequential learning problem. *Psychology of Learning and Motivation, 24,* 109–166. doi:10.1016/S0079-7421(08)60536-8

McDowell, J. J. (2004). A computational model of selection by consequences. *Journal of the Experimental Analysis of Behavior, 81,* 297–317. doi:10.1901/jeab.2004.81-297

McHale, G., & Husbands, P. (2004). GasNets and other evovalble neural networks applied to bipedal locomotion. In S. Schaal et al. (Eds), *From Animals to Animats 8: Proceedings of the Eigth International Conference on Simulation of Adaptive Behaviour (SAB'2004)* (pp. 163-172). Cambridge, MA: MIT Press.

McKinstry, J. L. (2008). Embodied models of delayed neural responses: spatiotemporal categorization and predictive motor control in brain based devices. *Neural Networks, 21*(4), 553–561. doi:10.1016/j.neunet.2008.01.004

McKinstry, J. L., Edelman, G. M., & Krichmar, J. L. (2006). A cerebellar model for predictive motor control tested in a brain-based device. *Proceedings of the National Academy of Sciences of the United States of America, 103*(9), 3387–3392. doi:10.1073/pnas.0511281103

McLaren, I. P. L., & Mackintosh, N. J. (2002). Associative learning and elemental representation: II. Generalization and discrimination. *Animal Learning & Behavior, 30,* 177–200.

McLaren, I. P. L., & Mackintosh, N. J. (2000). An elemental model of associative learning: I. Latent inhibition and perceptual learning. *Animal Learning & Behavior, 38,* 211–246.

McLaren, I. P. L., & Dickinson, A. (1990). The conditioning connection. *Philosophical Transactions of the Royal Society of London. Series B, Biological Sciences, 329,* 179–186. doi:10.1098/rstb.1990.0163

McLaren, I. P. L. (1994). Representation development in associative systems. In Hogan, J. A., & Bolhuis, J. J. (Eds.), *Causal mechanisms of behavioural development* (pp. 377–402). Cambridge, UK: Cambridge University Press. doi:10.1017/CBO9780511565120.018

McLaren, I. P. L. (1993). APECS: A solution to the sequential learning problem. In *Proceedings of the XVth Annual Convention of the Cognitive Science Society,* (pp. 717–722).

Melchers, K. G., Lachnit, H., Üngör, M., & Shanks, D. R. (2005). Past experience can influence whether the whole is different from the sum of its parts. *Learning and Motivation, 36,* 20–41. doi:10.1016/j.lmot.2004.06.002

Merletti, R., Farina, D., & Rainoldi, A. (2004). Myoelectric manifestations of muscle fatigue. In Kumar, S. (Ed.), *Muscle Strength.* Boca Raton, FL: CRC Press.

Meunier, M., Bachevalier, J., Mishkin, M., & Murray, E. A. (1993). Effects on visual recognition of combined and separate ablations of the entorhinal and perirhinal cortex in rhesus monkeys. *The Journal of Neuroscience, 13,* 5418–5432.

Meyer, J. A., Guillot, A., Girard, B., Khamassi, M., Pirim, P., & Berthoz, A. (2005). The Psikharpax project: Towards building an artificial rat. *Robotics and Autonomous Systems, 50*(4), 211–223. doi:10.1016/j.robot.2004.09.018

Milford, M., & Wyeth, G. (2008). Mapping a Suburb with a Single Camera using a Biologically Inspired SLAM System. *IEEE Transactions on Robotics, 24*(5), 1038–1053. doi:10.1109/TRO.2008.2004520

Milford, M., Wyeth, G., & Prasser, D. (2004). RatSLAM: A Hippocampal Model for Simultaneous Localization and Mapping. *Proc. IEEE International Conference on Robotics and Automation* (pp. 403-408). Pasadena, CA: IEEE Press.

Millenson, J. R., Kehoe, E. J., & Gormezano, I. (1977). Classical-conditioning of rabbits nictitating-membrane response under fixed and mixed CS-US intervals. *Learning and Motivation, 8,* 351–366. doi:10.1016/0023-9690(77)90057-1

Miller, N. E., & Dollard, J. (1941). *Social learning and imitation.* London: Kegan Paul, Trench, Trubner & Co.

Miller, R. R., & Matute, H. (1996). Biological significance in forward and backward blocking: Resolution of a discrepancy between animal conditioning and human causal judgment. *Journal of Experimental Psychology. General, 125,* 370–386. doi:10.1037/0096-3445.125.4.370

Miller, R. R., Barnet, R. C., & Grahame, N. J. (1995). Assessment of the Rescorla-Wagner Model. *Psychological Bulletin, 117,* 363–386. doi:10.1037/0033-2909.117.3.363

Miller, R. R., & Matzel, L. (1988). The comparator hypothesis: A response rule for the expression of associations. In Bower, G. H. (Ed.), *The psychology of learning and motivation* (*Vol. 22*, pp. 51–92). Orlando, FL: Academic Press.

Minsky, M. L., & Papert, S. A. (1969). *Perceptrons: An introduction to computational geometry*. Cambridge, MA: MIT Press.

Mishkin, M. (1982). A memory system in the monkey. [Biology]. *Philosophical Transactions of the Royal Society of London*, *298*, 83–95. doi:10.1098/rstb.1982.0074

Mitchell, C. J., Lovibond, P. F., & Condoleon, M. (2005). Evidence for deductive reasoning in blocking of causal judgments. *Learning and Motivation*, *36*, 77–87. doi:10.1016/j.lmot.2004.09.001

Mitchell, T. (1997). *Machine learning*. Burr Ridge, IL: McGraw Hill.

Mitchie, D., Spiegelhalter, D. I., & Taylor, C. C. (Eds.). Elder, J.F., IV. (Rev) (1994). Machine Learning, Neural, and Statistical Classification. *Journal of the American Statistical Association, 91*, 436-438.

Möller, R. (2001). Do Insects Use Templates or Parameters for Landmark Navigation. *Journal of Theoretical Biology*, *210*(1), 33–45. doi:10.1006/jtbi.2001.2295

Möller, R., & Vardy, A. (2006). Local visual homing by matched-filter descent in image distances. *Biological Cybernetics*, *95*(5), 413–430. doi:10.1007/s00422-006-0095-3

Möller, R. (2000). Modelling the Landmark Navigation Behavior of the Desert Ant *Cataglyphis*. Technical Report IFI-AI-00.24, Artificial Intelligence Lab, Dept. Computer Science, University of Zurich. Zurich.

Mondragón, E., Bonardi, C., & Hall, G. (2003). Negative priming and occasion setting in an appetitive Pavlovian procedure. *Learning & Behavior*, *31*, 281–291.

Monsell, S., Patterson, K. E., Tallon, J., & Hill, J. (1989). *Voluntary surface dyslexia: A new argument for two processes in reading?* Paper presented at the January meeting of the Experimental Psychology Society, London.

Montague, P. R., Dayan, P., & Sejnowski, T. J. (1996). A framework for mesencephalic dopamine systems based on predictive Hebbian learning. *The Journal of Neuroscience*, *16*, 1936–1947.

Moon, I., Lee, M., Chu, J., & Mun, M. (2005). Wearable emg-based hci for electric-powered wheelchair users with motor disabilities. In *Proceedings of IEEE International Conference on Robotics and Automation*, (pp. 2649-2654). Retrieved from http://ieeexplore.ieee.org/xpl/mostRecentIssue.jsp?punumber=10495

Moore, J. W., Desmond, J. E., & Berthier, N. E. (1989). Adaptively timed conditioned-responses and the cerebellum: A neural network approach. *Biological Cybernetics*, *62*, 17–28. doi:10.1007/BF00217657

Moore, J. W., & Stickney, K. J. (1980). Formation of attentional-associative networks in real-time - role of the hippocampus and implications for conditioning. *Physiological Psychology*, *8*, 207–217.

Moore, G. E. (1965, April 19). Cramming more components onto integrated circuits. *Electronics Magazine*, *38*(8), 4.

Moore, G. E. (1975). Progress in digital integrated electronics. *International Electron Devices Meeting*, 21, 11-13.

Morris, G., Nevet, A., Arkadir, D., Vaadia, E., & Bergman, H. (2006). Midbrain dopamine neurons encode decisions for future action. *Nature Neuroscience*, *9*, 1057–1063. doi:10.1038/nn1743

Morris, R. (1984). Developments of a water-maze procedure for studying spatial learning in the rat. *Journal of Neuroscience Methods*, *11*(1), 47–60. doi:10.1016/0165-0270(84)90007-4

Morris, R. G. M. (1994). The neural Basis of Learning with particular Reference to the Role of Synaptic Plasticity: Where Are We a Century after Cajal's Speculations? In Mackintosh, N. J. (Ed.), *Animal Learning and Cognition* (pp. 135–183). San Diego, CA: Academic Press.

Moss, H. E., Rodd, J. M., Stamatakis, E. A., Bright, P., & Tyler, L. K. (2005). Anteromedial temporal cortex supports fine-grained differentiation among objects. *Cereb Cortex*, *15*(5), 616–627. doi:10.1093/cercor/bhh163

Mumby, D. G., & Pinel, J. P. (1994). Rhinal cortex lesions and object recognition in rats. *Behavioral Neuroscience*, *108*(1), 11–18. doi:10.1037/0735-7044.108.1.11

Mundy, M. E., Honey, R. C., & Dwyer, D. M. (2007). Simultaneous presentation of similar stimuli produces perceptual learning in human picture processing. *Journal of Experimental Psychology. Animal Behavior Processes*, *33*, 124–138. doi:10.1037/0097-7403.33.2.124

Murray, E. A., & Bussey, T. J. (1999). Perceptual-mnemonic functions of perirhinal cortex. *Trends in Cognitive Sciences*, *3*, 142–151. doi:10.1016/S1364-6613(99)01303-0

Murray, E. A. (2000). Memory for objects in nonhuman primates. In Gazzaniga, M. S. (Ed.), *The new cognitive neurosciences*. London: The MIT Press.

Murray, E. A., Málková, L., & Goulet, S. (1998). Cross-modal associations, intramodal associations, and object identification in macaque monkeys. In Milner, A. D. (Ed.), *Comparative Neuropsychology* (pp. 51–69). Oxford: Oxford University Press.

Nehmzow, U. (2009). *Robot behaviour: Design, description, analysis and modelling*. London, UK: Springer Verlag.

Nehmzow, U., & Walker, K. (2005). Quantitative description of robot-environment interaction using chaos theory. *Robotics and Autonomous Systems*, *53*, 177–193. doi:10.1016/j.robot.2005.09.009

Nehmzow, U., & Owen, C. (2000). Robot Navigation in the Real World: Experiments with Manchester's *FortyTwo* in Unmodified, Large Environments. *Robotics and Autonomous Systems*, *33*, 223–242. doi:10.1016/S0921-8890(00)00098-1

Nilsson, N. J. (Ed.). (1984). *Shakey The Robot, Technical Note 323. AI Center, SRI International, Menlo Park CA., Nolfi, S., & Floreano, D. (2000) Evolutionary Robotics: The Biology, Intelligence, and Technology of Self-Organizing Machines*. Cambridge, MA: MIT Press.

Niv, Y. (2009). Reinforcement learning in the brain. *Journal of Mathematical Psychology*, *53*, 139–154. doi:10.1016/j.jmp.2008.12.005

Niv, Y., Daw, N. D., & Dayan, P. (2005). How fast to work: Response vigor, motivation and tonic dopamine. *Advances in Neural Information Processing Systems*, *18*, 1019–1026.

Niv, Y., & Schoenbaum, G. (2008). Dialogues on prediction errors. *Trends in Cognitive Sciences*, *12*, 265–272. doi:10.1016/j.tics.2008.03.006

Nixon, P. D. (2003). The role of the cerebellum in preparing responses to predictable sensory events. *Cerebellum (London, England)*, *2*, 114–122. doi:10.1080/14734220309410

Noether, E. A. (1918). Invariante variationsprobleme, *Nachr. v. d. Ges. d. Wiss. zu Götingen* 1918, 235-257. English translation: M.A. Tavel, Reprinted from "Transport Theory and Statistical Mechanics" 1(3), 183-207 (1971).

Norman, G., & Eacott, M. J. (2004). Impaired object recognition with increasing levels of feature ambiguity in rats with perirhinal cortex lesions. *Behavioural Brain Research*, *148*(1-2), 79–91. doi:10.1016/S0166-4328(03)00176-1

Norman, K. A., & O'Reilly, R. C. (2003). Modeling hippocampal and neocortical contributions to recognition memory: a complementary-learning-systems approach. *Psychological Review*, *110*(4), 611–646. doi:10.1037/0033-295X.110.4.611

O'Doherty, J., Dayan, P., Schultz, J., Deichmann, R., Friston, K., & Dolan, R. J. (2004). Dissociable roles of ventral and dorsal striatum in instrumental conditioning. *Science*, *304*, 452–454. doi:10.1126/science.1094285

O'Reilly, R. C. (1998). Six Principles for Biological Based Computational Models of Cortical Cognition. *Trends in Cognitive Sciences*, *2*(11), 455–462. doi:10.1016/S1364-6613(98)01241-8

Osterrieth, P. (1944). Filetest de copie d'une figure complex: Contribution a l'etude de la perception et de la memoire [The test of copying a complex figure: A contribution to the study of perception and memory]. *Archives de Psychologie, 30*, 286–356.

Page, M. P. A. (2000). Connectionist modelling in psychology: a localist manifesto. *The Behavioral and Brain Sciences, 23*, 443–467. doi:10.1017/S0140525X00003356

Palmeri, T. J., & Gauthier, I. (2004). Visual Object Understanding. Nature Reviews. *Neuroscience, 5*, 291–304. doi:10.1038/nrn1364

Patterson, K., Seidenberg, M. S., & McClelland, J. L. (1989). Connections and disconnections: acquired dyslexia in a computational model of reading processes. In Morris, R. G. M. (Ed.), *Parallel Distributed Processing - Implications for Psychology and Neurobiology*. Oxford: OUP.

Pavlov, I. P. (1927). *Conditioned Reflexes: An Investigation of the Physiological Activity of the Cerberal Cortex (G. V. Anrep Trans.)*. London: Oxford University Press.

Pearce, J. M. (1994). Similarity and discrimination: A selective review and a connectionist model. *Psychological Review, 101*, 587–607. doi:10.1037/0033-295X.101.4.587

Pearce, J. M., & Hall, G. (1980). A model for Pavlovian learning: Variations in the effectiveness of conditioned but not unconditioned stimuli. *Psychological Review, 87*, 532–552. doi:10.1037/0033-295X.87.6.532

Pearce, J. M. (1987). A model for stimulus generalization in Pavlovian conditioning. *Psychological Review, 94*, 61–75. doi:10.1037/0033-295X.94.1.61

Pearce, J. M. (1994). Similarity and discrimination: A selective review and a connectionist model. *Psychological Review, 101*, 587–607. doi:10.1037/0033-295X.101.4.587

Pearce, J. M. (2002). Evaluation and development of a connectionist theory of configural learning. *Animal Learning & Behavior, 30*, 73–95.

Pearce, J. M., & Hall, G. (1980). A model for Pavlovian learning: Variations in the effectiveness of conditioned but not unconditioned stimuli. *Psychological Review, 87*, 532–552. doi:10.1037/0033-295X.87.6.532

Pearce, J. M., & Wilson, P. N. (1991). Failure of excitatory conditioning to extinguish the influence of a conditioned inhibitor. *Journal of Experimental Psychology. Animal Behavior Processes, 17*, 519–529. doi:10.1037/0097-7403.17.4.519

Pearce, J. M., & Bouton, M. E. (2001). Theories of associative learning in animals. *Annual Review of Psychology, 52*, 111–139. doi:10.1146/annurev.psych.52.1.111

Pearce, J. M., & Hall, G. (1980). A model for Pavlovian learning: Variations in the effectiveness of conditioned but not of unconditioned stimuli. *Psychological Review, 87*, 532–552. doi:10.1037/0033-295X.87.6.532

Pearce, J. M. (1987). A model for stimulus generalization in Pavlovian conditioning. *Psychological Review, 94*, 61–73. doi:10.1037/0033-295X.94.1.61

Pearce, J. M. (1994). Similarity and discrimination: A selective review and a connectionist model. *Psychological Review, 101*, 587–607. doi:10.1037/0033-295X.101.4.587

Pearce, J. M., & Hall, G. (1980). A model for Pavlovian conditioning: Variations in the effectiveness of conditioned but not of unconditioned stimuli. *Psychological Review, 87*, 532–552. doi:10.1037/0033-295X.87.6.532

Pearce, J. M. (1987). A model for stimulus generalization in Pavlovian conditioning. *Psychological Review, 94*, 61–67. doi:10.1037/0033-295X.94.1.61

Pearce, J. M., & Bouton, M. E. (2001). Theories of associative learning in animals. *Annual Review of Psychology, 52*, 111–139. doi:10.1146/annurev.psych.52.1.111

Pearce, J. M., & Hall, G. (1980). A model for Pavlovian conditioning: Variations in the effectiveness of conditioned but not of unconditioned stimuli. *Psychological Review, 87*, 532–552. doi:10.1037/0033-295X.87.6.532

Pearson, R. (1999). *Discrete-time dynamic models*. Oxford, UK: Oxford University Press.

Pearson, K. G. (1976). The control of walking. *Scientific American, 235*, 72–86. doi:10.1038/scientificamerican1276-72

Pearson, M., Pipe, A., Melhuish, C., Mitchinson, B., & Prescott, T. (2007). Whiskerbot: A Robotic Active Touch System Modeled on the Rat Whisker Sensory System. *Adaptive Behavior, 15*(3), 223–240. doi:10.1177/1059712307082089

Peirce, J. W. (2007). The potential importance of saturating and supersaturating contrast response functions in visual cortex. *Journal of Vision (Charlottesville, Va.), 7*, 1–10. doi:10.1167/7.6.13

Peitgen, H., Jürgens, H., & Saupe, D. (1992). *Chaos and fractals—new frontiers of science*. New York, Berlin, Heidelberg, London: Springer Verlag.

Peña, D., Tiao, G., & Tsay, R. (Eds.). (2001). *A course in time series analysis*. New York, NY: Wiley.

Pfautz, P. L., & Wagner, A. R. (1978). Sensory preconditioning versus protection from habituation. *Journal of Experimental Psychology. Animal Behavior Processes, 4*, 286–295. doi:10.1037/0097-7403.4.3.286

Pfeifer, R., & Bongard, J. (2007). *How the body shapes the way we think: a new view of intelligence*. Cambridge, MA: MIT Press.

Philippides, A., Husbands, P., & O'Shea, M. (2000). Four Dimensional Neuronal Signaling by Nitric Oxide: A Computational Analysis. *The Journal of Neuroscience, 20*(3), 1199–1207.

Philippides, A., Husbands, P., Smith, T., & O'Shea, M. (2003). Structure based models of NO diffusion in the nervous system. In Feng, J. (Ed.), *Computational Neuroscience: a comprehensive approach* (pp. 97–130). London: Chapman and Hall/CRC Press. doi:10.1201/9780203494462.ch4

Platt, M. L. (2002). Neural correlates of decisions. *Current Opinion in Neurobiology, 12*, 141–148. doi:10.1016/S0959-4388(02)00302-1

Platt, M. L., & Huettel, S. A. (2008). Risky business: The neuroeconomics of decision making under uncertainty. *Nature Neuroscience, 11*, 398–403. doi:10.1038/nn2062

Plaut, D. C. (1995). Double dissociation without modularity: evidence from connectionist neuropsychology. *Journal of Clinical and Experimental Neuropsychology, 17*, 291–321. doi:10.1080/01688639508405124

Pomerleau, D. (1991). Efficient Training of Artificial Neural Networks for Autonomous Navigation. *Neural Computation, 3*, 88–97. doi:10.1162/neco.1991.3.1.88

Popper, K. (1999). *All Life is Problem Solving*. London: Routledge.

Postman, L. (1955). Association theory and perceptual learning. *Psychological Review, 62*, 438–446. doi:10.1037/h0049201

Prescott, T. J., Bryson, J. J., & Seth, A. K. (2007). Modelling natural action selection: Introduction to the theme issue. *Philosophical Transactions of the Royal Society of London. Series B, Biological Sciences, 362*(1485), 1521–1529. doi:10.1098/rstb.2007.2050

Prescott, T. J., Montes-Gonzalez, F., Gurney, K., Humphries, M. D., & Redgrave, P. (2006). A robot model of the basal ganglia: Behavior and intrinsic processing. *Neural Networks, 19*, 31–61. doi:10.1016/j.neunet.2005.06.049

Prescott, T. J., Redgrave, P., & Gurney, K. N. (1999). Layered control architectures in robots and vertebrates. *Adaptive Behavior, 7*, 99–127. doi:10.1177/105971239900700105

Preston, A. R., & Gabrieli, J. D. (2008). Dissociation between explicit memory and configural memory in the human medial temporal lobe. *Cerebral Cortex, 18*(9), 2192–2207. doi:10.1093/cercor/bhm245

Prokasy, W. F., & Papsdorf, J. D. (1965). Effects of increasing the interstimulus interval during classical conditioning of the albino rabbit. *Journal of Comparative and Physiological Psychology, 60*, 249–252. doi:10.1037/h0022341

RAE. (2009). *Autonomous systems: Social, legal and ethical issues*. The Royal Academy of Engineering No.

Ramsay, A., & Renault, J. (Eds.). (1999). *Groupoids in Analysis, Geometry, and Physics. Contemporary Mathematics 282*. Providence, RI: American Mathematical Society.

Randich, A., & LoLordo, V. M. (1979). Associative and non-associative theories of the UCS preexposure phenomenon: Implications for Pavlovian conditioning. *Psychological Bulletin, 86*, 523–548. doi:10.1037/0033-2909.86.3.523

Rangel, A., Camerer, C., & Montague, P. R. (2008). A framework for studying the neurobiology of value-based decision making. *Nature Reviews. Neuroscience, 9*, 545–556. doi:10.1038/nrn2357

Rankin, C. H. (2000). Context conditioning in habituation in the nematode C. elegans. *Behavioral Neuroscience, 114*, 496–505. doi:10.1037/0735-7044.114.3.496

Ratcliff, R. (1990). Connectionist models of memory: constraints imposed by learning and forgetting functions. *Psychological Review, 97*, 285–308. doi:10.1037/0033-295X.97.2.285

Redhead, E. S., & Pearce, J. M. (1995). Stimulus salience and negative patterning. *Quarterly Journal of Experimental Psychology, 48B*, 67–83.

Reeke, G. N., Sporns, O., & Edelman, G. M. (1990). Synthetic neural modeling: The "Darwin" series of recognition automata. *Proceedings of the IEEE, 78*(9), 1498–1530. doi:10.1109/5.58327

Reeve, R., Webb, B., Indiveri, G., Horchler, A., & Quinn, R. (2005). New technologies for testing a model of cricket phonotaxis on an outdoor robot. *Robotics and Autonomous Systems, 51*(1), 41–54. doi:10.1016/j.robot.2004.08.010

Reichardt, W. (1961). Autocorrelation, a principle for the evaluation of sensory information by the central nervous system. In Rosenblith, W. (Ed.), *Principles of sensory communication* (pp. 303–317). New York: Wiley.

Reil, T., & Husbands, P. (2002). Evolution of central pattern generators for bipedal walking in real-time physics environments. *IEEE Transactions on Evolutionary Computation, 6*(2), 10–21. doi:10.1109/4235.996015

Reiss, S., & Wagner, A. R. (1972). CS habituation produces a "latent inhibition effect" but not active conditioned inhibition. *Learning and Motivation, 3*, 237–245. doi:10.1016/0023-9690(72)90020-3

Rescorla, R. A. (1973). Evidence for a "unique stimulus" account of configural conditioning. *Journal of Comparative and Physiological Psychology, 85*, 331–338. doi:10.1037/h0035046

Rescorla, R. A. (2000). Associative changes in excitors and inhibitors differ when they are conditioned in compound. *Journal of Experimental Psychology. Animal Behavior Processes, 26*, 428–438. doi:10.1037/0097-7403.26.4.428

Rescorla, R. A. (2001). Unequal associative changes when excitors and neural stimuli are conditioned in compound. *The Quarterly Journal of Experimental Psychology. B, Comparative and Physiological Psychology, 54B*, 53–68. doi:10.1080/02724990042000038

Rescorla, R. A. (2002). Effect of following an excitatory-inhibitory compound with an intermediate reinforcer. *Journal of Experimental Psychology. Animal Behavior Processes, 28*, 163–174. doi:10.1037/0097-7403.28.2.163

Rescorla, R. A. (1967). Inhibition of delay in Pavlovian fear conditioning. *Journal of Comparative and Physiological Psychology, 64*, 114–120. doi:10.1037/h0024810

Rescorla, R. A. (1969). Pavlovian conditioned inhibition. *Psychological Bulletin, 72*, 77–94. doi:10.1037/h0027760

Rescorla, R. A. (1971). Summation and retardation test of latent inhibition. *Journal of Comparative and Physiological Psychology, 75*, 77–81. doi:10.1037/h0030694

Rescorla, R. A. (1972). Configural conditioning in discrete-trial bar pressing. *Journal of Comparative and Physiological Psychology, 79*, 307–317. doi:10.1037/h0032553

Rescorla, R. A. (1979). Aspects of the reinforcer learned in second-order pavlovian conditioning. *Journal of Experimental Psychology. Animal Behavior Processes, 5*, 79–95. doi:10.1037/0097-7403.5.1.79

Rescorla, R. A. (1997). Summation: Assessment of a configural theory. *Animal Learning & Behavior, 25*, 200–209.

Rescorla, R. A. (2000). Associative changes in excitors and inhibitors differ when they are conditioned in compound. *Journal of Experimental Psychology. Animal Behavior Processes, 26*, 428–438. doi:10.1037/0097-7403.26.4.428

Rescorla, R. A. (1968). Probability of shock in the presence and absence of CS in fear conditioning. *Journal of Comparative and Physiological Psychology, 66*, 1–5. doi:10.1037/h0025984

Rescorla, R. A. (1980). Simultaneous and successive associations in sensory preconditioning. *Journal of Experimental Psychology. Animal Behavior Processes, 6*, 207–216. doi:10.1037/0097-7403.6.3.207

Rescorla, R. A. (1988). Pavlovian conditioning: It's not what you think it is. *The American Psychologist, 43*, 151–160. doi:10.1037/0003-066X.43.3.151

Rescorla, R. A. (2003). Elemental and configural encoding of the conditioned stimulus. *The Quarterly Journal of Experimental Psychology, 56B*(2), 161–176.

Rescorla, R. A., & Wagner, A. R. (1972). A theory of Pavlovian conditioning: Variations in the effectiveness of reinforcement and nonreinforcement. In Black, A. H., & Prokasy, W. F. (Eds.), *Classical conditioning II: Current research and theory* (pp. 64–99). New York: Appleton-Century-Crofts.

Rescorla, R. A. (1985). Conditioned inhibition and facilitation. In Miller, R. R., & Spear, N. E. (Eds.), *Information processing in animals: Conditioned inhibition* (pp. 299–326). Hillsdale, NJ: Erlbaum.

Rescorla, R. A. (1985). Pavlovian conditioning analogues to Gestalt perceptual principles. In F.R. Brush., & J.B. Overmier (Eds.) *Affect, conditioning, and cognition: Essays on the determinants of behavior* (pp. 113-130). Hillsdale, NJ: LEA.

Reynolds, J. N., Hyland, B. I., & Wickens, J. R. (2001). A cellular mechanism of reward-related learning. *Nature, 413*, 67–70. doi:10.1038/35092560

Riabinina, O., & Philippides, A. (2009). A model of visual detection of angular speed for bees. *Journal of Theoretical Biology, 257*(1), 61–72. doi:10.1016/j.jtbi.2008.11.002

Rieke, F., Warland, D., van Steveninck, R. R., & Bialek, W. (1999). *Spikes: Exploring the Neural Code*. Cambridge, MA: MIT Press.

Robbins, H. (1952). Some aspects of the sequential design of experiments. *Bulletin of the American Mathematical Society, 58*, 527–535. doi:10.1090/S0002-9904-1952-09620-8

Roesch, M. R., Calu, D. J., & Schoenbaum, G. (2007). Dopamine neurons encode the better option in rats deciding between differently delayed or sized rewards. *Nature Neuroscience, 10*, 1615–1624. doi:10.1038/nn2013

Roesch, M. R., Singh, T., Brown, P. L., Mullins, S. E., & Schoenbaum, G. (2009). Ventral striatal neurons encode the value of the chosen action in rats deciding between differently delayed or sized rewards. *The Journal of Neuroscience, 29*, 13365–13376. doi:10.1523/JNEURO-SCI.2572-09.2009

Rolls, E. T., & Deco, G. (2002). *Computational Neuroscience of Vision*. New York: Oxford University Press Inc.

Rosenblatt, F. (1958). The perceptron: A probabilistic model for information storage and organization in the brain. *Psychological Review, 65*, 386–408. doi:10.1037/h0042519

Rosengren, R. (1971). Route Fidelity, Visual Memory and Recruitment Behaviour in Foraging Wood Ants of the *Genus Formica* (Hymenopteran Formicidae). *Acta Zoologica Fennica, 133*, 1–150.

Rosenstein, M. T., Collins, J. J., & De Luca, C. J. (1994). Reconstruction expansion as a geometry-based framework for choosing proper delay times. *Physica D. Nonlinear Phenomena, 73*, 82–98. doi:10.1016/0167-2789(94)90226-7

Rosenthal, O., & Behrmann, M. (2006). Acquiring long-term representations of visual classes following extensive extrastriate damage. *Neuropsychologia, 44*(5), 799–815. doi:10.1016/j.neuropsychologia.2005.07.010

Ross, R. T., & Holland, P. C. (1981). Conditioning of simultaneous and serial feature-positive discriminations. *Animal Learning & Behavior, 9,* 292–303.

Rossato, J. I., Bevilaqua, L. R. M., Izquierdo, I., Medina, J. H., & Cammarota, M. (2009). Dopamine control persistence of long-term memory storage. *Science, 325,* 1017–1020. doi:10.1126/science.1172545

Rumelhart, D. E., & McClelland, J. L. (Eds.). (1986). *Parallel Distributed Processing: Explorations in the Microstructure of Cognition (Vol. 1).* Cambridge, MA: MIT Press.

Rumelhart, D. E., Hinton, G. E., & Williams, G. E. (1986). Learning internal representations by error propagation. In Rumelhart, D. E., & McClelland, J. L. (Eds.), *Parallel Distributed Processing: Explorations in the Microstructure of Cognition. Cambridge, MA.* Bradford: MIT Press.

Rushworth, M. F. S., & Behrens, T. E. J. (2008). Choice, uncertainty and value in prefrontal and cingulate cortex. *Nature Neuroscience, 11,* 389–397. doi:10.1038/nn2066

Rushworth, M. F. S., Mars, R. B., & Summerfield, C. (2009). General mechanisms for making decisions? *Current Opinion in Neurobiology, 19,* 75–83. doi:10.1016/j.conb.2009.02.005

Saavedra, M. A. (1975). Pavlovian compound conditioning in the rabbit. *Learning and Motivation, 6,* 314–326. doi:10.1016/0023-9690(75)90012-0

Sakai, S., & Miyashita, Y. (1993). Memory and imagery in the temporal lobe. *Current Opinion in Neurobiology, 3,* 166–170.doi:10.1016/0959-4388(93)90205-D

Sakai, Y., & Fukai, T. (2008). The actor-critic learning is behind the matching law: Matching versus optimal behaviors. *Neural Computation, 20,* 227–251. doi:10.1162/neco.2008.20.1.227

Saksida, L. M. (2009). Remembering Outside the Box. *Science, 325*(5936), 40–41.doi:10.1126/science.1177156

Saksida, L. M., & Bussey, T. J. (2010). The Representational-Hierarchical View of Amnesia: Translation from Animal to Human. *Neuropsychologia, 48*(8), 2370–2384. doi:10.1016/j.neuropsychologia.2010.02.026

Saltelli, A., Campolongo, F., & Ratto, M. (2004). *Sensitivity analysis in practice.* New York, NY: Wiley.

Saltelli, A., Tarantola, S., & Campolongo, F. (2000). Sensitivity analysis as an ingredient of modeling. *Statistical Science, 15*(4), 377–395. doi:10.1214/ss/1009213004

Saltelli, A. (2005). Global sensitivity analysis: an introduction. In Hanson, K. M., & Hemez, F. M. (Eds.), *Sensitivity analysis of model output.* Los Álamos, NM: Los Álamos National Laboratory.

Samejima, K., & Doya, K. (2007). Multiple representations of belief states and action values in corticobasal ganglia loops. *Annals of the New York Academy of Sciences, 1104,* 213–228. doi:10.1196/annals.1390.024

Samejima, K., Ueda, Y., Doya, K., & Kimura, M. (2005). Representation of action-specific reward values in the striatum. *Science, 310,* 1337–1340. doi:10.1126/science.1115270

Sanderson, D. J., Pearce, J. M., Kyd, R. J., & Aggleton, J. P. (2006). The importance of the rat hippocampus for learning the structure of visual arrays. *The European Journal of Neuroscience, 24,* 1781–1788. doi:10.1111/j.1460-9568.2006.05035.x

Savastano, H. I., & Miller, R. R. (1998). Time as content in Pavlovian conditioning. *Behavioural Processes, 44,* 147–162.doi:10.1016/S0376-6357(98)00046-1

Schamjuk, N. A. (2009). Attentional and error-correcting associative mechanisms in classical conditioning. *Journal of Experimental Psychology. Animal Behavior Processes, 3,* 407–418. doi:10.1037/a0014737

Scheffield, F. D. (1965). Relation between classical conditioning and instrumental learning. In Prokasi, W. F. (Ed.), *Classical conditioning: A symposium. New-York.* Appleton-Century-Crofts.

Scheutz, M., & Crowell, C. R. (2007). *The burden of embodied autonomy: Some reflections on the social and ethical implications of autonomous robots.*, Dept Computer Science and Engineering, University of Notre Dame. Retrieved from http://hri.cogs.indiana.edu/publications/ethicsworkshoprevised.pdf

Schilling, M., Cruse, H., & Arena, P. (2007). Hexapod Walking: an expansion to Walknet dealing with leg amputations and force oscillations. *Biological Cybernetics, 96*, 323–340. doi:10.1007/s00422-006-0117-1

Schmajuk, N. A. (1997). *Animal learning and cognition: A neural network approach.* New York: Cambridge University Press.

Schmajuk, N. A. (2010). *Mechanisms classical conditioning: A computational approach.* New York: Cambridge University Press.

Schmajuk, N. A., & Kutlu, G. M. (2009). The computational nature of associative learning. *The Behavioral and Brain Sciences, 32*, 223–224. doi:10.1017/S0140525X09001125

Schmajuk, N. A., Lam, Y., & Gray, J. A. (1996). Latent inhibition: A neural network approach. *Journal of Experimental Psychology. Animal Behavior Processes, 22*, 321–349. doi:10.1037/0097-7403.22.3.321

Schmajuk, N. A., & Larrauri, J. A. (2006). Experimental challenges to theories of classical conditioning: Application of an attentional model of storage and retrieval. *Journal of Experimental Psychology. Animal Behavior Processes, 32*, 1–20. doi:10.1037/0097-7403.32.1.1

Schmajuk, N. A., & Larrauri, J. A. (2008). Associative models can describe both causal learning and conditioning. *Behavioural Processes, 77*, 443–445.

Schmajuk, N. A., Larrauri, J. A., & LaBar, K. S. (2007). Reinstatement of conditioned fear and the hippocampus: An attentional-associative model. *Behavioural Brain Research, 177*, 242–253. doi:10.1016/j.bbr.2006.11.026

Schmajuk, N. A., & Thieme, A. D. (1992). Purposive behavior and cognitive mapping: An adaptive neural network. *Biological Cybernetics, 67*, 165–174. doi:10.1007/BF00201023

Schmajuk, N. A. (1997). Stimulus configuration, long-term potentiation, and the hippocampus. *The Behavioral and Brain Sciences, 20*, 629–631. doi:10.1017/S0140525X97411597

Schmajuk, N. A., & Dicarlo, J. J. (1992). Stimulus configuration, classical conditioning, and hippocampal function. *Psychological Review, 99*, 268–305. doi:10.1037/0033-295X.99.2.268

Schmajuk, N. A., Lam, Y. W., & Gray, J. A. (1996). Latent inhibition: A neural network approach. *Journal of Experimental Psychology. Animal Behavior Processes, 22*, 321–349. doi:10.1037/0097-7403.22.3.321

Schmajuk, N. A., Lamoureux, J. A., & Holland, P. C. (1998). Occasion setting: A neural network approach. *Psychological Review, 105*, 3–32. doi:10.1037/0033-295X.105.1.3

Schneiderman, N., & Gormezano, I. (1964). Conditioning of the nictitating membrane of the rabbit as a function of CS-US interval. *Journal of Comparative and Physiological Psychology, 57*, 188–195. doi:10.1037/h0043419

Schneiderman, N. (1972). Response system divergencies in aversive classical conditioning. In Black, A. H., & Proasky, W. F. (Eds.), *Classical conditioning II: Current theory and research.* New York: Appleton-Century-Crofts.

Schneidermann, N. (1966). Interstimulus interval function of nictitating membrane response of rabbit under delay versus trace conditioning. *Journal of Comparative and Physiological Psychology, 62*, 397–402. doi:10.1037/h0023946

Schoenbaum, G., Roesch, M. R., Stalnaker, T. A., & Takahashi, Y. K. (2009). A new perspective on the role of the orbitofrontal cortex in adaptive behaviour. *Nature Reviews. Neuroscience, 12*, 885–892.

Schultz, W. (2006). Behavioral theories and the neurophysiology of reward. *Annual Review of Psychology, 57*, 87–115. doi:10.1146/annurev.psych.56.091103.070229

Schultz, W. (2002). Getting formal with dopamine and reward. *Neuron, 36*, 241–263. doi:10.1016/S0896-6273(02)00967-4

Schultz, W. (2007). Multiple dopamine functions at different time courses. *Annual Review of Neuroscience, 30*, 259–288. doi:10.1146/annurev.neuro.28.061604.135722

Schultz, W. (2009). Neuroeconomics: The promise and the profit. *Philosophical Transactions of the Royal Society of London. Series B, Biological Sciences, 363*, 3767–3769. doi:10.1098/rstb.2008.0153

Schultz, W., Dayan, P., & Montague, P. R. (1997). A neural substrate of prediction and reward. *Science, 275*, 1593–1599. doi:10.1126/science.275.5306.1593

Scilab Consortium. (1989-2004). *The Scilab programming language*. Retrieved from http://www.scilab.org.

Scoville, W. B., & Milner, B. (1957). Loss of recent memory after bilateral hippocampal lesions. *Journal of Neurology, Neurosurgery, and Psychiatry, 20*, 11–21. doi:10.1136/jnnp.20.1.11

Seidenberg, M. S., & McClelland, J. L. (1989). A distributed developmental model of word recognition and naming. *Psychological Review, 96*, 523–568. doi:10.1037/0033-295X.96.4.523

Sejnowski, T. J., Koch, C., & Churchland, P. S. (1988). Computational Neuroscience. *Science, 241*(4871), 1299–1306. doi:10.1126/science.3045969

Sejnowski, T. J., & Rosenberg, C. R. (1987). Learning and representation in connectionist models. In Gazzaniga, M. S. (Ed.), *Perspectives in memory research and training* (pp. 532–552). Cambridge, MA: MIT Press.

Seth, A. K., & Edelman, G. M. (2007). Distinguishing causal interactions in neural populations. *Neural Computation, 19*(4), 910–933. doi:10.1162/neco.2007.19.4.910

Shafir, S. (2000). Risk-sensitive foraging: The effect of relative variability. *Oikos, 88*, 663–669. doi:10.1034/j.1600-0706.2000.880323.x

Shallice, T. (1988). *From neuropsychology to mental structure*. New York: Cambridge University Press.

Shanks, D. R., & Darby, R. J. (1998). Feature- and rule-based generalization in human associative learning. *Journal of Experimental Psychology. Animal Behavior Processes, 24*, 405–415. doi:10.1037/0097-7403.24.4.405

Shanks, D. R. (2007). Associationism and cognition: human contingency learning at 25. *Quarterly Journal of Experimental Psychology, 60*, 291–309. doi:10.1080/17470210601000581

Shanks, D. R. (1995). *The Psychology of Associative Learning*. Cambridge, UK: Cambridge University Press. doi:10.1017/CBO9780511623288

Sherman, J. E., & Maier, S. F. (1978). The decrement in conditioned fear with increased trials of simultaneous conditioning is not specific to the simultaneous procedure. *Learning and Motivation, 9*, 31–53. doi:10.1016/0023-9690(78)90025-5

Shrager, Y., Gold, J. J., Hopkins, R. O., & Squire, L. R. (2006). Intact visual perception in memory-impaired patients with medial temporal lobe lesions. *The Journal of Neuroscience, 26*(8), 2235–2240. doi:10.1523/JNEUROSCI.4792-05.2006

Siciliano, B., & Khatib, O. (Eds.). (2008). *Springer Handbook of Robotics*. Berlin: Springer. doi:10.1007/978-3-540-30301-5

Siegel, S., & Domjan, M. (1971). Backward conditioning as an inhibitory procedure. *Learning and Motivation, 2*, 1–11. doi:10.1016/0023-9690(71)90043-9

Simen, P., & Cohen, J. D. (2009). Explicit melioration by a neural diffusion model. *Brain Research, 1299*, 95–117. doi:10.1016/j.brainres.2009.07.017

Skinner, B. F. (1938). *The behavior of organisms: An experimental analysis*. New York: Appleton-Century-Crofts.

Skinner, B. F. (1989). The Origins of Cognitive Thought. *The American Psychologist, 44*(1), 13–18. doi:10.1037/0003-066X.44.1.13

Smith, M. C. (1968). CS-US interval and US intensity in classical conditioning of the rabbit's nictitating membrane response. *Journal of Comparative and Physiological Psychology, 66,* 679–687. doi:10.1037/h0026550

Smith, M. C., Coleman, S. R., & Gormezano, I. (1969). Classical conditioning of rabbits nictitating membrane response at backward, simultaneous, and forward CS-US intervals. *Journal of Comparative and Physiological Psychology, 69,* 226–231. doi:10.1037/h0028212

Smith, L., Philippides, A., Graham, P., Baddeley, B., & Husbands, P. (2007). Linked local navigation for visual route guidance. *Adaptive Behavior, 15*(3), 257–271. doi:10.1177/1059712307082091

Smith, T. M. C., Husbands, P., & O'Shea, M. (2003). Local evolvability of statistically neutral GasNet robot controllers. *Bio Systems, 69,* 223–243. doi:10.1016/S0303-2647(02)00139-9

Smith, T. M. C., Husbands, P., Philippides, A., & O'Shea, M. (2002). Neuronal plasticity and temporal adaptivity: GasNet robot control networks. *Adaptive Behavior, 10*(3/4), 161–184.

Smith, L., Philippides, A., Graham, P., & Husbands, P. (2008). Linked Local Visual Navigation and Robustness to Motor Noise and Route Displacement. In M. Asada et al. (Eds.), *Proc. SAB'08: Animals to Animats X* (LNCS 5040, pp. 179-188). Berlin: Springer.

Sobol, I. (1993). Sensitivity estimates for nonlinear mathematical models. *Mathematical Modelling and Computational Experiment, 1,* 407–414.

Soto, F. A., Vogel, E. H., Castillo, R. D., & Wagner, A. R. (2009). Generality of the summation effect in causal learning. *Quarterly Journal of Experimental Psychology, 62,* 877–889. doi:10.1080/17470210802373688

Spence, K. W., Farber, I. E., & McFann, H. H. (1956). The relation of anxiety (drive) level of performance in competitive and non-competitive paired associates. *Journal of Experimental Psychology, 52,* 296–305. doi:10.1037/h0043507

Squire, L. R., Stark, C. E., & Clark, R. E. (2004). The medial temporal lobe. *Annual Review of Neuroscience, 27,* 279–306. doi:10.1146/annurev.neuro.27.070203.144130

Squire, L. R., & Zola-Morgan, S. (1983). The neurology of memory: The case for correspondence between the findings for human and nonhuman primate. In *The physiological basis of memory* (pp. 199–267). Academic Press.

Squire, L. R., & Zola-Morgan, S. M. (1991). The medial temporal lobe memory system. *Science, 253,* 1380–1386. doi:10.1126/science.1896849

Srinivasan, M. (2006). Small brains, smart computations: Vision and navigation in honeybees, and applications to robotics. *International Congress Series, 1291,* 30–37. doi:10.1016/j.ics.2006.01.055

Srinivasan, M., Chahl, J., Weber, K., Venkatesh, S., Nagle, M., & Zhang, S. (1999). Robot navigation inspired by principles of insect vision. *Robotics and Autonomous Systems, 26*(2-3), 203–216. doi:10.1016/S0921-8890(98)00069-4

Srinivasan, M., Zhang, S., Chahl, J., Stange, G., & Garratt, M. (2004). An overview of insect inspired guidance for application in ground and airborne platforms. *Proceedings of the Institution of Mechanical Engineers. Part G, Journal of Aerospace Engineering, 218,* 375–388. doi:10.1243/0954410042794966

Srinivasan, M. V. (2002). Visual Flight Control and Navigation in Honeybees, and Applications to Robotics. In Ayers, J., Davis, J. L., & Rudolph, A. (Eds.), *Neurotechnology for Biomimetic Robots* (pp. 593–610). Cambridge, MA: MIT Press.

Srinivasan, M., Thurrowgood, S., & Soccol, D. (2006). An optical system for guidance of terrain following in UAVs. *Proc IEEE International Conference on Advanced Video and Signal Based Surveillance* (AVSS '06), Sydney (pp. 51-56). Pasadena, CA: IEEE Press.

Staddon, J. E. R., & Cerutti, D. T. (2003). Operant conditioning. *Annual Review of Psychology, 54,* 115–144. doi:10.1146/annurev.psych.54.101601.145124

Stark, C. E., & Squire, L. R. (2000). Intact visual perceptual discrimination in humans in the absence of perirhinal cortex. *Learning & Memory (Cold Spring Harbor, N.Y.)*, *7*(5), 273–278.doi:10.1101/lm.35000

Stent, G. S. (1973). A physiological mechanism for Hebb's postulate of learning. *Proceedings of the National Academy of Sciences of the United States of America*, *70*, 997–1003.doi:10.1073/pnas.70.4.997

Stout, S. C., & Miller, R. R. (2007). Sometimes-competing retrieval (SOCR): A formalization of the comparator hypothesis. *Psychological Review*, *114*, 759–783. doi:10.1037/0033-295X.114.3.759

Sugrue, L. P., Corrado, G. S., & Newsome, W. T. (2004). Matching behavior and the representation of value in the parietal cortex. *Science*, *304*, 1782–1790. doi:10.1126/science.1094765

Sugrue, L. P., Corrado, G. S., & Newsome, W. T. (2005). Choosing the greater of two goods: Neural currencies for valuation and decision making. *Nature Reviews. Neuroscience*, *6*, 363–375. doi:10.1038/nrn1666

Sutton, R. S., & Barto, A. G. (1981). Toward a modern theory of adaptive networks: Expectation and prediction. *Psychological Review*, *88*, 135–170. doi:10.1037/0033-295X.88.2.135

Sutton, R. S. (1988). Learning to predict by the methods of temporal differences. *Machine Learning*, *3*, 9–44. doi:10.1007/BF00115009

Sutton, R. S., & Barto, A. G. (1998). *Reinforcement Learning: An Introduction*. Cambridge, MA: MIT Press.

Sutton, R. S., & Barto, A. G. (1990). Time derivative models of Pavlovian reinforcement. In Gabriel, M. R., & Moore, J. W. (Eds.), *Learning and computational neuroscience: Foundations of adaptive networks* (pp. 497–537). Cambridge, MA: MIT Press.

Sutton, R. S., & Barto, A. G. (1987). A temporal difference model of classical conditioning. In *Proceedings of the Seventh Annual Conference of the Cognitive Science Society* (pp. 355-378). Erlbaum.

Sutton, R. S., Maei, H. R., Precup, D., Bhatnagar, S., Silver, D., Szepesvari, C., & Wiewiora, E. (2009). Fast gradient-descent methods for temporal-difference learning with linear function approximation. *International Conference on Machine Learning*, *26*, 993-1000.

Suzuki, W. A. (2009). Perception and the medial temporal lobe: evaluating the current evidence. *Neuron*, *61*(5), 657–666.doi:10.1016/j.neuron.2009.02.008

Suzuki, W. A., & Baxter, M. G. (2009). Memory, perception, and the medial temporal lobe: a synthesis of opinions. *Neuron*, *61*(5), 678–679.doi:10.1016/j.neuron.2009.02.009

Suzuki, W. A., Zola-Morgan, S., Squire, L. R., & Amaral, D. G. (1993). Lesions of the perirhinal and parahippocampal cortices in the monkey produce long-lasting memory impairment in the visual and tactual modalities. *The Journal of Neuroscience*, *13*, 2430–2451.

Tait, R. W., & Saladin, M. E. (1986). Concurrent development of excitatory and inhibitory associations during backward conditioning. *Animal Learning & Behavior*, *14*, 133–137.

Tanaka, K., Saito, H., Fukada, Y., & Moriya, M. (1991). Coding Visual Images of Objects in the Inferotempral Cortex of the Macaque Monkey. *Journal of Neurophysiology*, *66*(1), 170–189.

Terry, W. S. (1976). Effects of priming unconditioned stimulus representation in short-term memory on Pavlovian conditioning. *Journal of Experimental Psychology. Animal Behavior Processes*, *2*, 354–369. doi:10.1037/0097-7403.2.4.354

The MathWorks. (2009). *Commercial Matlab website*. Retrieved from http://www.mathworks.co.uk/.

Theiler, J., & Lookman, T. (1993). Statistical error in a chord estimator of the correlation dimension: the rule of `five'. *Bifurcation and Chaos*, *3*, 765–771. doi:10.1142/S0218127493000672

Thompson, R. F., & Spencer, W. A. (1966). Habituation: A model phenomenon for the study of neuronal substrates of behavior. *Psychological Review*, 73, 16–43. doi:10.1037/h0022681

Thompson, R. F., Thompson, J. K., Kim, J. J., Krupa, D. J., & Shinkman, P. G. (1998). The nature of reinforcement in cerebellar learning. *Neurobiology of Learning and Memory*, 70, 150–176. doi:10.1006/nlme.1998.3845

Thorndike, E. L. (1911). *Animal Intelligence*. New York: Macmillan.

Thrun, T., Burgard, W., & Fox, D. (2005). *Probabilistic Robotics*. Cambridge, MA: MIT Press.

Thurnstone, L. L. (1930). The learning function. *The Journal of General Psychology*, 3, 469–493. doi:10.1080/00221309.1930.9918225

Timberlake, W. (1980). A molar equilibrium theory of learned performance. In Bower, G. H. (Ed.), *The psychology of learning and motivation* (*Vol. 14*, pp. 1–58). New York: Academic Press.

Tobler, P. N., Fiorillo, C. D., & Schultz, W. (2005). Adaptive coding of reward value by dopamine neurons. *Science*, 307, 1642–1645. doi:10.1126/science.1105370

Tobler, P. N., O'Doherty, J. P., Dolan, R. J., & Schultz, W. (2007). Reward value coding distinct from risk attitude-related uncertainty coding in human reward systems. *Journal of Neurophysiology*, 97, 1621–1632. doi:10.1152/jn.00745.2006

Tomsic, D., Pedreira, M. E., Romano, A., Hermitte, G., & Maldonado, H. (1998). Context- US association as a determinant of long-term habituation in the crab Chasmagnathus. *Animal Learning & Behavior*, 26, 196–209.

Tononi, G., Sporns, O., & Edelman, G. (1999). Measures of degeneracy and redundancy in biological networks. *Proceedings of the National Academy of Sciences of the United States of America*, 96, 3257. doi:10.1073/pnas.96.6.3257

Townsend, J. T. (2008). Mathematical psychology: Prospects for the 21st century: A guest editorial. *Journal of Mathematical Psychology*, 52, 269–280. doi:10.1016/j.jmp.2008.05.001

Trepel, C., Fox, C. R., & Poldrack, R. A. (2005). Prospect theory on the brain? Toward a cognitive neuroscience of decision under risk. *Brain Research. Cognitive Brain Research*, 23, 34–50. doi:10.1016/j.cogbrainres.2005.01.016

Tsai, H.-C., Zhang, F., Adamantidis, A., Stuber, G. D., Bonci, A., de Lecea, L., & Deisseroth, K. (2009). Phasic firing of dopaminergic neurons is sufficient for behavioral conditioning. *Science*, 324, 1080–1084. doi:10.1126/science.1168878

Tulving, E., & Schacter, D. L. (1990). Priming and human memory systems. *Science*, 247(4940), 301–306. doi:10.1126/science.2296719

Tulving, E. (1983). *Elements of episodic memory*. New York: OUP.

Tulving, E. (1972). Episodic and semantic memory. In Tulving, E. and Donaldson, W. (Eds.), *Organisation of memory*. New York: AP.

Tversky, A., & Kahneman, D. (1981). The framing of decisions and the psychology of choice. *Science*, 211, 453–458. doi:10.1126/science.7455683

Tyler, L. K., Stamatakis, E. A., Bright, P., Acres, K., Abdallah, S., & Rodd, J. M. (2004). Processing objects at different levels of specificity. *Journal of Cognitive Neuroscience*, 16(3), 351–362. doi:10.1162/089892904322926692

Ullman, S., Vidal-Naquet, M., & Sali, E. (2002). Visual features of intermediate complexity and their use in classification. *Nature Neuroscience*, 5(7), 682–687.

UN. (1999). *The world at six billion*. Population division of the Department of Economic and Social Affairs of the United Nations Secretariat. Retrieved from http://web.ukonline.co.uk/thursday.handleigh/demography/united-nations/19-supportratio.htm

Uttal, W. R. (2001). *The New Phrenology: The Limits of Localizing Cognitive Processes in the Brain.* Cambridge, MA: The MIT Press.

van Duuren, E., van der Plasse, G., Lankelma, J., Joosten, R. N. J. M. A., Feenstra, M. G. P., & Pennartz, C. M. A. (2009). Single-cell and population coding of expected reward probability in the orbitofrontal cortex of the rat. *The Journal of Neuroscience, 29,* 8965–8976. doi:10.1523/JNEUROSCI.0005-09.2009

Van Hamme, L. J., & Wasserman, E. A. (1994). Cue competition in causality judgements: The role of nonpresentation of compound stimulus elements. *Learning and Motivation, 25,* 127–151. doi:10.1006/lmot.1994.1008

van Strien, N. M., Scholte, H. S., & Witter, M. P. (2008). Activation of the human medial temporal lobes by stereoscopic depth cues. *NeuroImage, 40*(4), 1815–1823. doi:10.1016/j.neuroimage.2008.01.046

Vardy, A., & Moller, R. (2005). Biologically plausible visual homing methods based on optical flow techniques. *Connection Science, 17*(1), 47–90. doi:10.1080/09540090500140958

Vardy, A. (2006). Long-Range Visual Homing. In *Proceedings of the 2006 IEEE International Conference on Robotics and Biomimetics* (pp. 220-226).

Vargas, P., Moioli, R., Von Zuben, F., & Husbands, P. (2009). Homeostasis and Evolution Together Dealing with Novelties and Managing Disruptions. *International Journal of Intelligent Computing and Cybernetics, 2*(3), 435–454. doi:10.1108/17563780910982680

Vargas, P., Di Paolo, E., & Husbands, P. (2008). Exploring non-spatial GasNets in a delayed response robot task. In Bullock, S. (Eds.), *Proc. Artificial Life XI* (pp. 640–647). Cambridge, MA: MIT Press.

Vaughan, E., Di Paolo, E., & Harvey, I. (2004) The evolution of control and adaptation in a 3D powered passive dynamic walker. In J. Pollack, M. Bedau, P. Husbands, T. Ikegami, & R. Watson, (Eds), *Proceedings of the Ninth International Conference on the Simulation and Synthesis of Living Systems, Artificial Life IX* (pp. 139–145). Cambridge, MA: MIT Press.

Vedral, V. (2006). *Introduction to Quantum Information Science.* Oxford, UK: Oxford University Press. doi:10.1093/acprof:oso/9780199215706.001.0001

Vogel, E. H., Brandon, S. E., & Wagner, A. R. (2000). Stimulus representation in SOP II: An application to inhibition of delay. *Behavioural Processes, 110,* 67–72.

Vogel, E. H., Brandon, S. E., & Wagner, A. R. (2003). Stimulus representation in SOP: II. An application to inhibition of delay. *Behavioural Processes, 62,* 27–48. doi:10.1016/S0376-6357(03)00050-0

Vogel, E. H., Castro, M. E., & Saavedra, M. A. (2004). Quantitative models of Pavlovian conditioning. *Brain Research Bulletin, 63,* 173–202. doi:10.1016/j.brainresbull.2004.01.005

Vul, E., Harris, C., Winkielman, P., & Pashler, H. (2009). Puzzlingly High Correlations in fRMI Studies of Emotion, Personality, and Social Sciences. *Perspectives on Psychological Science, 4*(3), 274–290. doi:10.1111/j.1745-6924.2009.01125.x

Vuskovic, M., & Du, S. J. (2002). Classification of prehensile EMG patterns with simplified fuzzy ARTMAP networks. *Proceedings of International Joint Conference on Neural Networks, 3,* 2539–2544. Retrieved from http://medusa.sdsu.edu/Robotics/Neuromuscular/Our_publications/Hawaii/Paper.pdf.

Waelti, P., Dickinson, A., & Schultz, W. (2001). Dopamine responses comply with basic assumptions of formal learning theory. *Nature, 412,* 43–48. doi:10.1038/35083500

Wagner, A. R. (2003). Context-sensitive elemental theory. *Quarterly Journal of Experimental Psychology, 56,* 7–29. doi:10.1080/02724990244000133

Wagner, A. R., Logan, F. A., Haberlandt, K., & Price, T. (1968). Stimulus selection in animal discrimination learning. *Journal of Experimental Psychology, 76,* 171–180. doi:10.1037/h0025414

Wagner, A. R., Rudy, J. W., & Whitlow, J. W. (1973). Rehearsal in animal conditioning. *Journal of Experimental Psychology, 97,* 407–426. doi:10.1037/h0034136

Wagner, A. R. (1979). Habituation and memory. In Dickinson, A., & Boakes, R. A. (Eds.), *Mechanisms of learning and motivation: A memorial volume for Jerzy Konorski*. Hillsdale, NJ: Erlbaum Associates.

Wagner, A. R., & Rescorla, R. A. (1972). Inhibition in Pavlovian conditioning: Application of a theory. In Halliday, M. S., & Boakes, R. A. (Eds.), *Inhibition and learning*. San Diego, CA: Academic Press.

Wagner, A. R. (1978). Expectancies and the priming of STM. In Hulse, S. H., Fowler, W., & Honing, W. K. (Eds.), *Cognitive aspects of animal behavior*. Hillsdale, NJ: Erlbaum.

Wagner, A. R., & Brandon, S. E. (1989). Evolution of a structured connectionist model of Pavlovian conditioning (AESOP). In Klein, S. B., & Mowrer, R. R. (Eds.), *Contemporary learning theories: Pavlovian conditioning and the status of traditional learning theory*. Hillsdale, NJ: Erlbaum.

Wagner, A. R. (1969). Stimulus validity and stimulus selection in associative learning. In Mackintosh, N. J., & Honig, W. K. (Eds.), *Fundamental issues in associative learning*. Halifax, Canada: Dalhousie University Press.

Wagner, A. R., & Brandon, S. E. (2001). A componential theory of Pavlovian conditioning. In Mower, R. R., & Klein, S. B. (Eds.), *Handbook of contemporary learning theories*. Mahwah, NJ: Lawrence Erlbaum Associates, Inc.

Wagner, A. R. (1981). SOP: A model of automatic memory processing in animal behavior. In Spear, N. E., & Miller, R. R. (Eds.), *Information processing in animals: Memory mechanisms* (pp. 5–47). Hillsdale, NJ: Erlbaum.

Wagner, A. R., & Vogel, E. H. (2009). New and current views in basic conditioning: Theories of conditioning. In Squirre, L. (Ed.), *The new encyclopedia of Neuroscience*. New York: Elsevier.

Wagner, A. R. (1976). Priming in STM: An information-processing mechanism for self-generated or retrieval-generated depression in performance. In Tighe, T. J., & Leaton, R. N. (Eds.), *Habituation: Perspectives from child development, animal behavior and neurophysiology*. Hillsdale, NJ: Elrbaum.

Walter, W. G. (1950). An imitation of life. *Scientific American, 182*(5), 42–45. doi:10.1038/scientificamerican0550-42

Walter, W. G. (1951). A machine that learns. *Scientific American, 185*(2), 60–63.

Walter, W. G. (1953). *The Living Brain*. London: Duckworth.

Warrington, E., & James, M. (1991). *The Visual Object and Space Perception Battery*. Bury St Edmunds, UK: Thames Valley Test Company.

Warrington, E. K., & Weiskrantz, L. (1968). New method of testing long-term retention with special reference to amnesic patients. *Nature, 217*(132), 972–974. doi:10.1038/217972a0

Wasserman, E. A., & Miller, R. R. (1997). What's elementary about associative learning? *Annual Review of Psychology, 48*, 573–607. doi:10.1146/annurev.psych.48.1.573

Watkins, C. J. C. H., & Dayan, P. (1992). Q-Learning. *Machine Learning, 8*, 279–292. doi:10.1007/BF00992698

Watkins, C. J. C. H. (1989). *Learning from delayed rewards*. Ph.D. Thesis. University of Cambridge, England.

Webb, B. (2001). Can robots make good models of biological behaviour? *The Behavioral and Brain Sciences, 24*(6), 1033–1050. doi:10.1017/S0140525X01000127

Webb, B. (2009). Animals versus animats: or why not model the real iguana? *Adaptive Behavior, 17*(4), 269–286. doi:10.1177/1059712309339867

Webb, B., & Consi, T. (Eds.). (2001). *Biorobotics*. Cambridge, MA: MIT Press.

Webb, B., & Scutt, T. (2000). A simple latency dependent spiking neuron model of cricket phonotaxis. *Biological Cybernetics, 82*(3), 247–269. doi:10.1007/s004220050024

Wehner, R., Boyer, M., Loertscher, F., Sommer, S., & Menzi, U. (2006). Ant Navigation: One-Way Routes Rather Than Maps. *Current Biology, 16*, 75–79. doi:10.1016/j.cub.2005.11.035

Wehner, R., Michel, B., & Antonsen, P. (1996). Visual Navigation in Insects: Coupling of Egocentric and Geocentric Information. *The Journal of Experimental Biology, 199*, 129–140.

Weinstein, A. (1996). Groupoids: Unifying internal and external symmetry (a tour through some examples). *Notices of the American Mathematical Society, 43*(7), 744–752.

Wertheimer, M. (1923). Principles of perceptual organization. In Beardslee, D. S., & Wertheimer, M. (Eds.), *Readings in perception* (pp. 115–137). Princeton, NJ: Van Nostrand-Reinhold.

Weyl, H. (1928). *Gruppentheorie und Quantenmechanik.* Leipzig: S. Hirzel Verlag. English translation: The Theory of Groups and Quantum Mechanics. New York: Dover Publications.

Wheeler, M. (2005). *Reconstructing the Cognitive World.* Cambridge, MA: MIT Press.

Wheeler, J. A. (1990). Information, physics, quantum: The search for links. In Zurek, W. (Ed.), *Complexity, Entropy, and the Physics of Information.* Redwood City, CA: Addison-Wesley.

Whitlow, J. W. (1975). Short-term memory in habituation and dishabituation. *Journal of Experimental Psychology, 104*, 189–206.

Whitlow, J. W., & Wagner, A. R. (1972). Negative patterning in classical conditioning: Summation of response tendencies to isolable and configural components. *Psychonomic Science, 27*, 299–301.

Widrow, G., & Hoff, M.E. (1960). *Adaptive switching circuits.* Institute of radio engineers, Western Electronic show & convention, Convention record, Part 4, 96-104.

Williams, D. A., Dumont, J.-L., & Mehta, R. (2004). Conditions favoring superconditioning of irrelevant conditioned stimuli. *Journal of Experimental Psychology. Animal Behavior Processes, 30*, 148–159. doi:10.1037/0097-7403.30.2.148

Williams, D. A., Mehta, R., Poworoznyk, T. M., Orihel, J. S., George, D. N., & Pearce, J. M. (2002). Acquisition of superexcitatory properties by an irrelevant background stimulus. *Journal of Experimental Psychology. Animal Behavior Processes, 28*, 284–297.doi:10.1037/0097-7403.28.3.284

Williams, B. A. (1996). Evidence that blocking is due to associative deficit: Blocking history affects the degree of subsequent associative competition. *Psychonomic Bulletin & Review, 3*, 71–74.

Williams, D. A., & Braker, D. S. (1999). Influence of past experience on the coding of compound stimuli. *Journal of Experimental Psychology. Animal Behavior Processes, 25*, 461–474. doi:10.1037/0097-7403.25.4.461

Williams, D. A., Lawson, C., Cook, R., Mather, A. A., & Johns, K. W. (2008). Timed excitatory conditioning under zero and negative contingencies. *Journal of Experimental Psychology. Animal Behavior Processes, 34*, 94–105. doi:10.1037/0097-7403.34.1.94

Williams, D. R. (1965). Classical conditioning and incentive motivation. In Prokasy, W. F. (Ed.), *Classical conditioning: A symposium. New-York.* Appleton-Century-Crofts.

Wilson, M., & Kaufman, H. M. (1969). Effect of inferotemporal lesions upon processing of visual infomation in monkeys. *Journal of Comparative and Physiological Psychology, 69*(1), 44–48.doi:10.1037/h0027923

Wilson, M., Zieler, R. E., Lieb, J. P., & Kaufman, H. M. (1972). Visual Identification and Memory in Monkeys with Circumscribed Inferotemporal Lesions. *Journal of Comparative and Physiological Psychology, 78*(2), 173. doi:10.1037/h0032819

Wilson, P. N., & Pearce, J. M. (1989). A role for stimulus generalization in conditional discrimination learning. *The Quarterly Journal of Experimental Psychology. B, Comparative and Physiological Psychology, 41*, 243–273.

Wilson, P. N., & Pearce, J. M. (1990). Selective transfer of responding in conditional discriminations. *The Quarterly Journal of Experimental Psychology. B, Comparative and Physiological Psychology, 42*, 41–58.

Winters, B. D., Forwood, S. E., Cowell, R. A., Saksida, L. M., & Bussey, T. J. (2004). Double dissociation between the effects of peri-postrhinal cortex and hippocampal lesions on tests of object recognition and spatial memory: heterogeneity of function within the temporal lobe. *The Journal of Neuroscience, 24*(26), 5901–5908. doi:10.1523/JNEUROSCI.1346-04.2004

Wolf, A., Swift, J., Swinney, H., & Vastano, J. (1985). Determining Lyapunov exponents from a time series. *Physica, 16D*(3), 285–317.

Wolf, A. (2003). *Chaos analysis software.* Retrieved from http://www.cooper.edu/wolf/-chaos/chaos.htm.

Wood, G. (2003). *Living Dolls: A Magical History of the Quest for Mechanical Life.* London: Faber and Faber.

Wood, J., & Garthwaite, J. (1994). Model of the diffusional spread of nitric oxide - implications for neural nitric oxide signaling and its pharmacological properties. *Neuropharmacology, 33*, 1235–1244. doi:10.1016/0028-3908(94)90022-1

Wunderlich, K., Rangel, A., & O'Doherty, J. P. (2009). Neural computations underlying action-based decision making in the human brain. *Proceedings of the National Academy of Sciences of the United States of America, 106*, 17199–17204. doi:10.1073/pnas.0901077106

Wyeth, G., & Milford, M. (2009). Spatial Cognition for Robots: Robot Navigation from Biological Inspiration. *IEEE Robotics & Automation Magazine, 16*(3), 24–32. doi:10.1109/MRA.2009.933620

Yadid, G., & Friedman, A. (2008). Dynamics of the dopaminergic system as a key component in the understanding of depression. *Progress in Brain Research, 172*, 265–286. doi:10.1016/S0079-6123(08)00913-8

Yamaguchi, M. (2006). Complete solution of the Rescorla-Wagner model for relative validity. *Behavioural Processes, 71*, 70–73. doi:10.1016/j.beproc.2005.10.001

Young, M. E., & Wasserman, E. A. (2002). Limited Attention and Cue Order Consistency Affect Predictive Learning: A Test of Similarity Measures. *Journal of Experimental Psychology. Learning, Memory, and Cognition, 28*, 484–496. doi:10.1037/0278-7393.28.3.484

Zentall, T. R., Steirn, J. N., Sherburne, L. M., & Urcuioli, P. J. (1991). Common coding in pigeons assessed through partial versus total reversals of many-to-one conditional and simple discriminations. *Journal of Experimental Psychology. Animal Behavior Processes, 17*, 194–201. doi:10.1037/0097-7403.17.2.194

Zhang, L., & Cottrell, G. (2005). *Holistic processing develops because it is good.* Paper presented at the Proceedings of the 27th Annual Cognitive Science Conference, Stresa, Italy.

Zuse, K. (1969). *Rechnender Raum.* Braunschweig, Germany: Friedrich Vieweg & Sohn.

Zwarts, M. J., Bleijenberg, G., & Engelen, B. G. M. (2008). Clinical neurophysiology of fatigue. *Clinical Neurophysiology, 119*(1), 2–10..doi:10.1016/j.clinph.2007.09.126

About the Contributors

Eduardo Alonso is a Senior Lecturer at City University London. He is an expert on Artificial Intelligence in particular on the interdisciplinary bridges between machine learning and animal learning. He has published dozens of papers and contributions to Artificial Intelligence volumes (e.g., in The Cambridge Handbook of Artificial Intelligence, to appear in 2010, ISBN-10: 0521871425). His survey paper "AI and Agents: State of the Art", AI Magazine 23(3): Fall 2002, 25-30, is still recommended as a general reading at AAAI's AI Topics-Agents. He is the Public Understanding Officer of The Society for the Study of Artificial Intelligence and the Simulation of Behaviour, the eldest learned Artificial Intelligence society in Europe, and a member of the Society for Computational Modeling of Associative Learning. He is also a member of the EPSRC College.

Esther Mondragón held several research positions at the Department of Psychology at the University of York and at the Cognitive, Perceptual and Brain Sciences Unit at University College London. Her research focuses on Behavioural Neuroscience, specializing in the study of animal learning and cognition from the theoretical background of associative models of conditioning. She has published her work in, among others, Science, Learning and Behavior, and The Quarterly Journal of Experimental Psychology. She contributed to the book Occasion Setting (APA, 1998). Recently, she founded the Centre for Computational and Animal Learning Research that she co-chairs.

* * *

Marc Bellemare received his Bachelor of Science and subsequently his M.Sc. in Computer Science from McGill University. He is currently a member of the Reinforcement Learning and Artificial Intelligence (RLAI) group at the University of Alberta as a Ph.D. student under Professor Richard Sutton. He has held NSERC Canada Graduate Scholarships both at the M.Sc. and the Ph.D. level and his ongoing work is supported by iCORE. Marc's research investigates methods to extend conventional reinforcement-learning algorithms to long-lived robots.

David Bisset has worked in Domestic Robotics for 22 years. An academic for 10 years he headed the mobile robotics research lab at the University of Kent. In 1998 he and his team were recruited by James Dyson to start a robotics product group at Dyson Ltd. In 2000 the DC06 was announced but never came to market. He left Dyson in 2002. Since then he has acted as a consultant in Robotics and Embedded Systems and until 2009 Chaired the Domestic Group of EUROP the European Technology Platform for Robotics contributing to the Strategic Research Agenda for Robotics in Europe. He is now

Technical Director of Toby Churchill Ltd a global Assistive Technology company based in Cambridge and remains an expert adviser to EUROP.

Charlotte Bonardi completed a first degree in Natural Sciences and a PhD in Experimental Psychology at the University of Cambridge. From 1986-2004 she worked as a research fellow at the University of York Psychology department, and since 2004 has held a lectureship in psychology at the University of Nottingham. Her current research interests are conditional learning, timing, the function of the hippocampus, and the deficits in learning resulting from clinical conditions such as schizophrenia, personality disorder and Alzheimer's disease.

Tim Bussey is Senior Lecturer in the Department of Experimental Psychology at the University of Cambridge, and is a member of the MRC and Wellcome Trust Behavioural and Clinical Neuroscience Institute. He is a PI in the Cognitive Systems Neuroscience Laboratory (CSNLab; www.psychol.cam.ac.uk/csnlab). He received undergraduate degrees in Chemistry and Psychology from the University of Victoria and the University of British Columbia in Canada. He then did his PhD work with Trevor Robbins investigating the functions of the prefrontal and cingulate cortices in the rat. This was followed by a two-year postdoctoral fellowship with John Aggleton in Cardiff, and a three-year postdoctoral fellowship with Elizabeth Murray at the National Institutes of mental health in Bethesda, MD. He took up a lectureship in Cambridge in October 2000.

Rosie Cowell is a Research Scientist at the University of California, San Diego, in the Department of Psychology. Working in the area of cognitive neuroscience, her research uses computational modeling to investigate problems in visual cognition. Her investigations have ranged from studying the mechanisms of visual perception and recognition memory in the temporal lobe, to developing novel methods for analysing fMRI data from early visual cortex. The models of cognition that she builds are biologically inspired and, where possible, biologically constrained. She uses them to explain extant empirical data in the cognitive neuroscience literature and to provide new empirical predictions for experiments that include human behaviour, animal neuropsychology and fMRI.

Christopher S. Grand completed his first degree in Biology at the University of Sussex before conducting postgraduate research in the School of Psychology at the University of Cardiff. His postgraduate research included examining the role of similarity in human associative learning and the work that forms the basis of this chapter.

Robert C. Honey completed his first degree in Experimental Psychology at the University of Sussex before conducting postgraduate research in the Department of Psychology at the University of York. Following several postdoctoral positions in the Department of Psychology at the University of York and in the Department of Zoology at the University of Cambridge he received a Royal Society University Research Fellowship. Having brought this fellowship to the School of Psychology at Cardiff University, he now holds the position of Professor, and is Director of Postgraduate Research within the School of Psychology.

Huosheng Hu received the MSc degree in industrial automation from the Central South University, China in 1982, and the PhD degree in robotics from the University of Oxford, United Kingdom in

1993. Currently, He is a Professor in Department of Computing and Electronic Systems, University of Essex, U.K., leading the Human Centred Robotics Group. His research interests include autonomous mobile robots, human-robot interaction, evolutionary robotics, multi-robot collaboration, embedded systems, pervasive computing, sensor integration, RoboCup, intelligent control and networked robotics. He has published over 250 papers in journals, books and conferences, and received few best paper awards. He is a founding member of Networked Robots of IEEE Society of Robotics and Automation Technical Committee since 2001 and a member of the IASTED Technical Committee on "Robotics" for 2001-2004. He was a General Co-Chair of IEEE Int. Conference on Mechatronics and Automation, Harbin, China, 2007, Publication Chair of IEEE International Conference on Networking, Sensing and Control, London, 2007; Co-Chair of Special & Organised Sessions of IEEE International Conference on Robotics and Biomimetics, Sanya, China, 2007; Co-chair of International Program Committee, 1st International Conference on Human Body Simulation and Modelling, Shanghai University, China, 28–30 Oct. 2004, etc. Prof. Hu served as a member of the Editorial Advisory Board for the International Journal of Industrial Robots during 1997 to 2000, and is currently Editor-in-chief for the International Journal of Automation and Computing. He is a reviewer for a number of international journals such as IEEE Transactions on Robotics, Automatic Control, Neural Networks and the International Journal of Robotics Research. Since 2000 he has been a Visiting Professor at 6 universities in China - namely Central South University, Shanghai University, Wuhan University of Science and Engineering, Kunming University of Science and Technology, Chongqing University of Post & Telecommunication, and Northeast Normal University. He is a Chartered Engineer, a senior member of IEEE and ACM, and a member of IET, AAAI, IASTED and IAS.

Phil Husbands is Professor of Computer Science and Artificial Intelligence in the School of Informatics, University of Sussex. He is head of the Evolutionary and Adaptive Systems (EASy) group and co-director of the Centre for Computational Neuroscience and Robotics. His research interests include biologically inspired adaptive robotics, computational neuroscience and evolutionary systems. He has published more than 200 papers in these areas and is on the editorial board of eight international journals. He has degrees in Physics (BSc, University of Manchester), Computer Science (MSc, South Bank) and Artificial Intelligence (PhD, University of Edinburgh).

Dómhnall Jennings completed a BA and MA in Psychology and a PhD in Zoology at University College Dublin. From 2001 he worked as a research fellow at the Psychology Departments in the University of York and University of Nottingham. Since 2007 he has held a lectureship at the Institute of Neuroscience at Newcastle University. His research interests are broad within the field of animal behaviour and learning and focus on the interaction between learning and timing, learning deficits resulting from ageing and dementia.

Munir Gunes Kutlu got his Bachelor of Art degree in Psychology at Istanbul Bilgi University, Turkey, in 2006. From 2006 to 2008, he worked for Bogazici University Psychobiology Lab. In 2008, he moved to the USA to pursue a PhD degree in Cognitive Neuroscience at Duke University where he currently works as a research assistant in the Computational Neuroscience Lab.

Elliot Ludvig is currently a post-doc working with Rich Sutton in the Department of Computing Science at the University of Alberta. He obtained his Ph.D. in 2003 at Duke University in the Department of Psychological & Brain Sciences and, prior to that, a B.Sc. in Psychology at Concordia University in Montreal, Canada. His research aims to create and test quantitative models of learning, timing, and decision-making. He hopes to combine approaches from artificial intelligence and animal learning into a single coherent framework for understanding the mind and the brain.

I. P. L. McLaren, Professor of Cognitive Psychology in the School of Psychology. My interests are broadly in the area of Learning, Memory and Cognition, with an emphasis on Computational Modelling. I'm particularly interested in comparisons between humans and other species that attempt to identify common learning processes in each, and actively attempt to transfer research paradigms from infra-human to human and vice-versa to generate data that supports these comparisons. Recent projects I've been involved in include work on Peak-Shift (which reflects my interest in how automatic, associative processes can influence decision making), Categorisation in humans and pigeons, Subliminal Priming, Face Perception (particularly inversion effects), Perceptual Learning (how experience with stimuli can lead to expertise in discriminating between them) and Judgements of Recency and Frequency. If I had to identify a theme that unifies my work at the moment, it would be that our behaviour can best be described as some synthesis of rule-based symbolic action and associatively-based experience-driven reaction. I perform experiments that seek to dissociate these processes, and construct computational models that attempt to combine them in order to predict the results of the experiments. Qualifications: My post-school education was all at King's College, Cambridge in the UK. Here I studied Astrophysics, then Psychology at Undergraduate level, before taking a PhD under the supervision of Stephen Monsell (co-supervised by Nick Mackintosh) in the Department of Experimental Psychology (my thesis title was Association and Representation). I'm a Fellow of the Higher Education Academy, and a full member of the Experimental Psychology Society, the Psychonomic Society and the Cognitive Science society. Career: Post-PhD I became a research Fellow at King's College in Cambridge. Then spent two years as a Lecturer at Warwick University, back to Cambridge as a Lecturer and Senior Lecturer (and Fellow and Tutor at Emmanuel College) then to Exeter to take the Chair in Cognitive Psychology.

Ulrich Nehmzow is full Professor of Cognitive Robotics at the University of Ulster, Londonderry. He obtained his Diplom in Electrical Engineering and Information Science from the University of Technology at Munich in 1988, and his Ph.D. in Artificial Intelligence from the University of Edinburgh in 1992. After a post-doctoral position at Edinburgh University he became Lecturer in Artificial Intelligence at the University of Manchester in 1994, and Senior Lecturer (2001) and subsequently Reader (2004) in Mobile Robotics at the University of Essex. His research interests are scientific methods in robotics, robot learning, robot navigation, simulation and modelling in robotics, and novelty detection in mobile robotics, for instance for industrial applications. Ulrich Nehmzow is the founding chair and co-chair of the British conference on mobile robotics (TAROS), and member of the editorial board of Journal of Connection Science and the AISB journal. He is past secretary of the International Society for Adaptive Behavior. Ulrich Nehmzow died of cancer shortly after submitting his chapter, the 15th of April 2010. He was 48. He will be dearly missed.

Mohammadreza Asghari Oskoei received the M.Sc. degree in Control Systems from University of Tehran, Iran, in 1993, and the Ph.D. degree in Computer Science from the University of Essex, UK, in 2009. Currently, he is a Research Fellow in the School of Computer Science, University of Hertfordshire, London, UK, and his research interests are in the areas of adaptive systems, myoelectric control, machine learning, human-robot proximity, biomedical signal processing, and neuromuscular rehabilitation. He has published several papers in biomedical journals, and been reviewer for Elsevier Journal on Medical Engineering & Physics.

Keir Pearson is a neurophysiologist who received his Bachelor of Engineering (Electrical) from the University of Tasmania and his PhD in Physiology from Oxford University. He spent two years as a Junior Research Fellow at Merton College, Oxford, before joining the Physiology Department at the University of Alberta. He is currently a Professor and Chair of the Department of Physiology and former Director of the University Centre for Neuroscience. He has held a Tier I Canada Research Chair in Movement Physiology, and he is a Fellow of the Royal Society of Canada. His research program is focused on the nervous control of walking and functional recovery after spinal cord injury.

Andy Philippides is a lecturer in the School of Informatics, University of Sussex where he is a member of the Insect Navigation Group within the Centre for Computational Neuroscience and Robotics. His research interests include computational neuroscience, in particular neuromodulation in networks, visual navigation in insects using a combination of behavioural experiments, mathematical and robotic modelling, and adaptive behaviour in general. He has published 50 papers in these areas and has degrees in Mathematics (MA, Cambridge), Knowledge-Based Systems (MSc, Sussex) and Computational Neuroscience (DPhil, Sussex).

Fernando P. Ponce is a research associate at the Laboratory of Experimental Psychology at the University of Talca, Chile. His research interests include modeling basic learning through computer simulations and empirical work on habituation, sensitization and Pavlovian conditioning in humans. Ponce obtained B.A. degree in Psychology from Universidad de Talca in 2009.

Nick Ryman-Tubb has developed practical solutions for businesses using neural computers for 20-years. He founded and was CEO of the UK firm that now protects 1-in-7 of the world's mobile telephone subscribers from fraud using neural computers (www.neuralt.com). He developed anti-fraud systems for loan and credit card applications, city dealing and anti-money laundering. He is a well-known innovator, with successes such as the first neural computer to "taste champagne" and "sniff out explosives and drugs". Today, Nick is working with businesses like Retail Decisions (www.redplc.com), a card issuer and a world leader in card fraud prevention and payment processing, preventing around £600m in attempted fraudulent purchases for clients every year. Nick is also a Research Fellow at City University London researching state of the art neural-symbolic approaches at the Department of Computing (www.soi.city.ac.uk/neural).

Lisa Saksida completed an interdisciplinary PhD at the Centre for the Neural Basis of Cognition and the Robotics Institute at Carnegie Mellon University in 1999. She then held a Fogarty Fellowship at the National Institute of Mental Health, followed by a Pinsent Darwin Research Associateship at the University of Cambridge. She is now a Senior Lecturer in the Department of Experimental Psychology at the University of Cambridge and a Fellow of Newnham College. Her research focuses on the psychological processes underlying memory and perception, through a programme of theoretically-driven experimental research using several converging methods of enquiry including localised pharmacological methods, transgenic and knock-out mice, and computational modelling. She also has a particular interest in the development of translational methods for cognitive assessment.

Néstor A. Schmajuk graduated from the University of Buenos Aires and became an Associate Professor of Biomedical Engineering in Argentina. In 1986, he obtained a doctorate in Psychology from the University of Massachusetts and became a postdoctoral fellow at the Center for Adaptive Systems at Boston University. From 1988 until 1993, he was an assistant professor of psychology at Northwestern University. In 1992 he obtained a fellowship from the Royal Society to develop models of latent inhibition and the hip pocampus. In 1993 he moved to Duke University where he is a Professor. Dr. Schmajuk has developed neural network models of classical conditioning, operant conditioning, animal communication, spatial learning, cognitive mapping, and prepulse inhibition. Using these neural networks he has described the effects of hippocampal, cortical, and cerebellar lesions, as well as the results of the administration of dopaminergic and cholinergic drugs, in different sensory, learning and cognitive paradigms.

Anil K. Seth is a Reader in the School of Informatics at the University of Sussex. He is also an EPSRC Leadership Fellow and Co-Director of the Sackler Centre for Consciousness Science. He is a leading researcher in the fields of consciousness science and computational neuroscience, having published more than 35 journal papers in high-profile outlets; he is currently Editor-in-Chief of Frontiers in Consciousness Research and is Editor of the Scholarpedia chapter on consciousness. He holds degrees in Natural Sciences (MA, Cambridge, 1994), Knowledge-Based Systems (M.Sc., Sussex) and Computer Science and Artificial Intelligence (D.Phil., Sussex). Before returning to Sussex in 2006 he worked for nearly six years at The Neurosciences Institute in San Diego, where he collaborated with the Nobel laureate Gerald Edelman on research in consciousness science and neuro-robotics.

Edgar H. Vogel is an associate professor at the Faculty of Psychology in the University of Talca, Chile. His research focuses on theoretical and empirical analyses of Pavlovian conditioning and habituation. Since 2003, he works also as a research affiliate in the Department of Psychology at Yale University, where he conducts collaborative research with Allan R. Wagner. Vogel received his B.A. degree in Psychology from Universidad de Chile in 1993 and his Ph.D. degree in Behavioral Neuroscience from Yale University in 2001.

Index